AF771069

HOMICIDE

A Bibliography

2nd Edition

Bal K. Jerath, M.D., M.P.H., M.S.
Research Director
Diagnostic Technologies, Inc.
Associate Professor of Community Medicine
Medical College of Georgia
Augusta, Georgia

Rajinder Jerath, B.S.
Assistant Director of Research
Diagnostic Technologies, Inc.
Augusta, Georgia

CRC Press
Boca Raton Ann Arbor London Tokyo

Ref
Z
5703.4
.M87
J47
1993

Library of Congress Cataloging-in-Publication Data

Catalog record is available from the Library of Congress.

This book represents information obtained from authentic and highly regarded sources. Reprinted material is quoted with permission, and sources are indicated. A wide variety of references are listed. Every reasonable effort has been made to give reliable data and information, but the author and the publisher cannot assume responsibility for the validity of all materials or for the consequences of their use.

Neither this book nor any part may be reproduced or transmitted in any form or by any means, electronic or mechanical, including photocopying, microfilming, and recording, or by any information storage and retrieval system, without permission in writing from the publisher.

Direct all inquiries to CRC Press, Inc., 2000 Corporate Blvd., N.W., Boca Raton, Florida, 33431.

© 1993 by CRC Press, Inc.

International Standard Book Number 0-8493-8670-5

Printed in the United States 1 2 3 4 5 6 7 8 9 0

Printed on acid-free paper

Dedicated to all the authors whose contributions to the literature on homicide have made this reference work possible

PREFACE

The year 1991 has been the deadliest year in United States history. Homicide has claimed 25,000 lives, far in excess of the previous year. The U.S. homicide rate is the highest in the industrialized world. The rate is 10 per 100,000, compared to 5.5 in Britain and a microscopic 1.3 in Japan. In this country, murder is the leading cause of death among women in the workplace, and also for young African-American males aged fifteen to twenty-four years.

Homicide is the leading cause of premature mortality. Potential life-years lost before age sixty-five due to homicide adversely impact on our national productivity. The resulting drain on the economy is incalculably large. In the last four years arrests for homicides among juveniles have increased by 93%, while adult arrests for murder have increased by 16%. Criminologists predict these trends will continue for the next four years.

The literature on homicide is dispersed throughout virtually all areas of human endeavor. As homicide is the result of man killing man; its study logically includes examination of precipitating human factors such as, anger, frustration, mental make-up, socio-economic conditions, drug and alcohol abuse, distortion of human values, and gun use. This volume aims to meet the needs of the sociologist, criminologist, homicide detective, forensic pathologist, attorney, both prosecuting and defense, the judiciary, the lawmaker, from the local to the federal level, and the public health professional, among many others. For convenience, this compendium contains both contemporary and historical references in a single source.

A new emphasis on prevention and control of homicide has been reflected in the literature from the last five years. Our bibliographic research indicates that nearly 10% of current literature pertains to homicide prevention and control. Homicide must be attacked as a public health problem if prevention and control are to be achieved. Homicide should not be approached with a fatalistic attitude, but tackled as problem that begs solution.

The pool of analytic studies is a rich mine of data. For example, the homicide rate among African-Americans in the civilian population is twelve times greater than the death rate among African-Americans in the U.S. Army. Many other findings can be used as clues for the control of homicide. A positive correlation has been found between an increase in the legal drinking age and a reduction in adolescent deaths from virtually all categories of violent death. In one study of homicide victims, 40% tested positive for cocaine metabolites. Another study shows that 75% of homicides in this country are firearms-related, whereas in the other industrialized nations combined, guns account for only 25% of homicide deaths. In Washington, DC, the enactment of tough gun laws coincided with a sharp reduction in deaths from firearms. Hopefully, the synthesis of these various findings can lead researchers to new hypotheses and the forging of innovative, multidisciplinary, approaches leading to the reduction of homicide mortality.

The authors have extensively searched the world literature on homicide. References from hundreds of journals and publications have been included. All major indexes have been searched, including some, such as the Air University Library Index of Military Periodicals, the Index to United States Government Periodicals, and the Internationale Bibliographie der Zeitschriften Literatur (I.B.Z.), which are not universally available. As a further convenience, numerical codes for specific journals cited from the I.B.Z. have been decoded at the beginning of the book. Twenty-three indexes have been utilized in the compilation of this work. There is no other single source available which can provide the researcher with such a complete selection of homicide literature. Any abbreviations used are those found in the specific indexes.

Although every effort has been made to avoid errors, it is inevitable that some might slip through. Neither the authors nor the publisher can be held responsible for unforeseen problems arising from the use of this guide. It is assured that all errors are strictly inadvertent.

All essential elements of the ecology and epidemiology of homicide are reflected in the organization of the various chapter and subchapter headings. Chapters on the murderer, the victim, the mode, and the environments that produce all three, are included. This format guides the user to articles of particular interest to their specialty, and highlights the many components necessary for prevention in each. The entries have been compiled and converted to conform to the American Psychological Association (A.P.A.) style book guidelines. The subject index refers to specific key-word headings; the author index lists all entries by specific author. For articles with more than two authors, the principal author alone is listed in the index. For articles with two authors, both are listed separately.

The authors wish to thank all the reference librarians who provided valuable assistance during the research for this book. The reference staffs at the following libraries were of particular help: Caroliniana Library of the University of South Carolina, Columbia; Greenblatt Library of the Medical College of Georgia, Augusta; Reese Library of Augusta College, Augusta; Health Science Center Library of Emory University, Atlanta, Georgia; and the Library of Congress, Washington, D.C. The authors are indebted to the expert assistance provided by these individuals.

It is hoped that this bibliography meets the needs of its users. The authors appreciate any comments and suggestions readers may have.

The authors wish to express their sincere thanks to Mr. Joel Claypool at CRC Press, for his vital assistance in the preparation of this book. His patience, understanding, and cooperation have been essential to the success of this project. The authors also wish to acknowledge the valuable assistance of Mr. John M. Rockwell in the preparation of the manuscript.

Bal K. Jerath
Rajinder Jerath

HOMICIDE: A Bibliography

TABLE OF CONTENTS

CHAPTER 3 - THE MURDERER

CHAPTER 4 - THE VICTIM

CHAPTER 5 - MURDER MODES

CHAPTER 6 - CAUSES OF MURDER

CHAPTER 7 - INVESTIGATION

CHAPTER 8 - CASE REPORTS

CHAPTER 9 - HOMICIDE, SUICIDE, AND ACCIDENTS

CHAPTER 10 - LEGAL ASPECTS

CHAPTER 11 - ASSASSINATION

CHAPTER 12 - PREVENTION AND CONTROL

INDEXES SEARCHED

Abstracts for Social Workers
Published by:
National Association for Social Workers
Publication Department
2 Park Ave.
New York, NY 10016
Years - 1965-1977

Books in Print
Published by:
R.R. Bowker Company
1180 Avenue of the Americas
New York, NY 10016
Years - 1967-1991

Criminal Justice Periodical Index
Published by:
University Microfilms International
300 North Zeeb Rd.
Ann Arbor, MI 48106
Years - 1975-1991

Criminology and Penology Abstracts
Published by:
Kugler Publications BV
Amstelveen
The Netherlands
Years - 1964-1991

Dissertation Abstracts International
Published by:
University Microfilms International
300 Zeeb Ave.
Ann Arbor, MI 48106
Years - 1964-1991

Excerpta Medica
Forensic Science Abstracts
Published by:
Section 49
Database Division
100 BC
Amsterdam, The Netherlands
Years - 1975-1991

Humanities Index
Index to Legal Periodicals
Published by:
The H.W. Wilson Company
New York
Years - 1974-1991
1888-1991

Index Medicus
Published by:
National Library of Medicine
8600 Rockville Pike
Bethesda, MD 20209
Years - 1957-1991

International Bibliographie der Zeitschriften Literatur (I.B.Z)
Published by:
(International Bibliography of Periodical Literature (Covering all fields of knowledge).
Osnabruk. Felix Dietrich
Verlag
Years - 1911-1991

Monthly Catalog of United States Government Publications
Published by: U.S. Government Printing Office
Washington, D.C. 20402
Years - 1970-1991

National Library of Medicine Current Catalog
Published by:
National Library of Medicine
8600 Rockville Pike
Bethesda, MD 20209
Years - 1950-1991

Psychological Abstracts
Published by:
The American Psychological Association, Inc.
1400 North Uhle St.
Arlington, VA 22201
Years - 1929-1991

Public Affairs Information Service Bulletin (PAIS)
Published by:
Public Affairs Information Service, Inc.
11 W. 40th St.
New York, NY 10018
Years - 1971-1991

Reader's Guide to Periodical Literature
Published by:
The H.W. Wilson Company
New York, New York
Years - 1970-1991

Research on Violence
(a bibliography on criminal violence)
Published by:
University of Cambridge
Institute of Criminology
Year - 1974

Social Sciences Index
Published by:
The H.W. Wilson Company
New York, NY
Years - 1974-1991

Social Work Research and Abstracts
Published by:
National Association of Social Workers
Murray Hill Station
New York, NY

Years - 1977-1991

Sociological Abstracts (SA)
Published by:
Sociological Abstracts, Inc.
P.O. Box 22206
San Diego, CA 92122
Years - 1971-1991

The Index to U.S. Government Periodicals
Published by:
Infodata International, Inc.
175 E. Delaware Place
Suite 4602
Chicago, IL 60611
Years - 1988-1991

Air University Library Index to Military Periodicals
Published by:
Air University Library
Maxwell A.F.B., AL 36112-5564

Years - 1988-1991

IBZ Periodicals Referred to in this Book

1060 Afrika. Monatchrift fur Politik, Wirtschaft und Kultut in neuen Afrika. Munchen (Forts = Nr. 25284)

1127 Agricultura. Revista agropecuaria. Madrid

1227m Aktuelle Kriminologie. Melanges de criminologie. Essays in Criminology. Zum lojahrigen Bestehen der Deutschen Kriminologischen Gesellschaft und em 50. Geburtstag ihres Prasidenten, Prof. Dr. Armand Mergen. Hamburg, 1969.

1671 American Journal of Psychiatry. American Psychiatric Association. Baltimore , MD.

3647 Archiv fur Kriminologie. Monatsschrift fur naturwissenschaftliche Kriminalistik und Polizefarchiv. Lubeck.

3969 Archives of General Psychiatry. American Medical Association. Chicago, IL.

7430 The British Journal of Psychiatry. The British Journal of Mental Science. London.

9028 Canadian Medical Association Journal. Toronto.

11086 Deutsches Zentralblatt fur Krankenpflege. Gottingen.

11235 Diseases of the Nervous System. New York.

11290 Dokumente. Zeitschrift in Dienste ubernationaler Zusammenarbeit. Koln.

12599 Ethics. An international journal of social, political, and legal philosophy. Chicago, IL.

13029 Far Eastern Economic Review. Hongkong.

13157d Festschrift fur Erich zum 65. Geburtstag am 25. Januar 1968. Hrsg. von Heinz Brunotte u.a. Hanover, Berlin, Hamberg, 1968.

13586 Forschungen und Fortschritte (Erscheingestellt). Berlin.

18620 Journal of Criminal Law, Criminology, and Police Science. Baltimore.

20132 The Judical Review. Edinburgh.

21054 Juristenzeitung. Lubingen.

20957 Kriminalistic. Zeitschrift fur die gesamte kriminalistische Wissenschaft und Praxis. Hamburg.

20957k Krinalistische Akzente. Herrn Dr. Bernard Niggemeyer zum 69. Geburstag. Hrsg. von Herbert Schaffer. Grundlagen der Kriminalistik. Bd. 4. Hamburg 1968.

21397 Law Quarterly Review. London.

22424 Medico-legal Journal. Cambridge, England.

24232 Monatsschrift fur Kriminologie und Strafechtsreform. Koln.

25159 Neue juristische Wochenschrift. (nebst Beil.: Zeitschrift fur Rechstpolitik, Nr. 39163). Munchen.

25758 La Nouvelle Internationale, Paris.

26420 Med Omega. Journal of Death and Dying. Farmingdale, NY.

Baywood Publishing Company, Inc.

28414 Psychiatric Quarterly. Utica, NY

29027k Raubkrimalitat. Ursachen und vorbeugende Bekampfung. Vortrage gehalten anlablich der Arbeitstagung des Berufsverbandes Deutscher Psychologen in Mai 1966 in Kassel. Forschungsberichte zur forensischen Psychologie. H. 3. Berlin 1967.

30202 Revue internationale de criminologie et de police technique. Geneve.

30560 Revue de science criminelle et de droit penal compare. Paris.

32301 Scuola positiva. Rivista di criminologia e dirittp criminale. Milano.

37335 Weltwoche. Zurich

38593 Zeitschrift fur Ethnologie. Organ der Deutchen Gesellschaft fur Volkerkund. Braunschweig.

38667 Zeitschrift fur das gesamte Familiaenrecht. Ehe und Familie im privaten und offentichen Recht. Bielefeld.

38706 Zeitschrift fur die gesamte Strafrechtswissenschaft. Berlin.

Chapter 1
Introduction
General

(Social Research)

Staub, E. (1990) Moral exclusion, personal goal theory, and extreme destructiveness. *Social Issues, 46*(1), 47-64.

(Indicators - Homicide)

Huang, W.S., & Wellford, C.F. (1989) Assessing indicators of crime among international crime data series. *Criminal Justice Policy Review, 3*(1), 28-47.

(Homicide - Overview)

Homicide: A current overview. (1987) *Statistical Bulletin of the Metropolitan Insurance Company. 68*(4), 13-21.

(Homicide - Perspective)

Homicide: The public health perspective. (1986) *Bulletin of the New York Academy of Medicine, 62*(5), 373-624.

(Homicide - Patterns)

Tardiff, K. (1985) Patterns and major determinants of homicide in the United States. *Hospital and Community Psychiatry, 36*(6), 632-639.

(Worse than Death)

Coumo, M. (1984) A fate worse than death. *Corrections Digest, 15*(11), 4. Microforms and article copies available from UMI.

(Comments)

Mott, G., & Smith, J.C. (1983, June) Case and comment: Homicide. *The Criminal Law Review 1983*, 393-395.

(Homicide - General)

Willough, A. (1983, Jan.) Business as usual? *World Marxist Review, 26*, p. 72.

(Homicide - Response)

Barnett, A. (1982) Learning to live with homicide: A research note (attempt to find an explanation for the passive American response to increasing homicide). *Criminal Justice, 10*(1), 69-72.

(Murder Description)

Robbins, R. (1981, July 10) Describing the indescribable (review article). *Times Literary Supplement, 4084*, 779-780.

(Homicide - Vandalism)

Manslaughter - vandalism - damaging stop sign. (1980) *The Criminal Law Reporter: Court Decisions and Proceedings, 28*(12), 2283.

(Homicide - Blacks)

Winbush, R.A. (1980) Toward a macrocosmic view of crime in African-American communities. *Public Health Reports, 95*(6), 557.

(New Risk)

New risk. (1979) *Security World, 16*(8), 14,16. Article copies available from UMI.

(Homicide - Studies)

Frazier, S.H. (1974) Murder -- single and multiple. *Res Publ Assoc Res Nerv Ment Dis, 52*, 304-312.

(Homicide - Perfect)

Spenlingwimmer, U. (1972) An almost perfect murder? 20957. J 26, '72, 5, S. 236-239.

(Violence)

Palmer, S. (1972) *The violent society.* College & University Press.

(Homicide - Unsuccessful)

Stoller, J. (1970) The unsuccessful perfect murder. 20957. J. 24, '70. 5, S. 261-264.

(Homicide - Portfolio)

Cuthbert, T.M. (1970) A portfolio of murders: The Presidential address at the 129th annual meeting of the Royal Medico-Psychological Association, held in Middlesbrough, July 9, 1969. *British Journal of Psychiatry, 116*, 1-10.

(Astrology)

Watters, B. (1969) *The astrologer looks at murder.* Arcane Books.

(Homicide - Method)

Kentig, H.V. (1969) Murder and methods of diversion of suspicion. 1227m. '69, S. 125-132.

(Violence)

Wolfgang, M.E., & Ferracuti, F. (1967) *Subculture of violence.* New York: Barnes & Noble.

(Murder Book)

Sparrow, G. (1967) *Murder parade.* Roy Publishing.

(Death Attitudes)

Williams, M. (1966, Nov.) Changing attitudes to death: A survey of contributions in *Psychological Abstracts* over a thirty year period. *Human Relations, 19*, 405-423.

(Homicide - Typology)

Yoshimasu, S. (1966) RE: Typology of recurrent murder. 3647. Bd. 137, '66, H. 3-4, S. 84-90 (IBZ 1967).

(Homicide - Meaning)

Brophy, J. (1966) *Meaning of murder.* Crowell.

(Repression)

Graven, J. (1966) La repression de l'homicide en droit suisse. 30560. n. s., t. 21, '66, n. 2, p. 233-295. (IBZ 1969)

(Homicide - Invitation)

Gold, L.H. (1965) Invitation to homicide. *Journal of Forensic Sciences, 10*, 415-421.

(Sleepwalking)

Podolsky, E. (1964, Aug.) Somnambulistic homicide. *American Journal of Psychiatry, 121*, 191-192.

Theory

(Spouse-Murder)

Reed, W.S. (1990 Aug.) The case for legalizing limited "spousecide". *Advocate, 33*, p. 5

(Social Research)

Staub, E. (1990) Moral exclusion, personal goal theory, and extreme destructiveness. *Journal of Social Issues, 46*(1), 47-64.

(Police Killings)

Chamlin, M.B. (1989) Conflict theory and police killings. *Deviant Behavior, 10*(4), 353-368.

(Homicide - Causes)

Parker, R.N. (1989) Poverty, subculture of violence, and type of homicide. *Social Forces, 67*(4), 983-1007.

(Critical Mass)

Lester, D. (1989) The critical mass hypothesis. *Psychological Reports, 64*(1), 146.

(Homicide - Theory)

The evolution of family homicide. (1988) *Science News, 134*(19), p. 300.

(Homicide - Social Factors)

Messner, S.F. (1982) Societal development, social equality, and homicide: A cross-national test of the Durkheimian model. *Social Forces, 61*, 225-240.

(Homicide - Conflict Resolution)

Levi, K. (1980) Homicide as conflict resolution. *Deviant Behavior, 1*(3-4), 281-308.

(Homicide - Differences by Sex)

Ketner, L.G., & Humphrey, J.A. (1979-1980) Homicide sex role differences and role relationships. *Omega: Journal of Death & Dying, 10*(4), 379-387.

(Homicide - Ability to Kill)

Ambler, E. (1971) *Ability to kill.* New American Library.

(Homicide - Book)

Wellman, M.W. (1955) *Dead and gone.* Chapel Hill, NC: University of North Carolina Press.

(Homicide - An Approach)

Morris, A. (1955) *Homicide: An approach to the problem of crime.* Boston: Boston U. Press.

(Homicide - Article)

Murder. (1924, July) *Outlook, 54*, pp. 45-46.

Classification and Definition

(Misclassification)

Lapidus, G.D., et al. (1990) Misclassification of childhood homicide on death certificates. *American Journal of Public Health, 80*(2), 213-214.

(Homicide - Classification)

Higginbottham, S.F., Zamble, E. (1988) Categorization of homicide cases: Agreement, accuracy, and confidence of public assignments. *Canadian Journal of Criminology, 30*(4), 351-366.

(Homicide Rates)

Williams, K.R., & Flewilling, R.L. (1988) The social production of criminal homicide: A comparative study of disaggregated rates in American cities. *American Sociology Review, 53*(3), 421-431.

(Homicide - Legislation)

Higgins, J. (1986) The origins of the Homicide Act of 1957. *Journal of Medical Ethics, 12*(1), 8-12.

(Suicide - Incitement)

Homicide - incitement to suicide - definition of murder. (1986) *The Criminal Law Report: Court Decisions and Proceedings, 33*(14), 2288.

(Robbery-Murder)

Loftin, C. (1986) The validity of robber-murder classification in Baltimore. *Violence Victims, 1(3), 191-204.*

(Murder History)

Chunko, M.T. (1986) How to write a murder history. *Humanities, 7*(4), 16-18.

(Industrial Death)

Can an industrial death be murder? (conviction of Film Recovery Systems executives). (1985, July 15) *U.S. News and World Report, 99*, p. 14.

(Serial Murder)

Egger, S.A. (1984) A working definition of serial murder and the reduction of linkage blindness. *Journal of Police Science Administration, 12*(3), 348-357.

(Fetus)

Destruction of unborn fetus does not constitute murder. (1983) *The Family Law Report: Court Opinions, 9*(24), 2380-2382.

(Corporate Homicide)

Swigert, V.L., & Farrell, R.A. (1981) Corporate homicide: Definitional processes in the creation of deviance. *Law and Sociology Review, 15*(1), 161-182.

(Homicide - Typology)

McGurk, B.J. (1981) The validity and utility of a typology of homicides based on Megarqee's theory of a control. *Personality & Individual Differences, 2*(2), 129-136.

(Classification)

Rengier, R. (1980) Should murder be taken out of the category of intentional killing? Comparative essay about the laws of Austria, Switzerland, and Germany. 38706. bd. 92 '80, h. 2, s459-480 (IBZ 1981).

(Homicide - Definition)

Mewett, A.W. (1978) First degree murder. *Criminal Law Quarterly, 21*(1), 82-95.

(Homicide - Culpable)

Orchard, G.F. Culpable homicide. *New Zealand Law Journal,* (1977, Oct. 18), 411-415; (1977, Nov. 1), 447-456.

(Homicide - Philosophy)

The philosophy of classification of deaths. (1977) *Medical Legal Bulletin, 26*(2), 1-5.

(Homicide - Other)

English, P. (1977) Homicides other than murder. *Criminal Law Review 1977*, 79-90.

(Homicide - Article)

Elliot, D.W. (1977) Murder. *Criminal Law Review 1977*, 70-78.

(Homicide - Law)

Rubin, P.J. (1976) Homicide. *Main Law Review, 28*, 57-63 (Special Issue).

(Classification)

Presswalla, F. (1976) Classification of deaths. *New York State Journal of Medicine, 76*(9), 1531-1533.

(Golem Syndrome)

Bierer, G.S. (1976) Love-making -- an act of murder: The "Golem" syndrome. *International Journal of Social Psychiatry, 22*(3), 197-199.

(Homicide - Article)

Scott, E.M. (1975) The act of murder. *International Journal of Offender Therapy and Comparative Criminology, 19*(2), 154-163.

(Homicide - Classification)

Boudouris, J. (1974) A classification of homicides. *Criminology: An Interdisciplinary Journal, 11*(4), 525-540.

(Homicide - Studies)

Menninger, K. (1973) Murder. *Bulletin of the Menninger Clinic, 37*, 305-320.

(Homicide - General)

Bailey, F.L., & Rothblatt, H.B. (1973) *Crimes of violence, homicide, and assault*. Lawyer's Co-Op Press.

(Homicide - Book)

Turkus, B.B., & Feder, S. (1972) *Murder, inc.* New York: Manor.

(Homicide - Typology)

Verberne, T.J.P. (1972) Blackburn's typology of abnormal homicides: Additional data and a critique. *British Journal of Criminology, 12*(1), 88-89.

(Homicide - Principles)

Schipkowensky, P.N. (1971) The principles of homicide (French). *Ann Med Psychol, 1*, 773-775.

(Homicide - Phenomenology)

Matzler, A. (1969) Whom can we trust today? Phenomenology of homicide. 20957. J. 23, '69, 6, S. 312-314 (IBZ 1969).

(Homicide - Definition)

Riess, P. (1968) Fixing limits of murder and killings. 25159. J. 21, '68, H. 14, S. 628-631 (IBZ 1969).

(Homicide - Language)

Purver, J.M. (1967) Language of murder. *UCLA Law Review, 14*, 1306.

(Criminology - Theory)

Wolfgang, M.E., & Ferracuti, F. (1967) *Subculture of violence: Towards an integrated theory in criminology*. B&N.

(Homicide - Meaning)

Brophy, J. (1966) *Meaning of murder*. Crowell.

(Homicide - Violence)

Prevolnik, O. (1961) Murder as an act of violence (Serbian). *Neuropsihijatrija, 9*, 86-91.

(Homicide - Definition)

Cross, R. (1960) Need for re-definition of murder. *Criminal Law Review 1960*, 728.

(Homicide - Beginning)

Mueller, G.O.W. (1960) Where murder begins. *N H B J, 2*, 214.

(Murder Theory)

Palmer, S. (1960) *The psychology of murder*. New York: Crowell.

(Homicide - Legislation)

Wingersky, M.F. (1958) Death by definition. *DePaul Law Review, 7*, 172.

(Homicide)

Edwards, J. (1957) The Homicide Act of 1957: A critique. *British Journal of Delinquency, 8*(1), 49-61.

(Murder as Art)

Minty, L.M. (1957) Murder as a fine art. *Medical Legal Journal of Cambridge, 25*(1), 11-22

(Murder - First Degree)

Keedy, E.R. (1950) Problem of first degree murder: Fisher v. United States. *University of Pennsylvania Law Review, 99*, 267-292.

(Murder - First Degree)

Blinn, K.W. (1950) First degree murder - a workable definition. *J of Crim Law, 40*, 729-735.

(Homicide - Essay)

Gemelli, A. (1948) *Homicides: An interpretive essay*. Milan: A. Guiffre.

(Murder - Degrees)

Degrees of murder. (1948) Ir L T, 82, 187-188.

(Homicide - Book)

Mann, A. (1947) Homicide: Is it objective or subjective? (subjective view). *Kentucky Law Journal, 35*, 252-256.

(Felony Murder)

Clark, J.G. (1940) Modern felony murder doctrine. *Kentucky Law Journal, 28*, 215-218.

(Homicide - Book)

Roughead, W. (1938) Comfortable words about murder. *Jurid Review, 50*, 165-178.

(Murder - Degrees)

Degrees of murder and manslaughter. (1938) *West Virginia Law Quarterly, 44*, 194-205.

(Murder - Second Degree)

Pike, J.A. (1936) What is second degree murder in California? *Southern California Law Review 1936*, 1-25.

(Homicide - Legislation)

Hippenmeyer, R.S. (1935) Recommended change in statute defining homicide. *Wisconsin Law Review, 10*, 274-275.

(Murder - Degrees)

Killing no manslaughter. (1932) *L J, 74*, 289.

(Homicide - Emotional Crimes)

Helweg, H. (1932) On murder as a "normal" emotional crime. *Acta Psychiatr et Neur, 1932*, 7, 201-216.

(Murder - Degrees)

Degrees of murder (Ahmed Jabur Khabib v. Attorney General for Palestine, *Times*, March 29, 1930). (1930, April 5) *Justice of the Peace, 94*, 227.

(Murder Theory)

Raven, A. (1930, April) Theory of murder. *Sociology Review, 22*, 108-118.

(Homicide - Editorial)

Herzog, A.W. (1930) A new crime (editorial). *Medical Legal Journal, 47*, 39-40.

(Homicide - General)

Dell, R. (1929, Jan. 5) Killing no murder. *Nation (London), 44*, pp. 483-485.

(Murder - Degree)

Hearne, J.G., Jr. (1929) Murder, distinction between first and second degree: Inconsistency in some West Virginia cases. *West Virginia Law Quarterly, 35*, 287-290.

(Murder - Degrees)

Degrees of murder (Rex v. Davies). (1927) *Justice of Peace, 91*, 806-808.

(Killing)

Killing no murder? (1925, Feb.) *Spectator, 114*, 232.

(Homicide - Definition)

Hitchler, W.H. (1924) The new definition of murder in the first degree. *Dickinson Law Review, 29*, 63.

(Homicide - Definition)

Defining the crime of murder. (1921) *Journal of Criminal Law, 12*, 121-123.

(Homicide - Classification)

Dykes, D.O. (1912) Classification of homicide - a study in comparative law *American Law Review, 47*, 528; *Jurid Law Review, 24*, 177

History

(Fatal Diplomacy)

Frey, L., & M. (1990, August) Fatal diplomacy, 1541. *History Today, 40*, p. 10-15.

(Homicide - Politics)

Weisberger, B.A. (1990, July) The stolen election. *American Heritage, 41*(5), pp. 18-20.

(French Revolution)

Von Kuehnelt-Leddin, E. (1990, July 14) Reflections on the terror. *National Review, 41*(13), pp. 38, 40.

(Race Riot)

Nossiter, A. (1990, March 12) The case that refuses to die (G. Tyler, convicted of fatally shooting white boy during 1914 race riot in Destrehan, LA). *The Nation, 250*, 337-341.

(Assassination - Algiers)

McCully, W.C., Jr. (1990) Social Sciences -- History: Assassination in Algiers. *Library Journal, 115*(14), 236.

(Infanticide)

Hansen, E.D.R. (1990) 'Overlaying' in 19th-century England: Infant mortality or infanticide? *Human Ecology, 7*(4), 333-352.

(Appalachian Murders)

Gorn, E.J. (1990) Reviews of books: Feud. *American Historical Review, 95*(1), 266-267.

(Homicide - 19th Century)

Smith, B.A. (1990) Homicide in a nineteenth century rural community: The Talbot/Bell case of

1879. *Deviant Behavior, 11*(1), 17-43.

(Civil Rights)

Dray, P. (1989, Nov.) Back on the bus. *Mother Jones, 14*(9), pp. 37-39+.

(Soviet Executions)

All present and accounted for. (1989, April 24) *US News and World Report, 106*(16), p. 20.

(Murder in USSR)

Williamson, C., Jr. (1989, March 24) The right books. *National Review, 41*(5), p. 48.

(Mackenzie River Murders)

Foster, H., et al. (1989) Sins against the great spirit: The law, the Hudson Bay Co., and the Mackenzie River murders, 1835-1839. *Criminal Justice History: An International Annual, 10*, 23-76.

(Serial Murder)

Jenkins, P. (1989) Serial murder in the United States, 1900-1940: A historical perspective. *Journal of Criminal Justice, 17*(5), 377-392.

(Homicide - Athenian Law)

MacDowell, D.M. (1983) *Athenian homicide law in the age of the orators.* Manchester.

(Homicide - West Germany)

Monson, R.A. (1982) West German statute of limitations on murder: A political, legal, and historical exposition. *American Journal of Comparative Law, 30*, 605-625.

(Homicide - History)

Powell, E. (1981) Society and homicide in 13th-century England - J.B. Given - book review. *Michigan Law Review, 79*(4), 967.

(Homicides - Historical)

Part II: Notorious homicides through history. (1979) *Law Enforcement News, 5*(6), 8.

(Homicide - Historical)

Low murder clearance record has historical roots. (1979) *Law Enforcement News, 5*(5), 6, 14.

(Homicide - Historical)

McKee, C. (1978) Fantasies of mutiny and murder: A suggested psycho-history of the seamen in the United States Navy, 1798-1815. *Armed Forces & Society, 4*(2), 293-304.

(Homicide - India - Historical)

Thakur, U. (1978) *Introduction to homicide in India: Ancient and early medieval period.* South Asia Books.

(Homicide - Historical)

Wasserman, I.M. (1978) Religious affiliations and homicide: Historical results from the rural

South. *Journal of Sci Stud Relig, 17*, 415.

(Victorian Murderesses)

Hartman, M.S. (1977) *Victorian murderesses: A true history of thirteen respectable French and English women accused of unspeakable crimes.* Schocken.

(Fingerprints)

Lambourne, G.T.C. (1977) A brief history of fingerprints. *Journal of Forensic Science and Society, 17*(2-3), 95-98.

(Society and Homicide)

Given, J.B. (1977) *Society and homicide in 13th-century England.* Palo Alto, CA: Stanford Press.

(Violent Death)

Hanawalt, B.A. (1976) Violent death in fourteenth- and early fifteenth-century England. *Comparative Studies in Society and History, 18*(3), 297-320.

(Classic Crimes)

Roughead, W.N. (1975) *Classic crimes: A selection from works of William Roughead made by W.N. Roughead.* Hyperion.

(Parricide)

Foucault, M. (1975) *I, Pierre Reviere, having slaughtered my mother, my sister, and my brother: A case of parricide in the nineteenth century.* Pantheon.

(Historical Enigmas)

Williamson, H.R. (1974) *Historical Enigmas.* St. Martin.

(Homicide - Historical)

McCord, C.P. (1973) Some ancient mysteries reexplored, 3. Grigori Yehmovich Rasputin. *Journal of Occupational Medicine, 15*, 530.

(Infanticide - Historical)

Sinkulova, L. (1973) Infant mortality and infanticide in history. *Cesk Pediatr, 28*, 93-95.

(Murder - Witchcraft)

Marshburn, J.H. (1972) *Murder and witchcraft in England, 1550-1640: As recounted in pamphlets, ballads, broadsides, and plays.* Norman, OK: University of Oklahoma Press.

(Historical Concepts)

Green, T.A. (1972) Societal concepts of criminal liability for homicide in medieval England. *Speculum, 47*, 669-694.

(Homicide - Historical)

Altick, R.D. (1970) *Victorian studies in scarlet.* New York: Norton.

(Homicide - Historical)

Bawden, C.R. (1969) A case of murder in 18th-century Mongolia. 8333. vol. 32, '69, pt. 1 , p. 71-90 (IBZ 1970).

(Homicide - Historical)

Hurnard, N.D. (1969) *King's pardon for homicide before 1307.* London: Oxford Press.

(Murder - Historical)

Kennaugh, R.C. (1969) *Contemporary murder.* Tri-Ocean.

(Homicide - American Fiction)

Davis, D.B. (1968) *Homicide in American Fiction, 1798-1860: A study in social values.* Ithaca, NY: Cornell Press.

(Homicide - Historical)

Jarcho, S. (1968) Malaria and murder (J. Jones, 1878). *Bulletin of the New York Academy of Medicine, 44*, 759-760.

(Homicide - Historical)

Doumer, P. (1968) Unedited documents concerning the death of President Paul Doumer (French). *Brehant J. Presse Med, 76*, 1579-1582.

(Homicide - Historical)

Kaye, J.M. (1967) The early history of murder and manslaughter. 21397. vol. 83, '67, n. 332, p. 569-601 (IBZ 1969).

(Homicide - Historical)

Kielkowski, R. (1967) Extermination of the patients of the psychiatric hospital in Kobierzyn (Polish). *Przegl Lek, 23*, 68-78.

(Homicide - Racial)

Saller, K. (1967) Racial murder and the delusion of heroism in national socialism (Polish). *Przegl Lek, 23*, 13-20.

(Criminality - Modern)

Stein, A. (1967) Zur mordkriminalitat der Gegenwart (Re: Murder criminality of the present). 24232. J. 50, '67, H. 2, S. 86-90 (IBZ 1968).

(Homicide - Historical)

Leblond, S. (1965) The anatomists and the resurrectionists in Great Britain, II. Murder for anatomy. *Canadian Medical Association Journal, 93*, 113-120.

(Homicide - Historical)

Gluckman, L. (1964) Kerempa: The psychodynamics of a 19th-century murder. *New Zealand Medical Journal, 63*, 486-491.

(Homicide)

Wellman, M.W. (1955) *Dead and gone*. Chapel Hill, NC: University of North Carolina Press.

(Homicide - Self-Defense)

Historical development of self-defense as an excuse for homicide. (1951) *Kentucky Law Journal, 39*, 469-471.

(Manslaughter - Historical)

Coldiron, W.H. (1950) Historical development of manslaughter. *Kentucky Law Journal, 38*, 527-550.

(Homicide Statutes - History)

Keedy, E.R. (1949) History of the Pennsylvania statute creating degrees of murder. *University of Pennsylvania Law Review, 97*, 759-777.

(Homicide - Ancient Athens)

Hyde, W.W. (1918) Homicide courts in ancient Athens. *University of Pennsylvania Law Review, 66*, 319.

(Homicide - Historical)

Johnson, N.E. (1906) The early history of the crime of murder. *Brief, 6*, 269.

(Homicide - Historical)

Chapin, H.G. (1906) An historic murder. *American Law, 14*, 343.

Race, Religion, Philosophy, and Ethics

(Parricide - Buddhists)

Obeyesekere, G. (1989, June) The conscience of the parricide: A study of Buddhist history. *Man, 24*, 236-254.

(Ethnic Violence)

Homicide surveillance: High risk racial and ethnic groups - blacks and Hispanics, 1970-1983. (1987) *MMWR, 36*(38), 634-636.

(Homicide - Black)

Bell, C.C. (1987) Facts about black-on-black murder. *Journal of the National Medical Association, 79*(5), 471-472.

(Victims - Forgiveness)

Black mom has special Christmas wish for her son's slayer: Freedom (M. Henry wants freedom for E. Henderson). (1986, Dec. 22) *Jet, 71*, p. 6.

(Homicide - Jennifer Levin)

S & S signs book on Jennifer Levin killing (to be written by L. Wolfe). (1986, Dec. 5) *Publishers Weekly, 230*, p. 40

(Homicide - S. Bryant)

Trippett, F. (1986, Sept. 1) Troubled karma for the Krishnas (murder of S, Bryant). *Time, 128*, p. 20.

(Autobiography - J. Harris)

Alpern, D.M. (1986, July 28) A book from the pen (J. Harris' autobiography). *Newsweek, 108*, p. 24.

(Homicide - Black)

Bell, C.C., et al. (1986) Black-on-black homicide: The National Medical Association responsibilities. *Journal of the National Medical Association, 78*(12), 1139-1141.

(Ethics)

Murder, manslaughter, and responsibility (editorial). (1986) *Ethics, 12*(1), 3-4.

(Murder Writing)

Chunko, M. (1986, Aug.) How to write a murder history. *Humanities, 7*(4), 16-18.

(Philosophic Critique)

Leiman, S.Z. (1983) Therapeutic homicide: A philosophic and Halakhic critique of Harris' 'survival lottery'. *Journal of Medical Philosophy, 8*(3), 257-267.

(Homicide - Sociogenesis)

Hansmann, H.B., et al. (1982) Population heterogeneity and the sociogenesis of homicide. *Social Forces, 61*(1), 206-224.

(Homicide - Human Side)

Danto, B.L. (1982) *The human side of homicide.* New York: Columbia Press.

(Killing with Consent)

Pannain, B., et al. (1982) *Killing with consent of the victim - criminological and medicolegal aspects of criminal and legislative policy* (Italian). Naples: Edizioni Scientifiche Italiane

(Homicide - Blacks)

Klerman, G.L. (1980) Homicide among black males: Concluding remarks. *Public Health Reports, 95*(6), 561.

(Homicide - Black)

Thomas, C.W. (1980) Homicide among black males - final observation and summary. *Public Health Reports, 95*(6), 560.

(Homicide - Blacks)

Bowman, P.J. (1980) Toward a duel-market approach to black-on-black violence. *Public Health Reports, 95*(6), 555.

(Homicide - Philosophy)

Devine, P.E. (1980) Homicide revisited. *Philosophy, 55*, 329-347.

(Violence - US)

Scott, E.M. (1979) Violence in America: Violent people and violent offenders. *International Journal of Offender Therapy, 23*(3), 197-209.

(Homicide - Ethics)

Devine, P.E. (1978) *The ethics of homicide.* Ithaca, NY: Cornell Press.

(Utilitarianism)

Henson, R.G. Utilitarianism and the wrongness of killing. *Personalist, 58*, 84-87. (1977, Jan.); *Philosophy Review, 80*, 320-337 (1971, July).

(Morality)

Sullivan, S.J. (1976) *Killing in defense of private property: The development of a Roman Catholic moral teaching, thirteenth to eighteenth centuries.* American Academy of Religion Dissertation Service.

(Morality)

Greenwell, J. (1976) Catholic inconsistency on intentional killing. Humanist, 36, 20-23.

(Murder - Muslims)

Holy war? Trouble in the Muslim community, (1973, Feb.) *Newsweek, 81*, p. 41.

(Culture of Violence)

Gastil, R.D. (1971, June) Homicide and a regional culture of violence. *American Sociological Review, 36*, 412-427.

(Homicide - Supernatural)

Williams, G.L. (1949) Homicide and the supernatural. *Connecticut Bar Journal, 23*, 159-172.

(Child-Murder)

Immsberger, A. (1937) *Social and ethical problems in child-murder* (German). R.R. Willoughby.

Studies

(Murder Attempts)

Capatno, P. (1990, July 29) The town that could not forget. *New York Times Book Review*, p. 14.

(Homicide - Race)

Eisenberg, L. (1990) Rage, rage against the dying of the light: A lament for needless death. *J Dev Behav Pediatr, 11*(2), 81-85.

(Serial Murder)

Egger, S.A. (1990) *Serial murder: An elusive phenomenon*. Praeger.

(Homicide Rates - Factors)

Starke, E. (1990) Rethinking homicide: Violence, race, and the politics of gender. *International Journal of Health Service, 20*(1), 3-26.

(TV Homicide Programs)

Collins, M. (1989, Nov. 18) Extra! Extra!: Tabloid clones invade TV. *TV Guide, 37*(46), pp. 14-16.

(Firearms Law)

Handleman, W. (1989, Oct. 2) Perspectives. *Newsweek, 114*(14), p. 15.

(Homicide - Political)

Cockburn, A. (1989, June 26) Beat the devil. *Nation, 248*(25), pp. 874-875.

(Homicide - Race)

Keil, T.J., & Vito, G.F. (1989) Race, homicide severity, and application of the death penalty: A consideration of the Barnett scale. *Criminology, 27*(3), 511-531.

(Homicide - Studies)

Maxfield, M.G. (1989) Circumstances in supplementary homicide reports: Variety and validity. *Criminology, 27*(4), 671-695.

(Journalism and Murder)

Malcom, J. (1989, March 20) The journalist and the murderer: II., the murderer. *New Yorker, 65*(5), 49-82.

(Homicide)

Eberlie, W.F. (1988) R. vs. Alfred Arthur Rouse: Address to the society in 1931. *Medical Science and the Law, 28*(4), 296-300.

(Studies - Typology)

Silverman, D.C. (1988) Blitz rape and confidence rape: A typology applied to 1,000 consecutive cases. *American Journal of Psychiatry, 145*(11), 1438-1441.

(Crime Levels)

Lea, J., et al. (1987) *Law and order: Five years on.* Enfield, UK: Centre for Criminology, Middlesex Polytechnic.

(Homicide - Analysis)

Farrell, R.A., & Swigert, V.L. (1986) Adjudication in homicide: An interpretive analysis of the effects of defendant's and the victim's social characteristics. *Journal of Crime & Delinquency, 23*(4), 349-369.

(Homicide - Race)

Welte, J.W., & Abel, E.L. (1986) Homicide and race in Erie County, NY. *American Journal of Epidemiology, 124*(4), 666-670.

(Homicide - Race)

Abel, E.L., et al. (1985) Seasonal, monthly, and day-of-week trends in homicide as affected by race and alcohol. *Alcohol Clin Exp Res, 9*(3), 281-283.

(Homicide - Depression)

Hirose, S. (1979) Depression and homicide: A psychiatric and forensic study of four cases. *Acta Psychiatr Scand, 59*(2), 211-217.

(Religious Affiliations)

Wasserman, I.M. (1978, Dec.) Religious affiliations and homicide: Historical results from the rural south. *J Sci Stud Relig, 17,* 415-418.

(Homicide - Perspectives)

Kutash, I.L., et al. (1978) *Violence: Perspectives on murder and aggression.* Jossey-Bass.

(Violence - Understanding)

Simpson, M.L. (1977) Understanding lethal violence. *Intellect, 105*, 379-380.

(Homicide Reviews)

Fox, V. (1976) Reviews from: *Canadian Journal of Criminology and Corrections, Federal Probation, 40*(2), 71-72.

(Homicide - Madness)

Lunde, D.T. (1976) *Murder and madness.* SF Books.

(Crimes of Passion)

Lester, D., & G. (1975) *Crimes of passion: Murder and the murderer.* Nelson-Hall.

(Mass Murder - Psychopathology)

Fleszar-Szumigajowa, J. (1972) Psychopathology of mass murderers (Polish with English abstract) *Psychiatr Pol, 6*, 427-432.

(Psychiatric Studies)

Bromberg, W. (1971) *The mold of murder: A psychiatric study of homicide.* Greenwood.

(Homicide - Studies)

Wolfgang, M. (1969) *Studies in Homicide*, by D.R. Cressy (Ed.) Harper.

(Homicide - American Fiction)

David, D.B. (1968) *Homicide in American fiction, 1798-1860: A study of social values.* Ithaca, NY: Cornell Press.

(Incest and Murder)

AuClair, G. (1966) Murder, incest, and enigma: Comparative study of the press (French). *Revue Francaise de Sociologie, 7*(2), 215-228.

(Mass Murder)

Walsh, M.N. (1966) A contribution to the problem of recurrent mass homicide. *Journal of the Hillside Hospital, 15*(2), 84-93.

(Murder Psychology)

Palmer, S. (1962) *Psychology of murder.* Apollo.

(Homicide - Curriculum)

Boswell, C., & Thompson, L. (1962) *Curriculum of murder.* New York: Macmillan.

(Murder Victim)

MacDonald, J.M. (1961) *Murderer and his victim.* C.C. Thomas.

(Mental Illness)

Podolsky, E. (1959) Somnambulistic homicide. *Diseases of the Nervous System, 20*, 534-536.

(Homicide - Psychological Studies)

Bromberg, W. (1951) A psychological study of murder. *International Journal of Psychoanalysis, 32*, 117-127.

Books and Book Reviews

(Murder Stories)

Eckhoff, S.S. (1990, July 10) Mama was a dart board and other stories from the morgue. *Village Voice, 35*(28), p. 19.

(Homicide - Book Review)

Walsh, D. (1990) Homicide, by M. Daly and M. Wilson (book review). *British Journal of Criminology, 30*(3), 404-405.

(Murder in Queens)

One night in Queens. (1990, March 1) *New York Times Book Review*, p. 12.

(Homicide - Black America)

Smith, A.W. (1990) Book reviews: Homicide among black Americana. *Social Forces, 68*(3), 998-999.

(Serial Murders)

Broderick, J. (1990) Reference: Hunting humans. *Library Journal, 115*(5), 86.

(Sacramento Murder)

Lindheimer, S.K. (1990) Social sciences - law and crime: Human harvest. *Library Journal, 115*(5), 102.

(Murder - Religion)

Johnson, D. (1990) The lost world of Mormons. *New York Review of books, 37*(4), 28-31.

(Homicide - Conspiracy)

Lindheimer, S.K. (1990) Social sciences: Law and crime -- The Bluegrass conspiracy. *Library Journal, 115*(4), 103.

(Female Murderers)

Stuttaford, G. (1989, Dec. 1) Nonfiction: Terrifying love. *Publisher's Weekly, 236*(9), pp. 72-73.

(Murder Story)

Stuttaford, G. (1989, Oct. 13) Nonfiction: Sudden fury. *Publisher's Weekly, 236*(15), 40.

(Murder Attempts)

Stuttaford, G. (1989, Sept. 29) Nonfiction: The billionaires boy's club. *Publisher's Weekly, 236*(56), p. 56.

(Jack the Ripper)

Stuttaford, G. (1989, Sept. 1) Nonfiction: Jack the Ripper. *Publisher's Weekly, 236*(22), p. 44.

(Review - Book)

Goetting, A. (1989, Spring) Review of Homicide by M. Daly and M. Wilson. *Journal of Criminal Law and Criminology, 80*, 369-372.

(Mass Murderer)

Toolis, K. (1989) A case of knives. *New Statesman & Society, 2*(71), 35-36.

(Homicide - Book Review)

Strahlendrof, P.W. (1989) Homicide, by M. Daly and M. Wilson (book review). *Canadian Bar Review, 68*(6), 388-394.

(Homicide - Book Review)

Maio, K. (1989) Honeymoon with murder, by C.C. Hart (book review). *Wilson Library, 63*(7), 90.

(Book Review)

Chizwick, D. (1989) Homicide, by M. Daly & M. Wilson (review). *British Journal of Psychiatry, 155*(8), 275-276.

(Homicide - USSR)

Daniels, R.V. (1989) Stalin and the Kirov murder, by R. Conquest (book review). *Problems in Communism, 38*(5), 81-86.

(Homicide - Anthropology)

Otterbein, K.F. (1988) Book Reviews: General/Theoretic Anthropology. *American Anthropologist, 90*(4), 995-996

(Homicide - Review)

Beck, J.C. (1988) Book reviews. *New England Journal of Medicine, 319*(8), 524.

(Homicide - Review)

Maio, K. (1988) The bottom line is murder, by R. Eversz (book review). *Wilson Library, 63*(2), 82-83.

(Homicide - Encyclopedia)

Wilson, C., & Seaman, D. (1985) *The encyclopedia of modern murder, 1962-1982.* New York: Putnam.

(Review)

Cuomo, M.M. (1984) A fate worse than death. *Corrections Digest, 15*(11), 4. Microforms and article copies available from UMI.

(Homicide - General)

Moore, B. (1980) *From darkness to light.* Carlton.

(Homicide Story)

Danielson, L. (1979, July) Folklore and film: Some thoughts on Baughman. *Western Folklore, 38*, pp. 209-219.

(Homicide - General)

Buchanan, E.C. (1979) *Three years of murder.* Dutton.

(Review)

King, D.P. (1979) Book reviews. *Law Enforcement News, 5*(8), 12.

(Police Discretion)

Lundman, R.J. (1979) Organizational norms and police discretion: An observational study of police work with traffic law violators *Criminology, 17*(2), 159-171.

(Review)

Castro, I.M. (1978) Book review. *American Journal of Criminal Law, 6*(3), 349-350.

(Review)

McLeod, J. (1978) Book reviews. *International Journal of Criminology and Penology, 6*(4), 395-397.

(Homicide - General)

Christian, N. (1978) *Homicide zone four.* NAL.

(Murder Tales)

Ruotolo, A.K. (1978) *Murder & other fairy tales.* G & D.

(Murder Tales)

Sadler, E.J. (1977) *Murder in the afternoon.* Grand Rapids, MI: Zondervan.

(Reviews)

Recent books. (1977)*Police Journal, 50*(4), 401.

(Homicide - Money)

Thompson, T. (1977) *Blood & money.* New York: Dell.

(Review)

Fattan, E.A. (1977) Deterrence: A review of the literature. *Canadian Journal of Criminology and Corrections, 19*(2), 1-119.

(Review)

Gitchoff, G.T. (1977) Book reviews. *The Journal of Criminal Law and Criminology, 68*(1), 168-169.

(Review)

Books received and briefly noted. (1976) *Criminal Law Bulletin, 12*(3), 381-383.

(Reviews)

D'Amore, A.R.T. (1976) Book reviews. *Victimology, 1*(3), 468-469.

(Classic Crimes)

Roughead, W. (1975) *Classic crimes: A selection from works of William Roughead made by W.N. Roughead.* Hyperion.

(Criminology)

Wallace, W.S. (1975) *Murders and mysteries: A Canadian series.* Hyperion.

(Homicide - Books)

Gettinger, S. (1975) Books. *Corrections Magazine, 2*(6), 53.

(Reviews)

Lawder, L.E. (1975) Book reviews. *Law and Order, 23*(7), 63-65.

(Jack the Ripper)

Rumbelow, D. (1975) *The complete Jack the Ripper.* NYGS.

(Homicide - Manson)

Bugliosi, V., & Gentry, C. (1975) *Helter Skelter.* New York: Bantam.

(Murder Book)

Murder and the murderer. (1975) Nelson-Hall.

(Murderer - Child)

Adams, K.A. (1974) The child who murders: A review of theory and research. *Criminal Justice and Behavior, 1*(1), 51-61.

(Address - A. Hitchcock)

Hitchcock, A. (1974) Mr. Hitchcock's address to the Film Society of Lincoln Center, New York, on the 29th of April, 1974. *Film Comment, 10*(34), p. 5.

(Homicide - Review)

Lester, D. (1973) Murder: A review. *Corrective & Social Psychiatry & Journal of Applied Behavior Therapy, 19*(4), 40-50.

(Crimes of Violence)

Bailey, F.L., & Rothblatt, H.B. (1973) *Crimes of violence: Homicide and assault.* Lawyer's Co-op.

(Fourth Estate)

Deeley, P., & Walker, C. (1973) *Murder in the fourth estate.* McGraw.

(Ability to Kill)

Ambler, E. (1971) *Ability to kill.* NAL.

(Homicide - Casebook)

Wilson, C. (1970) *Casebook of murder.* Cowles.

(Homicide - U.S.)

Brearley, H.C. (1969) *Homicide in the United States.* Patterson-Smith.

(Homicidal Threats)

MacDonald, J.M. (1968) *Homicidal threats.* C.C. Thomas.

(Murder in Fiction - Social)

Davis, D.B. (1968) *Homicide in American fiction, 1798-1860: A study in social values.* Cornell Press.

(Homicide - Letter)

Szondi, L. (1968, Spring) A letter to Theodor Reik. *Amer Imago, 25,* pp. 21-26.

(Violence - Study)

Wolfgang, M.E., & Ferracuti, F. (1967) *Subculture of violence: Towards an integrated theory in criminology.* B&N.

(Murder - Novel)

Capote, T. (1966) *In cold blood.* New York: Random House.

(Factbook)

Dublin, L.I. (1965) *Factbook on man from birth to death.* New York: Macmillan.

(Murder - General)

Watters, B. (1964) *The astrologer looks at murder.* Arcane Books.

(Homicide Book)

McComas, J.F. (1962) *Graveside companion.* Astor-Honor.

(Homicide - Book)

Shew, E.S. (1961) *Companion to murder.* New York: Knopf.

(Homicide - Victims)

MacDonald, J.M. (1961) *Murderer and his victim.* C.C. Thomas.

(Homicide - Review)

Lowe, J.T. (1958) Murder and the reasonable man. *Criminal Law Review, 1958,* 453.

(Homicide Book)

Wellman, M.W. (1955) *Dead and gone.* Chapel Hill, NC: UNC Press.

(Murder - General)

Wertham, F. (1949) *Show of violence.* Greenwood.

(Shocking Crimes)

Hirsch, R. (1949) *Crimes that shook the world.* Books for Libraries.

(Murder - Unconscious)

Lehrman, P.R. (1937) Uber einige unbewusste komponenten beim mord (Some unconscious components of murder). *Int Z Psychoanal, 23*, 527-535.

(Homicide - Manslaughter)

Manslaughter - dangerous animals. *Just P, 96*, 198-199.

(Homicide - Blacks)

Brearley, H.C. (1930) The Negro and homicide. *Social Forces, 9*, 247-253.

(Murder Stories)

Pearson, E. (1926) *Murder at Smutty Nose and other murders.* Arden Library.

(Homicide in Novels)

Duke, W. (1926) Homicide in novels. *Jurid Rev, 38*, 271.

Chapter 2
Statistics
By People

(Homicide Data)

Fingerhut, L.A. & Kleinman, J.C. (1990) International and interstate comparisons of homicide among young males. *JAMA: The Journal of the American Medical Association, 263*(24), 3292-3295.

(Urban Homicide)

McLain, P.D. (1989) Urban black neighborhood environment and homicide: A research note on a decade of change in four cities--(1970-1980). *Bibl Urban Afr Q, 24*: 584-596.

(Life Years Lost)

Sienko, D.G., et al. (1989) Impact of homicide on years of potential life lost in Michigan's black population. *JAMA: The Journal of the American Medical Association, 261*(5), 686-687.

(Southern - Homicide)

Commentary and debate (1989) *American Journal of Sociology, 95*(1), 174-182.

(Workplace Violence)

Goerth, C.R. (1988) Violence in the workplace emerges as growing health and safety problem, *Occup Health Saf, 57*(5), 53.

(Premature Mortality)

Premature mortality due to homicides--United States, 1968-1985. (1988) *MMWR, 37*(35) ,543-545.

(Migrants - Violent Deaths)

Shai, D. et al. (1988) Violent deaths among Mexican, Puerto Rican and Cuban born migrants in the United States. *Soc Sci Med, 26*(2), 269-276.

(Black Homicide)

O'Carroll, P.W. (1988) Homicides among black males 15-24 years of age. (1970-1984).

MMWR CDC Surveill Summ, 37(1), 53-60.

(Elderly Offender)

Chressanthis, G.A. (1988) Criminal homicide and the elderly offender: A theoretical and empirical analysis. *Journal of Quantitative Criminology, 4*(2), 187-199.

(Undocumented Aliens - Crime)

Wolf, D. (1988) *Undocumented aliens and crime: the case of San Diego county.* University of California, San Diego, CA: Center of U.S. - Mexican Studies.

(Hispanic Men)

Kraus, J.F., et al. (1988) *Research conference on violence and homicide in Hispanic communities. September 14 and 15, 1987.* Los Angeles: UCLA Press.

(Homicide - Black Women)

Mann, C.R. (1987) Black women who kill. In R.L. Hampton (Ed.), *Violence in the black family: Correlates and consequences,* (157-186). Lexington, MA: Heath.

(Children - Homicide Patterns)

Paulson, J.A., et al. (1986) Violent death in children in a metropolitan county: changing patterns of homicide, 1958-1982. *Pediatrics, 78*(6), 1013-1020.

(Victims --Blood Types)

Lester, D. (1986) Distribution of blood types in a sample of homicide victims. *Psychological Reports, 58*(3), 802.

(Police Killings)

Another decline recorded in police officer killings. (July 1985) *FBI Law Enf Bull, 54*(7), 25.

(Crime Rise)

Rise in crime. (1985) *FBI Law Enf Bull, 54*(11), 20.

(Elderly Homicide)

Gibbs, T., et al. (1984) Homicide in the elderly population in South Carolina, 1970-1979. *J SC Med Assoc, 80* (1), 25-27.

(Crime Statistics)

Preliminary crime statistics. (1984) *FBI Law Enf Bull, 53*(12), 8.

(Youth - Deaths)

Violent deaths among persons 15 to 24 years of age-- United States. (1983). *JAMA, 250*(23), 3147-3148.

(Urban Homicide Rate)

Messner, S.F. (1983) Regional differences in the economic correlates of urban homicide rate: Some evidence on the importance of cultural context. *Criminology: An Interdisciplinary*

Journal, 21(4), 477-488.

(Pediatric Homicide Rate)

Jason, J., et al. (1983) Homicide as a cause of pediatric mortality in the United States. *Pediatrics, 72*(2), 191-197.

(Black Female Offenders)

McLain, P.D. (1982) Black female homicide offenders and victims: Are they from the same population? *Death Educ, 6*(3), 265-278.

(Officers Slain)

Decrease in number of officers slain. (1981) *FBI Law Enf Bull, 50*(10), 70.

(News Conference)

Haig, A.M., Jr. (1981) Secretary's news conference of October 7. *Dept. State Bull, 81*(2056), 66-71.

(Victims - Women)

Humphrey, J.A., et al. (1981-1982) Women who are murdered: An analysis of 912 consecutive victims. *Omega, 12*(3), 281-288.

(Karanga, Zimbabwe)

Aschwanden, R. (1981) Reality and symbolism of a murder according to the presentation/interpretation of Karanga (Zimbabwe). 38593. bd. 105: 81, h 1-2, s.125 ff (I.B.Z. 1982)

(Victimization - Statistics)

Akiyama, Y. (1981) Murder victimization: a statistical analysis. *FBI Law Enforcement Bull, 50*(3), 8-11.

(Capital Punishment - Effects)

Wasserman, I.M. (1981) Non-deterrent effect of executions on homicide rates. *Psychological Reports, 48*(1), 137-138.

(Black Child Killers)

Atlanta Murders (black child killers). (1980, Dec. 28) *Time, 116*, p. 28.

(Plot Against Blacks)

National plot to kill blacks? (1980, Nov. 7) *U.S. News, 89*, p. 7.

(Homicide - Black Children)

Lowther, W. (1980, Nov. 3) Murder the little children (crimes against blacks). *Macleans, 93*, pp. 43-44.

(Black Drug Abuse)

Homicide among black males: Highlights of the symposium sponsored by the alcohol, drug abuse, and mental health administration, Washington, D.C., May 13-14, 1980. (1980) *Pub Health Rep, 95*(6), 549-561.

(Data Collection)

Riedel, M. & Brown, J. (1980) Perils and pitfalls of systems that collect data on homicide. *Pub Health Rep, 95*(6), 552.

(NCHS Perspective)

Rice, D.P. (1980) Homicide from the perspective of NCHS statistics on blacks. *Pub Health Rep, 95*(6), 550-552.

(Black Males)

Thomas, C.W. (1980) Homicide among black males. Final observations and summary. *Public Health Rep, 95*(6), 560-561.

(Blacks - Costs)

Dennis, R.E. (1980) Homicide among black males. Social costs to families and communities. *Public Health Rep, 95*(6), 556-557.

(Black on Black Homicide)

Bowman, P.J. (1980) Toward a dual labor-market approach to black-on-black homicide. *Public Health Rep, 95*(6), 555-556.

(Black Males)

Homicide among black males. (1980) Highlights of the symposium sponsored by the alcohol, drug abuse, and mental health administration. *Public Health Rep, 95*(6), 549-561.

(Blacks - Causal Factors)

Akbar, N. (1980) Homicide among black males. Causal factors. *Public Health Rep, 95*(6), 554-556.

(Blacks - NCHS)

Rice, D.P. (1980) Homicide from the perspective of NACHS statistics on blacks. *Pub Health Rep, 95*(6), 550-551.

(Homicide - Black Males)

Sharman, P. (1980) Homicide among black males. *Pub Health Rep, 95*(6), 549.

(Bride Burnings)

Niesewand, P. (1979, July 16) Good man can be expensive to find; bride-burnings as a result of Indian dowry system. *Macleans, 99*(44), p. 16.

(Middle/Upper Class Patterns)

Green, E., & Wakefield, R.P. (1979) Patterns of middle and upper class homicide. *J Crim L, 70*, 172-181.

(Historical Trials)

Schuh, C. (1979) Justice on the northern frontier: Early murder trials of native accused. *Crim L Q, 22,* 74-111.

(Black-on-Black)

Jeff, M.F.E., Jr. (1979) *A study of black perceptions: A community survey on black-on-black homicides.* New Orleans: Tulane University School of Social Work.

(Prison - Patterns)

Wolfson, W.P. (1978) *The patterns of prison homicide.* University of Pennsylvania, 304p.

(Prison Homicide)

Sylvester, S., et al. (1977) In C. Chambers (ED.) *Prison homicide.* Spectrum.

(Canadian Indians)

Jilek, W. & Roy, C. (1976) Homicide committed by Canadian Indians and non-Indians. *Int J Offend Therapy 20,* No. 3, 201-216.

(Epidemiology - Homicide)

Herjanic, M. & Meyer, D.A. (1976) Notes on epidemiology of homicide in an urban area. *Forens Sci, 8*(3), 235-245.

(Regional/Cultural Homicide)

Bailey, W.C. (1976) Some further evidence on homicide and a regional culture of violence. *Omega: Journal of Death and Dying, 7*(2), 145-170.

(Cultural Blindness)

Shiloh, A. (1975) Psychological anthropology: A case study in culture blindness? *Current Anthropology, 16*(4), 618-620.

(Life Expectancy)

Vigderhous, G. (1975) Suicide and homicide as causes of death and their relationship to life expectancy: a cross-cultural comparison. *Soc Biol, 22*(4), 338-343.

(Eskimos - Patterns)

Bloom, J.D. (1975) Patterns of Eskimo homicide. *Bull Am Acad Psychiatry Law, 3*(3), 165-174.

(Anthropology of Homicide)

Thompson, S.I. (1975) Torture and execution of surrogate kinsmen in two societies: the Ainu and the Tupinamba. *J Soc Psychol, 95* (First Half), 19-26.

(Cultural Factors)

Loftin, C. & Hill, R.H. (1974) Regional subculture and homicide: An examination of the Gastil-Hackney thesis. *American Sociological Review, 39*(5), 714-724.

(Regional Factors)

Bailey, William C. (1974) Homicide and a regional culture of violence: Some further evidence. In M. Reidel & T.P. Thornberry (Eds.), *Crime and delinquency: Dimensions of deviance*. New York: Praeger.

(Psychiatric Epidemiology)

Shore, J.H. (1974) Psychiatric epidemiology among American Indians. *Psychiatric Annals, 4*(11), 56-66.

(Patterns of Violence)

Cameron, J.M. (1973) Changing patterns in violence. *Med Sci Law, 13*, 261-264.

(Genocide)

Hughes, B.R. (1973) Abortion: Perception and contemporary genocide myth: A comparative study among low-income pregnant black and Puerto Rican women. *Dissertation Abstracts International, 34*(6-A), 3542-3543.

(Amok Violence)

Westermeyer, J. (1973) On the epidemicity of Amok violence. *Arch Gen Psychiatry, 28*, 873-876.

(Sex Differences)

Lester, D. (1973) Sex differences in the homicide rate. *Psychol Rep, 33*, 250.

(Homicide/Suicide Trends)

Hirsch, C.S., et al. (1973) Homicide and suicide in the metropolitan county: I. Long-term trends. *JAMA: Journal of the American Medical Association, 223*(8), 900-905.

(Genocide - Birth Control)

Weisbord, R.G. (1973) Birth control and the black American: A matter of genocide? *Demography, 10*(4), 571-590.

(Violence - Society)

Palmer, S. (1972) *The Violent Society*. College & University Press.

(Subculture of Violence)

Moran, R. (1971) Criminal homicide: External restraint and sub-culture of violence. *Criminology, 8*(4), 357-374.

(Ghetto Violence)

Poussaint, A.F. (1970, Oct.) Why blacks kill blacks: Psychiatrist on ghetto violence. *Ebony, 25*, pp. 143-146.

(Navajo Homicide)

Levy, J., et al. (1969) Navajo criminal homicide. *Southwestern Journal of Anthropology, 25*(2),

124-152.

(Homicide - Subculture)

Wolfgang, M.E. & Ferracuti, F. (1967) Subculture of violence. *Towards an Integrated Theory in Criminology.* B & N.

(Maya Indian)

Nash, J. (1967) Death as a way of life: the increasing resort to homicide in a Maya Indian community. *American Anthropologist, 69*(5), 455-470.

(Homicide/Suicide)

Palmer, S. (1965) Murder and suicide in 40 non-literate societies. *Journal of Criminal Law, Criminology & Police Sci, 56*(3), 320-324.

(Arab Customs)

Canaan, T. (1964) . (Murder in the customs and morals of Arabs in Jordan). *38566* Bd. 80, 85-98.

(Western Tradition)

Wolin, S.S. (1963) Violence and the western political traditional *Amer. J Orthopsychiatry, 33,* 15-28.

(Black Homicide)

Pettigrew, T.F. & Spier, R.B. (1962) Ecological pattern of Negro homicide. *Amer. J Sociol, 67*(6), 621-629.

(Homicide - Subculture)

Wolfgang, M.E., & Ferracuti, F. (1961) (The Sub-culture of Violence: An Interpretive Analysis of Homicide). *R. Cienc Soc, 5*(2), 167-178.

(Victims - Children)

Adelson, L. (1961) Slaughter of the innocents: A study of forty-six homicides in which the victims were children. *New Engl J Med, 264,* 1345-1349.

(Homicide - Personality Disorder)

Parker S. (1960) The Wiitiko psychosis in the context of Ojibwa personality and culture. *Amer. Anthrop 62,* 603-623.

(Homicide - Urban)

Bensing, R.C., & Schroeder, O., Jr. (1960) *Homicide in an urban community.* C.C. Thomas.

(Urban Homicide)

Bullock, H.A. (1955) Urban homicide in theory and fact. *J. Crim Law Criminol, 45,* 565-575.

(Homicide - Westermark Society)

Munksgaard, E. *The Westermark Society, Transactions of the Westermark Society., Vol.*

II (1953); *The Westermark Society, transactions of the Werstermark Society, Vol. 1* (1947).

(Multiple Murder)

Berne, E. (1950) Cultural aspects of a multiple murder. *Psychiat. Quart. Suppl., 24,* 250-269.

(Homicide - Research Notes)

Garfinkel, H. (1949) Research note on inter- and intra-racial homicides. *Social Forces, 27,* 369-381.

(Criminality - Old Age)

Pollack, O. (1944) A statistical investigation of the criminality of old age. *J. Crim Psychopath, 5,* 745-767.

(Murderers)

Frankel, E. (1939) One thousand murderers. *J Crim Law, 29,* 672-688.

(Black Homicide)

Brearley, H.C. (1930) Negro and homicide. *Social Forces, 9,* 247-253.

(Church Membership)

Miner, J.R. (1929) Church membership and the homicide rate. *Human Biol, 1,* 562-564.

Statistics
By Place/U.S. Data

(Homicide - Trends)

Homicide. (1990) *Canadian Social Trends,* pp. 14-17

(U.S. Data)

Rokaw, W.M., et al. (1990) Comparing death certificate data with FBI crime reporting statistics on U.S. homicides. *Public Health Rep. 105*(5), 447-455.

(New York City Homicide)

Barrett, W. (1990, Oct. 2) Panic and the police panacea. *Village Voice, 35* (40), 11-12.

(Great Britain - Patterns)

Scott, K.W.M. (1990) Homicide patterns in the West Midlands. *Medicine, Science and the Law, 30,* 234-238.

(Contemplating Murder)

Brittan, D. (1990) Contemplating murder. *Technology Review, 93*(4), pp. 13-14.

(Drugs in Washington, DC)

Cassidy, J. (1989) War among Washington's blacks. *World Press Review, 36,*(5), 34.

(Homicide - US/Canada)

Lenton, R.L. (1989) Homicide in Canada and the U.S.A. - a critique of the Hagan thesis. *Can J Soc, 14*(2),163-178.

(Homicide Rates)

Smith, E., & Wong, S.K. (1989) Duskheim, individualism and homicide rate reexamined. *Sociol Spec., 9*(3),269-283.

(Urban/Rural Homicide)

Riddick, L., et al. (1989) Homicide in Alabama: An analysis of urban, suburban, and rural murders in the deep south. *Forensic Sci Int, 40*(2), 105-122

(Societal Statistics)

Messner, S.F. (1989) Economic distribution and societal homicide rates: Further evidence on the cost of inequality. *American Sociological Review, 54*(4), 597-611.

(Homicide - California)

Homicide in California, 1988. (1989) California Dept. of Justice Bur of Criminal Stats. and Special Services.

(Homicide - US vs. Canada)

Hagan, J. (1989) Comparing crime and criminalization in Canada and the U.S.A. *Canadian Journal of Sociology/Cahiers Canadiens de Sociologie, 14*(3), 361-371.

(Urban Homicide)

Barnett, A., & Schwartz, E. (1989) Urban homicide: Still the same. *Journal of Quantitative Criminology, 5*(1), 83-100.

(Hagan Thesis)

Lenton, R.L. (1989) Homicide in Canada and the U.S.A.: A critique of the Hagan thesis. *Canadian Journal of Sociology/Cahiers Canadiens de Sociologie, 14*(2), 163-178.

(Homicide - National)

Rokaw, W.M., et al. (1989) Comparability and utility of national homicide data from death certificates and police records. *Stat Med,8*(3), 390.

(Homicide - Western U.S.)

O'Carroll, P.W. & Mercy, J.A. (1989) Regional variation in homicide rates: Why is the west so violent? *Violence Victims, 4*(1), 17-25.

(Homicide - Canada)

Kennedy, L.W., et al (1988) Homicide from east to west: A test of the impact of culture and economic inequality on regional trends violent crime in Canada. *Edmonton, CAN: Center for Criminological Research,* 17p (Discussion Paper).

(Homicide - Yorkshire and Humberside)

Perry, M.J., et al (1988) Changing patterns of homicide in Yorkshire and Humberside. *Med Sci Law, 28*(3), 252-255.

(Homicide - New Orleans)

Lowry, P.W. et al. (1988) Homicide victims in New Orleans: Recent trends. *Am J Epidemiology, 128*(5), 1130-1136.

(Homicide Rates)

McCall, P.L. (1988) Social correlates of homicide and burglary rates for states, SMSA's and cities: A macro level analysis of 1960, 1970, and 1980. *Dissertation Abstracts International, A: The Humanities and Social Sciences, 49*(3), 626-A. Available from UMI.

(Homicide - Workplace)

Davis, H. (1988) The accuracy of industry data from death certificates for workplace homicide victims. *Am J Public Health, 78*(12), 1579-1581.

(Homicide - Atlanta)

Hanzlick, R., et al (1987) Demographics of Atlanta's homicide epicenter, 1984. *J Med Assoc Ga, 76*(12), 825-832.

(Homicide - U.S.)

Holinger, P.C., et al. (1987) Suicide and homicide in the United States: An epidemiologic study of violent death, population changes, and the potential for prediction. *American Journal of Psychiatry, 144*(2), 215-219.

(Homicide - Cities)

Perry, J.D., & Simpson, M.E. (1987) Violent crimes in a city: Environmental determinants. *Environment & Behavior, 19*(1), 77-90.

(Homicide - Statistics)

Loftin, C. (1986) The Validity of Robbery - Murder Classifications in Baltimore. *Violence and Victims, 1*(3), 191-204

(Homicide - Manhattan)

Tardiff, K., et al. (1986) A study of homicides in Manhattan, 1981. *Am. J. Public Health, 76*(2), 139-143.

(Homicide - U.S.)

Crime in the United States, 1985. (1986) *FBI Law Enf. Bull, 55*(9), 9-12.

(Homicide - Preliminary Statistics)

Preliminary crime statistics for 1985. (1986) *FBI Law Enf Bull, 55*(7), 15.

(Miami)

Two FBI agents killed, five wounded in Miami shootout. (1986) *Crime Control Digest, 20*(15), 10. Microforms and article copies available from UMI.

(Gary and Detroit)

Gary, Detroit top FBI's list of 25 deadliest cities list. (1985, Aug. 19) *Jet, 68*, p. 6.

(Homicide - US)

Gregory, M.C. (1985) Comparing U.S. and other homicide rates (letter). *West J Med, 143*(3), 389-390.

(Homicide - Chicago)

Block, C.R. (1985) Race/ethnicity and patterns of Chicago homicide 1965 to 1981. *Crime and Delinquency, 31*(1), 104-116, Charts and graphs. Microforms and article copies available from UMI.

(Homicide - U.S. Crime)

Crime in the United States 1984. (1985) *FBI Law Enf. Bull, 54*(9), 13-16.

(Homicide - Determinants)

Tardiff, K. (1985) Patterns and major determinants of homicide in the United States. *Hospital & Community Psychiatry, 36*(6), 632-639.

(Homicide U.S.)

Crime in the United States, 1983. (1984) *FBI Law Enf Bull, 53*(10), 15-18.

(Homicide - Florida)

Wilbanks, W. (1984) *Murder in Miami: An analysis of homicide patterns and trends in Dade county (Miami) Florida, 1917-1983*. Univ. Pr.

(Homicide - Urban)

Messner, S.F. (1983) Regional and racial effects on the urban homicide rate: The subculture of violence revisited. *American Journal of Sociology, 88*(5), 997-1007.

(Homicide - U.S.)

Jason, J., et al. (1983) A comparison of primary and secondary homicides in the United States. *American Journal of Epidemiology. 117*(3), 309-319.

(Homicide - U.S.)

Jason, J. et al. (1983) Epidemiological characteristics of primary homicides. *American Journal of Epidemiology, 117*(4), 419-428.

(Homicide - California)

Homicide in California, 1982. (1983) Prepared by the Division of Law Enforcement.

(Rape-Murders)

Ressler, R.K. (1983) Rape and rape-murder: One offender and twelve victims. *Am J Psychiatry, 140*(1), 36-40.

(Police Killings)

Wiessler, D.A. (1983) When police officers use deadly force. *U S News World Rep, 94*, p. 58-59.

(Homicide - U.S.)

Homicide - United States. (1982) *MMWR, 31*(44), 594, 600-602.

(Homicide - U.S.)

Crime in the United States stabilizes. (1982) *FBI Law Enforcement Bulletin, 51*(11), 12-15.

(Homicide - Prisons)

Lester, D. (1982) Suicide and homicide in U.S. prisons (letter). *Am J Psychiatry, 139*(11), 1527-1528.

(Homicide - Urban)

Messner, S.F. (1982) Poverty, inequality, and the urban homicide rate: Some unexpected findings. *Criminology: An Interdisciplinary Journal, 20*(1), 103-114.

(Homicide - Urban)

Smith, A. (1982, March) Why we are preyed upon (urban crime). *Esquire, 97*, p. 9.

(Homicide - El Salvador)

Whose figures? (1982, March) *Nation*, 234, p. 324-325.

(Homicide - Brazil)

Jorge, M.H. (1982) Mortality due to violent causes in the municipality of Sao Paulo, Brazil. IV - The situation in 1980. *Rev. Saude Publica, 16*(1), 19-41.

(Homicide - Iceland)

Gudjonsson, G.H., et al. (1982) Some criminological and psychiatric aspects of homicide in Iceland. *Med Sci Law, 22*(2), 91-98.

(Homicide - Capital Punishment)

Tifft, L. (1982) Capital punishment research, policy and ethics: Defining murder and placing murderers. *Crime and Social Justice, 1*, 61-68.

(Homicide - Parricide)

Post, S. (1982) Adolescent parricide in abusive families. *Child Welfare, 61*(7), 445-455.

(Boston Murders)

Rizzo, N.D. (1982) Murder in Boston: Killers and their victims. *International Journal of Offender Therapy and Comparative Criminology, 26*(1), 36-42.

(Homicide - Crime Rise)

Preliminary 1980 figures show rise in crime. (1981) *FBI Law Enf Bull, 50*(6), 7.

(Homicide - Crime Rise)

Reported crime up 9 percent last week. (1981) *Just Assist, 2*(1), 9.

(Homicide - National)

Around the nation. (1981) *Just Assist, 2*, 1-13.

(Homicide - Police Officers)

Thomas, W.J. & Boyer, F.W. (1981) Police officer survival during traffic stops. *FBI Enf Bull, 50*(2), 1-6.

(Homicide - California)

Homicide in California, 1980. (1981) California Dept. of Justice., Div. of Law Enforcement.

(Homicide - Regional Statistics)

Smith, M.D. & Parker, R.N. (1981) Type of homicide and variation in regional rates. *Soc Forces, 59*(1), 136-147.

(Homicide - Southern States)

Ruben, E.R., et al. (1981) Homicide in five southern states: A firearms phenomenon. *South Med J, 74*(3), 272-277.

(Homicide - Blacks)

Rose, H.M. (1981) The changing spatial dimension of black homicide in American cities. *J Environ Systems, 11*(1), 57-80.

(Homicide - California)

2,334 killings reported in Los Angeles County. (1981) *Crime Control Digest, 15*(1), 10. Microforms and article copies available from UMI.

(Homicide - Atlanta)

Atlanta murders (black child killers). (1980, Dec. 1) *Time, 116*, p. 28.

(Homicide - U.S.)

Crime in the United States, 1979. (1980) *FBI Law Enf Bull, 49*(12), 14-15 D.

(Homicide - Alaska)

Wolf, A.S. (1980) Homicide and blackout in Alaskan natives: A report and reproduction of five cases. *J Stud Alcohol, 41*, (5), 456-462.

(Homicide - Crime Rise)

Crime increase continues. (1980) *FBI Law Enf Bull, 49*(7), 17.

(Homicide - Crime Rise)

Crime up again. (1980) *Just Assist, 1*(5), 1.

(Homicide - Geographical)

Lester, D. (1980) Variation in suicide and homicide by latitude and longitude. *Perceptual & Motor Skills, 51*(3.2), 1346.

(Homicide/Suicide - Statistics)

Thomson, L.G. (1980) Homicide and suicide in Africa and England. *Med Sci Law, 20*(2), 99-103.

(Homicide/Suicide/Accidents - Relationships)

Wilbanks, W. (1980) Fatal accidents, suicide and homicide: are they related? *Paper presented at the First World Congress of Victimology.*

(Homicide - Victimization)

Rajan, V.N. (1980) Crime victimization research program and policy planning in developing countries. *Victimology, 5,*(2-4), 193-200.

(Homicide - Urban)

Barnett, A, et al. (1980) Urban homicide: Some recent developments. *Crim Justice, 8*(6), 379-385.

(Patterns - Violence)

Seiden, R.H., et al. (1980) Shifting patterns of deadly violence. *Suicide Life Threat Behav, 10*(4), 195-209.

(Statistics - U.S.)

Farley, R. (1980) Homicide trends in the United States. *Population, 35*(6), 1224.

(Social Demographics)

Braithwaite, J., et al. (1980) Effect of income inequality and social democracy on homicide: A cross-national comparison. *Brit. J Criminol, 20*, 45-53.

(Urban/Rural Spread)

Fischer, C.S. (1980) Spread of violent crime from city to countryside, 1955 to 1975. *Rur Sociol, 45*, 416-434.

(Homicide - Louisiana)

Bankston, W.B. & Allen, H.D. (1980) Rural social areas and patterns of homicide: An analysis of lethal violence in Louisiana. *Rur Sociol, 45,* 223-237.

(Homicide Rate - Decline)

Detroit rejoices as murder rate falls. (1980) *Crime Control Digest, 14*(2), 9-10. Article copies available from UMI.

(Homicide - St. Louis)

1979 Murder figures put St. Louis on top. (1980) *Crime Control Digest, 14*(14), 5-6.

Microforms and article copies available from UMI.

(Homicide - St. Louis)

St. Louis still tops in murder. (1980) *Law Enforcement News, 6*(8), 3, 11.

(Homicide - New York City)

New York City begins decade with record number of murders. (1980) *Security Systems Digest, 11*(1), 8. Article copies available from UMI.

(Homicide - Oklahoma)

Atterberry, A. (1980, May) Wild West in Idabel (murder of Henry Johnson and ensuing Oklahoma race riot). *Black Enterprise, 10, p.* 17.

(Homicide - Florida)

Hiaasen, C. & Messerschmidt, A. (1979, Sept. 20) Cocaine wars: Drug organizations in Dade County, Fl. *Roll Stone*, pp. 82-85.

(Homicide - Houston)

Williams, D.A. & Henkoff, R. (1979, Aug. 27) Houston: It's like Dodge City. *Newsweek, 94, p.* 26.

(Homicide - Atlanta)

Atlanta death house. (1979, Aug. 6) *Newsweek, 94, p.* 68.

(Homicide - Pennsylvania)

It was Pennsylvania gothic; crimes of the Johnston family of Chester county. (1979, Jan.) *Time, 113*, pp. 16-17.

(Homicide - New Orleans)

Levie, R.C. (1979) *A study of criminal homicide patterns and selected characteristics of victims and offenders in the city of New Orleans, 1971-1973.* The Louisiana State University and Agricultural and Mechanical College, 212p. Supervisor: Professor J.H. Jones, Jr.

(Homicide - Missouri)

Richardson, O. (1979) Pattern criminal indictments, information, and jury instructions for Missouri - some footnotes for a treatise. *Mo B J, 35,* 18-37+.

(Homicide - Fertility Rates)

Easterlin, R.A., et al. (1979) Homicide and fertility rates in the United States: A comment. *Soc Biol, 26*(4), 341-343.

(Homicide - Crime Rise)

Rise in crime. (1979) *FBI Law Enf Bull, 48*(12), 18.

(Homicide - Atlanta)

Six new killings send Atlanta reeling again. (1979) *Crime Control Digest, 13*(43), 8-9. Article copies available from UMI.

(Homicide - Texas)

Robert, L. (1979) *Differential sentencing patterns among criminal homicide offenders in Harris County, Texas.* Sam Houston State University.

(Homicide - New York City)

Young, R. (1978, Aug. 28) Dodge City, the deadliest precinct in town: Harlem precinct. *N Y, 11,* 43-46+.

(Homicide - Atlanta)

Leviton, J. (1978, June 12) Death inside the walls: Nine murders shake Atlanta federal prison. *People Weekly, 9,* 38-41.

(Homicide - Psychosocial Study)

Totman, J. (1978) *The murderers: A psychosocial study of criminal homicide.* R & E Research Associates.

(Homicide - Corn Consumption)

Mawson, A.R. & Jacobs, K.W. (1978) Corn consumption, tryptophan, cross-national homicides rates. *Journal of Orthomolecular Psychiatry, 7*(4), 227-230.

(Homicide - U.S.)

Crime is running rampant in the U.S. (1978) *Law Enforcement Journal, 8*(10), 5, 8. Article copies available from UMI.

(Homicide - U.S.)

Godwin, J. (1978) *Murder U.S.A.* New York: Ballantine.

(Homicide - Epidemiology)

Namekata, T. (1978) An epidemiologic study of homicides in Allegheny County, Pennsylvania (letter). *Am J Epidemiology, 108*(2), 158-159.

(Homicide - New Rochelle)

Season of savagery and rage: F.W. Cowan's shooting spree in New Rochelle. (1977, Feb. 28) *Time, 109,* 23-24.

(Homicide - Patterns)

Rushforth, N.B., et al. (1977) Violent death in a metropolitan county: Changing patterns in homicide, 1958-1974. *N Engl J Med, 297*(10), 531-538.

(Homicide - Detroit)

Across the nation: Detroit goes 7 days without killing. (1977) *Crime Control Digest, 11*(13), 7. Article copies available from UMI.

(Murder - Detroit)

Across the nation: Detroit almost had full week without a murder, Dept. says. (1977) *Crime Control Digest, 11*(11), 9. Article copies available from UMI.

(Homicide - Detroit)

Zimring, F.E. (1977) Determinants of the death rate from robbery: A Detroit time study. *J Legal Studies, 6,* 317-332.

(Homicide - Houston)

Lundsgaarde, H. (1977) *Murder in Space City: A cultural analysis of Houston homicidal patterns.* Oxford Pr.

(Homicide - Epidemiology)

Costantino, J.P., et al. (1977) An epidemiologic study of homicides in Allegheny County, Pennsylvania. *Am J Epidemiology, 106*(4), 314-324.

(Homicide - Detroit)

Fisher, J.C. (1976) Homicide in Detroit: The role of firearms. *Criminology, 14*(3), 387-400.

(Homicide - Washington, D.C.)

Across the states: District of Columbia. (1976) *Juvenile Justice Digest, 4*(21), 6.

(Homicide - California)

Roberson, C.E. (1976) *Patterns of victim involvement in criminal homicide: a case study of San Francisco, California.* United States International University, Chairman: Anwar S. Dil.

(Homicide - Michigan)

Keys, E. (1976) *The Michigan murders.* Pleasantville, NY: Readers Digest Pr.

(Firearms)

Fisher, J.C. (1976) Homicide in Detroit. The role of firearms. *USA Criminology, 14*(3), 387-400.

(Homicide - New York City)

Mathieson, D. & Passell, P. (1976) Homicide and robbery in New York City: An economic model. *The Journal of Legal Studies, 5*(1), 83-98.

(Homicide - Georgia)

Munford, R.S., et al. (1976) Homicide trends in Atlanta. *Criminology, 14*(2), 213-232.

(Homicide - Los Angeles)

Los Angeles County. (1975) *Juvenile Justice Digest, 3,(*22), 6.

(Homicide - Rates)

Doerner, W.G. (1975) Regional analysis of homicide rates in the United States. *Criminology,*

13, (1), 90-101.

(Homicide - U.S.)

Murder epidemic raging in U.S. (1975) *Law Enforcement Journal, 5*, (10), 15.

(Homicide - State Statistics)

Across the states. (1975) *Corrections Digest, 6*(16), 6.

(Murderer)

Wille, W.S. (1975) *Citizens who commit murder: A psychiatric study.* Green.

(Homicide - Urban)

Barnett, A., et al.. (1975) On urban homicide: A statistical analysis. *J Crim Justice, 3*(2), 85-110.

(Homicide - Rates)

Doerner, W.G. (1975) A regional analysis of homicide rates in the United States. *Criminology: An Interdisciplinary Journal, 13*(1), 90-101.

(Homicide - Los Angeles)

Skid Row slashers. Los Angeles murders. (1975, Feb. 10) *Time, 105*, p. 18.

(Homicide - Connecticut)

Hartford, Connecticut authorities. (1975) *Juvenile Justice Digest, 3*, (6), 6.

(Homicide - Chicago)

Block, R. (1975) Homicide in Chicago: A nine year study, 1965-1973. *J Crim Law Criminol, 66*(4), 496-510.

(Homicide - Fertility)

Lyster, W.R. (1974) Homicide and fertility rates in the United States. *Soc Biol, 21*(4), 389-392.

(Homicide/Suicide)

Lester, D. (1974) A cross-national study of suicide and homicide. *Behavior Science Research, 9*(4), 307-318.

(Homicide - U.S.)

Homicide in the United States. (1974) *State Bull Metropolitan Life Ins Co, 55*, 2-4.

(Homicide - Patterns)

Curtis, L.A. (1974) *Criminal violence: National patterns and behavior.* Lexington, MA: D.C. Heath & Co.

(Homicide - California)

Farrell, B. (1974, May) California inquest. *Harper, 248*, pp. 64-66+.

(Homicide - Detroit)

And in Detroit: Three murders a day. (1974, May 6) *U.S. News, 76*, 38.

(Homicide - San Francisco)

Fear in the streets of San Francisco: Zebra attacks. (1974, April 29) *Time, 103,* 18.

(Homicide - San Francisco)

Nothing personal; street shootings in San Francisco. (1974, Feb. 11) *Newsweek, 83,* p. 26.

(Homicide - Illinois)

Felony murder in Illinois. (1974) *U Ill L R 1974,* 685-694.

(Homicide - Memphis)

Meyer, G. (1974) *The Memphis murders.* LC 73-17880. Continuum Books.

(Homicide - Criminal Violence)

Curtis, LA. (1973) Criminal violence: Inquiries into national patterns and behavior. *Dissertation Abstracts International, 33*(12-A), 7052.

(Homicide - Rates)

Lester, D. (1973) Variation in homicide rate with latitude and longitude in the United States. *Perceptual and Motor Skills, 36*(2), 532.

(Homicide - Political Stability)

Lester, D. (1973) National homicide and suicide rates as a function of political stability. *Psychol Rep, 33*(1), 298.

(Homicide - Georgia)

Felony murder in Georgia: A lethal anachronism? (1973) *Ga SB J, 9,* 462.

(Homicide - Chicago)

Harding, R.W., Fahey, R.P. (1973) Killings by Chicago police, 1969-1970: An empirical study. *So Calif L Rev, 46,* 284.

(Homicide/Suicide - New Hampshire)

Humphrey, J.A. (1973) *Homicide, Suicide, and role relationships in New Hampshire.* University of New Hampshire.

(Homicide - New York City)

Helpern, M., et al. (1972) Changing patterns of homicide in New York City. *NY State J Med, 72,* 2154-2157.

(Homicide - Regional)

Gastil, R.D. (1971) Homicide and a regional culture of violence. *American Sociological Review, 36,* 412-417.

(Homicide - New York)

Helpern, M., et al. (1971) On the evolution of methods of homicides in New York. *Med Leg Domm Corpor* (Paris), *4,* 255-257.

(Homicide - Detroit)

Boudoris, J. (1970) *Trends in homicide, Detroit, 1926-1968.* Wayne State University.

(Homicide - Big Cities)

Big city murders: Clues to why they keep rising. (1970, Feb.) *U S News, 68,* 13.

(Homicide - U.S.)

Handel, K. (1970) (Homicide in the U.S.A.). 20959, J 23. '69, 2, S. 89-90.

(Homicide - U.S.)

Brearley, H.C. (1969) *Homicide in the United States.* Patterson Smith.

(Homicide - Epidemiology)

Lester, D. (1968) National motives and psychogenic death rates. *Science, 161,* 1260.

(Homicide - Chicago)

Voss, H.L. & Hepburn, J.R. (1968) Patterns in criminal homicide and police science. *Journal of Criminal Law, Criminology & Police Science, 59*(4), 499-508.

(Homicide - Mississippi)

Huie, W.B. (1968) Three lives for Mississippi. New York: NAL.

(Homicide - Manhattan)

West, D.J. (1968) A note on murders in Manhattan. *Med Sci Law, 8,* 249-255.

(Homicide - Wisconsin)

Derleth, A. (1968) *Wisconsin murders.* Arkham.

(Homicide - U.S.)

Homicide in the United States, 1950-1964. (1967) *Vital Health Statist, 20*(6), 33.

(Homicide - U.S.)

Langberg, R. (1967) Homicide in the United States. *Vital Health Statist, 20*(1), 33.

(Homicide - Patterns)

Morland, N. (1966) Pattern of murder. *Int. Pub Service, 6,* 25.

(Homicide - Baltimore)

Norton, S.M. (1966) Homicides in Baltimore. *Maryland Med J, 15,* 52.

(Homicide - Idaho)

First and second degree murder and their distinguishing requirements in Idaho. (1965) *Idaho L Rev, 2,* 77.

(Homicide - Comparison)

Pokorny, A.D. (1965) A comparison of homicides in two cities. *J Crim Law & Criminology, 56*(4), 479-487.

(Homicide - Alabama)

Cameron, A.H., & Asher, P. (1965) Cot deaths in Birmingham, 1958-1961. *Med Sci & L, 5,* 187.

(Homicide - Texas)

Pokorny, A.D. (1965) A comparison of homicides in two cities. *J Crim Law Criminol Police Sci, 56*(4), 479-487.

(Homicide - Minnesota)

Trenerry, W.N. (1962) *Murder in Minnesota: A collection of true cases.* Minneapolis: Minn. Historical Society.

(Homicide - Study)

Nat. Life Ins. Co. (La) 134 S 2d 337 (1962) *Tulane Law Review, 36,* 579.

(Homicide - West Virginia)

Frame, C.B. (1961) Automobile deaths and involuntary manslaughter in West Virginia. *W Va L Rev, 63,* 130.

(Homicide - Rates)

Homicide rate at record low. (1955) *Statist Bull Metropolitan Life Insurance Co, 36,* 8-10.

(Homicide/Suicide - Demographics)

Porterfield, A.L. (1949) Indices of suicide and homicide by states and cities: Some southern-non-southern contrasts with implications for research. *Amer. Sociol, 14*, 481-490.

(Homicide - International)

Roesner, E. (1939) (International homicide statistics). *Mschr Krim Biol, 30,* 65-88.

(Homicide - Texas)

Stumberg, G.W. (1938) Criminal homicide in Texas. *Tex L Rev, 16*, 305-334.

(Homicide - Wisconsin)

Stern, M. (1931) Study of unsolved murders in Wisconsin from 1924 to 1928. *J Crim Law, 21,* 513-536.

(Homicide - Rates)

Miner, J.R. (1929) Nativity and parentage of the population of the United States and the homicide rate. *Human Biol, 1,* 274-278.

(Homicide - South Carolina)

Brearly, H.C. (1929, Dec.) Homicide in South Carolina: A regional study. *Social Forces, 8,* 218-221.

(Homicide - Rhode Island)

Phelps, H.A. (1928) Rhode Island's threat against murder. *J Crim L, 18,* 552-567.

(Homicide - Statistics)

O'Brien, A. (1927) Statistics of murder. *Outlook* (Lond), *60*, 669.

(Homicide - Seattle)

Schmid, C.F. (1926) Study of homicides in Seattle, 1914-1924. *Social Forces, 4,* 745-756.

(Homicide - Massachusetts)

Stearns, A.W. (1925) Homicide in Massachusetts. *Amer. J Psychiat, 4,* 725-749.

(Homicide - Comparative Study)

Forster, H.A. (1917) Why the United States leads the world in the relative proportion of murders, lynchings, and other felonies and why the Anglo-Saxon countries not under the American flag have the least proportion of murders and felonies and know no lynchings. *Cent L J, 85,* 299; *Am L Rev, 51,* 239.

(Homicide - U.S.)

Garner, J.W. (1913) Homicide in American cities. *J Crim Law, 3,* 675-677.

(Homicide - Regional)

Denslow, V.B. (1910) Homicides, American and southern. *Social Economics, 8,* 163.

(Homicide - Article)

Homicide by necessity in America. (1908) *Law Journal, 28,* 432.

(Homicide - U.S.)

Cesare, L. (1906) Why has it increased in the United States. *N A Review, 165,* 641; *166,* 1.

Statistics
By Time

(Homicide Rates)

Land, K.C., et al. (1990) Structural covariates of homicide rates: Are there any invariances across time and social space? *American Journal of Sociology*, *95*(4), 922-963.

(Homicide - Victims)

Gartner, R. (1990) The victims of homicide: a temporal and cross-national comparison. *American Sociological Review, 55*(1), 92-106.

(Homicide - Rates)

Martinez-Schnell, V. & Waxweier, R.J. (1989) Increases in premature mortality due to homicide-United States, 1968-1985. *Violence and Victims, 4*(4), 287-293.

(Homicide -Blacks)

Leads from the MMWR: Impact of homicide on years of potential life lost in Michigan's black population. (1989) *JAMA, 261*(5), 686-687.

(Homicide - Blacks)

Impact of homicide on years of potential life lost in Michigan's black population. (1989) *MMWR, 38*(1), 4-6, 11.

(Homicide - Season)

Martinez, S.B. & Waxweiler, R.J. (1989) Increases in premature mortality due to homicide, United States, 1968-1985. *Violence Victims, 4*(4), 287-293.

(Homicide - Time of Month)

Lester, D., & Frank, M.L. (1988) Homicide at the beginning of the month. *Psychol Rep, 63*, 402-410.

(Homicide - Los Angeles)

Mercy, J.A., et al. (1986) Patterns of homicide victimization in the city of Los Angeles, 1970-1979. *Bull NY Acad Med, 62*(5), 427-445.

(Homicide - Regression)

Layson, S.K. (1986) United States time-series homicide regression with adaptive expectations. *Bull NY Acad Med, 62*(5), 589-600.

(Homicide - Trends)

Abel, E.L., et al. (1985) Seasonal, monthly, and day-of-week trends in homicide as affected by alcohol and race. *Alcoholism (NY), 9*(3), 281-283.

(Homicide - Trends)

Cook, P.J. (1985) Is robbery becoming more violent? An analysis of robbery murder trends since 1968. *J Crim Law Criminol, 76*(2), 480-489.

(Homicide - U.S.)

Tardiff, K. (1985) Patterns and major determinants of homicide in the United States. *Hosp. Community Psychiatry , 36*(6), 632-639.

(Homicide - Female Victims)

Frazer M.J. (1983) The female homicide victim: Trends in a metropolitan county from 1969 to 1980. *J Forensic Sci , 28*(3), 577-587.

(Homicide Surveillance)

Mercy, J.A. (1983) Homicide surveillance, 1970-1978. *MMWR Surveill Summ, 32*(2), 9.

(Homicide - Decline)

Boor, M. (1982) Reduction in deaths by suicide, accidents and homicide prior to United States presidential elections. *Journal of Social Psychology, 118*(1), 135-136.

(Homicide - Statistics)

1980 crime statistics. (1981) *FBI Law Enf Bull , 50*(11), 12-15.

(Homicide - Statistics)

Handel, K. (1981) Homicide in the 1980 crime statistics (FRG). *Die Neue Polizet, 35*(16), 139-140.

(Homicide - Demographics)

Smith, M.D. (1980) Type of homicide and variation in regional rates. Paper presented at 55th meeting of Southwestern Sociological Assn. April 2-5, Houston, Texas.

(Homicide - Patterns)

Rushforth, N.B., et al. (1977) Violent death in a metropolitan county. Changing patterns in homicide, 1958-1974. *N Engl J Med, 297*(10), 531-538.

(Homicide - U.S.)

Schwind, H.D. (1977) The trend in homicide and robbery in the USA (Germ).*Kriminaltstik, 31*(9), 383-387.

(Homicide - Statistics)

Final 1976 crime statistics show situation stabilizing. (1977) *Juvenile Justice Digest, 5,*(19), 6-7. Article copies available from UMI.

(Homicide - Statistics)

Leveling off of crime rate rise shown by preliminary 1976 figures. (1977) *Juvenile Justice Digest, 5*(7), 3-4. Article copies available from UMI.

(Crime Decline)

Serious crime declined 9% during 1st quarter, FBI says. (1977) *Crime Control Digest, 11*(27), 2. Article copies available from UMI.

(Homicide - Statistics)

Annual murders more than double U.S. battle death's in nations first three major wars. (1976) *FBI Law Enforcement Bulletin, 45,* (4), 31.

(Homicide - Increases)

Serious crime up 10 percent in 1975, attorney general says. (1976) *Crime Control Digest, 10*(35), 1-3.

(Homicide - Increases)

Serious crime up 10 percent in 1975, attorney general says. (1976) *Narcotics Control Digest, 6*(17), 1-3.

(Homicide Rates)

Archer, D. & Gartner, R. (1976) Violent acts and violent times: A comparative approach to postwar homicide rates. *American Sociological Review, 41*(6), 937-963.

(Homicide - Increases)

Serious crime up 11 percent in first 9 months of 1975. (1976) *Security Systems Digest, 7,* (1), 4.

(Homicide - Increases)

Serious crime up 10 percent in 1975. (1976) *Corrections Digest. 7*(17), 1-3.

(Homicide - Epidemiology)

Skousen, W.C. (1975) Murder rates continue climbing. *Law and Order, 23*(5), 6.

(Homicide - Juvenile Arrests)

American crime picture worsened by 18 percent last year, juveniles under 18 led in arrests. (1975) *Juvenile Justice Digest, 3*(22), 1-4.

(Homicide - U.S.)

Klebba, A.J. (1975) Homicide trends in the United States, 1900-1974. *Public Health Rep, 90*(3), 195-204.

(Homicide - Killing Ground)

Hogan, B. (1974) Killing ground, 1964-1973. *Crim L R, 74,* 387-401.

(Homicide - Police Killings)

Police killings in 1973 - a record year. (1974) *FBI Law Enforcement Bull, 43*(4), 13-15.

(Homicide - Statistics)

Simondi, M. (1970) Data on eighty cases of homicide. *Univ. Studi Firenze,* 135.

(Homicide - Study)

Murder 1957-1968. (1970) *Modern L Rev, 33*, 302.

(Homicide - United States - Statistics)

Homicide on the uptrend. (1968) *Statist Bull Metropolitan Life Ins Co, 49*, 5-7.

(Homicide - U.S.)

Homicide in the United States, 1950-1964; a study of homicide statistics showing trends for 1950-1964 and differences for selected periods by age, sex, color, marital status, nativity, and geographic area. (1967) Public Health Service Publication, 1000, Ser. 20, no. 6.

(Homicide - Regulation)

Baumann, J. (1964) RechtmaBigkeit von Mordgeboten? (Regularity of Homicide). 25159, S 1398-1405.

(Homicide - South Carolina)

Brearly, H.C. (1929, Dec.) Homicide in South Carolina: A regional study. *Social Forces, 8*, 218-221.

Statistics
By Place - Other Countries of the World

(Homicide - Indicators)

Rattner, A. (1990) Social indicators and crime rate forecasting. *Social Indicators Research, 22*(1), 83-96.

(Homicide - International)

Fingerhut, L.A. & Kleinman, J.C. (1990) International and interstate comparisons of homicide among young males. *JAMA, 263*(24), 3292-3295.

(Homicide - Switzerland)

Ward, C. (1990) Fringe benefits. *New Statesman & Society, 3*(86), 28.

(Homicide - Nordic Countries)

Gudjonsson, G.H., et al. (1990) Homicide in the Nordic countries. *Acta Psychiatr Scand, 82*(1), 49-54.

(Homicide - England and Wales)

Edwards, S.S.M. (1989) How safe is home - an analysis of homicide statistics in England and Wales 1982-1986 (meeting abstract). *Aggr Behav , 15*(1), 51-52.

(Homicide - Denmark)

Breiting, V.B., et al. (1989) Injuries due to deliberate violence in areas of Denmark. I. The extent of violence. *Forensic Sci Int, 40*(2), 183-199.

(Homicide - Netherlands)

Van Den Eshof, P. & Bergsma, H.H. (1989) Firearms homicide targeted by the crime analysis unit of the central criminal intelligence service. Victim often in (criminal) relationship with offender. *Algemeen Politieblad, 138*(10), 219-222.

(Homicide - Colombia)

Chepesiuk, R. (1989) Fighting anarchy in Colombia. *New Leader, 72*(14), 5-8.

(Homicide - Great Britain)

Norton, R.N. & Morgan, M.Y. (1989) Mortality from interpersonal violence in Great Britain. *Injury, 20*(3), 131-133.

(Homicide - India)

Bagley, C. (1989) Urban crowding and the murder rate in Bombay, India. *Percept Mot Skills, 69*(3), 1241-1242.

(Homicide - England)

Perry, M.J. & France, G. (1988) Changing patterns of homicide in Yorkshire and Humberside. *Med Sci Law, 28*(3), 252-255.

(Homicide - Northern Ireland)

More blood on their hands. (1988, Aug.) *Time* , *132*(7), p. 27.

(Homicide - Copenhagen)

Gottlieb, P., et al. (1988) Increasing rates of homicide in Copenhagen from 1959 to 1983. *Acta Psychiatr Scand, 77*(3), 301-308.

(Homicide - South Africa)

Duflou, J.A., et al. (1988) Homicide in Cape Town, South Africa. *Am J Forensic Med Pathol, 9*(4), 290-294.

(Homicide - Japan)

Merriman, D. (1988) Homicide and deterrence: The Japanese case. *International Journal of Offender Therapy and Comparative Criminology, 32*(1), 1-16.

(Homicide - El Salvador)

El Salvador; statements. (1988) *Dept. State Bull, 81*(2047), 68-69.

(Homicide - Germany)

Boose, C. (1987) Homicides in the federal city of Ulm in the first five decades following the 30 years' war. *Arch Kriminol, 179*(5-6), 166-170.

(Homicide - Copenhagen)

Gottlieb, P., et al. (1987) Psychotic homicides in Copenhagen from 1959 to 1983. *Acta Psychiatr Scand, 76*(3), 285-297.

(Homicide - Statistics)

Hoogendoorn, D. (1986) Homicide in the national statistics on the causes of death. *Ned Tijdschr Geneesld , 130*(23) 1066-1068.

(Homicide - Iceland)

Gudjohsson, G.H., et al. (1986) Changing characteristics of homicide in Iceland. *Med Sci Law, 26*(4), 299-303.

(Homicide - Sweden)

Lindqvist, P. (1986) Criminal homicide in northern Sweden 1970-1981: Alcohol intoxication, alcohol abuse and mental disease. *Int J Law Psychiatry, 8*(1),19-37.

(Homicide - Paris and Munich)

Terrorists hit targets in Paris and Munich: Trained exec slain. (1986) *Security Letter, part 1 16*(14), 2-3. Microforms and copies available from UMI.

(Homicide - Mexico)

U.S. "very frustrated" over Mexico's handling of search for DEA agent's murderers. (1986) *Narcotics Control Digest, 16*(15), 8-9. Microforms and article copies available from UMI.

(Homicide - Sweden)

Lindqvist, P. (1986) Criminal homicide in northern Sweden 1970-1981: alcohol intoxication, alcohol abuse and mental disease. *International Journal of Law & Psychiatry, 8*(1), 19-37.

(Homicide - South Africa)

Knobel, G.J. (1986) Effects of civil unrest on the incidence of violent and non-natural deaths. *S. Afr Med J, 70*(2), 83-88.

(Homicide - India)

Dikshit, P.C., et al. (1986) Comprehensive study of homicides in south Delhi, 1969-1979. *Med Sci Law, 26*(3), 230-234.

(Homicide - Greenland)

Hansen, J.P. (1985) Criminal homicide in Greenland. *Artic Med Res , 40* , 61-64.

(Homicide - Cambodia)

Blodgett, N. (1985) Cambodia case: Lawyer wants genocide trial. *American Bar Association Journal, 71,* 31. Illustrations, microforms and article copies available from UMI.

(Homicide - India)

Nagpaul, H. (1985) Patterns of homicide in north India: some sociological hypotheses.

International Journal of Offender Therapy and Comparative Criminology, 29(2), 147-158. Microforms and article copies available from UMI.

(Homicide - Singapore)

Kua, E.H., et al. (1985) Homicide in Singapore. *Med Sci Law, 25*(1), 26-28.

(Homicide - Ethiopia)

Jacobsson, L. (1985) Acts of violence in a traditional western Ethiopian society in transition. *Acta Psychiatri Scand, 71*(6), 601-607.

(Homicide - Canada)

Homicide in Canada, 1983: A statistical perspective. (1985) *Can Cent Just Stat, 84*(3), 84.

(Homicide - Greenland)

Jorgensen, B., et al. (1984) Accidents due to violence in Greenland (Danish). *Ugeskr. Laeg. 146*(44), 3398-3401, summary in Engl.

(Homicide - Phillipines)

Monjo, J.C. (1984) Recent situation in the Phillipines. *Dept. State Bull, 84*(2085), 37-39.

Homicide - England)

Stone, L. (1983) Interpersonal violence in English society 1300-1980. *Past, Present, 101,* 22-33.

(Homicide - Japan)

Tamura, M. (1983) Changes in the patterns of criminal homicide for recent three decades. *Reports of National Research Institute of Police Science*(Tokyo), *24*(2), 149-161.

(Homicide - Lebanon)

Schultz, G.P. (1983) Situation in Lebanon. *Dept. State Bull, 83*(2081), 44-45.

(Homicide - Chile)

Bushnell, J. (1981, April) United States and Chile. *Dept. State Bull, 81*(2049), 44-46.

(Homicide - Alberta,Canada)

Hackler, J., & Guald, A. (1981) Violent crime in Alberta, (Four Reports). *Criminal Justice Ab.CJA,* 181.

(Homicide - Possible Causes)

Illegal markets may influence murder rates. (1980) *Just Assist, 1*(1), 15.

(Homicide - Cuba)

Salas, L., & Wilbanks, W. (1979-1980) Homicide in Cuba: Placing the available data in a comparative framework. *Int Ann Criminol, 18,* 29-45.

(Homicide - New Mexico)

Serrill, M.S., & Kate, P. (1980) The anatomy of a riot: The facts behind New Mexico's bloody ordeal. *Corrections Magazine, 6*(2), 6-16.

(Homicide - Guyana)

Bargatze, F.O, et al. (1979) Guyana. *Med Serv Dig, 30*(2), 4-13.

(Homicide - Nigeria)

Emovon, A.C., et al. (1978) A survey of criminal homicide in Nigeria. *Scand J Soc Med, 6*(2), 55-58.

(Homicide - Italy)

Merli, S. & Anaclerio, M. (1978) Homicide in the casuistics of the Roman Medicolegal Institute from 1966 to 1975. (Italian with summary in English and German) *Zacchia, 14*(1), 73-96.

(Homicide - Italy)

Terrorism in Italy: a new dimension. (1978) *Security Management, 22*(11), 42-45. Microforms and article copies available from UMI.

(Homicide - Ancient England)

Hammer, C.I., Jr. (1978, Feb.) Patterns of homicide in a medieval university town: Fourteenth-century Oxford. *Past & Present, 78*, 3-23.

(Homicide - England)

Samuels, A. (1977) Homicide today. *Justice Peace 1977, 141*(48), 701-702.

(Homicide - Canadian Indians)

Jilek, W.G., & Roy, C. (1976) Homicide committed by Canadian Indians and non-Indians. *International Journal of Offender Therapy and Comparative Criminology, 20*(3), 201-216.

(Homicide - Greenland)

Hart Hansen, J.P. (1976) Criminal homicide in Greenland. *Circumpolar Health*, 548-554.

(Homicide - Japan)

Usui, T., et al. (1976) Mortality statistics of homicide, Japan. *Bull Inst Pub Health, 25*(1), 24-40.

(Homicide - Scotland)

Gillies, H. (1976) Homicide in the west of Scotland. *Fr J Psychiatry, 128*, 105-127.

(Homicide - Sudan)

Malik, M.O.A., & Sawi, O. (1976) A profile of homicide in the Sudan. *Forens Sci, 7*(2), 141-150.

(Homicide - Nigeria)

Emovon, A.C., et al. (1975) A survey of criminal homicide in Nigeria. *Int J Soc Psychiatry, 21*(3), 214-219.

(Homicide - Australia)

Vinson, T. (1974) Homicides and serious assaults in New South Wales. *Anglo-Amer Law Rev, 3*(1), 29-36.

(Homicide - Yugoslavia)

Jovanovic, R. (1974) Drustvene Karakteristike Izvrsilaca Ubistava Na Teritoriji Severoistocne Srbije U Peridou Od 1967. Do 1972. Godine (Social Characteristics of Homicides in North East Serbia From 1967 to 1972). *Sociologija, 16*(3-4), 431-452.

(Homicide - Germany)

Stein, A. (1973) (Homicides of the year 1968). 24232 J, 53, H. 8, S. 374-378.

(Homicide - Hong Kong)

Wong, M., & Singer, K. (1973) Abnormal homicide in Hong Kong. *British Journal of Psychiatry, 123*(574), 295-298.

(Homicide - Norway/France)

Lester, D. (1973) External restraints, suicide, and homicide: comparison of Norway and France. *Percept Mot Skills, 36,* 646.

(Homicide - Singapore)

Chao, T.C. (1973) Homicides and suspected homicides in Singapore. *Med Sci Law, 13*(2), 98-102.

(Homicide - Sudan)

Fleuhr-Lobban, C. (1973) An anthropological analysis of homicide in an Afro-Arab state, the Sudan. *Dissertation Abstracts International, 34*(6-B), 2426.

(Homicide - U.S.S.R./U.S.)

Connor, W.D. (1973) Criminal homicide, U.S.S.R./U.S.A.: Reflections on Soviet data in a comparative framework. *J Crim L, 64,* 111.

(Homicide - Laos)

Westermeyer, J. (1972) A comparison of Amok and other homicide in Laos. *Am J Psychiatry, 129,* 703-709.

(Homicide - Germany)

Kiel, F. (1972) Homicides in Germany involving American soldiers. *Beitr Gerichtl Med, 29,* 218-222.

(Homicide - Egypt)

Wagih, I.M., et al. (1970) A biometrical and medico-legal assessment of homicide in Alexandria, 1965-1968. *J Egypt Med Assoc, 53,* 722-729.

(Homicide - Germany)

Rasch, W. (1970) Epoch dependent changes in homicide pattern. *Beitr Gerichtl Med, 27,* 127-134.

(Homicide - Japan)

Oishi, F. (1970) Statistical report on handling of cases of unnatural death occurring in Shizuoka Prefecture, 1967-1968. *J Tokyo Med Coll, 28,* 105-111.

(Homicide - Singapore)

Ting, S.K. (1969) Post-mortem survey of homicides in Singapore, 1955-1964. *Singapore Med J, 10,* 243-247.

(Homicide - Nigeria)

Asuni, T. (1969) Homicide in Western Nigeria. *Brit. J Psychiat, 115,* 1105-1113.

(Homicide - England)

Ashworth, A.J. (1969) Short note on the English murder rate. *Crim L R , 1969,* 645.

(Homicide - Italy)

Gambassini, L., et al. (1969) Analysis of death, from violent causes, of Italian children under 15 years of age during the years 1958-1964. *Minerva Pediat, 21,* 281-291.

(Homicide - New Guinea)

Burton-Bradley, B.G. (1968) The amok syndrome in Papua and New Guinea. *Med J Aust, 1,* 252-256.

(Murder - Germany)

Hentig, H.V. (1968) *Der muttermord und sieben andere verbechensstudien.* Neuwied: Luchterhand.

(Homicide - Japan)

Oishi, F. (1967) Statistical data compiled from reports on the occurrence of unexpected deaths in the Shizuoka prefecture of Japan for three years from 1964-1966. *J Tokyo Med Coll, 25,* 235-239.

(Homicide - Philippines)

Polsky, A. (1967) Crime in the Philippines. Murder in Manila. *13029, 58*(257), 409-412.

(Homicide - Poland)

Fleszar-Szumigajowa, I., et al. (1966) Analysis of homicide in forensic psychiatric material. *Neurol Neurochir Psychiat Pol, 16,* 1185-1192.

(Homicide - Latin America)

Homs, J.A. (1965) Argueologia panamericana; los padres del panamericanismo cientifico. *Humboldt, Hamburg, 6*(23), 64-74.

(Homicide - Scotland)

Gillies, H. (1965) Murder in the west of Scotland. *Brit. J Psychiat, 111,* 1087-1094.

(Homicide - Brazil)

Porto, H.A.M. (1965) Homicido e homicido qualificado: As cicunstancias qualificadoras no anteprojeto do codigo penal, elaborado pelo Ministro Nelson Hungria. *Justitia*(Sao Paulo), *49*, 131-139.

(Murder - Germany)

Unruh, C. (1965) Der giftmord, tat, tater, opfer. *Streafrecht, Strafverfahren, Kriminologie, 9*, 156.

(Homicide - Mexico)

Favre, H. (1965) Notas sobre el homicido entre los chamulas. *ICAHA, 15*, 173-190.

(Homicide - England)

Morris, T., & Cooper, L.B. (1964) *Calendar of murder: Criminal homicide in England since 1957.* Fern hill.

(Homicide - Somalia)

Santiapichi, S. (1963) *Il prezzo del sangue e l'omicido nel diritto somalo.* Milan: Instituto Universitario della Somalia.

(Homicide - Germany)

Gainham, S. (1962) Murder in Munich. *Spec. 208.* 819-820.

(Homicide - India)

Driver, E.D. (1961) Interaction and criminal homicide in India. *Soc Forces, 40,* 153-158.

(Homicide - Pakistan)

Qureshi, A.N., & Khan, M.K. (1961) Some aspects of epidemiology of traumas in the former Punjab Province, Pakistan. *I Pakistan J Health, 11,* 82-100.

(Homicide - Peru)

Bramon Arias, L.A. (1958) El homicidio en el Codigo penal peruano. *Rev de Derecho y Ciencias Politicas* (Lima), *22*(1/3), 68-100.

(Homicide - Ceylon)

Gunasekara, N.D. (1956) Homicide in Ceylon. *Ceylon Med J, 3,* 140-163.

(Homicide - Mexico)

Viqueira, C. (1954) Alcoholismo, Brujeria y homicido en dos comunidades rurales de Mexico. *America indigena, Mexico, 14*(1), 7-36.

(Homicide - England/Australia)

Turner, A.L. (1949) Constructive murder in England and Australia. *U Western Aust Ann L*

Rev, 1, 295-302.

(Homicide - Ireland)

Fisher, J.R. (1923) Authorized murders in Ireland, and elsewhere. *Spec., 130,* 52-53

General Epidemiology

(Homicide - International Comparison)

Fingerhut, L.A., & Kleinman, J.C. (1990) International and interstate comparisons of homicide among young males. *JAMA, 263*(24), 3292-3295.

(Homicide Rates)

Gartner, R. (1990) The victims of a homicide: A temporal and cross-national comparison. *American Sociological Review, 55*(1), 92-106.

(Homicide - Risk)

Helzlsouer, K.J., & Gordis, L. (1990) Risks to health in the United States. *Daedalus, 119*(4), 193-206.

(Homicide - Ethnic)

Balkwell, J.W. (1990) Ethnic inequality and the rate of homicide. *Social Forces, 69*(1), 53-70.

(Homicide - Family)

Lewis, D. (1990, Aug.) When love turns violent. *Glamour, 88*(8), pp. 234-235.

(Homicide - Rates)

Lester, D. (1989) National suicide and homicide rates: Correlates versus predictors. *Soc Sci Med 29*(11), 1249-1252.

(Homicide - Colombia)

Delpar, H. (1989) The assassination of Gaitan - public life and urban violence in Colombia, by H. Braun. *Lat Am Res, 24*(1),261-274.

(Homicide - Black)

Mitchell, M.A., & Daniels, S. (1989) Black on black homicide: Kansas City's response. *Public Health Rep, 104*(6), 605-608.

(Vancouver Study)

Martinoff, M.J. (1989, June) "A tale of two cities'": A Vancouverite's perspective. *American Rifleman, 137*(6), pp. 12-13.

(Homicide - Evolution)

Daly, M., & Wilson, M. (1989) Homicide and cultural evolution. *Ethnology and*

Sociobiology,10(1-3), 99-110

(Homicide - Memphis)

Harruff, R.C., et al. (1988) Cocaine and homicide in Memphis and Shelby county: An epidemic of violence. *J Forensic Sci, 33*(5), 1231-1237.

(Homicide - Time of Month)

Frank, M.L. (1988) Homicide at the beginning of the month. *Psychol Rep, 63*(2), 402.

(Homicide Mortality - U.S.)

Premature mortality due to homicide United States, 1968-1985 (book review). (1988) *JAMA: The Journal of the American Medical Association, 260*(14), 2021-2026.

(Homicide - Statistics)

Lester, D. (1988) The birthday blues for males and females. *Psychol Rep. 62*(2), 638.

(Homicide - Children)

Blaster, M.J., et al. (1986) Epidemiologic analysis of a cluster of homicides of children in Atlanta. *JAMA, 251*(24), 3255-3258.

(Homicide - Los Angeles)

Epidemiologic notes and reports: Homicide, Los Angeles, 1970-1979. (1986) *JAMA, 255*(24), 3348, 3350-3351.

(Homicide - Epidemiology)

Rosenberg, M.L., et al. (1986) Homicide: Epidemiologic analysis at the national level. *Bull NY Acad Med, 62*(5), 376-399

(Homicide - Epidemiology)

Welte, J.W., et al. (1986) Homicide and race in Erie County, New York. *Am J Epidemiology, 124*(4), 666-670.

(Chicago Homicide)

Block, C.R. (1986) *Homicide in Chicago: Aggregate and time series perspective on victim, offender, and circumstances (1965-1981).* Chicago: Loyola University Center for Urban Policy.

(Homicide - Singapore)

Heong, S.Y.M. (1985, July) Homicide in Singapore: A study of the incidence, nature, and prevention of culpable homicide in Singapore. *Malaya Law Review, 27*, 113-143.

(Homicide - Epidemiology)

Michaud, P.A. (1985) Violent deaths among adolescents in Switzerland from epidemiology to prevention. *Pediatrician, 12*(1), 28-36.

(Homicide - Atlanta)

Blaster, M.J. (1983-1985) Epidemiologic characteristics of child homicides in Atlanta, 1970-1980. *Pediatrician,12*(1), 63-67.

(Homicide - Honolulu)

Armstrong, R.W., et al. (1984) Epidemiologic patterns of homicides in the city & county of Honolulu, 1977-1983. *Hawaii Med J, 43*(7), 230-236.

(Homicide - Epidemiology)

Jason, J. (1984) Centers for disease control and the epidemiology of violence. *Child Abuse Negl, 8*(3), 279--283.

(Homicide - Epidemiology)

Disease Researchers Studying Epidemiology of Violence. (1984) *Criminal Justice News Letter, 15*(17), 5-6

(Homicide - Epidemiology)

Jason, J., et al. (1983) Epidemiologic characteristics of primary homicides. *American Journal of Epidemiology, 117*(4), 419-428.

(Homicide - Sanctions)

Felson, R.B., & Ribner, S.A. (1981, June) Attributional approach to accounts and sanctions for criminal violence. *Social Psychology Quarterly, 44*, 137-142.

(Homicide - Trends)

Klebba , A.J. (1981) Comparison of trends for suicide and homicide in the United States, 1900-1976. *SP Medical and Scientific Books (Jamaica)*, 127-150.

(Homicide - Epidemiology)

Holinger, P.C. (1980) Violent deaths as a leading cause of mortality: An epidemiologic study of suicide, homicide, and accidents. *American Journal of Psychiatry, 137*(4), 472-476.

(Homicide - Statistics)

Riedel, M., & Brown, J. (1980) Perils and pitfalls of systems that collect data on homicide. *Public Health Rep, 95*(6), 552.

(Homicide - Patterns)

Seiden, R.H., & Freitas, R. (1980) Shifting patterns of deadly violence. *Suicide & Life-Threatening Behav, 10*(4), 195-209.

(Homicide - Statistics)

Sherman, L.W., & Langworthy, R.H. (1980) Measuring homicide by police officers. *J Crim Law Criminol, 70*(4), 546-560.

(Homicide - Epidemiology)

Loys, F., & Mercy, J.A. (1980) The epidemiology of homicide in the city of Los Angeles, 1970-79. Washington, DC: U.S. Government Printing Office.

(Homicide - Trends)

Holinger, P.C. (1979) Violent deaths among the young: Recent trends in suicide, homicide, and accidents. *Am J Psychiatry, 136*(9), 1144-1147.

(Homicide - Epidemiology Classification)

Wright, R.K., & Davis, J.H. (1977) Studies in the epidemiology of murder: a proposed classification system. *J Forensic Sci, 22*(2), 464-470.

(Homicide - Statistics)

Block, R. (1977) *Violent Crime.* Lexington, MA: D.C. Heath.

(Homicide - Prison)

Sylvester, S.F., et al (1977) *Prison Homicide.* Halsted Press.

(Crimes - Punishment)

Molinari, F. (1977) Fines in the punishment of crimes. Observations and evaluation of statistical data (Italian with summaries in English and French). *Quad Crim Clin, 19*(1), 36-37.

(Homicide - International)

Kohler, G., & Alcock, N. (1976) An empirical table of structural violence. *Journal of Peace Research, 13,* (4), 343-356.

(Homicide - Urban Epidemiology)

Herjanic, M., et al. (1976) Notes on epidemiology of homicide in an urban area. *Forensic Sci, 8*(3), 235-246.

(Homicide - Cause)

Stross, J.K., et al. (1976) An epidemic of mysterious cardiopulmonary arrests. *N Engl J Med, 295*(20), 1107-1110.

(Homicide - Method)

Annual gun deaths triple revolutionary war casualties. (1976) *Crime Control Digest, 10*(1), 6.

(Homicide - Statistics)

Price, R. (1976) Chilling murder statistics in book. *Law Enforcement Journal, 6,* 1

(Sinusoidal Analysis)

Banks, J., & Vatz, D. (1976) Sinusoidal pattern analysis in criminal incidence. *Criminology, 14*(2), 251-258.

(Homicide/Suicide - Epidemiology)

Berman, A.L. (1975) The epidemiology of life-threatening events. *Suicide 5*,(2), 67-77.

(Patterns and Perceptions)

Fritz, K.A. (1975) *Patterns and perceptions of homicide in detective novels.* New Haven, CT: Yale Press.

(Homicide Rates)

Lester, D. (1973) Mortality rates and aggression management. *Psychological Reports, 33*(3), 865-866.

(Homicide/Suicide - Age Dependency)

Lester, D. (1973) Suicide, homicide, and age dependency ratios. *Aging and Human Development, 4*(2), 127-132.

(Homicide - International)

Homicide - international comparison. (1972) *State Bull Metropolitan Life Ins Co, 53,* 6-8.

(Homicide - Patterns)

Wiegand, G. (1970) (Re: Murder and killing criminality 1967 and 1968). 33325, *22*(4), 71-78.

(Homicide - Patterns)

Hepburn, J., & Voss, H.L. (1970) Patterns of criminal homicide. *Criminology, 8*(1), 21-45.

(Homicide - Statistics)

Rangol, A.J. (1969) (Murder statistics). 24232, J, *52*(6-7), 274-292.

(Homicide - Deviants)

Spruill, V.J., et al. (1969) Differences in leadership stereotypes between deviants and normals. *J Soc Psychol, 79,* 255-256.

(Homicide - Patterns)

Moorland, N. (1966) Pattern of murder. *Int Pub Service, 6,* 25.

(Homicide Rates)

Field, P.B. (1963) Mortality rates and aggression management indices. *J Health Hum Behav, 4,* 99-114.

(Homicide - Prevention)

Jayewardene, C.H. (1961) Influence of medical progress on homicide rates. *Ceylon Med J, 6,* 73-79.

(Deadly Quarrels)

Richardson, L.F. (1960) Statistics of deadly quarrels. Wright, Quincy, and Lienau, E.C., Ed.

(Homicide - Survey)

Survey of felony murder. (1955) *Temp L Q, 28,* 453-466.

Chapter 3
The Murderer
General Characteristics

(Murderer - Juvenile)

Newman, J. (1990, Oct.) Dressed to kill. *Seventeen, 49*(10), p. 32.

(Serial Killer)

Rosenbaum, R. (1990, Sept.) Dead reckoning. *Vanity Fair, 53*(9), pp. 190-197.

(Freed Killer)

Stuttaford, G. (1990, Aug. 17) Freed to kill (book review). *Publishers Weekly*, p. 58.

(Murderers Interviewed)

Diski, J. (1990, March 30) Aftermath. *New Statesman and Society*, p. 34.

(Killer)

Fowler, K. (1990). The serial killer. *RCMP Gazette, 52(3*), 1-11.

(Criminal Profile)

Pinizzotto, A.J., & Finkel, N.J. (1990) Criminal personality profiling: An outcome and process study. *Law and Human behavior, 14*(3), 215-233.

(Murderer Differentiation)

Jeilburn, A.B., Jr. (1990) Differentiation of death-row murderers and life sentence murderers by antisociality and intelligence measures. *Journal of Personality Assessment, 54*(3-4), 617-627.

(Murderers - Who's Who)

Walsh, D. (1990) The new murderers Who's Who, by J.H. Gaute and R. Odell (book review). *British Journal of Criminology, 30*(3), 404-405.

(Murderer - Montreal)

Wallace, B., et al. (1989, Dec. 18) The masking of a mass killer. *Macleans, 102*(5), p.22.

(Case Report)

MacPherson, M. (1989, May) The roots of evil. *Vanity Fair, 52*(5), pp.140-149.

(Multiple Murderer)

Ritter, B.J. (1989) Multiple murderers: The characteristics of the person and the nature of their crimes (Dissertation). *Dissertations Abstracts International, A: Humanities and Social Sciences, 49*(7). Available through UMI, Ann Arbor, MI. (Order # DA8819738).

(Murderer - Research)

Breault, K.D. (1988) The murderer and his murder- A review of research, by D. Lester (book review). *Contemporary Sociology, 17*(3), 366.

(Serial Killers)

Norris, J. (1988) *Serial Killers.* New York: Doubleday.

(Multiple Murderer)

Gee, D.J. (1988) A pathologist's view of multiple murder. *Forensic Science International, 38*(1-2), 53-65.

(Domestic Profile)

Kalischman, S.C. (1988) MMPI profiles of men and women convicted of domestic homicide. *Journal of Clinical Psychology, 44*(6), 847-853.

(Homicide - Filicidal Men)

Campion, J.F., et al. (1988) A study of filicidal men. *Journal of American Psychiatry, 145*(9), 1141-1144.

(Murderer - Juvenile)

Lewis, D.O. (1988) Intrinsic and environmental characteristics of juvenile murderers. *Journal of the American Academy of Child and Adolescent Psychiatry, 27*(5), 582-587.

(Murderer - Nurse)

Reed, D., & Moore, K. (1988) *Deadly medicine: The chilling story of a pediatric nurse who murdered scores of her infant patients.* New York: St. Martin's.

(Homicide - Criminal Culpability)

Marasco, M. (1988) The state of domination in the criminal subject for the purpose of attributing culpability. *Minerva Psichiatr, 29*(20), 87-93.

(Women Killing Children)

Silverman, R.A., & Kennedy, L.W. (1988) Women who kill their children. *Violence and Victims, 3*(2), 113-127.

(Homicide - Gang Delinquency)

Curry, G.D., & Spergel, I.A. (1988) Gang homicide, delinquency, and the community. *Criminology, 26*(3), 381-405.

(Homicide - Under 21)

Montecinos, M., et al. (1987) The characteristics of homicides in subjects under 21 of the metropolitan region. (English translation). *Rev Med Chil, 115(10)*, 995-1000.

(Killer Sheep)

Murray, L.A., et al. (1987) Rambut- The killer sheep. *Med Sci. Law, 27*(2), 95-97.

(Murderers - Wanted)

Nichols, H. (1986, Sept./Oct.) Wanted again. *American West*, pp. 22-31.

(Homicide - Remembering Victim)

We remember. (1986, Sept.-Oct.) *Post Life*, pp. 2-3.

(Homicide - Profile)

Douglas, J.E., & Burgess, A.E. (1986) Criminal profiling: A viable investigative tool against violent crime. *FBI Law Enforcement Bulletin, 55*(12), 9-13.

(Murderers - Characteristics)

Wilcox, D.E. (1986) Characteristics of seventy-one convicted murderers. *American Journal of Forensic Psychiatry, 7*(2), 48-52.

(Homicidality- Karyotype)

Kazamatsuri, H., et al. (1985) Homicidality in a woman with a 47,XXX karyotype. *Journal of Clinical Psychiatry, 46*(8), 346-347.

(Murderer - Typology)

Holcomb, W.R., et al. (1985) The development and cross-validation of an MMPI typology of murderers. *J Pers Asses, 49*(3), 240-244.

(Serial Killer)

Holmes, R.M., and Deburger, J.E. (1985) Profiles in terror: The serial murderer (typology of serial murderers and characteristics of U.S. offenders). bibl *Federal Probation, 49*, 29-34.

(Psychosocial- Profile)

Lewis, D.O. (1985) Biopsychosocial characteristics of children who later murder: A prospective study. *American Journal of Psychiatry, 142*(10), 1161-1167.

(Murderers - Male)

Men who murdered: Chapter 1. (1985) *FBI Law Enforcement Bulletin, 54*(8), 2-6.

(Behavioral Predictors)

Holcomb, W.R., et al. (1984) Cognitive and behavioral predictors of MMPI scores in pretrial psychological evaluations of murderers. *Journal of Clinical Psychology, 40*(2), 592-597.

(Murderer - Race)

Holcomb, W.R., et al. (1984) Are separate black and white MMPI norms needed? An IQ-controlled comparison of accused murderers. *Journal of Clinical Psychology, 40*(1), 189-193.

(Personality - Identifying)

Kodman, F. (1984) Identifying the CBK personality. *Social Behavior and Personality, 12*(2), 139-142.

(Terminating Executioner)

Conrad, J.P. (1984) Terminating the executioner: How the empiricist can help. *Federal Probation, 48*(2), 59-62.

(Juvenile Criminals)

Tarter, R.E., et al. (1984) Neuropsychological, personality, and familial characteristics of physically abused delinquents. *Journal of the American Academy of Child Psychiatry, 23*(6), 668-674.

(Murderer - Personality)

Holcomb, W.R., et al. (1983) The inter-domain among personality and cognition variables in people who commit murder. *J Pers Assess, 47*(5), 524-530.

(Killers - Childhood)

Langevin, R., et al. (1983) Childhood and family background of killers seen for psychiatric assessment: A controlled study. *Bull Am Acad Psychiatry Law, 11*(4), 331-341.

(Murderer Types)

Anderson, W.P., et al. (1983) Accused murderers: Five MMPI personality types. *Journal of Clinical Psychology, 39*(5), 761-768.

(Mass murder)

Mass murder studied. (1983) *Criminal Justice Newsletter, 14*(17), 3.

(Murderers - Iran)

Roohanna, R.S.S. (1982) A survey of the psychosocial aspects of murderers in Iran. *Forensic Science International, 19*(1), 51-66.

(Murderers - Differences)

Mohan, V., et al. (1982) Sex differences in the adjustment of murderers. *Indian Journal of Criminology, 10*(1), 53-55.

(Murderer - Personality)

Kundu, R., et al. (1982) Some affective personality qualities of murderers: A research note. *Personality Study & Group Behavior, 2*(1), 36-43.

(Mutilator - Characteristics)

Henderson, M. (1982) An empirical classification of convicted violent offenders. *The British Journal of Criminology, 22*(1), 1-20.

(Murderer - Characteristics)

Fay, C.B. (1982) The mutilator. *Australian Police Journal, 36*(1), 3-55.

(Murderers - Diagnosis)

Langevin, R., et al. (1982) Diagnosis of killers seen for psychiatric assessment. A controlled study. *Acta Psychiatrica Scandinavica, 66*(3), 216-228,

(Murderer - Characteristics)

Braga, A., et al. Statistical information on 200 perpetrators of homicide. (1981) *Rass Penititenziaria Crim, 3*(3-4), 439-462.

(Reference Work)

Bottiger, L.E. (1982) The murder's vade mecum (Clinical research). *British Medical Journal, 285*(6357), 1819-1821.

(Criminal Behavioral System)

Hoenack, S.A., & Weiter, W.C. (1980) Structural model of murder behavior and the criminal behavior system. *A R, 70*, 327-341.

(Offender Profiles)

Ressler, R.K., et al. (1980) Offender profiles: A multidisciplinary approach. il *FBI Law Enforcement Bulletin, 49*(4), 16-20.

(Murderer - Study)

Bigger, A.B., Jr. (1979) Death by murder: A study of women murderers. *Death Education, 3*(1), 1-9.

(Real-Life Criminals)

Real-life criminals inspire authors through the ages: First of four parts. (1979) *Law Enforcement News, 5*(19), 13.

(Murderers - Legends)

Legend is a one-armed murderer. (1979) *Law Enforcement Journal, 8*(10), 2. Copies available through UMI, Ann Arbor, MI.

(Murderers - Listing)

Gaute, J.H., & Odell, R. (1979) *The murderer's who's who.* London: Methuen.

(Homicide - Twentieth Century)

'Jekyll-and-Hyde' criminals enter the twentieth century. (1979) *Law Enforcement News, 5*(4), 6,10.

(Homicide - 20th Century)

Murder in the 20th century: These will kill you. (1979) *Law Enforcement News, 5*(8), 13,16.

(Murderers)

Murderers (letter). (1979) *Medical Journal of Australia, 1*(7), 283-284.

(Murderers - Personality)

Parker, N. (1979) Murderers: A personal series. *Medical Journal of Australia, 1*(2), 36-39.

(Homicide - Personality types)

McGurk, B.J. (1978, April) Personality types among normal homicides. *British Journal of Criminology, 18*, 146-161.

(Murderers - Characteristics)

Keltikangas-Jarvinen, L. (1978) Personality characteristics of homicides and assaulters. *Psychiatr Fenn, 1978*, 65-71.

(Murderer - Impulsive)

Heilbrun, A.B., Jr., et al. (1978) Impulsive and premeditated homicide: An analysis of subsequent parole risk of the murderer. *Journal of Criminal Law and Criminology, 69*(1), 108-114.

(Murder of Inmates)

Confessed killer gives Congress details on inmate murders at federal prison in Atlanta. (1978) *Corrections Digest, 9*(16), 7-8. Article copies available through UMI, Ann Arbor, MI.

(Murderers - Rehiring)

What should you do if a murderer asks for his job back? (1978) *Protection Management*, pp. 2, 4.

(Escaped Convicts)

Vacationing family murdered by two escaped convicts. (1978) *Corrections Digest, 9*(16), 10.

(Homicide - Psychosocial Study)

Totman, J. (1978) *A psychosocial study of criminal homicide*. R &E Research Associates.

(Murder - New York)

Raab, S. (1978) Murder by 'strangers' drop in New York. *Quarterly Journal of Corrections, 2*(1), 57.

(Murderer - True Story)

Cullen, T. (1977) *The mild murderer: The true story of the Dr. Crippen case*. HM.

(Murderers)

Freeman, L., & Freeman, T. (1977) *The murderers*. Bobbs.

(Murderers - Types)

Simon, R.I. (1977) Type A, AB, B murderers: Their relationship to the victims and the criminal justice system. *Bulletin of the American Academy of Psychiatry and Law, 5*(3), 344-362.

(Multiple Murderer)

Cheney, M. (1976) *Massacre: The calculated killings of a multiple murderer. New York:* Walker.

(Multiple Murderer)

William, A. (1976) *Starkweather: The story of a mass murderer.* HM.

(Murders - Los Angeles)

Skid row slasher: Los Angeles murders. (1975, Feb. 10) *Time, 105*, p. 18.

(Murderer - Portrait)

Thornton, W.E., & Pray, B.J. (1975) The portrait of a murderer. *Diseases of the Nervous System, 36*(4), 176-178.

(Homicide - Pathologies)

Landau, S.M. (1975) Pathologies among homicide offenders: Some cultural profiles. *The British Journal of Criminology, 15*(2), 157-166.

(Crimes of Passion)

Lester, D. & Lester, G. (1975) *Crime of passion: Murder and the murderer.* Chicago: Nelson, Hall.

(Sexual Aggressors)

Drvota, S., & Student, V. (1975) Dangerous sexual aggressors. *Ceskoslovenska Psychiatrie, 71*(1), 33-37.

(Crimes of Passion)

Gorder, E. (Ed.). (1975) *Murder my love: The great crimes of passion.* Chicago: Playboy Press.

(Assassin - Political)

Hassel, C.V. (1974) The political assassin. *Journal of Police Science Administration, 2*(4), 399-403.

(Murderers - Body Image)

Lester, D., & Perdue, W.C. (1974) Body image of the murderers. *Journal of General Psychology, 90*(2), 187-189.

(Manson Murders)

Bugliosi, V. (1974) *Helter Skelter: The true story of the Manson murders.* New York: Norton.

(Murderers - Personality)

Perdue, W.C., et al. (1974) Racial differences in the personality of murderers. *Percept Mot Skills, 38*, 726.

(Murderers - Attempted Suicide)

Lester, D. (1974) Murderers who have attempted suicide. *Psychological Reports, 35*, 238.

(Murderer - Psychiatry)

Citizens who commit murder: A psychiatric study. (1974) Green.

(Mass Murderer)

Mind of the mass murderer. (1973, Aug.) *Time, 102*, pp. 56-57.

(Murderer - Characteristics)

Wiesenthal, S. (1973) *The murderers among us*. New York: Bantam.

(Murderer - Physical examination)

Naeve, W., & Lohmann, E. (1973) Methodology and conclusiveness of physical examinations of living persons immediately after criminal offenses. *Journal of Legal Medicine, 72*(2), 79-99.

(Murder Suspects)

Anatomy of a murder suspect; Yuba City, Ca. (1971, June 14) *Time, 97*, p. 24.

(Doctors - Criminal)

Barzun, J. (1971) Doctors criminal and criminous. *New England Journal of Medicine, 284*, 710-713.

(Murderer - Making of)

Lagner, H.P. (1971) The making of a murderer. *American Journal of Psychiatry, 127*, 950-953.

(Murderers)

Gaddis, T.E. (1970) *Killer*. New York: Macmillan.

(Homicide- Offenders)

Hepburn, J.R. (1970). *Violent offenses and violent offenders*. Session 34. (SA 1970 p. 12, Supp. 7).

(Homicide- Repetitive)

Shaw, R.S. (1970) Murderers who repeat. *New England Journal of Medicine, 282*, 1435.

(Murderers - Parole)

Stanton, J.M. (1969) Murderers on parole. *Crime and Delinquency, 15*, 149.

(Murderers- Biography)

Block, E.B. (1968) *Fabric of guilt: True stories of criminals caught in the net of circumstantial evidence*. New York: Doubleday.

(Murderers - I.Q.)

Kahn, M.W. (1968) Superior performance IQ of murderers as a function of overt act or diagnosis. *Journal of Social Psychology, 76*, 113-116.

(Murderers - Attitude)

May, A.E. (1968) An assessment of homicidal attitudes. *British Journal of Psychiatry, 114*, 479-480.

(Assassins)

Sparrow, G. (1968) *The great assassins*. London: Long.

(Murderers)

Roughead, W. (1968) *The murderer's companion*. New York: Norton.

(Murderers - Unknown)

Wiesenthal, S. (1967) *The murderers among us*. Edited with a profile of the author by J. Wechsberg. London: Heinemann.

(Mass Murderers)

Steiger, B. (1967) *Mass murderer*. Award.

(Murderers - Suicides)

Dorpat, T.L. (1966, June) Suicide in murderers. *Psychiatry Digest, 27*, 51-55.

(Murders - World's Worst)

Franklin, C. (1966) *World's worst murders*. Chicago: Taplinger.

(Murderer - Amnesia)

Meyerson, A.T. (1966) Amnesia for homicide (pedicide): Its treatment with hypnosis. *Archives of General Psychiatry, 14*(5), 509-515.

(Murderers - Sadists)

Ulonska, K. (1966) Der verhinderte morder. Vom flagellanten zum sadisten und morder (The impeded murder. From flagellant to sadist and murderer). 20957. J. 20, '66, 3, S. 149-180 (IBZ 1971).

(Murders - Youthful)

Peter, F.R. (1966) Jegendlicher doppelmorder (Persistence leads to success). 20957. J. 20, '66, 1, S. 33-36 (IBZ 1967).

(Murderer - Psychiatry)

Keil, F.W. (1965) The psychiatric character of the assailant as determined by autopsy observations of the victim. *Journal of Forensic Science*, 19, 263-271.

(Medical Quacks)

Curran, W.J. (1964) Medical quacks and murder with words. *New England Journal of Medicine, 270*, 728.

(Preventive Interaction)

Blackman, N., & Weiss, J.M. (1963) The sudden murderer, III. Clues to preventive interaction.

Archives of General Psychiatry, 8(3), 289-294.

(Murderer - Characteristics)

McComas, J.F. (1962) *Graveside companion.* Astor-Honor.

(Murderer - Psychology)

Palmer, S. (1962) *Psychology of murder.* (Original title: *Study of murder*). (ISBN 0-8152-0050-1, A50).

(Murderer - Characteristics)

Shew, E.S. (1962) *Second comparison to murder.* New York: Knopf.

(Murderer and Victim)

MacDonald, J.M. (1961) *Murderer and his victim.* C.C. Thomas.

(Murderer - Unknown)

Reik, T. (1945) *The unknown murderer.* (Translation by K. Jones). New York: Prentice-Hall.

(Murderers - Personality)

Cassity, J.H. (1941) Personality study of 200 murderers. *Journal of Criminal Psychopathology, 2*, 296-304.

(Murderers)

Frankel, E. (1939) One thousand murderers. *Journal of Criminal Law and Criminology, 29*, 672-675.

(Murderers - Motives)

Roesner, E. (1936) Murder: Its perpetrator, motives, and victim. (With a bibliography on the problem of murder). German. *Z Strafrechtswiss, 56*, 327.

(Murderers - Backgrounds)

Gillin, J.L. (1935, Dec.) Social backgrounds of sex offenders and murderers. *Social Forces, 14*, 232-239.

(Murderer and Victims)

The murderer and his victim's insurance money. (1930) *Sol J, 74*, 32.

(Murderer)

Lynd, R. (1924, July) Murderer. *New Statesman, 23*, 433-435.

The Murderer
Children and Youth

(Trial of Child)

A fifth-grader stands trial for murder (from the *New York Times*). (1990, April 4) *Los Angeles Daily Journal,* p.6.

(Murderers - Teens)

Ads, violence, and values. (1990, April 2) *Advertising Age, 61*(14), p. 12.

(Youth Crimes)

Darnton, N. (1990, March 5) Street crimes of passion (youth violence over stylish clothes). *Newsweek, 115,* p. 58.

(Homicide - Juvenile)

Malmquist, C.P. (1990) Book forum: Children and adolescents-- Juvenile homicide. *American Journal of Psychiatry, 147*(5), 671.

(Murderers - Children)

Ewing, C.P. (1990) *Kids who kill.* Lexington, MA: Heath.

(Homicide - Juvenile)

Dossantos, E. (1990) Juvenile homicide by E.P. Bendek and D.G. Cornel (book review). *J Clin Psych 51*(5), 216.

(Murderers - Adolescents)

Malmquist, C.P. (1990) Depression in homicidal adolescents. *Bulletin of the American Academy of Psychiatry and the Law, 18*(1), 23-36.

(Murderers - Youth)

Myers, W.C., & Kemph, J.P. (1990) DSM-III-R classification of murderous youth: Help or hindrance? *J Clin Psychiatry, 51*(6), 239-242.

(Homicide - Juvenile)

Toupin, J., & Morisette, L. (1990) Juvenile homicide: A case control study. *Med Law, 9*(3), 986-994.

(Patricide - Boy)

Myers, W.C., Caterine, A. (1990) Tarasoff and threats of patricide by a 9-year-old boy. *American Journal of Psychiatry, 147*(4), 535-536.

(Juvenile Intervention)

Grant, C.A. (1989) Juveniles who murder: Insights for intervention. *Nurs Ment Health Serv, 27*(12), 4-11.

(Homicide - Juvenile)

Benedeck, E.P., & Cornell, D.G. (Eds.). (1989) *Juvenile homicide*. Washington, D.C.: American Psychiatric Press.

(Patterns - Delinquency)

Goetting, A. (1989) Patterns of homicide among children (perspectives on delinquency). *Criminal Justice and Behavior, 16*, 63-80.

(Teen-age ax-murderers)

Feld, B.C. (1989) Bad law makes hard cases: Reflections on teen-aged ax-murderers, judicial activism, and legislative default (Minnesota). *Law and Inequality: A Journal of Theory and Practice, 8*, 1-101.

(Homicide - Juvenile)

Seidel, D.R. (1989) Juvenile Homicide by E. Benedek and D. Cornell (book review). *The Bulletin of the American Academy of Psychiatry and Law, 17*, 247.

(Murderers - Adolescents)

Strehlow, U. (1989) Follow-up of adolescent homicide perpetrators committed in accordance with section 63 of the federal penal code: Four case reports. *Z Kinder Jugenpsychiatr, 17*(4), 211-215.

(Problem Behavior)

Haggery, R.J. (1989) Problem behavior in adolescence. *Acta Paediatr Jpn Overs Ed, 31*(2), 107-114.

(Murderer - Teenager)

White youths nabbed in a 'prank' killing of Black. (1988, Dec. 19) *Jet*, p. 32.

(Homicide - Childhood)

Muscat, J.E. (1988) Characteristics of childhood homicide in Ohio, 1974-84. *Am J Public Health, 78*(7), 822-824.

(Murderers - Juveniles)

Girets, G. (1988) Young murderers. *Ann Pediatr* (Paris), *35*(9), 681-685.

(Murderers - Juveniles)

Lewis, D.O., et al. (1988) Intrinsic and environmental characteristics of juvenile murderers. *J Am Acad Child Adolesc Psychiatry, 27*, 582-587.

(Murderer- Characteristics)

Myers, W.C., & Kempf, J.P. (1988) Characteristics and treatment of four homicidal adolescents. *Journal of American Academy of Child and Adolescent Psychiatry, 27*(5), 595-599.

(Adolescent Homicides)

Cornell, D.G., et al. (1988) MMPI profile of adolescents charged with homicide. *Behav Sci Law, 6*(3), 401-407.

(Juvenile Killer)

Hackett, G. (1987, Sept. 21) Indiana killer, Italian martyr (Italians show sympathy for juvenile killer P. Cooper). *Newsweek, 110*, p. 37.

(Homicide - Juvenile)

Salholz, E. (1987, May 11). In Detroit, kids kill kids (searching students for weapons used in school-related attacks). *Newsweek, 109*, p. 74.

(Juvenile Homicide)

Cornell, D.G., et al. (1987) Juvenile homicide: Prior adjustment and a proposed typology. *Am J Orthopsychiatry, 57*(3), 383-393.

(Narcissistic adolescent)

Marohn, R.C. (1987) John Wesley Hardin, adolescent killer: The emergence of a narcissistic behavior disorder. *Adolescent Psychiatry, 14*, 271-296.

(Juvenile Homicide)

Rowley, J.C., et al. (1987) Juvenile homicide: The need for an interdisciplinary approach (Special issue: Homicidal behavior). *Behavioral Sciences and the Law, 5*(1), 1-10.

(Murderer - Child)

Boy, 13, charged in slaying Georgia principal with pencil (case of K.L. Jones in Bethlehem). (1986, Dec. 15) *Jet, 71*, p. 14.

(Murderers - Children)

Press, A. (1986, Nov. 24) Children who kill. *Newsweek, 108*, pp. 93-94.

(Murderers - Adolescents)

Murders by people underage 18. (1986) *Corrections Digest, 17*(3), 5. Microforms and article copies available from UMI.

(Homicide - Juvenile)

Shapiro, W. (1985, Dec. 2) Kids who kill (Detroit). *Newsweek, 106*, p. 55.

(Punishment - Child)

How do you punish a criminal child? (murder of 9 yr. old A. Wilson by juveniles in Beloit, Wi.). (1985, Aug. 26) *Newsweek*, pp. 58-59.

(Murderer - Adolescent)

Lubow, A. (1985, May 13) In a deadly explosion of teenage unhappiness, one life is cut short, another blighted by murder (K. Costas stabbed by B. Protti Orinda, Ca.). *People Weekly, 23*,

155-156+.

(Murderers - Adolescents)

Two D.C. boys held in death of 7-year-old (case of C.E. Arthur). (1985, April 29) *Jet, 68*, p. 13.

(Murderers - Children)

Three Florida kids charged in death of retarded boy (case of T. Davis). (1985, March 4) *Jet, 67*, p. 32.

(Murderers - Children)

Florida officials probe kids' fight that killed retarded six-year-old (West Palm Beach). (1985, Jan. 28) *Jet, 67*, p. 38.

(Adolescent - Case Report)

Restifo, N.P. (1985) Three case reports of a single homicidal adolescent (letter). *Am J Psychiatry, 142*(3), 388.

(Murderers - Prospective Study)

Lewis, D.O., et al. (1985) Biopsychosocial characteristics of children who later murder: A prospective study. *Am J of Psychiatry, 142*(10), 1161-1167.

(Homicide - Under Fourteen)

Scarella, M. (1985) Notes on a recent case of homicide involving under fourteens: Considerations on the role of families and institutions (Translated from Italian). *G. Neuropsichiatr. Eta Evol., 5*(1), 51-66.

(Adolescent Killing)

Corson, D. (1984) Lying and killing: Language and the moral reasoning of twelve- and fifteen-year-olds by social group. *Adolescence, 19*(74), 473-482.

(Homicide -Children and Adolescent)

Goldenring, J.M. (1984) On homicide in children and adolescents (letter). *Am J Public Health, 74*(6), 623-624.

(Homicide - Teenage)

Copeland, A.R. (1984) Homicide during teenage years- the ten year metro Dade County experience from 1973-1982. *Forensic Sci Int, 25*(3), 167-173.

(Murderers - Children)

Zimring, F.E. (1984) Youth homicide in New York: A preliminary analysis. *The Journal of Legal Studies, 13*(1), 81-99. Charts and graphs. Microforms and article copies available from UMI.

(Aggressive Adolescent)

Martinius, J. (1983) Homicide of an aggressive adolescent with right temporal lesion: A case report. *Neurosci Biobehav Rev, 7*(3), 419-422.

(Killer - Rapist)

Ressler, R.K., et al.. (1983) Rape and rape-murder: One offender and twelve victims. *Am J of Psychiatry, 140*(1), 36-40.

(Murderers - Children)

Lewis, D.O., et al. (1983) Homicidally aggressive young children: Neoropsychiatric and experiential correlates. *American Journal of Psychiatry, 140*(2), 148-153.

(Murderer - Child)

Macleod, R.J. (1982, Aug.) A child is charged with homicide: His family responds. *British Journal of Psychiatry, 141*, 199-201.

(Juvenile Homicide)

Marohn, R.C., et al.. (1982) Juvenile delinquents and violent death. *Adolescent Psychiatry, 10*, 47-170.

(Murderers - Adolescent/ Teen)

Teen convicted of murder in case that shocked Vermont into rewriting law. (1982) *Juvenile Justice Digest, 10*(10), 4. Microforms and article copies available from UMI, Ann Arbor, MI.

(Murderers - Youths)

Eigen, J.P. (1981, Fall) Punishing youth homicide offenders in Philadelphia. *Journal of Criminal Law, 72*, 1072-1093.

(Adolescent Homicide in Scotland)

Fiddes, D.O. (1981) Scotland in the seventies: Adolescents in care and custody: A survey of adolescent murder in Scotland. *Journal of Adolescence, 4*(1), 47-65.

(Homicide - Youth)

Petti, T.A., & Davidman, L. (1981) Homicidal school-age children: Cognitive style and demographic features. *Child Psychiatry Hum Dev, 12*(2), 82-89.

(Murderers - School-Age)

Petti, T.A., et al. (1981) Homicidal school-age children: Cognitive style and demographic features. *Child Psychiatry and Human Development, 12*(2), 82-89.

(Juvenile Violence)

Stranger to stranger murders testimony to mounting violence. (1981) *Juvenile Justice Digest, 9*(9), 1,6. Microforms and article copies available from UMI.

(Homicide - Juvenile)

Sorrels, J., Jr. (1980, April) What can be done about juvenile homicide? *Crime and Delinquency, 26*, 152-161.

(Homicidal Children)

Pfeffer, C.R. (1980) Psychiatric hospital treatment of assaultive homicidal children. *American Journal of Psychotherapy, 34*(2), 197-207.

(Murder - Premeditated)

Bernstein, J.I. (1980) Premeditated murder by an eight-year-old boy. *International Journal of Offender Therapy and Comprehensive Criminology, 23*(1), 47-56.

(Children - FGR)

Weber, W. (1980) Thrust injuries by children. *Verletzung von Kinderhand Z. Rechsmed, 85*(1), 63-71.

(Murderers - Children)

Child given 114 years in prison for 2nd-degree murder conviction. (1979) *Juvenile Justice Digest, 7*(12), 8. Article copies available from UMI.

(Murderer - Adolescent)

Rosner, R., & Rosner, W.M., et al. (1979) Adolescents accused of murder and manslaughter: A five year descriptive study. *Bulletin of American Academy of Psychiatry and Law, 7*(4), 342-351.

(Child Killer)

Montagno, M., & Jones, J.C. (1978, Feb. 13) Child killer: Oakland County, Mich. *Newsweek, 91*, p. 9+.

(Narcissism)

McCarthy, J.B. (1978) Narcissism and the self in homicidal adolescents. *American Journal of Psychoanalysis, 38*(1), 19-29.

(Boys - Hitmen)

Two boys, 13 and 14, hired as 'hit men' to blast crook's rival. (1978) *Juvenile Justice Digest, 6*(7), 7-8. Article copies from UMI.

(Juvenile Murderers)

Hayes, J.R. (1978) Intellectual characteristics of juvenile murderers vs. status offenders. *Psychological Reports, 43*(1), 80-82.

(Vandalism - Theory)

Allen, V.L., & Greenberger, D.B. (1978) An aesthetic theory of vandalism. *Crime & Delinquency, 24*(3), 309-321.

(Murderers - Children)

Sorrels, J.M. (1977, July) Kids who kill. *Crime and Delinquency, 23*, 312-320.

(Murderers - Youth)

Chicago murder statistics show youth account for more deaths. (1977) *Juvenile Justice Digest, 5*(10), 4. Article copies available from UMI.

(Murderers - Characteristics)

Mecir, J. (1977) Homicidal behavior among persons under age of nineteen. *Acta Universitatis Carolinae Medica, Monographia, 70,* 1-100.

(Child as Killer)

Bush, S. (1976, Nov.) Child as killer; study by B. Corder, et al. *Psychology Today, 10,* p. 29+.

(Young Murderers)

Evseeff, G.S. (1976) A potential young murderer. *Journal of Forensic Science, 21*(2), 441-450.

(Murderers - Characteristics)

Gardiner, M. (1976) *The deadly innocents: portraits of children who kill.* New York: Basic Books.

(Young Murderers)

Walshe-Brennan, K.S. (1976) An analysis of homicide by young persons in England and Wales. *Acta Psychiatr Scand, 54*(2), 92-98.

(Murderer - Coed)

Cheney, M. (1976) *The coed killer.* New York: Walker.

(Murderers - Young)

Eight-year-old murderer kils again 13 years later. (1976) *Corrections Digest, 7*(20), 10.

(Murderers - Juvenile)

1975 serious crimes up 10%; juvenile involvement rises. (1976) *Juvenile Justice Digest, 4*(17), 1-3.

(Murderers - Over 18)

Mecir, J. (1976) Murdering behavior of persons older than nineteen years (Czech.), with English abstract). *J Cesk Psychaitr, 72*(6), 374-383.

(Murder - Case Report)

Morgan, T. (1975, Jan. 19) They think I can kill because I'm 14. *New York Times Magazine,* pp. 9-11+. Discussion of article in issue of Feb. 16, 1975.

(Murderers - Youth)

King, C.H. (1975, Jan.) Ego and the integration of violence in homicidal youth. *American Journal of Orthopsychiatry, 45,* 134-145.

(Murderer - Juvenile)

Colorado Springs-- A sixteen year old boy . . . . . (1975) *Juvenile Justice Digest, 3*(19), 8.

(Murderer - Youth)

Youth sentenced for triple slayings. (1975) *Juvenile Justice Digest, 3*(11), 3.

(Murderers - Children)

Child murderers commonplace now; Recession sparking more child abuse. (1975) *Juvenile Justice Digest, 3*(4), 2.

(Young Murderers)

Walshe-Brennan, K.S. (1975) Children convicted of homicide. *Ulster Medical Journal, 44*(1), 39-44.

(Murderers - Youth)

Walsh-Brennan, K.S. (1975) Community factors in young murderers. *Community Health, 6*(5), 252-256.

(Murderers - Juvenile)

Two Florida boys murder one 4- year old boy, seriously injuring his six- year old sister. (1975) *Juvenile Justice Digest, 3*(4), 2-3.

(Murderers - Adolescent)

Schipkowensky, N. (1975) Adolescent murderers through love (German). *Acta Paedopsychiatrica, 41*(4-5), 187-202.

(Fratricide)

Paluszny, M. & McNabb, M. (1975) Therapy for a six year old who committed fratricide. *Journal of American Academy of Child Psychiatry, 14*(2), 319-336.

(Murderous Children)

Tooley, K. (1975) The small assassins: Clinical notes on a subgroup of murderous children. *Journal of the American Academy of Child Psychiatry, 14*(2), 306-318.

(Homicide - Children)

Schacter, M. (1975) Attempts to homicide and homicides committed by subjects under 20 years: Clinical and psychodiagnostic investigations (French). *Acta Paedopsychiatrica, 41*(4-5). 174-187.

(Murderers - Adolescents)

Miller, D., & Looney, J.G. (1975) Determinants of homicide in adolescents. *Adolescent Psychiatry, 4*, 231-254.

(Murderer - Juvenile)

Szewczyk, H. (1974) Manslaughter committed by juveniles with early childhood brain damage. *Psychiatr Neorol Med Psychol, 26*(7), 385-394.

(Murderer - Adolescent)

Bakowski, A. (1974) A 14 year old murderer disguised in a girl's dress (Polish). *Arch Med Sodowej Krym, 24*(2), 299-302.

(Murderers - Children)

Adams, K.A. (1974) The child who murders: A review of theory and research. *Criminal Justice and Behavior, 1*(1), 51-61.

(Murderers - Children)

Walshe-Brennan, K.S. (1974) Child murderers: An analysis. *Criminologist, 9*(32), 3-12.

(Murderers - Adolescent)

Kido, M. (1973) An EEG study of delinquent adolescents with reference to recidivism and murder. *Folia Psychiatr Neorol Jap, 27,* 77-84.

(Murderers - Juveniles)

Russell, D.H. (1973) Juvenile murderers. *International Journal of Offender Therapy and Comparative Criminal, 17*(3), 235-239.

(Murderers - Children)

Colligan, D. (1973, Sept.) Children who kill, and why: Views of L. Adelson. *Science Digest, 74,* pp. 31-35.

(Children - Batterers)

Adelson, L. The battering child. *Criminologist 1973*, 26-33 (1973, Aug. 27); *JAMA, 222,* 159-161 (1972, Oct. 9).

(Murderers - Children)

Wilson, P. (1973) *Children who kill.*. London: Joseph.

(Murderers - Juvenile)

Szymusik, A., et al. (1972, March-April) Juvenile homicides and sex offenses. *Psychiatr Pol, 6,* 143-149.

(Murderers - Children)

Haulser, K. (1972) Mord durch kindeshand. Problems bei einem strafunmundigen gewalttater (Homicide by children. Problems with a brutal minor under age for law purposes). 20957. J. 26, '72, 2, S. 89-92 (IBZ 1973).

(Murderers - Underage)

Matzler, A. (1972) Minderjahrige morder. Eine kriminologische bertrachtung (Underage murderer. A criminologic evaluation. II. 20957. J. 26, '72, 6, S. 273-277 (IBZ 1973).

(Murderers - Adolescent)

Duncan J.W., et al. (1971, May) Murder in the family: A study of some homicidal adolescents.

American Journal of Psychiatry, 127, 1498-1502.

(Juvenile Aggression)

Malmquist, C.P. (1971, Oct.) Premonitory signs of homicidal aggression in juveniles. *American Journal of Psychiatry, 128,* 461-465.

(Murderers - Youths)

Briguet-Lamarre, M. (1971, May) Passage to the act of murder in children and adolescents (French). *Rev Neuropsychiatr Infant, 19,* 225-233.

(Murderers - Minors)

Mecir, J. (1969) Murderous behavior in children. *Rev Czech Med, 15,* 111-117.

(Murderers - Minors)

Mecir, J. (1968, Oct.) Homicidal actions of minors against parents. *Cesk Psychiat, 64,* 319-325 (Czech).

(Violence - Psychology)

Anthony, H.S. (1968) The association of violence and depression in a sample of young offenders. *British Journal of Criminology, 8*(4), 346-365.

(Murderers - Adolescents)

Colin, M., et al. (1967, Nov.) Clinical study of five adolescents who have committed murder. *Ann Med Leg, 47,* 643-645 (French).

(Murderers - Youth)

Ansprenger, F. (1966, June 22) Mord and Morder. 11290. H. 3, S. 168-170 (IBZ 1967).

(Murderers - Children)

Podolsky, E. (1965, May) Children who kill. GP 31-98-102.

(Murderers - Adolescents)

Smith, S. (1965) The adolescent murderer. 3969. vol 13, n. 4, 310-319 (IBZ 1969).

(Murderers - Adolescents)

Marten, G.W. (1965, Oct.) Adolescent murders. *Southern Medical Journal, 58,* 1217-1220.

(Murderers - Adolescents)

Mecir, J. (1965, June) Homicidal attempts by minors and the connection with their sexual activity. *Cesk Psychiatr, 61,* 176-179 (Czech).

(Murderers - Adolescents)

Smith, S. (1965, Oct.) The adolescent murderers. A psychodynamic interpretation. *Archive of General Psychiatry, 13,* 310-319.

(Murderers - Juvenile)

Jaklewicz, H. (1964, March/April) Psychiatric and social conditioning in juvenile crimes.

Neurol Neurochir Psychiat Pol, 14, 303-307 (Polish).

(Murders - Sex)

Michaux, M.H., & Michaux, W.W. (1963) Psychodiagnostic follow-up of a juvenile sex murderer: R. Lindner's "Charles" thirteen years later. *Psychoanalytic Review, 50*(1), 93-112.

(Murderers - Juvenile)

Legrun, A. (1963, July) Handwriting patterns of juvenile murderers. *Prax Kinderpsychol, 12*, 181-188.

(Murderers - Children)

Sargent, D. (1962) Children who kill: A family conspiracy. *Social Work, 7*(1), 35-42.

(Aggression - Children/Adolescents)

Easson, W.M., & Steinhilber, R.M. (1961, Jan.) Murderous aggression by children and adolescents. *AMA Archives of General Psychiatry, 4*, 1-9.

(Murderers - Children)

Fiori, A. & Marigo, M. (1961, March/April) Six homicides by means of E-605 committed by a minor. *Minerva Medicolegale, 81*, 54-62.

(Murderers - Adolescents)

Woods, S.M. (1961, Dec.) Adolescent violence and homicide. Ego disruption and the 6 and 14 dysrhythmia. *Archives of General Psychiatry, 5*, 528-534.

(Murderers - Children)

Michaels, J.J. (1961, Nov.) Enuresis in murderous aggressive children and adolescents. *Archives of General Psychiatry, 5*, 490-493.

(Murderers - Adolescent)

Stutte, H. (1958) Paranoide hafte psychosen (verfogungs- unschulds- Grossenwahn) bei jugendlichen Mordern. English translation, Paranoid confinement psychoses (persecution complex, delusions of innocence and grandeur). *Zschr Kinderpsychiatr. Basel, 25*(1-2), 80-89.

(Murderers)

Schilf, E. (1953) Beitrage zur kinderpsychologie, II. Zwei kinder als morder. (Contributions to child psychology, II. Two children as murderers). *Psychiat Neurol med Psychol, 5*, 316-328.

(Murderers - Juvenile)

Precker, M.S. (1950) The treatment of juvenile offenders in murder cases. *Journal of Criminal Law and Criminology, 41*, 49-54.

(Murderers - Group Studies)

Growdon, C.H. (1950) *A group study of juvenile homicide*. Columbus, OH: State Bureau of Juvenile Research.

(Murderers - Juvenile)

Thom, D.A. (1949, July) Juvenile delinquency and criminal homicide. *Journal of Maine Medical Association, 40*, 176-180.

(Murderers - Juvenile)

Hobbs, A.W. (1944, April) Juvenile murderers. *Canadian Behavioral Review, 22*, 377-379.

(Murderers - Juvenile)

Patterson, R.M. (1943) Psychiatric study of juveniles involved in homicide. *American Journal of Orthopsychiatry, 13*, 125-130.

(Murderer - Youth)

Fontes, V. (1942) A case of deliberate homicide executed by a youth of 14. *Crianca Portung, 1*, 131-140.

(Murderers- Adolescents)

Karr, M.L. (1941) A study off adolescent who kill. *Smith College Stud Social Work, 12*, 199-200.

(Murderers - Adolescents)

Begon, L. (1940, Oct. 5) Murder by children and adolescents. *Nature, 146*, p. 456.

(Murderers - Children/Adolescents)

Bender, L., & Curran, F.J. (1940) Children and adolescents who kill. *Journal of Criminal Psychopathology, 1*, 297-322.

(Homicide - Degrees)

Homicide by minor, degrees of homicide, juvenile delinquency. (People v. Murch) (N.Y.) 189 N E 200. (1934, May) *St. John's Law Review, 8*, 358-359.

(Murderers - Youth)

Arado, C.C. (1932, Sept./Oct.) Murder by abandoned colored youths. *Journal of Criminal Law, 23*, 469-473.

(Murderers -Youth)

Seelig, E. (1932) Young murderers. *Vjsch f Jugendkd, 2*, 112-119.

(Murderers - Youth)

Holler, E. (1930) A youthful type of murderer. *Bl f Gefangniskunde, 61*, 60-76.

(Murderers - Youth)

Bridgman, O. (1929) Four young murderers. *Juvenile Research, 13*, 90-96.

The Murderer
Males

(Murderers - Sons)

Smith, J.M. (1990, June 10). Mothers: Tired of taking the rap. *new York Times Magazine*, p. 32.

(Homicides - British Columbia)

Shroeder, A. (1990, March) Eric, Tyrone, and Michael. *Saturday Night, 105*(2), pp. 25-36.

(Murderers - Male)

Fingerhut, L.A., & Kleinman, J.C. (1990) International and interstate comparison of homicide among young males. JAMA, 263(24), 3292-3295.

(Murderer - Biography)

Baker, J.N., & Murr, A. (1989, Sept. 25) 'I told them I'd be back'. *Newsweek, 114*(13), 22.

(Murderers - Husbands or Lovers)

Smith, P. (1989, July 7). Perfect murderers (men who kill their wives or lovers). *New Statesman Soc, 2*, 14-16.

(Serial Killer - Bundy)

Nobile, P. (1989, July) The making of a monster. *Playboy, 36*(7), 41-45.

(Murderers - Men)

Rule, A. (1989, Feb.) Final attraction: Men who charm women - - to death. *Redbook, 172*(4), 104-106+.

(Murderer - Husband or Lover)

Came, B. (1989, Feb.) Victims in the home. *Macleans, 103*(43), pp. 104-106+.

(Green River Murderer)

Ryan, M. (1987, Aug. 24) A killer on the loose (Green River serial murderer). *People Weekly, 28*, 24-29.

(Homicide - Lennon)

Gaines, J.R. (1987, March 9) The killer takes his fall (M. Chapman, murderer of John Lennon). *People Weekly, 27*, 60-62+.

(Homicide - Workplace)

Davis, H. (1987) Workplace homicide of Texas males. *American Journal of Public Health, 77*(10), 1290-1293.

(Spouse Abuse)

Virkkunen M., & Kallio, E. (1987) Low blood glucose nadir in the glucose tolerance test and homicidal spouse abuse. *Aggressive Behavior, 13*(2), 59-66.

(Lady-Killer)

A lady-killer stalks Atlanta (murders of elderly blacks). (1986, April 28) *Time, 127*, p. 38.

(Homicide - Domestic/Non-domestic)

Daniel, A.E., & Holcomb, W.R. (1985) A comparison between men charged with domestic and non-domestic homicide. *Bulletin of American Academy of Psychiatry and the Law, 13*(3), 233-241.

(Murderers - Males)

Devasia, V.V., Devasia, L. (1984) Victim-offender relationship in female homicide by male: A study conducted in Maharashtra. *Indian Journal of Social Work, 145*(3), 317-323.

(Murderer - Male)

Ressler, R.K., et al. (1983) One offender and twelve victims. *American Journal of Psychiatry, 140*(1), 36-40.

(Child Killer)

Montagno, M., & Jones, J.C. (1978, Feb. 13) Child killer: Oakland County, Mich. *Newsweek, 91*, p. 9+.

(Serial Killers)

Morrison, H.L. (1979) Psychiatric observations and interpretations of bite mark evidence in multiple murders. *Journal of Forensic Science, 24*(2), 492-502.

(Murderers - Mothers)

Schetky, D.H. (1978) Preschoolers responses to murder of their mothers by their fathers: A study of four cases. *Bulletin of the American Academy of Psychiatry and Law, 6*(1), 45-47.

(Murderer - Male)

Deiker, T.E. (1974) Characteristics of males indicted and convicted of homicide. *Journal of Social Psychology, 95*, 151-152.

(Offenders)

Landau, S.F., et al. (1974, Sept.) Homicide victims and offenders: An Israeli study. *Journal of Criminology and the Law, 65*, 390-396.

(Murderers - Male)

Delker, T.E. (1973) WAIS characteristics of indicted male murderers. *Psychological Reports, 32*(3, part 2), 1066.

(Sadists - Males)

Grabowska, H., et al. (1972, March/April) Case of a 14-year old sadist murder of a four year old girl. *Psychiatr Pol, 6*, 219-221.

(Murderers - Male)

Mohr, J.W. (1971, Feb.) Violence as a function of age and relationship with special reference to matricide. *Canadian Psychiatric Association Journal, 18*, 29-32.

(Murderers - Male)

Gribble, L. (1968) *They had a way with women.* Roy.

(Murderers - Psychology)

Berg, I.A., & Fox, V. (1947, Aug.) Factors in homicide committed by 200 males. *Journal of Social Psychology, 26*, 109-119.

(Murderers - Men)

Berg, I.A., & Fox, V. (1946) Factors in homicide committed by 200 males. *American Psychologist, 1*, 461.

(Murderers - Men)

Rosanoff, A.J. (1943) The thirty condemned men. *American Journal of Psychiatry, 99*, 484-495.

(Murderers - Men)

Banay, R.S. (1943) A study of twenty-two men convicted of murder in the first degree. *Journal of Criminal Law and Criminology, 34*, 106-11.

The Murderer
Women

(Battered Women)

Greenwald, J.P., et al. (1990, Spring) Psychological self-defense jury instructions: Influence on verdicts for battered women defendants. (Special Issue: Spouse Abuse) *Behavioral Sciences and the Law, 8*, 171-180.

(Homicide - Females)

Dorban, P.T. (1990) Female homicide. *Ir J Psychology Med, 7*(1), 64-70.

(Murderers - Women)

Occupational homicides among women - - United States, 1980-1985. (1990) *MMWR, 39*(32), 544, 551-552.

(Criminality - Female)

Best, J., & Luckenbill, D.F. (1990) Male dominance and female criminality: A test of Harris' theory of deviant type-scripts. *Sociological Inquiry, 60*(1), 71-86.

(Self-Defense - Female)

Carpenter, T. (1989, Dec. 31) The final self-defense. *New York Times Book Review,* , p. 17.

(Female Homicide)

Mann, C.R. (1989, Nov. 2) Female homicide and substance abuse: Is there a connection? *Women and Criminal Justice, 1*, 87-109.

(Murderers - Women)

Browne, A., & Williams, K.R. (1989, Feb.) Exploring the effect of resource availability and the likelihood of female-perpetrated homicides. *Law and Society Review, 23*, 75-94.

(Parricide - Women)

Dorban, P.T., & O'Connor, A. (1989, Jan.) Women who kill their parents. *British Journal of Psychiatry, 154*, 27-33.

(Murderers - Women)

Walker, L.E. (1989) *Terrifying love: Why battered women kill and how society responds.* New York: Harper & Row.

(Murderer - Female)

Wright, L., & Baker, J. (1988, Nov. 28) Death at the rooming house. *Newsweek, 112*(22), p. 47.

(Murderer - Female)

Kleinman, D. (1988, Nov.) A deadly silence. *Ladies Home Journal, 105*(11), 70-82.

(Murderers - Nurses)

Yorker, B.C. (1988) Nurses accused of murder. *American Journal of Nursing, 88*(10), 1327-1332.

(Murderers - Black Women)

Mann, C.R. (1987) Black women who kill, in R.L. Hampton, (Ed.), *Violence in the Black Family: Correlates and consequences*, pp. 157-186. Lexington, MA: Heath.

(Murderer - Woman)

Chicago woman kills her son over a card game (L. White). (1986, Dec. 1) *Jet, 71*, p. 14.

(Murderer - Mother)

Mom who killed one child wants sterilization as plea bargain in 2nd's death (case of D.A. Williams). (1986, Aug. 4) *Jet, 70*, p. 38.

(Murderer - T.Broome)

Grogan, D. (1986, July 14) Driven by drugs and fear, an American model kills her tormenting Italian playboy. *People Weekly, 26*, 34-46+.

(Battered Women)

Campbell, J.C. (1986, July) Nursing assessment for risk of homicide in battered women. *ANS, 8*(4), 36-51.

(Murderer - Women)

Browne, A. (1986) Assault and homicide: When battered women kill, in M.J. Saks and L. Saxe (Eds.), *Advances in Applied Psychology (Volume 3)*, pp. 57-79. Hillsdale, NJ: Lawrence Erlbaum Associates.

(Girls who kill)

Russell, D.H. (1985) Girls who kill. *International Journal of Offender Therapy and Comparative Criminology, 29*(2), 171-176.

(Battered Women)

Cohen, M.F. (1985) Domestic Violence. *Medicine and the Law, 4*(1), 19-27.

(Homicide/Suicide - Female)

Fishbain, D.A., et al. (1985) Female homicide - suicide perpetrators: A controlled study. *Journal of Forensic Science, 30*(4), 1148-1156.

(Battered women)

Blackman, J., & Brickman, E. (1984) The impact of expert testimony on trials of battered women who kill their husbands. *Behavioral Sciences and the Law, 2*(4), 413-422.

(Murderer - Female)

Wilbanks, W. (1983) The female homicide offender in Dade County, Florida. *Criminal Justice Review, 8*(2), 9-14. Microforms and article copies available through UMI.

(Murderer- Female)

Husain, A., et al. (1983) A study of young-age and midlife homicidal women admitted to a psychiatric hospital for pretrial evaluation. *Canadian Journal of Psychiatry, 28*(2), 109-113.

(Murderers - Women)

Wilbanks, W. (1983) Female homicide offenders in the U.S. *International Journal of Women's Studies, 16*(4), 302-310.

(Murderers - Black Females)

McLain, P.D. (1982-83) Black females and lethal violence: Has time changed the circumstances under which they kill? *Journal of Death and Dying, 13*(1), 13-25.

(Murderer - Female)

Kromm, J. (1982) Occupational therapy in the assessment of a woman accused of murder. *Psychiatric Quarterly, 54*(2), 85-96.

(Murderers - Wives)

Jones, A. (1980, Oct./Nov.) She had to die! (R. Snyder's 1927 murder of husband: excerpt from *Women who kill*). *American Heritage, 31*, pp. 20-31.

(Victims - Women)

McCall, C. (1980, Jan. 7) Enigma of Ted Bundy: Did he kill 18 women or has he been framed? *People Weekly, 13*, pp. 14-19.

(Murderers - Women)

Jones, A. (1980) *Women who kill.* HR & W.

(Murderer - Female)

Borowitz, A.I. (1980) *The woman who murdered Black Satin: The Bermondsey Horror.* Columbus, OH: OSU Press.

(Murderers - Women)

Biggers, T.A. (1979) Death by murder: A study of women murderers. *Death Education, 3*(1), 1-9.

(Murderer - Mother)

Woman murders daughter to stop her life as a prostitute. (1978) *Juvenile Justice Digest, 6*(18), 10. Article copies available through UMI.

(Murderer - Mother)

Woman murders daughter to stop her from returning to Boston and her life as a prostitute. (1978) *Crime Control Digest, 12*(39), 6. Artocle copies available from UMI.

(Murderers - Women)

Totman, J. (1978) *The murderess: A psychosocial study of criminal homicide.* R & E Research Associates.

(Battered Women)

Dvoskin, J. (1978) Legal alternatives for battered women who kill their abusers. *Bulletin of American Academy of Psychiatry and the Law, 6*(3), 335-354.

(Battered Wives)

Fiora-Gormally, N. (1978) Battered wives who kill. Double standard out of the court, single standard in? *Law and Human Behavior, 2*(2), 133-165.

(Murderers - Mothers)

Riehl, A., et al. (1978) Women convicted for killing their own children. *Mschr Krimonol Strafrechtsref, 61*(1), 51-61.

(Murderers - Women)

The female of the species. (1978) *The Police Journal, 51*(2), 209.

(Murderers - Mothers)

Bush, S. (1976, Nov.) Child killers: The murderer is often the mother, study by D. Kaplun and R. Reich. *Psychology Today, 10,* 28.

(Murderers - Women)

Krouse, A.N., et al. (1975) Why women kill. *J Commun, 25*(2), 98-105.

(Murderers - Women)

Parker, E. (1974, July) The victims of mentally disordered female offenders. *British Journal of Psychiatry, 125,* 51-59.

(Murderers - Mothers)

Desseigne, F., et al. (1974) Mothers who kill their children. *Ann Med Psychol, 2*(1), 238-248.

(Murderers - Women)

Rosenblatt, E., & Greeland, C. (1974) Female crimes of violence. *Canadian Journal of Criminology and Corrections, 16*(2), 173-180.

(Prisoners - Women)

D'Alessandro, B., et al. (1972, July-Sept.) On the adreno-ovarian androgenic function in women in prison, I. (preliminary note) (Italian). *Quad Criminol Clin, 14,* 329-338.

(Murderers - Women)

Sparrow, G. (1971) *Women who murder.* New York: Tower.

(Murderers - Women)

Geis, G., & Soler, J. (1973) Response of female homicide offenders to press coverage of their trials. *Journalism Quarterly, 48*(3), 558-560.

(Murderers - Mothers)

Turbe-Becker, E. (1970) Homicide by mothers. *Beitr Gerichtl Med, 27,* 166-175. German with English abstract.

(Murderers - Mothers)

Myers, S.A. (1970, Dec.) Maternal filicide. *American Journal of Disabled Children, 120,* 534-536.

(Murderers - Women)

Cole, K.E., et al. (1968, July) Women who kill: A sociopathological study. *Archives of General Psychiatry, 19,* 1-8.

(Murderers - Women)

Feix, G. (1967) Zur Personlichkeit der Moderin. 13586, J. 41, 1967, H. 7, S. 205-209.

(Murderers - Mothers)

Tuteur, W., & Glotzer, J. (1966, July) Further observations on murdering mothers. *Journal of*

Forensic Science, 11, 373-383.

(Murderer - Mother)

Zumpe, L. (1966) Killing and attempting to kill one's own children by psychotic mothers. *Arch Psychiat Nervenkr, 208*, 198-208 (German).

(Murderers - Women)

Gribble, L. (1965) *Such women are deadly*. New York: Arco.

(Murderer - Women)

Brown, W. (1963) *Women who died in the Chair*. New York: Macmillan.

(Murderers - Mothers)

Tuteur, W., & Glotzer, J. (1959, Nov.) Murdering mothers. *American Journal of Psychiatry, 116*, 447-452.

(Women - Criminal Instigators)

Pilmes, R. (1953) Women as criminal instigators. *Nervenarzt, 24*, 248-251.

(Murderers - Young Women)

Ellis, A. (1951) A young woman convicted of manslaughter. *Case Reports in Clinical Psychology, 2*(1), 9-34-A.

(Homicides - Female)

Morton, J.H. (1934) Female homicides. *Journal of Ment Sci, 80*, 64-74.

(Murderer - Women)

Winckelmann, W. (1934) *Observations on 50 murderesses in the penitentiary at Jauer*. Berlin: Schotz.

(Murderers - Women)

Heindle, R. (1934) Women as murderers. *Arch Krim Anthrop, 95*, 61-63.

(Murderess - Young)

Plaut, P. (1931) Eine dreizehnjahrige kindesmorderin (A thirteen-year-old child murderess). *Krim Monatsh, 5*, 221-224.

(Lefebvre Case)

Bonaparte, M. (1929) The Lefebvre case: Psychoanalysis of a murderess. *Imago, 15*, 15-62.

The Murderer
Murderers in the Family

(Carol Stuart Case)

Brown S.A. (1990, Oct. 29) After the lies and the anger, the murder of Carol Stuart leaves a legacy of hope. *People Weekly, 34*(17), pp. 48-49.

(Killing Sister's Boyfriend)

Kunen, J.S., et al. (1990, June 4) Brando's son faces murder one. *People Weekly, 33*(22), 23-24.

(Murderer - Spouse)

Jacobi, M., & Wright, R. (1990, May) The perfect marriage that ended in murder. *Good Housekeeping, 210*(5), 166-167+.

(Boston Murderer)

Brudnoy, D. (1990, Feb. 5) Stranger than Wolfe. *National Review, 42*(2), 23-24.

(Murder - Family)

Kaye, N.S., et al. (1990) Families, murder, and insanity: A psychiatric review of paternal neonaticide. *Journal of Forensic Science, 35*(1), 113-139.

(Murderers - Parents)

Bourget, D. (1990) Homicidal parents. *Canadian Journal of Psychiatry, 35*(3), 233-238.

(Marital Homicide)

Goetting, A. (1989, Autumn) Patterns of marital homicide: A comparison of husbands and wives. *Journal of Comprehensive Family Studies, 20*, 341-354.

(Murderer - Wife)

Salholz, E., & Murr, A. (1989, Aug. 14) Arsenic and old lace. *Newsweek, 114*(7), 24.

(Murderers - Spouses)

Mercy, J.A., & Saltzman, L.E. (1989, May) Fatal violence among spouses in the United States, 1976-1985. *American Journal of Public Health, 79*, 595-599.

(Murderer - Mother)

Egginton, J. (1989, April) The bad mother. *Good Housekeeping, 208*(4), pp. 119, 247+.

(Homicide - Family)

Evolution and family homicide (letter). (1989) *Science, 243*(4890), 462-464.

(Case Report - Bob Marshall)

McGinniss, J. (1988, Dec. 1) Blind Faith. *Rolling Stone, 540*, pp. 69-79+.

(Patricide)

Detroit boy who shot, killed father is cleared. (1988, Oct. 24) *Jet, 75*(4), p. 28.

(Murderer - Mother)

Silverman, R.A., & Kennedy, L.W. (1988) Women who kill their children *Violence Victims, 3*(2), 113-127.

(Homicide - Evolutionary)

Daly, M., et al. (1988) Evolutionary social psychology and family homicide. *Science, 242*(4878), 519-524.

(Homicide - Domestic)

Kalischman, S.C. (1988) MMPI profile of women and men convicted of domestic homicide. *Journal of Clinical Psychology, 44*(6), 847-853.

(Murderers - Parents)

Goetting, A. (1988) When parents kill their young children: Detroit 1982-1986. *Journal of Family Violence, 3*(4), 339-346.

(Murderer - Mother)

Brower, M. (1987, Sept. 14) Unmasking a murderous mother, crime writer Ann Rule closes the book on another psychopath (case of D. Downs). *People Weekly, 28,* 125.

(Intimate Homicide)

Silverman, R.A., et al. (1987) Intimate homicide: An analysis of violent social relationships. (Special issue: Homicidal behavior) *Behavioral Sciences and the Law, 5*(1), 37-47.

(Matricide - Diagnosis)

Lowenstein, L.F. (1987) The diagnosis and treatment of a potential matricidal and fratricidal adolescent in a therapeutic community. *Criminologist, 11*(1), 44-45.

(Murderer - Son)

Johnson, T.E. (1986, Sept. 15) Brother's keepers - - and son's (author J. Wideman's son accused of murder in Flagstaff, Ariz.). *Newsweek, 108,* 35.

(Matricidal Men)

Campion, J., et al. (1985) A study of 15 matricidal men. *American Journal of Psychiatry, 142*(3), 312-317.

(Battered Wife)

Buda, M.A., & Butler, T.L. (1985) The battered wife syndrome: A back door assault on domestic violence. *Social Action and the Law, 10*(3), 63-71.

(Domestic Homicide)

Blinder, M.G. (1984) The domestic homicide. *Family Therapy, 11*(3), 185-198.

(Murderer - Wife)

Family man (A. Toto puts up bail for his wife after she is arrested for attempting to murder him in Allentown, PA). (1983, March 14) *Time, 121*, p. 33.

(Kinship)

Daly, M., et al. (1982) Homicide and kinship. *American Anthropologist, 84*(2), 372-378.

(Parricide)

Benefits frozen for kids who kill parents. (1982) *Juvenile Justice Digest, 10*(19), 6. Article copies available from UMI.

(Homicide - Spouse)

Wallacker, B.E. (1981) Poet as jurist: Po Chu-i and a case of conjugal homicide. *Harvard Journal of Asiatic Studies, 41*, 507-526.

(Conjugal Violence)

Marcus, M.I. (1981) Conjugal violence: The law of force and the force of law. *California Law Review, 69*, 1657-1733.

(Matricide - Son)

Green, C.M. (1981) Matricide by sons. *Medical Science and the Law, 21*(3), 207-214.

(Spouse Murder)

Bach, G.R. (1980) Spouse killing: The final abuse. *Journal of Contemporary Psychotherapy, 11*(2), 91-103.

(Murder - Movies)

Nash, J.R. (1979) Gamblers, wife choppers, killers provide grist for the movie mill (last of four parts). *Law Enforcement News, 5*(22), 13.

(Murderer- Mother-in-law)

Nobile, P. (1978, Aug. 7) Case of the murderous mother-in-law: Conspiracy to commit murder (trial of H. Ritz in New York City). *N Y, 11*, pp. 24-30.

(Battered Wives)

Footlick, J.K., & Sciolino, E. (1978, Jan. 30) Wives who batter back. *Newsweek, 91*, p.54.

(Murderer - Husband)

Schetky, D.H. (1978) Preschoolers' responses to murder of their mothers by their fathers: A study of four cases. *Bulletin of the American Academy of Psychiatry and the Law, 6*(1), 45-57.

(Murderers - Fathers)

Scharbach, H. (1978) Three cases of fathers murdering their sons (French). *Nautes Fra Evol Psychiatr, 43*(3), 609-624.

(Murder - Familial)

McCully, R.S. (1978) The laugh of Satan: A study of a familial murder. *Journal of Personal Assessment, 42*(1), 81-91.

(Parricide)

Corder, B.F., et al. (1976) Adolescent parricide: A comparison with other adolescent murder. *American Journal of Psychiatry, 133*(8), 957-961.

(Marital Homicide)

Chimbos, P.D. (1976) *Marital violence: A study of interspouse homicide.* Toronto: York University Press.

(Murder - Family Victims)

Foucault, M. (1975, Aug. 29) Pierre Riviera, having slaughtered my mother, my sister, and my brother. *Nat R, 27*, 950.

(Crimes - Father/Son)

Bizarre case of father and son: Crimes linked to J. Kallinger and son, Michael. (1975, Feb. 3) *Time, 105*, 13-14.

(Murderer - Mother)

Mother charged in shooting death of son in hospital after overdose. (1975) *Narcotic Control Digest, 5*(18), 2.

(Victims - Family)

California youth held for family murder. (1975) *Juvenile Justice Digest, 3*(4), 3.

(Maternal Violence)

Forrest, T. (1974) The family dynamics of maternal violence. *Journal of the American Academy of Psychoanalysis, 2*(3), 215-230.

(Murderers - Parents)

Scott, P.D. (1973, April) Parents who kill their children. *Medical Science and the Law, 13*, 120-126.

(Murder by Parents)

Uszkiewiczowa, L. (1971) Child murder by parents in light of the medico-forensic material. *Psychiatr Pol, 5*, 125-132.

(Child Killer)

Myers, S.A. (1967, Aug.) The child slayer: A 25-year survey of homicides involving preadolescent victims. *Archives of General Psychiatry, 17*, 211-213.

(Matricide)

McKnight, C.K., et al. (1966, April) Matricide and mental illness. *Canadian Psychiatric*

Assessment Journal, 11, 99-106.

(Matricide)

Scheri, D.J. (1966, Oct.) A study of adolescent matricide. *Journal of the American Academy of Child Psychiatry, 5*, 569-593.

(Parricide)

Sutte, H. (1964, Feb./March) Attempted parricide by a 16-year old girl. *Acta Paedopsychiat, 31*, 95-99. (German)

(Homicide - Psychodynamics)

Cormier, B.M. (1962) Psychodynamics of homicide committed in a marital relationship. (French) *Psychiat J Soc Ther, 8*(4), 187-194.

(Double Murderers)

Sulestrowska, H. (1962, July/Aug.) Retrospective personality evaluation of a double murderer: Father of a schizophrenic boy. *Neurol Neurochir Psychiat Pol, 32*, 627-630.

(Murderer - Sons)

Meerloo, J.A. (1959) The case of the murderous son. *American Practitioner, 10*(7), 1109.

(Homicides - Husband/Wife)

Wolfgang, M.E. (1956) Husband-Wife homicides. *Journal of Social Therapy, 2*, 263-271.

(Matricide)

Wertham, F. (1941) The matricidal impulse: Critique of Freud's interpretation of *Hamlet. Journal of Criminal Psychopathology, 2*, 455-464.

(Criminal Act - Housewife)

Doi, M. (1940) Die tat einer Mandschurischen hausfrar infolge von besessenheitswahn (The criminal act of a Manchurian housewife due to obsession). *Arb Psychiat Inst Sendai, 7*, 18-39.

(Murderer - Mother)

Kinberg, O. (1934) Murder of her own child by a woman in a state of extreme psychological adjustment. *Svenska Larkartidn, 31*, 969-987.

The Murderer
Murderers and Mental Illness

(Depression - Homicidal)

Malmquist, C.P. (1990, March) Depression in homicidal adolescents. Journal of American Academy of Psychiatry and the Law, 18, 32-36.

(Insanity - Homicidal)

McGovern, C.M. (1990) Homicidal insanity, 1800-1985 , by J. Colaizzi, book review. *Journal of American History, 76*(4), 1238-1239.

(Slaughter)

Baker, J.N., et al. (1989, Jan. 30) Death on the playground. *Newsweek, 113*(5), p. 35.

(Homicide - Sadistic)

Simonsen, J. (1989) A sadistic homicide. *American Journal of Forensic Medical Pathology, 10*(2), 159-163.

(Hungorford Massacre)

Appleby, L., & Wessely, S. (1988) Public attitude to mental illness: The influence of the Hungerford massacre. *Medical Science and Law, 28*(4), 291-295.

(Murderers)

Feldman, M., et al. (1986) Filicidal abuse in the histories of 15 condemned murderers. *Bulletin of the American Academy of Psychiatry and Law, 14*(4), 345-352.

(Stress Disorder)

Harry, B., & Resnick, P.J. (1986) Post-traumatic stress disorder in murderers. *Journal of Forensic Science, 31*(2), 609-613.

(Malingered Amnesia)

Parwatikar, S.D., et al. (1985) The detection of malingered amnesia in accused murderers. *Bulletin of the American Academy of Psychiatry and the Law, 13*(1), 97-103.

(Figlicide)

Fazzari, G., et al. (1985) On a criminological study concerning cases of female and male figlicide crimes committed by insane individuals (Italian). *Rivista Sperimentale di Freiatra e Medicina Legale delle Alienazoni Mentali, 109*(1), 87-99.

(Homicide by Psychotics)

Benezech, M., et al. (1984) Homicide by psychotics in France: A five year study. *Journal of Clinical Psychiatry, 45*(2), 85-86.

(Hillside Strangler)

Watkins, J.G. (1984) The Bianchi (Hillside Strangler) case: Sociopath or multiple personality. *International Journal of Clinical and Experimental Hypnosis, 32*(2), 67-101.

(Mothers - Filicidal)

Husain, S.A., & Daniel, A. (1984) A comparative study of filicidal and abusive mothers. *Canadian Journal of Psychiatry, 29*(7), 596-598.

(Offenders - Mental Illness)

Haynes, R.L., & Marques, J.K. (1984) Patterns of suicide among hospitalized mentally disordered offenders. *Suicide and Life Threatening Behavior, 14*(2), 113-125.

(Mental Illness)

Friedman, S. (1983) Predicting psychiatric admission from an emergency room. *The Journal of Nervous and Mental Disease, 171*(3), 155-158.

(Mentally Disordered)

Quinsey, V.L., et al. (1983) Assertion and over-controlled hostility among mentally disordered murderers. *Journal of Consultative Clinical Psychology, 51*(4), 550-556.

(Post-Traumatic Stress Disorder)

Grant, B.L. (1983) Guilty verdict in a murder committed by a veteran with post-traumatic stress disorder. *Bulletin of the American Academy of Psychiatry and the Law, 11*(4), 355-358.

(Murderer - Mentally Ill)

Benezech, M. (1983) Mentally ill murderers in France. *International Criminology Policy Review, 38*(371), 226-229.

(Murderers - Psychiatric Evaluation)

Langevin, R. (1982) Diagnosis of killers seen for psychiatric evaluation: A controlled study. *Acta Psychiatr Scand, 66*(3), 216-228.

(Predicting Homicide)

McDonald, A. (1981) A study of homicide: The validity of predictive test factors. *Canadian Journal of Psychiatry, 26*(8), 549-554.

(Homicidal Offenses)

Spiel, W. (1981) Homicidal offenses as viewed by children and adolescents (a study in child psychiatry). *Osterreichische Richterzeitung, 59*(8), 145-151.

(Homicide - Psychiatry)

Kermani, E.J. (1981) Violent psychiatric patients: A study. *American Journal of Psychotherapy, 35*(2), 215-225.

(Murderer - Psychosis)

Fellion, G., et al. (1980) From fantasy to reality: On criminal and cannibalistic actions (French). *Ann Med Psychol, 138*(5), 596-602.

(Murderers - Psychiatric Evaluation)

Bloom, J.D. (1980) Forensic psychiatric evaluation of Native Alaska homicide offenders. *International Journal of Law and Psychiatry, 3*, 163-171.

(Murderers - Mentally Ill)

Grunberg, F., et al. (1977, June) Homicide and deinstitutionalization of the mentally ill. *American Journal of Psychiatry, 134*, 685-687.

(Murderers - Schizophrenics)

Nakatani, Y. (1977) Homicide committed by latent schizophrenic patients. *Seishin Shinkeigaku Zasshi, 82*(6), 353.

(Murderers - Schizophrenics)

Browne, W.J., & Palmer, A.J. (1975) A preliminary study of schizophrenic women who murdered their children. *Hospital and Community Psychiatry, 26*(2), 71, 75.

(Matricide)

Oberdalhoff, H.E. (1974) Matricide in a schizophrenic psychosis: Case report (German). *Confinia Psychiatrica, 17*(2), 122-131.

(Arson - Schizophrenics)

Virkkunen, M. (1974) On arson committed by schizophrenics. *Acta Psychiatr Scand, 50*, 152-160.

(Murderer - Psychiatric Patient)

Turns, D.M., et al. (1973) An attendant is murdered: The state hospital responds. *Psychiatric Quarterly, 47*(4), 487-494.

(Dangerous Patients)

Dangerous patients. (1973, Feb. 3) *British Medical Journal, 1*, 247-248.

(Murderer - Psychopathology)

Szymusik, A. (1972) Studies on the psychopathology of murderers. *Polish Medical Journal, 11*, 752-757.

(Criminals - Mentally Disturbed)

Hafner, H., et al. (1972) Violent mentally disturbed criminals in West Germany: An epidemiological study (German). *Nervenarzt, 43*, 285-291.

(Murderers - Analysis)

Lachman, J.H. (1969) The murderers - before and after. 28414. vol. 43, 1969, n. 1, pp. 1-11

(IBZ 70).

(Murderer - Schizophrenia)

Blackburn, R. (1968, Oct.) Emotionality, extroversion, and aggression in paranoid and non-paranoid schizophrenic offenders. *British Journal of Psychiatry, 114,* 1301-1302.

(Mental Illness)

Becker, W. (1967, Sept. 29) The compulsive criminal in today's society (German). *Med Klin, 62,* 1522-1525.

(Murderers)

Kahn, M.W. (1967) Correlates of Rorschach reality adherence in the assessment of murderer who plead insanity. *Journal of Projective Techniques and Personality Assessment, 31*(4), 44-45.

(Murderers)

Deford, M.M. (1966) *Murderers sane and mad.* New York: Avon. (1965) New York: Abelard.

(Murderers - Mental Illness)

McKnight, C.K., et al. (1966, April) Mental illness and homicide. *Canadian Psychiatric Assessment Journal, 11,* 91-98.

(Murderers - Mental Illness)

Varma, L.P., et al. (1966, May) Characteristics of murder in mental disorder. *American Journal of Psychiatry, 122,* 1296-1298.

(Murderers - Manic Depression)

Hudgens, R.W. (1965, Aug.) Murder by a manic depressive. *International Journal of Neuropsychiatry, 1,* 381-383.

(Murderers - Psychiatric Study)

Merland, A., et al. (1964, May/June) Considerations of homicide based on the study of 298 psychiatric expertises for first-degree murder, willful homicide, and attempted murder. *Ann Med Leg, 44,* 289-297 (French).

(Psychopathic Personalities)

McCartney, J.L. (1964, Dec.) Two psychopathic personalities. *Medical Trial Techniques Quarterly, 11,* 65-71.

(Manic Murderers)

Podolsky, E. (1962, July) The manic murderer. *Journal of National Medical Association, 54,* 483-485. Also in *Medicolegal Journal, 27,* 162-165 (1959).

(Homicide)

Bromberg, W. (1961) *The mold of murder: A psychiatric study of homicide.* New York: Grune and Stratton, and Greenwood.

(Mass Murderers)

Galvin, J.A., & MacDonald, J.M. (1959) Psychiatric study of a mass murderer. *American Journal of Psychiatry, 115*(12), 1057-1061.

(Mental Illness)

Podolsky, E. (1959) The maniac murderer. *Medicolegal J, 27*, 162-165.

(Murderers - Paranoid)

Podolsky, E. (1956) The paranoid murderer. *Samiksa, 10*, 65-69.

(Murderers - Husbands)

Kurland, A.A., et al. (1955) A comparative study of wife murderers admitted to a state psychiatric hospital. *Journal of Social Therapy, 1*(2), 7-15.

(Murderers - Institutionalized)

Cruvant, B.A., & Waldrop, F.N. (1952) The murderer in the mental institution. *Annals of the American Academy of Political and Social Sciences, 284*, 35-44.

(Murderers - Psychology of)

Eliasberg, W. (1952) He murdered to get hanged: A pre-analytical case history of 1783. *Psychoanalysis Review, 39*, 164-167.

(Murderers - Psychoanalytical Study)

Karpman, B. (1951) Psychoanalytic study of a case of murder. *Psychoanalytic Review, 38*, 245-270.

(Psychopathic Personalities)

Molina, M.F. (1947) Study of a psychopathic personality in Guatemala. *Psychiatry, 10*, 31-36.

(Murder - Insanity)

Cohen, L.H., & Coffin, T.E. (1946, Nov.) Pattern of murder in insanity: A criterion of the murderer's abnormality. *Journal of Criminal Law, 37*, 262-287; abstract, *Eug R, 39*, 77 (1947, July).

(Psychopathic Personalities)

Uribe-Cualla, G. (1946) Psychopathic personality of a murderer (Spanish). *Rev Med legal Columbia, 8*(45-46), 146-159.

(Murderers - Psychopathic Analysis)

Lafora, G.R. (1942) Psychopathological analysis of the strangler Gregorio Cardenas (Spanish). *Criminalia, Mexico, 9*, 106-117.

(Schizophrenic Murder)

Wilmanns, K. (1940) Murder in the early stages of schizophrenia (German). *Z ges Neurol u Psychiat, 170*, 583-562.

(Homicide - Schizophrenia)

Schipowensky, N. (1938) *Schizophrenia and homicide*. (German). Berlin: Springer.

(Paranoid Murderer)

Case R: A paranoid schizophrenic murderer (German). (1936) *Allg Z Psychiat, 105*, 79.

(Murderer - Schizophrenic)

Kinberg, O. (1935) Murder of her own illegitimate child committed by a schizoid woman in a state of psychological maladjustment (Swedish). *Svenska Lakartidn, 32*, 582-596.

(Family Homicide)

Kinberg, O. (1934) Family murder by a schizoid under emotional confusion (Swedish). *Svenska Lakart, 31*, 480-512.

(Murder Attempts)

Kinberg, O. (1934) A young man's attempt at murder of his fiancee during a state of confused consciousness (Swedish). *Svenska Lakart, 31*, 1321-1338.

(Murderers - Psychopathic)

Rosch, A. (1934) *Murder and attempted murder in psychopathy* (German). Giessen: Meyer.

The Murderer
Psychology

(Offender type)

Fraboni, M., et al. (1990) Offense types and two-point MMPI code profiles: Discrimination between violent and non-violent offenders. *Journal of Clinical Psychology, 44*(6), 774-777.

(Massacre - Stockton, Ca.)

Caputo, P. (1989, Dec.) Death goes to school: a psychological autopsy of an American nightmare. *Esquire, 112*(6), 136-155.

(Serial Murderers)

Leibman, F.H. (1989) Serial murderers: Four case histories. *Federal Probation, 53*(4), 41-45.

(Murderers - Psychology)

Lewis, D.O., et al. (1989) Biopsychosocial characteristics of children who later murder: A prospective study. *American Journal of Psychiatry, 142*(10), 1161-1167.

(Murderous Science)

Mitchell, P. (1989) Murderous science (letter). *Australia and New Zealand Journal of Psychiatry, 23*(1), 15-16.

(Bundy and Media Violence)

Bundy indicts sexual violence in media. (1989) *Broadcasting, 116*(5), 96.

(Perfect Murderers)

Smith, P. (1989) Perfect murderers. *New Statesman, 2*(57), 14-16.

(Homicide - Social Psychology)

Daly, M., & Wilson, M. (1988, Oct. 28) Evolutionary social psychology and family homicide. *Science, 242*, 519-524.

(Murderers - Profiles)

Kalischman, S.C. (1988) MMPI profiles of women and men convicted of domestic homicide. *Journal of Clinical Psychology, 44*(6), 847-853.

(Adolescent Psychiatry - Expert Viewpoint)

Strehlow, U., et al. (1988) Homicides by adolescents and young adults from the viewpoint of the adolescent psychiatry expert. *Z Kinder Jugenpsychiatr, 16*(2), 80-86.

(Murderers - Profiles)

Kalichman, S.C. (1988) Emperically derived MMPI profile subgroups of incarcerated homicide offenders. *Journal of Clinical Psychology, 44*(5), 733-738.

(Murderer - Psychology)

Wilkes, J. (1987, June) Murder in mind (views of homicide expert D. Archer). *Psychology Today, 21*, pp. 26-28+.

(Fears of Killer)

Fears of a serial killer (Edmonton, Alberta). (1987, April 13) *Macleans, 100*, p. 14.

(Homicidal Behavior)

Meer, J. (1987, March) Murder in mind: Neurological disorders and homicidal behavior (study of death row juveniles by D.O. Lewis). *Psychology Today, 21*, p. 62.

(Murderer - Psychopathic)

Koludrovic, M., et al. (1986) Psychopathic murderers and their victims. *Vojnosanit Pregi, 43*(3), 198-203.

(Murderers - Women)

Korbin, J.E. (1986) Childhood histories of women imprisoned for fatal child maltreatment. *Child Abuse and Neglect, 10*(3), 331-338.

(Crime Scene Analysis)

Ressler, R.K. (1986) Sexual killers and their victims: Identifying patterns through crime scene analysis. *Journal of Interpersonal Violence, 1*(3), 288-308.

(Murderer - Lack of Remorse)

Waggoner, D. (1985, Sept. 23) A remorseless murderer goes free after seven years, refusing to promise that he won't kill again (case of T. Streleski who murdered Stanford professor K.W. deLeeuw). *People Weekly, 24*, pp. 60-62+.

(Murderer's Dreams)

Szymusic, A., et al. (1985) The murderer's dreams. World Psychiatric Association Symposium: Psychopathology of dream and sleeping. *Psychiatria Fennica* (1985 supplement), 145-148.

(Murderers - MMPI typology)

Holcomb, W.R., et al. (1985) The development and cross-validation of an MMPI typology of murderers. *Journal of Personality Assessment, 49*(3), 240-244.

(Murderers - Psychological Types)

Lester, D. (1984) Psychological types of murderers. *Research Communications in Psychology, Psychiatry, and Behavior, 9*(4), 439-441.

(Murderer - Psychology)

Michaud, S.G., et al. (1983, March) When one murders: Ted Bundy talks about the unthinkable (excerpt from the only living witness). *Esquire, 99*, pp. 76-78+.

(Murderer - Study of)

Mass murderer studied. (1983) *Criminal Justice Newsletter, 14*(17), 3.

(Murderers - Personality)

Anderson, W.P., & Holcomb, W.R.. (1983) Accused murderers: five MMPI personality types. *Journal of Clinical Psychology, 39*(5), 761-768.

(Murderers - Intelligence)

Holcomb, W.R., & Adams, N. (1982) Racial influences on intelligence and personality measures of people who commit murder. *Journal of Clinical Psychology, 38*(4), 793-796.

(Murderers - Frustration Reactions)

Mani, K. (1982) Frustration reactions among murderers and non-criminals. *Indian Journal of Criminology, 10*(2), 116-119.

(Murderer - Lustful)

Hazelwood, R.R., & Douglas, J.E. (1980) Lust murderer. *FBI Law Enforcement Bulletin, 49*(4), 18-22.

(Stereotypes and Dispositions)

Boris, S.B. (1979, Aug.) Stereotypes and dispositions for criminal homicide. *Criminology, 17*, 139-158.

(Homicide - Rorschach Testing)

Bukowski, N.T. (1979) The Rorschach in homicides. *PSICO, 16*, 5-27.

(Murderer - Personality)

Keltikangas-Jarvinen, L. (1978) Personality characteristics of homicides and assaulters. *Psychiatria Fenn, 1978*, 65-71.

(Murder and Aggression)

Kutash, I.L (1978) *Violence: Perspectives on murder and aggression.* Behav. and Social Sci. Ser.

(Murderers - Hostility)

Lester, D., & Wright, T. (1978) Murderers and over-controlled hostility. *Psychology Reports, 43*, 1202.

(Shy Murderers)

Lee, M., et al. (1977, Nov.) Shy murderers. *Psychology Today, 11*, pp. 68-70+.

(Psychiatric Evaluation)

Uhlin, D.M. (1977) The use of drawings for psychiatric evaluation of a defendant in a case of homicide. *Mental Health and Society, 4*(1-2), 61-73.

(Murderers - Sociopsychological Investigation)

Walshe-Brennan, K.S. (1977) A sociopsychological investigation of young murderers. *The British Journal of Criminology, 17*(1), 58-63.

(Murderers - Psychiatric Study)

Wille, W.S. (1975) *Citizens who commit murder: A psychiatric study.* New York: Green.

(Murderers' Mind)

Abrahamsen,D. (1975) *The murdering mind.* New York: Harper-Row.

(Murderers - Personality)

Perdue, W.C., & Lester, D. (1974) Tempermentally suited to kill: The personality of murderers. *Corrective Psychiatry and Journal of Behavior Technology Methods and Therapy, 20*(1), 13-15.

(Murder and Aggression)

Lester, D., et al. (1974) Murder and the control of aggression. *Psychology Reports, 34*(3), 706.

(Murderers - Body Image)

Lester, D., et al. (1974, April) Body images of murderers. *Journal of General Psychology, 90*, 187-189.

(Murderers - Psychology)

Boyanowsky, E.O., et al. (1974) Film preferences following a murder. *Communication Research, 1*(1), 32-43.

(Murderers - Rorschach Stimuli)

Lester, D., et al. (1973, Oct.) Movement responses of murderers to Rorschach stimuli. *Perception and Motor Skills, 37,* 668.

(Murderer's Mind)

Guttmacher, M.S. (1973) *Mind of the murderer.* Grove.

(Murderers)

Goldstein, R.L. (1972, Dec.) Those who kill without thinking. *American Journal of Psychiatry, 129,* 766-777.

(Dangerous Patients)

Releasing potentially dangerous patients. (1972, Aug.) *Journal of Royal College of General Practitioners, 22,* 496-497.

(Murderers - Anger/fear)

McKie, R.R. (1972) A clinical study: Relationships of anger and fear to aggression in murderers and non-violent offenders. *Dissertation Abstracts International, 32*(12-B), 7317-7318.

(Criminals - Impulsive)

Bauer, G. (1971, Aug. 6) Violent impulsive criminals: Analysis of their development and behavior (German). Munch Med Woehenschr, 113, 1089-1096.

(Homicide - Sex)

Staak, M. (1971, Summer) Psychopathological and medicosocial aspects of homicide in sexual relations between strangers on chance acquaintances (French). Med Leg Domm Corpor, 4(258-261).

(Murder - Mississippi)

Senseless killing: High school graduate J. Collier of Drew, Miss. (1971, June 7) *Time, 97,* 13-14.

(Murder Story)

Conroy, F. (1970, Nov.) Manson wins! A fantasy. *Harper, 241,* pp. 53-59.

(Murderers - Sadistic)

Brittain, R.P. (1970, Oct.) The sadistic murderer. *Med Sci Law, 10,* 198-207.

(Murderers)

Lachman, J.H., et al. (1969) The murderers: Before and after. *Psychiatric Quarterly, 43*(1-11)

(Murderers)

Murderers, madmen, and mores. (1968, Jan.) *Stanford Law Review, 1,* 134-136.

(Homicidal Threats)

MacDonald, J.M. (1968) *Homicidal Threats.* Springfield, IL: Thomas.

(Guilty Minds)

Biggs, J., Jr. (1967) *The guilty mind: Psychiatry and the law of homicide.* Baltimore: Johns Hopkins.

(Murderers - Personality)

Evaluation of the criminal's personality in regard to the qualifying indications of homicide. (1966) 24232. J. 49, (1966), H. 5, S. 204-211.

(Murderers - Mental Illness)

Meyerson, A.T. (1966, May) Amnesia for homicide (pedicide): Its treatment with hypnosis. *Archives of General Psychology, 14*, 509-515.

(Jealous Murderers)

Podolsky, E. (1965, Winter) Jealous murderer. *Journal of Forensic Medicine, 12*, 35.

(Murderers - Psychology)

Kothe, K. (1964, Jan.) From behavioral psychology: Case of a young murderer (German). *Psychiat Neurol Med Psychol, 16*, 24-27.

(Murderers - Emotions)

Von Hentig, H. (1963) The feeling of well-being in the murderer after his deed (German). *Psychiat Neurol, 146*, 16-28.

(Murderers - Psychology)

Reinhardt, J.M. (1962) *Psychology of strange killers.* Springfield, IL: Thomas.

(Murderer - Personality)

Ferracuti, F. (1961, Fall) The personality of the murderer. *Quad Crimin Clin, 3*, 419-456.

(Murderers - Characteristics)

De Baudouin, H.,et al. (1961) Study of a population of 97 confined murderers: Medicolegal, clinical, psychological, and EEG study (French). *An Medicopsychol, 119*(1), 625-686.

(Homicide - Psychiatric Study)

Bromberg, W. (1961) *The mold of murder: A psychiatric study of homicide.* Westbury, CT: Greenwood.

(Murderers - Comparative Analysis)

Weiss, J.M., et al. (1960, June) The sudden murderer: A comparative analysis. *AMA Archives of General Psychiatry, 2*, 669-678.

(Murderers - Psychoanalytic Treatment)

Williams, A.H. (1960) A psychoanalytic approach to the treatment of the murderer. *International Journal of Psychoanalysis, 41*, 532-539.

(Murderers - Psychoanalysis)

Brandt, R.J. (1958) From the psychoanalysis of a murderer (German). *Psyche-Stutig, 12*(1), 18-32.

(Murderer's Mind)

Neustatter, W.L. (1957) *The mind of the murderer.* New York: Philosophical Library.

(Murderer - Psychology)

Von Hentig, H. (1957, Nov./Dec.) Pre-murderous kindness and post-murderous grief. *Journal of Criminal Law, 48,* 368.

(Axe Murderer)

MacCrandle, A.M. (1956, Nov.) Enigma of Natal's axe-murderer. *Contemp Rev, 190,* 291-294.

(Murderers' Reminiscences)

Hollis, C. (1955, July 8) Murderers' reminiscences. *Spec, 195,* 37-39.

(Murderer's Mind)

Podolsky, E. (1954) Mind of the murderer. *Journal of Criminal Law and Criminology, 45,* 48-50.

(Murderer - Psychology)

Wittman, P., & Astrachan, M. (1949) Psychological investigation of a homicidal youth. *Journal of Clinical Psychology, 5,* 88-93.

(Murderer - Motivation)

Greene, J.E., et al. (1948) Inferences concealing the motivations of a murderer: A psychological study of displaced aggression. *American Psychologist, 3,* 335.

(Criminal Psychology)

Bernaldo De Quiros, C. (1945) A paleolithic survival in the criminal psychology of a woman (Spanish). *Criminalia, Mexico, 11,* 579-586.

(Murderers - Personality Types)

Abrahamsen, D. (1944) The dynamic connection between personality and crime and the detection of the potential criminal illustrated by different types of murder. *Journal of Criminology and Psychopathology, 5,* 481-488.

(Murder - Psychopathological Aspects)

London, L.S. (1944) Psychopathological aspects of murder. *Journal of Criminology and Psychopathology, 5,* 795-812.

(Homicide - Character)

Bramblet, H.H. (1943, Nov.) Character of deceased and un-communicated threats by deceased in homicide cases. *Kentucky Law Journal, 32,* 84-86.

(Murderer - Psychology)

Ludtke, W. (1939) The psychology of a murder. *Kriminalistic, 13*, 106-108.

(Murderer's Attitude)

Schilder, P. (1936, Oct.) Attitude of murderers towards death. *Journal of Abnormal Psychology, 31*, 348-363.

(Child Killer)

Jungling, A. (1935) *Casuistic contributions on multiple child murder: Considerations on the psychology and penal evaluation of child murder in general.* English trans. published by R.R. Willoughby.

(Murder - Emotionally Determined)

Ummersbach, H. (1934) Emotionally determined murder (German). *Krim Monatsh, 8*, 175-179.

(Tripp Case)

Remy, K.H. (1934) The Tripp case: A contribution to the criminal psychology of sex murder. English trans. published by Willoughby.

(Homicide - Psychology of)

Petzelt, K. (1932) *The psychology of homicide and homicidal attempts from sexual motives.* Breslau: Med. Diss.

(Murderers - Psychological Problems)

Erismann, T. (1932) The psychological problems of the Halsmann murder case. *Ber Kongr dtsch Ges Psychol, 12*, 322-331.

(Murderers - Casuistic Psychology)

Brennecke, H. (1932) A casuistic contribution to the psychology of the murderer. *Montssch f Krimppsychol u Strafrechtsref,23*, 402-415.

(Murderers - Evaluation)

Tersiev (1930) The evaluation of their own acts by condemned murderers. *Montssch f Krimpsychol u Strafrechtsref, 4, 198-207.*

(Murderer's - Mind)

Dearden, H. (1930) *The mind of the murderer.* New York: Sears.

(Murderers)

Frenkel, H. (1929) The murderer who is not motivated by personal gain. *Montssch f Krimppsychol u Strafrechtsref, 20*, 607-617.

The Murderer
Epilepsy

(Murderers - Epilepsy)

Shaw, E.D., et al. (1986) A case of suicidal and homicidal ideation and akathisia in a double-blind neuroleptic crossover study. *Journal of Clinical Psychopharmacology, 6*(3), 196-197.

(Murderer - Epileptic)

Acuda, S.W. (1980) Epilepsy, automatisms, and homicide (Summary in English). *African Journal of Psychiatry, 6,* (3-4), 35-38.

(Murderer - Epilepsy)

Singer, L, et al. (1978) Resort to homicide and arson in amnesia in epilepsy. *Ann Med Psychol, 136*(4),609-617.

(EEG Examination)

Roman, I., et al. (1975) Contribution to the study of the value of EEG in psychiatric legal examination. *Rev Roum Med-Neurol Psychiat, 13*(1), 3-19.

(Homicide - Epileptic Seizure)

Brewer, C. (1971, April) Homicide during a psychomotor seizure: The importance of air-encephalography in establishing insanity under the McNaghten rules. *Medical Journal of Australia, 1*, 857-859.

(Murderers - Epileptic)

Schipkowensky, N. (1970) Reactive epilepsy and murder: Killing during a pathological attack. *Acta Med Inst Sup Med Sofia, 49*(2), 49-58. *Also in Nauch Tr Vissh Med Inst Sofiia,* 44, 1-6 (1965).

(Murderers - EEG Studies)

Sayed, Z.A., et al. (1969, Oct.) An EEG and psychiatric study of thirty-two insane murderers. *British Journal of Psychiatry, 115*, 1115-1124.

(Murderers - Epileptic)

Livingston, S. (1964, April 13) Epilepsy and murder. *JAMA, 188,* 172.

(Murderers - Epileptic)

Podolsky, E. (1962) The epileptic murderer. *Medicolegal Journal, 30*, 176-179.

The Murderer
Occupations

(Organized Crime)

Pooley, E. (1990, Jan. 29) Death of a hood: The bloody end of big bad guys. *New York, 23*(4), pp. 26-33.

(Murderers - Nurses)

Yorker, B.C. (1988, Oct.) Nurses accused of murder. *American Journal of Nursing, 88*, 10, 1327-1332.

(Murderers - Physicians)

Steenfeldt-Foss, O.W. (1987) Physicians as murderers. *Tidsskr Nor Laegeforen, 107*, (34-36), 3019-3020.

(Murderer - Executive)

Levine, R. (1986, Jan.) Executive murder: Conviction of film recovery systems executives in murder of employees. *Omni, 8*, p. 18.

(Police Homicides)

Vasquez, J. (1985) Police homicides by misidentity. *FBI Law Enforcement Bulletin, 54*(3), 22-25.

(Murderers - Physicians)

Beynon, H. (1982, Jan.) Doctors as murderers. *The Criminal Law Review 1982,* 17-28.

(Police Brutality)

Anderson, G.M (1982, Jan. 23) Addressing police brutality. *America, 146*, pp. 51-54.

(Murderer - Mafia Hitmen)

Italy's top anti-terrorist expert assassinated by mafia hitmen. (1982) *Organized Crime Digest, 3*(9), 6. Microforms and article copies available from UMI.

(Police - Deadly Force)

Fyfe, J.J. (1981) Observations on police deadly force. *Crime and Delinquency, 27*(3), 376-389.

(Murderers - Police Officers)

Two policemen found guilty of attempting to murder fellow officers. (1978, July)) *AELE Law Enforcement Legal Liability Reporter, 67*, 3.

(Murderers - Professional)

Nash, J.R. (1977) The hit man: It's only business. *Law Enforcement Journal, 7*(7), 2. Article copies available from UMI.

(Police Assaults)

Hattery, L.H. (1977) Enlightening report on police assaults. *Systems, Technology, and Science for Law Enforcement and Security, 9*(6), 1-2.

(Murderers - Security Guards)

Security guard held in slayings. (1976) *Crime Control Digest, 10*(23), 5.

(Murder - Cop)

Daley, R. (1976) *To kill a cop.* Crown.

(Murderer - Coed)

Cheney, M. (1976) *The coed killer.* New York: Walker.

(Murderer - Physician)

Manslaughter charges against doctors. (1975, May) *British Medical Journal, 2*(5965), 287-288.

(Murderer - Musician)

Gray, C., & Heselitine, P. (1973) *Carlo Gesualdo, Prince of Venosa: Musician and murderer.* Dover Books.

(Murderers - Nazi)

Dicks, H.V. (1972) *Licensed mass-murderer: A sociopsychological study of some SS killers.* New York: Basic books.

(Murderers - Medical)

Furneaux, R. (1967) *Medical murderer.* Abelard.

Chapter 4
The Victim

(Victims - Journalists)

Janeway, M. (1990, Oct. 28) An early victim of the cold war (book review). *New York Times Book Review*, p. 3.

(Victims - Women)

Came, B. (1990, Oct. 22) Victims in the home. *Macleans, 103*(43), p.18.

(Victims - Students)

Campus ripper. (1990, Sept. 10) *Time, 136*(11), p. 43.

(Victims - Police)

Boylen, M., & Little, R. (1990) Fatal assaults on United States law enforcement officers. *Police Journal, 63*(1), 61-77.

(Victims)

Brown, L., et al. (1990) *Victim support: Families of murder victims project* (Final report). London: Victim Support National Office.

(Victims - Female)

Humphries, D., & Caringella-MacDonald, S. (1990) Murdered mothers, missing wives: Reconsidering female victimization. *Social Justice, 17*(2), 71-89.

(Victims - Police)

Young, T.J. (1990) Felonious murder of police by ambush. *Psychology Reports, 67*(1), 206.

(Victim - John Lennon)

Stuttaford, G. (1989, July 14) Nonfiction: Who killed John Lennon? *Publisher's Weekly, 236*(2), p. 64.

(Victims)

Welte, J.W., & Abel, E.L. (1989) Homicide: Drinking by the victim. *Journal Stud Alcohol, 50*(3), 197-201.

(Victims - Women)

Kay, T., & Kent, J.H. (1989) Women victims of domestic violence. *British Medical Journal, 299*(6711), 1339.

(Victim - Black)

Marshall, M. (1988, Dec.) Why famous blacks died young. *Ebony, 44*(2), pp. 88-94.

(Victims - Police)

Hill, K.Q., & Clawson, M. (1988) The health hazards of 'street-level' bureaucracy mortality among the police. *Journal of Police Science and Administration, 16*(4), 243.

(Victim - Adolescent)

Smith, D. (1986, July 14) A death in hell's kitchen (murder of 15 year old T. Burke). *New York, 19,* pp. 21-22.

(Victim - Unknown)

Carlson, P. (1986, April 7) The death of an unknown boy (found dead by a roadside in Thayer, Co., Nebraska). *People Weekly, 25,* 34-39.

(Victims - Black and Hispanic)

Blacks, Hispanics are murder victim risks. (1986) *Law Enforcement News, 11*(6), 3. Article copies available from UMI.

(Victim-Offender Analysis)

Morgan, F., & Kratkowski, P.C. (1986) The victim-offender relationship in homicide cases: An analysis of 1979-83. *Journal of Police and Criminal Psychology, 2*(1), 52-63.

(Victims - Elderly)

Copeland, A.R. (1986) Homicide among the elderly: The metro Dade County experience 1979-1983. *Medical Science and the Law 1986, 26*(4), 259-262.

(Victims)

Lester, D. (1986) Distribution of blood types in a sample of homicide victims. *Psychology Reports, 58*(3), 802.

(Victims - City Residents)

Durkin, M. (1986) On residential status of New York City homicide victims (letter). *American Journal of Public Health 1986, 76*(8), 1034.

(Victims)

Abel, E.L. (1986) Guns and blood alcohol levels among homicide victims. *Drug and Alcohol Dependence, 18*(3), 253-257.

(Officers Killed)

Nineteen-eighty-six preliminary officer killed statistics. (1986) *FBI Law Enforcement Bulletin,*

55(11), 24.

(Victims - Students)

Cabanis, D., et al. (1985) Student tragedy: Forensic-psychiatric and legal-medicine aspects of an unusual crime (German). *Z Rechtmed 1985, 95*(2), 137-144.

(Victims - Psychiatric Patients)

Hillard, J.R., et al. (1985) Accidental and homicidal death in a psychiatric emergency room population. *Hospital and Community Psychiatry, 36*(6), 640-643.

(Victim and Perpetrator)

Szewczyk, H., et al. (1984) A comparative study of relations between perpetrator and victim in homicide (German). *Psychiatrie Neurologie und Medizinische Psychologie, 36*(2), 84-90.

(Victims - Dade County, Fl.)

Copeland, A.R. (1984) The right to keep and bear arms: A study of civilian homicides committed against those involved in criminal acts in metropolitan Dade County from 1957 to 1982. *Journal of Forensic Sciences, 29*(2), 584-590

(Victim - Prisoner)

Simonsen, J. (1984) Fatal subarachnoid hemorrhages in relation to minor injuries in Denmark from 1967 to 1981. *Forensic Science International, 24*(1), 57-63.

(Black-on-Black Homicide)

Poussaint, A.F. (1983) Black-on-Black homicide: A psychological-political perspective. Second International Institute proceedings on Victimology. *Victimology 1983, 8*(3-4), 161-169.

(Victim - Female)

Frazer, M. (1983) The female homicide victim: Trends in a metropolitan county from 1969 to 1980. *Journal of Forensic Science, 28*(3), 577-587.

(Victims - Black Females)

McLain, P.D. (1982) Cause of death - homicide: A research note on Black females as homicide victims. *Victimology 1982, 7*(1-4), 204-212.

(Victims - Los Angeles)

Budd, R.D. (1982) The incidence of alcohol use in Los Angeles County homicide victims. *American Journal of Drug and Alcohol Abuse 1982, 9*(1), 105-111.

(Victim and Murderer)

Krishna, K.P. (1982) Murdered and the murderer. *Indian Journal of Social Work, 43*(1), 83-90.

(Victims)

Rajan, V.N. (1981) Victims of homicide. *Indian Journal of Criminology, 1*(4), 154-158.

(Victimization Analysis)

Akiyama, Y. (1981) Murder victimization: A statistical analysis. *Law Enforcement Bulletin, 50*(3), 8-11.

(Victimization - Psychology)

Gulotta, G. (1980) Victimization and interpersonal misunderstandings in dyadic systems. *Victimology 1980, 5*(2-4), 110-114.

(Victims - Violent Death)

Braucht, G.N., et al. (1980) Victims of violent death: A critical review. *Psychological Bulletin, 87*(2), 309-333.

(Homicide - Defendants/Victims)

Demayo, A.V., & Gensheimer, L.K. (1979, Dec.) Ten years of homicides: A study of homicide defendants and victims in the New Haven County superior court between 1967 and 1977. *Conn B J, 53*, 516-529.

(Victim - Hostage)

Berg, S., et al. (1979) Determination of the duration of length of time of incarceration before killing the hostage. 3647, bd. 164, '79, h 5-6, s. 153-161 (IBZ 1982).

(Organized Crime)

Long list of organized crime dealings detailed by the FBI. (1979) *Security Systems Digest, 10*(13), 4-5 (Article copies available from UMI).

(Homicide - Florida)

Wilbanks, W. (1979) Homicide victimization rates in Dade County, Florida. *Victimology 1979, 4*(2), 305-307.

(Victim - Spouse)

Chimbos, P.D. (1978) *Marital violence: A study of interspouse homicide.* R & E Research Associates.

(Victims - Self-Defense)

Character and prior conduct of the victim in support of a plea of self-defense. (1977, Summer) *La Law Review, 37*, 1166-1174.

(Victimology)

Lewin, J.R. (1977) Book Review. *Victimology: An International Journal, 2*(1), 137-139.

(Victim Compensation)

Sato, D., et al. (1977) A study on the victims of crimes causing death or bodily injury - second (final) report. *Bull Criminol Res Dep 1977*, 1-3.

(Aggrieved Party)

Aggrieved Party: Transient guest. (1976, Aug.) *Pennsylvania Search and Seizure Bulletin*, pp. 5-6.

(Victims - Stranger)

Stranger murders up in New York City. (1976) *Criminal Justice Newsletter, 7*(13), 8.

(Victims - Unidentified)

Unidentified murder victim. (1976) *Fingerprint and Identification Magazine, 57*(9), 13.

(Victims and Offenders)

Landau, S.F., et al. (1974, Sept.) Homicide victims and offenders: An Israeli study. *Journal of Criminal Law, 65*, 340-346.

(Criminalistic Aspects)

Smerling, M. (1974) Forensic and criminalistic aspects of a case of cutting into pieces of a murder victim (German). *Inst Forens Med Berlin Arch Kriminol, 153*(5-6), 129-140.

(Homicide - Victims)

Avison, N.H. (1974) Victims of homicide. *International Journal of Criminology and Penology,* 2(3), 225-227.

(Attempted Suicide)

Ford, C.V., et al. (1974) Chronic pain in a victim of attempted suicide. *International Journal of Psychiatry in Medicine, 5*(3), 283-293.

(Victim - Fetus)

Groves, R.E. (1972, May 18) Is abortion murder? *Nursing Times, 68*, 624-625.

(Victim - Fetus)

Lins, G, & Schafer, A. (1972) Forensic problems in a case of abortion by shooting (German). *J Leg Med, 71*(2), 108-113.

(Victims - Fetus)

Is the intentional killing of an unborn child homicide (California's law to punish the willful killing of a fetus. (1971, Jan.) *Pacific Law Journal, 2*, 179.

(Victims)

Houts, M. (1970) *They asked for death.* New York: Cowles.

(Victims - Case Report)

Lefkowitz, B., & Gross, K.G. (1969) *Victims: The Wylie-Hoffert murder case and its strange aftermath.* New York: Putnam.

(Victims - Pregnant Women)

Rocco, R., et al. (1963, Sept.) Penetrating wound of the abdomen in pregnancy: Lesion and death of a fetus *in utero* (Portuguese). *Rev Ginec Obstet, 113*, 97-100.

(Abortion)

Chaumont, A.J. (1961, Jan./Feb.) Injury and abortion: Spontaneous abortion with fatal sequelae after minor physical violence (French). *Ann Med Leg, 41*, 1113-1137.

(Victims - Characteristics)

MacDonald, J.M. (1961) *Murderer and his victim.* New York: C.C. Thomas.

(Victims)

Hitchler, W.H. (1948, Oct.) Killer and his victim in felony-murder cases. *Dick Law Review, 53*, 3-11.

(Victims)

Roesner, E. (1938) Murderers and their victims (German). *Mschr KrimBiol, 29*, 161-185., 209-228.

(Victims' Letters)

Maclachlan, C.F.M. (1926, Sept.) "Letters of slains". *Jurid Review, 38*, 309-313.

The Victim
Characteristics/Age/Occupation

(Victim - Rabbi)

Bierman, J. (1990, Nov. 19) Murder of a rabbi. *Macleans, 103*(47), p. 24.

(Victim - Lawyer)

Norman, J.R. (1990, Nov. 12) Death in Sausalito. *Forbes, 146*(11), pp. 180-186.

(Victims - Students)

Kunen, J., et al. (1990, Sept. 17) A killer on the campus. *People Weekly, 34*(11), pp. 38-43.

(Victims - U.S. Journalists)

Stein, M.L. (1990, May 19) Journalists as part of the story. *Editor and Publisher, 123*(20), pp. 26.

(Victims)

Gartner, R. (1990) The victims of homicide: A temporal and cross-national comparison. *American Sociological Review, 55*(1), 92-106.

(Victim - Journalist)

Cridland, N.C. (1990) History: The Polk conspiracy. *Library Journal, 115*(13), 123.

(Victims - Elderly)

Sperry, K. (1990) Anterior thoracic wall trauma in elderly homicide victims: The CPR defense. *American Journal of Forensic Medicine and Pathology, 11*(1), 50-55.

(Victims - Journalists)

Smyth, F. (1989, April 4) Under fire. *Village Voice, 34*(14), pp. 19-20.

(Victims- Schoolchildren)

Baker, J.N., et al. (1989, Jan. 30) Death on the playground. *Newsweek, 113*(5), p. 35.

(Victim - Bolivian Activist)

O'Sullivan, M. (1989, Jan. 7) Tribute to a Latin American martyr. *America, 160*(1), pp. 8-11+.

(Victims - Age)

Christoffel, K.K., et al. (1989) Age-related patterns of violent death, Cook, County, Ill., 1977 through 1982. *American Journal on Disabled Children, 143*(12), 1403-1409.

(Victims - Peace Officer)

Moorman, C, & Williams, G. (1989) Peace officers murdered in California -- 1988. *Journal of California Law Enforcement 1989, 23*(1), 11-17.

(Victimology)

Bell, C.C., et al. (1988) Need for victimization screening in a Black psychiatric population. *Journal of National Medical Association, 80*(1), 41-48.

(Victim - Priest)

Brockman, J.R. (1987, March 14) A torch held on high (legacy of murdered priest R. Grande in El Salvador). *America, 156*, pp. 214-216+.

(Victims - Police)

Law enforcement officers killed - 1986. (1987) *FBI Law Enforcement Bulletin, 56*(6), 30.

(Victims - Children)

Gary, M., & Diotte, K. (1986, Aug. 25) The children's murderers (Canada). *Macleans, 99*, pp. 39-40.

(Victim - Black Sheriff)

Black sheriff killed during attempted arrest (O. Bell in Mississippi). (1986, May 26) *Jet, 70*, p.36.

(Victims - Elderly)

Kivela, S.L., et al. (1986) Mortality from violent causes among the elderly population in Finland from 1951-1979. *Scandinavian Journal of Society and Medicine, 14*(1), 31-38.

(Victim - Psychiatrist)

Annis, L.V., et al. (1986) A psychiatrist's murder in a mental hospital. *Hospital and Community Psychiatry, 37*(5), 505-506.

(Victims - Sex and Age)

Lester, D. (1986) The distribution of sex and age among victims of homicide: A cross-national study. *International Journal of Social Psychiatry, 32*(2), 47-50.

(Victims - Elderly)

Copeland, A.R. (1986) Homicide among the elderly: The metro Dade County experience, 1979-1983. *Medical Science and the Law, 26*(4), 259-262.

(Victims - Officers)

Nineteen-eighty-six preliminary officer-killer statistics. (1986) *FBI Law Enforcement Bulletin, 55*(11), 30.

(Victims - Black Males)

Black males most likely murder victims: A report. (1985, May 27) *Jet, 68,* p. 37.

(Victim - Police)

Lester, D. (1985) Murder of police officers in American cities, victimization rates, and public attitudes to safety. *Psychological Reports, 57*(2), 534.

(Victims - Inmates)

Jayewardene, C.H., & Doherty, P. (1985) Individual violence in Canadian penitentiaries. *Canadian Journal of Criminology, 27*(4), 429-439.

(Victims - Mexican Officers)

IACO director outraged by murder of 22 Mexican officers. (1985) *Narcotics Control Digest, 15*(24), 2.

(Victims - Peace Corp Volunteers)

Hargarten, S.W., & Baker, S.P. (1985) Fatalities in the Peace Corp: A retrospective study from 1962 through 1983. *JAMA, 254*(10), 1326-1329.

(Victim - Youth)

Zimring, F.E. (1984) Youth homicide in New York: A preliminary analysis. *The Journal of Legal Studies, 13*(1), 81-99 (Article copies available from UMI).

(Victims - Law Enforcement Officers)

Moorman, C.B., & Wemmer, R.C. (1983, May) Law enforcement officers murdered in California: 1980-1981. *Police Chief, 50*, 42-44.

(Victim - Police Officer)

Holy terror (policeman murdered by religious cult in Memphis). (1983, Jan. 24) *Time, 121*, p.

27.

(Victims - Elderly)

Kunkle, S., et al. (1982-1983) Murder of the elderly: An analysis of increased vulnerability. *Journal of Death and Dying, 13*(1), 27-34.

(Victims - Police)

Lester, D. (1982) Police officers killed and the guns used by criminals. *Psychology Reports 1982, 50*(3, pt. 2), 1206.

(Victims - Police)

Police homicides - Newark officer no-billed in Guardian Angel deaths. (1982, May) *Police Magazine,* 5, 42.

(Victim - Police)

Zunno, I.A., et al. (1982) The risk of murder for police. *National Criminal Offense Review, 37*(354), 6-8.

(Victims - Women)

Humphrey, J. (1982) Women who are murdered: An analysis of 912 consecutive victims. 26420, Vol. 12, 181-182, n 3, p. 281 (IBZ 1982).

(Case Reports - Boston Murders)

Rizzo, N.D. (1982) Murder in Boston: Killers and their victims. *Journal of Offender Therapy and Comparative Criminology 1982, 26*(1), 36-42.

(Victims - Police)

Margarita, M. (1982) *Criminal violence against police.* Ann Arbor, MI: Dissertation Abstracts.

(Victims - Elderly)

Wilbanks, W. (1981/1982) Trends in violent death among the elderly. *International Journal on Aging Hum Dev, 14*(3), 167-175.

(Victimization)

Akiyama, Y. (1981) Murder victimization: A statistical analysis. *FBI Law Enforcement Bulletin, 50*(3), 8-11.

(Victims - Hikers)

Death trail (murder of hikers in Point Reyes National Seashore, Ca.) (1980, Dec. 15) *Time, 116,* p. 24.

(Victims - Police)

Margarita, M. (1980, Nov.) Killing the police: Myths and motives. *Annals of American Academy of Political and Social Science 1980,* 63-71.

(Victims - Tourists)

Trumbull, R. (1980, July 28) Blood on the sands of paradise (attacks on tourists in Hawaii). *Macleans, 93*, pp. 23-24.

(Victim - Doctor - Tarnower Murder)

Death of the diet doctor (J. Harris' arrest in connection with H. Tarnower murder in Purchase, N.Y.) (1980, March 24) *Time, 115*, p. 27.

(Victims - Regional Characteristics)

Hudson, R.P., et al. (1980, Winter) Regional variations in the characteristics of victims of violence. *International Journal of Social Psychology, 26*, 300-320.

(Homicide - Stress)

Humphrey, J.A. (1980) Stressful life events and criminal homicide offender-victim relationships. *Victimology 1980, 5*(2-4), 115-120.

(Victims - Police)

Lester, D. (1980) The police as victims: Analysis of murdered police officers. Paper presented at the First World Congress of Victimology, held in Washington, D.C., August 20-24, 1980.

(Victims - Officials)

Organized crime spawns new breed of criminals who are killing officials. (1980) *Narcotics Control Digest, 10*(9), 10. Article copies available from UMI.

(Victims - Government Informants)

Mancini, J. (1979, Dec. 17) License to die: Murder of government informant C. Welcome after testifying in PCP prosecution in New York City. *New York, 12*, pp. 71-74.

(Victim - District Judge)

Assault: Shooting of U.S. district judge J.H. Wood. (1979, June 11) *Time, 113*, p. 24.

(Victim - Terrorist)

Death of a terrorist: Murder of Abu Hassan in Beirut. (1979, Feb. 5) *Time, 113*, pp. 111-112.

(Victims - Law Enforcement Officials)

Moorman, C.B., & Wemmer, R. (1979) California law enforcement officers murdered -- 1978. *California Law Enforcement Journal, 13*(4), 179-182.

(Victims - Gem Merchants)

Two more gem merchant deaths suspected in New York City: Police task force called up. (1979) *Security Systems Digest, 10*(7), 6. Copies available from UMI.

(Victims - Police)

Bradlee, B., Jr. (1979) *The ambush murders: The true account of the killing of two California policemen*. Los Angeles: Dodd.

(Victims - Juveniles)

Russell, D.H. (1979) Ingredients of juvenile murder. Paper presented at the International Congress of Social Psychiatry, Athens, Greece, 1974. *International Journal of Offender Therapy and Comparative Criminology, 23*(1), 65-72.

(Victims - Physicians)

Revitch, E. (1979, June) Patients who kill their physician. *Journal of the Medical Society of New Jersey, 76*(6), 429-431.

(Victims - Police Officers)

Moorman, C.B. (1978) Peace officers murdered in California, 1973-1977: Awareness and learning points survey. *Journal of California Law Enforcement, 13*(2), 62-69.

1(Victims - Police)

Lester, D. (1978) A study of civilian-caused murders of police officers. *International Journal of Criminology and Penology, 6*(4), 373-378.

(Victim - Reporter)

They finally got me: Killing of reporter D.F. Bolles. (1976, June 28) *Time, 107*, pp. 19-20.

(Victim - Mail Carrier)

Middle-class teenage gang plots murder, executes postman, dumps body, steals car for joyride. (1976) *Juvenile Justice Digest, 5*(23), 8. Article copies available from UMI.

(Victims - Psychiatric Illness)

Herjanic, M., & Meyer, D.A. (1976) Psychiatric illness in homicide victims. *American Journal of Psychiatry, 133*(6), 691-693.

(Victims - Elderly)

Savage thugs invade apartment, torture old man to death, force son to turn over savings. (1976) *Security Systems Digest, 6*(24), 5.

(Victims - Narcotic Abusers)

Monforte, J.R., & Spitz, W.U. (1975) Narcotic abuse among homicide victims in Detroit. *Journal of Forensic Science, 20*(1), 186-190.

(Victims)

Parker, E. (1974) The victims of mentally disordered female offenders. *British Journal of Psychiatry, 124*(7), 51-59.

(Victims - Bystanders)

Pecar, J. (1972) Involved bystanders: Examination of a neglected aspect of criminology. *International Journal of Contemporary Sociology, 9*(2-3), 81-87.

(Victims - Police Officers)

Suddenly this summer: Murder of two New York cops. (1971, June 7) *Newsweek, 77*, p. 29.

(Victims - Negroes)

Robins, L.N. (1968, June) Negro homicide victims: Who will they be? *Transaction, 5*(7), pp. 15-19.

(Victims - Journalists)

Kosyra, H. (1968) The murder of journalist Piotr Nokolicz. 3674. Ed. 142, '68, H. 3-4, S. 65-72 (IBZ 70).

(Victims - Police)

Cardarelli, A.P. (1968) An analysis of police killed by criminal action: 1961-1963. *Journal of Criminal Law, Criminology and Police Science, 59*(3), 447-453.

(Victims - Children)

Myers, S.A. (1967) The child slayer: A 25-year survey of homicides involving preadolescent victims. *Archives of General Psychiatry, 17*(2), 211-213.

(Victims - Nurses)

Nath, S. (1964) Murder of a nurse. 20957, J. 18, '64, 3, S. 164-165 (IBZ 1965).

(Victims - Insane)

Tovo, S. (1964, May/June) On homicide of the insane (Italian). *Minerva Medicoleg, 84*, 48-89.

(Victims - Sorcerers)

Collomb, H., et al. (1964) Difficulties of the psychiatrist apropos of the murderer of a sorcerer (French). *Bull Soc Med Aft Noire Lang Franc, 9*, 415-417.

(Victims - Children)

Zachau-Christiansen, B., & Jensen, J. (1963) Violent deaths in childhood in a Danish medical district. *Acta Paedist, 140*, 135-136.

(Victims - Police)

Killing of an officer was manslaughter (Jones v. State (Miss) 155 So. 430). (1934, Nov.) *B Di J Temp L Q, 9*, 100-102.

(Victims - Doctors)

Lambton, A. (1934, May 3) Murder of a doctor. *Saturday Review, 157*, 572-573.

Victims
Infants and Children

(Infanticide)

Attinger, J. (1990, Aug. 20) The littlest victims. *Time, 136*(8), pp. 44-45.

(Infanticide)

Sacrificing children (Christian Scientists' case; from the *Morning News Tribune*) (editorial). (1990, July 18) *The Los Angeles Daily Journal, 103*, p. 6.

(Victim - Baby)

Vogeler, W. (1990, June 21) Manslaughter conviction upheld in death of baby. *The Los Angeles Daily Journal, 103*, p. 1.

(Homicide - Children)

Marshall, J.C. (1990, May 17) Merit of the children. *Nature, 345*(6272), pp. 215-216.

(Victims - Infants/Children)

Jenish, D.A. (1990, March 26) Justice: Rumor and scandal. *Macleans, 103*(13), pp. 55-58.

(Infanticide - Muslims)

Giladi, A. (1990) Some observations on the infanticide in medieval Muslim society and review. *International Journal of Medieval Studies, 22*(2), 185-200.

(Murdered Children)

Silverman, R.A., et al. (1990) Murdered children - a comparison of racial differences across 2 jurisdictions. *Journal of Criminal Justice, 18*(5), 401-416.

(Neonaticide)

Kaye, N.S., et al. (1990) Families. murder, and insanity: A psychiatric review of paternal neonaticide. *Journal of Forensic Science, 35*(1), 133-139.

(Manslaughter - Infant)

Sargeant, G. (1990) Pit bull owner gets prison term for manslaughter. *Trial, 26*(2), 14.

(Violent Death - Children)

Christoffel, K.K. (1990) Violent death and injury in U.S. children and adolescents. *American Journal of the Diseases of Children, 144*(6), 697-706.

(Pediatrics - Fatalities)

Beaver, B.L., et al. (1990) Characteristics of pediatric firearm fatalities. *Journal of Pediatric Surgery, 25*(1), 97-100.

(Neonaticide)

Green, C.M., & Manohar, S.V. (1990) Neonaticide and hysterical denial of pregnancy. *British*

Journal of Psychiatry, 156(1), 121-123.

(Homicide - Childhood)

Lapidus, G.D., et al. (1990) Misclassification of childhood homicide on death certificates. *American Journal of Public Health, 80*(2), 213-214.

(Victims - Infants)

Egginton, J. (1989, April) The bad mother (M. Tinning kills nine infants in Schenectady, NY). *Good Housekeeping, 208*, p. 119+.

(Women - Medical Care)

Ruley, D.A., Jr. (1989) Compelled medical treatment of pregnant women (letter). *JAMA 1989, 261*(12), 1729-1730.

(Victims - Children)

Gausche, M., et al. (1989) Violent deaths in the pediatric age group: Rural and urban differences. *Pediatric Emergency Care, 5*(1), 64-67.

(Victims - Teens)

Lions Rogers faces suit in death of teenagers. (1988, Dec. 12) *Jet, 75*(11), p. 46.

(Victim - Female Child)

Trippett, F., et al. (1988, Oct. 31) The death of Dayana. *Time, 132*(18), p. 19.

(Infanticide)

Wilson, S. (1988, Oct.) Infanticide, child abandonment, and female honour in nineteenth-century Corsica. *Comp Stud Soc Hist, 30*, 762-783.

(Victims - Children)

Steacy, A., & Laderette, B. (1988, Aug. 1) Murder in a small town. *Macleans, 101*(32), pp. 44-46.

(Infanticide)

Jones, P. (1988, July) "There was a woman": La Ilorona in Oregon. *Western Folklore, 47*, 195-211.

(Victims - Infants/Children)

Clover, C.J. (1988, Spring) The politics of scarcity: Notes on the sex ratio in early Scandinavia. *Scand Stud, 60*, 147-188.

(Victim - Child)

Fiala, R., & LaFree, G. (1988) Cross-national determinants of child homicide. *American Sociological Review, 53*(3), 432-445.

(Child-Murder)

Wilson, P.R. (1988) Stranger child-murder: Issues relating to causes and controls. *Forensic*

Science International, 36(3-4), 267-277.

(Victims - Infants)

Reed, D., & Moore, K. (1988) *Deadly medicine: The chilling story of a pediatric nurse who murdered scores of her infant patients.* New York: St. Martins.

(Victim - Child)

Hurt, H. (1987, Dec.) Little Blue of Chester, Nebraska (child found dead by roadside). *Readers Digest, 131,* 73-78.

(Victim - Children)

Korbin, J.E. (1987) Incarcerated mothers' perceptions and interpretations of their fatally maltreated children. *Child Abuse & Neglect, 11*(3), 397-407.

(Victims - Children)

Larson, O.W., et al. (1987) Child maltreatment among U.S. east coast migrant farm workers. *Child Abuse & Neglect, 11*(2), 281-291.

(Victims - Mom and Children)

Despondent welfare mom kills kids, leaps to death (case of L. Belizaire). (1986, Oct. 6) *Jet, 71,* p. 28.

(Victim - Baby)

Detroit mom accused of high seas murder admits killing baby, FBI says (case of C.A. Washington). (1986, Aug. 25) *Jet, 70,* p. 18.

(Child-Murders)

Gray, M. (1986, Aug. 11) The horror of child murders (A. Parrot of Toronto). *Macleans, 99,* pp. 40-41.

(Victim - Baby)

College mom who killed baby could get 20 years (case of C.Y. Frazier, N.C.). (1986, May 12). *Jet, 70,* p. 5.

(Homicide - Children)

Paulson, J.A., & Rushforth, N.B. (1986) Violent death in children in a metropolitan county: Changing patterns of homicide, 1958-1982. *Pediatrics, 78*(6), 1013-1020.

(Child Neglect)

Hoffmeyer, O. (1986) Child abuse and child neglect with fatal result (German). *Munch Med Wochenschr, 128*(4), 44-48.

(Child Abuse)

Knight, B. (1986) The history of child abuse. *Forensic Science International, 30*(2-3), 135-141.

(Homicide - Child)

Blaser, M.J. (1986) Epidemiologic characteristics of child homicides in Atlanta, 1970-1980. *Pediatrics, 77*(4), 518-522.

(Victim - Child)

Showers, J., et al. (1986) Criminal disposition of persons involved in 72 cases of fatal child abuse. *Med Sci Law, 26*(3), 243-247.

(Victim - Child)

Jacob, G. (1986) Damage patterns in severe child abuse with and without fatal sequele. *Monatsschr Kinderheild, 134*(6), 307-315.

(Abortion)

Frazier, H.C. (1986) Burns, abortions, and dying declaration. *Med Law, 5*(5), 431-440.

(Child-Murder)

Hollander, N. (1986) Homicides of abused children prematurely returned home. *Forensic Science International, 30*(2-3), 85-91.

(Infanticide - Britain)

Rose, L. (1986) *Massacre of the innocent: Infanticide in Britain 1800-1939.* London: Routledge, Chapman, & Hall.

(Infanticide)

Tooley, M. (1986) *Abortion & infanticide.* London: Oxford U. Press.

(Infant Death)

Emerick, S.J., et al. (1986) Risk factors for traumatic infant death in Oregon, 1973 to 1982. *Pediatrics, 77*(4), 518-522.

(Childhood Homicide)

Abel, E.L. (1986) Childhood homicide in Erie County, New York. *Pediatrics, 77*(5), 709-713.

(Infanticide)

Ulbricht, O. (1985, Sept.-Dec.) The debate about founding hospitals in Enlightenment Germany: Infanticide, illegitimacy, and infant mortality. *Central European History, 18*, pp. 211-256.

(Victim - Child)

Winslow, P.C. (1985, April 1) A small town murder (J. Hays accused of murdering her illegitimate child in Tralee, Ireland). *Macleans, 98*, pp. 6-7.

(Violent Death)

Rivara, F.P. (1985) Epidemiology of violent deaths in children and adolescents in the United States. *Pediatrician, 12*(1), 3-10.

(Homicide - Childhood)

Hodge, D., 3rd, & Ludwig, S. (1985) Childhood homicide: Emergency department recognition. *Pediatric Emergency Care, 1*(1), 3-6.

(Children and Guns)

Schetky, D.H. (1985) Children and handguns. American Journal of the Diseases of Children, 139(3), 229-231.

(Child Abuse)

Krugman, R.D. (1985) Fatal child abuse: Analysis of 24 cases. *Pediatrician, 12*(1), 68-72.

(Infanticide)

Tedeschi, M. (1984, Nov.) Infanticide & its apologists. *Commentary, 78*, pp. 31-35.

(Child Abuse - Norway)

Grunfeld, B., et al. (1984) Fatal child abuse -- child killing in Norway: A review of the years 1950-1979. *Tidssker Nor Laegeforen, 20*(5), 289-292.

(Homicide - Childhood)

Christoffel, K.K. (1984) Homicide in childhood: A public health problem in need of attention. *American Journal of Public Health, 74*(1), 68-70.

(Victims - Children)

Regnery: Many missing children may be serial murder victims. (1984) *Justice Assistance News, 4*(10), 4. Microforms and article copies available from UMI.

(Homicide - Childhood)

Christoffel, K.K., et al. (1983) Homicide death rates in childhood in 23 developed countries: U.S. rates atypically high. *Child Abuse & Neglect, 7*(3), 339-345.

(Victim - Child)

Case, M.E.S., & Nanduri, R. (1983) Laceration of the stomach by blunt trauma in a child: A case of child abuse. *Journal of Forensic Sciences, 28*(2), 496-501.

(Victim - Child)

Cordier, J. (1983) The child, privileged victim of crimes of passion (French). *Victimology, 8*(1-2), 131-136.

(Child Homicide)

Jason, J. (1983) Child homicide spectrum. *American Journal of Disease Control, 137*(6), 578-581.

(Pediatric Homicide)

Janson, J., et al. (1983) Homicide as a cause of pediatric mortality in the United States. *Pediatrics, 72*(2), 191-197.

(Childhood Homicide)

Christoffel, K.K., et al. (1983) Homicide in childhood: Distinguishable patterns of risk related to developmental levels of victims. *American Journal of Forensic Medicine & Pathology, 4*(2), 129-137.

(Infanticide)

Batten, M. (1983) Slaughter of the innocents: The evolution of infanticide. *Science Digest, 91*, 38+.

(Infanticide)

Varge, A.C. (1982, Dec.) Ethics of infant euthanasia. *Thought, 57*, pp. 438-448.

(Infanticide)

Wilkey, I., et al. (1982) Neonaticide, infanticide, and child homicide. *Medical Science and the Law, 22*(1), 31-34.

(Victims - Female Children)

Miller, B. (1981) *The endangered sex: Neglect of female children in rural North India*. Ithaca, NY: Cornell U. Press.

(Child Murder)

Srch, M. (1981) Child murder Summary in English and Russian. *Cesk Pediatr, 36*(6), 345-347.

(Child Murders)

Rodregra, H. (1981) Case analyses of child murders. Sociological and social medicine aspects (German). *Med Welt, 32*(13), 432-435.

(Fatal Child Abuse - Statistics)

Christoffel, K.K., et al. (1981) Epidemiology of fatal child abuse: International mortality data. *Journal of Chronic Diseases, 34*(2-3), 57-64.

(Feticide - Legality)

Feticide is still legal in Louisiana. (1980, Spring) *Loyola Law Review, 26*, 422-430.

(Deaths - Children)

Creighton, S. (1980) Deaths from non-accidental injury in children (letter). *British Medical Journal, 281*(6233), 147.

(Child Killers - Hanging)

R.I. congressman says hang child abusers who kill. (1980) *Juvenile Justice Digest, 8*(5), 3.

(Infanticide)

Quay, E.A. (1980) *And now infanticide*, 2nd. ed. Sun Life.

(Victims - Runaway Youths)

Behind growing worry over runaway youths; result of John Gacy mass murders. *U.S. News, 86*,

86, p. 63.

(Infanticide - Mothers)

Peneva, M., & Alexandrova, M. (1979) Infanticide committed by mothers (Bulgarian with English summary). *Nevrol Psikhiatr Nevrokhir, 18*(1), 32-35.

(Birth Defects - Infanticide)

Partick, J.G. (1979, April 3) Little murders: Question of birth defects and infanticide. *New Times, 10*, 32-35+.

(Infanticide)

Kohl, M., ED. (1978) *Infanticide and the value of life*. Prometheus.

(Victim - Child)

Huntington, R.W., 3rd, et al. (1977) Unusual form of child abuse (letter). *Journal of Forensic Science, 22*(1), 5-6.

(Female Infanticides)

Harris, M. (1977) Why men dominate women: Female infanticide and overpopulation. *New York Times Magazine*, p. 46+.

(Victims - Children)

They all trusted their killer: Child killings in Oakland County, Michigan. (1977, April 4) *Time, 109*, 20.

(Victims - Children)

Davidson, B. (1977, Sept.) Town that lives in terror; child murders in Birmingham, MI in Oakland County. *Good Housekeeping, 185*, pp. 136-137+.

(Murder Fetus)

Homicide - murder - fetus - assault on mother. (1976, March) *Law Enforcement Legal Review, 45*, 7.

(Murder - Unborn Fetus)

Homicide - murder - death of unborn fetus. (1976, Feb.) *Law Enforcement Legal Review, 44*, 7.

(Victims - Children)

Kaplun, D., et al. (1976) The murdered child and his killers. *American Journal of Psychiatry, 133*(7), 809-813.

(Child Abuse)

Palmer, C.H., & Weston, J.T. (1976) Several unusual cases of child abuse. *Journal of Forensic Sciences, 21*(4), 851-855.

(Child Abuse)

Helpern, M. (1976) Fatalities from child abuse and neglect: Responsibility of the medical examiner and coroner. *Pediatr Ann, 5*(3), 42-57.

(Infanticide)

Turbe-Becker, E. (1975) Physical negligence and subsequent exitus of infants (German with English abstract). *Med Klin, 70*(10), 417-426.

(Infanticide)

Arboleda-Florez, J. (1975) Infanticide: Some medicolegal considerations. *Canadian Psychiatric Association Journal, 20*(1), 55-60.

(Abortion)

Stubblefield, P.G. (1975) Abortion vs. manslaughter. *Archives of Surgery, 110*(7), 790-791.

(Victims - Children)

Dormann, U. (1975) Special statistics: Successful homicidal offenses against children during 1968-1974 (German and French). *Kriminalistik 1975*, 29(10), 465.

(Infanticide)

Dimaio, V.J.M., & Bernstein, C.G. (1974) A case of infanticide. *Journal of Forensic Science, 19*(4), 744-754.

(Infanticide)

Baxter, S.J., & Rees, B. (1974) The immunological identification of fetal haemoglobin in bloodstains in infanticide and associated crimes. *Medical Science and the Law, 14*(3), 163-167.

(Infanticide - Fantasy)

Bloch, D. (1974) Fantasy and the fear of infanticide. *Psychoanalytic Review, 61*(1), 5-31.

(Battered Child - Homicide)

Levine, L.J. (1973, Nov.) The solution of a battered-child homicide by dental evidence: Report of a case. *Journal of the American Dental Association, 87*, 1234-1236.

(Infanticide - Psychiatric Aspects)

Smoczynski, S. (1973) The forensic psychiatric aspect of infanticide (polish). *Psychiatria Polska, 7*(4), 433-436.

(Infanticide)

Scott, P.D. (1973) Parents who kill their children. *Medical Science and the Law, 13*(2), 120-126.

(Abortion or Murder)

Non-consensual destruction of the fetus - abortion or murder? (1971, Fall) *UCLA-Alaska Law Review, 1*, 80.

(Unborn Infants)

Non-consensual killing of an unborn infant: A criminal act? (1971, Winter) *Buffalo Law*

Review, 20, 535.

(Infanticide - India)

Pakrasi, K., & Sasmal, B. (1971) Infanticide and variation of sex ratio in a caste population in India. *Acta Med Auxol* (Milan), *3*(3), 217-228.

(Homicides - Fetus)

Fetus as a legal entity -- facing reality. (1971) *San Diego Law Review, 8,* 126.

(Infanticide)

Meldmann, J.A. (1968, Summer) Legal concept[ts of human life: The infanticide doctrines. *Marquette Law Review, 52,* 105.

(Victims - Infants)

Bonnet, E.F. (1970, April-June) Homicide followed by criminal incineration of cadavers of newborn infants. Medicolegal considerations. *Zacchia, 6,* 226-257.

(Victim - Fetus)

Killing of a viable fetus is murder. (1970, Spring) *Maryland Law Review, 30,* 137.

(Neonaticide)

Walther, G., et al. (1970) Problems in the diagnosis of homicide in newborns (German) *Z Rechtsmed, 67,* 109-118.

(Homicides - Children)

Otsuka, F., et al. (1967) Case studies of homicide in children. *Bulletin of Osaka Medical School Supplement, 12,* 385+.

(Victims - Children)

Myers, S.A. (1967) The child slayer: A 25-year survey of homicides involving preadolescent victims. *Archives of General Psychiatry, 17*(2), 211-213.

(Infanticide)

Deadman, W.J. (1964) Infanticide. 9028. vol. 91, '64, n. 10, p. 558-560 (IBZ 1966).

(Infanticide)

Proving live birth in infanticide. (1963, Spring) *Wyoming Law Review, 17,* 237.

(Homicide - Children)

Gatti, R. (1963, Sept.-Oct.) Homicide involving children. *Minerva Medicoleg, 83,* 134-141.

(Victims - Children)

Bakwin, H. (1960, Oct.) Homicidal deaths in infants and children. *Journal of Pediatrics, 57,* 568-570.

(Victims - Children)

Bergen, M.E. (1958) The effect of severe trauma on a four-year-old child: Psychoanalytic study of the child (New York). *Psychoanalytic Studies of Children, 13*, 407-429.

(Female Infanticide)

Hirschmann, J., & Schmitz, E. (1957) Structural analysis of the female infanticide (German). *J Bone Surg Am, 39*(6), 1-20.

(Infanticide)

Delay, J., et al. (1957) Contribution a l'etude de l'infanticide pathologique. *Semaine Des Hospitaux de Paris, 33*(69), 6.

(Infanticide - Ceylon)

Gunasekara, N.D. (1956, May) Infanticide in Ceylon. *Ceylon Med Journal, 3*, 140-163.

(Infanticide - Manifestations)

Schwade, E.D., & Otto, O. (1953, March) Infanticide as manifestation of thalamic or hypothalamic disorder with abnormal electroencephalographic findings. *Wisconsin Medical Journal, 52*, 171-174.

(Infanticide - Uncommon Methods)

Miloslavich, E.L. (1951, Sept.-Oct.) Uncommon methods of infanticide. *Journal of Criminal Law, 42*, 414-416.

(Infanticide - Eskimos)

Garber, C.M. (1947) Eskimo infanticide. *Science Monthly, 64*, 98-102.

(Infanticide - Law)

Cameron, R.G. (1947, July) Criminal law - subject of infanticide (People v. Chavez (CA) 176 Pac. 2d. 92). *Southern California Law Review, 20*, 357-360.

(Abortion)

Abortion - murder - removal of dead fetus (Rex v. Trim, 1943, V L R 109). (1944) *Australian Law Journal*, 17, 305-306.

(Infanticide)

Davidson, G.M. (1941) Medicolegal aspects of infanticide. *Journal of Criminal Psychopathology, 2*, 500-511.

(Infanticide)

Matheson, J.C.M. (1941) Infanticide. *Medicolegal Review, 9*, 135-152.

(Infanticide)

Elo, O. (1940) Caustic contribution to the question of grounds for mercy in infanticide (German). *Acta Soc Med, 28*, 1-243.

(Infanticide)

The Infanticide Act, 1938. (1938, Dec.) *Modern Law Review, 2*, 229.

(Infanticide)

Pfister-Amende, M. (1937) Psychiatric examination of two cases of infanticide (French). *Schweiz Arch Neurol Psychiat 1937*(2), 39.

(Infanticide)

Infanticide or murder? (1929, Nov. 23) *Sol J, 73*, 772.

Victims
Family/Relatives

(Wife-murder)

Sedgwick, J. (1990, June) A case of wife-murder. *Esquire, 113*(6), pp. 195-205.

(Victims - Family/Relatives)

Streshinsky, S. (1990, March) Angela: A history of innocence, hope, despair, and mass murder. *Glamour, 88*(6), pp. 268-271+.

(Wife-killing)

Besse, S.K. (1989, Summer) Crimes of passion: The campaign against wife-killing in Brazil, 1910-1940. *Journal of Social History, 22*, 653-656.

(Victim - Wife)

Hopkins, E. (1989, April 20) Nowhere to run (R. Linton murdered by her husband in Yonkers, NY). *Rolling Stone*, pp. 72-74+.

(Victims - Parents)

Dorban, P.T., & O'Connor, A. (1989, Jan.) Women who kill their parents. *British Journal of Psychiatry, 154,* 27-33.

(Victims - Women)

Kay, T., et al. (1989) Women victims of domestic violence (letter). *British Medical Journal, 299*(6711), 1339.

(Homicide - Marital)

Goetting, A. (1989) Patterns of marital homicide: A comparison of husbands and wives. *Journal of Comprehensive Family Studies, 20*(3), 341-354.

(Victims - Family)

Roos, J.L., et al. (1989) Psychiatric aspects of family killings. *South African Medical Journal, 75*(3), 121-123.

(Victim - Spouse)

McGinniss, J. (1988, Dec. 1) Blind Faith. *Rolling Stone, 540,* pp. 69-79+.

(Victim - Wife)

Husband tosses wife 18 stories in heated dispute (J. Burgos). (1987, Oct. 26) *Jet, 73,* 32.

(Victims - Wives)

Nadelhaft, J. (1987, Fall) Wife torture: A known phenomenon in nineteenth-century America. *Journal of American Culture, 10,* pp. 39-59.

(Filicide)

Bourget, D., et al. (1987) Affective disorder and homicide: A case of familial filicide, theoretical and clinical considerations. *Canadian Journal of Psychiatry, 32*(3), 222-225.

(Victims - Father and Son)

Chicago's Flukey Stokes met same tragic end as his son. (1986, Dec. 8) *Jet, 71,* p. 18.

(Victim - Ex-Wife)

Plummer, W. (1986, Aug. 18) Christiana Henry's ex-husband didn't kill her the first time; her fear is he'll never stop trying (attempted murderer P. Henry paroled). *People Weekly, 26,* pp. 73-74+.

(Victim - Black Adopted Child)

Male couple charged in death of adopted child (Black child abused by Black adoptive parents in Oakland, CA). (1986, July 7) *Jet, 70,* p. 54.

(Victim - Brother)

Staples, B. (1986, March 30) A brother's murder. *New York Times Magazine,* p. 72.

(Fratricide)

Marchand, P., et al. (1986) The determinism of a fratricide. *Annals of Medical Psychology, 144*(5), 531-534.

(Victims - Family)

Straus, M.A. (1986) Medical care costs of intra-family assault and homicide. *Bulletin of NY Academy of Medicine, 62*(5), 556-561.

(Battered Women)

Kuhl, A.F. (1986) Implications of justifiable homicide verdicts for battered women. *Response to the Victimization of Women and Children, 9*(2), 6-10.

(Victims - Family)

Hammer, J. (1985, Nov. 18) Driven by his long-buried raged, a 17-year-old honor student lethally lashes out at his family (case of J. Justice in Kenmore, NY). *People Weekly, 24,* pp. 127-130.

(Victim - Son)

Houston doctor kills son, charged with murder (J.H. Pendleton). (1985, Aug. 5) *Jet, 68*, p. 10.

(Victims - Spouse)

Jordan, N. (1985, July) Till murder us do part. *Psychology Today, 19*, p. 7.

(Victim - Mother-in-law)

Moore, G. (1985, Jan.) The case of the murdered mother-in-law (N. Carter wrongfully imprisoned). *Reader's Digest, 126*, pp. 98-103.

(Battered Women)

Levit, H.I. (1985) The battered woman. *American Journal of Forensic Psychology, 3*(2), 9-14.

(Uxoricide)

Lescovelli, M., et al. (1985) On a statistical study and psychopathological hypotheses as regards cases of uxoricide committed by male and female psychiatric patients (Italian). *Rivista Sperimentale di Freniatria e Medicina Legale delle Allieazioni Mentali, 109*(1), 73-86.

(Victim - Spouse)

Edwards, S.S.M. (1985) A sociolegal evaluation of gender ideologies in domestic violence, assault, and spousal homicides. *Victimology, 10*(1-4), 186-205.

(Battered Women)

New Jersey admits expert testimony on 'battered woman syndrome'. (1984) *The Criminal Law Reporter: Court Decisions, 35*(19), 2329-2330. Also in *Family Law Reporter: Court Opinions, 10*(42), 1577-1578.

(Domestic Violence)

Goldberg, W.G., & Tomlanovich, M.C. (1984) Domestic violence victims in the emergency department: New findings *Journal of American Medical Association, 251*(24), 3259-3264.

(Victims - Spouses)

Wallacker, B.E. (1981, Dec.) Poet as jurist Po Cha-i and a case of conjugal homicide. *Harvard Journal of Asiatic Study, 41*, 507-526.

(Victim - Wife)

Custody: Father loses rights by killing mother. (1981) *Juvenile and Family Law Digest, 13*(7), 214. Microforms and article copies available from UMI.

(Victims - Fiance and Daughter)

Demaret, K. (1979, July 2) Her fiance and daughter dead, Priscilla Davis leaves murder mansion. *People Weekly, 12*, pp. 26-28.

(Victim - Wife)

McCall, C. (1978, Dec. 18) Heiress Sasha Bruce dies, her husband is accused: There the riddle begins. *People Weekly, 10,* pp. 30-33.

(Victims - Offspring)

Kamiyama, S., & Aoki, T. (1978) A case of homicidal electrocution by father (Japanese, summary in English). *Journal Leg Med, 32*(2), 88-93.

(Victims - Family)

Foucalt, M. (1975) *I, Pierre Reviere, having slaughtered my mother, my sister, and my brother: A case of parricide in the nineteenth century.* New York: Pantheon

(Homicide - Family)

Burgess, A.W. (1975) Family reaction to homicide. *American Journal of Orthopsychiatry, 45*(3), 391-398.

(Victims - Kin)

Perdue, W.C., & Lester, D. (1973) Those who murder kin: A Rorschach study. *Perceptual and Motor Skills, 36*(2), 606.

(Victims - Relatives)

Watson, J., et al. (1971) Murder in the family: a study of some homicidal adolescents. 1671. vol. 127, '71, n. 11, p. 1498-1502 (IBZ 1972).

(Homicide - Relatives)

Geilen, G. (1964) Silence of relative in a homicide plot (German). 38667. J. 11, '64, S. 385-392 (IBZ 1972).

(Victims - Parents)

Drechsler, J. (1957) Faults in education in relation to murder of parents (German). *Psychol Rdsch, 8,* 136-144.

Victims in Parricide

(Patricide)

Myers, W.C., et al. (1990) Terasoff and threats of patricide by a nine-year-old boy (letter). *American Journal of Psychiatry, 147*(4), 535.

(Patricide)

Singhal, S., & Dutta, A. (1990) Who commits patricide? *Acta Psychiatr Scand, 82*(1), 40-43.

(Patricide - Buddhist)

Obeyesekere, G. (1989, June) The conscience of the patricide: A study in Buddhist history. *Man, 24*, pp. 236-254.

(Patricide - Study)

Cravens, J.M., et al. (1985) A study of 10 men charged with patricide. *American Journal of Psychiatry, 142*(9), 1089-1092.

(Patricide)

Van Ginneken, J. (1984) Patricide: On the background of Freud's 'mass psychology and ego analysis'. *Psyche, 38*(12), 1124-1148.

(Double Parricide)

Mass, R.L., et al. (1984) Double parricide - matricide and patricide: A comparison with other schizophrenic murders. *Psychiatry Quarterly, 56*(4), 286-290.

(Parricide)

Benefits frozen for kids who kill parents. (1982) *Juvenile Justice Digest, 10*(19), 6. Microforms and article copies available from UMI.

(Parricide)

Post, S. (1982) Adolescent parricide in abusive families. *Child Welfare, 61*(7), 445-455.

(Parricide)

Parents murdered, baby spared. (1981) *Narcotics Control Digest, 11*(25-26), 8. Microforms and article copies available from UMI.

(Victims - Parents)

Russell, F. (1979, June 8) Murder strikes home: Murder of parents by J. Bradley, Jr. in Westwood, Ma. *National Review, 31*, pp. 744-745.

(Patricide)

Tucker, L.S., Jr., et al. (1977) Mother-son *folie a deax*: A case of attempted patricide. *American Journal; of Psychiatry, 134*(10), 1146-1147.

(Parricide - Constitutionality)

Ryu, P.K. (1977) Is the crime of parricide unconstitutional? *Rev Jur UPR, 46*, 555-572.

(Parricide - Reactive)

Tanay, E. (1976) Reactive parricide. *Journal of Forensic Science, 21*(1), 76-82.

(Parricide - France)

Devaux, C, et al. (1974) Inquiry into parricide in France (French). *Annales Medico-Psycholgiques, 1*(2), 161-168.

(Patricide - Psychology)

Tanay, E. (1973) Adolescents who kill parents: Reactive parricide. *Australian and New Zealand Journal of Psychiatry, 7*(4), 263-277.

(Parricide)

Tuovinen, M. (1973) On parricide. *Psychiatria Fennica, 1973*, 141-146.

(Parricide - Psychological Aspects)

Rozycka, M., & Thille, Z. (1972) The psychopathological aspect of parricide (Polish). *Psychiatira Polska, 6*(2), 159-168.

(Patricide - Causes)

Matuszewicz, T., et al. (1971) Patricide as an expression of emotional disorders in a subject with a tumor in the parietal region of the brain (Polish). *Psychiatr Polska, 5*, 105-112.

(Parricide)

Sadoff, R.L. (1971) Clinical observations in parricide. *Psychiatric Quarterly, 45*, 65-69.

(Patricide)

Purini, T. (1970, Jan.-June) Patricide by hanging (Italian). *Minerva Medicoleg, 90*, 24-31.

(Parricide)

Porot, M., et al. (1968) Parricide (French). *Rev Neuropsychiatr Infant Suppl.*, 59-63.

(Parricide - Adolescent)

Petit, G., et al. (1967) Parricide committed by an adolescent followed by suicide: Apropos of a case (French). *Ann Med Leg, 47*, 685-690.

(Parricide)

Bourgeois, M., et al. (1967, April) The parricide and his father (French). *Ann Medicopsychol, 125*, 595-600.

(Victims - Parents)

Takomura, S. (1966) The Japanese father- and mother-murder. 20957. J. 20. '66, 3 S, 164 (IBZ 1967).

(Parricide - Case Report)

Vereeken, J.L. (1965) A case of parricide. *Psychotherapy and Psychosom, 13*, 364-379.

(Parricide - Attempt)

Sutte, H. (1964, Feb.-March) Attempted parricide by a 16-year-old girl (German). *Acta Paedopsychiat* (Basel), *31*, 95-99.

(Victims - Parents)

Beukenkamp, C. (1960, Sept.) Phantom patricide. *AMA Archives of General Psychiatry, 3*, 282-288.

(Victims - Parents)

DeWaele, J.P. (1957) Two Rorschach tests of a parricide: Contribution to the study of the dangerous state of mind (French). *Acta Neurologica et Psychiatrica Belgica, 57*(3), 263-302.

(Parricide - Psychiatric Study)

Gonzalez Garcia, F. (1947) A psychiatric study of a parricide (Spanish). *Rev Med Leg Columbia, 9*, 111-124.

(Parricide)

Bautista, A.L. (1940, Jan.) Liability of a stranger who participates in the crime of parricide. *Philadelphia Law Journal, 19*, 326-328.

(Parricide)

Richmond, F.C. (1931) Mental examination of fourteen-year-old boy parricide. *Med Leg Journal, 47*, 6-12.

(Parricide Statute)

Smythe, J.G., Jr. (1921, Nov.) Mississippi's parricide statute. *Mississippi Law Journal, 4*, 132-134.

Victims in Matricide

(Victims - Mothers)

Mouridsen, S.E. (1988) Children who kill: A case study of matricide *Journal of Child Psychology and Psychiatry, 29*(4), 511-515.

(Matricide)

Lipson, C.F. (1986) A case report of matricide (letter). *American Journal of Psychiatry, 143*(1), 112-113.

(Matricidal Men)

Campion, J., et al. (1985) A study of 15 matricidal men. *American Journal of Psychiatry, 142*(3), 312-317.

(Matricide)

Dreyfuss, L., et al. (1984) a case of matricide, questions posed (with videotape recording) [French]. *Ann Med Psychol, 142*(9), 1192-1205.

(Matricide)

Green, C,M. (1981) Matricide by sons. *Medical Science and the Law, 21*(3), 207-214.

(Matricidal Defendant)

Frank, B., & Robins, J.E., Jr. (Eds.) (1976) Matricidal defendant: Perpetrator or victim? *Federal Probation, 40*(4), 78-79. Article copies available from UMI.

(Matricide)

Rossi, R. (1975) Mastermind and execution of a matricide: a psychoanalytic viewpoint (Italian). *Archivio di Psicologia, Neurologia e Psichiatria, 36*(3), 363-377.

(Matricide)

Rubinstein, L.H. (1969, June) The theme of Electra and Orestes: A contribution to the psychopathology of matricide. *British Journal of Medical Psychology, 42*, 99-108.

(Matricide)

McKnight, C.K., et al. (1966) Matricide and mental illness. *Canadian Psychiatric Association Journal, 11*(2), 99-106.

(Matricide - Sacrifice)

Skinner, J. (1961) Ritual matricide: A study of the origins of sacrifice. *Amer. Imago, 18*, 71-102.

(Matricide)

Winfield, D.L., & Ozturk, O. (1959) Electroencephalographic findings in matricide. *Diseases of the Nervous System, 20*(4), 176-178.

(Matricide - Psychodynamics)

Dalma, G. (1945) "Via del Maltempo" of Onofrio Fabrizi - psychodynamism of matricide. *Psicoanaly appl Med Pedag Sociol 1945*(1), 70-87.

(Victim - Mother)

Bunker, H.A. (1944) Mother-murder in myth and legend: A psychoanalytic note. *Psychoanalysis Quarterly, 13*, 198-207.

(Matricide)

Hill, D., et al. (1943) A case of matricide. *Lancet, 244*(part 1), 526-527.

Victims in Feticide

(Feticide)

Homicide - Death of a fetus. (1982) *The Criminal Law Reporter: Court Decisions, 32*(6), 2116.

(Feticide - Legality)

Killer of unborn child can be prosecuted under murder statute. (1982) *The Family Law Reporter: Court Opinions, 8*(31), 2457-2458.

(Feticide)

Feticide is still legal in Louisiana. (1980, Spring) *Loyola Law Review, 26*, 422-430.

(Feticide - California)

Feticide in California: A proposed statutory scheme. (1979, Summer) *UCD Law Review, 12*, 723-742.

Victims in Filicide

(Filicide)

Bourget, D., et al. (1987) Affective Disorder and homicide: A case of familial filicide, theoretical and clinical considerations. *Canadian Journal of Psychiatry, 32*(3), 222-225.

(Filicide)

Feldman, M., et al. (1986) Filicidal abuse in the histories of 15 condemned murderers. *Bulletin of the American Academy of Psychiatry in the Law, 14*(4), 345-352.

(Filicide)

Chueng, P.T. (1986) Maternal filicide in Hong Kong, 1971-1985. *Medical Science and the Law, 26*(3), 185-192.

(Filicide)

Lesnick, O.M. (1986) Multitherapeutic approach to clinical treatment for a child at risk for maternal filicide. *Child Abuse & Neglect, 10*(3), 407-410.

(Filicide - Study)

Husain, A., et al. (1984) A comparative study of Filicidal and abusive mothers. *Canadian Journal of Psychiatry, 29*(7), 597-598.

(Filicide - Incest)

Green, C.M. (1982) Filicidal impulses as an anniversary reaction to childhood incest. *American Journal of Psychotherapy, 36*(2), 264-271.

(Filicide)

Kressel, G.M. (1981) Sororicide/filicide: Homicide for family honor. *Current Anthropology, 22*(2), 141-158.

(Filicide - Somnambulance)

Luchins, D.J., et al. (1978) Filicide during psychotropically induced somnambulism: A case report. *American Journal of Psychiatry, 135*(11), 1404-1405.

(Filicide - Motivation)

Rascovsky, A. (1974) Filicide and the unconscious motivation for war. *Adolescent Psychiatry, 3*, 54-67.

(Filicide)

Podolsky, E. (1958) The psychodynamics of filicide and matricide. *Diseases of the Nervous System, 19*(11), 475-477.

Victims of Sex Abuse

(Victims - Women)

Revitch, E. (1980) Gynocide and unprovoked attacks on women. *Corrective and Social Psychiatry and Behavior Technology, Methods and Therapy, 26*(1), 6-11.

(Victimization - Women)

Bowker, L.H. (1979) the criminal victimization of women. *Victimology, 4*(4), 371-384.

(Victims - Women)

Murder figures for women showing violent trend. (1976) *Criminal Justice Digest, 4*(6), 13.

(Gynecocide)

Geha, R. (1975, Spring) For the love of Medusa: A psychoanalytic glimpse into gynecocide. *Psychoanalytic Review, 62*, 49-77.

(Female Victims)

Zahn, M.A. (1975) The female homicide victim. *Criminology: An Interdisciplinary Journal, 13*(3), 400-415.

(Victims - Teenage Boys)

Houston horrors: sexual abuse and killing of teenage boys. (1973, Aug. 20) *Time, 102*, p. 24.

(Victims - Prostitutes)

Fernandez, E.A. (1968) Death of a call girl (German). 20957. J. 22, '68, 2, S. 111-112 (IBZ 1969).

(Victims - Women)

Gribble, L. (1968) *They had a way with women.* Roy Publishers.

(Sex Murders)

Revitch, E. (1965) Sex murder and the potential sex murderer. 1123. vol. 26, '65, n. 10, p. 640-648 (IBZ 1967).

(Sexual Assault)

Jayewardene, C.H. (1963, Oct.-Dec.) Murder and sexual assault of an old woman. *Zacchia, 26*, 460-462.

(Victims - Women)

Meyers, A.F., et al. (1946) Men who kill women, Part I. *Journal of Clinical Psychopathology and Psychotherapy 1946*(7), 441-472.

(Victims - Fair Women)

Warning for fair women. (1912) AMS Press.

Mass Murder

(Slaying - International)

The talk of the town: Notes and comment. (1990, July 2) *New Yorker, 66*(20), pp. 21-22.

(Mass Murder - USSR)

Chelminski, R. (1990, May) Katyn: Anatomy of a massacre. *Reader's Digest, 136*(817), pp. 69-78.

(Barbarians)

Saporito, B. (1990, May) Barbarians at the gate, by J. Helyar & B. Burrough (book review). *Fortune, 121*(5), pp. 117-118.

(University Murder - Quebec)

Golden, J., & Breslauer, H.J. (1990, May) Violence and the University. *Society, 14*(2), pp. 5-7.

(Mass Murder and J. List)

Memorandum on a mass murder (letter sent by J. List to his pastor). (1990, April 9) *Newsweek, 115*, p. 25.

(Mass Murder - Romania)

Nelan, B.W., et al. (1990, Jan. 1) Slaughter in the streets. *Time, 135*(1), pp. 34-37.

(Mass Murder)

Grabosky, P.N. (1990) They wrought mayhem: An insight into mass murder (A. Kapardis). *Aust NZ J C, 23*(3), 207.

(Mass Murder)

Turque, B., & Colin, M. (1989, Dec. 18) Massacre in Montreal. *Newsweek, 114*(25), p. 39.

(Mass Murder)

Shepherd, R. (1989, Fall) The Hungerford massacre (speech given at the Royal Society of Medicine, London). *Medico-Legal Journal, 57*, 197-215.

(Schoolyard Murder)

Mathis, N. (1989) Schoolyard gun spree leaves 6 dead, 30 injured. *Education Week, 8*(18), 1.

(Mass Murder - Texas)

This is war: A.L. King's mass murder rampage in Daingerfield, TX. (1980, July 7) *Time, 116*, p. 18.

(Mass Murder - El Salvador)

Mass murder at the cathedral; shooting of protesters calling for release of Popular Revolutionary Bloc prisoners in El Salvador. (1979, May 21) *Time, 113*, p. 61.

(Shooting Spree - San Diego)

It was Monday: B. Spencer's shooting spree in San Diego. (1979, Feb. 12) *Time, 113*, p. 25.

(Mass Murder - New Orleans)

Gambino, R. (1977) *Vendetta: A true story of the worst lynching in America, the mass murder of Italian-Americans in New Orleans in 1891, the vicious motivations behind it, and the tragic repercussions that linger to this day.* New York: Doubleday.

(Mass Murder)

Williams, A. (1976) *Starkweather: The story of a mass murderer.* New York: Houghton.

(Mass Murders - Houston)

Olsen, J. (1975) *The man with the candy.* New York: PB.

(Massacre - Germany)

Massacre at Lebach arms depot in Federal Germany. (1974) *International Criminology and Police Review, 28*(279), 154-161.

(Mass Murderers - Juvenile)

Bretzfeld, K. (1936) Juvenile mass murderers (German). *Arch Kriminol, 98*, 57-70; *97*, 205-210 (1935).

(Mass Murder)

Polke. (1934) The mass-murderer Denke (German). *Arch Krim Anthrop, 95*, 8-30.

Genocide

(Genocide - Indonesia)

Ireland, D. (1990, June 12) Hidden history. *Village Voice, 35*(24), p. 8.

(Genocide - Armenia)

Corn, D. (1990) The slaughterhouse province: An American diplomat's report on the Armenian genocide, 1915-1917 (Book review by L.A. Davis). *Nation, 250*(21), pp. 748-749.

(Genocide)

Thompson, J.P., & Quets, A.G. (1990) Genocide and social conflict: A partial theory and a comparison. *Research in Social Movements, Conflicts, and Change, 1990*, 245-266.

(Genocide - Ethiopia)

Zeiler, J.A. (1989, Fall) Genocide convention - intentional starvation - Ethiopian famine in the Eritrean war for independence: The applicability of the Genocide Convention to government-imposed famine in Eritrea. *Ga J International and Comparative Law, 19*, 589-612.

(Genocide - General)

Staub, E. (1989) *The roots of evil: The origins of genocide and other violence.* London: Cambridge Press.

(Genocide)

Kuper, L. (1989) The prevention of genocide: Cultural and structural indicators of genocidal threat. *Ethic and Racial Studies, 12*(2), 157-173.

(Genocide - History)

Dadrian, V.N. (1988) The anticipation and prevention of genocide in International Conflicts: Some lessons from history. *International Journal of Group Tensions, 18*(3), 205-214.

(Genocide)

Pfafflin, F. (1986) The connection between eugenics, sterilization, and mass murder in Germany from 1933 to 1945. *Medical Law, 5*(1), 1-10.

(Genocide - Psychopathology)

Charny, I.W. (1986) Genocide and mass destruction: Doing harm to others as a missing dimension in psychopathology. *Psychiatry, 49*(2), 144-157.

(Genocide)

Dietz, P.E. (1986) Mass, serial, and sensational homicides. *Bulletin of New York Academy of Medicine, 62*(5), 477-491.

(Genocide - General)

Geberth, V.J. (1986) Mass, serial, and sensational homicides: The investigative perspective. *Bulletin of New York Academy of Medicine, 62*(5), 492-496.

(Murder - Nazis)

Degwitz, R. (1985) Medical thinking and way of acting in the National Socialist era (German with English summary). *Forschr Neurol Psychiatr, 53*(6), 212-225.

(Mass Murder)

Scharfetter, C. (1984) An objective of the education of mankind: Delegated destructiveness (mass murder of psychiatric patients in Hitler's Germany) [German]. *Schweiz Arch Neurol Neurochir Psychiatr, 134*(2), 279-293.

(Peoples Temple)

Fatal prophesy is fulfilled (murder of People's Temple members A. and J. Mills in Berkeley, CA.) (1980, March 10) *Newsweek, 95*, p. 46.

(Genocide)

Wishny, S.L. (1980) Children of the holocaust and their relevancy to probation: Presentence investigations and case planning. *Federal Probation, 44*(4), 12-15.

(Genocide)

Mant, A.K. (1978) Genocide. *Journal of Forensic Science Soc, 18*(1-2), 13-17.

(Genocide)

Pilisuk, M., et al. (1976) Torture and genocide as public health problems. *American Journal of Orthopsychiatry, 46*(3), 388-392.

(Genocide - Case Report)

Rappaport, E.A. (1976) Adolf Eichmann: The traveling salesman of genocide. *International Review of Psychoanalysis, 3*(1), 111-119.

(Genocide - Blacks)

Turner, C., et al. (1973, Dec.) Fears of genocide among Black Americans as related to age, sex, and region. *American Journal of Public Health, 63*, 1029-1034.

(Genocide - Population Control)

Sal, F.T. (1973, Fall) Regional viewpoints on population growth: Perspectives of the genocide issue. *International Journal of Health Services, 3*, 753-758.

(Genocide - Fear)

Darity, W.A., et al. (1972, Nov.) Family planning, race consciousness and the fear of race genocide. *American Journal of Public Health, 62*, 1454-1459.

(Genocide)

Lowinger, P. (1971, Oct.) Science, medicine, and genocide. *American Journal of Psychiatry, 128*, 497-498.

(Genocide - Factors)

Dadrian, V.N. (1971) Factors of anger and aggression in genocide. *Journal of Human Relations, 19*(3), 394-417.

(Genocide)

New crime of genocide. (1969, Aug. 16) *British Medical Journal, 3*, 422.

(Genocide - Criminology)

Genocide and criminology (German). (1967, Sept.) *Med Mschr, 21*, 387-388.

(Genocide - History)

Cormier, B.M. (1966, Feb.) On the history of men and genocide. *Canadian Med Ass Journal, 94*, 276-291.

Victims
Precipitated Homicide

(Spousal Homicide)

Showalter, C.R., et al. (1980) The spousal homicide syndrome. *International Journal of Law & Psychiatry, 3*(2), 117-142.

(Murderer/Victim Relationship)

Palmer, S., & Humphrey, J.A. (1980) Offender-victim relationship in criminal homicide followed by offender's suicide, North Carolina, 1972-1977. *Suicide & Life Threatening Behavior, 10*(2), 106-118.

(Provocation)

Ca, D. (1977) A study on the victims of crimes causing death or bodily injury - second (final) report. *Bull Criminol Res Dep 1977*, 1-3.

(Homicide - Precipitated)

Dietz, P.E. (1977) Medical criminology notes No. 1: Victim-precipitated criminal homicide. *Bulletin of the American Academy of Psychiatry and Law 1977*(5), 367-370.

(Case Report)

Two Oklahoma escaped convicts killed in police shootout after murdering eight. (1978) *Corrections Digest, 9*(11), 9-10. Article copies available from UMI.

Chapter 5
Murder Modes
Unusual Methods

(Mail Bomb - Murder))

Carlson, M., et al. (1990, Jan 1) Murder by mail. *Time, 135*(1), 33.

(Homicide - Electrocution)

Al-Alousi, L.M. (1990) Homicide by electrocution. *Medicine, Science and the Law, 30,* 239-246.

(Murder - Vaginal)

Fain, D.B., et al. (1989) Vaginal "fisting" as a cause of death. *Am J Forensic Med Pathol, 10*(1), 73-75.

(Homicide - Clubbing)

Groups march on Portland city hall in protest of recent racial slaying. (1988, Dec. 5) *Jet, 75*(10), 17.

(Homicide - Hanging)

Vieira, D. N., (1988) Homicidal hanging. *Am J Forensic Med Pathol, 9*(4), 287-289.

(Hanging - Mode)

Lew, E. O. (1988) Homicidal hanging in a dyadic death. *Am J Forensic Med Pathol, 9*(4), 283-286.

(Burning Homicide)

Frazier, H.C. (1987) "She went up in flames": Evidence of burn homicide. *Med Law, 6*(1), 69-77.

(Drowning - Mode)

Copeland, A.R. (1986) Homicidal drowning. *Forensic Sci Int, 31*(4), 247-252.

(Murdering In Sleep)

Ur, A. (1986) Murdering while asleep (letter). *Br Med J (Clin Res), 293*(6555), 1172.

(Murder In Sleep)

Fenwick, P. (1986) Murdering while asleep (editorial). *Br Med J (Clin Res), 293*(6547), 574-575.

(Fatal Fire)

Stickevers, J. (1986) Investigation of fatal fires: Views of the fire investigator (Part 1). *FBI Law Enf Bul, 55*(8), 1-5.

(Homicide - Bathtub)

Devos, C., et al. (1985) Deaths in the bath. *Med Sci Law, 25*(3), 189-200.

(Electrocution - Bathtub)

Schneider, V. (1985) Electrocution in the bathtub. *Arch Kriminol, 176*(3-4), 89-95.

(Bathtub Murder)

Weiler, G., et al. (1985) Death by electricity in the bathtub. Demonstration by formed local as well as linear electric mark. *Arch Kriminol, 176,*(3-4), 82-88.

(Homicide - Fire)

Copeland, A.R. (1985) Homicide by fire. *Z Rechtmed, 95*(1), 59-65.

(Homicide - Bathtub)

Pueschel, K. et al. (1985) Electrocutions in the bathtub, Hamburg, 1971-1983. *Arch Kriminol, 176*(3-4), 96-100.

(Electrocution)

Maxeiner, H. (1985) Survival of a homicide attempt by electric current (German with English abstract). *Beitr Gerichtl Med, 43*, 399-402.

(Homicide - Arsenic)

Massey, E.W. et al. (1984) Arsenic: Homicidal intoxication. *South Med J, 77*(7), 848-851.

(Blanket Suffocation)

Missliwetz, J., et al. (1984) A blanket as noise silencer (German with English abstract). *Beitr Gerichtl Med, 42*, 133-137.

(Murder/Suicide)

Allen, N.H. (1983) Homicide followed by suicide: Los Angeles, 1970-1979. *Suicide Life Threat Behav, 13*(3), 155-165.

(Death Styles - Canadian Indians)

Jarvis, G.K., et al. (1982) Death styles among Canadian Indians. *Can Soc Sci Med, 16*(14), 1345-1352.

(Homicide - Electrocution)

Kosa, F., & Viragos-Kis, E. (1981) Sudden death after 'domestic electric treatment' (German with

English abstract). *Arch Kriminol, 167*(1-2), 43-51,

(Victim Injury - Weapon)

Relationship shown between weapon type used to commit crime and victim injury-death. (1979) *Security Systems Digest, 10* (2), 2-4.

(Murder by Nail)

Ljunggren, B. et al. (1977) The good old method of the nail. *Surg Neurol, 7*(5), 288-292.

(Homicide - Accidental)

Foodman, A. et al. (1977) Adolescents who commit accidental homicide. The emotional consequences to the individual, family and community. *J Am Acad Child Psychiatry, 16*(2), 314-326.

(Manslaughter - By Neglect)

Manslaughter by neglect. (1977) *Br Med J, 1*(6062), 722-723.

(Electric Current)

Carlsson, L., et al. (1976) Attempted murder with electric current: Criminal-technical investigation. *Arch Kriminol, 157*(1-2), 30-36.

(Manslaughter - By Heat Stroke)

MacPherson, R.K. (1976) A case of manslaughter by heat stroke. *Med J Aust,2*(25), 926-927; *Med J Aus, 2*(26), 18-25.

(Mode - Heat Stroke)

Mullaly, P.R. (1976) Manslaughter by heat stroke. A note on the trial (editorial). *Med J Aust, 2*(25), 926-927; *Med J Aus, 2*(26), 18-25.

(Lynching - Psychiatric)

Raschka, L.B. (1976) Lynching: A psychiatrist's view. *Can Psychiatr Assoc J, 21*(8), 577-580.

(Lynching - Causes)

Miller, G. (1975) *Invitation to a lynching*. New York: Doubleday.

(Tear Gas Pen Gun)

Smialek, J.E., et al. (1975) Accidental death with tear gas pen gun: A case report. *Journal of Forensic Science, 20*(4), 708-713.

(Killing Under Foot)

Reh, H., et al. (1975) Injuries in killings by trampling under foot (German with English abstract). *Beitr Gerichtl Med, 33*, 148-153.

(Homicide - Bathtub)

Schneider, V. (1974) Criminal submersion in bathtubs. *Med Leg Dommage Corpor, 7*(4), 397-399.

(Criminal Electrocution)

Schneider, V. (1973) Remarkable cases of electric current induction for criminal purposes. *Arch Kriminol, 151,* 149-158.

(Homicide - Assault)

Bailey, F.L., & Rothblatt, H.B. (1973) *Crimes of violence: Homicide and assault.* Lawyers Co-Op.

(Witchcraft - England)

Marshburn, J.H. (1972) *Murder and witchcraft in England, 1550-1640, as recounted in pamphlets, ballads, broadsides, and plays.* Norman, OK: U of Oklahoma Press.

(Murder Via the Ear)

Huizinga, E. (1971) Murder through the ear. *Pract Otorhinolarryngol Basel, 33,* 361-365.

(Bathtub Murder)

Kosa, F. et al. (1970) (Murder in the bathtub). 3647, *146,* (3-4), 99-108 (IBZ 1971).

(Drowning - Head Injuries)

Oishi, F. (1970) A typical case of homicide with drowning and head injuries. *J Tokyo Med Coll, 28,* 541-548.

(Petrol Fires)

Nelson, D.F. (1970) Petrol fires in closed rooms. *Journal of Forensic Sci Soc, 10,* 3-6.

(Burns - Medicolegal Aspects)

Dell'erba, A. (1967) Medicolegal aspects of death caused by burns. *A. Zacchia, 3,* 13-52.

(Inferno - A Cloak)

Eckert, W.G. (1966) Masquerade by inferno. *J Florida Med Ass, 51,* 963.

(Solving Train Murder)

Patel, A. (1966) ("Watchfulness shows results": Difficulty in solving a murder in a moving train). 20957, *20*(12), 657-658 (I.B.Z. 1967).

(Homicide by Pepper)

Adelson, L. (1964) Homicide by pepper. *J Forensic Sci, 9,* 391-395.

(Murder Mode)

Lipsig, F. (1962) *Murder, family style.* New York: Collier.

(Weapon - Blunt Instrument)

Portiglatti, B.M. (1962, Sept.-Oct.) Homicide with a blunt instrument (Italian). *Minerva Medicoleg, 82,* 303-315.

(Murder By Stomping)

Huntington, R.W., Jr., et al. (1961) The stomped pancreas death. *Amer J Surg, 102,* 728-731.

(Battered Child - Starvation)

Adelson, L. (1960) Homicide by starvation: The nutritional variant of the "battered child." *JAMA, 186,* 458-460.

(Killing by Witchcraft)

Burchell, E.M. (1957) Mandate to kill by witchcraft. *S A L J, 74,* 382.

(Murder By Animal Hair)

Prokop, O. (1952) Murder by means of animal hair. *Deutsche Ztschr ges gericht Med, 41,* 240-242.

(Somnambulistic - Homicide)

Morris, N. (1951) Somnambulistic homicide: Ghosts, spiders, and North Koreans. *Res Judicatae, 5,* 29-33.

(Show of Violence)

Wertham, F. (1949) *Show of violence.* Westport, CT: Greenwood.

(Malice - Deadly Weapon)

Barney, C.E. (1938) Malice, presumption of malice from use of deadly weapon. *Neb L B, 17,* 231-235.

(Psychopathic Frenzy)

Amir, M. (1936) (The forensic importance of psychopaths in the Dutch Indies: amok and Atjesi assassination). *Arch Antrop crim, 56,* 571-579.

(Homicide - Bootlegging)

Manslaughter by "bootlegging". (1921) *25 Law Notes, 105*(1921), 54 *Chi Leg N,* 116.

(Manslaughter - Sports)

Manslaughter by violence on the football field. (1898) 32 *Ir L T,* 539.

Murder By Automobile

(Bishop's Murder)

Bishop's death prompts calls for democracy. (1990, Oct. 22) *Christianity Today, 34*(15), 63-64.

(Manslaughter - DUI)

Lions' Rogers faces suit in death of teenagers. (1988, Dec. 12) *Jet, 75*(11), 46.

(Vehicular Homicide)

Copeland, A.R. (1986) True vehicular homicide. *Am J Forensic Med Pathol, 7*(4), 305-307.

(DUI Murder)

Brandt, A.A. et. al. (1985) Drunken injured drivers: Are they getting away with murder? *Con Med, 49*(6), 377-379.

(Pushing Mode)

Gayda, M.,et al. (1985) The "pushing on" in the tube. *J Med Leg Droit Med, 28*,(1), 57-61.

(Car Murder - Conviction)

Philpott, T. (1983, May 9) CMA upholds conviction in car murder. *Air Force Times, 43*, p. 50.

(Vehicular Death)

Homicide death by auto statute, applicability to stillborn fetus. (1982) *IACP Law Enforcement Legal Review, 118*, 10.

(Vehicular Homicide)

Death of fetus by auto ruled not a homicide. (1982) *The Family Law Reporter Court Opinions, 8*(19), 2274-2275.

(Vehicular Homicide)

Michalowski, R.J., Jr. (1975) Violence in the road: The crime of vehicular homicide. *J Res Crim and Delinquency, 12*, 30-43.

(Highway Murders)

Critchley, T.A., & James, P.D. (1971) *The maul and the pear tree: The Ratcliffe highway murders, 1811*. Crane-Russak Co.

(Traffic Laws)

Traffic laws commentary. (1969) Washington, D.C.: U.S. Government Printing Office (Written by National Highway Traffic Safety Administration, U.S. Department of Transportation.

(Suicide/Homicide - Auto)

MacDonald, J.M. (1964) Suicide and homicide by automobile. *Amer J Psychiat, 121*, 366-370.

(Vehicular Manslaughter)

Manslaughter by motor cars. (1942) *Fortnightly L J, 12,* 118-121.

(DUI Murder)

Riesenfeld, S.A. (1936) Homicide committed through the operation of a motor vehicle while intoxicated. Calif Veh Code 510, 502.*Calif L Rev, 24,* 55..

(Manslaughter - Vehicular)

Manslaughter by automobile (Commonwealth v. Mayberry, 290 Pa. 195). (1928) *E F Temp L Q, 2,* 389-390.

Murder Modes
Medical

(Homicide by Steroid)

Pope, H.G., et al. (1990) Homicide and near-homicide by anabolic steroid users. *J Clin Psychiatry, 51*(1), 28-31.

(Insulin Murder)

Haibach, H., et al. (1987) Homicide by insulin administration. *J Forensic Sci, 32*(1), 208-216.

(Hypoglycemia)

Bidot-Lopez, P., et al. (1987) Hypoglycemia: Facetious or felonious? *Hospital Practitioner, 22*(15), 128-132.

(Life Support - Disconnection)

Towers, B. (1982) Irreversible coma and withdrawal of life support: Is it murder if the IV line is disconnected? *J Med Ethics, 8*(4), 203-205.

(Medical Murder)

Camp, J. (1982) *One hundred years of medical murder.* London: Bodley Head.

(Murder - Medical)

Kosa, F., et al. (1981) Sudden death after 'domestic electric treatment' (German). *Arch Kriminol, 167*(1-2), 43-51.

(Ricin Poisoning)

Knight, B. (1979) Ricin - a potent homicidal poison. *Br Med J, 6159,* 350-351.

(Alcohol/Drugs - Violent Death)

Haberman, P.W. et al. (1978) Alcohol, other drugs and violent death. *New York: Oxford Univ Press, 134,* 111.

(Anesthetic Drugs - Homicide)

Maltby, J.R., (1977) Criminal use of anesthetic drugs (letter). *Anaesthesia, 32*(2), 212-213.

(Phenprocoumon Murder)

Schneider, V. et al. (1975) Attempted murder with phenprocoumen (marcumar) (German) *Dtsch Med Wochenschr, 100*(37), 1838-1841.

(Anesthetic Drugs - Poisoning)

Maltby, J.R. (1975) Criminal poisoning with anesthetic drugs: Murder, manslaughter, or not guilty. *Forens Sci, 6*(1-2), 91-108.

(Digitalis Murder)

Meijier, F.L. (1972) A crime with the use of digitalis. *Ned Tijdschr Geneeskd, 116,* 2297-2300.

(Tattoos - Murder)

Baker, S.P. et al. (1971) Tattoos, alcohol, and violent death. *J Forensic Sci, 16,* 219-225.

(Homicide - Amphetamine Abuse)

Retterstol, N. (1971, Dec.) Homicide related to amphetamine abuse (Nor.). *N Tidsskr Nor Laegeforen, 91*, 2578-2579.

(Medical Murderer)

Furneaux, R. (1966) Medical murderer. *Abelard.*

(Murder - Medicine)

Davison, M.H. (1964) Medicine, murder and man. *Medicoleg J, 32,* 28-39.

(Insulin - Murder)

Schweisheimer, W. (1963) Murder and suicide by insulin (German). *Med Klin, 58,* 1046-1047.

(Alcohol Death)

Chetta, N.J., et al. (1960) The effects of alcohol in traumatic deaths. *J Louisiana Med Soc, 112,* 833-837.

(Chloroform Murder)

Fairchild, D.S. (1906) Alleged murder by inhalation of chloroform to sleeping unconscious victim. *Med Leg, 24,* 19.

Murder Modes - Shooting

(Bloodiest Year)

Hackett, G. (1990, July 16) The bloodiest year yet? *Newsweek, 116*(3), 24.

(Guns)

Death by gun, one year later. (1990, May 14) *Time, 135*(20), 30-31.

(Firearm Availability)

Vadakan, V. (1990) Homicide rates and firearm availability. *J Am Med Assoc, 264*(17), 2210.

(Firearms - Pediatric)

Beaver, B.L., et al. (1990) Characteristics of pediatric firearm fatalities. *J Pediatr Surg, 25*(1), 97-100.

(Vancouver Study)

Martinoff, M.J. (1989, June) "A tale of two cities": A Vancouverite perspective. *American Rifleman, 137*(6), 12-13.

(Firearms - Family)

Firearm associated homicide among family members, relatives, or friends. (1989) *Ohio MMWR, 38*(15), 253-356.

(Projectile Guns)

Lignitz, E., et al. (1988) Death caused by projectile guns - a retrospective analysis of 34 cases in Berlin and Hamburg. *Arch Kriminol, 182*(3-4), 83-93.

(Firearms Injuries)

Mercy, J.A., & Houk, V.N. (1988) Firearm injuries: A call for science. *New England Journal of Medicine, 319*(19), 1283-1285.

(Shooting Pattern)

Frazer, M. (1987) An unusual pattern of gunshot injury linking two homicides to the same assailant. *J Forensic Sci, 32*(1), 262-265.

(Firearms - Defect)

King, S. (1986, Jan.) A manufacturer's defect or murder? *Fire Engineer, 139*, 31-32.

(Firearm Accidents)

Morrow, P.L., & Hudson, P. (1986) Accidental firearm fatalities in North Carolina, 1976-80. *Am J Public Health, 76*(9), 1120-1123.

(Handguns and Children)

Schetky, D.H. (1985) Children and handguns. *Am J Dis Child, 139*(3), 229-231.

(Weapons' Role)

Sarvesvaran, R., et al. (1985) The role of the weapon in the homicide drama. *Med Law, 4*(4), 315-326.

(Shooting - Double Death)

Sellier, K. (1984) Unexpected effect of a shot from a 7.65 Browning cartridge: Double death. *Arch Kriminol, 174*(3-4), 87-88.

(Blankets as Silencers)

Missliwetz, J., & Wieser, I. (1984) Blankets as silencers. *Beitr. Gerichtl Med, 42,* 133-137. Summary in Engl. (Germ).

(Shooting Death - Retrial)

Yvorra, J. (1984, Aug.) The return of tragedy (retrial involving shooting death of a central Pennsylvania fire chief). *Fire Command, 51*, 20-21.

(Air Gun Homicide)

Green, G.S., & Good, R. (1982) Homicide by use of a pellet gun. *Am J Forensic Med Pathol, 3*(4), 361-365.

(Homicide - Shooting)

Green, G.S. (1982) Homicide by use of a pellet gun. *Am J. Forensic Med Pathol, 3*(4), 361-365.

(Murder Rate -Gun Link)

Michigan academic links guns to high murder rate. (1981) *Crime Control Digest, 15*(1), 6-7. Microforms and article copies available from UMI.

(Identification -Weapon)

De Pietro, O. (1980) Identification of the murderer's weapon (short barrel shotgun) from the skin imprint of the muzzle plate. (Italian with English summary). *Zacchia, 16*(1), 57-63.

(Gun Deaths)

Duncan, D. (1979, April) Gun Deaths - some real, dead cases. *Chr Cent, 96,* 469-471.

(Violence - Firearms)

Danto, B.L. (1979) Firearms and violence. *Int J Offend Therapy, 23,* (2), 135-146.

(Zebra Murders)

Mann, E.B. (1978, Aug.) Gun in the zebra murders. *Field and Stream, 83,* 20+.

(Hokum - Handguns)

Drooz, R.B. (1977) Handguns and hokum; A methodological problem. *J Am Med Assoc, 238*(1), 43-45.

(Traceability - Gunshots)

Kijewski, H. (1977) Traceableness of smoldering elements on gunshot entries following the effect of water and fire. *Arch Kriminol, 159*(1-2), 23-30.

(Rifle Wounds)

Dimaio, V.J.M., & Zumwalt, R.E. (1977) Rifle wounds from high velocity, center fire hunting ammunition. *Journal of Forensic Science, 22*(1), 132-140.

(Costs - Handgun Control)

Phillips, L.,et al. (1976) Handguns and homicide: Minimizing losses and the costs of control. *J Leg Studies, 5*(2), 463-478.

(Detroit - Firearms)

Fisher, J.C. (1976) Homicide in Detroit: The role of firearms. *Criminology, 14,* 387-400.

(Air Gun Death)

Barnes, F.C. et al. (1976) A death from an air gun. *J Forensic Sci, 21*(3), 653-658.

(Handgun Problem)

Browning C.H. (1976) Handguns and homicide. A public health problem. *JAMA, 236*(19), 2198-2200.

(Homicide - Guns)

Guns: Bicentennial note. (1976) *Crime and Delinquency, 22*(2), 247.

(Air Rifle)

Dimaio, V.J. (1975) Homicidal death by air rifle. *J Trauma , 15*(11), 1034-1037.

(Ballistics Study)

Mattoo, B.N. et al. (1975) *Principles of forensic ballistics, I and II.* Forensic Science Labs.

(Firearms - Denmark)

Hart-Hansen, J.P.H. (1974) Fatalities from firearms in Denmark. *Forens Sci,* (Lausanne)*4*(3), 239-245.

(Stun Gun)

Markert, K., et al. (1974) Lethal mouth shot with a device to stun animals. Also a contribution on the forensic relevance of bolt-shot injuries (German). *Kriminalist Forens Wissensch, 17,* 107-124.

(Handgun - Peculiarities)

Schmidt Orndorff, H., et al. (1974) Peculiarities of certain .22 caliber revolvers (Saturday night specials). *J Forensic Sci, 19*(1), 48-53.

(Firearms - Relationships)

Yearwood, J.H. (1974) Firearms and interpersonal relationships in homicide: Some cross-national comparison. In *Crime and delinquency: Dimensions of deviance.* Praeger.

(Bolt Projectile)

Gowda, B.C. (1972) A bolt as a projectile: Report of a case. *Forensic Sci 1,* 107-109.

(Gun Control - Effectiveness)

Seitz, S.T. (1972) Firearms, homicides and gun control effectiveness. *Law and Soc Rev, 6,* 595.

(Gunshots - Mouth)

Fatteh, A. (1972) Homicidal gunshot wound of mouth. *J Forensic Sci Society, 12*(2), 347-349,

(Shotgun - Dissimulation)

Chaumont, A.J. et al. (1971) Dissimulation of a corpse, dead from a shotgun blast, in a well. *Med Leg Domm Corpor (Paris), 4,* 161-162.

(Murder Reconstruction)

Fourcade, J. et al. (1971) Medicolegal reconstruction of a murder by shotgun. *Med Leg Domm Corpor (Paris), 4,* 182-183.

(Air Rifle)

L'Epee, P. et al. (1971) Fatal wounds caused by a compressed air rifle. *Med Leg Comm Corpor* (Paris), *4,* 176-177.

(Firearms - Criminology)

Jarosch, K. (1969) Criminology of the use of firearms. *Beitr Gerichtl Med, 26,* 126-129.

(Stun Gun - Shooting)

Obersteg, J.I., & Hegglin, O. (1958) (Cattle shooting apparatus from the medicolegal viewpoint). *C L of M L,* 163-167.

(Homicide - Firearms)

Brearley, H.C. (1931) Firearms and homicide. *Sociol and Social Res, 15,* 456-462.

(Firearms - Identification)

Wigmore, J.H. (1931) Identification of bullet and firearm. *Ill L Rev, 25,* 692-693.

(Explosives)

Finlason, W.F. (1916) Homicide caused by explosives. The Remerhaven explosion. *L J, 11,* 53

Murder Modes - Strangulation

(Strangulation)

Young, J., & Demaret, K. (1989, Jan. 16) The victim of a savage attack, a minister's wife is condemned to a long death in life. *People Weekly, 31*(2), pp. 50-57.

(Strangulation - Ligature)

Ueno, Y., et al. (1989) A homicidal strangulation by ligature, disguised as a suicidal hanging. *Jpn J Leg Med, 43*(1), 46-51.

(Strangulation - Sexual)

Biak, S.O. et al. (1988) Ligature strangulation of a woman during sadomasochistic sexual activity. *Am J Forensic Med Pathol, 9*(3), 249-251.

(Unusual Hanging)

Cooke, C.T. et al. (1988) Unusual hanging deaths. *Am J Forensic Med Pathol, 9*(4), 277-82.

(Hanging - Homicide)

Vieria, D.N., et al (1988) Homicidal hanging. *Am J Forensic Med Pathol, 9*(4), 287-289.

(Hanging - Dyadic Death)

Lew, E.O. (1988) Homicidal hanging in a dyadic death. *Am J Forensic Med Pathol, 9*(4), 283-286.

(Strangulation)

Sperry, K. (1988) An unusual deep lingual hemorrhage as a consequence of ligature strangulation. *Journal of Forensic Science, 33*(3), 806-811.

(Strangulation Injuries)

Maxeiner, H. (1987) Injuries to laryngeal articulations in strangulation and throttling (German with English abstract). *Arch Kriminal, 179*(1-2), 38-44.

(Strangulation Cases)

Srivasteva, A.K. et al. (1987) A study of fatai strangulation cases in Varanasi (India). *Am J Forensic Med Pathol, 8*(3), 806-811.

(Choke-Hold Deaths)

Koiwai, E.K. (1987) Deaths allegedly caused by the use of "choke holds" (shime-waza). *J Forensic Sci, 32*(2), 419-432.

(Strangulation Diagnosis)

Madea, B. et al. (1985) Strangulation - murder or suicide? *Arch Kriminol, 176*(1-2), 1,7.

(Strangulation Hemorrhage)

Maxeiner, H. (1985) Soft tissue hemorrhage within the larynx following strangulation. *Z*

Rechtsmed, 94(2), 127-35.

(Strangulation - Amputation)

Katsumata, Y. et al. (1984) A case of strangulation with post mortem amputation of the penis. *J Forensic Sci, 29*(3), 934-937.

(Asphyxiation - Masking Homicide)

Brinkmann, B., et al. (1984) Identification of mechanical asphyxiation in cases of attempted masking of the homicide. *Forensic Sci Int, 26(4), 235-245.*

(Asphyxiation - Hematoma)

Maxeiner, H. (1984) Internal hematoma of the larynx. *Arch Kriminol, 174*(1-2), 51-56.

(Strangulation Injuries)

Missliwetz, J. (1983) Injuries of the larynx and hyoid bone in strangulation and throttling. *Arch Kriminol, 172*(1-2), 29-31.

(Strangulation Determination)

Zabusov, I. et al. (1982) Determination of strangulation during life. *Sud Med Ekspert, 25*(3), 52-53.

(Strangulation - Rare Type)

Molin, I. (1982) Rare mechanism of strangulation asphyxia. *Sud Med Ekspert, 25*(3), 53.

(Strangulation Deaths)

Madro, R. (1981) Death by strangulation - suicide or homicide? *Arch Med Sadow Kryminol, 31*(2), 139-143. Polish with summaries in English and Russian.

(Strangulation - Homicidal)

Harm, T., & Rajs, J. (1981) Types of injuries and interrelated conditions of victims and assailants in attempted and homicidal strangulation. *Forensic Science International, 18*(2), 101-123.

(Strangulation - Hostages)

Berg, S., et al. (1979) Determination of the duration of fettering in case of murder of hostages. *Arch Kriminol, 164*(5-6), 153-161.

(Animal Violence)

Maetzsch, T., & Kleiber, M. (1979) Animal violence simulating a sex crime (German). *Arch Kriminol, 164*(3-4), 78-82.

(Gagging -Suffocation)

Jaklinski, A., & Tomaszewska, Z. (1978) Two cases of homicide in consequence of suffocation by gagging. *Kat Zak Med Sael, Am, Lubin Pol - Arch Med Sadow Kryminol, 28,* (2), 147-149.

(Strangulation - Vital Reactions)

Brinkmann, B. (1978) Vital reactions of the pulmonary circulation in fatal strangulation (German). *J Leg Med, 81*(2), 133-146.

(Strangulation Marks)

Sorgel, H.J. (1978) Radiographic demonstration of a strangulation mark on the neck (German). *Z Aerztl Fortbild, 72*(1), 39-40.

(Suffocation Murder)

Dotter, C.T. (1977) Murder by suffocation. *Dent Radiogr Photogr, 50*(2), 34.

(Strangulation - Fractures)

Hansch, C.F. (1977) Throat-skeleton fractures by strangulation. *J Leg Med, 79*(2), 143-147.

(Encephalopathy - Strangulation)

Dooling, E.C., et al. (1976) Delayed encephalopathy after strangling. *Arch Neurol, 33*(3), 196-199.

(Hanging - Sexual)

Wright, R.K., & Davis, J. (1976) Homicidal hanging masquerading as sexual asphyxia. *J Forens Sci, 21*(2), 387-389.

(Strangulation - Evidence)

Althoff, H. (1975) Studies on the evidential value of microtraces in cases of death by strangulation. *Arch Kriminol, 155*(1-2), 46-58, Figs 6, tables 2.

(Hanging - Unusual)

Graev, M. (1974) An unusual case of homicidal hanging (Italian). *1st Med Leg Assicur, U Macerata Minerva Med Leg, 94*(1), 17-20.

(Strangulation - Morbidity)

Green, M.A. (1973) Morbid anatomical findings in strangulation. *Forens Sci, 213*, 317-323.

(Suffocation - Plastic Bag)

Polson, C.J., & Gee, D.J. (1972) Plastic bag suffocation. *Z Rechtsmed, 70*(3), 183-190.

(Suffocation - Historical)

Christison, R. (1972) Medicolegal contributions of historical interest. Case IV, Murder by suffocation. *Forensic Sci, 1,* 119-131.

(Throttling - Delayed Asphyxia)

El-Guindy, M.K., et al. (1971) Delayed asphyxia: a cause of death in interrupted hanging and throttling. *J Egypt Med Assoc, 54,*410-416.

(Strangulation - Ocular Accidents)

Douche, C. (1971) Ocular accidents following a strangulation attempt. *Ann Ocul (Paris), 204,*

749-752.

(Strangulation Danger)

Geertinger, P., et al. (1971) Strangle hold on adult women in Copenhagen with particular attention to an estimation of the danger. *Ugeskr Laeger, 133,* 19-23.

(Hanging - Unusual)

Paldauf, E. (1970) Unusual case of death by hanging. *Beitr Gerichtl Med, 27,* 263-266.

(Pillowcase - Smothering)

Luke, J.L. (1969) Recovery of intact respiratory epithelium from a cloth pillowcase four days following its utilization as a smothering instrument. *J Forensic Sci, 14,* 398-401.

(Strangulation - Boston)

Frank, G. (1968) *Boston Strangler.* New York: Signet.

(Sash Bands - Noose)

Nishizawa, S., et al. (1968) Expert opinion on an example of a noose made of a sash band with an Inataba or Imanae knot at the back of the neck. *J Tokyo Med Coll, 26,* 145-201.

(Strangulation - Dissimulation)

Umani Ronchi, G. (1967) A case of attempted dissimulation of a homicidal strangulation by throwing the victim out of a window. *Zacchia, 3,* 522-531.

(Strangulation - Lesions)

Nathan, F. (1967) On the absence of cutaneous lesions of the neck in cases of strangulation. *Minerva Medicoleg, 87,* 299-302.

(Garroting - Hanging)

Nakajima, M., et al. (1967) Expert opinion on an example of garroting by means of a man's silk muffler tied tightly around the neck. *J Tokyo Med Coll, 25,* 663-669.

(Strangulation - Study)

Luke, J.L. (1967) Strangulation as a method of homicide: Study 1965-1966 in New York City. *Arch Path (Chicago), 83,* 64-70.

(Strangulation - Necklace)

Nakajima, M., et al. (1966) Expert testimony on an extra-ordinary type of homicidal strangulation with a thin 18-karat gold necklace. *J Tokyo Med Coll, 24,* 303-313.

(Strangulation - Perverted)

Carella, A., et al. (1965) Perverted sexual attack on an 18-month-old girl and murder of the victim by atypical strangulation. Examination of the victim. *Minerva Medicoleg, 85,* 79-81.

(Strangulation - Carotid Thrombosis)

Mackintosh, R.H. (1965) Unilateral manual strangulation (with special reference to carotid thrombosis). *Med Sci Law, 5,* 117-118.

(Hanging - Theory)

Olbrycht, J.S. (1964) Contributions on the theory of death by hanging. *Deutsch Z Ges Gerichtl Med, 54,* 407-423.

(Strangulation - Atypical)

Carella, A. (1962) Two cases of homicide by atypical strangling. *Zacchia, 25,* 88-98.

(Hanging - Case)

Radian, I., & Radovici, L. (1957) (A case of homicide by hanging). *Ann Med Leg, 37*(5), 232-236.

Murder Modes - Sharp Weapons

(Tool-marks - Homicide)

Takizawa, H.,et al. (1989) Tool-marks and peculiar blunt force injuries related to an adjustable wrench. *J Forensic Sci, 34*(1), 258-262.

(Violence - Homicidal)

Barlow, H.D., & Barlow, L.S. (1988) More on the role of weapons in homicidal violence. *Med Law, 7*(4), 347-358.

(Fatal Stabbings)

Murray, L.A., et al. (1987) Hilts and knives: A survey of ten years of fatal stabbings. *Med Sci Law, 27*(3), 182-184.

(Sharp Force Fatalities)

Ormstad, K., et al. (1986) Patterns in sharp force fatalities - a comprehensive forensic medical study. *J Forensic Sci, 31*(2), 529-542.

(Sharp Weapons - Survival)

Thoresen, S.O., & Rognum, T.O. (1986) Survival time and acting capability after fatal injury by sharp weapons. *Forensic Sci Int, 31*(3), 181-187.

(Sharp Force - Medical Study)

Ormstad, K., et al. (1986) Patterns in sharp force fatalities - a comprehensive forensic medical study. *J Forensic Sci, 31* (2), 529-542.

(Saw - Homicide)

Bratzke, H., et al. (1985) Unusual injuries caused by blows with a sash saw. *Arch Kriminol, 175*(5-6), 151-155.

(Weapons - Blunt Force)

Zugibe, F.T., & Costello, J.T. (1985) Identification of a murder weapon by a peculiar blunt force in injury pattern and histochemical analysis. *J Forensic Sci, 30*(1), 239-242.

(Blunt Trauma)

Eriksson, A. (1984) Homicidal blunt trauma with isolated laceration of the small bowel mesentery. *Z Rechtsmed, 93*(2), 143-146.

(Corpse Dismemberment)

Krauland, W., et al. (1980) Defensive dismemberment of a corpse. *Arch Kriminol, 166*(1-2), 1-17 (Germ).

(Needles - Intracranial)

Abbassioun, K., et al. (1979) Intracranial sewing needles: Review of 13 cases. *J Neurol Neurosurg Psychiatry, 42*(11), 1046-1049.

(Stab Wounds - Data)

Kapusz, N. (1976) Data on stab wounds of the human thorax (German). *Kriminal Forens Wiss, 26,* 97-99, Fig 1.

(Axe - Injury)

Chandu, L.R. (1974) Homicidal axe injury of the head. *Forensic Sci, 3*(3), 279-281.

(Dynamics of Stabbings)

Von Weber, et al. (1974) Elucidation of the dynamics of stabbing . *Med Fak Rheinl Westf Techn Hochschule, Aachen Kriminalistik, 28*(1), 24-26, fig 8, table 1.

(Head Wounds - Statistics)

Weber, W. (1974) Quantitative investigations concerning penetrating wounds of the human skull. *Z Rechtsmed, 74*(2), 111-116.

(Poisoned Arrows - Survey)

Maital, C.K., et al. (1973) A survey on the use of poisoned arrows in Kenya during the period 1964-1971. *East Afr Med J, 50,* 100-104.

(Stabbings - Body Tissues)

Weber, W., et al. (1973) Stabbing dynamics in human body tissues. *Z Rechtsmed 73,* 295-300.

(Throat Cutting)

Durante, F. (1969, Jan.-March) A case of throat-cutting associated with atypical attempted strangulation (Italian). *Zacchia, 5,* 137-147.

(Animal Slaughter Weapons)

Danek, E. (1965) Animal slaughter apparatus as a murder weapon (German). 20957. J. 19, '65, 7, S. 380 (IBZ 1966).

(Arrow Poison)

Mello, J.P. (1965) Offensive weapons of the world, Kenya: Arrow poison. *Med Sci Law, 5,* 44-45.

(Slaughtering Devices)

Simon, G. (1964, Oct.-Dec.) Lethal injuries caused by slaughtering devices (German). *Acta Med Leg Soc* (Liege), *17,* 73-77.

(Offensive Weapons - Global)

Mello, J.P. (1964) Offensive weapons of the world: Offensive weapons used in East Africa. *Med Sci Law, 4,* 129-130.

(Throat Cutting - Unusual)

Faraone, G. (1962) An unusual means of homicidal throat-cutting. *Zacchia, 25,* 224-232.

(Cutting Instruments and Acid)

Lopes, C., & Tavares, R. (1959) A case of homicide in which a hammer, cutting instrument, and sulfuric acid were used. *Gaz Med Port, 12,* 325-326.

(Scissors - Homicide)

Tarsitano, F. (1954) Murder by means of scissors. *Minerva Medicoleg, 74,* 85-90.

Poisoning

(Sodium Azide Poisoning)

Howard, J.D., et al. (1990) Death following accidental sodium azide ingestion. *Journal of Forensic Sciences, 35,* 135-196.

(Accidental Poisoning)

Ferslew, K.F., et al. (1990) A fatal interaction of methocarbamol and ethanol in an accidental poisoning. *Journal of Forensic Sciences, 35*(3), 477-482.

(Cornish Tea - Murder)

Whittington-Egan, R. (1990) A cornish tea (tale of murder in the 1930's). (Great Britain) *New Law Journal, 140,* 982(1).

(Clay Pits - Homicide)

Whittington-Egan, R. (1990) The man from the clay pits (murder case from 1921). (Great

Britain) *New Law Journal, 140,* 798(1).

(Poisoning)

Whittington-Egan, R. (1989, Nov. 24) A poisonous partnership (Murder by poisoning). *New Law Journal, 139,* 1614.

(Rat Poison - Homicide)

McCurdy, W. (1988) An attempted homicide using d-con trademark rat poison. *Anal Toxicol, 12*(1), 51-52.

(Phosphoglucomutase Poisoning)

Franco, M.A., et al. (1988) Identification of a phosphoglucomutase 1 (PGM 1) variant in a case of murder/suicide. *J Forensic Sci, 33*(4), 1050-1051.

(Product Tampering)

Dietz, P.E. (1988) Dangerous information: Product tampering and poisoning advice in revenge and murder-manuals. *J Forensic Sci, 33*(5), 1206-1217.

(Lead Poisoning)

Flood, A.U., et al. (1988) The distribution of lead in human hemopoietic tissue and spongy bone after lead poisoning and Ca-EDTA chelation therapy: Observations made by atomic absorption spectroscopy, laser microbeam mass analysis, and electron microbeam x-ray analysis. *Archives of Toxicology, 62*(4), 295-300.

(D-Con Poisoning)

McCurdy, W. (1988) An attempted homicide using d-con trademark rat poison. *J Anal Toxicol, 12*(1), 51-52.

(Arsenic Poisoning)

Madge, A.G. (1987) Poisoning by arsenic. *J R Soc Health, 107*(2), 72-73.

(Poisoning - Homicidal)

Adelson, L. (1987) Homicidal poisoning. A dying modality of lethal violence? *Am J Forensic Med Pathol, 8*(3), 245-251.

(Poisoning - Criminal)

Dunckelmeyer, E. (1986) Rare forms of criminal administration of poisons, I. *Arch Kriminol, 178*(1-2), 35-43.

(Poisoning by Place)

Fechner, G., et al. (1985) Homicidal poisoning - a study from the catchment area of the Institute for Forensic Medicine of the University of Munster. *Beitr Gerichtl Med, 43,* 145-148.

(Temazepam Homicide)

Verweij, A.M., et al. (1985) An unusual benzophenone of 3-hydroxydiazepam (temazepam).

Arch Kriminol, 176(1-2), 17-20.

(Strychnine Poisoning)

Kloppel, A., et al. (1985) Double murder by strychnine poisoning. *Arch Kriminol, 176*(5-6), 153-158.

(Naptha Injection)

Case, M.E., et al. (1985) Homicide by intravenous injection of naptha. *J Forensic Sci, 30*(1), 208-212.

(Tubocurarine Poisoning)

Siegel, H., et al. (1985) The medical and scientific evidence in alleged tubocurarine poisonings. A review of the so-called Dr. X case. *Forensic Sci Int, 29*(1-2), 29-76.

(Arsenic Murder)

Mackell, M.A., et al. (1985) An unsuspected arsenic poisoning murder disclosed by forensic autopsy. *Am J Forensic Med Pathol, 6*(4), 358-361.

(Homicide by Lye)

Jonsson, J., et al. (1984) Homicidal intoxication by lye and parachlorcresol containing disinfectants. *Am J Forensic Med Pathol, 5*(1), 57-63.

(Arsenic Murder)

Wold, D., & Heyman, A. (1984) Arsenic: Homicidal intoxication. *South Med J, 77*(7), 848-851.

(Thallium Poisoning)

Metter, D., et al. (1984) Hair findings in a series of 6 thallium poisoning. *Beitr Gericht Med, 42,* 379-385.

(Parachlorcresol Poisoning)

Jonsson, J., & Voigt, G.C. (1984) Homicidal intoxications by lye and parachlorcresol containing disinfectants. *Am J. Forensic Med Pathol, 5*(1), 57-63.

(Cyanide Murder)

Weiler, G., et al. (1983) An unusual cyanide murder. *Arch Kriminol, 172*(1-2), 16-20.

(Poisoning - Alcohol)

Oseanmi, W.O. (1983) The fatal blood alcohol level in acute alcohol poisoning. *Med Sci Law, 23*(1), 25-30.

(Homicide - Arsenic)

Bednarczyk, L.R., et al. (1982) Case report: an arsenic murder. *J Anal Toxicol, 6*(5), 260-261.

(Cyanide - Vaginal Administration)

Drasch, G., et al (1982) A case of vaginal cyanide administration. *Arch Kriminol, 170,* (1-2),

21-28.

(Homicide - Carbon Monoxide)

Akaishi, S. (1982) Homicidal and camouflaged carbon monoxide poisoning in Japan. *Z Rechtsmed, 88*(4), 297-304.

(Uxoricide - Poisoning)

Di Girolamo, F., et al. (1981) Uxoricide in Italy (Italian). *Rass Penititenziaria Crim, 3*(3-4), 481-497.

(Dimethylnitrosomine Poisoning)

Cooper, S.W., & Kimbrough, R.D. (1980) Acute Dimethylnitrosomine poisoning outbreak. *J Forensic Sci, 25*(4), 874-882.

(Gevisol Murder)

Voigt, G.E. (1980) Murder and attempted murder with Gevisol or Ivisol. *Beitr GerMed, 38,* 227-229.

(Alcohol and Drug Abuse)

Gary, L.E. (1980) Role of alcohol and drug abuse in homicide. *Pub Health Rep, 95*(6), 553-554.

(Self-Poisoning - Hexapropymate)

Robbins, G., & Brown, A.K. (1978) Hexapropymate self-poisoning. *British Medical Journal, 1*(6127), 1593.

(Heroin Homicide)

Homicide: Murder; Heroin: Malice. (1978) *Law Enforcement Legal Review, 76,* 9.

(Carbon Monoxide Homicide)

Tomaszewska, Z., & Trojanowska, M (1977) Homicide per CO intoxication (Summary in Russian and English). *Arch Med Sadow Kryminol, 27*(4), 321-323.

(Poisoning - Europe)

Brzezinski, Z.J. (1977) Poisoning in the European region. *WHO Reg Off Europe, Copenhagen, Den Acta Pharmacol Toxicol Suppl, 41*(2), 470-484.

(Amines Intoxication)

Holmgren, P., & Lindquist, O. (1975) Lethal intoxications with centrally stimulating amines in Sweden 1966-1973. *Z Rechtsmed, 75*(4), 265-273.

(Thallium Murder)

Irvine, A., & Johnson, H. (1974) R vs. Young - murder by thallium. *Med Leg J (Cambr), 42*(3), 76-90.

(Rodenticide Poisoning)

Fischbach, R. (1973) Homicide through poison using a rodenticide containing thallium. *Arch*

Kriminol, 151(3-4), 91-95.

(Beer/Nicotine Poisoning)

Kosa, F., et al. (1972) Murder and attempted murder with beer-added nicotine solution. *Arch Kriminol, 150,* 84-92.

(Beer/Nicotine Murder)

Kosa, F., et al. (1972) Homicide with nicotine solution mixed into beer. *Orv Hetil, 113,* 1925-1927.

(Poisoning - Sodium Chlorate)

Jansen, H., et al. (1972) Homicidal chronic sodium chlorate poisoning. *Forensic Sci, 1,* 103-105.

(LSD - Homicide)

Reich, P., et al. (1972) Homicide during a psychosis induced by LSD. *JAMA, 219,* 869-871.

(Amphetamine Abuse)

Ellinwood, E.H., Jr. (1971) Assault and homicide associated with amphetamine abuse. *Am J Psychiatry, 127,* 1170-1175.

(Cyanide Detection)

Tewari, S.N., et al. (1971) A new detection method for traces of cyanides from their metabolites in decomposed human body tissues in forensic studies (German). *Arch Kriminol, 147,* 22-31.

(Barbiturate Identification)

Bonnichsen, R., et al. (1970) Identification of small amounts of barbiturate sedatives in biological samples by a combination of gas chromatography and mass spectrometry (German) *Zacchia, 6,* 371-385.

(Calor Gas - Homicide)

Baldock, D.V. (1970) Attempted murder by calor gas. *J Forensic Sci Soc, 10,* 175-178.

(Carbon Monoxide Murder)

Borodin, S.V. (1969) (Murder by poisoning with carbon monoxide of the exhaust). *32917, 39*(7), 127-129.

(Acetic Acid Homicide)

Laufer, M. (1969) Homicide using acetic acid. *Zbl Allg Path, 112,* 522-526.

(Poisoning - Acute)

Roche, L., et al. (1969) Death in acute poisoning. *Bull Med Leg, 12*(5), 222-232.

(Arsenic - Per Os)

Montagna, M., et al. (1968) Acute arsenic poisoning per os: A study of the cases reported in literature with special attention to chronological problems. *Zacchia, 4,* 516-542.

(Strychnine Homicide)

Jaulmes, P., et al. (1968) A case of criminal strychnine poisoning. *Med Leg Comm Corpor (Paris), 1,* 219-220.

(Mixer Woman)

Dangl, J. (1968) (The poison mixer woman). 20957. J. 22, '68, 7, S. 395-397 (IBZ 1970).

(Murderer's Mode)

Holden, I.G. (1968) Homicidal poisoning. *Med Sci Law, 6,* 22-26.

(Poisoning - Carbon Monoxide)

Canale, M. (1968) "Mord durch vegiftung mit dem kohlenoxyd der auspuffgase". 20957. J. 22, '68, 1, S. 567 (IBZ 1970).

(Homicide - Poisoning)

Wagner, H.J. (1967) Der giftmord (Murder by poison). 11086. J. 11, '67, H. 6, S. 242-243 (IBZ 1968).

(Veronal Murder)

Herold, K. (1967) Spouse's murder with veronal. *Deutsch Gesundh, 22,* 810-811.

(Strychnine Murder)

Bogan, J., et al. (1966) Homicidal poisoning by strychnine. *J Forensic Sci Soc, 6,* 166-169.

(Chlorinated Hydrocarbons)

Bonnichsen, R., et al. (1966) Poisoning by volatile compounds. II Chlorinated aliphatic hydrocarbons. *J Forensic Sci, 11,* 414-427.

(Warfarin Murder)

Pribilla, O. (1966) Murder caused by warfarin. *Arch Toxik, 21,* 235-249.

(Organophosphorus Murder)

Svraka, L., et al. (1966) Four cases of murder with organophosphorus compound. *Arch Hig Rada, 17,* 447-453.

(Arsenic Homicide)

Kapczynska, M., et al. (1966) Four cases of homicidal arsenic poisoning. *Wiad Lek, 19,* 45-47.

(Poisoning - Uxoricide)

Perdue, W.C. (1966, Dec.) A preliminary investigation into uxoricide. *Dis Nerv Syst, 27,* 808-811.

(Poisoning - E-605)

Petersohn, F. (1965) Case reports on unusual E 605 poisonings. *Arch Toxik, 21,* 168-174.

(Lysergic Acid Homicide)

Knudsen, K. (1964) Homicide after treatment with lysergic acid diethylamide. *Acta Psychiat*

Scand, 40(180), 389+.

(Nicotine Homicide)

Fazekas, I., et al. (1964) Three cases of homicide (murder) with nicotine solution. *Orv Hetil, 105,* 1694-1697.

(Parathion Murder)

Calabrese, A., et al. (1964) Criminal poisoning by means of administration of parathion mixed with a medicinal substance. *Zacchia, 27,* 471-477.

(Parathion Murder)

Van Hecke, W. (1964) A case of murder by parathion (E 605) which nearly escaped detection. *Med Sci Law, 4,* 197-199.

(Nicotine Homicide)

Fazekas, I.G. (1964) Murders with nicotine. *Deutsch Z Ges Gerichtl Med, 55,* 40-46.

(Homicide - Phosphorous)

Zeidenrust, J., et al. (1964) Fatal phosphorous poisoning elucidated by exhumation three and half years after burial. *Med Sci Law, 4,* 120-121.

(Trichloroethylene Poisoning)

LeBreton, R., et al. (1963) A case of criminal poisoning by trichloroethylene. *Ann Med Leg (Paris), 43,* 281-283.

(Atropine Murder)

Berg, S., & Fischer, K. (1962) Quantitative data in group poisoning (attempted murder with atropine). *Deutsch Z Ges Gerichtl Med, 53,* 44-50.

(Zinc Phosphide Poisoning)

Vasileva, R. (1962) Medicolegal studies of zinc phosphide poisonings. *Nauch Tr Vissh Med Inst Sofiia, 41*(4), 67-77.

(Parathion Poisoning)

Hristic-Sojic, L., & Stupar, P. (1961) A case of homicidal parathion poisoning (German). *Arch Hig Rada, 12,* 195-198.

(Homicide - Poisoning)

Cleveland, F.P. (1958) Homicidal poisoning. *Temp L Q, 31,* 323.

(Poisoning - Metaldehyde)

Ludin, M. (1958) Murder by metaldehyde poisoning (German). *Schweis Med Wschr, 88*(16), 381-384.

(Poisoning - Art of)

Hilton, R. (1956) Art of poisoning. *Contemp R, 189,* 119-122.

(Thallium Poisoning)

Matthys, R. (1955) Criminal poisoning by thallium; 9 cases. *Ann Med Leg, 35,* 237-275.

(Mercurous Chloride Poisoning)

Thomas, F. (1953) Criminal poisoning by means of administration of corrosive mercurous chloride enema; case. *Ann Med Leg, 33,* 123-129.

(Uxoricide - Psychodynamics)

Rosenzweig, S., et al. (1942) The psychodynamics of an uxoricide. *American Journal of Orthopsychiatry, 12,* 283-294.

(Arsenic Murders)

Byloff, F. (1930) Die Arsenmorde in Steiermark (The arsenic murders in Styria). *Montassch f Krimpsychol u Strafrechtsref, 21,* 1-4.

(Murderers - Doctors)

Sanders, H.T. (1930) (The psychology of poison-murders committed by doctors). *Arch f Krimin, 86,* 33-55.

(Arsenic Murder)

Arsenic for homicides. (1929) *Sol J, 73,* 668.

(Poisoning in Pantry)

Roughead, W. (1927) Poison in the pantry: Or Dr. Pritchard revisited. *Jurid Rev, 39,* 115.

(Arsenic Murder)

Freeman, W.M. (1920) Arsenic; A case report. *Sol J, 73,* 622.

(Prussic Acid Poisoning)

Roughhead, W. (1915) The Eaglesham case, poisoning with prussic acid. *Jurid Rev, 27,* 76.

Chapter 6
Causes of Murder
General

(Murder - Clothing)

Newman, J. (1990) Dressed to kill. *Seventeen, 49*, 10, pp. 32.

(Promoting Murder)

Stud, B. (1990) My life with the thrill kill cult: tabooed love boys. *Melody Maker, 66*(66), pp. 46-47.

(Homicide - Stress)

Busuttil, A., & McCall-Smith, A. (1990) Fright, stress, and homicide. *Journal of Criminal Law, 54*(2), 257-270.

(Media - As Cause)

Lester, D. (1989) Media violence and suicide and homicide rates. *Percpt Mot Skills, 69*(3 pt. 1), 894.

(Causes - General)

Parker, R.N. (1989) Poverty, subculture of violence, and type of homicide. *Social Forces, 67*(4), 983-1007.

(Television - Risk)

Centerwall, B.S. (1989) Exposure to television as a risk factor for violence. *Am J Epidemiol, 129*(4), 643-652.

(Psychiatric Evidence)

Gudjonsson, G.H., et al. (1989) Psychiatric evidence: A study of psychological issues. *Acta Psychiatr Scand, 80*(2), 165-169.

(Homicide - Causes)

Baron, L & Straus, M. (1988) Cultural and economic sources of homicide in the United States. *The Sociological Quarterly, 29*(3), 371-390.

(Homicide - Music)

Wass, H. et al. (1988-1989) Adolescents' interest in and views of destructive themes in rock music. *Omega, 19*(3), 177-186.

(Murder)

Wilson, P.R. (1988) 'Stranger' child-murder: Issues relating to causes and controls. *Forensic Sci Int, 36*(3-4), 267-277.

(Murder - Etiologies)

Mitlohner, M. (1987) Etiology of homicide and possibilities of its prevention. *Cesk Zdrav, 35*(3), 133-139.

(Homicide Antecedents)

Straus, M.A. (1986) Domestic violence and homicide antecedents. *Bull NY Acad Med, 62*(5), 446-465.

(Homicide - Cause)

Martin, R.L. et al. (1985) Mortality in a follow-up of 500 psychiatric outpatients. II Cause-specific mortality. *Arch Gen Psychiatry, 42*(1), 58-66.

(Crime-Victims)

Kahn, M. (1984) Victims of crime. *ADAMHA N,* (10), 8.

(Causes - Research)

Messner, S.F. (1982) Societal development, social equality, and homicide: A cross-national test of the Durkheimian method. *Social Forces, 61*(1), 225-240.

(Homicidal - Causes)

Petti, T.A. & Davidman, L. (1981) Homicidal school-age children: Cognitive style and demographic features. *Child Psychiatry and Hum Dev, 12*(2), 82-89.

(Homicide - Causes)

Homicide search - plain view. (1981, Nov.) *Narcotics Law Bulletin*, 7. Article copies available from UMI.

(Causes - Criminal Violence)

Felson, R.B., et al. (1981) An attributional approach to accounts and sanctions for criminal violence. *Social Psychology Quarterly, 44*(2), 137-142.

(Causes - Guns)

Gun-toting kids a problem. (1981) *Juvenile Justice Digest, 9*(21), 10. Article copies available from UMI.

(Remarks)

Klerman, G.L. (1980) Concluding remarks. *Pub Health Rep, 95*(6), 581.

(Observations)

Thomas, C.W. (1980) Final observations and summary. *Pub Health Rep, 95*(6), 560-561.

(Causes - Stress)

Humphrey, J.A. (1980) Stressful life events and criminal homicide offender-victim relationships. *Victimology, 5*(2-4), 115-120.

(Causes - General)

Akbar, N. (1980) Causal factors. *Public Health Reports, 95*(6), 554.

(Motives)

Bakoczi, A. (1980) Motives for homicide (Hungarian). *Az emberoles inditekai, Kriminol Kriminal Tanulmanyok, 17*, 81-130.

(Murder and Mass Media)

Phillips, D.P. (1980) Airplane accidents, murder, and the mass media: Toward a theory of imitation and suggestion. *Social Forces, 58*(4), 1001-1024.

(Offender Therapy)

Russell, D.H. (1979) Ingredients of juvenile murder. *International Journal of Offender Therapy and Comparative Criminology, 23*(1), 65-72. Article copies available from UMI.

(Causes - Grief)

Washbrook, R.A.H. (1979) Bereavement leading to murder. *International Journal of Offender Therapy and Comparative Criminology, 23*(1), 57-64. Article copies available from UMI.

(Hospital Negligence)

Gregory, D.R. (1979) Hospital negligence results in murder. *Legal aspects in Medical Practice, 7*(2), 58.

(Violent Death)

Srch, M., et al. (1979) Immune complexes in sudden and violent deaths (Czech with English abstract). *Cesk Patol, 24*(2), 20-22.

(Causes - Study)

Chimbos, P.D. (1978) *Marital violence: A study of interspouse homicide.* R & E Research Associates.

(Humane Treatment)

The price of humane treatment (editorial). (1977) *British Medical Journal, 2*(6099), 1374.

(Homicide - Intentional)

Rutkowski, R., et al. (1977) Intellectual efficiency and intentional homicide (Polish with English abstract). *Psychiatr Pol, 11*(5), 533-538.

(Homicidal Aggression)

Planansky, K., et al. (1977) Homicidal aggression in schizophrenic men. *Acta Psychiatr Scand, 55*(1), 65-73.

(Causes - Immorality)

Man kills “immoral persons”. (1976) *Crime Control Digest, 10*, 20.

(Causes - Early Release)

Early-out ‘good time’ inmate charged with killing three within one week of release. (1976) *Corrections Digest, 7*(22), 10.

(Porphyria)

Trafford, P.A. (1976) Homicide in acute porphyria. *Forensic Science, 7*(2), 113-120.

(Causes - Passion)

Lester, D., & Lester, G. (1975) *Crime of Passion: Murder and the murderer.* New York: Nelson-Hall.

(Homicide - Altruistic)

Scherrer, P., et al. (1975) 'Altruistic homicide or accompanied suicide: apppropos of a case (French). *Annals Med Psychol, 2*(4), 734-744.

(Homicide Book)

Bailey, F.L., & Rothblatt, H.B. (1973) *Crimes of violence: Homicide and assault.* Lawyers Co-op.

(Homicide - Laos)

Westermeyer, J. (1973, Autumn) Grenade-amok in Laos: A Psychosocial perspective. *International Journal of Social Psychiatry, 19*, 251-260.

(Homicide - Causes)

Lester, D. (1973) Status integration and homicide. *Psychological Reports, 32*(3, part 1), 774.

(Homicide - Causes)

Bates, G.M., Jr. (1972) Homicidal acts of war. *American Journal of Psychiatry, 129*, 766.

(Homicide - Causes)

Ambler, E. (1971) *Ability to kill.* New American Library.

(Homicide - Causes)

Two problems in causation (Regina v. Smith, 1959, 2 W L R 623). (1969, Sept.) *Modern Law Review, 22*, 514.

(Homicide - Causes)

Bandini, T., et al. (1968) (100 legal-medical opinions of the thema-intended murder). 20957. J. 22, '68, 10, S. 567 (IBZ 1970)

(Homicide - Causes)

Lustgarten, E. (1968) *Business of murder.* New York: Scribners.

(Theories of Homicide)

Al-Saadi, H. (1968) *Theorie generale de l'homicide; etude theorique et ptatique comparee entre les droits Irakian, Francias, and Italien* text in Arabic). Bagdad: al-Ma'arif Press.

(Homicide Book)

MacDonald, J.M. (1968) *Homicidal threats.* C.C. Thomas.

(Causes - Violent Culture)

Wolfgang, M.E., & Ferracuti, F. (1967) *Subculture of violence: Towards an integrated theory in criminology.* B & N.

(Motives)

Goudsmit, W. (1966) Moord en ambivalentie. 25017. J. 8, '66, N. 3, S. 142-148 (IBZ 1967).

(Homicide - Invitation)

Gold, L.H. (1965, Oct.) Invitation to homicide. *Journal of Forensic Science, 10*, 415.

(Murderers - Analyses)

Leudl, F. (1965) Analyse eines mordes (analysis of a murder). 20957. J. 19, '65, 7, S. 372-374 (IBZ 1966).

(Homicide - Motives)

Kosyra, H. (1965) (The problem of homicide motives). 3647. Bd. 135, '65, H. 3-4, S. 70-72.

(Homicide - Causes)

Confessions and causation (Regina v. Smith, 1959, 2 Q B 35). (1959, Oct.) *Law Quarterly Review, 75*, 464.

(Homicide - Motives)

Camps, F.E. (1959) Motives for murder. *Texas Rep Biol Med, 17*, 287-295.

(Etiology)

Duncan, G.M., et al. (1958) Etiological factors in first-degree murder. *JAMA, 168*(13), 1755-1758,

(Homicide - Causes)

Williams, G. (1957) Causation in homicide. *Criminal Law Review 1957*, 429, 510.

(Homicide - Causes)

Camps, F.E. (1957) Causation in homicide - a medical view. *Criminal Law Review 1957*, 576.

(Homicide - Causes)

Hoedemarker, E.D. (1948) "Irresistible impulse" as a defense in criminal law; a criticism based on modern psychiatric concept. *Washington Law Review, 23*, 1-7.

(Homicide - Causes)

Provocation in murder cases (Rex v. Prince, 1941) 3 All E R 37. *Law Quarterly Review, 57, 441-442.*

(Homicide - Motives)

Gummersbach, H. (1935) (The motives for murder and "motivated murder"). *Arch Krim, 96*, 58-76, 143-155.

(Homicide - Causes)

Homicide, proximate cause (State v. Leopold, Conn. 147, Atl. 118). (1930, June) *Illinois Law Review, 25*, 208-210.

(Murder - Sports)

Murder for sport. (1924, Sept. 13) *Saturday Review, 138*, pp. 256-257.

Causes - Psychiatric

(Homicide - Stress)

Busuttil, A. & McCall Smith, A. (1990) Fright, Stress and homicide. *Journal of Criminal Law, 54*(2), 257-270.

(Murder-Suicide and Homicide)

Rosenbaum, M. (1990) The role of depression in couples involved in Murder-Suicide and Homicide. *American Journal of Psychiatry, 147*(8), 1036-1039.

(Killers - Psychopathic)

Petzal, D.E. (1990) Endangered tradition: Stockton, revisited. *Field & Stream (South Edition), 95*(1), 14, 18.

(Murder - Menace)

Meloy, R.J. (1989, Spring) Mass murder: America's growing menace (book reviews). *Journal of Psychiatry & Law, 17,* 85-108.

(Fantasy Role)

Prentky, R.A. et al. (1989) The presumptive role of fantasy in serial sexual homicide. *Am J Psychiatry, 146*(7), 887-891.

(Mexican - Religious Killing)

Voodoo in Mexico. (1989, April 24) *U.S. News & World Report, 106*(16), pp. 16.

(White House Cases)

Shore, D. et al. (1989) Murder and assault arrests of White Houses cases: clinical and demographic correlates of violence subsequent to civil commitment. *Am J Psychiatry, 146*(5), 645-651.

(Transient Psychosis)

Dorban, P.T. (1989) Medicine and the law: Steroid-induced psychosis. *Lancet, 8664,* 694.

(Sexual Homicide)

Prentky, R.A. et al. (1989) The presumptive role of fantasy in serial sexual homicide. *Am J Psychiatry, 146*(7), 887-891.

(Necrophilia)

Rosman, J.P. & Resnick, P.J. (1989) Sexual attraction to corpses: A psychiatric review of Necrophilia. *Bull Am Acad Psychiatry Law, 17*(2), 153-163.

(Psychiatric - Evidence)

Gudjonsson, G.H. et al. (1989) Psychiatric evidence: A study of psychological issues. *Acta Psychiatr Scand, 80*(2), 165-169.

(Homicidal - Mental)

Meloy, J.R. (1988) Violent and homicidal behavior in primitive mental states. *J Am Acad*

Psychoanal, 16(3), 381-394.

(Murder - Psychiatric)

Daradkeh, T.K. (1988) The psychiatric aspects of murder and attempted murder in Jordan, 1976-1985. *Med Sci Law, 28*(1), 57-61.

(Depression)

Acland, P.R. (1988) Hypercalcemia and depression. *Med Sci Law, 28*(2), 139-141.

(Murderers)

Lewis, D.O. et al. (1988) Intrinsic and environmental characteristics of juvenile murderers. *J Am Acad Child Adolesc Psychiatry, 27,* 582-587.

(Homicide - Insanity)

Colaizzi, J. (1988) *Homicidal insanity, 1800-1985.* Tuscaloosa, AL: University of Alabama Press.

(Behavior Development)

Rydelius, P.A. (1988) The development of antisocial behavior and sudden violent death. *Acta Psychiatr Scand, 77*(4), 398-403.

(Psychiatric)

McEwan, S.A. (1988) Neuropsychiatric liability associated with a patient's prospective commission of a dangerous tort. *J Neurol Orthop Med Surg, 9*(1), 85-88.

(Criminologic Psychiatry)

Benezech, M. (1987) Object loss in criminologic psychiatry or passion according to Werther. *Ann Med Psychol (Paris), 145*(4), 329-339.

(Cause - Psychiatric)

Applebaum, P.S. (1987) In the wake of Ake: The ethics of expert testimony in an advocate's world. *Bull Am Acad Psychiatry Law, 15*(1), 15-25.

(Homicide: Affective Disorder)

Bourget, D. et al. (1987) Affective disorder and homicide: a case of familial filicide theoretical and clinical considerations. *Can J Psychiatry, 32*(3), 222-225.

(Homicidal - Schizophrenics)

Tanay, E. (1987) Homicidal behavior in schizophrenics. *J Forensic Sci, 32*(5), 1382-1388.

(Sleep-Walking - Murder)

On serious violence during sleep-walking (letter). (1986) *Br J Psychiatry, 149,* 120-122.

(Homicide - Depression)

Rosenbaum, M. & Bennett, B. (1986) Homicide and depression. *Am J Psychiatry, 143*(3), 367-370.

(Murderer - 'Crime of Passion')

Beyaert, F.H. (1985) Psychiatric expertise of the partner murderer: when can one infer a 'crime of passion'? *Rev Med Suisse Romande, 105*(1), 17-22.

(Homicide - Psychiatric Institution)

Modestin, J. et al. (1985) Homicide in a psychiatric institution. *Br J Psychiatry, 146,* 321-324.

(Homicidal)

Hillard, J.R. et al. (1985) Accidental and homicidal death in a psychiatric emergency room population. *Hosp Community Psychiatry, 36*(6), 640-643.

(Mass Media)

Levy, R. (1985) Terrorism and the mass media. *Mil Intel, 11*(4), 34-38.

(Homicidal - Behavior)

Cornelius, J.R. et al. (1984) Paranoia, homicidal behavior, and seizures associated with phenylpropanolamine. *Am J Psychiatry, 141*(1).

(Schizophrenic Homicide)

Sun, J.W. (1984) Schizophrenic homicide - report of 6 cases. *Chung Hua Shen Ching Ching Shen Ko Tsa Chih, 17*(3), 140-142.

(Psychotic)

Taylor, P.J. & Gunn, J. (1984) Risk of violence among psychotic men, violence and psychosis, I.. *Br Med J, 288*(6435), 1945-1949.

(Aggression)

Valzelli, L. (1984) Reflections on experimental and human pathology of aggression. *Prog Neuropsychpharmacol Biol Psychiatr., 8*(3), 311-325.

(Homicidal - Behavior)

Cornelius, J.R. et al. (1984) Paranoia, homicidal behavior and seizures associated with phenylpropanolamine. *Am J Psychiatry, 141*(1), 120-121.

(Murder - Psychiatry)

Smith, C.E. (1984) The art of forensic psychiatry: A montage of murder cases. *J Forensic Sci, 29*(1), 209-218.

(Schizophrenic - Homicide)

Ishigaki, K. (1984) Criminality in schizophrenics (Japanese, summary in English). *Iryo, 38*(12), 1160-1163.

(Homicide - Responsibility)

Sobczyk, P. et al. (1983) Irresponsibility and limited responsibility in homicide. *Psychiatr Pol, 17*(3), 215-220.

(Psychopathic Murderer)

Herbert, W. (1982) The case of the missing hormones (serotonin deficit in brains of psychopathic murderers research by Markku Linnoila and Matti Virkunen). *Science News, 122*, 282.

(Causes - Psychiatric)

Gudjonsson, G.H. (1982) Some criminological and psychiatric aspects of homicide in Iceland. *Medical Science and the Law, 22*(2), 91-98.

(Causes - Psychiatric)

Cox, M. (1982) "I took a life because I needed one': Psychotherapeutic possibilities with the schizophrenic offender-patient. *Psychother & Psychosom, 37*(2), 96-105.

(Cause - Psychotic State)

Mitterauer, B., et al. (1982) The role of genetic disposition in the formation of reactive-psychotic states leading to extreme violence: A study of a case of arson with ensuing double murder and extended suicide. *Journal of Legal Medicine, 89*(1), 25-42.

(Homicide - Mental Retardation)

Coid, J. (1982) Suggestibility, low intelligence, and a confession to a crime. *British Journal of Psychiatry, 139*, 436-438.

(Causes - Schizophrenia)

Arieti, S., et al. (1981) Multiple murders of a schizophrenia patient: A psychodynamic interpretation. *Journal of the American Academy of Psychoanalysis, 9*(4), 501-524.

(Causes - Psychiatric Illness)

Obejide, A.O. (1981) Some clinical aspects of criminology: A study of criminal psychiatric patients at the Lantoro long-stay psychiatric institution, Abeokuta, Nigeria. *African Journal of Psychiatry, 7*(1-2), 11-16.

(Psychiatric Studies)

Petursson, H., et al. (1981) Psychiatric aspects of homicide. *Acta Psychiatrica Scandinavia, 64*(5), 363-372.

(Psychiatric)

Fottrell, E. (1981) Violent behavior by psychiatric patients. *Br J Hosp Med, 25*(1), pp 28-38.

(Mental - Homicide)

Petursson, H. & Gudjonsson, G.H. (1981) Psychiatric aspects of homicide. *Acta Psychiatr Scand, 64*(5), 363-372.

(Psychiatrists' Reports)

Bentil, J.K. (1981) Homicide and evidence and reports of psychiatrists. *Sol J, 125*, 89-91.

(Homicide - Psychiatry)

Pisztora, F. (1980) Forensic and psychiatric expertise in homicides committed in atypical mental states caused by affective disorders (Hungarian). *Morphol Igazsagugyi Orv Sz, 20*(4), 304-308.

(Insanity Defense)

Easson, W.M. (1980) Myxedema psychosis: Insanity defense in homicide. *Journal of Clinical*

Psychiatry, 41(9), 316-318.

(Murder)

Torrey, E.F. (1980, Oct.) Sweeney-Lowenstein madness. *Psychology Today, 14*, p. 14+.

(Murder - Cannibalism)

Benezech, M. et al. (1980) Cannibalism and vampirism in a schizophrenic patient who committed numerous murders. *Bordeaux Med. 13*(23), pp 1261-1265.

(Mental Disease)

Vandusen, K. (1980) Challenge of chronic physical and mental disease to environmental sanitarians. *Pub Health Rep, 95*(3), 223-231.

(Genocide - Psychology)

Charny, I.W. (1980) A contribution to the psychology of genocide: Sacrificing others to the death we fear ourselves. *Israel Yearbook on Human Rights, 1980*, 90-108.

(Homicide - Psychiatric Assessment)

Bluglass, R. (1979) The psychiatric assessment of homicide. *British Journal of Hospital Medicine, 22*(4), 366-377.

(Homicide - Depression)

Hirose, S. (1979) Depression and homicide. A psychiatric and forensic study of four cases. *Acta Pschiatr Scand, 59*(2), 211-217.

(Multiple - Murders)

Morrison, H.L. (1979) Psychiatric observations and interpretations of bite-mark evidence in multiple murders. *J Forensic Sci, 24*(2), 492-502.

(Cause - Schizophrenia)

Capasso, G., et al. (1979) Medicolegal significance of the initial stage of schizophrenia (Italian with English and French summaries). *Osp Psichiatr, 47*(1), 130-134.

(Crime - Depression)

Somasundaram, O. (1979) Depressive illness and crime. *Indian Journal of Criminology, 7*(2), 153-156.

(Homicide - Psychiatry)

Grunberg, F., et al. (1978) Homicide and community-based psychiatry. *Journal of Nervous and Mental Disease, 166*(12), 868-874.

(Insanity Defense)

Sadoff, R.L. (1978) Heavier burden put on insanity defense. *Legal Aspects of Medical Practice, 6*(6), 14.

(Aggression)

Mikolajcak, J., & Hagen, D.Q. (1978) Aggression in psychiatric patients in a VA hospital. *Mil Med, 143*(6), 402-405.

(Homicide - Depression)

Martini, M. (1977) Homicide during depression (case report) (Italian with English and French summary). *Rass Studi Psychiatr, 66*(5), 992-998.

(Homicide - Mentally Ill)

Grunberg, F., et al. (1977) Homicide and deinstitutionization of the mentally ill. *American Journal of Psychiatry, 134*(6), 685-687.

(Homicide - Psychiatric Aspects)

Medlicott, R.W. (1976) Psychiatric aspects of murder and attempted murder. *New Zealand Medical Journal, 83*(555), 5-9.

(Reactive Parricide)

Tanay, E. (1976) Reactive parricide. *Journal of Forensic Science, 21*(1), 76-82.

(Homicide - Psychiatry)

Fagiani, M.B., & Fornari, U. (1976) The dynamics of a homicide: Psychiatric or psychological examination? (Italian) *Ann Freniat Sci Affini, 89*(4), 367-385.

(Psychiatric Study)

Pakola, R., et al. (1976) A psychiatric study of violent behavior in lifers. *Bulletin of the American Academy of Psychiatry and the Law, 4*(1), 58-66.

(Murder - Madness)

Lunde, D.T. (1976) *Murder and madness.* Stanford, CA: Stanford U. Alumni Association.

(Homicide - Psychiatry)

Editorial: Psychiatry and homicide. (1976) *British Medical Journal, 1*(6021), 1300.

(Provocation)

Recent judicial decision: Provocation and psychiatry. (1975) *The Police Journal, 48*(2), 153-154.

(Psychopathic Personality)

Blair, D. (1975) Medicolegal implications of the terms 'psychopath','psychopathic personality', and 'psychopathic disorder' (Part 2). *Medical Science and the Law, 15*(2), 110-123.

(Homicidal Children)

Walshe-Brennan, K.S. (1974) Psychopathology of homicidal children. *Royal Society Health Journal, 94*(6), 274-277.

(Schizophrenic Psychosis)

Krstic, B. (1974) Disintegration phenomenon and its criminogenic value in homicides committed in acute schizophrenic psychosis (Serbo-Croatian). *Socijalna Psihijatrija, 2*(4), 311-316.

(Pre-Homicidal Psychotic)

Erdreich, M. (1974) The psychotic pre-homicidal in society. *Soc, 1*(5-6), 356-363.

(Deviant Behavior)

Winslow, R.W., & V. (1974) *Deviant reality: Alternative world views.* Boston: Allyn & Bacon.

(Psychopathology)

Finney, J.C., et al. (1973, Dec.) Phases of psychopathology after assassination. *American Journal of Psychiatry, 130,* 1379-1380.

(Personality Disorder)

Medical testimony in a second-degree murder case of a personality disorder (dissocial type), showing the direct and cross-examinations of the psychiatrists and the charge to the jury. (1973, Spring) *Medical Trial Techniques Quarterly, 19,* 491-530.

(Homicide - Depression)

Reinhardt, J.M. (1973) The dismal tunnel: Depression before murder. *International Journal of Offender Therapy and Comparative Criminology, 17*(3), 246-249.

(Mental Health)

Shelton, J.L., & Sanders, R.S. (1973) Mental health intervention in a campus homicide. *Journal of the American College Health Association, 21*(4), 346-350.

(Homicide - Psychosis)

Psychosis, psychiatry, and homicide. (1972, May 8) *JAMA, 220,* 864-865.

(Parricide - Psychopathology)

Rozycka, M., et al. (1972, March-April) Psychopathological aspects of parricide (Polish with English abstract). *Psychiatr Pol, 6,* 159-168.

(Homicide - Psychosis)

Reich, P., & Hepps, R.B. (1972) Homicide during psychosis induced by LSD. *JAMA, 219*(7), 869-871.

(Homicide - Psychiatry)

Dawson, E.B., et al. (1972) Relationship of lithium metabolism to mental hospital admission and homicide. *Diseases of the Nervous System, 33,* 546-558.

(Neonaticide)

Medvecky, J., & Kapka, J. (1972) Psychiatric aspects of neonaticide committed by mothers (Czech). *Ceskoslovenska Psychiatrie, 68*(1), 16-22.

(Homicide - Psychopathology)

Szymusik, A. (1972) Psychopathology of homicide (Polish with English abstract). *Folia Med Cracov, 14,* 3-28.

(Mass Murderers)

Evseeff, G.S., et al. (1972) A psychiatric study of a violent mass murderer. *Journal of Forensic Science, 17,* 371-376.

(Psychopathology)

Szymusik, A. (1971) Studies on the psychopathology of homicides (Polish with English abstract). *Przegl Lek, 27,* 529-531.

(Homicide - Superstitions)

Drogowski, M., et al. (1969, Sept.-Oct.) Homicide with the background of superstition (Polish). *Psychiat Pol, 3*, 605-608.

(Genocide - Psychopathology)

Federn, E. (1969, Aug.) Clinical remarks on the psychopathology of genocide (German). *Psyche, 23*, 629-639.

(Homicide - Mental Distress)

Szewczyk, H. (1969, July) "Mental distress" as a motive for homicide (German). *Psychiatr Neurol Med Psychol, 21*, 262-266.

(Patricide - Psychosis)

Holfield, H., et al. (1969, May) Patricide as the central conflict of a psychogenic psychosis (German). *Nervenarzt, 40*, 203-209.

(Psychosis)

Danielczyk, W. (1969, April) Sequelae of a disulfiram psychosis (German). *Nervenarzt, 40*, 188-191.

(Homicide - Psychiatric Study)

Tanay, E. (1969, March) Psychiatric study of homicide. *American Journal of Psychiatry, 125*, 1252-1257.

(Homicide - Psychopathology)

Isaacs, E.R. (1969, Jan.) Modern concepts of the crime of murder: A psychopathological study. *Medicolegal Bulletin, 189*, 1-4.

(Homicide - Psychiatry)

Wilmer, H.A. (1969) "Murder, you know". *Psychiatric Quarterly, 43*, 414-447.

(Psychopathic Behavior)

Rascovsky, A., et al. (1968) On the genesis of acting out and psychopathic behavior in Sophocles' *Oedipus*. *International Journal of Psychoanalysis, 49*, 390-394.

(Psychiatric Aspects)

MacDonald, J.M. (1968) *Homicidal threats*, with a chapter by M. Mead. Springfield, IL: C.C. Thomas.

(Psychiatry)

Steigleder, E. (1968) *Morder und totschlager; die forensischmedizinische beurteilung von nicht gelteskranken tatern als psychopathologischen problem.* Stuttgart: Enke.

(Homicide - Schizophrenic)

Schipkowensky, N. (1967) The fields of force in schizophrenic homicides (French). *Evolution Psychiatrique, 32*(1), 89-113.

(Homicide - Mental Illness)

Hrbicek, S., et al. (1967) Psychiatric problems of murder (Czech). *Cesk Psychiat, 63*, 325-329.

(Homicide - Schizophrenia)

Fennelly, J.J. (1967) A schizophrenic murder. *Journal of the Irish Medical Association, 60*, 177-178.

(Paranoid Schizophrenia)

Yanovskaya, E.V. (1966) Catamnestic study of patients suffering from a paranoid form of schizophrenia, who have committed dangerous acts for delirious reasons (Russian). *Zhurnal Nevropatologii i Psikhiatrii, 66*(9), 1392-1397.

(Mental Illness)

McKnight, C.K., et al. (1966) Mental illness and murder. *Canadian Psychiatric Association Journal, 11*(2), 91-98.

(Homicide - Pathophysiology)

Podolsky, E. (1965) Organic brain conditions and homicide. *Corrective Psychiatric and Journal of Social Therapy, 11*(2), 91-94.

(Mental Illness)

Borzyk, D., et al. (1964, July-Aug.) Homicides from the psychiatric point of view (Polish). *Neurol Neurochir Psychiat Pol, 14*, 589-592.

(Homicide - Insanity)

Tovo, S. (1964, May-June) On homicide of the insane (Italian). *Minerva Medicolegal, 84*, 48-89.

(Threat of Death)

Fiorentini, H. (1963, May-June) The threat of death apropos of psychiatric expertise (French). *Ann Med Leg* (Paris), *43*, 257-277.

(Necrophilia)

Pride, D.E. (1963, April) Necrophilia complicating a case of homicide. *Medical Science and the Law, 3*, 121-131.

(Murder - Insanity)

Lanzkron, J. (1963, Feb.) Murder and insanity: A survey. *American Journal of Psychiatry, 119*, 754-758.

(Child Psychiatry)

Kenyon, F.E. (1962) Emergencies in child psychiatry. *Journal of Mental Science, 108*(455), 419-426.

(Matricide)

Camba, R., & Dede, G. (1962) On 2 cases of paranoid schizophrenic matricide (Italian). *Rass Med Sarda, 14*, 243-261.

(Mental Illness)

Podolsky, E. (1961, April) Somnambulistic homicide. *Med Sci and Law, 1*, 260.

(Mental Illness)

Somnambulistic homicide. (1961) *British Medical Journal, 5239*, 1616.

(Causes of Murder)

Gibson, E., Klein, S. (1961) Murder. *Stud Causes Delinqu Treatm Offenders 1961*, 4.

(Homicide - Psychiatric Studies)

Bromberg, W. (1961) *The mold of murder: A psychiatric study of homicide.* Westport, CT: Greenwood.

(Amnesia and Homicide)

O'Connell, B. (1960) Amnesia and homicide. *British Journal of Delinquency, 10*(4), 262-276.

(Mental Disease)

Satten, J., et al. (1960) Murder without apparent motive: A study in personality disorganization. *American Journal of Psychiatry, 117*, 48-53.

(Mental Illness)

Shiphovenski, N. (1960) *Epileptic psychosis and homicide (Bulgarian).* Nauch Tr Vissh Med Inst Sofia, 39(6), 81-103.

(Homicide - Psychopath)

William, J.E.H. (1958) Psychopath and the defense of diminished responsibility (Regina v. Dunbar, 1957, 3 W L R 330; Regina v. Spriggs, 1958, 2 W L R 162; Regina v. Matheson, 1958, 1 W L R 474). *Modern Law Review, 31*, 544.

(Homicide - Insanity)

Gibbens, T.C.N. (1958) Sane and insane homicide. *Journal of Criminal Law, 49*, 110.

(Homicide - Schizophrenic)

Sheehan-Dare, H. (1955) Homicide during a schizophrenic episode. *International Journal of Psychoanalysis, 36*, 43-52.

(Psychopathic Personality)

Smykal, A., & Thorne, F.C. (1951) Etiological study of psychopathic personality. II. Asocial type. *Journal of Clinical Psychology, 1951*(7), 299-316.

(Homicide - Psychiatric Study)

McDermaid, G., & Winkler, E.G. (1950) Psychiatric study of homicide cases. *Journal of Clinical Pathology, 1950*(11), 93-146.

(Homicidal Schizophrenia)

Velasquez, J.O. (1950) Homicidal schizophrenia (Spanish). *Rev Med y Cir, Barranquilla, 17*, 27-46.

(Crime - Psychopathology)

Karpman, B. (1948) *Case studies in the psychopathology of crime. Vol. III: Cases 10-13.* Washington, DC: Medical Science Press.

(Pattern of Insanity)

Cohen, L.H., & Coffin, T.E. (1947) The pattern of murder in murder: A criterion of the murderer's abnormality. *Journal of Criminal Law and Criminology, 37*, 262-287.

(Homicide - Mental Capacity)

Feld, V. (1946) Premeditation and mental capacity (Fisher v. United States, 66 Sup. Ct. 1318). *Columbia Law Review, 46*, 1005-1012; *Southern California Law Review, 20*, 95-99.

(Homicide - Paranoid)

Gross, K. (1936) Concerning paranoid murder (German). *Jb Psychiat Neurol, 53*, 85.

(Homicide - Paranoid)

Lima, A., & Guerner, F. (1935) Homicide by a paranoiac (Portuguese). *S. Paulo, 1*, 232-237.

(Homicide - Psychiatry)

East, W.N. (1935) Homicide from the point of view of the psychiatrist. *Medicolegal and Criminology Review, 3*, 61.

(Homicide - Hysteria)

Marx, A.M. (1929) Murder in a hysterical twilight state (German). *Arch f. Krimin, 1929*, 4, 85.

(Homicidal Impulse)

Abely, P. (1929) Dementia praecox of rapid growth. Homicidal impulse: First symptom (Italian). *Ann Med Psychol, 87*(2), 345-357.

(Homicidal Impulse)

Sizaret, A., & Bastie, J. (1929) Homicidal impulse: Initial symptom of a dementia praecox with rapid development (French). *Bull Soc Clin Med Ment, 22*, 166-169.

Psychological

(Extreme Emotion)

Hall, H.V. (1990) Extreme emotion. *The University of Hawaii Law Review, 12,* 39-82.

(Homicide - Hypothesis)

Lester, D. (1989) The critical mass hypothesis and homicide. *Psychol Rep, 64*(1), 146.

(Homicide - Status Integration)

Lester, D. (1989) Status Integration and homicide: Note. *Psychol Rep, 65*(2), 594.

(Homicide - Sexual)

Prentky, R.A. et al. (1989) The presumptive role of fantasy in serial sexual homicide. *Am J Psychiatry, 146,* 887-891.

(Non-survivor)

Miller, T.W. et al. (1989) The adult non-survivor of child abuse. *J Ky Med Assoc, 87*(3), 120-124.

(Homicide - Football)

White, G F. (1989) Media and violence: the case of professional football championship games. *Aggressive Behavior, 15*(6), 423-433.

(Homicide - Child)

Vaughn, J.B. (1989) The rise of child abuse as an extra-legal factor affecting the criminal law of homicide. *Quarterly Journal of Ideology, 13*(2), 35-47.

(Murder - Facing)

Gampel, Y. (1988) Facing war, murder, torture, and death in latency. *Psychoanal Rev, 75*(4), 499-509.

(Homicide - Stressful)

Humphrey, J. A. & Palmer, S. (1987) "Stressful life events and criminal homicide". *Omega, 17*(4), 299-308.

(Homicide - Psychological)

Ndetei, D.M., et al. (1987) Some social-psychological characteristics of criminal homicide in Kenya. *East Afr Med J, 64*(1), 17-30.

(Homicide - Psychosis)

Trixler, M., et al. (1987) Homicide committed in acute paranoid psychosis. *Morphol Igazsagugyi Orv Sz, 27*(2), 11-15.

(Homicide - Neurological)

Hidden histories on death row (neurological disorders and homicidal behavior; study of death row juveniles by Dorothy Otnow Lewis. (1987) *Sci News, 132,* 287.

(Stress - Life Threat)

Pynoos, R.S., et al. (1987) Life threat and post-traumatic stress in school-age children. Annual meeting of the American Psychiatric Association. *Archives of General Psychiatry, 44*(12), 1057-1063.

(Homicide - Personality)

Hart, C.J. (1987) The relevance of a test of speech comprehension deficit to persistent aggressiveness. *Personality & Individual Differences, 8*(3), pp 371-384.

(Murder in Mind)

Wilkes, J. (1987) Murder in mind. *Psychology Today, 21*(6), 26-32.

(Violence - Sleep-Walking)

Bartholomew, A.A. (1986) On serious violence during sleep-walking. *British Journal of Psychiatry, 148,* 476-477.

(Homicide - Study)

Cook, P.J. & Zarkin, G.A. (1986) Homicide and economic conditions: A replication and critique of M. Harvey Brenner's new report to the U.S. Congress. *Journal of Quantitative Criminology, 2*(1), 69-80.

(Homicide and Depression)

Rosenbaum, M., et al. (1986) Homicide and depression. *Am J Psychiatry, 143*(3), 367-370.

(Mass Murderers)

Ritts, M. (1986) Why mass murderers kill (interview with E. Leyton). *por Macleans, 99,* 6-7.

(Murderers - Childhood)

Feldman, M., et al. (1986) Filicidal abuse in the histories of 15 condemned murderers. Special issue: child forensic psychiatry. *Bulletin of the American Academy of Psychiatry & the Law, 14*(4), 345-352.

(Shooting - Fantasy)

Montanile, J. (1986) Bernard Goetz as group fantasy object. *Journal of Psychohistory, 14*(1), 55-63.

(Death - Imagery)

Lewis, C.N. (1986) Caravaggio's imagery of death and illusion. *American Imago, 43*(3), 261-272.

(Genocide - Psychopathology)

Charny, I.W. (1986) Genocide and mass destruction: Doing harm to others as a missing dimension in psychopathology. *Psychiatry, 49*(2), 144-157.

(Murder Psychology)

Lowenstein, L.F. (1986) The psychology of the young murderer. *Contemporary Review, 249*(1447), 97-104.

(Psychological - Study)

Benezech, M. (1985) Introduction to the medico-psychological study of Marie Besnard. *Ann Med Psychol (Paris), 143*(5), 409-448.

(Avilocide)

Bornstein, S., et al. (1985) Apropos of a new case of avilocide. *Ann Med Psychol Paris, 143*(4), 391-395.

(Conflict - Murder)

Bluestone, H., et al. (1984) Murder: the ultimate conflict. *Am J Psychoanal, 44*2), 147-167.

(Homicidal - Habitually)

Virkkunen, M. (1983) Serum cholesterol levels in homicidal offenders. A low cholesterol level is connected with a habitually violent tendency under the influence of alcohol. *Neuropsychobiology, 10*(2-3), 65-69.

(Black-on-Black Homicide)

Poussaint, A.F., et al. (1983) Black-on-on black homicide: A psychological political perspective. *Victimology, 8*(3-4), 161-169.

(Homicide - Psychopathology)

Psychopathology of homicide. (1981) C.C. Thomas.

(Causes - Psychosocial Factors)

Bartol, C.R. (1980) *Criminal behavior: A psychosocial approach.* Englewood Cliffs, NJ: Prentice-Hall.

(Causes - Stressful Life Events)

Humphrey, J.A., et al. (1980) Stressful life events and criminal homicide offender-victim relationships. Paper presented at the first World Congress of Victimology, held in Washington, DC, August 20-24, 1980. *Victimology, 5*(2-4), 115-120.

(Murderer - Psychology)

Whittington, S.N. (1980) *The psychology of murder and of murderers.* American Institute of Psychology.

(Causes - Altruistic)

Fink, W.L., et al. (1979) Altruistic murder-suicide: A case report and clinical indications. *Hospital and Community Psychiatry, 30*(8), 558-559.

(Murder - Emotional)

Middendorf, W. (1978) Emotional homicide: A criminological study based on the case of Adolf D. , Part II. (German). *Arch Kriminol, 162*(3-4), 65-85.

(Murder - Emotional)

Middendorf, W. (1978) Affective killing: A criminological study based on the case of Adolf D. (German). *Arch Kriminol, 162*(1-2), 34-42.

(Homicide - Psychodynamics)

Tanay, E. (1978) Psychodynamic differentiations of homicide. *Bulletin of the American Academy of Psychiatry and Law, 6*(4), 364-373.

(Homicide - Biological)

Breier, S., et al. (1978) Contribution to the problem of the correlation between biological and psychological factors in homicide (Author's translation). *Cesk Psychiatr, 74*(5), 267-284.

(Homicide - Psychology)

Askenasy, H. (1978) *Homicide: Psychological aspects - are we all Nazis?*

(Homicide - Psychodynamics)

Riley, D., & Cohen, H. (1977) Psychodynamics in a case of homicide. *International Journal of Offender Therapy, 21*(1), 26-30.

(Childhood)

Spiel, W. (1977) Extreme psychogenic shock states in childhood. *Pschiatr Neurol Med Psychol Beih,* 22-23, 307-312.

(Homicide - Analysis)

King, C.H. (1975) The ego and the integration of violence in homicidal youth. *American Journal of Orthopsychiatry, 45*(1), 134-145.

(Psychoanalysis)

Karan, M. (1975) Psychoanalytic approach to the problems of blood feud (Serbo-Croatian). *Anali Zaovda za Mentalno Zdravlje, 7*(1), 63-73.

(Gynecocide)

Geha, R. (1975) For the love of Medusa: A psychoanalytic glimpse into gynecocide. *Psychoanalysis Review, 62*(1), 49-77.

(Homicide - Neurotic Pride)

Ruotolo, A.K. (1975) Neurotic pride and homicide. *American Journal of Psychoanalysis, 35*(1), 1-16.

(Murder and Madness)

Lunde, D.T. (1975, July) Our murder boom; excerpt from *Murder and Madness. Psychology Today, 9*, 35-40+; discussion, (1975, Nov.), 8+.

(Homicide - Disturbed Communications)

Blackman, N., et al. (1974) Disturbed communications -- a contributing factor in sudden murder. *Mental Health Soc, 1*(5-6), 345-355.

(Homicide - Psychology)

Damio, W. (1974) *Urge to kill.* Pinnacle Books.

(Homicide - Status Integration)

Lester, D. (1973, June) Status integration and homicide. *Psychology Reports, 32*, 774.

(Homicide - Psychodrama)

Moreno, J.L. (1973) Note on indications and contra-indications for acting out in psychodrama. *Group Psychotherapy and Psychodrama, 26*(1-2), 23-24.

(Homicide - Psychology)

Abrahamsen, D. (1973) *The murdering mind.* New York: Harper-Row.

(Psychological Examination)

Munnich, I. (1973) Psychological examination of a murderer guilty twice of infanticide (Hungarian). *Magyar Psichological Szmele, 28*(2), 213-220.

(Mass-Murder - Psychology)

Westermeyer, J. (1973) Grenade-amok in Laos: A psychosocial perspective. *International Journal of Social Psychiatry, 19*(3-4), 251-260.

(Crimes of Passion)

Corder, E. (1973) *Crimes of passion.* Chicago: Playboy Press.

(Neonaticide)

Brovovsky, M., & Falit, H. (1971) Neonaticide: Clinical and psychodynamic considerations. *Journal of the American Academy of Child Psychiatry, 10*(4), 673-683.

(Psychological Murder)

Pouget, R., & Reynaud, E. (1971) Evolution of ideas on pathological murder (French). *Annales Medico-Psychologiques, 2*(5), 665-698.

(Homicide - Psychodynamics)

Cormier, B.M., et al. (1971) The psychodynamics of homicide committed in a specific relationship. *Canadian Journal of Criminology and Corrections, 13*(1), 1-8.

(Murderesses - Psychosocial Study)

Totman, J.M. (1970) The murderess: *A psychosocial study of the process of criminal homicide.* University of California- Berkeley.

(Dreams)

Lower, R.B. (1969) On Raskolnikov's dreams in Dostoyevsky's *Crime and Punishment. J Amer Psychoanal Ass, 17*, 728-742.

(Homicide - Cyclophrenia)

Schipkowensky, N. (1968) Affective disorders: Cyclophrenia and murder. *Int Psychiat Clin, 5*, 59-75.

(Homicide - Threats)

MacDonald, J.M. (1968) *Homicidal threats.* A chapter by Margaret Mead. Springfield, IL: C.C. Thomas.

(Psychiatric Expertise)

Vinek, Z., et al. (1967) Problems of psychiatric expertise in murder cases under unsure circumstances (Croatian). *Neuropsihijatrija, 15,* 155-160.

(Psychology)

Lujan, J.A. (1966) *El homicidio emocional por Jose Angel Lujan y tiburcio de la carcova.* Buenos Aries: Abeledo-Perrot.

(Murderer's Mind)

Neustatter, W.L. (1965) The state of mind in murder. *Lancet, 1,* 861-863.

(Psychoanalysis)

Quiros Cuaron, A. (1965) *Psicoanalisis del magnicidio por Alphonso Quiros Cuaron y Samuel Maynes Puente.* Mexico City: Editorial Juridia Mexicana.

(Homicide - Psychology)

Villavicencio, V.M. (1964) *Psicologia del homicida.* Lima.

(Murderer - Psychology)

Sturup, G.K. (1964) The psychology of murderers. *Journal of the Irish Medical Association, 54,* 27-32.

(Murderer - Juvenile)

Von Kothe, K. (1964) From the field of behavioral psychology: The case of a juvenile murderer. *Psychiatrie, Neurologie & Medizinische Psychologie, 16*(1), 24-27.

(Threat to Kill)

MacDonald, J.M. (1963, Aug.) The threat to kill. *American Journal of Psychiatry, 120,* 125-130.

(Homicide - Psychology)

Ferracutti, F. (1963) Psychology of the criminal homicide. *Rev Jur UPR, 32,* 569.

(Homicide - Psychology)

Palmer, S. (1962) *Psychology of murder.* Apollo Books.

(Homicide - Psychodynamics)

Salzman, L. (1962) Psychodynamics of a case of murder. *Comprehensive Psychiatry, 3*(3), 152-169.

(Homicide - Marriage)

Cormier, B. (1962) Psychodynamics of homicide committed in a marriage relationship. *Correct Psychiat J Soc Ther, 8*(4), 187-194.

(Mental Illness)

Palmer, S. (1960) Frustration, aggression, and murder. *Journal of Abnormal Social Psychology, 60,* 430-432.

(Mental Illness)

Irresistible impulse. (1960) *British Medical Journal, 5181,* 1283-1284.

(Mass Murderers)

Kahn, M.W. (1960) Psychological test study of a mass murderer. *Journal Project Techn, 24*, 148-160.

(Psychological Factors)

Rose, G.J. (1960) Screen memories in homicidal acting out. *Psychoanalysis Quarterly, 29*, 328-343.

(Mental Illness)

Lamb, J.F. (1959) Hysterical amnesia not a form of insanity. *Lancet, 2*, 729-730.

(Crime - Fear)

Heuyer, G., et al. (1956) Crime caused by fear (French). *Ann Med Leg, 36*(3), 136-144.

(Murder - Family Psychology)

Schafroth, H.J. (1954) *Additions to the problem of murder delicti in the family* (German). Zurich: Inaug. Diss.

(Psychosocial Study)

Fontes, V., et al. (1953-1954) A psychosocial clinical case of an eleven-year-old girl who killed two others (Portuguese). *Crianca Portugal, 13*, 129-142.

(Homicide - Nervous Shock)

Treitel, G.H. (1954) Nervous shock and homicide. *Law Q Review, 70*, 168-169.

(Homicide - Psychology)

Evidence of uncommunicated threats in excusable homicide cases. (1951) *Arkansas Law Review, 5*, 207-213.

(Psychology)

Hanau, G. (1951) *Murder emotionally activated in a person with diminished awareness* (German). Munich: Inaug. Diss.

(Homicide - Mental Retardation)

Schachter, M., & Cotte, S. (1946-1947) Clinical psychological study of a youthful feebleminded criminal (French). *Crianca Portug 1946-1947*, 61-70.

(Murder - Emotionally Activated)

Gummersbach, H. (1934) Murder emotionally activated (German). *Krim Monatsh, 8*, 124-128.

(Criminal Psychology)

The practice of criminal psychology: Zurich premeditation and German deliberation (German). *Psychol Rundchau, 2*, 379-381.

(Rape/Murder - Psychology)

Morf, G. (1930) The psychology of murder (German). *Psychol Rundchau, 2*, 143-144.

(Murder - Psychology)

Bjerre, A. (1927) *Psychology of murder: A study in criminal psychology.* Finch Press.

(Respectability)

Jesse, F.T. (1924) Respectability as a motive for murder. *World Today, 44*, 117-120.

(Homicide - Psychology)

Coutts, W.A. (1914) Killing by influence on the mind alone. *Cent Law Journal, 78*, 291.

(Temptation)

Temptation to kill. (1910, July 30) *Spectator, 105*, 162-163.

Drugs and Alcohol

(Violence and Alcohol)

Goodman, S. (1990, Oct.) Agony without ecstasy: Alcohol and violence. *Current Health, 17*(2), pp. 28-29.

(Homicide - Drugs)

Zinsmeister, K. (1990, June) Growing up scared. *Atlantic, 265*(6), pp. 49-66.

(Violent Deaths and Drugs)

Poklis, A., et al. (1990) Phencyclidine and violent death in St. Louis: A survey of medical examiners' cases from 1977-1986. *American Journal of Drug and Alcohol Abuse, 16*(3-4), 265-274.

(Homicide - Drugs)

Drugs blamed for record year for homicides. (1989, Dec. 27) *Chicago Daily Law Bulletin*, p. 1, column 5.

(Murder Capital)

Tidwell, M. (1989, July) Murder capital. *Progressive, 53*(7), p. 46.

(Homicide - Drugs)

Notes and comment (drug murders in Washington, DC). (1989, April 17) *The New Yorker, 65*. pp. 29-30.

(Murderer - Todd Bridges)

Todd Bridges tells how Hollywood destroyed his life and God is rebuilding it. (1989, April 10) *Jet, 76*(1), pp. 28-30.

(Violent Deaths and Drugs)

Milhizer, E.R. (1989, March) Involuntary manslaughter and drug overdose deaths: A proposed methodology. *Army Lawyer*, pp. 10-17.

(Homicide - Drugs)

Martz, L., et al. (1989, Jan. 16) A tide of drug killings. *Newsweek, 113*(3), pp. 44-45.

(Homicide Victim - Drinking)

Welte, J.W., & Abel, E.L. (1989). Homicide - drinking by the victim. *Journal of the Study on Alcohol, 50*(3), 197-201.

(Cocaine-Induced Psychosis)

Strauss, A. (1989) Homicidal psychosis during the combined use of cocaine and an over-the-counter cold preparation (letter). *Journal of Clinical Psychiatry, 50*(4), 147.

(Homicide - Drugs)

Bailey, D.N., et al. (1989) Cocaine- and methamphetamine-related deaths in San Diego County: Homicides and accidental overdoses. (1987). *Journal of Forensic Science, 34*(2), 407-422.

(Homicide - Drugs)

Spitz, W.U. (1989) Drugs and homicide (letter). *American Journal of Forensic Medicine and Pathology, 10*(1), 90.

(Homicide - Crack)

Goldstein, P.J., et al. (1989) Crack and homicide in New York City, 1988: A conceptually based event analysis. *Contemporary Drug Problems, 16*, 651-687.

(Lust to Kill)

Simon, R.J. (1989) The lust to kill - a feminist investigation of sexual murder, by D. Cameron and E. Frazer (Book review). *Cont Psycho, 34*(5), 502-503.

(Homicide - Drugs)

Slaughter in the streets. (1988, Dec. 5) *Time, 132*(23), p. 51.

(Violent Deaths and Drugs)

Schmalzbach, O.R. (1988) Drug-related homicide by juveniles: Is there prevention? *Australian Journal of Forensic Science, 2171*, 8-12.

(Homicide - Study)

Laubichler, W., et al. (1988) Homicide with special reference to alcoholic intoxication and relation to time of day. *Arch Krimol, 181*(5-6), 172-181.

(Homicide - Cocaine)

Harruff, R.C., et al. (1988) Cocaine and homicide in Memphis and Shelby County: An epidemic of violence. *Journal of Forensic Sciences, 33*(5), 1231-1237.

(Murder - Crack)

Machine-gunman, high on crack, pumps 26 fatal bullets into boy, 3 (murder of L. Harris in Brooklyn). (1987, Dec. 7) *Jet, 73*, p. 63.

(Violent Deaths and Crack)

Rosenbaum, R. (1987, Feb. 15) Crack murder: A detective story (solving the murder of a crack dealer in Brooklyn). *New York Times Magazine*, 24-30+.

(Violent Deaths and Drugs)

Johnson, T.E. (1987, Feb. 9) Urban murders on the rise (cocaine-related killings). *Newsweek, 109*, p. 30.

(Homicide - Drugs)

Abel, E.L., et al. (1987) Drugs and homicide in Erie County, NY. *International Journal of Addiction, 22*(2), 195-200.

(Narcotics Laws)

Clawson, P.M. (1987) Ex-Hell's Angel tells senators about corrupt police; describes drug trafficking by bikers. *Narcotics Control Digest, 13*(7), 2-3. Article copies available from UMI.

(Murder - Drug Dealer)

Forever stylish, drug dealer Flukey Stokes goes out with a bang. (1986, Dec. 8) *People Weekly, 26*, 172-173.

(Narcotics Laws)

Constructive possession of narcotics - NY. (1986, Feb.) *Narcotics Law Bulletin*, 6. Article copies available from UMI.

(Organized Crime)

Bodies of two alleged mobsters found buried in a cornfield. (1986) *Organized Crime Digest, 7*(6), 2. Article copies available from UMI.

(Homicide - Alcohol)

Abel, E.L., et al. (1986) Alcohol and homicide: A comparison between Erie County, New York, and Los Angeles County, California. *American Journal of Drug and Alcohol Abuse, 12*(1-2), 121-129.

(Victims - Alcohol Levels)

Abel, E.L., et al. (1986) Guns and blood alcohol levels among homicide victims. *Drug and Alcohol Dependency, 18*(3), 253-257.

(Violent Deaths and Alcohol)

Goodman, R.A., et al. (1986) Alcohol use and interpersonal violence: Alcohol detected in homicide victims. *American Journal of Public Health, 76*(2), 144-149.

(Homicide - Drugs)

McBride, D.C., et al. (1986) Drugs and homicide. *Bulletin of the NY Academy of Medicine, 62*(5), 497-508.

(Violent Deaths and Drugs)

Garriot, J.C., et al. (1986) Detection of cannaboids in homicide victims and motor vehicle fatalities. *Journal of Forensic Science, 31*(4), 1274-1282.

(Narcotics Laws)

All 47 Senate democrats co-sponsoring Comprehensive Narcotics Control Act of 1986. (1986)

Crime Control Digest, 20(38), 1-5; *Narcotics Control Digest, 16*(19), 5-9. Article copies available from UMI.

(Narcotics Law)

Bill seeks "popper" regulation. (1986) *Narcotics Control Digest, 16*(15), 10. Article copies available from UMI.

(Narcotics Laws)

Bosarge, B. (1986) Senate democrats introduce bill resurrecting cabinet "drug czar" proposals. *Crime Control Digest, 20*(33), 10-12. Article copies available from UMI.

(Narcotics Laws)

Congress, President speeding ahead to get massive anti-drug legislation enacted quickly. (1986) *Juvenile Justice Digest, 14*(18), 8-10. Article copies available from UMI.

(Narcotics Laws)

Congress sends $1.7 billion anti-drug bill to Reagan. (1986) *Crime Control Digest, 20*(38), 1-2. Article copies available from UMI.

(Camarena Case)

DEA gets a break in year-old Camarena murder case. (1986) *Narcotics Control Digest, 16*(17), 9-12. Article copies available from UMI.

(Murder - Drug Agents)

Drug traffickers torture and kill 17 Mexican police officers. (1986) *Narcotics Control Digest, 16*(4), 8. Article copies available from UMI.

(Police Scandal)

Miami police officers charged with murder in drug scandal. (1986) *Criminal Justice Newsletter, 17*(2), 2-3.

(Narcotics Laws - California)

California Attorney General urges enactment of package of strong anti-drug bills. (1986) *Narcotics Control Digest, 16*(18), 7-8.

(Homicide - Drugs)

Legal decisions: Homicide. (1986) *Inside Drugs Law, 3*(3), 15.

(Homicides - Barbiturates)

Goodman, R.A. (1986) Drug use and interpersonal violence: Barbiturates detected in homicide victims. *American Journal of Epidemiology, 12*(1-2), 121-129.

(Drugs and Police)

Dade police investigators say greed motivated Miami officers running drug-homicide ring. (1986) *Narcotics Control Digest, 16*(1), 6-8.

(Violence and Alcohol)

Moller-Madsen, B., et al. (1986) Alcohol involvement in violence: A study from a Danish community (German). *Z Rechtsmed, 97*(2), 141-146.

(Violent Death and Drugs)

Hayman, J.A, (1986) Head injury associated with barbiturate suicide. *American Journal of Forensic Medicine and Pathology, 7*(1), 78-80.

(Violent Deaths and Alcohol)

Abel, E.L., et al. (1985) Seasonal, monthly, and day-of-week trends in homicide as affected by alcohol and race. *Alcoholism: Clinical and Experimental Research, 9*(3), 281-283.

(Murder - Drug Agents)

Mexicans trying to piece together details of massacre of 22 narcotics agents. (1985) *Narcotics Control Digest, 15*(23), 10. Article copies available from UMI.

(Drugs - Mexico)

Drugs: The bodies in Primavera Park (murders of Americans in Mexico). (1985, July 1) *Newsweek, 106*, p. 41.

(Murders - Quebec)

Wilson-Smith, A. (1985, June 24) The fallen angels case (murders of Hell's Angels members in Quebec). *Macleans, 98*, p. 51.

(Homicide - Narcotics Officers)

IACP director outraged by murder of 22 Mexican officers. (1985) *Narcotics Control Digest, 15*(24), 2. Article copies available from UMI.

(Violent Deaths and Alcohol)

MADD pushes for murder charges in fatal drunk driving cases. (1985) *Criminal Justice Newsletter, 16*(24), 2-3.

(Violent Deaths and Drinking Age)

Hingson, R., et al. (1985) Effects of Massachusetts raising its legal drinking age from 18 to 20 on deaths from teenage homicide, suicide, and non-traffic accidents. *Pediatr Clin North Am, 32*(1), 221-232.

(Violent Deaths and Alcoholism)

Rouzioux, J.M., et al. (1985) Role of acute alcoholism in violent deaths: Statistics of the Lyon Medico-Legal Institute (1981-1982) (French with English abstract). *Presse Med, 14*(18), 1017-1023.

(Fatal Accidents and Alcohol)

Berkelman, R.L., et al. (1985) Fatal injuries and alcohol. *American Journal of Preventive Medicine, 1*(16), 21-28.

(Violent Deaths and LSD)

Bratzke, H., et al. (1985) Acts of violence and LSD use. *Beitr Gerichtl Med, 43*, 179-186.

(Violent Deaths and Alcohol)

Abel, E.L., & Zeidenberg, P. (1985) Age, alcohol, and violent death: A postmortem study. *Journal on the Study of Alcohol, 46*(3), 228-231.

(Drugs and Terrorism)

Westrate, D.L. (1985) Drug trafficking and terrorism. *Drug Enforcement, 12*(1), 19-24.

(Deaths - Heroin)

Schneider, V., et al. (1985) Heroin deaths. Cadaver disposal - defensive cadaver dismemberment. *Arch Kriminol, 175*(5-6), 145-150.

(Masculinity as Murder)

Green, J.J. (1984) Macbeth masculinity as murder. *American Imago, 41*(2), 155-180.

(Narcotics Trafficking)

Henze, P.B. (1984) Bulgaria: An interlocking web of narcotics trafficking, terrorism, and subversion. *Security Systems Digest, 15*(13), 4-8.

(Narcotics Law)

Sen. Hawkins introduces bill calling for death penalty for drug-related murders. (1984) *Crime Control Digest, 18*(17), 6. Article copies available from UMI.

(Alcohol Use)

Adverse social consequences of alcohol and alcoholism. (1984) *Alc Health & Res W, 9*(1), 32-37.

(Homicide - Alcohol)

Kramarz, E. (1983) Alcohol as the psychopathology of homicide and robberies (Polish). *Ann Acad Med Stetin, 29*, 305-321.

(Homicide - Drugs)

Senay, E.C., & Wettstein, R.. (1983) Drugs and homicide: A theory. *Drug and Alcohol Dependency, 12*(2), 157-166.

(Drugs and Mafia)

Judge murdered by Mafia as crackdown on heroin traffickers continues in Sicily. (1983) *Narcotics Control Digest, 13*(16), 7. Article copies available from UMI.

(Violent Deaths and Alcohol)

Virkkunen, M. (1983) Serum cholesterol levels in homicidal offenders: A low cholesterol level is connected with a habitually violent tendency under the influence of alcohol. *Neuropsychobiology, 10*(2-3), 65-69.

(Violent Deaths and Drugs)

Monforte, J.R., et al.. (1983) Toxicological and pathological findings in fatalities involving pentazocine and tripelennamine. *Journal of Forensic Science, 28*(1), 90-101.

(Homicide and Drugs)

Daly, M. (1982, Nov. 1) The cadet and the surfer (cocaine-related murder of R. Rasmussen in

New York City). *New York, 15*, pp. 44-52.

(Drug Trafficking)

Heffernan, R., et al. (1982) Homicides related to drug trafficking. *Federal Probation Quarterly, 46*(3), 3-7. Article copies available from UMI.

(Violent Deaths and PCP)

Budd, R.D., & Lindstrom, D.M. (1982-1983) Characteristics of victims of PCP-related deaths in Los Angeles County. *Journal of Toxicology and Clinical Toxicology, 19*(9), 997-1004.

(Homicide - Drugs)

Edland, J.F. (1982) Homicide by barbiturates and alcohol. *Journal of Forensic Science, 27*(4), 942-943.

(Violent Deaths and Alcohol)

Langevin, R., et al. (1982) The role of alcohol, drugs, suicide attempts, and situational strains in homicide committed by offenders seen for psychiatric assessment: A controlled study. *Acta Psychiatr Scand, 66*(3), 229-242.

(Causes - Alcohol)

Budd, R.D. (1982) The incidence of alcohol use in Los Angeles County homicide victims. *American Journal of Drug and Alcohol Abuse, 9*(1), 105-111.

(Violent Deaths and Alcohol)

Wilbanks, W. (1981) Does alcohol cause homicide? *Journal of Crime & Justice 1981, 4*, 149-170.

(Violent Deaths and Alcohol)

Lockhart, J. (1981) Book review of drinking, homicide, and rebellion in colonial Mexican villages, by W.B. Taylor. *Journal of Interdisciplinary History, 11*(4), 757-758.

(Homicide and Drugs)

Gary, I.E. (1980) Role of alcohol and drug abuse in homicide. *Public Health Reports, 95*(6), 553-554.

(Violent Deaths and Alcohol)

Lester, D. (1980) Alcohol and suicide and homicide. *Studies on Alcohol, 41*(11), 1220-1223.

(Violence and Alcohol)

Evans, C.M. (1980) Alcohol, violence, and aggression. *British Journal of Alcohol and Alcoholism, 15*(3), 104-117.

(Causes - Drugs)

Karten, R. (1979, May) Jesus died for your sins: Colombian coke dealers in Queens, NY. *Feature*, pp. 36-41.

(Violent Deaths and Alcohol)

Marek, Z., & Zaranek, S. (1979) Alcohol as a victimogenic factor in cases of violent death

(Polish with English and Russian abstracts). *Arch Med Sadow Kryminol, 29*(3), 183-189.

(Violence and Alcohol)

Roslund, B., & Larson, C.A. (1979) Crimes of violence and alcohol abuse in Sweden. *International Journal of Addiction, 14*(8), 1103-1115.

(Causes - Drugs)

Offenkrantz, W. (1978-1979) A hypothesis about heroin addiction, murder, prostitution, and suicide: Acting our parenting conflicts. *Int J Psychoanal Psychother, 7*, 602-608.

(Heroin)

Homicide - murder - heroin - malice. (1978, Oct.) *IACP Law Enforcement Legal Review, 76*, 9.

(Alcoholism)

Moser, L. (1978) A psychological evaluation of the alcohol problem in judicial statistics (German). *Blutalcohol, 15*(5), 339-355.

(Alcohol-Related Deaths)

Riddick, L., & Luke, J.L. (1978) Alcohol-related deaths in the District of Columbia: A postmortem study. *Journal of Forensic Science, 23*(3), 493-502.

(Homicide - DUI)

Bates, M.L.D. (1977) Murder convictions for homicides committed in the course of driving while intoxicated. *Cumberland Law Review, 1977, 8*, 477-494.

(Violent Deaths and Alcohol)

Simpson, H.M., & Heayn, B. (1976) Alcohol and other drug testing in traffic deaths: A report on current practices in Canada. *Canadian Society of Forensic Science Journal, 9*(1), 27-41.

(Violent Deaths and Drugs)

Weissman, J.C. (1975) Imposing homicide liability for death-producing drug law violations. *Western Law Review, 12*(1), 102-121.

(Violent Deaths and Alcohol)

Davis, J.H. (1975) Alcohol as a precursor to violent death. *Journal of Drug Issues, 5*(3), 270-275.

(Amnesia - Alcohol-Induced)

Ikeda, T. (1975) Pathological alcohol intoxication and amnesia: From the psychiatric tests of an accused murderer (Japanese). *Kyushu Neuropsychiatry, 21*(2), 80-94.

(Poisoning - Anesthetics)

Maltby, J.R. (1975) Criminal poisoning with anesthetic drugs: Murder, manslaughter, or not guilty? *Forensic Science, 6*(1-2), 91-108.

(Violent Deaths and Alcohol)

Haberman, P.W., & Baden, M.M. (1974) Alcoholism and violent death. *Quarterly Journal on the Study of Alcohol, 35*(1), 221-231.

(Violent Deaths and Drugs)

Riedel, M., & Thornberry, T.P. (Eds.) (1974) Murders in a drug using population, by M.A. Zahn and M. Bencivengo. *Crime and Delinquency: Dimensions of Deviance*. New York: Praeger.

(Violent Deaths and Drugs)

Zahn, M.A., et al. (1974) Violent death: A comparison between drug users and non-drug users. *Addict Dis, 1*(3), 283-295.

(Violent Deaths and Alcohol)

Virkkunen, M. (1974) Alcohol as a factor precipitating aggression and conflict behavior leading to homicide. *British Journal on Addiction, 69*(2), 149-154.

(Violent Deaths and Alcohol)

Goodwin, D.W. (1974) Alcohol in suicide and homicide. *Quarterly Journal of Studies on Alcohol, 34*(1, part A), 144-156.

(Alcohol Factors)

Slater, H.W. (1974) On the etiology of criminal homicides - the alcohol factor. *Journal of Police Science Administration, 2*(1), 50-53.

(Alcohol and LSD)

Sadow, R.L. (1973, Aug. 27) LSD, alcohol, and homicide. *JAMA, 225*, 1123.

(Violent Deaths and LSD)

Klamt, R.R. (1973, April 9) Homicide and LSD. *JAMA, 224*, 246.

(Violent Deaths and LSD)

Klepfisz, A., et al. (1973, Jan. 22) Homicide and LSD. *JAMA, 223*, 429-430.

(Violent Deaths and Alcohol)

Baker, S.P., et al. (1971) Tattoos, alcohol, and violent death. *Journal of Forensic Science, 16*, 219-225.

(Violent Deaths and LSD)

Williams, L.N. (1969, Aug. 9) LSD and manslaughter. *Lancet, 2*, 332.

(Violent Deaths and Alcohol)

Medina, E. (1966) Alcohol, accidents, and violence. *Rev Med Chile, 94*, 651-653.

(Violent Deaths and Medications)

Brzezicki, E. (1966) Unexpected, sudden, and sometimes dangerous behavior following ingestion of modern antihistaminic and tranquilizing drugs (paragnomen) (French). *Ann Medicopsychol, 124*, 652-660.

(Violent Deaths and Alcohol)

Le Roux, L.C., et al. (1964) Violent deaths and alcohol intoxication. Journal of Forensic Medicine, 11, 131-147.

(Violent Deaths and Alcohol)

Wilentz, W.C., & Brady, J.P. (1961) The alcohol factor in violent deaths. *American Practitioner, 12*, 829-835.

(Violent Deaths and Alcohol - Native Americans)

Baker, J.L. (1959) Indians, alcohol, and homicide. *Journal of Social Therapy, 5*, 270-275.

(Criminal Law - Intoxication)

Crist, R.G. (1948, Oct.) Criminal law - intoxication as a defense - burden of proof (Commonwealth v. Chapman (PA) 58 Atl. 2d. 433). *Dick Law Review, 53*, 61-62.

(Homicide - DUI)

Brock, J.C. (1947) Drunken driving and murder. *Kentucky Law Journal, 36*, 138-141.

(Homicide - Degrees)

Degree of drunkenness necessary to reduce a murder from first degree to second degree (Mullendore v. State (TN) 191 S W 2d 149). (1946) *Tennessee Law Review, 19*, 486-487.

(Homicide - Mitigation)

Coleman, S. (1940) Intoxication in mitigation of murder. *Journal of Criminal Law, 31*, 72-77.

(Violent Deaths and Alcohol)

Voluntary drunkenness as a defense to murder (State v. Roach, N.J. 197 Atla 33). *Virginia Law Review, 24*, 926-927.

(Homicide and Alcohol)

Grinnell, F.W. (1937) Drunkenness and manslaughter -- should the Commonwealth have an appeal on certain questions of law in criminal cases? *Massachusetts Law Quarterly, 22*, 23-24.

(Homicide - Degrees)

Justifiable homicide, defense of intoxicating liquor illegally possessed (State v. Shannon (Iowa) 243 N W 507). *Virginia Law Review, 19*, 301-302 (1933); *Iowa Law Review, 18*, 386-387.

(Violent Deaths and Alcohol)

Arado, C.C. (1932) Homicides committed in drunken brawls. *Journal of Criminal Law, 23*, 473-478.

(Homicide - DUI)

Manslaughter: Owner permitting intoxicated friend to drive auto (State v. Hopkins, 147 Wash. 198, 265 Pac. 481). (1929) *Yale Law Journal, 38*, 392-393.

(Homicide and Alcohol)

Stroud, D.A. (1920) Constructive murder and drunkenness. *Law Quarterly Review, 36*, 268.

(Homicide and Alcohol)

Collier, N.C. (1910) Intoxication as affecting criminality in homicide cases. *Cent Law Journal, 70*, 102.

Sexual Motives

(Dangerous Love)

Donovan, J.B. (1990, Sept. 4) Warning: Someone you love may be dangerous. *Woman's Day, 53*(13), pp. 76-77+.

(Homicide - Sexual)

Money, J. (1990) Forensic sexology: Paraphilic serial rape (blastophilia) and lust murder (erotophilia). *American Journal of Psychotherapy, 44*(1), 26-36.

(Homicide - Sexual)

Prentky, R.A., et al. (1989) The presumptive role of fantasy in serial sexual homicide. *American Journal of Psychiatry, 146*(7), 887-891.

(Sexual Violence)

Buzash, G.E. (1989) The "rough sex" defense. *Journal of Criminal Law and Criminology, 80*(3), 557-584.

(Sexual Politics)

Caputi, J. (1989) The sexual politics of murder. *Gender & Society, 3*(4), 437-456.

(Sexual Deviancy)

Quinsey, V.L. (1988) Sexual deviancy. *Current Opinions in Psychiatry, 1*(6), 688-690.

(Homicide - Sexual)

O'Brien, R.M. (1988) Exploring the intersexual nature of crimes. *Criminology, 26*(1), 151-170.

(Assault - Elderly)

Pollock, N.L. (1988) Sexual assault of older women. *Annals of Sex Research, 1*(4), 523-532.

(Homicide - Beheading)

Ex-boyfriend beheads teen girl with samurai sword in New York (E. Rodrique kills J. Mentor) (1987, June 8) *Jet, 72*, p. 17.

(Homicide - Sexual)

Burgess, A.W., et al. (1987) Sexual homicide: A motivational model. *Journal of Interpersonal Violence, 1*(3), 251-272.

(Sexual Aggression)

Raboch, J., et al. (1987) Sexual aggressivity and androgens. *British Journal of Psychiatry, 151*(9) 398-400

Steacy, A. (1986, Sept. 15) Corpse on a quiet street (murder of Vancouver, B.C. prostitute). *Macleans, 99*, p. 33.

(Rape/Mutilation)

Ressler, R.K., et al. (1986) Murderers who rape and mutilate. *Journal of Interpersonal Violence, 1*(13), 273-287.

(Homicide - Sexual)

Geberth, V.J. (1986) The investigation of sex-related homicides. *Law and Order, 34*(7), 41-48. Article copies available from UMI.

(Homicide - Sexual)

Pondelickova, J., et al. (1986) Sexually motivated killing of the victim: Characteristics of a group of 50 offenders. (English Abstract). *Cesk Psychiatr, 82*(6), 396-401.

(Sexual Violence)

Sadoff, R.L. (1986) Sexual violence. *Bulletin of the NY Academy of Medicine, 62*(5), 466-476.

(Murder Appeal)

Frame, R. (1985, June 14) News media takes a high profile in well-publicized rape case (case of G. Dotson compared to S. Linscott's murder appeal). *Christianity Today, 29*, p. 58+.

(Homicide - Sexual)

Wilber, C.G. (1985) A case of lust murder. *American Journal of Forensic Pathology and Medicine, 6*(3), 226-232.

(Homicide - Sexual)

Walter, R. (1985) Homosexual panic and murder. *American Journal of Forensic Pathology and Medicine, 6*(1), 49-51.

(Homicide - Sexual)

Classifying sexual homicide crime scenes: Interrater reliability (Chapter 3). (1985) *FBI Law Enforcement Bulletin, 54*(8), 12-17.

(Homicide - Sexual)

Lane, R.C. (1984) Robert Linder and the case of Charles, a teen-age sex murderer: "Songs my mother taught me". *Current Issues in Psychoanalytic Practice, 1*(2), 65-83.

(Sex Offenders - Comparison)

West, D.J. (1984) Violent and non-violent sex offenders. *Australian Journal of Forensic Science, 16*(3), 104-112.

(Homicide - Motive)

Kosa, F., et al. (1983) Sexual frustration as motive for homicide (German). *Arch Kriminol, 172*(3-4), 79-88.

(Homicide - Sadistic)

Reay, D.T., et al. (1983) Sexual abuse and death of an elderly by 'fisting'. *American Journal of Forensic Medicine and Pathology, 4*(4), 347-349.

(Rape/Murder)

Ressler, R.K., et al. (1983) Rape and rape-murder: One offender and twelve victims. *American Journal of Psychiatry, 14*(1), 36-40.

(Sexual Aggression)

Nacci, P.L., & Kane, T.R. (1983) Incidence of sex and sexual aggression in federal prisons. *Federal Probation, 47*(4), 31-36.

(Homicide - Sexual)

Hazelwood, R.R., et al. (1982) Sexual fatalities: Behavioral reconstruction in equivocal cases. *Journal of Forensic Science, 27*, 4, 763-773.

(Homicide - Sexual)

Kippax, D.E. (1982) The lust murder of Edward. *Australian and New Zealand Journal of Psychiatry, 16*(3), 161-168.

(Homicide and Transsexuals)

Milliken, A.D. (1982) Homicidal transsexual: Three cases (summary in French). *Canadian Journal of Psychiatry, 27*(1), 43-46.

(Homicide - Sexual)

Pfafflin,F. (1982) The urge to commit a sexual murder (German). Nervenarzt, 53(9), 547-550.

(Homicide - Sexual)

Wilbanks, W. (1981) A test of Verkko's static and dynamic "laws" of sex and homicide. *International Journal of Women's Studies, 4*(2), 173-180.

(Sexual Crimes)

Kyburz, H.R. (1978) Explanation of sexual crime-learning from predescendents in police files (German). *Kriminalistic, 32*(9), 419-424.

(Necrophilia)

Bartholomew, A.A., et al. (1978) Homosexual necrophilia. *Medical Science and Law, 18*(1), 29-35.

(Murderers - Wives)

Killing excuse: Wives murdering husbands because of abuse. (1977, Nov. 28) *Time, 110*, p. 108.

(Murder)

Lewis, C.N., et al. (1977) Murder will out. *Journal of Nervous and Mental Disease, 164*(4), 273-279.

(Motivation - Romance)

Youth kills four blacks over unhappy romance. (1977) *Juvenile Justice Digest, 5*(17), 6. Article copies available from UMI.

(Homicide - Sexual)

Swigert, V.L., et al. (1976) Sexual homicide: Social, psychological, and legal aspects. *Archive on Sexual Behavior, 5*(5), 391-401.

(Sexual Assault)

Sexual assault, robbery, murder are tactics of man and youth in string of East Coast crimes. (1975) *Juvenile Justice Digest, 3*(2), 8-9.

(Murder - Love)

Schipkowensky, N. (1975) Adolescent murderers through love (German). *Acta Paedopsychiatr* (Basel), *41*(4-5), 187-202.

(Sexual Violence)

Bailey, F.L., & Rothblatt, H.B. (1973) *Crimes of violence: Rape and other sex crimes.* Rochester, NY: Lawyer's Co-op.

(Sex Murder)

Gorder, E. (1973) *Murder my love: The great crimes of passion.* Chicago: Playboy Press.

(Homicide - Sexual)

Szymusik, A., et al. (1972) Juvenile homicides and sexual offenders (Polish). *Psychiatrica Polska, 6*(2), 143-149.

(Homicide - Sexual)

Staak, M. (1972) Situations of homicide in heterosexual and homosexual transient partnerships (German with English abstract). *Z Rechtsmed, 71*, 39-46.

(Homicide - Sexual)

Holzer, F.J. (1971) Sex murderer Zingerle (German). *Arch Kriminol, 148*(5), 94-105.

(Homicide - Sexual)

Holzer, F.J. (1971) Sex murderer Zingerle (German). *Arch Kriminol, 148*(4), 14-23.

(Sex Murder)

Nass, G. (1966) *Criminological judgment of murder delicti for sexual reasons* (German). Luchterhand.

(Sex Murder)

Misra, P.C. Ein lustmord. 20957. J. 20, '66, 9, S. 489-490.

(Homicide - Sexual)

Revitch, E. (1965) Sex murder and the potential sex murderer. *Diseases of the Nervous System, 26*(10), 640-648.

(Motives - Lust)

Podolsky, E. (1965) The lust murderer. 32424. vol. 33, '65, n. 4, p. 174-178 (IBZ 1965).

(Homicide - Sexual)

Helldorfer, H. (1964) Pertaining to the criminology of a sex murder (German). 20957. J. 18, '64, 8, S. 387-390 (IBZ 1966).

(Sex Murder)

Rasch, W. (1964) *Murder of the partner in sex* (German). Stuttgart: Enke.

(Homicide - Sexual)

Von Hentig, H. (1963) Sexual acts after and before murder (German). *Deutsch Z Ges Gerichtl Med, 53*, 211-218.

(Sex Murder)

Schwartz, W.A. (1961) *Sex fiend: A doctor's realistic report on the darker side of love and sexual impulses gone wild.* Derby, CT: Monarch Books.

(Sexual Assault)

Podolsky, E. (1961, April) The lust murder. *Indian Medical Journal, 55*, 81-83.

(Rape/Murder)

Motta, E. (1960, March-April) Homicide committed during theft or rape by minors under 21 (Italian) *Rass Studi Psichiat, 49*, 202-212.

(Sex Murder)

Miller, R.F., Jr. (1948, Oct.) Sexual acts as provocation in Pennsylvania. *Dick Law Review, 53*, 43-45.

(Homicide - Prostitutes)

Kuhn, R. (1948) A murder attempt on a prostitute by a depressive fetishist and sodomist (German). *Mschr Psychiat Neurol, 116*, 66-124.

(Homicide - Adultery)

Hernandez Quiros, A. (1946) Extenuation in homicide prompted by conjugal infidelity (Spanish). *Criminalia* (Mexico), *12*, 13-40.

(Sex Murder)

Lyly, J. (1912) *Warning for fair women.* AMS Press.

Provocation

(Revenge)

Magnuson, E. (1987, Dec. 21) David Burke's deadly revenge (fired USAir employee causes PSA jet to crash). *Time, 130*, p. 30.

(Revenge)

Houston man waits in dark, kills assailant (B. Gibson slays man who had robbed him of his social security money). (1987, Aug. 24) *Jet, 72*, p. 12.

(Women Who Kill)

Women right to kill men who brutalize them (Committee on Domestic Violence and Incarcerated Women). (1987, July 13) *Jet, 72*, p. 28.

(Provocation)

Miethe, T.D. (1984) The impact of victim provocation on judgments of legal responsibility: An experimental assessment. *Journal of Criminal Justice, 12*(4), 407-414.

(Violent Behavior)

Silver, B.J., et al. (1984) The 1980 objectives for the nation for control of stress and violent behavior: Progress report. *Public Health Reports, 99*(4), 374-384.

(Murder - Premeditated)

Premeditated murder by detective precludes city's civil liability. (1978, July) *AELE Law Enforcement Legal Liability Reporter, 67*, 8-9.

(Provocation)

Spencer, M. (1978, June 22) Provocation and the reasonable man. *New Law Journal, 128*, 615-617.

(Provocation)

Orchard, G.F. (1974) Provoked provocation. *NZ UL Review, 6*, 63-68.

(Provocation)

Ashworth, A.J. (1973) Self-induced provocation and the homicide act. *Criminal Law Review 1973*, 483-492.

(Provocation)

Brett, P. (1970) Physiology of provocation. *Criminal Law Review 1970*, 634.

(Provocation)

White, S. (1970) Note on provocation. *Criminal Law Journal 1970*, 446.

(Homicide - Sudden)

Ruotolo, A.K. (1968) Dynamics of sudden murder. *American Journal of Psychoanalysis, 28*, 162-176.

(Homicide - Premeditated)

Blackman, N. (1965) "Premeditated murder" trials -- a juxtaposition. *Psychiatry Digest, 26*(6), 51-58.

(Homicide - Intent)

Yahuda, J. (1960, Oct. 28) Intention in murder. *Legal Times, 230*, 244; reply by G. Williams, Nov. 11.

(Homicide - Intent)

Ritz, W. (1959) Felony murder transferred intent and the Palszgraf doctrine in the criminal law. *Washington & Lee Law Review, 16*(3), 169.

(Homicide - Provocation)

Steyn, J.V. (1958, Nov.) Basis of provocation reexamined. *S A L J, 75*, 383.

(Homicide - Provocation)

Manslaughter and the adequacy of provocation: the reasonableness of the reasonable man. (1958, May) *University of Pennsylvania Law Review, 106*(5), 1021.

(Homicide - Provocation)

Campbell, I.D. (1956, Nov.) Anatomy of provocation. *Vict U C L Review, 2*(11), 7.

(Homicide - Provocation)

Williams, G. (1954) Provocation and the reasonable man. *Criminal Law Review 1954*, 10, 740-754.

(Homicide - Provocation)

Pilmes, R. (1953) Women as criminal instigators: Three cases of women who were successful (German). *Nervenarzt, 24*, 248-251.

(Homicide - Premeditated)

First degree murder -- premeditation and deliberation (Jones v. United States, 175 F., 2d, 544). (1949-1950) *Arkansas Law Review, 4*(1), 92-94.

(Homicide - Premeditated)

Hitchler, W.H. (1950) Willful, deliberate, and premeditated killing. *Pennsylvania Bar Association Quarterly, 22*, 84-89.

(Manslaughter - Provocation)

State v. Martin (SC) 57 SE 2d. 55 - Manslaughter provocation - criminal and forceful relations and spouse (case report). (1950) *University of Pittsburgh Law Review, 11*(3), 709-711.

(Homicide - Provocation)

Provocation in murder cases. (1949, Nov. 5) *Sol J, 93*, 685.

(Homicide - Provocation)

Homicide and provocation. (1942, Feb. 28) *Ir L T, 76*, 57-59.

(Homicide - Provocation)

Slaying upon provocation (Rex v. Uddin, The Times, Sept. 14, 1929). (1929, Sept. 21) Sol J, 73, 604.

(Homicide - Provocation)

Homicide, manslaughter, provocation (State v. Cline (WV) 130 S E 91). (1925) *West Virginia Law Quarterly, 32*, 75-76.

Environmental Causes

(Overcrowding)

Jarrell, S., & Howsen, R.M. (1990) Transient crowding and crime - the more strangers in an area, the more crime, except for murder, assault, and rape. *American Journal of Economic Studies, 49*(4), 483-494.

(Homicide at Work)

Liss, G.M., & Craig, C.A. (1990) Homicide in the workplace in Ontario: Occupations at risk and limitations of existing data sources. *Canadian Journal of Public Health, 81*(1), 10-15.

(Domestic Violence)

Kellerman, A.L. (1990) Domestic violence and the internist's response: Advocacy or apathy? *Journal of General Internal Medicine, 5*(1), 89-90.

(Homicide - Home)

Edwards, S.S.M. (1989) How safe is home - an analysis of homicide statistics in England and Wales, 1982-1986: Meeting abstract. *Aggressive Behavior, 15*(1), 51-52.

(Urban Crowding)

Bagley, C. (1989) Urban crowding and the murder rate in Bombay, India. *Perceptual Motor Skills, 69*(12), 1241-1242.

(Environmental Characteristics)

Lewis, D.O., et al. (1988) Intrinsic and environmental characteristics of juvenile murderers. *Journal of the American Academy of Child and Adolescent Psychiatry, 27*, 582-587.

(Homicide at Work)

Kraus, J.F. (1987) Homicide while at work: Persons industries, and occupations at high risk. *American Journal of Public Health, 77*(10), 1285-1289; editorial by P.E. Dietz, 1273-1274.

(Homicide - Situational Factors)

Felson, R.B., et al. (1983) Situational factors in dispute leading to criminal violence. *Criminology, 21*(1), 59-74.

(Homicide - Geographic Factors)

Lester, D. (1980) Variation in suicide and homicide rates by latitude and longitude. *Perceptual Motor Skills, 51*(3, part 2), 1346.

(Homicide - Ecological Factors)

Myers, H.P. (1980) *An ecological study of Southern homicide.* Tallahassee: FSU Press.

(Homicide - Environmental)

Block,R. (1980) Community, environment, and violent crime. *Criminology, 17*(1), 46-57.

(Homicide - Lunar Effect)

Lunar effect related to murder and aggression to slight degree. (1978) *Security Letter, 8*(14), 4.

Article copies available from UMI.

(Homicide - Situational Factors)

Luckenbill, D.F. (1977) Criminal homicide as a situated transaction. *Social Problems, 25*(12), 176-185.

(Homicide - Environmental Factors)

Kumasaka, Y., et al. (1975) Crimes in New York and Tokyo: Sociocultural perspectives. *Community Mental Health Journal, 11*(1), 19-26.

(Homicide - Environment)

Arocha, J. (1975) *Environmental and economic determinants of homicide in a coffee-growing municipio.* New York: Columbia University.

(Sociolegal Analysis)

Swigert, V.L. (1975) *Criminal homicide: A sociolegal analysis.* Albany: SUNY.

(Lunar Cycle)

Lynch, R. (1974) Letter: Comments on "homicides and the lunar cycle". *American Journal of Psychiatry, 131*(2), 230.

(Homicide - Lunar Cycle)

Pokorny, A.D., et al. (1974) The questionable relationship between homicides and the lunar cycle. *American Journal of Psychiatry, 131*(7), 827-829.

(Lunar Influence)

Lieber, A.L., et al. (1972) Homicides and the lunar cycle: Toward a theory of lunar influence on human emotional disturbances. *American Journal of Psychiatry, 129*(7), 69-74.

(Homicide - Situational)

Shoham, S. (1972) Points of no return: Some situational aspects of violence, In R.S. Parker (Ed.), *The Emotional Stress of War, Violence, and Peace.* Pittsburgh: Stanwix House.

(Seasonal Variation)

Cerbus, G. (1970) Seasonal variation in some mental health statistics: Suicides, homicides, psychiatric admissions, and institutional placement of the retarded. *Journal of Clinical Psychology, 26*(1), 61-63.

(Homicide - Situational)

Staak, M. (1970) Homicide as a situation-dependent affect (German with English abstract). *Beitr Gerichtl Med, 27,* 144-146.

(Sociological Study)

Gertsenzon, A.A. (1969-1970, Winter) Attempt at a concrete sociological study of the elements of a crime. *Soviet Review, 10,* 35-43.

(Meteorological Effects)

Pokorny, A.D. (1966) Sunspots, suicide, and homicide. *Diseases of the Nervous System, 27*(5),

347-348.

(Environmental Influences)

Pokorny, A.D., et al. (1966) Geomagnetic fluctuations and disturbed behavior. *Journal of Nervous and Mental Disease, 143*(8), 140-151.

(Homicide - Seasonal)

Petersen, G. (1965) On New Year's shootings (Danish). *Ugeskr Laeg, 127*, 1688-1689.

(Meteorological Factors)

Pokorny, A.D., et al. (1964) Homicide and weather. *American Journal of Psychiatry, 120*, 806-808.

(Environmental Factors)

Pokorny, A.D. (1964) Moon phases, suicide, and homicide. *American Journal of Psychiatry, , 121*, 66-67.

(Social Factors)

Littunen, Y., & Gaier, E.L. (1963) Social control and social integration. *International Journal of Social Psychiatry, 9*(3), 165-173.

(Motion Picture Effects)

Llinas, P.A. (1943) An adolescent homicide: The influence of motion pictures and of home and social environment (Spanish). *Rev Med leg Columbia, 6*, 40-47.

Social Causes

(Death Threats)

Jennings, L. (1990, June 13) Death threats linked to desegregation efforts in Duval. *Education Week, 9* (38), 7.

(Growing Up)

Zinsmeister, K. (1990, June) Growing up scared. *Atlantic, 265*(6), pp. 49-66.

(Social Sciences)

Lindheimer, S.K. (1990, April 15) Social Sciences: Law & crime - the sleeping lady. *Library Journal, 115*(7), 108.

(Vengeance)

Otterbein, K. (1990, March) Book reviews: Social/cultural anthropology -- Vengeance is their reply. *American Anthropologist, 92*(1), 245-246.

(Aggression)

Lester, D. (1990) Social correlates of lethal aggression. *Psychological Reports, 66*(2), 146.

(Hawkins Slaying)

N.Y.gunman surrenders in Hawkins slaying; Blacks riot on Brooklyn Bridge. (1989, Sept. 18) *Jet, 76*(24), pp. 7-8.

(Blacks in Washington, DC)

Cassidy, J. (1989, May) War among Washington's Blacks. *World Press Review, 36*, p. 34.

(Homicide - Washington, DC)

Notes and comments (drug murders in Washington, D.C.). (1989, April 17) *The New Yorker, 65*, pp. 29-30.

(Inequality and Homicide)

Messner, S.F. (1989) Economic discrimination and societal homicide rates: Further evidence on the costs of inequality. *American Sociological Review, 54(*4), 597-611.

(Southern Homicide)

Corzine, J., & Huffcorz, L. (1989) On cultural explanations of southern homicide - comment: Note. *American Journal of Sociology, 95*(1), 178-182.

(Killing Not Racial)

Racial link ruled out in killing of NY woman. (1988, Aug. 1) *Jet, 74*(18), p. 18.

(Homicide - Integration)

Lester, D. (1988, June) Status integration and homicide. *Psychology Reports, 62*, 1006.

(Race Riots)

Britt, D.W., & Allen, L. (1988) Homicides and race riots. *Journal of Community Psychology, 16*(4), 119-131.

(Homicide - Juveniles)

Poinsett, A. (1987, Dec.) Why our children are killing one another. *Ebony, 43*, p. 88+.

(Guardian Angels)

Why are there Angels in the Dells? (Guardian Angels in Wisconsin) (1987, Aug. 24) *Newsweek, 110*, p. 12.

(Homicide - Black Youth)

Black Nashville youth killed by whites over $2 vase at flea market (K. Majors). (1987, June 15) *Jet, 72*, p. 36.

(Homicide - Blacks)

Black women report of sex, torture, murder at the hands of a Philadelphia 'bishop' (G. Heidnik case). (1987, April 13) *Jet, 72*, 6-7.

(Idaho Fugitive)

Riley, M. (1987, Jan. 26) In Idaho: A killer becomes a mythic hero (C. Dallas). *Time, 129*, 10-11.

(Homicide and Stress)

Humphrey, J.A., & Palmer, S. (1987) Stressful life events and criminal homicide. *Omega, 17*(4), 299-308.

(Social Characteristics)

Ndetei, D.M., et al. (1987) Some sociopsychological characteristics of criminal homicide in Kenya. *East Africa Medical Journal, 64*(1), 17-30.

(Homicide - New Guinea)

Knauft, B.M. (1987) Reconsidering violence in simple human societies: Homicide among the Gebusi of New Guinea. *Current Anthropology, 28*(4), 457-482.

(Racist Slaying)

Racist killer convicted of slaying of slaying interracial couple (J.P. Franklin). (1986, March 10) *Jet, 69*, p. 16.

(Violence - Social Aspects)

Loftin, C. (1986) Assaultive violence as a contagious social process. *Bulletin of the New York Academy of Medicine, 62*(5), 550-555.

(Prison Overcrowding)

Ekland-Olson, S. (1986) Crowding, social control, and prison violence: Evidence from post-Ruiz years in Texas. *Law & Society Review, 20*(3), 389-421.

(Poverty - Detroit)

McDowell, D. (1986) Poverty and homicide in Detroit, 1926-1978. *Violence and Victims, 1*(1), 23-24.

(Economic Change)

Brenner, M.H., & Swank, R.T. (1986) Homicide and economic change: recent analyses of the Joint Economic Committee report, 1984. *Journal of Quantitative Criminology, 2*(1), 81-103.

(Sociophysiological Aspects)

Sikka, K.D. (1985) Offenders against life: Some sociophysiological aspects. *Indian Journal of Social Work, 46*(2), 243-258.

(Homicide - Sociological)

Nagpaul, H. (1985) Patterns of homicide in North India: Some sociological hypotheses. *International Journal of Offender Therapy and Comparative Criminology, 29*(2), 147-158.

(Male Syndrome)

Wilson, M., & Daly, M. (1985) Competitiveness, risk-taking, and violence: The young male syndrome. Northwestern University symposium on human sociobiology: New research and theory (1981, Evanston, IL). *Ethology and Sociobiology, 6*(1), 59-73.

(Destructiveness - Delegated)

Scharfetter, C. (1984) Ein anliegen der menscheitserziehung: Delegierte destructiveness

(German). *Schweizer Archiv fur Neurology Neurochirurgie und Psychiatrie, 134*(2), 279-293.

(Victims - Solicitation)

Solicitation to commit murder - multiple victims. (1984) *The Criminal Law Reporter: Court Decisions, 34*(23), 2431.

(Individualism)

Messner, S.F. (1984) Durkheim and individualism revisited: Response to Chandler. *Social Forces, 63*(2), 574-575.

(Homicide - Rurality)

Wilkinson, K.P. (1984) A research note on homicide and rurality. *Social Forces, 63*(2), 445-452.

(Poverty and Violence)

Williams, K.R. (1984) Economic sources of homicide: Re-estimating the effects of poverty and inequality. *American Sociological Review, 49*(2), 283-289.

(Homicide - Black-on-Black)

Herndon, W. (1984) Black-on-Black homicide called epidemic. *ADAMHA News, 10*(8), 11.

(Black-on-Black Violence)

Poussaint, A.F. (1983) Black-on-Black violence: A psychological and political perspective. *Victimology, 8*(3-4), 161-169.

(Mass Media)

Phillips, D.P. (1983) The impact of mass media violence on U.S. homicides. *American Sociological Review, 48*(4), 560-568.

(Homicide - Social Ecology)

Massey, C.R. (1983) The social ecology of homicide in Dade County, FL: A modified lifestyle.routine activities perspective. *Dissertation Abstracts International, 43*(12).

(Racial Influences)

Holcomb, W.R., et al. (1983) Racial influences on intelligence and personality measures of people who commit murder. *Journal of Clinical Psychology, 38*(4), 793-796.

(Social Factors)

Messner, S.F. (1982) Societal development, social equality, and homicide: A cross-national test of a Durkheimian model. *Social Forces, 61*(1), 225-240.

(Social Factors)

Hansmann, H.B., et al. (1982) Population heterogeneity and the sociogenesis of homicide. *Social Forces, 61*(1), 206-224.

(Homicide - Press Freedom)

Lester, D. (1981) Freedom of the press and personal violence: A cross-national study of suicide and homicide. *Journal of Social Psychology, 114*(2), 267-269.

(Black-on-Black)

Bowman, P.J. (1980) Toward a duel-market approach to Black-on-Black homicide. *Public Health Reports, 95*(6), 555-556.

(Homicide - Blacks)

Jeff, M.F. (1981) Why Black-on-Black homicide? *Urban League Review, 6*(1), 25-34.

(Genocide - Rural Tones)

Farrell, W.C., Jr., et al. (1979) Determinants of genocide fear in a rural Texas community: A research note. *American Journal of Public Health, 69*(6), 605-607.

(Social Aspects)

Rowe, D. (1978) How language, image, and myth influence behavior. *International Journal of Offender Therapy and Comparative Criminology, 22*(2), 133-139.

(Sociological Aspects)

Henry, A.F., & Short, J.F. Jr. (1977) *Suicide and homicide: Some economic, sociological, and psychological aspects of aggression.* New York: Arno.

(Violence and TV)

Somers, A.R. (1976) Violence, television, and the health of American youth. *New England Journal of Medicine, 294*(15), 811-816.

(Transcultural Attitudes)

Weiss, J.M., et al. (1975) Transcultural attitudes - toward homicide and suicide. *Suicide, 5*(4), 223-227.

(Social Realities)

Wilt, G.M. (1974) *Towards an understanding of the social realities of participants of homicides.* Detroit: Wayne State.

(Sociological Analysis)

Janowska, H. (1974) *Homicides and their perpetrators: Sociological analysis* (Polish). Warsaw: Panstwowe Wydawnictwo Naukowe.

(Sociopsychiatric Analysis)

Bartoszewski, J., & Halaunbrenner-Lisowsk, J. (1973) Sociopsychiatric analysis of infanticides committed in the Warsaw region from 1962 to 1971 (Polish). *Psychiatria Polska, 7*(4), 427-432.

(Violent Society)

Palmer, S. (1972) *The violent society.* College and University Press.

(Homicide - Union Link)

Murder with a union link? (1970, Jan. 6) *US News and World Report, 68*, p. 6.

(Social Problems)

Wolfgang, M.E., (Ed.). (1967) *Studies in homicide.* New York: Harper-Rowe.

(Sociological Analysis)

Wolfgang, M.E. (1961) Sociological analysis of criminal homicide. *Federal Probation, 25*, 48.

(Sociological Phenomenon)

Gillin, J.L. (1952) Murder as a sociological phenomenon. *Annals of the American Academy of Political and Social Sciences, 284*, 20-25.

Religious and Cultural Causes

(Cultural Vengeance)

Otterbein, K. (1990) Social/cultural anthropology -- vengeance is their reply. *American Anthropologist, 92*(1), 245-246.

(Homicide - Zulu Leader)

Hexham, I., & Powe-Hexham, K.O. (1989, June 16) Zulu spiritual leader murdered (the Londaukosi Shembe). *Christianity Today, 33, p. 65.*

(Buddhism and Parricide)

Obeyesekere, G. (1989, June) The conscience of the parricide: A study in Buddhist history. *Man, 24*, 36-54.

(Violence)

Parker, R.N. (1989, June) Poverty, subculture of violence, and type of homicide. *Social Forces, 67*, 983-1007.

(Homicide - Lynches)

Cerio, G. (1989, May 8) Deaths in the name of life (R. & J. Lynch accused of murder and kidnapping in Delaware). *Newsweek, 113*, p. 29.

(Homicide - Religious)

Van Belzen, J.A. (1989) Religion, psychopathology, and murder: Historical and cultural-psychological notes on a controversy (Dutch). *Amsterdams Sociolgisch Tijdschrift, 16*(1), 115-128, reply, 129-131.

(Human Sacrifice)

Graulich, M. (1988) Double immolations in ancient Mexican sacrificial ritual (including ritual decapitation). *Hist Relig, 27*, 393-404.

(Human Sacrifice)

Williams, C. (1988) Asante: Human sacrifice or capital punishment? An assessment of the period 1807-1874 (with discussion). *International Journal of African History Studies, 21*(3), 433-441+.

(Satanist)

Webster, S.L. (1987) Double homicide by a 17-year-old self-described Satanist. *American Journal of Forensic Psychology, 5*(4), 5-20.

(Satanic Murder)

Green, M. (1986, Dec. 1) A boy's love of Satan ends in murder, a death sentence, and grisly memories (case of S. Sellers). *People Weekly, 26*, pp. 154-155+.

(Homicide - Religious Cult)

Johnson, T.E. (1986, Nov. 10) Yahweh's way (sect implicated in Opo-Locka, FL murder). *Newsweek, 108*, p. 13.

(Cultural Correlates)

Rotton, J. (1986) Determinism redux: Climate and cultural correlates of violence. *Environment & Behavior, 18*(3), 346-368.

(Catholic Workers)

Brockman, J.R. (1985, Dec. 7) The passion and death of Mary and Felipe (Catholic workers M. and F. Barreda murdered by the Contras in Nicaragua). *America, 153*, 404-406.

(Mormon Bombings)

Plummer, W. (1985, Nov. 4) Mysterious bombings kill two in Salt Lake City -- and rock the Mormons (M. Hoffman implicated in forged documents case). *People Weekly, 24*, pp. 121-123.

(Mormon Bombings)

Wilentz, A. (1985, Oct. 25) Utah docudrama (bombings connected to controversy surrounding documents challenging the origins of Mormonism). *Time, 126*, p. 48.

(Missionary - El Salvador)

Costello, G.M. (1985, Aug.,) The prime of Miss Jean Donovan(murdered missionary in El Salvador). *U.S. Catholic, 50*, 48-51.

(Church Leaders)

Mumper, S. (1985, Jan. 18) Political insurgents murder Phillipines church leaders. *Christianity Today, 29*, p.52.

(Homicide - India)

Sondhi, S. (1983, Jan.) Dowry deaths in India. *Ms, 11*, p. 22.

(Cannibalistic Acts)

Fellion, G., et al. (1980) From fantasy to reality: Appropos of a transition to criminal and cannibalistic acts (French). *Ann Med Psychol, 138*(5), 596-608.

(Ritualism - India)

Indian police note revival in ritualistic thuggery practice. (1980) *Law Enforcement News, 6*(1), 6.

(Homicide - Supernatural Beliefs)

Aremu, L.O. (1980) Criminal responsibility for homicide in Nigeria and supernatural beliefs. *Int and Comp Lit Quarterly, 29*(1), 112-131.

(Human Sacrifice)

Wimmer, W. (1979) An archaic murder motive (German). *Kriminalistic, 31*(12), 555-556.

(Cultural Factors)

Weiss, J.M. A., & Perry, M.E. (1976) Transcultural attitudes towards antisocial behavior: The worst crimes. *Social Science and Medicine, 10*(11-12), 541-545.

(Sorcery - Premeditated Murder)

Obeyesekere, G. (1975) Sorcery, premeditated murder, and the canalization of of aggression in Sri Lanka. *Ethnology, 14*(1), 1-23.

(Homicide - Sorcery)

O'Regan, R.S. (1974) Sorcery and homicide in Papua New Guinea. *Australian Law Journal, 48*(2), 76-82.

(Religion)

Whitt, H.P., et al. (1972) Religion, economic development, and lethal aggression. *American Sociological Review, 37*(2), 193-201.

(Homicide - Witchcraft)

Scobie, A. (1965) *Murder for magic: Witchcraft in Africa.* London: Cassell.

(Religious Factors - Uganda)

Boccarsino, R. (1963) The religious and social reparation of a murder by the Atsholi in Uganda. 131570. '63, S. 193-199 (IBZ 1967).

(Cultural Factors)

Foot, D. (1959) Ritual murder. *Medicolegal Journal, 27*, 103-113.

(Religious Factors)

Sprague, H.B. (1958) The murder of the penultimate Puritan. *Transactions of the American Physician, 71*, 50-61.

(Homicide - Social Contact)

Svalstoga, K. (1956) Homicide and social contact in Denmark. *American Journal of Sociology, 62*, 37-41.

(Murder in Temple)

Minty, L.M. (1949, Feb.) Murder in the temple. *Sol J, 16*, 39-42.

(Murder - Fanaticism)

Herbertz, R. (1930) A murder resulting from fanaticism for truth (German). *Psychol Rundschau, 2*, 279-284.

Medical

(Halcion-related Psychosis)

Seager, S. (1990, Sept. 4) Man blames Halcion in wife's slaying; suits, complaints, say sleeping pill induces violence; 1st California criminal case. *The Los Angeles Daily Journal, 103*, p. 1.

(Steroid Use)

Pope, H.G., Jr., & Katz, D.L. (1990) Homicide and near-homicide by anabolic steroid users. *Journal of Clinical Psychiatry, 51*(1), 28-31.

(Steroid Use)

Conacher, G.N., et al. (1989) Violent crime possibly associated with anabolic steroid use (letter). *American Journal of Psychiatry, 146*(5), 679.

(Munchausen Syndrome)

Connelly, P.J., et al. (1989) Munchausen syndrome: New cause for concern (letter). *Journal of Clinical Psychiatry, 59*(2), 73.

(Medical Ethics)

Gaylin, W., et al. (1988, April 8) Doctors must not kill. *JAMA, 259*(14), 2139-2140.

(Atypical Rape)

Pontius, A.A. (1988) Limbic system - frontal lobes' role in subtypes of of 'atypical rape'. *Psychology Reports, 63*(3), 879-888.

(Murderer - Nurse)

Gates, D. (1987, Nov. 30) Long Island's 'angel of death' (male nurse R. Angels charged with murder of patients at Good Samaritan Hospital in West Islap. NY). *Newsweek, 110*, p. 35.

(Medical Case)

Brown, S.R., et al. (1987) Primary hypothyroidism, hypercalcemia, paranoid delusions, homicide and attempted murder. *Journal of Forensic Science, 32*(5), 1460-1463.

(Homicide - Insulin Injection)

Haibach, H., et al. (1987) Homicide by insulin administration. *Journal of Forensic Science, 32*(1), 208-216.

(Homicide - Suspicions)

Barber, J. (1986, Sept. 22) Suspicions of murder (potentially lethal doses of digoxin administered at Toronto Western Hospital). *Macleans, 99*, p. 50.

(AIDS)

An attempted murder with a cup of AIDS? (inmates spike corrections officer R. Elliot's coffee with AIDS-infected blood serum in Lake Butler, FL) (1986, Aug. 11) *Newsweek, 108,* p. 24

(Hospital Death)

Binder, G. (1986) Unnatural death in the hospital - some issues of legal evaluation (German with

English abstract). *Zentrlbl Chir, 111*(12), 748-751.

(Capgras Syndrome)

Woytassek, L.E., et al. (1985) Capgras syndrome in court. *Nebraska Medical Journal, 70*(11), 392-394.

(Homicide - 47, XXX Karyotype)

Kazamatsuri, H., et al. (1985) Homicidality in a woman with a 47, XXX karyotype. *Journal of Clinical Psychiatry, 146*(8), 346-347.

(Fatal Medicine)

Hartmann, H., et al. (1985) Fatal incidents in medical activity and their legal evaluation (German with English Abstract). *Beitr Gerlichtl Med, 43*, 31-35.

(Homicide - Inpatient)

Cournos, F. (1985) Staff reaction to an inpatient homicide. *Hospital & Community Psychiatry, 36*(6), 664-666.

(Naptha Injection)

Case, M.E., et al. (1985) Homicide by intravenous injection of naptha. *Journal of Forensic Science, 30*(1), 208-212.

(Manslaughter - Drug Overdose)

Involuntary manslaughter - drug overdose. (1984) *The Criminal Law Reporter: Court Decision, 35*(21), 2388.

(Euthanasia)

MacKinnon, P. (1984) Euthanasia and homicide. *The Criminal Law Quarterly, 26*(4), 483-508.

(Hospital Deaths)

Riley, S. (1983, March 7) Baby deaths without answers (deaths at Toronto's Hospital for Sick Children). *Macleans, 96*, p. 20.

(Holocaust)

Lifton, R.J. (1982) Medicalized killing in Auschwitz. *Psychiatry, 45*(4), 283-297.

(Cause - Aneurysm)

Krauland, W., et al. (1982) Aneurysms of the cerebral arteries at the base of the brain and trauma. *Beitr Gerichtl Med, 40*, 145-161.

(Insulin as Weapon)

Bauman, W.A., et al. Insulin as a lethal weapon. *Journal of Forensic science, 26*(3), 594-598.

(Epilepsy)

Acuda, S.W. (1980) Epilepsy, automatisms, and homicide - a case report (summary in French). *African Journal of Psychiatry, 6*(3-4), 35-38.

(Murderous Propensity)

Hinton, J.W,, et al. Test faking relating to a hormonal index of murderous propensity.

International Journal of Offender Therapy and Comparative Criminology, 23(3), 257-261.

(PMS and Murder)

Singh, S., & A. (1979) The relationship between PMS and murder. *Indian Journal of Criminology, 7*(2), 149-152.

(Biological Factors)

Breier, S., et al. (1978) Contribution to the problem of the correlation between biological and psychological factors in homicide (Czech, with English and Russian summaries). *Cesk Psychiatr, 74*(5), 267-284.

(Homicide - Porphyria)

Trafford, P.A. (1978) Homicide in acute porphyria. *Police Surg, 14*, 65-77.

(Murder - Cardiac Death)

Davis, J.H. (1978) Can sudden cardiac death be murder? *Journal of Forensic Science, 23*(2), 384-387.

(Unexplained Deaths)

Kroll, P., et al. (1977) Denying the incredible: Unexplained deaths in a VA hospital. *American Journal of Psychiatry, 134*(12), 1376-1380.

(Manslaughter - Cerebral Lesions)

Szewczyk, H. (1974) Manslaughter committed by juveniles with cerebral lesions contracted in early childhood (German). *Psychiatrie, Neurologie, and medizinishe Psychologie, 26*(7), 385-394.

(Quackery)

Holder, A.R. (1972, Nov. 27) Homicide by Quackery. *JAMA, 222*, 1219-1220.

(Insulin Murders)

Taylor, L.B. (1970) Insulin murders. *Today's Health, 48*(12), 50-53+.

(Medical Psychosis)

Train, G.J., & Winkler, E.G. (1962) Homicidal psychosis while under ACTH: Corticosteroid therapy for pemphigus vulgaris during involution. *Psychomatics, 3*(4), 317-322.

(Insulin Poisoning)

Birkinshaw, V.J., et al. (1958) Investigations in a case of murder by insulin poisoning. *British Medical Journal, 5094*, 463-468.

(Murder - Puberty)

Petrova, A.E. (1930) A murder committed during the period of puberty (German) *Montassch f. Krimpsychol u Strafrechtsref, 21*, 592-607.

(Murder)

Murder by acceleration of death (Rex v. Davies). *Law Times, 164*, 348-349 (1927, Nov. 5); *Law Notes, 31*, 217 (1928).

Jealousy

(Revenge Killings)

Lamar, J.V., Jr. (1986, Sept. 1) "Crazy Pat's" revenge (postman P.H. Sherrill kills co-workers in Edmond, OK). *Time, 128*, p. 19.

(Jealousy)

Sommavilla, F. (1977) Criminologic and clinical aspects of jealousy crimes in old age (Italian with English abstract). *Med Mil, 127*(5-6), 513-519.

(Jealousy)

Psarska, A.D. (1970) Jealousy factor in homicide in forensic psychiatric material (Polish). *Psychiat Pol, 4*, 9-15; *Pol Medical Journal, 9*, 1504-1510.

(Jealousy)

Mowat, R.R. (1966) *Morbid jealousy and murder*. Barnes and Noble.

(Jealousy)

Podolsky, E. (1965) The jealous murderer. *Journal of Forensic Medicine, 12*(1), 35-40.

(Jealousy)

Podolsky, E. (1961) Jealousy as a motive in homicide. *Diseases of the Nervous System, 22*(8), 438-441.

(Provocation - Adultery)

Miller, H.B., Jr. (1949, March) Manslaughter - adultery as provocation. *Kentucky Law Journal, 37*, 288-293.

(Murder - Jealousy)

Ortiz Velasquez, J. (1945) A psychological study of a murderer activated by jealousy (Spanish). *Ann Acad Med Medellin 1945*(1), 639-643.

(Crimes - Jealousy)

Di Frisco, S. (1934) The state of doubt and the state of certainty in relation to crimes caused by jealousy (Italian). *Arch Antrop Crim, 54*, 708-713.

Political

(Political Vengeance)

Masland, T. (1990, Oct. 29) Israel's cycle of vengeance. *Newsweek, 116*(18), p. 53.

(South Africa Murder)

Gevisser, M. (1990, Oct. 2) Mummie dearest. *Village Voice, 35*(40), pp. 31-34.

(South Africa)

South Africa: The halo slips. (1990, Sept. 22) *Economist, 316*(7673), p. 49.

(Indonesia Murders)

Still waiting. (1990, June 1) *Commonwealth, 117*(11), 340-341.

(Psychosis)

State of psychosis. (1990, May 25) *New Statesman & Society, 3*(102), p. 5.

(Murder of Journalists)

Saltzman, J. (1990, March) The riskiest profession. *USA Today: The Magazine of the American Scene, 118*(2538), p. 53.

(Terrorism - Egypt)

Mulligan, J.E. (1990, Feb. 17) The blood of martyrs: The seed of hope and commitment. *America, 162*(6), pp. 145-146.

(Terrorism - Arab)

Israel: Ambushing the peace bus. (1990, Feb. 10) *Economist, 314*(7641), pp. 41-42.

(Sandinistas)

Bozell, L.B., III. (1990, Feb. 5) Murder in Masatape. *National Review, 42*(2), pp. 22-23.

(Students Murdered)

The warlords. (1989, June 26) *Nation, 248*(25), pp. 871-872.

(Party's Rights)

The party's inhuman rights. (1989, June 17) *Economist, 311*(7607), p. 40.

(Political Killings)

Thomsen, J.L., et al. (1989, June 17) Medicolegal investigation of political killings in El Salvador. *Lancet, 8651*, pp. 1377-1379.

('Greenkill' Case)

Bardolph, R. (1988) Book reviews: Code name Greenkill. *Journal of American History, 75*(3), 1035.

(Apartheid)

Gunning for apartheid. (1988, Nov. 28) *Time, 132*(22), p. 73.

(South Africa - Death Row)

South Africa: On and off death row. (1988, Nov. 26) *Economist, 309*(7578), pp. 44-49.

(Con Man)

Farber, M.A. (1987, June 21) The con man (FBI informant M. Raymond). *New York Times Magazine*, p. 34+.

(Rodrigo Rojas)

Sinnott, J.P. (1986, Aug. 27) At the funeral of Rodrigo Rojas (Chile). *Christian Century, 103*, 733-734.

(U.S. - Chile Relations)

Chile: A grisly murder strains U.S. relations (murder of R. Rojas de Negri). (1986, July 21) *Newsweek, 108*, p. 26.

(D.C. Mayor's Aide)

Aide to D.C. Mayor Barry strangled, burned in home (P.R. Gee). (1986, July 7) *Jet, 70*, p. 54.

(Terrorism)

Vought, D.B., & Fraser, J.H., Jr. (1986, July) Terrorism: The search for working definitions. *Military Review, 66*(7), 70-76.

(Political Murders)

Lyons, H.A., & Harbinson, H.J., Jr. (1986) A comparison of political and nonpolitical murders in Northern Ireland. *Medical Science and Law, 26*(3), 193-198.

(H. Liu Case)

Smith, P. (1985, May 18) In Taiwan, many questions remain. *Nation, 240*, 587-590.

(Khitrichenko Case)

High noon (Soviet diplomat V. Khitrichenko murdered in India). (1985, April 1) *Time, 125*, p. 46.

(Murder - Reporter)

Hitchens, C. (1985, Feb. 16) Minority report (suspicious murder of American reporter G. Polk during Greek Civil War). *Nation, 240, p. 166.*

(H. Liu Case)

Ellison, K.A. (1985, Feb. 4) A deadly style of diplomacy (murder of H. Liu). *Macleans, 98*, p. 37.

(Terrorists - El Salvador)

Reagan, R (1985) U.S. citizens killed by terrorists in El Salvador. *Department of State Bulletin, 85*(2101), 82-87.

(Political Killings)

Political killings by government of their citizens: Hearing, Nov. 16-17, 1983. (1984) Washington, DC: U.S. Government Printing Office.

(Presidential Elections)

Boor, M., & Fleming, J. (1984) Reductions in suicide and accident levels prior to presidential elections are independent of unemployment levels. *Journal of Social Psychology, 124*(1), 119-121.

(Terrorists - Arab)

Reagan, R. (1983) Terrorist attack against U.S. forces in Beirut. *Department of State Bulletin, 83*(2081), 40-43.

(Black-on-Black Homicide)

Poussaint, A.F. (1983) Black-on-black homicide: A psychological-political perspective. *Victimology, 8*(3-4), 161-169.

(Anti-Khomeini Leader)

Killing one's enemies (Bethesda, MD slaying of anti-Khomeini group leader. (1980, Aug. 4) *Time, 116*, p. 38.

(Murder - Saudi Arabia)

Mather, I. (1980, Sept. 22) Keeping an eye on scandal (implications of murder surrounding British expatriates Richard and Penny Arnot in Saudi Arabia). *Macleans, 93*, pp. 33-34.

(Kidnapping)

Middendorff, W. (1974) New developments in hostage-taking and kidnapping. Criminologic experience and criminal policy needs. Parts I. and II. (German) *Polizeiblatt, 37*(10), 146-150; *37*(11), 166-170.

(Homicide - Political)

Zellweger, E. (1970) Murder of hostages -- a political crime (German)? 37335. J. 38, '70, N. 16, S. 1 (IBZ 1971).

(Deaths of Hostages)

High cost in blackmail: Kidnappings and deaths of hostages at San Rafael, CA and Uruguay. (1970, Aug. 25) *National Review, 22*, p. 880+.

(Violence - Political)

Brennis, S. (1968) Violences et crimes politiques (violence and political crimes). 25758. Vol. 11, '68, n. 9, p. 126-132 (IBZ 1971).

(Political Homicide)

Spett, K. (1968, Jan.-Feb.) Mentally ill as perpetrators of political homicide (Polish). *Psychiat Pol, 2*, 77-80.

(Political Murder)

Brundi. (1965) Politischer mord. 1060. J. 7, '65, S. 51-52 (IBZ 1966).

(Political Homicide)

Friedrich, P. (1962) Assumptions underlying Tarascan political homicide. *Psychiatry, 25*(4), 315-327.

Robbery

(Robbery/Murder - New York)

Wadler, J., et al. (1990, Sept. 24) Death of an out-of-towner. *People Weekly, 34*(12), pp. 74-80.

(Children - Ransom)

Muller-Kuppers, M. (1988) The ransom paid for children (German). *Z Kinder Jugenpsychiatr, 16*(2), 59-60.

(Robbery Victims)

Zimring, F.E., Zuel, J. (1986) Victim injury and death in urban robbery: A Chicago study. *The Journal of Legal Studies, 15*(1), 1-40. Article copies available from UMI.

(Robbery/Murder)

Cook, P.J. (1985) Is robbery becoming more violent? An analysis of robbery/murder trends since 1968. *The Journal of Criminal Law and Criminology, 76*(2), 480-498.

(Motivation - Rape/Robbery)

East Coast, father and son rape, robbery team arrested. (1975) Juvenile Justice Digest, 3(3), 6.

(Motivation - Ransom)

Businessman kidnapped, murdered despite payment of ransom. (1975) Security Systems Digest, 6(21), 3.

(Homicide - Related Offenses)

Arthur, C. (1972, Spring) Homicide, assault, kidnapping, and related offenses. *Oregon Law Review, 51*, 459.

(Robbery/Murder)

Spenlingwimmer, U. (1971) Robbery murder solved after 42 years (German). 20957. J. 25, '71, 8 S. 426-428 (IBZ 1973).

(Robbery/Murder)

Fattah, E.B. (1967) The place of robbery/murder in the hierarchy of crime (German). 24232. J. 50, '67, H. 2, S. 49-60 (IBZ 1968).

(Robbery/Murder)

Murder done in the course of theft (Regina v. Jones, 1959 2 W L R 190). (1959, April) *Law Quarterly Review, 75*, 164.

(Homicide - Insurance)

Jordan, E. (1945, July) Murder for insurance money. *Insurance Law Journal 1945*, 387-390.

Causes - Epilepsy

(Epilepsy - Violence)

Hindler, C.G. (1989) Epilepsy and violence. *British Journal of Psychiatry, 155*(8), 246-249.

(Temporal Lobe Epilepsy)

Pontius, A.A. (1989) Subtypes of limbic system dysfunction evoking homicide in limbic psychotic trigger reaction and temporal lobe epilepsy - evolutionary constraints. *Psychology Reports, 65*(2), 659-671.

(Epileptic Case)

Martinius, J., & Strunk, P. (1979) Homicide of an aggressive adolescent with right temporal lobe lesion: A case study (German). *Z Kinder Judend Psychiatr, 7*(3), 199-207.

(Epileptic Homicide)

Bartholomew, A.A., et al. (1978, Dec.) Epileptic homicide (letter). *British Journal of Psychiatry, 133*, 564-565.

(Parricide and Epilepsy)

Neyraut-Sutterman, T. (1970) Parricide and epilepsy: Apropos of an article by Freud on Dostoevski (French). *Rev Fr Psychoanal, 34*, 635-652.

(Epileptic Seizure)

Schipkowensky, N. (1970) Epileptic seizures and homicide. 3. Homicide during pathological drowsiness (German). *Nauchni Tr Vissh Med Inst Sofia, 49*, 49-58.

(Epilepsy and Crime)

Bogicevic, D. (1968) Epileptics and crime (Croatian). *Neuropsihijatrija, 16*, 37-44.

(Epilepsy - Murder)

Drink, epilepsy, murder, and amnesia. (1960, Feb.27) *Brit Med J*, 5173, 565-567.

(Neurological Illness)

Winkler, E.G., & Train, G.J. (1959, July-Sept.) Acts of violence with EEG changes. *Journal of Clinical and Experimental Psychopathology, 20*, 223-230.

Causes - Self-Defense

(Assailant Killed)

Quinn, J. (1989, March 15) Anchor saved as her B.F. shoots and kills assailant. *Variety, 334*(8), p. 44.

(Police Shooting)

Langworthy, R.H. (1986) Police shooting and criminal homicide: The temporal relationship. *Journal of Quantitative Criminology, 2*(4), 377-388.

(Precipitated Homicide)

Dietz, P.E. (1977) Medical criminology notes, 1: Victim-precipitated criminal homicide. *Bulletin of the American Academy of Psychiatry and Law, 5*(3), 367-370.

(Killing - Defense)

Sullivan, S.J. (1976) *Killing in defense of private property: The development of a Roman Catholic moral teaching, thirteenth to eighteenth centuries.* Scholars Press.

Money or Property

(Doctors)

Kass, L.R. (1989, Winter) Neither for love or money: Why doctors must not kill. *Public Interest, 94*, 25-46.

(Emeralds - Mystique)

Ward, F. (1989) The timeless mystique of emeralds. *National Geographic, 178*(1), pp. 38-69.

(Dowry Deaths)

McCoid, C.H. (1989) *Dowry deaths in India: A materialistic analysis.* East Lansing, MI: Michigan State University.

(Family Murder)

Wadler, J. (1987, July 6) Family business: Murder would settle it and Debra Banister knew who to ask (hit man J.W. Hearn). *People Weekly, 28*, pp. 57-58+.

(Forger Guilty)

Wilentz, A. (1987, Feb. 2) A Latter-Day forger (Mormon M. Hoffman pleads guilty to murder). *Time, 129*, p. 32.

(Dowry Murders)

Bordewich, F.M. (1986, July) Dowry murders (India). *Atlantic, 258*, p. 21+.

(Hitmen)

Hammer, J., & Demaret, K. (1986, May 26) Want ads in *Soldier of Fortune* magazine lead a blundering gang of alleged killers to their victims. *People Weekly, 25*, pp. 38-40+.

(Burnt Wife Syndrome)

Das Gupta, S.M., et al. (1984, Jan.) Burnt wife syndrome. *Annals of Academy of Medicine of Singapore*, 37-42.

(Dowry Murders)

Khan, M.Z., & Ray, R. (1984) Dowry death. *Indian Journal of Social Work, 45*(3), 303-315.

(Homicide and Property Crimes)

Stack, S. (1983) Homicide and property crime: The relationship to anomie. *Aggressive Behavior, 9*(4), 339-344.

(Money)

Dietz, M.L. (1983) *Killing for profit: The social organization of felony homicide*. Nelson-Hall.

(Theft and Criminality)

D'Hondt, W., & Vadewiele, M. (1983) Senagalese adolescents and the need to control theft and criminality. *Journal of Adolescence, 6*(4), 329-332.

(Homicide - Money)

Thompson, T. (1977) *Blood and money*. Dell.

(Property)

Murderer's interest in his victims property. (1956, Fall) *Alabama Law Review, 9*, 58.

(Hitmen)

Turkus, B.B., & Feder, S. (1972) *Murder, Inc*. Manor Books.

(Property)

Potter, R.L. (1961) Acquisition of property by homicide. *University of Detroit Law Journal, 38*, 360.

(Property)

Woerner, W.F. (1924) Self-made heirship through murder. *St. Louis Law Review, 10*, 34.

Animosity

(Israel and Palestine)

Masland, T. (1990, Oct. 29) Israel's cycle of violence. *Newsweek, 116*(18), p. 53.

(Family Murder)

Schroeder, A. (1990, March) Eric, Tyrone, and Michael. *Saturday Night, 105*(2), pp. 25-36.

(Victim - Judge)

Kasindorf, J. (1988, Aug. 1) Last judgment. *New York, 21*(30), pp. 24-33.

(PSA Crash)

Hackett, G. (1987, Dec. 21) Settling a score (murders aboard PSA airliner linked to USAir ex-employee D. Burke). *Newsweek, 110*, p. 43.

(Vengeance)

Hackett, G. (1987, Aug. 17) Pennsylvania gothic (death of K. Umstadter in alcohol-related traffic accident results in her brother murdering the driver in Honesdale). *Newsweek, 110*, p. 27.

(C. Armstrong Case)

Chicago publisher fatally shot and his son wounded (case of C. Armstrong). (1985, April 8) *Jet, 68*, p. 11.

(Implied Malice)

Murder - use of human shield - implied malice. (1978) *The Criminal Law Reporter: Court Decisions and Proceedings, 23*(10), 2221-2222.

(Overcontrolled Hostility)

Lester, D., et al. (1978, Dec.) Murderers and overcontrolled hostility. *Psychology Reports, 43*(3, pt. 2), 1202.

(Duress)

Mewett, A.W. (1975) Duress and mens rea. *The Criminal Law Quarterly, 17*(4), 352-354.

(Personal Violence)

Yager, J. (1975) Personal violence in infantry combat. *Archives of General Psychiatry, 32*(2), 257-261.

(Blood Revenge)

Karan, M. (1972) Blood revenge and position of psychiatry in the study of the phenomenon (Croatian with English abstract). *Neuropsihijatrija, 20*, 363-367.

(Hostility and Aggression)

Blackburn, R. (1972) Dimensions of hostility and aggression in abnormal offenders. *Journal of Consulting and Clinical Psychology, 38*(1), 20-26.

(Motive - Malicious)

Murder indicators particularly "malicious" and "base" motives. 20171. J. 11, '71, H. 12, S. 626-

631 (IBZ 1972).

(Motives - Malicious)

Schaffstein, F. (1966) Explanation of the concept "malicious killing" as murder indicators. 5564K. '66, S. 419-431 (IBZ 1966).

(Resentment)

Salwa, W. (1965) The role of the feeling of resentment in the criminal acts of some killers (Polish). *Neurol Neurochir Psychiat Pol, 15*, 325-330.

(Murder - Perjury)

Hogan, J.C. (1961, Dec.) Murder by perjury. *Fordham Law Rev, 30*, 285.

(Intimacality)

Mazza, A., & Benassi, P. (1961, June 30) Psychopathological and developmental aspects of morbid jealousy and its relation to criminality (Italian). *Riv Sper Freniat, 85*, 285-313.

(Malice)

Williams, G. (1960) Constructive malice revived. *Modern Law Review, 23*, 605.

(Malice)

Murdock, L.B. (1934, Oct.) Malice aforethought (Ramsey v. State of Florida, 154 So 855). *Journal of Criminal Law, 25*, 454-457.

(Malice)

Garrigues, J.E. (1922) Murder and malice - express and implied. *Cent L J, 94*, 114.

(Malice)

Brown, W.F.W. (1909) Constructive murder and felonious intent: The place of malice in crimes. *Law Magazine and Review, 34*, 453.

No Motive or Impulsive

(Beyond Reason)

Walter, S.G. (1990) Social Sciences: Law & Crime -- beyond reason. *Library Journal, 115*(7), 107.

(Winetka Tragedy)

Bultman, J. (1989, May) Diary of a tragedy (L. Dann's shooting spree in Winetka, IL school in 1988). *Parents, 64*, 105-110.

(Impulsive)

Best friend killed in argument over cockroach. (1988, Aug. 29) *Jet, 74*, p. 12.

(Motiveless)

Holcomb, W.R., & Daniel A.E. (1988) Homicide without apparent motive. *Behavioral Science and Law, 6*(3), 429-437.

(Murder - No Motive)

Serial murders: hearing, July 12, 1983, on patterns of murders committed by one person, in large numbers with no apparent rhyme, reason, or motivation. (1983) Hearing before United States Senate, Committee on the Judiciary, Subcommittee on Juvenile Justice. Washington, DC: U.S. Government Printing Office.

(Necrophilia)

James, I.P. (1979, Jan.) Necrophilia, murder, and high intelligence (letter). *British Journal of Psychiatry, 134*, 125-126.

(Necrophilia)

Fullerton, A.G. (1978, Oct.) Necrophilia, murder, and high intelligence (letter). *British Journal of Psychiatry, 133*, 382-383.

(Motiveless)

Gallemore, J.L., Jr., et al. (1976) Motiveless public assassins. *Bulletin of the American Academy of Psychiatry and Law, 4*(1), 51-57.

(Killing Urge)

Damio, W. (1974) *Urge to kill.* Pinnacle Books.

(No Motive)

Burkart, F. (1972) A senseless murder (German). 20957. J. 26, '72, 1, S. 34-36 (IBZ 1973).

(Murder Motives)

Szymusik, A. (1971, Sept.) Motives of murder and the personality of murderers (Polish with English abstract). *Przegl Lek, 27*, 579-581.

(Manslaughter - Involuntary)

Amboss, M., et al. (1971, March) Involuntary manslaughter through violation of medical legal responsibility (German). *Dtsch Gesundheitsw, 26*, 465-468.

(Motiveless)

Shenken, L.I. (1964) The implications of ego psychology for a motiveless murder. *Journal of the American Academy of Child Psychiatry, 3*(10), 741-744.

(Impulsive)

Lander, J., et al. (1963) Homicide, acting out, and impulse. *American Journal of Orthopsychiatry, 33*(10), 928-930.

(Motiveless)

Podolsky, E. (1956) Notes on motiveless murder. *International Journal of Social Psychiatry, 1*(4), 42-45.

(Murders - Unmotivated)

Guiraud, P. (1931) Unmotivated murders (French). *L'Evolution Psychiatrique 1931*, 23-34.

(Motiveless)

Absence of motive. (1927, July 23) *Justice of the Peace, 91*, 561-562.

Chapter 7
Investigations
General

(Jesuit - Murder)

Bennett, P. (1990, Nov.) Burying the Jesuits. *Vanity Fair, 53*(11), pp. 110-123.

(Arabs Deaths)

Masland, T. (1990, Oct. 29) Israel's cycle of vengeance. *Newsweek, 116*(18), pp. 53.

(Criminalistic Traces)

Markiewicz, J. & Chlobowska, Z. (1990) Specific features of poisoning (Symposium of forensic sciences 'Criminalistic Traces"). *Forensic Science International, 46, pp* 3-5.

(Photographer's Death)

Photographer's death abroad is investigated. (1989, Oct. 28) *Editor &I Publisher, 122,* (43), p. 39.

(Murder - Witness)

Royal, J. (1989, Oct.) The littlest victim. *Life, 12*(11), p. 39.

(TV Investigation)

Jacoby, T. (1989, June 12) Murder they broadcast. *Newsweek, 113*(24), p. 58.

(Investigative Journalism)

Indiana, G. (1989, April 11) Blood Simplistic. *Village Voice, 34*(15), pp. 57-58.

(Supervision - Investigation)

Geberth, V.J. (1989) Supervision and management of a homicide investigation. *Law and Order, 37*(11), 85-92.

('Disappeared' Victims)

Raymond, C. (1989) Forensic experts tackle task of identifying thousands of 'disappeared' victims (news). *JAMA, 26*(10), 1388-1389.

(Injuries - Finding)

Pollak, S. (1989) Pattern of finding in injuries caused by "survival". *Arch Kriminol, 183*(1-2),

11.

(Murder - Prove)

Carl, L.C. (1989) Statistics alone can't prove murder (letter). *Am J Nurs, 89*(7), 931.

(Homicide - Validity)

Maxfield, M.G. (1989) Circumstances in supplementary homicide reports: Variety and validity. *Criminology, 27,* 671-695.

(Spectacle)

Indiana, G. (1988, Oct.) Spectacle: Hurting. *Village Voice, 33*(10), pp. 1327-1332.

(Cover-up)

Stalker, J. (1988) *The stalker affair: The shocking true story of six deaths and a notorious cover-up.* New York: Viking.

(Nurses Accused)

Yorker, B.C. (1988) Nurses accused of murder. *American Journal of Nursing, 88*(10), 1327-1332.

(Swamp - Murder)

Murphy, G.K. (1988) Birchall and Benwell. Murder in a Canadian swamp. *Am J Forensic Med Pathol, 9*(3), 255-257.

(Workplace - Homicide)

Davis, H. (1988) The accuracy of industry data from death certificates for workplace homicide victims. *Am J Pub He, 78*(12), 1579-1581.

(Killer - Search)

Corelli, R. (1987, Oct.) Search for a serial killer (Ontario). *Macleans, 100,* pp 54.

(Dream)

Green, M. (1987, May 25) A vision of murder (S. Linscott tried for murder on basis of dream). *People Weekly, 27,* pp. 30-32.

(Scene - Investigation)

Wecht, C.H. (1987) Homicide investigation - importance of scene visit by forensic pathologist. *Leg Med, 45,* 331-338.

(Criminal - Energy)

Bohm, E., et al. (1987) Criminal and kinetic energy in homicides caused by blunt forces (German). *Beitr Gerichtl Med, 45,* 331-338.

(Expert Evidence)

Gerber, P. (1987) Playing dice with expert evidence: The lessons to emerge from Regina v. Chamberlain. *Med J Aust, 147*(5), 243-247.

(Mexico - Reporters)

Alter, J. (1986, Nov. 17) Reporters under the gun (Mexico). *Newsweek, 108*, pp 62.

(Crime - Scene)

Wagner, G.N. (1986) Crime scene investigation in child-abuse cases. *Am J Forensic Med Pathol, 7*(2), 94-99.

(Trial -Evidence)

Prichard, J.G., et al. (1986) Implications of trombiculid mite bites: Report of evidence in a murder trial. *J Forensic Sci, 31*(1), 301-306.

(Organized - Crime)

Did Carmine Persico fire the shot that killed Al Anastasia? (1986) *Organized Crime Digest, 7*(6), 6. Microforms and article copies available from UMI.

(Sensational - Homicides)

Geberth, V.J. (1986) Mass serial and sensational homicides. *Law and Order, 34*(1), 20-22. Microforms and article copies available from UMI.

(Trace Evidence)

Petraco, N. (1986) Trace evidence - the invisible witness. *J Forensic Sci, 31*(1), 321-328.

(Splatt - Case)

Davis, R.J. (1986) The Splatt case. *J Forensic Sci Soc, 26*(3), 219-221.

(Gang - Investigations)

Doughtie, J.A. (1986) Motorcycle gang investigations: a team effort. *FBI Law Enf Bul, 55*(8), 19-22.

(Interrogation - Miranda)

Higginbottham, J. (1986) Interrogation: Post Miranda refinements (part I). *FBI Law Enf Bul, 55*(2), 23-30.

(Searches)

Anderson, W. (1985, Fall) Inventory searches. *Mil Law Review, 110*, 95-114.

(Raids - Quebec)

Burke, D. (1985, Aug. 5) New raids on the Angels (murders of Hell's Angers members in Quebec). *Macleans, 98*, pp 41.

(Murder - Scene)

Supreme court reaffirms Mincey v. Arizona, Rejects warrantless murder scene searches. (1985) *Search and Seizure Law Report, 12*(2), 108.

(Search - Murder Scene)

There is no "Murder Scene" exception to the search warrant requirement. (1985) *Criminal Law*

Bulletin, 21(3), 254-255. Microforms and article copies available from UMI.

(Court - Warrant)

Triewasser, J. (1985) Supreme Court briefs: Warrant, Warrant, Who's Got the Warrant? *Law Enforcement News, 11*(5), 7, 12. Microforms and article copies available from UMI.

(Crime Scenes)

Classifying sexual homicide crime scenes: Inter-rater reliability: Chapter 3. (1985) *FBI Law Enf Bul, 54*(8), 12-17.

(Interviewing Techniques)

Interviewing techniques for homicide investigations: chapter 5. (1985) *FBI Law Enf Bul, 54*(8), 26-31.

(Crime Scene)

Crime scene and profile characteristics of organized and disorganized murders: Chapter 4. (1985) *FBI Law Enf Bul, 54*(8), 18-25.

(Investigations - Forensic Anthropologist)

Sauer, N.J., et al. (1984) Clarifying the role of forensic anthropologist in death investigations. *J Forensic Sci, 29*(4), 1253-1259.

(Approach - Forensic)

Davis, J.H., et al. (1984) A forensic science approach to a starved child. *J Forensic Sci, 29*(2), 663-669.

(Murder - Revealed)

Mehrotra, V.K., et al. (1984) Murder revealed by a broken piece of glass bangle: A case report. *Med Sci Law, 24*(3), 179-180.

(Unsuccessful Murder)

Prathnadi, S. (1983) An unsuccessful murder. *J Forensic Sci, 28,* (1), 285-286.

(Computer Track)

National computer bank sought to track mass murderers. (1983) *Juvenile Justice Digest,11*(14), 2. Microforms and article copies available from UMI.

(Mass Murder Cases)

Police in Washington, Illinois dealing with mass murder cases. (1983) *Crime Control Digest, 17*(47), 9-10. Microforms and article copies available from UMI.

(Findings - Incidental)

Jones, A.M. & Chapman, A.J. (1983) Intramural ventricular fibroma of the heart. Incidental findings in a homicide victim. *Am J Forensic Med Pathol, 4,* (1), 73-77.

(Homicidal Aggression - Diagnosis)

Lewis, D. O., et al. (1983) Homicidally aggressive young children: Neuropsychiatric and experiential correlates. *American Journal of Psychiatry, 140*(2), 148-153.

(Forensic Odyssey)

Buikstra, J.E. (1982) A forensic odyssey. *Criminal Justice Review, 7*(1), 7-10. Microforms and article copies available from UMI.

(Detectives - Training)

Forensic archaeology training may be just what your homicide detective needs. (1982) *Training Aids Digest, 7*(12), 5-6. Microforms and article copies available from UMI.

(Evidence - Photographs)

Admission of gruesome photographs in homicide prosecutions. (1982-1983) *Creighton L Rev, 16,* pp 73-89.

(Psychiatric Evaluation)

Langevin, R., et al. (1982) Diagnosis of killers seen for psychiatric assessment: A controlled study. *Acta Psychiatrica Scandinavica, 66*(3), 216-228.

(Investigation - Woman Killer)

Kromm, J., et al. (1982) Occupational therapy in the assessment of a woman accused of murder. *Psychiatric Quarterly, 54*(2), 85-96.

(Investigation - No Body)

Homicide - Sufficiency of evidence - Failure to find victim's body. (1982)*The Criminal Law Reporter Court Decisions, 32*(2), 2033.

(Evidence - Scientific)

Dowling, D.C. (1982) Scientific evidence; a vital role in homicide cases. *Trial 18*, pp 34-37.

(Homicide - Cop)

Hirschfield, N. (1982) *Homicide cop: The true story of Carolann.* Berkeley Pub.

(Forensic Medicine)

Buikstra, J.E. (1982) A Forensic Odyssey. *Criminal Justice Review, 7*(1), 7-10. Microfilms and article copies available from UMI.

(Investigation - Psychiatrist)

Danto, B.L. (1982) The psychiatrist and violent death investigation. *The American Journal of Forensic Medicine and Pathology, 3*(1), 29-33.

(Homicide Investigation - News Media)

Geberth, V.J. (1981) The news media in homicide investigation. *Law and Order, 29*(7), 46-53.

(Investigation - Handwriting)

Totty, R.N. (1981) A case of handwriting on an unusual surface. *Journal of the Forensic Science Society, 21*(4), 349-350.

(Investigation - Death Scene)

Beyer, J.C., et al. (1981) Homicide investigation. Death scene checklist. *FBI Law Enforcement Bulletin, 50*(8), 14-18.

(Investigation - Homicide)

Gossweiner-Saiko, T. (1981) General data on the nature and functions of interrogation in homicidal offenses. *Rundschau Gendarm, 33*(12), 3-5 & *34*(1), 4-5.

(Homicidal Investigation)

Southwestern Law Enforcement Institute (1981) *Homicide investigation techniques personal experience accounts of professionals & experts.* C.C. Thomas.

(Detecting - Method)

Helpern, M. (1981) History of the methods of detecting murder. *Am J Forensic Med Path, 2*(1), 61-65.

(Handwriting - Surface)

Totty, R.N. (1981) A case of handwriting on an unusual surface. *J Forensic Sci Soc, 21(4), 349-350.*

(Death Scene)

Beyer, J.C. & Enos, W.F. (1981) Death scene checklist. *FBI Law Enf Bul, 50*(8), 14-18.

(Bloodstain Morphology)

Legault, D.E. (1980) An unusual bloodstain morphology. *J Can Soc Forensic Sci, 13*(2), 36-37.

(Scene - Search)

Fox, R.H. et al. (1980) Search of the homicide scene. *Legal Med, 1980,* 21-29.

(Informers)

Gettinger, S. (1980) Informer. *Corrections Magazine, 6*(2), 17-19.

(Forensic Service)

Tabakman, M. (1980) Forensic medical service in the U.S.S.R. *Am J Forensic Med Pathol, 1*(3), 271-276.

(Forensic Pathology)

Raekallio, J. (1980) Estimation of time in forensic biology and pathology. An Introductory review. *Am J Forensic Med Pathol, 1*(3), 213-218.

(Magrath, G.B. - A Tribute)

Tedeshchi, L.G. (1980) George Burgess Magrath. Tribute to a resting lion. *Am J Forensic Med Pathol, 1*(2), 169-172.

(Investigation)

Fox, R.H., Sr. et al. (1980) Search of the homicide scene. *Leg Med,* pp 21-29.

(Warrant Requirement)

"Homicide scene" exception to the fourth amendment warrant requirement: a dead issue? (1980) *J Crim L, 71,* 289-299.

(Murder Scene Searches)

Warrantless murder scene searches in the aftermath of Mincey v Arizona (98 Sup. Ct. 2408). (1980) *Wash U L Q, 58, 367-408.*

(Buried Body)

Boyd, R.M. (1979) Buried Body cases. *FBI Law Enf Bul, 48*(2), 1-7.

(Crime Scene)

Geberth, V. (1979) The homicide crime scene, Parts I and II. *Law Order, 27*(7), 38-40, 42-46, 48 & *27*(8), 28-38.

(Searches - Warrantless)

Sholder, J.M. (1979) Murder scene warrantless searches: a proposal. *Arizona Law Rev. 21*(3), 777-793.

(Hostage Murder Investigation)

Berg, S. et al. (1982) Determination of the duration of length of time of incarceration before killing the hostage. 3647. bd. 164, '79, h. 5-6, s. 153-206 (IBZ 1982).

(Investigation - FBI)

Fratianno, J. (1978, Feb. 20) Nabbing the .22 cal killers: FBI informer. *Time, 111*, p. 27.

(Homicide - England)

Forbes, T.R. (1977) Inquests into London and Middlesex homicides, 1673-1782. *Yale J Biol Med, 50*(2), 207-220.

(Squeal Man)

Flusser, M. (1977) *The Squeal Man.* Morrow.

(Homicide - Sudan)

Malik, M.O.A. & Sawi, O. (1976) A profile of homicide in the Sudan. *Forensic Sci* (Lausanne), *7*(2), 141-150.

(Homicide - Iceland)

Hansen, J.P.H. & Bjarnason, O. (1974) Homicide in Iceland 1946-1970. *Forens Sci, 4*(2), 107-

117.

(Gunpowder Residue)

Barnes, F.C. & Helson, R.A. (1974) An empirical study of gunpowder residue patterns. *J Forensic Sci, 19*(3), 448-462.

(Homicide - Pathology)

Adelson, Lester. (1974) *The pathology of homicide: a vade mecum for pathologist, Prosecutor and Defense Counsel.* C.C. Thomas.

(Detection of Murder)

Kilgor, D.G., Jr. (1974) President's pages. Will murder out? *J SC Med Assoc, 70*(11), 367-368.

(Homicide Investigation)

Cawley, D.F. (1974) Homicide Investigation. *Police Chief, 41*(4), 67.

(Railway Fatalities)

Jaegermann, K. & Packo, Z. (1974) Fatal casualties on the railways (Analysis of post mortem material, 1957-1972). *Zakl Med Sad Am, Krakow Arch Med Sadowej Krym, 24*(1), 15-32.

(Parricide in France)

Devaux, C., et al. (1974) Investigation concerning parricide in France. *Ann Med Psychol (Paris), 1,* 161-168.

(Murder - Prediction)

How to tell who will kill. (1973, June 4) *Newsweek, 81,* p. 69-70.

(Crime Reporting)

Uniform crime reporting (January - March 1973). (1973) U.S. Dept. of Just (Washington DC).

(Time to Speak)

Brownlie, A.R. (1972) There is a time to speak. *J Forensic Sci Soc, 12,* 335-337.

(Police Killings)

Burnham, J. (1971, June 15) What language do you speak? Working in reports to police killings in New York. *Nat R, 23,* p. 633.

(Murder - Medical Education)

Anderson, P.C. (1968) Murder in medical education. *JAMA, 204,* 21-25.

(Witnesses)

Rosenthal, A.M. (1964) *Thirty-eight Witnesses.* McGraw.

(Investigation - Doctors)

Hardwick, J.M.D. (1961) *Doctors on trial.* London: Jenkins.

(Investigation - Forensic)

Miloslavich, E.L. (1952) Forensic pathologic and criminalistic analysis of obscure murder cases. *J Crim L, 42*, 689-693.

(Inquests - Trials)

Inquest after inconclusive assize trial. (1930) *Just P, 94*, 137.

(Evidence)

No body. R. v. Lord, *The Times*, Sept. 24, 1929. (1929, Oct. 5) *Just P, 93*, 662-663.

(Investigation - Evidence)

Walker, R.C. (1915) Circumstantial evidence in homicide cases. *Va L Rev, 20*, 721.

Laboratory Techniques

(Murder Chemistry)

Furtsch, T.A. (1990) Cooke, Josian, Parson (1827-1894) - Murder, chemistry and theology at Harvard: Meeting abstract. *Abs Par Acs, 199*, 13.

(B Gene Forensic)

Vuorio, A.F., et al. (1990) Amplification of the hypervariable region close to the apolipoprotein B Gene: Application to forensic problems. *Biochem Biophys Res Commun, 170*(2), 616-620.

(Cocaine - Examiner's)

Hood, I., et al. (1990) Cocaine in Wayne County medical examiner's cases. *J Forensic Sci, 35*(3), 591-600.

(Unusual Identification)

Clark, E.G.I., et al. (1990) The identification of maternity in an unusual pregnancy-related homicide. *J Forensic Sci, 35*(1), 80-88.

(Injury - Vehicle)

Smock, W.S., et al. (1989) The forensic pathologist and the determination of driver versus passenger in motor vehicle collisions. The need to examine injury mechanism, occupant kinematics, vehicle dynamics, and trace evidence. *Am J Forensic Med Pathol, 10*(2), 105-114.

(Infant)

Cashelle, A.W., et al. (1989) Radiologic contributions to the investigation of fatal infant abuse. *New Engl J Med, 321*(15), 1045-1046.

(Dental Identification)

Rothwell, B.R., et al. (1989) Dental identification in serial homicide: the Green River murders. *J Am Dent Assoc, 119*(3), 373-379.

(Investigation - Princess)

Bramwell, N.H., et al. (1989) The bones in the Abbey: are they the murdered princes? A review of the evidence. *Am J Forensic Med Pathol, 10,* (1), 83-87.

(Acid Death)

Chela, A., et al. (1989) Death due to hydrofluoric acid. *Am J Forens Med Path, 10*(1), 47-48.

(Evidence - DNA)

Werett, D. & Lygo, J. (1989) The role of DNA profiling in the courts. *Law Society's Gazette, 86*(13), 35-38.

(Blood Examination)

Stuttaford, G. (1989) Nonfiction: blood warning. *Publishers Weekly, 236*(4), 209-210.

(DNA)

Lewin, R. (1989) DNA typing is called flawed. *Science, 245*(4916), 355.

(DNA Typing)

Michelmore, P. (1989) The startling Shelly Prine Case. *Readers's Digest, 135*(807), 179-186.

(Microscopy Identification)

Adelman, H.C., et al. (1988) Identification of wooden instrument by scanning electron microscopy from splinters left in victim. *J Forensic Sci, 33*(3), 787-796.

(Cranial Gunshots)

Risse, M., et al. (1988) The hydrodynamic effect of gunshots in cranial explosive shots. *Arch Kriminol, 182*(3-4), 75-82.

(Database - Investigative)

Bel Bruno, R. (1988) Elementary my dear R:Base. *Personal Computing, 12*(12),44.

(Blood Alcohol)

Kleiber, M., et al. (1988) Are toxicologic studies of stored blood alcohol samples necessary in the future also (German)? *Beitr Gerichtl Med, 46,* 171-173.

(Vertebral - Arteries)

Leinzinger, E.P. (1988) Change in the flow relations in the vertebral arteries in head-neck movements (German). *Beitr Gerichtl Med, 46,* 451-469.

(Forearm - Strangulation)

Denk, W., et al. (1988) Mechanism of action of forearm strangulation technique. *Z Rechtsmed, 100*(2-3), 165-176.

(DNA Murder)

Dabbs, D., et al. (1988) The use of DNA profiling in linking serial murders. *Med Leg Bull, 37*(6), 1-10.

(Bones - Teeth)

Ubelaker, D.H., et al. (1988) Alterations in human bones and teeth as a result of restricted sun exposure and contact with corrosive agents. *J Forensic Sci, 33*(2),540-548.

(SIDS or Murder)

Dimaio, V.J. (1988) SIDS or Murder? (Letter). *Pediatrics, 81*(5), 747-748.

(Peter Tosh's Murder)

More intrigue involved in Peter Tosh's murder. (1987, Oct. 26) *Jet, 73,* p. 32.

(Murder - School Principal)

Freedman, S.G. (1987, May 31) Murder hits home (murder of school principal W.M. Donahue of Highland Park, NJ). *NY Times Magazine,* p. 20+.

(Usual Murder)

Pearson, N. (1987, Feb.) Murder as usual (Mt. Pleasant, IA). *Progressive, 51,* p. 50.

(Ricochet Marks)

Sellier, K. (1987) Double ricochet marks (German). *Z Rechtsmed, 98*(4), 241-244.

(Investigation Witness)

Ober, W.B. (1987) The trial of Spencer Cowper. Expert witness to the rescue. *Am J Forensic Med Pathol, 8*(2), 172-178.

(Chloropicrin - Intoxication)

Gonmori, K., et al. (1987) A case of homicidal intoxication by chloropicrin. *Am J Forensic Med Pathol, 8*(1), 45-50.

(Entomology - Forensic)

Goff, M.L., et al. (1987) Forensic entomology in the Hawaiian Islands, three case studies. *Am J Forensic Med Pathol, 8*(1), 45-50.

(Immunoprecipitation - Court)

Ouchterlony, O. (1987) Carl Prausnitz memorial lecture. Immunoprecipitation in court - the Chamberlain case. *Int Arch Allergy Appl Immunol, 82*(3-4), 233-237.

(Decisions - False Evidence)

Gossweiner-Saiko, T. (1987) Erroneous decisions based on false evidence. A criminalistic debate in forensic practice for forensic practice (German). *Arch Kriminol, 179*(5-6), 171-182.

(Cadaver Fingerprints)

Klose, W., et al. (1987) Visualization of latent fingerprints on the cadaver hand by dactyloscopic procedures (German). *Arch Kriminol, 179*(3-4), 104-109.

(Pre-ceramic - Homicide)

Rohrer-Ertl, O., et al.. (1987) Two cases of homicide from the pre-ceramic era of Arabia Petracea (German with English abstract). *Gegenbaurs Morphol Jahrb, 133*(3), 507-537.

(Injury - Assault)

Imajo, T. (1987) Diffuse axonal injury by assault. *Am J Forensic Med Pathol, 8*(3), 217-219.

(Gunshot - Pattern)

Frazer, M. (1987) An unusual pattern of gunshot of gunshot injury linking two homicides to the same assailant. *J Forensic Sci, 32*(1), 262-265.

(Bite Mark)

David, T.J. (1986) Adjunctive use of scanning electron microscopy in bite mark analysis: a three dimensional study. *J Forensic Sci, 31*(3), 1126-1134.

(Histological Findings)

Pueschel, K., et al.. (1986) Histological and ultra-structural findings in parotid gland following parathion poisoning (German with English abstract). *Beitr Gerchtl Med, 44,* 477-485.

(X-Ray - Bone)

Fischbeck, H.J., et al. (1986) Detection of bullet residue in bone using proton- induced x-ray emission (PIXE) analysis. *J Forensic Sci, 31*(1), 79-85.

(Evidence - Revisited)

Starrs, J.E. (1986) Once more unto the breech: the firearms evidence in the Sacco and Vanzetti case revisited: part I. *J Forensic Sci, 31*(2), 630-654.

(Evaluation - Violent)

Tomilin, V.V., et al. (1986) Physico-technical methods of examination to improve medico-legal expert evaluation of violent death. *Sud Med Ekspert, 29*(2), 15-19.

(Murder Weapon)

Zugibe, F.T. & Costello, J.T. (1986) Identification of the murder weapon by intricate patterned injury measurements. *Journal of Forensic Sciences, 31*(2), 773-777. Microforms and article copies available from UMI.

(Demonstration - Injection)

Hood, I., et al.. (1986) Immunohistochemical demonstration of homicidal injection site. *Arch Pathol Lab Med, 110*(10), 973-974.

(Malicious Overdose)

Levy, W.J., et al. (1985) Unusual problems for the physician in managing a hospital patient who received a malicious insulin overdose. *Neurosurgery, 17*(6), 992-996

(Bite Mark)

Berstein, M.L. (1985) Two bite mark cases with inadequate scale reference. *Journal of Forensic Sciences, 30*(3), 958-964. Microforms and article copies available from UMI.

(Crime Scenes)

Dingeman, R.H. (1985) Blood spatters at crime scenes tell all. *The Police Chief, 52*(3), 49. Microforms and article copies available from UMI.

(Berwid Case)

Lehrman, N.S. (1985) The Berwid case (letter). *NY State J Med, 85*(5), 198-199.

(Skeletal Remains)

Frayer, D.W., et al. (1985) Stab wounds and personal identity determined from skeletal remains: a case from Kansas. *J Forensic Sci, 30*(1), 232-238.

(Bodies - Location)

Rodriguez, W.C., et al. (1985) Decomposition of buried bodies and methods that may aid in their location. *J Forensic Sci, 30*(3), 836-852.

(Prehistoric - Homicide)

Murad, T.A., et al. (1985) An analysis of a prehistoric homicide from Northern California. *J Forensic Sci, 30*(3), 948-952.

(Bone - Differentiation)

Owsley, D.W., et al. (1985) Case involving differentiation of deer and human bone fragments. *J Forensic Sci, 30*(2), 572-578.

(Blood - Characterization)

Brinkmann, B., et al (1985) Characterization of micro-traces of blood. *Z Rechtsmed, 94*(3), 237-244.

(Skin Matching)

Perper, J.A., et al. (1985) Matching the lost skin of a homicide suspect. *Forensic Sci Int, 29* (1-2), 77-82.

(Detective Analyst)

Lorenzer, A. (1985) The analyst as detective, the detective as the analyst. *Psyche* (Stuttgard), *39*(1), 1-11.

(Suffocation - Airways)

Maxeiner, H., et al. (1985) Suffocation death by occlusion of the airways with sand. *Z Rechtsmed, 94*(3), 173-189.

(Fingerprint)

Rho, Y.M. (1985) Importance of examination of the clothed victim. Fingerprinting identification of assailant from skin fragment on knifing victim's clothing. *Am J Forensic Med Pathol, 6*(1), 19-20.

(Fingerprints - Enhanced)

Nutt, J. (1985) Chemically enhanced bloody fingerprints. *FBI Law Enf Bul, 54*(2), 22-25.

(FBI Serology)

Murch, R.S. (1985) FBI serology unit: services, policies and procedures. *FBI Law Enf Bul, 54*(3), 15-21.

(Evidence - Fiber)

Deadman, H.A. (1984) Fiber evidence and the Wayne Williams trial (conclusion). *FBI Law Enf Bul, 53*(3), 12-20.

(Cartridge - Evidence)

Schrecker, P. (1984) Identification of cartridge case head-stamps. *Crime Lab Digest, 11*(3), 51-52.

(Clothing - Indication)

Oehmichen, M., et al. (1984) Cytologic findings as indications: morphologic and immunohistochemical identification of human brain tissue on the clothing of a murderer. *Arch Kriminol, 173*(5-6), 129-141.

(Diagnosis - Asphyxia)

Katsumata, Y., et al. (1984) Detection of thyroglobulin in bloodstains as in the diagnosis of mechanical asphyxia. *Journal of Forensic Sciences, 29*(1), 299-302. Microforms and article copies available from UMI.

(Clothing - Murderer's)

Oehmichen, M. et al. (1984) Cytologic findings as indications: morphologic and immunohistochemical identification of human brain tissue on the clothing of a murderer. *Arch Kriminol, 173*(5-6), 129-141.

(Skulls - Matching)

McKenna, J.J., et al. (1984) A method of matching skulls with photographic portraits using landmarks and measurements of the dentition. *J Forensic Sci, 29*(3), 787-797;*J Forensic Sci, 28*(3), 572-576. Article copies available from UMI.

(Postmortem Records)

Rudnick, S.A. (1984) The identification of a murder victim using a comparison of the postmortem and antemortem records. *J Forensic Sci, 29*(1), 349-354. Article copies available from UMI.

(Skeleton Studies)

Taylor, J.V., et al. (1984) Metropolitan Forensic Anthropology Team (MFAT) studies in identification: 1. Race and sex assessment by discriminant function analysis of the post cranial analysis of the post cranial skeleton. *J Forensic Sci, 29*(3), 798-805.

(Reconstruction Crime)

Weber, W. (1984) Forensic contribution to the reconstruction of a murder crime in Aachen 1734. *Beitr Gerichtl Med, 42,* 373-378.

(Investigation - Skull)

Taylor, J.V., et al. Metropolitan Forensic Anthropology Team (MFAT) case studies in identification: 2. Identification of a Vietnamese trophy skull. (1984) *J Forensic Sci, 29*(4), 1081-1086.

(Dental Records)

Rudnick, S.A. (1984) The identification of a murder victim using a comparison of the postmortem and antemortem dental records. *J Forensic Sci, 29*(1), 39-354.

(Plastic Bags)

Von Bremen, U.G. & Blunt, L.K.R. (1983) Physical comparison of plastic garbage bags and sandwich bags. *Journal of Forensic Sciences, 28*(3), 644-654.

(Rope Identification)

Laux, D.L. (1983) Identification of a rope by means of a physical match between the cut ends. *Journal of Forensic Sciences, 28*(2), 468-481. Microforms and article copies available from UMI.

(Powder - Handgun)

Dehaan, J.D. (1983) Homicide with a black powder handgun. *Journal of Forensic Sciences, 28*(2), 468-481. Microforms and article copies available from UMI.

(Assaults - Women)

Deming, J.E., et al. (1983) Forensic science aspects of fatal sexual assaults on women. *Journal of Forensic Science, 28*(3), 572-576. Article copies available from UMI.

(Orbital - Criminologic)

Pollak, S., et al. (1983) Criminologic aspects of indirect orbital roof fractures. *Arch Kriminol, 172*(5-6), 159-165.

(Skeletal Age)

Meindl, R.S., et al. (1983) Skeletal age at death: Accuracy of determination and implications for human demography. *Hum Biol, 55*(1), 73-87.

(Assailant Marks)

Irons, F., et al. (1983) Two bite marks on assailant. Primary Link to homicide conviction. *Am J Forensic Med Pathol, 4*(3), 177-180.

(Investigation - Weapon)

Makarenko, T.F., et al. (1982) Use of spectrum analysis for determination of the objects used for inflicting the injuries. *Sud Med Ekspert, 25*(4), 54.

(Investigation - Blood)

Unusual blood evidence in a homicide a century ago. (1982) *Am J Forensic Med Pathol, 3*(3), 231-239.

(Investigation - Death Time)

Van de Voorde, H. et al. (1982) Determination of the time of death by fungal growth. *Z Rechtsmed, 89*(2), 75-80.

(Self-inflicted Justice)

Longwell, C.R., et al. (1981) A case of self inflicted justice. *J Forensic Sci, 26*(1), 210-215.

(Weapon Investigation)

De Pietro, O. (1980) Identification of the murderer's weapon (short barrel shotgun) from the skin imprint of the muzzle plate. *Zacchia, 16*(1), 57-63.

(Investigation - Chewing Gum)

Sperber, N.D. (1981) Chewing gum - an unusual clue in a recent homicide investigation. *Int J Orthod, 19*(2), 7-8.

(Investigation - Denture Evidence)

Webster, G, et al. (1981) Denture evidence in a case of alleged culpable homicide. *Med Sci and the Law, 21*(2), 134-136.

(Investigation - Blood)

Warner, E. (1980) Sex typing of dried blood: science in the courtroom? *Criminal Law Bulletin, 16*(4), 325-357. Article Copies available from UMI.

(Homicide - Survivors)

Danto, B., et al. (1980) *Homicide and Survivors.* Thanatology Service Services.

(Murder Arrest)

ATF Dynamite tagging program leads to first murder arrest. (1980) *Security Systems Digest, 10*(13), 10. Article copies available from UMI.

(Warrantless Searches)

Murder scene warrantless searches: A proposal. (1980) *Ariz L Rev, 21,* 776-793.

(Victim Identification)

Winney, T.J. (1979) The murder of Brian Harry Kavanagh. Homicide involving an unusual identification of the victim. *Aust Police J, 33*(3), 161-180.

(Identification - Fibers)

Mitchell, E.J. & Holland, D. (1979) An unusual case of identification of transferred fibers. *J Forensic Sci Soc, 19*(1), 23-26.

(Evidence Collecting)

Hall, R. F. (1979) Latent skin print identification solves homicide. *FBI Law Enf Bul, 48*(10), 9-11.

(Medico-Legal Investigation)

Srch, M. (1979) Medico-legal investigations of 66 homicides. *Soud Lek, 24*(1), 7-14.

(Investigative - Strategies)

Littlejohn, R.F. (1979) Modern investigative strategies. *Law Order, 27*(9), 20-22, 24.

(Murder Tracing - Fibers)

Mitchell, E.J. & Holland, D. (1979) An unusual case of identification of transferred fibers. *J Forens Sci Society, 19*(1), 23-26.

(Homicide - Evidence)

Evidence admissibility of evidence of a homicide victim's character where the defendant pleads self-defense. (1979) *Suffolk U L Rev, 13,* 1135-1149.

(Gun Deaths)

Duncan, D. (1979) Gun deaths - some real dead cases. *Christian Cent 96,* 469-471.

(Investigation Errors)

Matzler, A. (1978) Sources of error in police investigations. *Dusseldorf Kriminalistik, 32*(6), 247-251.

(Investigation - Deaths)

Schaper, F. (1978) The practice of investigating deaths. *Laatzen Kriminalist, 10*(10), 431, 433, 435.

(Criminal Investigation)

Schultz, D.O. (1978) *Criminal investigation techniques. A concise introduction to the procedures and methods of investigating crimes.* Gulf Publishing Co.

(Chewing Gum - Investigation)

Sperber, N.D. (1978) Chewing gum: An unusual clue in a recent homicide investigation. *J Forensic Sci, 23*(4), 792-796.

(Biochemical Reconstruction)

Raekallio, J., e al. (1978) Biochemical reconstruction of three cases of death - results of international cooperation. *Forensic Sci, 12*(1), 25-32.

(Murder)

Tallberg, M. (1978) *Don Bolles: An investigation into his murder.* Popular Library.

(Homicide - Evidence)

Black, T. (1978) New evidence on the efficiency of sanctions as a deterrent to homicide. *Soc Sci Q, 58,* 616-631.

(Spermatozoa - Corpses)

Starostin, N.N., et al. (1978) Spermatozoa preservation in the mouth and vagina of corpses. *Sud Med Ekspert, 21*(2), 48.

(Homicide Investigation)

Snyder, L. (1977) Homicide Investigation: practical information for coroners, police officers, and other investigators. *CC Thomas,*

(Corrosion - Rifle Brass)

Shanahan, R. (1977) Corrosion of new, fired, .22 caliber long-rifle brass cartridge cases buried in soil. *J Forensic Sci, 22*(3), 614-627.

(Forensic/Criminalistic Aspects)

Smerling, M. (1977) Forensic and criminalistic aspects on falling from a height. Report on a larger series (125 cases). *Arch Kriminol, 160*(1-2), 39-50.

(Ballistics)

Price, G. (1977) Forensic ballistics. *Med Sci Law, 17*(3), 164-166.

(Blood Luminol Tests)

Thornton, J.I. & Murdock, J.E. (1977) Photography of luminol reaction in crime scenes. *Criminologist, 10*(37), 15-19.

(Blood - Signs)

MacDonnell, H.L., et al. (1977) Detection and significance of blood in firearms. *Leg Med Ann, 7,* 183-199.

(Morphology of Injuries)

Pollack, S. (1977) Morphology of injuries by humane killer (livestock stunner) (German). *Z Rechtsmed, 80*(2), 153-165.

(Murder - Tracking)

Gelb, B. (1976) On the track of murder. *Ballantine.*

(Felony Murder - Evidence)

Felony murder - underlying felony - sufficiency of evidence. (1976) *The Criminal Law Reporter: Court Decisions and Proceedings, 19,* 17.

(Blood Grouping from Teeth)

Schmechta, H. (1976) Identification of the ABO blood group from human teeth *Kriminalist Forens Wiss, 23,* 97-109.

(Investigational Error)

Klingner, G. (1976) Errors in investigational procedure. *GFR Kriminalistik, 30*(1), 17-18.

(Insulin - Post Mortem Blood)

Oksanen, A. (1976) Insulin in post mortem blood: a comment. *Z Rechtsmed, 77*(4), 311-312.

(Electric Current)

Carlsson, L. (1976) Attempted murder with electric current. Criminal technical investigation. *Arch Kriminol, 157*(1-2), 30-36.

(Investigation - Fundamentals)

Nickels, E.M. (1975) Fundamentals of homicide investigation. *Police Law Quart, 4*(2), 11-18.

(Murder - Tracking)

Gelb, D. (1975) *On the tract of murder: behind the scenes with a homicide commando squad..* New York: Morrow.

(Investigation and Forensic Experts)

Grieschat, H., et al. (1975) Special problems in the initial stages of homicide. Investigation and cooperation of medical examiners. *Krim Forens, 19,* 88-96.

(Murders - EEG Studies)

Okasha, A., et al. (1975) Psychosocial and electroencephalographic studies of Egyptian murderers. *Br J Psychiatry, 126,* 34-40.

(Murder - Dismemberment)

Harris, J.E. & Pontius, A.A. (1975) Dismemberment murder: in search of the object. *Journal of Psychiatry and Law, 3*(1), 7-23.

(Comparative Toxicology)

Sturner, W.Q. & Garriot, J.C. (1975) Comparative toxicology in vitreous humor and blood. *Forensic Sci, 8*(4), 126-131.

(Air Rifles)

Dimaio, V.J.M. (1975) Homicidal death by air rifle. *J Trauma, 15*(11), 1034-1037.

(Thallium - Human Head Hair)

Goetz, H. & Stoeppler, M (1975) Contribution to the determination of thallium in human hair forensic cases with flameless atomic absorption spectrometry . *Arch Toxicol. 34*(1), 17-26.

(Homicide - Evidence)

Evidence-proof of prior events admissible generally and specifically to demonstrate corpus delicti because the relevance of and the need for the evidence outweighed its prejudicial impact. (1974) *Tex L Rev, 52,* 585-593.

(Investigation Techniques)

Hughes, D.J. (1974) *Homicide, investigative techniques.* C.C. Thomas.

(Homicide - Evidence)

Evidence - other crimes - balancing relevance and need against unfair prejudice to determine the admissibility of other unexplained deaths a proof of the corpus delicti and the perpetrator's identity. (1974) *Rutgers Camden L J, 6,* 173-188.

(Investigation - Homicide)

Cawley, D.F. (1974) Homicide investigation. *Police Chief, 41*(4), 67.

(Homicide - Evidence)

Evidence of prior similar incidents is admissible to show the corpus delicti of murder. (1974) *U Cin L Rev, 43,* 437-443.

(Medicolegal Activity)

Medjbeur, T. (1974) Medicolegal activity in Oran from the end of 1963 to the beginning of 1972. *Med Leg Damage Corp, 7*(3), 227-234.

(Clinical and EEG Studies)

Driver, M.V., et al. (1974) Clinical and EEG studies of prisoners charged with murder. *British Journal of Psychiatry, 125,* 583-587.

(Exploratory Study)

Cobb, S.E. (1974) An exploratory study of episodic violent behavior in selected groups of subjects. *Dissertation Abstracts International, 34*(10-A), 6768-6769.

(Investigation - Unusual)

Larson, C.P. (1974) Unusual methods of human identification used in three cases. *J Forensic Sci, 19*(2), 402-405.

(Clotting Disturbances)

Encke, A. (1974) Pathophysiology of polytrauma: clotting disturbances. *Langenbecks Arch Chir, 337*(Kong), 179-182.

(Homicide - Evidence)

Evidence - proof of particular facts - evidence that defendant may have committed similar crimes is admissible to prove corpus delicti of murder. (1974, March) *Harvard Law Review, 87*, 1074-1081.

(Murder - Handwriting)

Harvey, R. & Mitchell, R.M. (1973) The Nicola Brazier murder: the role of handwriting in a large scale investigation. *J Forensic Sci Soc, 13*(3), 157-168.

(Evidence - Homicide)

Evidence - presumptions - application of the deadly weapons presumption in West Virginia. (1973) *W Va L Rev, 75,* 287.

(Victim Identification)

Suzuki, T. (1973) Reconstitution of a skull. *Inst Crim Police Rev, 28*(266), 76-80.

(Police Illegality)

Baade, H.W. (1973) Illegally obtained evidence in criminal and civil cases: a comparative study of a classic mismatch. Parts I and II. *Texas Law Rev. 51*(7), 1325-1362 & *52*(4), 621-702.

(Investigation - Cooking Fats)

Lloyd, J.B., et al. (1973) Gas chromatographic characterization of cooking fats with reference to a case of murder. *J Chromatography, 77,* 228-232.

(Gunpowder - Detection)

Tewari, S.N. (1973) A new microchemistry reagent for the demonstration of gunpowder residues in cases of firearm use. *Arch Kriminol, 152,* 96-100.

(Fingerprints - On a Body)

Weiss, K.G., et al. (1972) Visual detection of assailants fingerprints on skin of deceased. *Beitr Gerichtl Med, 29*, 223-226.

(Chromatography)

Tewari, S.N. & Bhatt, N. (1972) Separation and identification of metal-dithizonates by thin-layer chromatography and its application in toxicological analysis. *Agra Chromatographia, 5*(10), 624-626.

(Pediatric Forensic)

Forensic aspects of pediatric problems. (1972) *Inform Newsletter, 4*(3), Entire issue.

(Investigation - Murder)

Oughton, F. (1971) *Murder investigation.* Elektra Books.

(Laboratory Investigation)

Bohn, G., et al. (1971) Mass spectrometric and gas chromatographic detection of parathion in autopsy material after murder by poisoning. *Z Rechtsmed, 68,* 45-52.

(Blood Stains)

Fukae, T. (1971) Species identification of blood stains at the crime scene. *Jap J Leg Med, 25,* 361-365.

(Murder - Evidence)

Frankel, S. (1971) Beyond a reasonable doubt. *LC 73-1634521, Stein & Day.*

(Investigating Officer)

Collinson, J.G. (1970) The role of the investigating officer. *J Forensic Sci Soc, 10,* 199-203.

(Evidence)

Tushnet, L. (1970) The weight of evidence. *JAMA, 212,* 137-138.

(Murder - Suspects)

Dead man's finger: J.A. Yablonski murder suspects held. (1970, Feb. 2) *Newsweek, 75,* p. 22.

(Investigation - Pneumoencephalography)

Chrzanowski, R., et al. (1970) Results of pneumoencephalography in a group of murderers. *Pol Med J, 9,* 758-764.

(Criminology)

Holyst, B. (1970) Probleme criminologique et criminalistique de la tentative de meurtre. 30202. vol. 24, '70, n. 1, p. 29-34 (IBZ 1971).

(Examination - Pneumoencephalographic)

Chrzanowski, R., et al. Results of pneumoencephalographic examinations in a group of homicides. (1969) *Psychiat Pol, 3,* 437-442.

(Evidence - Killings)

Roper, M.K. (1969) Survey of the evidence for intrahuman killing in the pleistocene (with discussion). *Cur Anthropology, 10*(pt. 2), 427-459.

(Evidence - Mineral Studies)

Smale, D., et al. (1969) Heavy mineral studies as evidence in a murder case in outback Australia. *J Forensic Sci Soc, 9,* 123-128.

(Investigation - Mass Photography)

Chapman, A. (1969) Mass photography in murder investigation. *J Forensic Sci Soc, 9,* 177-184.

(Evidence - New)

Williams, L.N. (1969) Fresh evidence a year later. *Lancet, 1,* 305.

(Pathologist - Investigation)

Bhaskaran, C.S. (1969) Role of forensic pathologist in homicide investigation. *J Indian Med Ass, 52,* 171-173.

(Investigation - Spectral Analysis)

Anan'ev, G.V. (1968) Study of the strangulation mark by the method of spectral emission analysis. *Sudebnomed Ekspert, 11,* 8-12.

(Homicide - Fiction)

Davis, D.B. (1968) *Homicide in American fiction 1798-1860: a study in social values.* Ithaca,

NY: Cornell U Pr.

(Investigation - Teeth Marks)

Furness, J. (1968) A new method for the identification of teeth marks in cases of assault and homicide. *Brit Dent J, 124*(6), 261-266.

(Homicidal Threat)

MacDonald, J.M. (1968) *Homicidal Threats.* C.C. Thomas.

(Investigation - Instructions)

Matzler, A. (1968) (Instruction sheet solves "Murder"). 20957, *5,* 259-260.

(Investigation - Stab Wound)

Hendry, W.T., et al. (1967, Oct.) Stab wound of medulla by handle of metal comb. *Med Sci Law, 7,* 213-215.

(Electroencephalography)

Bonkalo, A. (1967) Electroencephalography in criminology. *Canadian Psychiatric Association Journal, 12*(3), 281-286.

(Investigations - Arsenic)

Shapiro, H.A. (1967) Arsenic content of human hair and nails: Its interpretation. *J Forensic Med, 14,* 65-71.

(Murders - Children)

Luke, J.L., et al. (1967) Pediatric forensic pathology. Death by homicide. *J Forensic Sci, 12,* 421-430.

(Homicide - Anthropological Aspects)

Carriero, F. (1967) Comprehensive anthropological analysis of a case of homicide. Criminogenetic considerations. *Zacchia, 3,* 288-297.

(Homicide - Investigation)

Snyder, L. (1967) *Homicide Investigation.* CC Thomas.

(Investigation Mistakes)

Kirwan, W.E. (1966) Mistakes in homicide investigation. *Med Trial Techn Quart, 12,* 23-43.

(Murder - Investigation).

Williams, E. (1966) *Beyond belief: a chronicle of murder and its detection.* New York: Random House.

(Homicide - Photographs)

Admissibility of photographs of the corpse in homicide cases. (1966) *W & M L Rev, 7,* 137.

(Poisoning - Arsenic)

Adelson, L. (1966) Homicidal arsenic poisoning. Medicolegal investigation of four cases. *Postgrad Med, 39*(A), 46-60.

(Investigation - Homicide)

Rasch, W. (1966, Jan.) Cases of extended suicide. *Deutsch Z Ges Gerichtl Med, 57,* 124-133.

(Homicide - Murderous Intent)

Brown, B. (1965) Murderous intent and the "lesser offenses". *NZ L J,* 537.

(Cruentations)

Brittain, R.P. (1965) Cruentations in legal medicine and in literature. *Med Hist, 9,* 82-88.

(Murderous Evidence - Cloth Fiber)

Muir, A.A. (1965) (A routine case for the criminal technical examination institute: Murderer convicted through cloth fibers on a rape). 20957. J. 19, '65, 10, S. 546 (IBZ 1966).

(Evidence - Footprints)

Edberg, S., et al. (1965) The use of footprints for identification in infanticide: Report of a case. *J Forensic Sci, 10,* 225-231.

(Investigation - Double Murder)

Chapman, A. (1964) A double murder, the police investigation. *J Forensic Sci Soc., 4,* 124-129.

(Homicide - Infant Death)

Petersohn, F. (1964) The importance of starch demonstration in the internal organs for evaluation of the viability and the cause of death in newborn infants. *Deutsch Z Ges Gerichtl Med, 55,* 215-224.

(Forensic Medicine - Human Cells)

Jelacic, O. (1964) Possibility of identification of human cells on a deadly weapon after a prolonged delay. *Acta Med Leg Soc, 17,* 19-22.

(Thallotoxicosis)

Haasman, R., et al. (1964, Jan.) Thallotoxicosis: A social menace. *Journal of Forensic Science, 10*, 116-118.

(Expertise - Medicolegal)

Lemoigne, M., et al. (1963) Reflections on medicolegal and toxicological expertise. *Ann Med Leg, 43,* 214-217.

(Homicide - Evidence)

Evidence: The "split-verdict act" in Pennsylvania (Commonwealth v. McCoy (PA) 172 A 2d. 795). (1962, Winter) *Temple Law Quarterly, 35,* 211.

(Laboratory Investigation)

Podolsky, E. (1962) The electrophysiology of homicide. *Dis Nerv System, 23,* 146-148.

(Laboratory Tests)

Winkler, G.E. & Kove, S.S. (1962) The implications of electroencephalographic abnormalities in homicide cases. *J Neuropsychiatry, 3,* 322-330.

(Electrophysiology - Homicide)

Podolsky, E. (1961) The electrophysiology of homicide. *J Forensic Med, 8,* 161-164.

(Homicide Investigation)

Dieckmann, E. (1961) *Practical Homicide Investigation.* CC Thomas.

(Investigation Guide)

Southwestern Law Enforcement Institute. Homicide investigation techniques: Personal experience accounts of professionals and experts. (1961) CC Thomas.

(Homicide - Corpus Delicti)

Proof of the corpus delicti by circumstantial evidence where the body is never found. (1961) *W Va L Rev, 63,* 156.

(Homicide - Tests)

Subjective or objective test of presumptions in murder cases. (1961) *L Q Rev, 77,* 1.

(Homicide - Reference)

Shew, E.S. (1961) *A second companion to murder; a dictionary, 1900-1950.* London: Cassell

.**(Homicide - Murder Conviction)**

Murder conviction upheld despite lack of direct evidence of corpus delicti (People v Scott). (1961) *Colum L Rev, 61,* 740.

(Homicide - Investigation)

Southwestern Law Enforcement Institute. *Homicide investigation techniques.* (1961) CC Thomas.

(Homicide - Evidence)

Zeanah, O. (1961) Homicide evidence. *Ala Law, 22,* 125.

(Homicide - Corpus Delicti)

Corpus delicti - body missing (People v Scott). (1961) *NDL Rev, 37,* 117.

(Homicide - Evidence)

Evidence-proof of murder without a body - sufficiency of circumstantial evidence to prove the corpus delicti in a murder prosecution. (1960) *Will L Rev, 5,* 685.

(Murder - Detection)

Kessler, W.F. & Weston, W.B. (1960) *Detection of murder.* Arco.

(Homicide - Manslaughter)

Tresher, R.L. & O'Neil, T.N. (1960) Medical care for dependent children: Manslaughter liability of the Christian Scientist. *U Pa L Rev, 109,* 203.

(Medicolegal)

Havard, J.D.J. (1960) The detection of secret homicide: a study of medico-legal system of investigation of sudden and unexplained deaths. *Cambridge Studies in Criminology, 11,* 253.

(Medicolegal)

Leoncini, F. (1960) *Medicina legale delitti contro la persona in generale, l'omicidio e le sue diverse forme, indagini medico-legali in casi di infanticidio* (Italian). Firenze: Editrice Universitaria.

(Homicide - Onus of Proof)

Fridman, G.H.L. (1959) Onus of proof in cases of murder. *Crim Law Review 1959,* 557.

(Homicide - Witnesses)

Lansdown, A.V. (1958) Failure of defense to call supporting witnesses. *S A L J, 75,* 338.

(Investigation - Blood)

Recine, H. (1958) (Forensic hemothanatology: Relations between pH, blood platelet count and time of death). *Minerva Med Leg, 78*(4), 148-150.

(Investigation - Blood)

Santini, M. (1958) (Postmortem changes in blood sugar; experimental study and case reports). *Minerva Med Leg, 78*(4), 141-145.

(Evidence - Forensic Medicine)

Schroeder, O., Jr. (1958) The camera as a witness. *Med Leg J, 26*(2), 47-50.

(Detection - Diagnosis)

Hegglin, O. (1957) Uber totung und selbstmord durch bolzenschussapparate. *Freiburg i Br,* 31p.

(Homicide - Corpus Delicti)

Conviction for murder when no direct evidence of corpus delicti. (1955) *Law Q Rev, 71,* 168-169.

(Homicide - Body)

Eddy, J.P. (1955, Feb. 11) Murder without a body. *Law Times, 219,* 69-70.

(Homicide - Body)

Harrison, W.R. (1955) Murder without a body - the forensic science aspect. *Crim L R, 1955,* 158-169.

(Murder - Detection)

Kessler, W.F. & Weston, P.B. (1953) *Detection of murder.* Arco.

(Murder - Evidence)

Morris, N. (1952) Corpus delicti and circumstantial evidence. *Law Q Rev, 68,* 391-396.

(Homicide - Evidence)

Evidence - criminal law - homicide - admissibility of the deceased's good reputation (Lee v Commonwealth). (1949) *Tulane Law Review, 23,* 407-409.

(Homicide - Evidence)

Storey, J.D. (1949) *Ark L Rev, 3,* 464-466.

(Medicolegal Aspects)

Dutra, F.R. (1949) Medicolegal aspects of conflagrations. *J Crim L, 39,* 771-777.

(Homicide - Self-Defense).

Miller, J.M., Jr. (1949) *Wash & Lee L Rev, 6,* 224-229.

Homicide - Evidence)

Kirschner, L. (1949) Intent-evidence-weight and sufficiency - nature of means (State v Salter, Ohio). *U Cin L Rev, 18,* 114-115.

(Homicide - Evidence)

Winshel, D.B. (1949, April) Evidence - circumstantial - sufficiency (Commonwealth v. Wentzel (PA) 61 Atl 2d. 309). *Temple Law Quarterly, 22,* 451-453.

(Homicide - Examination)

Helpern, M. (1946) Postmortem examination in cases of suspected homicide. *J Crim L, 36,* 485-522.

(Homicides - Proofs)

Doyle, F.T. (1946) Marshalling of proofs in homicide cases. *J Crim L, 36,* 473-484.

(Investigation Kit)

O'Neill, M.E. & Wilson, C.M. (1940) Homicide investigation kit. *J Crim Law, 31,* 357-363.

(Cooling Time Test)

Koranda, H. (1939) Cooling time, a desirable test (Golden v Commonwealth (KY) 121 SW 2d. 21). *J Crim L, 30,* 130-132.

(Detection Problems)

Hentig, H V. (1938) Some problems regarding murder detection. *J Crim L, 29,* 108-118.

(Reversible Error)

Murder, evidence, res gestae, reversible error (Commonwealth v Fugmann (PA) 198 Atl 99). (1938) *L R S Temp L Q, 12,* 518-519.

(Homicide - Charges)

Corpus delicti absent in homicide charges. (1936) *So African L T., 5,* 47.

(Mitigating Evidence)

Lindauer, H.D. (1935) Evidence in mitigation or excuse after proof of homicide (People v Madison (CA) 46 Pac 2d. 159). *J Crim L, 26,* 617-618.

(Homicides - Body)

Right to have bodies exhumed so that bullets may be used in ballistic test (Quinn v State (OK) 16 Pac. 2d. 591). (1934) *Law Notes, 37,* 155-175.

(Homicide - Corpus Delicti)

Corpus delicti in murder. (1934) *W J D Scot L Rev, 50,* 101-105.

(Homicide - Evidence)

Jelliffe, S.E. (1934) "What, no pictures?" *J Crim Law, 24,* 1019-1024.

(Homicide - Confession)

Wharton, I. L. Corroboration of confession, homicide while in the commission of a felony (People v Lytton (NY) 178 NE 290). *St. John's L Rev, 7,* 328-332 (1933, May); *N Y U L Q Rev, 9,* 373-374 (1932, March).

(Coronor's Evidence)

Evidence, coroner's inquest, admissibility in homicide cases to prove the cause of death (State v Hayden). (1931, Dec.) *Tulane Law Review, 6,* 142-143.

(Murder - Body)

Finding of a body in cases of murder. (1931) *Ir L T, 64,* 139-140; *Fortnightly L J,* 31.

(Sociological Investigations)

Eyrich, M. (1930) (Criminal-biological and sociological investigations of murderers and homicides). *Bl F Gefungnisk, 61,* 247-262.

(Ballistics)

Buxton, J.J., Jr. (1930) The science of ballistics: judicial applications. *34 Law Notes,* 24.

(Admitting Evidence)

Admitting evidence of the character of the accused as ground for reversal (People v Zackowitz (NY) 172 NE 466) (1930) *Va L Rev, 17,* 190-191, *R L St John's L Rev, 5,* 121-123.

(Murder - Confessions)

Murder in first degree, evidence, confessions (People v Fisher (249 NY 419, 164 NE 336). (1929) *St. John's L Rev, 3,* 284-285.

(Coroner's Inquests)

Permitting Commonwealth to introduce transcript of all evidence of coroner's inquest held erroneous (Canterbury v. Commonwealth (KY) 1 SW 2d. 976). (1928) *Ky L J, 17,* 61-63.

Investigation
Case Reports

(Unquiet Grave)

Jones, M., Jr. (1990, Oct. 8) Reopening an unquiet grave. *Newsweek, 116*(15), p. 72.

(Unsolved - Murder)

Belated justice, (1990, Aug. 13) *Time, 136*(7), p. 36.

(Homicide - Tragedy)

Bergman, B. (1990, May 21) Anatomy of a tragedy (inquest into R.Reid's slaying of wife and two sons in Winnipeg, Man. in June 1989). *Maclean's, 103,* p. 20.

(Menendez - Coroner)

Seager, S. (1990, May 16) California coroner: 14 shots hit the Menendez (Jose and Maria Menendez). *The Los Angeles Daily Journal, 103,* p. 8.

(Iraqi - Arms)

Bierman, J. (1990, April 23) A doomsday gun mystery: The murder of a Canadian-born arms expert may be linked to Iraqi plans to build a super canon (G. Bull). *Macleans, 103,* pp. 22-24.

(Montreal)

Came, B. (1990, April 9) A death in the family. *Macleans, 103*(15), pp. 57-59.

(Riddles)

Jenish, D.A. (1990, March 19) The case of riddles. *McLean's, 41*(12), pp. 42-43.

(My Lai Case)

Wilson, W. (1990, Feb.) "I had prayed to God that this thing was fiction..." *American Heritage, 41*(1), pp. 44-53.

(Mail Bomb)

Anderson, C.E. (1990) FBI studies assassin's message; mail bomb letter writer threatens deceased journal chairman. *ABA Journal, 76*(2), 14.

(Pregnancy - Related)

Clark, E.G.I., et al. (1990) The identification of maternity in an unusual pregnancy related homicide. *Journal of Forensic Sciences, 35,* 80-89.

(Theresa Terry - Investigation)

Where is the black queen? (1990) *Time, 136*(6), p. 37.

(Psychic Detective)

Tropkin, A. (1990) Psychic plays detective. *Soviet Life, 126*(4), 60-62.

(Microscopic Studies)

Knight, B. (1990) Tales of murder and detection: murder, under the microscope. *New Scientist, 126*(1715), 62-62.

(Jimmy Hoffa Murder)

Headley, L., & Hoffman, W. (1989, Nov.) The hit on Jimmy Hoffa. *Playboy, 36*(11), p. 74-80.

(Green River Murders)

Sachs, A. (1989, July 31) Stalking the Green River killer. *Time, 134*(5), p. 57.

(Detected by TV)

Gross, K., et al. (1989, June 19) In hiding for 18 years, a wanted man is caught by the FBI and a TV Posse. *People Weekly, 31*(24), pp. 69-72.

(Killer - Found)

Gross, K. (1989, June 5) A devoted brother believes he's found little Billy Ruff's killer 31 years after the crime (C. Ruff links cousin R.Ruff to 1957 murder in Colonie, N.Y.). *People Weekly, 31,* pp. 69-70.

(New Evidence)

Chin, P., & Grant, M. (1989, March 6) Convicted of murdering one of his children, James Richardson hopes the truth will set him free. *People Weekly, 31*(9), pp. 191-197.

(Investigation - Insects)

Lord, W. D. & Rodriguez, W.C., III (1989) Forensic entomology: the use of insects in the investigation of homicide and untimely death. *Prosecutor, Journal of the National District Attorneys Association, 22,* 41-48.

(Journalistic - Investigation)

Wood, S.A. (1989) Journalists are public figures. *Editor & Publisher, 122*(14), 5.

(Victim - Polk)

Stuttaford, G. (1989) Nonfiction. *Publishers Weekly, 235*(14), 117.

(Investigations - Warrants)

Court media cannot see warrant during investigation. (1989) *Editor & Publisher, 122*(16), 46.

(Overdose - Deaths)

Bailey, D.N., & Shaw, R.G. (1989) Cocaine- and methamphetamine-related deaths in San

Diego County, 1987: Homicides and accidental overdoses. *Journal of Forensic Sciences, 34*(2), 407-422.

(Self-Defense)

Zugibe, F.T., et al. (1989) Gunshot wound to the back of the head - self defense vs. homicide. *J Forensic Sci Soc, 29*(4), 255-259.

(Murdered - Music)

Goodyear, J.E. (1989) Murdered to the music of Bob Dylan. *Am J Forensic Med Pathol, 10*(4), 349-352.

(Lisa Steinberg - Case)

Lisa Steinberg's tortures. (1988, Dec. 30) *National Review, 40*(25), p. 19.

(Blind Faith)

McGinniss, J. (1988, Dec. 1) Blind faith. *Rolling Stone, 540,* pp. 67-69.

(Necklace Identification)

Phillips, V.M., & Lang, I.R. (1988) The identification of a 'necklace' murder victim. *J Forensic Odonto Stomatol, 6*(2), 55-66.

(Multiple Murder)

Gee, D.J. (1988) A pathologist's view of multiple murder. *Forensic Sci Int, 38*(1-2), 53-65.

(Hospital Homicide)

Maul, M.R. (1988) Tracking hospital homicide. *Quill, 76,* 16-21.

(Hypnosis - Case Report)

Coons, P.M. (1988) Misuse of forensic hypnosis: a hypnotically elicited false confession with the apparent creation of a multiple personality. *Int J Clin Hypn, 36*(1), 1-11.

(Medicolegal - Investigation)

Sauer, N.J., et al. (1988) Medicolegal investigation of an eighteenth century homicide. *Am J Forensic Med Pathol, 9*(1), 66-73.

(Eighteenth Century)

Sauer, N.J., et al. (1988) Medicolegal investigation of an eighteenth century homicide. *Am J. Forensic Med Pathol, 9*(1), 66-73.

(Mother's Murder)

Georgia sisters indicted for their mother's murder (R. Golden and Collier). (1987, Nov. 2) *Jet, 73,* p.47.

(Bodies - Find)

Find 7 bodies in Philly, jail tenant (case of H. Graham). (1987, Aug. 31) *Jet, 72,* p. 18.

(Injuries - Neck)

Maxeiner, H. (1987) Local vital reaction following injuries of the neck. *Z Rechtsmed, 99*(1), 35-54.

(Larynx Hemorrhage)

Oehmichen, M. (1987) Reactive changes in soft tissue hemorrhage inside the larynx. *Beitr Gerichtl Med, 45,* 73-78.

(Physician - Murderer)

Sterkowicz, S. (1987) The physician and mass murderer Joachim Mrugowsky. *Przegl Lek, 44*(1), 126-131.

(Gunshot - Pattern)

Frazer, M. (1987) An unusual pattern of gunshot injury linking two homicides to the same assailant. *J Forensic Sci, 32*(1), 262-265.

(Mask)

Zugibe, F.T., et al. (1987) The man in the mask. *J Forensic Sci, 32*(3), 810-817.

(Vision - Victim)

Kelley, J. (1987) Etta Smith's inspiration cost her four days in jail (vision of victim's body in Pacoima section of Los Angeles). *People Weekly, 27,* p. 33.

(Injuries - Kick)

Bohm, E. (1987) Morphology and biomechanics of kick injuries. *Beitr Gerichtl Med, 45,* 319-329.

(Murderer - Charged)

Walder, J. (1986, April 28) Playing with fire (G.E. Meek believed to be murderer of P. Jenning and parents). *People Weekly, 25,* pp. 76-78+.

(Killers - Solved)

Fleischer, L. (1986, March 7) Solved (story behind S. Kirkpatrick's forthcoming A cast of killers). *Publisher's Weekly, 229,* p. 93.

(Murderer Apprehension)

Fincher, J. (1986, Feb.) A face from the grave (skull reconstruction aids apprehension of murderer E.C. Finn in Stillwater, OK.). *Read Dig, 128,* pp. 199-200.

(Spouses - Involvement)

Trillin, C. (1986, Jan. 6) Rumors around town (question of T. Bird's and L. Anderson's involvement in death of their spouses in Emporia, KA.). *New Yorker, 61,* pp. 35-36+.

(Eyewitness - Memory)

Yuille, J.C., & Cutsall, J.L. (1986) A case study of eyewitness memory of crime. *Journal of*

Applied Psychology, 71(2), 291-301.

(Investigation - Jury)

Grand jury investigating Hare Krishna members. (1986) *Organized Crime Digest, 7*(9), 4-5. Microforms and article copies available from UMI.

(Backlash)

Lucas case backlash hits two Louisiana detectives. (1986) *Law Enforcement News, 12*(8), 1-4. Microforms and article copies available from UMI.

(Serial Murder)

Serial murder investigation project underway in Texas. (1986) *Crime Control Digest, 20*(37), 2-3. Microforms and article copies available from UMI.

(Serial Murder)

Serial murder probers close in with computer. (1986) *Law Enforcement News,12*(7), 3,7. Microforms and article copies available from UMI.

(Serial Murder)

Serial murder probers meet. (1986) *Law Enforcement News, 12*(11), 3,6. Microforms and article copies available from UMI.

(Killer - Solution)

Solution may be near in green river killer probe. (1986) *Law Enforcement News, 12*(3), 3. Microforms and article copies available from UMI.

(Homicide - Cannibalism)

McClain, J.L., et al. (1986) Human cannibalism: A case report. *Am J Forensic Med Pathol, 7*(2), 172-173.

(Suspect)

Elmer-Dewitt, P. (1985, Oct. 15) Taking a byte out of crime (murder suspect R. Ramirez identified through automated fingerprint identification system). *Time, 126,* pp. 96-97.

(Kidnappers - Apprehension)

Cramer, R.B. (1985, Oct.) The ballad of Johnny France (sheriff who captured the abductors of K. Swenson). *Esquire, 104*, 110-112+.

(Torso - Identified)

Headless torso identified as Chicago school teacher (D. Tapper). (1985, Sept. 23) *Jet, 69,* p. 26.

(Stalking - Killer)

Stengel, R. (1985, Sept. 9) Stalking the serial killer (suspect R. Ramirez in Calif.). *Time, 126,* p. 43.

(Hillside Strangler)

O'Brien, D. (1985, Sept.) "The Hillside Strangler" (excerpt from two of a kind). *Good Housekeeping, 201,* pp. 75-78+.

(Implicating)

Starr, M. (1985, Feb. 18) Boston: murder she heard? (F. James overhears conversation implicating teenage boys in attempted murder of her daughter). *Newsweek, 105,* p. 34.

(Political Suspects)

Treen, J. (1985, Jan. 28) Sorting the suspects in a political murder (Taiwanese agents implicated in murder of H. Liu). *Newsweek, 105,* 38.

(Bodies - Location)

Rodriguez, W.C. et al. (1985) Decomposition of buried bodies and methods that may aid in their location. *J Forensic Sci, 30*(1), 232-238.

(Homicide - Prehistoric)

Murad, T.A., et al. (1985) An analysis of a prehistoric homicide from Northern California. *J Forensic Sci, 30*(3), 984-1052.

(Bone - Differentiation)

Owsley, D.W., et al. (1985) Case involving differentiation of deer and human bone fragments. *J Forensic Sci, 30*(2), 572-578.

(Hypnosis - Murder)

Harris, R. (1985) Murder under hypnosis. *Psychol Med, 15*(3), 447-505.

(Lucas Murder)

More questions arise about Lucas murder "Confessions" as Lubbock, Texas, drops charges. (1985) *Crime Control Digest, 19*(35), 10. Microforms and article copies available from UMI.

(FBI - Search)

FBI joins Green River search. (1985) *Law Enforcement News, 11*(16), 3. Microforms and article copies available from UMI.

(Killer - Data)

Los Angeles sheriff upset over release of critical data on "night stalker" serial killer. (1985) *Crime Control Digest, 19*(35), 4. Microforms and article copies available from UMI.

(Narcotics - Massacre)

Mexicans trying to piece together details of massacre of 22 narcotics agents. (1985) *Narcotics Control Digest, 15*(23), 10. Microforms and article copies available from UMI.

(Injury - Weapon)

Zugibe, F.T., et al. (1985) Identification of a murder weapon by a peculiar blunt force injury pattern and histochemical analysis. *J Forensic Sci, 30*(1), 239-242.

(Dade County Homicide)

Copeland, A.R. (1985) Homicide in childhood. The Metro-Dade county experience from 1956-1982. *Am J Forensic Med Pathol, 6*(1), 21-24.

(Crime Scene)

Crime scene and profile characteristics of organized and disorganized murders: Chapter 4. (1985) *FBI Law Enf Bul, 54*(8), 18-25.

(Lacerations - Trauma)

Errikson, A. (1984) Homicidal blunt abdominal trauma with isolated lacerations of the small bowel mesentery. *Z Rechtsmed, 93*(2), 143-146.

(Hit and Run)

No liability for arrest of female obstructing investigation of a hit-and-run accident. (1984) *AELE Liability Reporter, 135,* 3. Microforms and article copies available from UMI.

(Witness - Child)

Pynoos, R.S., & Spencer, E. (1984) The child as witness to homicide (experience of children who have witnessed the homicide of a parent and are then legally compelled to testify; legal and psychological issues). *J Social Issues, 40,* 87-108.

(Dade County Study)

Copeland, A.R., et al. (1984) The right to keep and bear arms - A study of civilian homicides committed against those involved in criminal acts in metropolitan Dade County from between 1957-1982. *Journal of Forensic Sciences. 29*(2), 584-590. Microforms and article copies available from UMI.

(Murders Solved)

Lucas-Led California tour helps solve 15 gruesome murders. (1984) *Crime Control Digest, 18*(37), 4. Microforms and article copies available from UMI.

(Dingo Murder)

Cameron, J.M. (1984) The dingo murder in retrospect. *Med Leg J, 52*(3), 164-179.

(Bangle Piece Revealed)

Mehrotra, V.K., & Yadav, A.Y. (1984) Murder revealed by a broken piece of glass bangle: a case report. *Med Sci Law, 24*(3), 179-180.

("Identity Evidence")

Morris, J.R. (1984) MRE 404(b) and "Identity evidence": a case study in "Whodunit?" *Advocate, 16*(1), 51-69.

(Suspects - Sought)

Suspects sought in"Snuff-Film" slayings of teenage girls. (1983) *Crime Control Digest, 17*(33), 10. Microforms and article copies available from UMI.

(Investigative - Challenge)

Gilbert, J.N. (1983) The stranger homicide: investigative challenge. *Law and Order, 31*(11), 73-77. Microforms and article copies available from UMI.

(Confessions)

Johnson, R.S., Jr. (1983) Corroboration of confessions. *Advocate, 15*(6), 325-337.

(Investigation - Fatal Vision)

Goldstein, W. (1983) 1970 Murder spree probed in *Fatal Vision* (J. MacDonald case). *Publisher's Weekly, 223*, 69-70.

(Death Scene)

Beyer, J.C. & Enos, W.F. (1981) Death scene checklist. *FBI Law Enf Bul, 50*(8), 14-18.

(Manhunt - Atlanta)

Morganthau, T. & Smith, V.E. (1980, Dec. 1) Atlanta goes on a manhunt (black children). *Newsweek, 96*, p. 40+.

(Investigation - CIA)

Lowther, W. (1980, June 23) Murder incorporated II (investigation of former CIA agents for training Libyan assassins). *Macleans, 93*, p. 29.

(Murder Suspect)

Brecher, J. (1980, Aug. 18) Murder suspect in the cabinet (Manpower minister E.Tekere accused of murder of white Zimbabwe farmer). *Newsweek, 96*, pp. 49-50.

(Pathologist's Defense Contribution)

Usher, A. (1980) The contribution of the defense pathologist. *Med Sci Law, 20*(4), 246-249.

(Murder - France)

McDonald, M. (1980) L'affaire in the corridors of power (scandal concerning official investigation into murder of J. De Broglie in France). *Macleans, 93*, p. 25+.

(Convicted Murderer)

Grescoe, P. (1979, Nov. 19) Bad things come in small packages; attempt to clear J. Lewis of convicted murder in British Columbia. *Macleans, 92*, p. 33+.

(Corpus Delicti)

Higginbotham, R.D. (1979, June 10) Confessions and corroboration: Don't let the 'corpus delicti' climb out of the coffin. *Army Law, 27*, 50-83.

(Hypnosis - Polygraph)

Mutter, C B. (1979) Regressive hypnosis and the polygraph: A case study. *American Journal of Clinical Hypnosis, 22*(1), 47-50.

(Murder - Unsolved)

From the files of murder unsolved. (1979) *Law Enforcement Journal 8*(4), 6. Article copies available from UMI.

(Murders - Unsolved)

Unsolved murder cases are grist for the rumor mill. (1979) *Law Enforcement News, 5*(7), 13, 16.

(Witness - Murder)

Wohlfert, L. (1978, Sept. 11) In a few violent hours, Melanie Cain's life turns from cover girl to murder witness. *People, 10,* pp. 36-38.

(Assassin - Investigation)

Assassins' trail: O. Letelier case. (1978, Aug. 14) *Time, 112,* p. 14.

(Investigation - Case Report)

Branch, T. (1978, July 16) Letelier investigation. *NY Times Magazine,* pp. 26-30+.

(Murders - Aftermath)

Breu, G. (1978, Feb. 20) Medics; aftermath of the Nelson murders; Winnebago County, Il. *People Weekly, 9*, pp. 57-58.

(Skeletons)

Sivaram, S., & Wadhera, C.K. (1977) Identity from skeleton, a case study. *Int Crim Pol Rev, 32*(308), 158-160.

(Son Of Sam)

Man hunt for Son of Sam goes on. (1977, Aug. 15) *Time, 110,* pp. 13-15.

(Son Of Sam)

Axthelm, P., & Lallande, A. (1977, June 20) Hunting the Son of Sam; New York City killer. *Newsweek, 89*, p. 86.

(Nationwide - Search)

Nationwide child search ends in Canada. (1975) *Juvenile Justice Digest, 3*(16), 4.

(Autopsy Data)

Bonte, W. (1975) Tool marks in bones and cartilage. *J Forensic Sci, 20*(2), 315-325.

(Pathologists Reports)

Jackson, R. (1975) Francis Camps: famous case histories of the celebrated pathologist Robert Jackson. London: Hart Davis.

(Criminal Dismemberment)

Bonte, W. (1974) Experimental characterization of individual saw marks in another case of criminal dismemberment. *Z Rechtsmed, 74,* 145-154.

(Homicidal Offenses)

Holzhausen, G., & Hofmann, V. (1974) The forensic stand-by service of Leipzig, preliminary results of an evaluation. *Kriminalist Forens Wissensch, 17,* 41-48.

(Dragnet)

Zebra dragnet. (1974, May 6) *Newsweek, 83,* p. 50.

(Murder - Wife/Daughter)

Solve it yourself: John Cali solves murder of wife and daughter. (1973, Aug. 20) *Newsweek, 82,* p. 31-32.

(Murder - Suspected)

Lowther, W. (1973, April 3) Trail of blood; suspected murderer T.R. Bundy. *Macleans, 91,* p. 62.

(CID Files)

Andrews, A. (1973) *Intensive inquires: Seven chief constables open CID files on their most remarkable murder investigations.* St Martin.

(Homicide - Suicide)

Rittner, C. (1973) Homicide or suicide. A contribution to the evidence of forensic pathologic findings in the case of death by violence. *Z Rechtsmed, 72,* 240-244.

(Investigation - Suffocation)

Christison, R. (1972) Archives of the forensic sciences. Murder by suffocation. *For Sci, 1,* 119-131.

(Autopsy - Child)

Petersohn, R. (1972) Findings related to forensic medicine of a child's corpse which was wrapped in plastic for 3 years. *Beitr Gerichtl Med, 29,* 351-358.

(Double Homicide)

Malik, K. (1972) Differential-diagnostic difficulties in a case of double homicide. *Psychiatr Pol, 6,* 93-96.

(Homicide - At Sea)

Bowen, D.A. (1972) Homicide at sea. *Med Sci Law, 12,* 184-187.

(Arthur Hoffman Investigation)

Hofmann, W., et al. (1971) (Criminal-technical investigation in the homicide case of Arthur Hoffman). 20957, *25*(5), 243-250.

(Murder - Parkman-Webster)

Sullivan, R. (1971) *The disappearance of Dr. Parkman: The Parkman-Webster Murder.* New York: Little, Brown.

(Sex Murderer)

Reker, E. (1971) (The sex murderer. Attempts at a criminological evaluation). 20957, *25*(2), 88-92.

(Investigation - Fragments)

Suter, H. (1971) Fragments from a murder investigation (German). 20957. J. 25, '71, 1, S. 6-10; J. 24, '70, 12, S. 610-616 (IBZ 1972).

(Evidence - Quality)

Logan, A. (1970) Against the evidence: The Becker-Rosenthal Affair. New York: McCall.

(Killers Caught)

Sanders, B. (1969) *They caught these killers.* Roy.

(Mineral Studies - Evidence)

Smale, D. I., & Trueman, N.A. (1969) Heavy mineral studies as evidence in murder case in outback Australia. *J Forensic Sci Soc, 9,* 123-128.

(Murder Investigation)

Aebersold, M. (1968) (A murder is solved. Successful cooperation between court of inquiry and police). 20957, *22*(11)584-587.

(Robbery - Case Report)

Beck R. (1967) (The robber-murderer after 20 years of permanence). 29027k. '67, S. 130-141 (IBZ 1969).

(Detection - Thirty Years Later)

Langauer, J. (1967) (Crime does not pay. Train assassinations of 30 years ago - attempted murder on a policeman). 20957. J. 21, '67, 1, S. 48-50 IBZ 67.

(Investigation - YWCA Hostel)

The investigation at the YWCA hostel, Birmingham, Haughton. (1965, Jan.-March) *Acta Med Leg Soc, 18,* 73-76.

(Investigation - Murder)

Kosyra, H. (1964) Washschussel unterm bett. 20957. J. 18, '64, 7, S. 367-368.

(Murder - Stepson)

Meese, F. (1964) Explanation of a murder of a stepson (German). 20957. J. 18, '64, 7, S. 351-357 (IBZ 65).

(Witnesses)

Rosenthal, A.M. (1964) *Thirty-eight witnesses.* McGraw-Hill.

(Spanish Fly)

Teare, D. (1962) Cause of death - Spanish Fly. *What's New, 229,* pp. 17.

(Herodes Murder)

Fairchild, W.D. (1961) Preparation of the evidence in the Herodes murder case. *Ala L Rev, 13,* 343.

(Murder Weapon)

Kobiela, J., & Socha W. (1959) Identification of the criminal weapon. *Acta Med Leg Soc, 12,* 91-104.

(Obscure Murders)

Miloslavich, E.L. (1952) Forensic pathologic and criminalistic analysis of obscure murder cases. *J Crim L, 42,* 689-693.

(Electroencephalography)

Hill D., & Pond, D.A. (1952) Reflections on one hundred capital cases submitted to electroencephalography. *J Ment Sci, 98,* 23-43.

(Straiton Murder)

Brown, A.A. (1947) The Straiton Murder Case; a study in detection. *Jurid Rev, 59,* 44-49.

(Evidence - Rouse Case)

Questionable evidence in the Rouse case. (1931) *Just P, 95,* 131-132.

(Dying Declaration)

Dying declaration, effect of religious belief upon competency of witness. (1930) Marshall v State, Ala. 121 So 72. *Ala L J, 5,* 168-170, *Mich L Rev, 28* 454-455.

Investigation
Autopsy

(Forensic Medicine)

McLay, W.D.S. (1990) Clinical forensic medicine. *J R Soc Med, 83*(12), 809.

(Skeletal Remains)

Kashyap, V.K., et al. (1990) A puzzle of skeletal remains: how forensic science and medicine succeeded in unraveling a complex and controversial murder case. *Med Sci Law. 30*(4), 322-328.

(Skeletal - Remains)

Haglund, W.D., et al. (1990) Recovery of decomposed and skeletal human remains in the 'Green River Murder' investigation. Implications for Medical Examiner/Coroner and Police. *Am J Forensic Med Pathol., 11*(1), 35-43.

(Sitting Corpse)

Spitz, W.U. (1989) The case of the sitting corpse. Accident or homicide? *Am J Forensic Med Pathol, 10*(3), 242-244.

(Podmore Case)

Murphy, G.K. (1989) The Podmore case. *Am J Forensic Med Pathol, 10*(3), 247-250.

(Injuries - Cerebral)

Maxeiner, H. (1989) Extra and intracranial injuries of the cerebral arteries as a sequele of assault. *Z Rechtsmed, 102*(2-3), 191-198.

(Body - Concealment)

Hawley, D.A., et al. (1989) Concealment of the body in drug deaths. *J Forensic Sci, 34*(2), 495-499.

(Woodchipper - Evidence)

Grogan, D.W. (1988, Aug. 1) The lady vanishes and a woodchipper leave just a shred of evidence. *People Weekly, 30*(5), pp. 83-90.

(Strangulation Marks)

Metter, D. (1988) Strangulation marks in homicides caused by choking? On an irritant blood strain picture. *Arch Kriminol, 182*(1-2), 43-51.

(Burned Cadaver)

Magerl, H., et al. (1988) The concrete case - burned cadaver in an automobile. *Beitr Gerichtl Med, 3,* 313.

(Burn Deaths)

Maxeiner, H. (1988) Circumstances and findings in 202 burn deaths. *Beitr Gerichtl Med, 46,* 313-325.

(Skeletal - Identification)

Salgado, M.S., et al. (1988) Identification from skeletal remains. *Forensic Sci Int, 36*(1-2), 73-80.

(Victim - Decomposition)

Skinner, M.F., et al. (1988) Case report in forensic anthropology: Animal and insect factors in decomposition of homicide victim. *J Can Soc Forensic Sci, 21*(1-2), 71-81.

(Multiple Murder)

Gee, J.J. (1988) A pathologist's view of multiple murder. *Forensic Sci Int, 38*(1-2), 53-65.

(Cremation - Bodies)

Eckert, W.G., et al. (1988) Investigation of cremations and severely burned bodies. *Am J Forensic Med Pathol, 9*(3), 188-200.

(Polygamy Murder)

Abramson, P. (1987, Dec. 21) A hand from the grave (E. LeBaron and the polygamy murders case). *Newsweek, 110,* p. 45.

(Dismemberment - Criminal)

Denk, W., et al. (1987) Aspects, findings and problems in criminal cadaver dismemberment. *Arch Kriminol, 179*(1-2), 24-30.

("Transit - Cadaver")

Lignitz, E., et al. (1987) Defensive cadaver dismemberment - a further case of a "transit cadaver". *Arch Kriminol, 179*(5-6), 136-148.

(Trauma - Tetanus)

Murphy, G.K. (1987) Homicidal death following blunt trauma in a vulnerable host, with secondary infections including local tetanus. *Am J Forensic Med Pathol, 8*(3), 259-262.

(Perpetrator - Behavior)

Brinker, H. (1987) The behavior of the perpetrator in cases of missing persons with a hidden or removed cadaver. *Arch Kriminol, 179*(5-6), 129-135.

(Victims - Lakes)

Dix, J.D. (1987) Missouri's lakes and the disposal of homicide victims. *J Forensic Sci, 32*(3), 806-809.

(Postmortem - Jonestown)

Thompson, R.L., et al. (1987) Postmortem findings of the victims of the Jonestown tragedy. *J*

Forensic Sci, 32(2), 433-443.

(Skull Wounds)

Madea, B. (1986) Determining the sequence of occurrence in case of multiple gunshot wounds of the skull. *Z Rechtsmed, 97*(3), 213-218.

(Laryngeal - Death)

Maxeiner, H. (1986) Hemorrhages of the laryngeal muscles in various causes of death. *Beitr Gerichtl Med, 44,* 307-312.

(Injury - Severity)

Allen, R.B. (1986) Measuring the severity of physical injury among assault and homicide victims. *Journal of Quantitative Criminology, 2*(2), 139-156.

(Bites - Evidence)

Prichard, J.G., et al. (1986) Implications of trombiculid mite bites: report of a case and submission of evidence in a murder trial. *J Forensic Sci, 31*(1), 301-306.

(Patterned Injury)

Rao, V.J. (1986) Patterned injury and its evidentiary value. *J Forensic Sci, 31*(2), 768-772.

(Weapon Identification)

Zugibe, F.T., et al. (1986) Identification of the murder weapon by intricate patterned injury measurements. *J Forensic Sci, 31*(2), 773-777.

(Larynx)

Maxeiner, H. et al. (1986) Instructions for the complete preparation of the larynx. *Z Rechtsmed, 96*(1), 11-16.

(Detection - Burial)

Wehr, K. (1986) Detection of E 605 several years after burial. *Z Rechtsmed,, 96*(1), 11-16.

(Hidden Corpse)

Brinker, H. (1986) Missing persons with hidden corpse. Criminalistic and criminologic aspects for practice and research. *Arch Kriminol, 177*(1-2), 1-8.

(Exhumation - Criminologic)

Brinkmann, B., et al. (1986) Exhumation by reason of the criminal process. A comparative criminologic study. *Arch Kriminol, 177*(3-4), 65-75.

(Cadaver Remains)

Helmer, R. (1986) Identification of the cadaver remains of Josef Mengele. *Arch Kriminol, 177*(5-6), 130-144.

(Postmortem - du Pont)

Donahue, C. (1985, Oct. 28) The death of Alfred I. du Pont - a postmortem (suspicion of foul play). *Forbes, 136,* 62.

(Attacks - Neck)

Pollak, S., et al. (1985) Hematomas of the tongue musculature in attacks on the neck. *Beitr Gerichtl Med, 43,* 109-116.

(External - Morphologic)

Janssen, W. (1985) Morphologic demonstration in death caused by external factors. *Beitr Gerichtl Med, 43,* 109-116.

(Laryngeal - Hemorrhages)

Maxeiner, H. (1985) Hemorrhages in internal laryngeal soft tissues. *Beitr Gerichtl Med, 43,* 103-116.

(Bone Recognition)

Walters, E.E., et al. (1985) From bone to recognition. *Law and Order. 33*(12), 40-43. Microforms and article copies available from UMI.

(Crime Suspect)

Homolacova, A. (1985) Removal of tissues and organs for transplantation purposes from the bodies of cadavers when the examining physician suspects a crime. *Cesk Zdrav, 33*(10), 435-438.

(Perforations - Caused)

Missliwetz, J., et al. (1985) Perforations of the vaginal and rectal areas - self-inflicted or caused by another hand? *Arch Kriminol, 176*(5-6), 146-152.

(Poisoning)

Mackell, M.A., et al (1985) An unsuspected arsenic poisoning murder disclosed by forensic autopsy. *Am J forensic Med Pathol, 6*(4), 358-36.

(Skeletal - Remains)

Frayer, D.W., & Bridgens, J.G. (1985) Stab wounds and personal identity determined from skeletal remains: A case from Kansas. *J Forensic Sci, 30*(1), 232-238.

(Proof - Causes)

Janssen, W. (1985) Morphologic proof of death from external causes. *Beitr Gerichtl Med, 43,* 41-47.

(Differentiation - Bone)

Owsley, D.W., et al. (1985) Case involving differentiation of deer and human bone fragments. *J Forensic Sci, 30*(2), 572-578.

(Postmortem - Evaluation)

Szathmary, S.C., et al. (1985) Evaluating the formation of adipocere. Investigation of postmortem decomposition of lipids by HPLC, capillary-GC, GC-MS and NMR (1H -- and 13C - NMR). *Z. Rechtsmed. 94*(4), 273-287.

(Larynx)

Maxeiner, H. (1985) Hemorrhaging in the larynx area. *Beitr Gerichtl Med, 43,* 103-108.

(Administrator - Visit)

Lawn, J.C. (1985) Visit with the administrator. *Drug Inf., 12*(1), 2-6.

(Thorax - Study)

Morar, J.J. (1984) Homicidal penetrating incised wounds of the thorax. An autopsy study of 52 cases. *S Afr Med J, 65*(10), 385-389.

(Bangkok - Hospital)

Tosayanond, S. (1984) Homicide: A study at Siriraj Hospital, Bangkok. *Med Sci Law, 24*(3), 222-226.

(Scientist Assassins)

Behavioral Scientists want to help Secret Service identify assassins, dangerous people. (1984) *Security Systems Digest, 15*(6), 2-3. Microforms and article copies available from UMI.

(Exhumation - Lee Harvey Oswald)

Norton, L.E., et al. (1984) The exhumation and identification of Lee Harvey Oswald. *Journal of Forensic Sciences, 29*(1), 19-38. Charts; Illus Microforms and article copies available from UMI.

(Pedal Morphology)

Smerecki, C.J., & Lovejoy, O.C. et al. (1984) Identification via pedal morphology. *The Police Chief, 51*(4), 52-54. Illus Microforms and article copies available from UMI.

(Skin - Fingerprint)

Nagata, T. (1984) Fingerprint imprinted on skin surface. *Nippon Hoigaku Zasshi, 38*(1), 9-12.

(Injuries - Fatal)

Hulejova, T., et al. (1984) Analysis of cases of deliberate injuries with a fatal outcome during 1972-1981 from autopsy material of the institute of Forensic Medicine at the Medical School Hospital in Martin. *Soud Lek, 29*(3), 40-45.

(Intoxications - Disinfectants)

Jonsson, J., & Voigt, G.E. (1984) Homicidal intoxications by lye and parachlorcresol containing disinfectants. *Am J Forensic Med Pathol, 5*(1), 57-63.

(Emmett Dunne Case)

Emson, H.E. (1983) The case of Emmett Dunne. A personal reminiscence. *Am J Forensic Med Pathol, 4*(3), 225-228.

(Murder - Unsuccessful)

Prathanadi, S. (1983) An unsuccessful murder. *J Forensic Sci, 28*(1), 285-286.

(Asphyxia - Infanticide)

Dirnhofer, R., & Sigrist, T.H. (1983) Intrapartem death of infanticide? A contribution on intrapartal asphyxia. *Z Rechtsmed, 91*(2), 145-151.

(Investigation - Bite Marks)

Irons, F., et al.. (1983) Two bite marks on assailant. Primary link to homicide conviction. *Am J Forensic Med Pathol, 4*(2), 177-180.

(Forensic Medicine)

Palinkosev, Z. (1982) Forensic medical aspects of cruelty. *Srp Arh Celok Lek, 110*(3), 379-385.

(Dismemberment)

Schneider, V., et al. (1982) Remarkable findings in the criminal dismemberment of a corpse. *Z Rechtsmed 89*(2), 131-143.

(Human Bodies)

Clark, M.A., & Jones, J.W. (1982) Studies on putreactive ethanol production. I: Lack of spontaneous ethanol production in intact human bodies. *J Forensic Sci. 27*(2), 366-371.

(Postmortem Injuries)

Tomaszewska, Z., & Gaisor, M. (1981) A case of the postmortem injuries caused by animals or due to the scalping of the corpse by the murder in order to impede the identification. *Arch Med Sadow Kryminol, 31*(2), 147-150.

(Exploder - Ammunition)

Amatuzio, J.C., & Coe, J.I. (1981) Homicide by exploder ammunition. *Am J Forensic Med Path, 2*(2), 111-113.

(Denture - Evidence)

Webster, G., et al. (1981) Denture evidence in a case of alleged culpable homicide. *Med Sci Law 21*(2), 134-136.

(Clues - Case)

Loetterle J., & Schellmann, B. (1981) The criminal's "visiting card" for the victim: Highly characteristic clues in a murder case. *Arch Kriminol, 167*(3-4), 83-86.

(Investigation - Strangulation)

Adebahr, G. (1981) Value of cyanosis and petechiae in strangulation and concurrent severe anemia (author's transl.) *Z Rechtsmed, 86*(2), 123-128.

(Evidence - Denture)

Webster, G., et al. (1981) Denture evidence in a case of alleged culpable homicide. *Med Sci Law, 21*(2), 134-136.

(Forensic Medicine - Early)

Forbes, T.R. (1981) Early forensic medicine in England: the Angus murder trial. *J Hist Med Allied Sci, 36*(3), 296-309.

(Impeding Identification)

Tomaszewska, Z., et al. (1981) A case of the postmortem injuries caused by animals or due to the scalping of the corpse by the murderer in order to impede the identification. *Arch Med Sadow Kryminol, 31*(2), 147-150.

(Stress - Injuries)

Cebelin, M.S., & Hirsch, C.S. (1980) Human stress cardiomyopathy. Myocardial lesions in victims of homicidal assaults without internal injuries. *Hum Pathol, 11*(2), 123-132.

(Evidence - Bite)

Glass, R.T., et al.. (1980) Bite mark evidence: A case report using accepted and new techniques. *J Forensic Sci, 25*(3), 638-645.

(Georgi Markov - Death)

Crompton, R., & Gall, D. (1980) Georgi Markov - death in a pellet. *Med Leg J, 48*(2), 51-62.

(Forensic Medicine Center)

Eckert, W.G., et al. (1980) The Milton Helpern International center for the Forensic Sciences. A reference center in forensic medicine. *Am J Forensic Med Pathol, 1*(1), 9-18.

(Autopsy - Intracerebral Clot)

Smialtek, J.E., et al. (1980) Ethanol in Intracerebral clot. Report of two homicidal cases with prolonged survival after injury. *Am J Forensic Med Pathol, 1*(2), 149-150.

(Firearm - Identification)

Goddard, C.H. (1980) A history of firearms identification to 1930. *Am J Forensic Med Pathol, 1*(2), 155-168.

(Autopsy)

Krauland, W., et al. (1980) Forensic corpse dissection. Anatomy of a criminal procedure. *Arch Kriminol, 166*(1-2), 1-17.

(Investigation - Skull Fractures)

Bonte, W. (1980) Identification of fracture patterns in skull injuries. *Arch Kriminol, 166*(3-4), 83-88.

(Dental Evidence)

Solheim, T. (1980) Unusual dental forensic cases in Norway. *Am J Forensic Med Pathol, 1*(3), 197-203.

(Homicide and Dentist)

Sims, B.G. (1980) Homicide and the dentist. *Med Leg J, 48*(1), pp. 25-43.

(Hostage - Murder)

Berg, S., et al. (1979) Estimating the duration of binding in a hostage murder. *Arch Kriminol, 164*(5-6), 153, 161.

(Rape - Post-Mortem)

Ito, M. (1979) Postmortem examinations of Japanese rape victims. *Victimology, 4*(4), 390-394.

(Dismembering)

Gerchow, J. (1978) On the problem of defensive dismembering of a dead body by a person not involved in the previous homicide. *Z Rechtsmed, 81*(2), 151-156.

(Saw Marks)

Andahl, R.O. (1978) The examination of saw marks. *J Forensic Sci Soc. 18*(1-2), 31-46.

(Gunshot Wounds)

Stone, I.C., et al. (1978) Gunshot wounds: visual and analytical procedures. *J Forensic Sci, 23*(2), 361-367.

(Murder - Sudden Deaths)

Davis, J.H. (1978) Can sudden cardiac death be murder? *J Forensic Sci, 23*(2), 384-387.

(Identification - Human Relations)

Warren, C.P. (1978) Personal identification of human remains: An overview. *J. Forensic Sci, 23*(2), 388-395.

(Investigation - Examples)

Bettscha, W. (1978) Juvenile homicides - Study of 80 cases of homicides or attempted homicides. *Act Paedops, 43*(4), 179-180.

(Radiological Identification)

Martel, W., et al. (1977) The accuracy of radiologic identification of humans using skeletal landmarks: A contribution to forensic pathology. *Radiology, 124*(3), 681-684.

(Body Disposal)

Girod, H. (1977) Some phenomenological and investigative technical aspects of homicide with body disposal. *Krim Forens Wiss, 29,* 83-91.

(Dismemberment)

Saravanapavanandan, N. (1977) Reconstruction of a dismembered decapitated body. *Ceylon Med*

J, 22(3), 142-146.

(Tooth Marks)

Bang, G. (1976) Analysis of tooth marks in a homicide case. Observations by means of visual description, stereophotography, scanning electron microscopy and stereometric graphic plotting. *Acta Odontal Scand, 34*(1), 1-11.

(Fire Arms and Explosives)

Knight, B. (1976) Forensic problems in practice; XII. Injuries from firearms and explosives. *Practitioner, 217*(1302), 975-982.

(Death Scene)

Knight, B. (1976) Forensic problems in practice. VI. The doctor at the scene of death. *Practitioner, 216*(1296), 721-724.

(Evidence - Dog Bites)

Vale, G.L, et al. (1976) Unusual three-dimensional bite mark evidence in a homicide case. *J Forens Sci, 21*(3), 642-652.

(Odontology - Victim Identification)

Sivaram, S. (1976) Forensic odontology in identification of a murder victim in India. *Forensic Sci, 7* (1), 67-69.

(Manner of Dying)

Blinderman, A. (1976) The coroner describes the manner of dying in New York City, 1784-1816. *Amer J Med, 61*(1), 103-110.

(Hospital Deaths)

Unnatural causes; investigation of suspicious deaths of patients in the Ann Arbor Veterans Hospital. (1975, Sept. 1) *Newsweek, 86,* p. 19.

(Investigation - Fragmented Corpse)

Klages, U. (1975) Steeping of mummified cadaver parts in a case of corpse fragmentation. *Arch Kriminol, 155*(5-6), 148-154.

(Identification - Reconstruction)

Haarhoff, K., et al. (1975) Identification of a burned torso and reconstruction of homicide. *Arch Kriminol, 156*(5-6), 145-152.

(Coroners and Manslaughter)

Coroners and manslaughter. (1975) *Br Med J, 3*(5975), 108-109.

(Coroner's Jury)

Editorial: Restrictions on coroners' juries. (1975) *Br Med J, 3*(5978), p 265.

(Investigation Problems)

Grieschat, H., et al. (1975) Special problems of first approach to homicide cases and cooperation of medical examiner. *Krim Forens, 19,* pp. 88-96.

(Dismemberment)

Harris, J.E., & Pontius, A.A. (1975) Dismemberment murder: In search of the object. *J Psychiat Law, 3*(1), 7-23.

(Death - Unnatural)

Mueller, B. (1974) What does the pathologist do in reference to the German Federal Law, if autopsy gives hints for non-natural death? *Beitr Pathol, 153*(1), 91-98.

(Anatomic Abnormality)

Taylor, H.L. (1974) The sternal foramen: the possible forensic misinterpretation of an anatomic abnormality. *J Forensic Sci, 19*(4), 730-734.

(Homicide - Pathology)

Adelson, L. (1974) *The pathology of homicide: A vade mecum for pathologist, prosecutor and defense counsel.* CC Thomas.

(Strangulation - Pathology)

Green, M.A. (1974) Morbid anatomical findings in strangulation. *Forens Sci 213,* 317-323.

(Criminal Dismemberment)

Bonte, W., et al. (1973, May) Analysis of saw marks in cases of criminal dismemberment (English abstract). *Z Rechtsmed, 72,* 180-193.

(Forensic Science)

Bradford, L.W., et al. (1973) Teamwork in the forensic sciences: report of a case. *J Forensic Sci, 18,* 31-39.

(Exhumation)

Zientarski, A. (1973) Exhumation of murdered POW's at the Czarne camp. *Przegl Lek, 30,* 56-60.

(Bite Marks)

Luntz, L.L., & Luntz, P. (1973) A case in forensic odontology: a bite-mark in a multiple homicide. *Oral Surg, 36*(1), 72-78.

(Practical Investigation)

Snyder, L. (1973) *Homicide investigation: practical information for coroners, Police Officers, and other Investigators.* CC Thomas.

(Saw Marks)

Bonte W., et al. (1973) Identification of saw marks in criminal cadaver dismemberment. *Beitr*

Gerichtl Med, 31, 168-169.

(Odontology - Forensic Medicine)

Luntz, L.L., & Luntz, P. (1973) A case in forensic odontology: a bite-mark in a multiple homicide. *Oral Surg, 30,* 72-78.

(Stab Injuries)

Bonte, W. (1972) Aspects of identification of tool marks in stab injuries. *Arch Kriminol, 149,* 77-96.

(Forensic Medicine)

Goodman, J. (1972) *Posts-mortem.* New York: St. Martin.

(Evidence - Bite Marks)

Levine, L.J. (1972) The value of bite mark evidence in homicide cases. *Police, 16*(12), 32-34.

(Forensic Medicine)

International reference organization in forensic medicine and science. (1970) *Homicide, 6*(6), 15.

(Odontology)

Owens, J.F. (1970) Forensic odontology with case report. *Irish J Med Sci, 3,* 137-147.

(Autopsy Reports)

Bailey, G. (1969) *The fatal chance: Twelve cases from the notebook of a crime pathologist.* With a forward by Edgar Lustgarten. London: Peter Davies

(Autopsy - Complete)

Arcadio, F., et al. (1969) Unexpected findings during autopsy of a series of collective deaths (3 dead). Necessity of practicing complete and systematic autopsy. Value of collaboration among physicians, magistrates. police or gendarme departments. *Med Leg Domm Corpor.* 2, 276-277.

(Dental Reports)

From the Scottish Press: A murder case in which dental evidence was decisive. (1968) *Brit Dent J, 124,* 252.

(Post Mortem Examination)

Wagner, H.J. (1968) On the dependence of causality on the extent of ordered examinations. (Case history contribution) *Deutsch Z Ges Gerichtl Med, 62,* 160-163.

(Criminal Incineration)

Bonnet, E.F. (1968) Murder followed by criminal incineration of the cadavers of adults or minors. Medicolegal consideration. *Zacchia, 4,* 435-478.

(Strangulation - Examination)

Permiakov. A.V. (1968) Histologic evidence of strangulation asphyxia. *Sudebnomed Ekspert,*

11, 12-14.

(Coroners Inquest)

Adler, J.N. (1967) Coroners' inquests: the impact of Watts. *UCLA L Rev, 115*, 97.

(Post Mortem Examination)

Rasch, W. (1966) Cases of extended suicide. *Deutsch Z Ges Gerichtl Med, 57*, 124-133.

(Injuries - Homicidal)

Labrooy, E.B. (1965) Counter-irritation marks produced by traditional Chinese medical practice. Their recognition and distinction from homicidal injuries. *J Forensic Sci, 10*, 94-103.

(Capital Criminals)

Podolsky, E. (1965) The vivisection of capital criminals for the advancement of medical knowledge. *Nebraska Med J, 50*, 275-277.

(Heart - Punctures)

Fazekas, I.G. (1963) Experimental data explaining multiple heart punctures in cases of a single portal of entry from the medicolegal point of view. *Ann Med Leg, 43, pp* 478-480.

(Diagnosis - Murder/Epilepsy)

Walker, A.E. (1961) Murder or epilepsy? *J Nerv Ment Dis, 133*, 430-437.

(Forensic - Medicolegal)

Coroner's procedure in homicide. (1959) *British Medical Journal, 5113*, 59.

(Corpse Disposal)

Vacancy for a victim (how to dispose of a corpse). (1958) *Strix Spec, 201*, 614.

(Hit-Run Murders)

Beddoe, H.L. (1958) Hit-run murders: Examination of the body. *J Crim L, 49*, 280.

(Criminal Investigation)

Browne, D.G. (1952) *The scalpel of Scotland Yard: The life of Sir Bernard Spilsbury*. New York: Cutton.

(Postmortem Examination)

Helpern, M. (1938) The postmortem examination in homicides. *Am J Med Jur, 1*, 165-176.

(Body Exhumation)

Abbey, S.C. (1932) Exhumation of a body of deceased on motion of defendant (Sexton v Commonwealth (KY) 39 SW 2d. 229). *J Crim Law, 22*, 749-752.

(Finding of a Body)

Finding of a body in cases of murder. (1931) *Fortnightly L J, 31*, 131.

(Murder Evidence)

The finding of a body in cases of murder. (1930) *Ir L T*, 139.

(Corpses)

The corpse as evidence of murder. (1929) *Sol J, 73,* 619.

Investigation
Psychological

(Psychological)

Wortis, J. (1990) Getting away with murder. *Biol Psychi, 28*(7), 555.

(Psychiatric - Neonaticide)

Kaye, N.S., et al. (1990) Families, murder and insanity: a psychiatric review of paternal neonaticide. *J Forensic Sci, 35*(910), 133-139.

(Psychic Power)

Grant, R. (1989, May) Psych Out! *Redbook, 173*(1), 140-142.

(False Confession)

Gudjonsson, G.H., & Lebegue, B. (1989) Psychological and psychiatric aspects of a coerced-internalized false confession. *J Forensic Sci Soc, 29*(4), 261-269.

(Testimony)

Zabow, T. (1989) Psychiatric evidence in extenuation: Assessment and testimony in homicide defendants. *Med Law, 8*(6), 631-639.

(Forensic Psychiatry)

Gottlieb, P, et al. (1987) The practice of forensic in cases of homicide in Copenhagen, 1959-1983. *Acta Psychiatr Scand, 76*(5), 514-522.

(Under 18)

Murders by people under age 18. (1986) *Corrections Digest, 17*(3), 5. Microforms and article copies available from UMI.

(Offender - Relationship)

Morgan, F., & Kratkowski, P.C., at. (1986) An analysis of the victim-offender relationship in homicide cases. *Journal of Police and Criminal Pathology, 2*(1), 52-63.

(Serial Murder)

Serial murder investigation project underway in Texas. (1986) *Crime Control Digest, 20*(37), 2-3.

(Serial Murder)

Serial murder probers close in with computer. (1986) *Law Enforcement News, 12*(7), 3,7.

Microforms and article copies available from UMI.

(Serial Murder)

Serial murder probers meet. (1986) *Law Enforcement News, 12*(11) 3,6. Microforms and article copies available from UMI.

(Jeffery MacDonald - Murders)

Nasser, T.J., & Stonibaugh, P. (1986) The Jeffery MacDonald murders: A look at the evidence. *The Police Chief, 52*(3), 96-99. Microforms and article copies available from UMI.

(Case Evidence)

Knapman, L. et al. (1986) Case and comment: Evidence. *The Criminal Law Review,* 394-397.

(Gangland Style)

Was the Phoenix maitre D slain gangland style because he testified against Spilotro? (1986) *Organized Crime Digest, 7*(6), 10. Microforms and article copies available from UMI.

(Police Killings)

Police killings down 50 percent since 1970, study finds. (1986) *Criminal Justice Newsletter, 17*(21), 5-6.

(Patterned Injury)

Rao, V.J., et al. (1986) Patterned injury and its evidentiary value. *Journal of Forensic Sciences, 31*(2), 768-772. Microforms and article copies available from UMI.

(Police Shootings)

Turco, R.N. (1986) Police shootings: Psychoanalytic viewpoints. *International Journal of Offender Therapy and Comparitive Criminology, 30*(1), 53-58. Microforms and article copies available from UMI.

(Homicides - Sensational)

Geberth, V.J. (1986) Mass, serial, and sensational homicides. *Law and Order, 34*(1), 187-200. Microforms and article copies available from UMI.

(Green River Case)

Solution may be near in Green River Killer Probe. (1986) *Law Enforcement News, 12*(3), 3. Microforms and article copies available from UMI.

(Psychiatrist's Murder)

Roman, D.D., & Annis, L.V. (1986) Behavioral and situational clues to a psychiatrist's murder by her brother. *International Journal of Offender Therapy and Comparitive Criminology, 30*(2), 177-182. Microforms and article copies available from UMI.

(Bone Recognition)

Walters, E.E., et al. (1985) From bone to recognition. *Law and Order, 33*(12), 40-43.

Microforms and article copies available from UMI.

(Proof - Blood)

Barnard, J. (1985) Proof of hospital-performed blood alcohol tests in evidence. *American Journal of Trial Advocacy, 9*(1), 43-52. Microforms and article copies available from UMI.

(Serial Murder)

Liebert, J.A. (1985) Contributions of psychiatric consultation in the investigation of serial murder. *International Journal of Offender Therapy and Comparitive Criminology, 29*(3), 187-200. Microforms and article copies available from UMI.

(Paul Castellano - Case)

Paul Castellano assassinated in New York City. (1985) *Organized Crime Digest, 6,* 12. Supplement. Microforms and article copies available from UMI.

(Psychics - Police)

Lucas, W. (1985) Police use of psychics: A waste of resources and tax money. *Campus Law Enforcement Journal, 15*(4), 1,6. Illus Microforms and article copies available from UMI.

(Forensic Hypnosis)

O'Connor, D.J., Jr. (1985) Application of forensic hypnosis to court-martial. *Naval Law Rev, 34,* 49-73.

(Evidence - Criminal)

Cox, F.N. (1984) Psychological test evidence in the criminal courts. A case study. *Med Law, 3*(2), 163-170.

(Homicide - Survivor)

Danto, B.L. (1984) A psychiatric view of another survivor of homicide. The cop who kills. *Am J Forensic Med Pathol, 5*(3), 257-263.

(Investigation - Ten Years Later)

Lewis, C.N., et al. (1982) Psychological resolution of homicide after 10 years. *J Pers Assess, 46*(6), 647-657.

(Mental Illness - Pneumoencephalography)

Gierowski, J., et al. (1982) Fractional pneumoencephalography and the mental state of criminal offenders. *Psychiatr Pol, 16*(1-2), 31-37.

(Investigation - Psychological)

Geberth, V.J. (1981) Psychological profiling: practical homicide investigation. *Law and Order, 29*(9), 46-48, 52.

(Bite Marks)

Morrison, H.L. (1979) Psychiatric observations and interpretations of bite mark evidence in multiple murders. *J Forens Sci, 24*(2), 492-502.

(Guilt - Murder)

Devine, P.E. (1979) Conscious acceptance of guilt in the necessary murder. *Ethics, 89,* pp. 221-239.

(Role Interference)

Humphrey, J.A. (1978) Role interference: An analysis of suicide victims, homicide offenders, and non-violent individuals. *J Clin Psychiatry, 39*(8), 652-655.

(WAIS Differences)

Wagner, E.E., et al (1977) WAIS differences between murderers and attackers referred for evaluation. *Percept Mot Skills, 44*(1), 125-126.

(Sociopsychological Investigation)

Walshe-Brennan, K.S. (1977) Sociopsychological investigation of young murderers. *Brit J Criminol, 17,* pp. 58-63.

(Murderers - Adolescent)

Schachter, M. (1975) Attempted homicide and homicides committed by subjects under 20 years. Clinical and psychodiagnostic investigations (Author's Trans.). *Acta Paedopsychiatr, 41* (4-5), 174-187.

(Murder - Detection)

Lester, D., et al. (1974) The detection of attempted suicides and murderers using the Rorschach. *J Psychiatr Res, 10*(2), 101-103.

(Jack Ruby - Psychiatric Exam)

Tuter, W. (1974) Dialogue in Dallas. Psychiatric examination of Jack Ruby. *M H, 58,* 6-10.

(Homicidal Behavior)

Shagoury, P. B. (1972) An exploratory investigation of homicidal behavior. *Dissertation Abstracts International, 32,* (10-B), 6061.

(Rorschach Test)

Durand De Bousingen, R. (1971) Trial comparison between clinical history and psychological tests, particularly projective tests (Rorschach especially and T.A.T.) in adolescent and child murderers. *Rev Neuropsychiatr Infant, 19,* 219-223.

(Rorschach Test)

Sethi, B.B., et al. (1971) Rorschach as a measure of psychopathology in murder. *Indian J Psychiat, 13*(4), 243-247.

(Murder - Pathologic)

Pouget, R., et al. (1971) Evolution of ideas concerning pathologic murder. *Ann Med Psychol,*

2, 665-598.

(Psychiatrist's Role)

Marcus, E.H. (1970) Psychiatrist's role in murder cases. *Calif S B J, 45,* 502.

(History - Homicidal Wounds)

Simpson, K. (1969) Homicidal and suicidal wounds of the throat by A. S.Taylor. Some Medico-legal comments. *Guy Hosp. Rep, 118,* pp 495-517.

(Homicide - Threats)

MacDonald, J.M. (1968) *Homicidal Threats.* CC Thomas.

(Painting - Diagnosis)

Marinow, A. (1965) The diagnostic value of the spontaneous painting in a homicide offense. Simulation by drawing. *Conf Psychiat, 8,* pp. 229-336.

(Testimony - Psychiatric)

Teuteur, W. (1964) Murder and attempted murder - practical hints for psychiatric testimony. *J Forensic Sci, 9,* 492-500.

(Psychology of Murder)

Palmer, S. (1962) *Psychology of Murde*r. Orig. Title *Study of Murder.* Apollo Eds..

(Psychology of Murder)

MacDonald, J.M. (1961) *The murderer and his victim.* C.C. Thomas.

(Psychology of Matricide)

Royer, P., & Vanet, G. (1961) Diagnostic problems. Apropos of a matricide. *Rev Med Nancy, 86,* 1104-1115.

(Investigation - Hypnosis)

Ehrenreich, G.A. (1960) Headache, necrophilia, and murder. A brief hypnotherapeutic investigation of a single case. *Bull Menninger Clin, 24,* 272-287.

(Mental Tests)

Palmieri, V.M., & Romano, C. (1959-1960) The results of the use of mental tests on murderers in prison. *Deutsch Z Ges Gerichtl Med, 49,* 619-620.

(Psychiatric Tests)

Brown, B. (1959) Emergence of the psychical test of guilt in homicide, 1200-1550. *Tasmanian U L Rev, 1,* p 231.

(Psychiatric Investigation)

Cassity, J.H. (1958) *The quality of murder, a psychiatric and legal evaluation of motives and responsibilities involved in the plea of insanity as revealed in outstanding murder cases of this century.* New York: Julian Press.

(Truth Drug)

Walton, H.B., & Doherty, C. (1954) "Truth Drug". *Crim L R,* 423-434.

(Adultery - Murder)

Confession of adultery and murder (Holmes v Director of Public Prosecution, 1946 A C 588). (1947) *Law Q Rev, 63,* 4-5.

Investigation
Homicide or Suicide

(Homicide/Suicide - Child)

Fain, D.B., & McCormick, G.M.,II. (1988) An unusual case of child abuse homicide/suicide. *J Forensic Sci, 33*(2), 554-557.

(Simulation Suicide)

Madea, B., et al. (1987) Simulation of a suicide to hide a homicide in a case of autoerotic accident. *Arch Kriminol, 179*(5-6), 149-153.

(Investigation - Homicide/Suicide)

Raekallio, J. (1986) Differentiation between suicides and homicides through biochemical timings of injuries. *Beitr Gerichtl Med, 44,* 47-49.

(Investigation - Homicide/Suicide)

McCorkell, S.J., et al. (1986) Nail gun injuries: Accident, homicide or suicide? *Am J Forensic Med Pathol, 7*(3), 192-195.

(Investigation - Homicide/Suicide)

Santoro, J.P., et al. (1985) The murder-suicide. A study of the post-agressional suicide. *Am J Forensic Med Pathol, 6*(3), 222-225.

(Investigation - Homicide/Suicide)

Lidberg, L., et al. (1985) Homicide, suicide and CSF 5-HIAA. *Acta Psychiatr Scand, 71*(3), 230-236.

(Suicide - Homicide)

Reeves, J.H.G., Jr., (Ed.) (1979) *Perceptions of justices of the Peace in Relation to Curriculum of the Justice of the Peace Training center for Suicide and Homicide Investigations and Inquests.* East Texas State University.

(Stab - Heart)

Haarhoff, K., & Weiler, G. (1975) Stab in the heart: self-inflicted injury or crime? (German.)

Arch Kriminol, 155(3-4), 103-109.

(Murder or Suicide)

Bonte, W., & Bode, G. (1975) A foreign Body in the throat - murder or suicide? (German) *Arch Kriminol, 156*(5-6), 160-168.

(Suicide)

Kangas, R.R. (1972) Investigation of suicides. *Milit Police J, 21*(6), 22-24.

(Diagnosis - Murder/Suicide)

Picton, B. (1971) *Murder, suicide or accident; the forensic pathologist at work.* London: Hale.

(Homicide - Suicide)

Pokorny, A.D. (1965) Human violence; a comparison of homicide, aggravated assault, suicide, and attempted suicide. *J Crim Law Criminol Police Sci, 56*(4), 488-497.

(Murder - Suicide)

Medico-legal investigation in murder and suicide: proceedings...November 2-3, 1962. (1963) Boston University Law-Medicine Research Institute.

(Diagnosis - Violent Death)

Guareschi, G. (1951) Criteria for differential diagnosis of suicide, homicide and accident in lesions due to explosives. *Minerva Medicoleg, 71,* 89-96.

(Homicide/Suicide)

Cololian, P. (1934, March 9) La jalousie des emotifs homicide et suicide. *Ann Pol et Litt, 102,* 263.

(Suicide v. Murder)

Roughhead, W. (1932) Queen's evidence; or, suicide versus murder. *Jurid Rev., 44,* 139.

Chapter 8
Case Reports
General

(Case Report - Danny Chamoun Murder)

Lebanon: Blood overlooked. (1990, Oct. 27) *Economist, 317*(7678), pp. 44-45.

(Murder - South Africa)

Nemeth, M. (1990, Oct. 1) Peace on trial. *Macleans, 103*(40), p. 34.

(Murder - John Reisbach)

Kasindorf, J. (1990, Sept. 17) Nightmare on Jane Street. *New York, 23*(36), pp. 30-38.

(Trial - USSR)

Skvorecky, J. (1990, Aug. 16) The theater of cruelty. *New York Review of Books, 37*(13), p. 41-44.

(Murder Mysteries)

Gross, A. (1990, Aug.) Can these mysteries be solved. *Ladies' Home Journal, 107*(8), pp. 104-106+.

(Murder Attempts)

Ray, K. (1990, July 22) Blood evidence. *New York Times Book Review*, p. 21.

(The Victim)

Stuttaford, G. (1990, July 13) Nonfiction: Murder of innocence. *Publisher's Weekly, 237*(28), pp. 46-47.

(Drug Killings)

Stuttaford, G. (1990, July 6) Nonfiction: Painted Black. *Publisher's Weekly, 237*(27), pp. 55-56.

(Murder - Brazil)

Stuttaford, G. (1990, July 6) Nonfiction: The world is burning. *Publisher's Weekly, 237*(27), p. 53.

(Murder Story)

Stuttaford, G. (1990, July 6) Nonfiction: Deadly masquerade. *Publishers Weekly, 237*(27), p. 57.

(Case Report - Wife-murder)

Sedgwick, J. (1990, June) A case of wife-murder. *Esquire, 113*, pp. 199-206.

(Documentaries)

Tate, G. (1990, May 15) Steele blaming the victim. *Village Voice, 35*(20), p. 53.

(Case Report - Wife-murder

Jacob, M., & Wright, R. (1990, May) The perfect marriage that ended in murder. *Good Housekeeping, 210*, pp. 166-167.

(Infanticide - Cultural Aspects)

Special section: The cultural and legal aspects of infanticide. (1990, Spring) *Pacific Basin Law Journal, 8*, 1-90.

(Murder Hector Oqueli)

Woddis, R. (1990, Jan. 19) The nature of madness. *New Statesman & Society, 3*(84), p. 8.

(Murder - Howard Beach)

Hynes, C.J., & Drury, B. (1990) *Incident at Howard Beach: The case for murder.* New York: Putnam.

(Zani Murders)

Preston, G.A. (1990) Social Sciences: Law and crime - - the Zani murders. *Library Journal, 115*(8), 99.

(Case Study - Hospital Murder)

Copeland, A.R. (1990) Homicide in the hospital. *Journal Med Leg Droit Med, 33*(3), 159-164.

(White House Case)

Shore, D., et al. (1990) Violent crime arrest rates of White House Case subjects and matched control subjects. *American Journal of Psychiatry, 147*(6), 746-750.

(Drinking Death)

Spencer, G. (1989, Dec. 18) Panel orders parents to stand trial for 'drinking' death of teenage son (New York). *New York Law Journal, 202.*

(Murder-Suicide)

Trillin, C. (1989, Oct. 30) American Chronicles: Knowing Johnny Jenkins. *New Yorker, 65*(37), pp. 79-97.

(Murder - California)

Clegg, P. (1989, Aug. 23) A debt can never be repaid (murder case). *Los Angeles Daily*

Journal, 102, p.6, col. 3.

(Murder-Suicide)

Ex-Angels' reliever D. Moore shoots wife, kills self. (1989, Aug. 7) *Jet, 76*, p. 48.

(Celebrity Obsession)

Toufexis, A. (1989, July 31) A fatal obsession with the stars (murder of actress R. Schaeffer and other incidents). *Time, 134*, pp. 43-44.

(Celebrity Obsession)

Axthelm, P. (1989, July 31) An innocent life, a heartbreaking death (murder of actress R. Schaeffer). *People Weekly, 32*, pp. 60-62+.

(Case Report - F. Fowle)

Moore, T. (1989, July 31) Death of a bard (F. Fowle stabbed to death in Forsyth, GA.). *US News and World Report, 107*, pp. 20-25.

(Case Report - Newspaper Editor)

Murray, W. (1989, July 31) To the left of zero (Mexican newspaper editor H.F. Miranda killed in Tijuana). *The New Yorker, 65*, pp. 57-66.

(Case Report - Drugs/Porn)

Sager, M. (1989, July 31) The devil and John Holmes: drugs, porn, and the murders on Woodland Ave. *Rolling Stone*, pp. 50-52+.

(Case Reports - Cocaine Murders)

Kasindorf, J. (1989, July 24) The 'Cotton Club' murder: Cocaine and hitmen in Hollywood - - a 1980's film noir (B. Evans implicated in murder of R. Radin; cover story). *New York, 22*, pp. 24-33.

(Civil Rights Murders)

Kornbluth, J. (1989, July 23) The 1964 civil rights murders: The struggle continues (honoring J. Chaney, M. Schwerner, and A. Goodman; cover story). *The New York Times Magazine*, pp. 16-19+.

(Police Hunt)

DC police hunt for suspect in slaying of coed and her brother (murder of M. Shiferaw). (1989, July 23) *Jet, 76*, p. 52.

(Civil Rights Murders)

Munk, E. (1989, July 18) Mississippi Yearning. *Village Voice, 34*(29), pp. 35-39.

(Canadian Murder)

Turbide, D. (1989, July 17) Murder on the prairie (Canadian TV show depicts C. Thatcher's 1983 murder of his wife). *Macleans, 102*, pp. 45-46.

(Voodoo Murder)

Two Blacks face charges in voodoo scheme (charges against J. and L. Ivy in voodoo scheme against Judge T. Gardner in Mississippi). (1989, July 17) *Jet, 76*, pp. 52-53.

(Triple Murder)

Honor trio killed by KKK in Mississippi vote drive (M. Schwerner, J. Chaney, and A. Goodman). (1989, July 10) *Jet, 76*, pp. 6-7.

(Murder Capital)

Tidwell, M. (1989, July) Murder capital (Washington, DC). *Progressive, 53*, p. 46.

(Case Report - Hearns' Brother)

'Hitman' Hearns' brother charged in shooting of 'girl friend' in Michigan. (1989, June 26) *Jet, 76*, pp. 51-52.

(Murder - Rural Brazil)

Steif, W. (1989, June) Rural workers face murder (Brazil). *The Progressive, 53*, p. 26.

(Drug Violence)

Goldstein, P., & Brownstein, H. (1989, Summer) The drug-violence nexus (crack-related violence). *New Perspectives Quarterly, 6*, 24.

(Case Report - Wrongful Conviction)

Hill, D. (1989, May 8) 'Because I was a nobody' (wrongful jailing of R.D. Adams as depicted in *The Thin Blue Line*). *TV Guide, 37*, pp. 20-22.

(Lynch's Accused)

Cerio, G. (1989, May 8) Deaths in the name of life (R. and J. Lynch accused of murder and kidnapping in Delaware). *Newsweek, 113*, p. 29.

(Murder)

Gallagher, J.E., et al. (1989, March 6) No happy ending. *Time, 133*(10), p. 56.

(Murder)

Savadis, G.P. (1989, Winter) Ill met by moonlight. *Grand St, 8*, pp. 229-230.

(Murder - Nigeria)

Kastfelt, N. (1989, Jan.) Rumors of Maitatsine: A note on political culture in northern Nigeria. *African Affairs, 88*, 83-90.

(Fjord Murder)

Giertsen, J.C., et al. (1989) The fjord murders. *American Journal of Forensic Medicine and Pathology, 10*(2), 124-129.

(Pepper Aspiration)

Cohle, S.D., et al. (1989) Fatal pepper aspiration. *American J Dis Child, 142*(6), 633-636.

(Neonaticide)

Saunders, E. (1989) Neonaticides following 'secret' pregnancies: Seven case reports. *Public Health Reports, 104*(4), 368-372.

(Puppy Love)

A serious case of puppy love. (1988, Nov. 28) *Time, 132*(22), p. 24.

(Murder of Heir)

Woman found guilty in murder of media heir. (1988, Nov. 19) *Editor and Publisher, 121*(47), p. 20.

(Desperados)

Shannon, E. (1988, Nov. 7) Desperados. *Time, 132*(19), pp. 84-93.

(Spinner's Descent)

O'Malley, M. (1988, Nov.) Spinner's descent. *Saturday Night, 103*(11), pp. 42-53.

(Political)

Klher, H. (1988, Nov.) Political book notes. *Washington Monthly, 20*(10), p. 59.

(Texas Murder Case)

Texas police chief honored by PNG. (1988, Oct.) *Antiques & Collecting Hobbies, 3*, p. 84.

(Reporter's Murder)

California man charged with reporter's murder. (1988, Sept. 3) *Editor and Publisher, 121*(36), p. 42.

(Threat Against Judge)

Threats ignored as judge sets charges in publisher murder. (1988, Sept. 17) *Editor and Publisher, 121*(38), p. 4.

(Nurses Accused)

Yorker, B.C. (1988) Nurses accused of murder. *American Journal of Nursing, 88*(10), 1327-1328, 1332.

(Case Report - Murder of Children)

Goetting, A. (1988) When parents kill their children: Detroit 1982-1986. *Journal of Family Violence, 3*(4), 339-346.

(Pepper Aspiration)

Cohle, S.D., et al. (1988) Fatal pepper aspiration. *Am J Dis Child, 142*(6), 633-636.

(Workplace Homicide)

Davis, H. (1988) The accuracy of workplace data from death certificates for workplace homicide victims: Note. *American Journal of Public Health, 78*(12), 1579-1581.

(Teen Tragedy)

Mitchell, C., & Burdick, T. (1987, Dec.) A teenager's tragedy: Birth and death in a Florida town (M.Clark charged with murder of her newborn child in Golden Gate). *Ms, 16*, pp. 60-63.

(Case Report - Irwin Schiff)

Daly, M. (1987, Oct. 19) The Fat Man: The life and high times of Irwin Schiff (cover story). *New York, 20*, pp. 46-61.

(Killing Spree)

They shoot only in America, don't they? (M. Ryan killing spree in Hungerford, England) (1987, Aug. 31) *Newsweek, 110*, p. 34.

(Case Reports - V. Harris)

Jacobs, S. (1987, Fall/Winter) The death of Vinson P. Harris. *Southern Exposition, 15*, pp. 45-49.

(Case History - Cover-up)

Abramson, P. (1987, June 22) Bitter memories of murder (movie *River's Edge* recalls murder and cover-up by Milpitas, CA teens). *Newsweek, 109*, p. 25.

(Unsolved Murder)

Ryan, M. (1987, June 8) Blood and money: The unsolved murder of a Long Island woman leads to a novel suit against her husband (case of M.S. Schwartz). *New York, 20*, pp. 38-44.

(Case Report - G. Heldnik Case)

House of horrors (murderer G. Heldnik in Philadelphia). (1987, April 6) *Time, 129*, p. 34.

(Claude Dallas Case)

Stuart, R.P. (1987, March) Claude Dallas update. *Outdoor Life*, 179, p. 49.

(Murder in Family)

Rocher, L. (1987, Jan.-March) Can a murderer inherit his victim's estate? British responses to troublesome questions in Hindu law. *Journal of the American Oriental Society, 107*, 1-10.

(Forensic Entomology)

Goff, M.L., & Odom, C.B. (1987) Forensic entomology in the Hawaiian Islands: Three case studies. *American Journal of Forensic Medicine, 8*(1), 45-50.

(Glyn Turman's Son)

Glyn Turman's son stabbed to death in Santa Monica, CA. (1986, Dec. 15) *Jet, 71*, p. 55.

(Case Reports - Patrick Duffy's Parents)

Labrecque, R. (1986, Dec. 8) A world away from Dallas, Patrick Duffy's parents are slain in their Montana tavern (S. Wentz and K. Miller charged). *People Weekly, 26*, pp. 68-70.

(Death in New York City)

Stone, M. (1986, Nov. 10) East Side Story: Robert Chambers, Jennifer Levin, and a death that shocked the city. *New York, 19*, pp. 42-53.

(Star's Brother)

Football star's brother found murdered in LA (E.M. Lofton, brother of J. Lofton). (1986, Nov. 3) *Jet, 71*, p. 46.

(Murder-Suicide Revenge)

Woman kills ex-roomate in revenge murder-suicide (case of C.M. Piccot of New Orleans). (1986, Sept. 29) *Jet, 71*, p. 13).

(Case Reports - Youth Gang Member)

Sullivan, R. (1986, Aug. 28) Leader of the Pack (murder of L.A. youth gang member M. Miller). *Rolling Stone*, pp. 50-52+.

(Case Reports - Molester Murdered)

Trillin, C. (1986, Aug. 11) Outdoor life (teenager L. Connor shoots molester E. Dyer). *New Yorker, 62*, pp. 63-73.

(Case Reports - Stephenson Murder)

Reed, S.K. (1986, July 21) A teenage game of war and revenge ends in the stabbing death of an innocent drifter (murder of M. Stephenson by D. Kurtsman and J. Tramel in Santa Barbara). *People Weekly, 26*, pp. 47-48+.

(Murder - Mob)

Murder in a cornfield (mob murder of T. Spilotro). (1986, July 7) *Newsweek, 108*, p. 27.

(Murderer - Capture)

France, J., & McConnell, M. (1986, June) Murder at Big Sky (J. France captures the Nicholas in Montana; condensation of book). *Reader's Digest, 128*, pp. 138-144+.

(Child Tragedy)

Kerridge, R. (1986, June) A London tragedy: Death of a child (review article). *Encounter, 67*, pp. 66-69.

(Monster of Florence)

Moody, J. (1986, March 24) The monster of Florence (killer who strikes once a year haunts lovers). *Time, 127*, p. 54.

(Gangland Politics)

Gangland politics: Marcos crony A. Pacificador implicated in murder of E. Javier. (1986, Feb. 24) *Time, 127*, p. 33.

(Case Reports - Mclean Murder)

Hammer, J. (1986, Feb. 24) The struggle for custody of a 7-year-old boy ends in an explosion of gunfire and death (K. Hayden shoots ex-wife J. Mclean). *People Weekly, 25*, pp. 38-44.

(Case Reports - D. Fossey)

Brower, M. (1986, Feb. 17) The strange death of Diane Fossey. *People Weekly, 25*, pp. 46-48.

(Murder - Revenge)

Levin, E. (1986, Jan. 27) A little boy's murder and the father's revenge leave a quiet French valley in turmoil (G. Villemin killed in Vologne River valley town). *People Weekly, 25*, pp. 91-92+.

(Family Attacked)

No escape (C. Goldmark and family attacked in Seattle by D. Rice). (1986, Jan. 13) *Time, 127*, p. 23.

(Organized Crime)

Mafia 'soldier' claims Gotti was involved in Castellano hit. (1986) *Organized Crime Digest, 7*(9), 11-12. Microforms and article copies available from UMI.

(Police - Illegality)

Police illegality results in exclusion of witness' testimony. (1986) *The Criminal Law Reporter: Court Decisions, 38*(17), 2323-2325.

(Weapon Possession)

Homicide, felony murder, possession of a weapon. (1986) *The Criminal Law Reporter: Court Decisions, 38*(14), 2273.

(Colombian Judge)

Colombian judge murdered. (1986) *Narcotics Control Digest, 16*(6), 6-7. Article copies available from UMI.

(Case Reports - Leclair Killing)

Borowitz, A. (1986) Finale marked presto: The killing of Leclair. *Musical Quarterly, 72*(2), 228-238.

(Airliner Sabotage)

Murphy, G.K. (1986) A brilliant ball of fire: The sabotage of United Airlines Flight 629. *American Journal of Forensic Medicine and Pathology, 7*(1), 59-61.

(Manslaughter)

Soloman, S., et al. (1985, Dec.) Case and comment: Manslaughter. *The Criminal Law Review*, 787-790.

(Massacre in Columbia)

Columbia/US extradition treaty may have sparked massacre. (1985) *Narcotics Control Digest, 15*(23), 6. Article copies available from UMI.

(J.D. Merrett Case)

Murphy, G.K. (1985) Murders for profit. The case of John Donald Merrett. *American Journal of Forensic Medicine and Pathology, 6*(4), 325-328.

(Berwid Case)

Lehrman, N.S. (1985) The Berwid case. *New York State Journal of Medicine, 85*(5), 198-199.

(Split Reality)

Split reality of murder: Chapter 2. (1985) *FBI Law Enforcement Bulletin, 54*(8), 7-11.

(Medieval Justice)

Saul, N. (1984, Aug.) Murder and justice, medieval style: The Pashley case. *History Today, 34*, 30-35.

(Legacy)

Frankel, C. (1984, Spring) A legacy. *American Scholar, 53*, 159-166.

(Dual Modality)

Moar, J.J. (1984) Homicide by dual modality: A case report. *South African Medical Journal, 65*(4), 137-138.

(Merrett Case)

Murphy, G.K. (1984) Murder for profit: The case of John Donald Merrett. *American Journal of Forensic Medicine and Pathology, 6*(4), 325-328.

(Crime Severity)

Severity of crime. (1984) *Sold Sup J, 1*(5), 301.

(Letting Die)

Kamm, F.M. (1983, Oct.) Killing and letting die: methodology and substantive issues. *Pacifist Philosophy Quarterly, 64*, 297-312.

(Murder Case)

Torre, C., et al. (1983) A case of murder by impalement (German). *Z Rechtsmed, 91*(1), 83-84.

(Lust Murder)

Kippax, D.E. (1982) The lust murder of Edward. *New Zealand Journal of Psychiatry, 16*(3), 161-168.

(Case Report - John Lennon)

John Lennon (special issue). (1981, Jan. 22) *Rolling Stone*, p. 8+.

(Shorty's Murder)

McNamara, J.D. (1981) Shorty's murder. *Crime Control Digest, 15*(10), 4. Microforms and article copies available from UMI.

(Captain Colthurst Case)

Henry, W.D. (1981) The case of Captain Colthurst. *Practitioner, 225*(1353), 418-420.

(Murder Surge)

Surge in murders, search for solution (with interviews with M. Beard and N. Knox). (1980, Dec. 22) *U.S. News and World Report, 89*, pp. 22-24.

(Unlicensed Killing)

Posner, M. (1980, Dec. 22) Unlicensed to kill. *Macleans, 93*, p. 30.

(Murders - Missionaries)

Nissen, B. (1980, Dec. 15) Missionary murders (four American women). *Newsweek, 96*, p. 517+.

(Murder - American Nuns)

Death on a twisting dirt road (murder of American Nuns and Catholic lay worker in El Salvador). (1980, Dec. 15) *Time, 116*, p. 54.

(Murder - Monk)

Lindsey, R. (1980, Dec. 7) Case of the missing monk (R. LaScola charged in murder of Georgia Thera). *New York Times Magazine*, pp. 82-84+.

(Case Report - Crimes of Passion)

Deming, A., & Sullivan, S. (1980, Dec. 1) Philosopher's crime of passion (case of L. Althusser). *Newsweek, 96*, pp. 55-56.

(Murder - Case Report)

Marx and murder (case of L. Althusser). (1980, Dec. 1) *Time, 116*, p. 47.

(Racist Rifleman)

Racist rifleman (arrest of J.P. Franklin). (1980, Nov. 10) *Time, 116*, p. 22.

(Murder - Black Children)

Lowther, W. (1980, Nov. 3) Murder the little children (crimes against Blacks). *Macleans, 93*, pp. 43-44.

(Murder - Robbie Wayne)

Chambers , M.J. (1980, Nov.) Murder of Robbie Wayne, age six. *Reader's Digest, 117*, pp. 215-219+.

(Case Report - Double Murder)

Parker, N. (1980, Nov.) Personality change following accidents: a report of a double murder.

British Journal of Psychiatry, 137, 401-409.

(Case Report - Cuban Diplomat)

Member states condemn killing of Cuban diplomatic attache (New York City). (1980, Nov.) *UN Chronicles, 17*, 18.

(Offenders - Vietnam Vets)

Franks, L. (1980, Oct. 25) Soldiers' pay (sentencing of Vietnam veteran W.R. Felde). *Nation, 231*, p. 397.

(Case Report - Sweeney)

Torrey, E.F. (1980, Oct.) Sweeney-Lowenstein madness. *Psychology Today, 14*, p. 14+.

(Case Report - Family Murder)

Williams, D.A., & Huck, J. (1980, Sept. 15) All in the family (R. LaScola charged in murder of Georgia Thera) *Newsweek, 96*, p. 42.

(Case Report - Thera)

Doctor and the money monk (R. LaScola's alleged murder of Georgia Thera). (1980, Sept. 15) *Time, 116*, p. 27.

(Case Report - Stratton)

Hopkins, T. (1980, Aug. 25) Curse of the *Playboy* bunny (case of D. Stratton). *Macleans, 93*, p. 18.

(Case Report - Bakhtiar)

Hit men strike again (attacks on S. Bakhtiar and S.E. al Bitar). (1980, Aug.4) *Newsweek, 96*, p. 32+.

(Case Report - White Killer)

Assagai, M. (1980, April) Killers: alive to kill another day (plea bargaining used in murder case against self-confessed White killers of Blacks in California). *Encore, 9*, pp. 24-25.

(Case Report - Jim Jones)

Crawford-Mason, C., & Faber, N. (1980, March 17) Mills family murders: Could it be Jim Jones' last revenge? *People Weekly, 13*, pp. 41-42.

(Murder Style)

Murder American style (views of J. Godwin). (1980, Feb.) *Futurist, 14*, pp. 72-73.

(Murder - Newness)

Curtis, L.A. (1980, Jan. 26) What's new in murder. *New Republic, 182*, pp. 19-21.

(Homicide News)

Police news. (1980) *Law Enforcement, 9*(1), 9. Article copies available from UMI.

(Case Report - Dora)

Crasilneck, H.B. (1980) The case of Dora. *American Journal of Clinical Hypnosis, 23*(2), 95-97.

(Case Study - Stanley Setty)

Murphy, G.K. (1980) The case of Stanley Setty. *American Journal of Forensic and Medical Pathology, 1*(3), 245-247.

(St. Valentine's Day Massacre)

Eckert, W.G. (1980) The St. Valentine's Day massacre. *American Journal of Forensic and Medical Pathology, 1*(1), 67-70.

Case Report - Georgi Markov)

Crompton, R., et al. (1980) Georgi Marcov: Death in a pellet. *Medical and Legal Journal, 48*(2), 51-62.

(Murder - Planning)

Brown, L.P. (1980) Crime specific planning: The Atlanta experience. *Police Chief, 48*(7), 53-59. Microforms and article copies available from UMI.

(Case Report - Domer)

Eckert, W.G. (1980) The murder masquerade: The Domer case. *American Journal of Forensic and Medical Pathology, 1*(1), 71-72.

(Hall-Mills Murder)

Kunstler, W.M. (1980) *The Hall-Mills murder case: The minister and the choir singer.* Rutgers University Press.

(Murder - Medical)

Levitt, L. (1980) *The healer: A true story of medicine and murder.* New York: Viking.

(Murder)

Trilling, D. (1980) *A respectable murder.* New York: Harcourt, Brace.

(Murder - Greek Village)

Bullets used to save face in small Greek villages. (1980) *Law Enforcement News, 6*(5), 6.

(Case Report - Wife Killing)

Jennes, G. (1979, Aug. 20) Poet James Lewisohn wants out of prison but not out of guilt for killing his wife. *People Weekly, 12*, pp. 28-29.

(Case Report - Ernest Giles, Jr.)

Sanders, C.L. (1979, Aug.) Ernest Giles, Jr. #175318. *Ebony, 34*, pp. 92-94+.

(Case Report - Stepdaughter's Murder)

Rein, R.K. (1979, Aug. 6) Stepdaughter's murder began Fred Kassab's 9-year crusade to see his son-in-law on trial. *People Weekly, 12*, pp. 89-92.

(Gun Deaths)

Duncan, D. (1979, April 25) Gun deaths: Some real, dead cases. *Christian Century, 96*, pp. 469-471.

(Case Report - Union Hotel Shooting)

Read, S. (1979, April) Shootout at the Union Hotel. *Journal of the West, 18*, pp. 77-78.

(Case Report - Hit Man)

William, D., & Shannon, E. (1979, March 19) Tales of a hitman (case of C. Allen). *Newsweek, 93*, pp. 43-44.

(Body Snatcher)

Ballantyne, C., & Lewis, P. (1979, Feb. 19) Death of a body-snatcher (H. U. Lenzlinger). *Macleans, 92*, pp. 33-34.

(Case Report - Esposito)

Pepper, C. B. (1979, Feb. 18) Possessed: Murder of A. Esposito by the Red Brigade. *New York Times Magazine*, pp. 29-32+.

(Case Report - Female Murderer)

Scobie, W. (1979, Jan. 22) She looked like a lot of trouble (T.C. Davis case). *Macleans 92*, p. 22.

(Citizen)

Krajick, K. (1979) A solid citizen for 100 years. *Corrections Magazine, 5*(1), 37.

(Case Report - Atlanta Prison)

Bureau of prisons has no plans to shut down Atlanta prison despite official recommendation. (1979) *Corrections Digest, 10*(10), 7-8.

(Educational Films)

High-impact juvenile film series released by MTI teleprograms. (1979) *Juvenile Justice Digest, 7*(2), 9-10. Article copies available from UMI.

(Torture Killings)

Civilian informant force charged in torture killings. (1979) *Law Enforcement News, 5*(16), 6.

(Case Report - Son of Sam)

Speir, W.E. (1979) Son of 'Son of Sam': A travesty in two acts. *The Police Chief, 46*(4), 8.

(Goilala Tribe)

Goilala tribe moves to city, carrying its own crime wave. (1979) *Law Enforcement News, 5*(15), 6.

(Slayings - Moscone-Milk)

White gets 7 years, 8 months for the Moscone-Milk slayings. (1979) *Corrections Digest, 10*(14), 3. Article copies available from UMI.

(St. Valentine's Day Massacre)

Chamberlain, C. (1979) St. Valentine's Day massacre 50 years ago. *Law Enforcement Journal, 8*(3), 7. Article copies available from UMI.

(Case Report - Rape & Murder)

Buchanan, E. (1979) *Carr: Five years of rape and killing*. New York: Dutton.

(Homicide)

Mishkin, B.D. (1979) Police news. *Law Enforcement Journal, 8*(10), 12. Article copies available from UMI.

(Moscone/Milk Murder)

Crime; murders of G. Moscone and H. Milk. (1978, Dec. 11) *People Weekly, 10*, p. 161.

(Sid Vicious Case)

Segell, M. (1978, Nov. 30) Sid Vicious accused. *Rolling Stone*, p. 9+.

(Case Report - Letelier)

Fox, C. (1978, Nov. 27) Death of a diplomat: Making the connections (murder of O. Letelier by DINA). *Macleans, 91*, p. 39,

(Case Report - M.G. Thevis)

Killing for smut; capture of M.G. Thevis. (1978, Nov. 27) *Time, 112*, p. 33.

(Case Report - T.R. Bundy)

Pinsky, M. (1978, Nov. 27) Just an excitable boy? T.R. Bundy. *New Times, 11*, pp. 52-53+.

(Case Report - Cullen Davis)

Axthelm, P. (1978, Nov. 20) Racehorse for Cullen Davis. *Newsweek, 92*, pp. 83-84.

(Case Report - Polygamy and Murder)

Fox, C. (1978, Nov. 6) Gospel of polygamy and murder: Murder of Rulon Allred. *Macleans, 91*, p. 6.

(A Love Story)

Rosenbaum, R. (1978, Oct. 30) Sid Vicious and Nauseating Nancy: A love story. *New York, 11*, pp. 66-69.

(Reilly's Life)

Life of Reilly. (1978, Oct. 16) *New Times, 11*, p. 53.

(Case Report - Valerie Percy)

Who killed Valerie Percy? (1978, Oct. 14) *Newsweek, 84*, p. 20+.

(Case Report - T.C. Davis)

Who do you want next? T.C. Davis case. (1978, Sept. 4) *Time, 112*, p. 16.

(T.C. Davis Case)

Lubow, A., & Donosky, L. (1978, Sept. 4) Murder that wasn't (T.C. Davis case). *Newsweek, 92*, p. 25.

(Case Report - Letelier)

Buckley, W.F., Jr. (1978, Sept. 1) Letelier and Pinochet. *National Review, 30*, p. 1103.

(Case Report - Joey Thomas' Murder)

Young, R. (1978, Aug. 28) Case of Joey Thomas, innocent victim. *New York, 11*, p. 46.

(Case Report - Melanie Cain)

Adventures of Melanie Cain. (1978, Aug. 21) *Time, 112*, p. 19.

(Case Report - Hoffa)

Keerdoja, E., et al. (1978, June 13) Who killed Hoffa? *Newsweek, 92*, p. 17.

(Case Report - Zebra Murder)

Shield, J. (1978, May 8) Why Nick? Zebra murder victim Nick Shields. *Newsweek, 91*, p. 23.

(Case Report - Letelier)

Who killed Letelier? (arrest of M.V. Townley). (1978, April, 24) *Time, 111*, p. 29.

(Case Report - LeBaron)

Bradlee, B., Jr. (1978, March 6) Mormon Manson: Deaths attributed to sect leader E. LeBaron. *New Times, 10*, pp. 38-40+.

(Murders - Household)

Carrol, R., & Collings, A. (1978, Feb. 6) Pinter meets Christie: Murders involving the W. Scott-Elliot household. *Newsweek, 91*, p. 50+.

(C. Hargis Case)

Greenberg, P. S. (1978, Feb. 6) Thirteen ways to leave your lover: C. Hargis case. *New Times, 10*, pp. 6-7.

(Case Report - Donald Lang)

Simon, S. (1978, Feb.) What do you do with Donald Lang? *Progressive, 42*, pp. 26-27.

(Case Report - Roy Lyle)

Boeth, R., & Gram, D. (1978, Jan. 16) Ron Lyle's last fight? *Newsweek, 91*, pp. 29-30.

(Murder Story - Beretta)

Adams, N.M. (1978, Jan.) Tracing Beretta, A47469 (condensation). *Reader's Digest, 112*, pp. 203-206+.

(Case Report - Ceorge Wallace)

Rappeport, J.R. (1978) Gov. Wallace, Arthur Bremer, and Dr. Rappeport, Part I. Inside Arthur Bremer: Portrait of the assailant. *Maryland State Medical Journal, 27*(3), 35-38.

(Case Report - George Wallace)

Taylor, B. (1978) Gov. George Wallace, Arthur Bremer, and Dr. Rappeport, Part 2. Jonas R. Rappeport, M.D.: The man behind the Bremer report. *Maryland State Medical Journal, 27*(3), 39-43.

(Case Report - McEvoy's Murder)

He calmly adjusted the cylinder and fired into McEvoy's head. (1978) *Juvenile Justice Digest, 6*(13), 10. Article copies available from UMI.

(Goodbar Murder)

Fosburgh, L. (1978) *Closing Time: True story of the Goodbar murder.* New York: Dell.

(Murder Story)

Phillips, S. (1978) *No heroes, no villains: The story of a murder.* New York: Random.

(Case Report - Evelyn Foster)

Goodman, J. (1978) *The burning of Evelyn Foster.* New York: Scribner.

(Case Report - Dr. Clements)

Camp, J. (1978) The murderous Dr. Clements. *GBR Med Leg Journal, 46*(3), 72-84.

(Case Report - D. Long)

Footlick, J.K., & Sciolino, J. (1977, Nov. 7) Silent one: Case of D. Long. *Newsweek, 90*, p. 89+.

(Case Report - M.V. Jackson)

Connor, L.S. (1977, Nov.) Six million dollar murder: Murder of M.V. Jackson. *Saturday Evening Post, 249*, pp. 54-55+.

(Letelier-Moffitt Case)

Stein, J. (1977, Nov.) Letelier-Moffitt mystery. *Progressive 41*, pp. 36-39.

(Case Report - P. Jaroslawicz)

Steele, R., & Agrest, S. (1977, Oct. 10) Diamonds and death: Murder of P. Jaroslawicz. *Newsweek, 90*, pp. 35-36.

(Son of Sam)

Tucker, C. (1977, Oct. 1) The night TV cried wolf: Son of Sam coverage. *Saturday Review, 5*, p. 56.

(Case Report - David Berkowitz)

David Berkowitz Story. (1977, Sept. 2) *Commonwealth, 104*, pp. 547-548.

(Case Report - Homer Phillips)

Clayton, E.T. (1977, Sept.) Strange murder of Homer Phillips. *Ebony, 32*, pp. 160-162+.

(Case Report - LeBaron)

Deadly messenger of God: E. LeBaron. (1977, Aug. 29) *Time, 110*, p. 31.

(Son of Sam)

Sam told me to do it ... Sam is the devil. (1977, Aug. 22) *Time, 110*, pp. 22-23+.

(Son of Sam)

Axthelm, P., et al. (1977, Aug. 22) Sick world of Son of Sam. *Newsweek, 90*, pp. 16-20.

(Son of Sam)

Rosenblatt, R. (1977, Aug. 20) Killer captured: Son of Sam case. *New Republic, 117*, pp. 40-41.

(Case Report - Son of Sam)

Axthelm, P. (1977, Aug. 15) City under siege: Son of Sam case. *Newsweek, 90*, p. 18+.

(Son of Sam)

Notes and comments on press treatment of Son of Sam story. (1977, Aug. 15) *New Yorker, 53*, pp. 21-22 and Sept. 5, 1977, pp. 19-22.

(Case Report - Reilly)

Keerdoja, E. (1977, July 25) New life for Reilly. *Newsweek, 90*, p. 6.

(Case Report - Sheik Zahaby)

Repentance, retreat, and murder: Case of Sheik Zahaby. (1977, July 18) *Time, 110*, p. 32.

(Son of Sam)

Mathews, T., et al . (1977, July 11) Hunting the Son of Sam. *Newsweek, 90*, pp. 18-21.

(Case Report - Son of Sam)

Son of Sam is not sleeping. (1977, July 11) *Time, 110*, p. 61.

(Case Report - Sister Maureen)

Breslin, C. (1977, July) Sister Maureen: Not guilty and not free. *Ms, 6*, p. 22.

(Murder of R. Grande)

Moran, E. (1977, May 7) Witness to justice: Murder of R. Grande. *America, 136*, pp. 410-414.

(Case Report - Mafia Killer)

New Mafia killer: A silenced .22. (1977, April 18) *Time, 109*, p. 22.

(De Feo Murders)

Hoffman, P. (1977, April) Our dream house was haunted: Scene of De Feo murders and home of G.L. Lutzes. *Good Housekeeping, 184*, p. 119+.

(Letelier-Moffitt Murder)

Landau, S., & Stavins, R. (1977, March 26) Letelier/Moffitt murder: This is how it was done. *Nation, 224*, pp. 358-360.

(Case Report - Letelier)

Lynch, K. (1977, March 18) Blow-up: Murder of O. Letelier. *National Review, 29*, p. 320.

(Case Report - Sister Maureen)

Breslin, C. (1977, March) Nun on trial for infanticide: Case of Sister Maureen. *Ms, 5*, pp. 68-71+.

(Death of a Wireman)

Death of a wireman: Murder of F. Chin. (1977, Feb. 21) *Time, 109*, p. 19.

(Case Report - Reporter)

Lindsey, R. (1977, Feb. 20) Anatomy of a reporter's murder: D.F. Bolles. *New York Times Magazine*, pp. 11-14+.

(Case Report - Teferi Benti)

And then there were sixty: Execution of Teferi Benti. (1977, Feb. 14) *Time, 109*, p. 37.

(Case Report - J. de Brogile)

Case of the peculiar prince: Murder J. deBrogile. (1977, Jan. 17) Time, 109, p. 32.

(Case Report - Police Chief)

Former police chief subject of federal grand jury inquiry. (1977) *Crime Control Digest, 11*(7), 5-6. Article copies available from UMI.

(Case Report - General)

Mishkin, B.D. (1977) Police news. *Law Enforcement Journal, 7*(4), 5. Article copies available from UMI.

(Case Report - Drug Kingpin)

Slain narcotics kingpin an informant? (1977) *Narcotics Control Digest, 7*(17), 6. Article copies available from UMI.

(Case Report - Locust Grove)

Locust Grove suspect tells AIM he is weary but fears surrender. (1977) *Juvenile Justice Digest, 5*(15), 9. Article copies available from UMI.

(Case Report - Afternoon Murder)

Siadler, E.J. (1977) *Murder in the Afternoon.* Grand Rapids, MI: Zondervan.

(Detective Story)

Flusser, M. (1977) *The squeal man: The story of Matt Bonora, suburban homicide detective.* New York: Morrow.

(Case Report - Diamond Thieves)

Broker fingered colleagues for 'hits' by diamond thieves. (1977) *Security Systems Digest, 8*(22), 5. Article copies available from UMI.

(Murder Story)

Allen, W. (1977) *Starkweather.* New York: Avon.

(Case Report - Dr. Crippen)

Cullen, T. (1977) *The mild murderer: The true story of Dr. Crippen's case.* New York: HM.

(Case Report - Girl Scout's Slaying)

Convicted rapist charged for Locust Grove Girl Scout killings. (1977) *Juvenile Justice Digest, 5*(12), 10. Article copies available from UMI.

(Identical Murders)

Bradshaw, E.S. (1977) The carbon copy murders or murder in triplicate. *The Police Journal, 50*(3), 260-279.

(Case Report - Business Partners)

Former business partner sought in slaying of four security execs. (1977) *Security Systems Digest, 8*(15), 3. Article copies available from UMI.

(Case Report - J. Roselli)

Williams, D.A., et al. (1976, Dec. 23) Swim in the bay: J. Roselli. *Newsweek, 88*, p. 38.

(Case Report - Murder)

Greenwood, W., & Smith, J.C. (1976, Nov.) Case and comment: Murder. *Criminal Law Review*, 690-691.

(Case Report - Letelier Murder)

Winn, P. (1976, Oct. 9) Motives for murder: Why Letelier died now. *Nation, 223*, pp. 326-328.

(Parricide)

Cockburn, A. (1976, Oct.) Mom and pop murders; parricide. *Esquire, 84*, p. 70+.

(Case Report - Chicago)

Chu, D., & Barnes, J. (1976, Sept. 13) Ray Yablun's luck: Chicago coin dealer. *Newsweek, 88*, p. 18+.

(Case Report - Jesse Burkett)

Blank, J.P. (1976, Sept.) Conscience of Chris Burkett: Reprieve of F.L. Pitts and W. Lee in Jesse Burkett murder case. *Reader's Digest, 109*, pp. 84-88.

(Case Report - G. Levasseur)

Cain and Abel: Killing of G. Levasseur by brother Phillipe. (1976, Aug. 23) *Time, 108*, p. 32.

(Case Report - J. Roselli)

Deep six for Johnny: Murder of J. Roselli. (1976, Aug. 23) *Time, 108*, pp. 23-25.

(Case Report - Reilly)

Keiffer, E. (1976, July) We always knew Peter didn't kill his mother; case of P. Reilly. *Good Housekeeping, 183*, pp. 76-77+.

(Case Report - J. Emory)

Cut-rate osteopath: Case of J. Emory. (1976, June 21) *Time, 107*, p. 45.

(Case Report - Genoa Murder)

Death before lunch: Murder of Genoa Chief Prosecutor F. Coco. (1976, June 21) *Time, 107*, p. 39.

(Case Report - D.M. Leone)

Common man: murder of Dominick M. Leone by C. Hopkins; Baltimore. (1976, May 1) *Nation, 222*, p. 516.

(Frankie Silver)

Young, P.D. (1976, May) Why Frankie Silver swung. *Ms, 4*, pp. 120-122.

(Case Report - D. Dawson)

Greenfield, M. (1976, April 12) Death by friendly fire: Failure of criminal rehabilitation (case of Danny Dawson). *Newsweek, 87*, p. 112.

(Bishop Murders)

Bishop murders. (1976, March 22) *Time, 107*, p. 18+.

(Murders by Hospital Staff)

Death follows art: Murders committed by members of hospital staff. (1976, March 22) *Time, 107*, p. 47.

(Case Report - Peter Reilly)

Footlick, J.K., & Agrest, S. (1976, March 1) Case of Peter Reilly. *Newsweek, 87*, p. 62.

(Case Report - Mullendore Murder)

Kwitney, J. (1976) *The Mullendore murder case*. New York: Warner.

(Case Reports - Murderesses)

Hartman, M.S. (1976) *Victorian murderesses: A true story history of 13 respectable French & English women accused of unspeakable crimes*. New York: Schocken.

(Murder in Prison)

Lewisberg inmates indicted for murder of fellow prisoner. (1976) *Corrections Digest, 7*(20), 4.

(Rape/Murder)

Inmate on work-release kills five and rapes four. (1976) *Crime Control Digest, 10*(36), 2-3.

(Abduction and Murder)

Banker's wife abducted, slain. (1976) *Security Systems Digest, 7*(2), 4-5.

(Case Report - Mosley)

Mosley murder charges dropped. (1976) *Juvenile Justice Digest, 4*(22), 4.

(Famous Murder Stories)

Kelly, T. (1976) *Murders: The capital's famous murder stories.* Washington, DC: Washingtonian.

(Case Report - General)

Texas police. (1976) *Juvenile Justice Digest, 4*(4), 8.

(Case Report - P. Pasolini)

Stevens, M., & Gilbert, S. (1975, Nov. 17) Death imitates art: case of P. Pasolini. *Newsweek, 86*, p. 64.

(Case Report - Kallinger)

Bell, A. (1975, Nov.) Wife of the accused; B. Kallinger. *Esquire, 84*, pp. 132-135+.

(Killer Society)

Killer society; views of D.T. Lunde. (1975, Sept. 13) *Nation, 221*, p. 196.

(Case Report - Exorcism Killing)

Cockburn, A. (1975, Aug.) Night of the forty demons: Exorcism killing (case of M. Taylor). *Esquire, 84*, p. 34+.

(Murder by Mistake)

Murder by mistake: B. Cabanes killed by bomb. (1975, June 30) *Time, 105*, p. 48.

(Police Murdered)

Cop carnage: Murders of policemen. (1975, June 30) *Time, 105*, p. 26

(Case Report - Murder of a Don)

Demise of a Don (S. Giancana). (1975, June 30) *Time, 105*, p. 26.

(Case Report - Ginette Vidal)

Carroll, R., & Sullivan, S. (1975, May 19) Femme fatale: Case of Ginette Vidal. *Newsweek, 85*, p. 46.

(Ruppert Family Murders)

Calio, J., & Lowell, J. (1975, April 14) Silent slaughter: Ruppert family murders. *Newsweek, 85*, p. 46.

(Case Report - Mullendore Murder)

Kwitney, J. (1975, April 7) Mullendore murder case - review. *Business Week*, p. 12+.

(Case Report - J. Little)

Pinsky, M. (1975, April) In the heat of the night: J. Little case. *Progressive, 39*, p. 9.

(Case Report - Pere Menard)

Lusky, M.H. (1975, Spring) Pere Menard, author. *Texas Quarterly, 18*, 104-116.

(Case Report - Edelim)

Margulies, M.B. (1975, Spring) Dying after Edelim. *Colom Forum, 4*, p. 48-50.

(Case Report - A. Gossage)

Sibling castaways: A. Gossage case. (1975, March 3) *Time, 105*, p. 22.

(Case Report - Murder Suspects)

Footlick, J.K., & Smith, S. (1975, Feb. 17) Did the bikers do it? *Newsweek, 85*, pp. 63-64.

(Case Report - Kallingers)

Bizarre case of father and son: Crimes linked to J. Kallinger and son Michael. (1975, Feb. 8) *Time, 105*, pp. 13-14.

(Case Report - Kallinger Case)

Family affair: Case of J. Kallinger. (1975, Feb. 3) *Newsweek, 85*, pp. 18-19.

(Shooting Siege)

Pride of Olean: Shooting siege by high school senior A. Barbaro. (1975, Jan. 13) *Newsweek, 85*, p. 27.

(Case Report - G.A. Taylor)

Freedom to kill: Case of G.A. Taylor. (1975, Jan. 9) *Time, 105*, p. 19.

(Case Report - John Cali)

Moore, G. (1975, Jan.) Ordeal of John Cali. *Reader's Digest, 106*, p. 77-82.

(Case Report - Violent Family)

Kuhn, M.A. (1975) Domestic battleground: The violent family image. *Criminal Justice Digest, 3*(11), 6-9.

(Case Report - Alice Crimmins)

Gross, K. (1975) *The Alice Crimmins case*. New York: Knopf.

(The Torture Doctor)

Franke, D. (1975) *The torture doctor: the incredible but true story of Herman W. Mudgett, the most fiendish killer in the annals of American crime*. New York: Hawthorn.

(Classic Crimes)

Roughead, W. (1975) *Classic Crimes*. New York: Random.

(Case Report - Leopold/Loeb)

Higdon, H. (1975) *Crime of the century: The Leopold & Loeb case*. New York: Putnam.

(Case Report - L.A. Slasher)

L.A. slasher strikes again. (1975) *Crime Control Digest, 9*(5), 7.

(Crimes - Classic)

Roughead, W.N. (1975) *Classic crime: A selection from works of William Roughead made by W.N. Roughead.* New York: Hyperion.

(Death of a Nurse)

Editorial: Death of a nurse. (1975) *British Medical Journal, 4*(5995), 425.

(Gunmen - Rampage)

Gunmen go on rampage. (1975) *Crime Control digest, 9*(49), 5.

(Case Report - Lord Duncan)

Murder for mayfair: Charges against Lord Duncan. (1974, Nov. 25) *Time, 104*, p. 58+.

(Case Report - Defeo Murders)

Rich kid: Defeo murders. (1974, Nov. 25) *Newsweek, 84*, p. 43.

(Case Report - Ivan the Ripper)

Ivan the Ripper. (1974, Nov. 11) *Newsweek, 84*, p. 55.

(Case Report - Joyce Cary)

Seltzer, A.J. (1974, Autumn) Speaking out of both sides of the horse's mouth: Joyce Cary vs. Gully Jimson. *Contemporary Literature, 15*, pp. 448-502.

(Murder Story)

Earnshaw, T.K., & Pace, P.J. (1974, Aug. 30) Let the hand receiving it be ever so chaste. *Modern L Review, 37*, pp. 481-496.

(Murder - Bourgeois Style)

Futch, J.D. (1974, Aug. 30) Mass murder, bourgeois style. *National Review, 26*, p. 980.

(A. King's Murder)

Murder in a church: Shooting of A. King. (1974, July 20) *Nation, 219*, pp. 35-36.

(Case Report - Shooting of A. King)

That certain smile: Shooting of A. King. (1974, July 15) *Newsweek, 84*, p. 30.

(Case Report - Shooting of A. King)

Third King tragedy: Shooting of A. King. (1974, July 15) *Time, 104*, p. 20.

(A. King's Murder)

Another King tragedy: Shooting of A. King. (1974, July 8) *Newsweek, 84*, pp. 33-34.

(Case Report - Zebra Killers)

Zebra killers. (1974, April 29) *Newsweek, 83*, p. 27.

(Case Report - Banquo's)

Blythe, J.H. (1974, April) His horses go about: The circumstance of Banquo's death and the escape of Fleance. *Notes and Queries, 21*, pp. 131-132.

(Case Report - Dominici)

Laborde, J. (1974) *The Dominici affair, translated from the French by M. Walman*. New York: Morrow.

(Case Reports - Enigmas)

Williamson, H.R. (1974) *Historical enigmas*. New York: St. Martin.

(Case Report - Houston 'Candy Man')

Olsen, J. (1974) *The man with the candy: The story of the Houston mass murders*. New York: S&S.

(Case Report - Raskolnikov's Motives)

Wasiolek, E. (1974) Raskolnikov's motives: Love and murder. *American Imago, 31*(3), pp. 252-269.

(Case Report - Jack the Ripper)

Bell, D. (1974) Jack the Ripper: Final solution. *Criminologist, 9*(33), 40-61.

(Jack the Ripper)

Davis, J. (1974) Jack the Ripper: The handwriting analysis. *Criminologist, 9*(33), 62-69.

(Criminality - Travel)

Krefft, S. (1974) Criminality in air travel (kriminalitat in der luftahrt). *Arch Kriminol, 153*(3-4), 84-96.

(Percy Murder)

Percy lead #273. (1973, Dec. 10) *Time, 102*, p. 29.

(Murderers - Education)

Murchison, J. (1973, Oct.) Never too late to learn. *American Educator, 9*, 28-31.

(Case Report - Nagaraju Case)

Reddy, K.S. (1973, Aug.) Identification of dismembered parts: The medicolegal aspects of the Nagaraju case. *Forensic Science, 2*, 351-374.

(Case Report - W.D. Archerd)

Taylor, L.B., Jr. (1973, July) Perfect crime: Case of W.D. Archerd. *Saturday Evening Post, 245*, pp. 26-28+.

(Richie Murder Case)

Clemons, W. (1973, June 4) Richie, by T. Thompson (review). *Newsweek, 81*, p. 101.

(Murder - G. Jayne)

Boyle, R.H., & Higgins, A. (1973, June 4) End of a bloody bad show (case of G. Jayne). *Sports Illustrated, 38*, pp. 36-38+.

(Case Report - B. Dewevre)

Notary and the miner's daughter (Brigitte Dewevre case). (1973, May 14) *Time, 101*, p. 54.

(Murder - W.R. Judd)

Dobkins, J.D., & Hendricks, R.J. (1973) *Winnie Ruth Judd: The Trunk murders and the strange events afterward.* New York: G&D.

(Case Report - Gunshot Wound)

Fatteh, A. (1972, April) Homicidal gunshot wound of mouth. *Forensic Science Soc, 12*, 347-349.

(Medicolegal Case Report)

Cameron, J., et al. (1972) R. vs. Payne. *Med Leg J, 40*, 18-26.

(Hosein and Hosein)

Hudson, W.M. (1972) R. vs. Hosein and Hosein. *Med Leg J, 40*, 130-143.

(Murder Story)

Turkus, B.B., & Feder, S. (1972) *Murder, Inc.* New York: Manor Books.

(Supernatural Phenomena)

Von Daniken, E. (1972) *Gods from outer space.* Bantam.

(Ballroom Murders)

Ballroom murders: The J. List family. (1971, Dec. 20) Newsweek, 78, p. 30+.

(Case Report - Charles Manson)

Sanders, E. (1971, Nov.) Charlie and the devil: Excerpts from *The Family*. *Esquire, 76*, pp. 105-112+.

(Case Report - Woodstock Murder)

French, A.L. (1971, Autumn) Richard II and the Woodstock murder. *Shakespeare Quarterly, 22*, 337-344.

(Case Report - P.M. Newell)

Rosemary's babies: Case of Patrick Michael Newell. (1971, July 19) *Newsweek, 78*, p. 22.

(Case Report - Corona)

Corona in court. (1971, June 14) *Newsweek, 77*, p. 37.

(Case Report - Murder of Police)

Mourning the police. (1971, June 7) *Time, 97*, p. 8.

(Case Report - Highway Murder)

Critchley, T.A., & James, P.D. (1971) *The maul and the pear tree: The Ratcliffe Highway murders of 1811.* New York: Crane-Russek.

(Case Report - R. vs. Cray, et al)

R. vs. Cray, and others. (1971) *Med Leg J, 39*, 4-16.

(Double Murder)

Dittrich, K., et al. (1971) A double murder (German). 20957. J. 25, '71, 11, S. 584-588 (IBZ 1971).

(Case Report - Ohta Family)

Tarot murders; case of the Ohta family. (1970, Nov. 2) *Newsweek, 76*, p. 32+.

(Case Report - Ben Chaney)

Mok, M. (1970, June 19) Ben Chaney at eleven and at seventeen; with report by M. Mok. *Life, 68*, pp. 26-29.

(Case Report - Sharon Tate Murders)

Singer, M. (1970, April) Fragments from the shooting gallery: Sharon Tate murders. *Ramp Mag, 8*, pp. 16-18.

(Case Report - Sharon Tate)

Maas, P. (1970, April) Sharon Tate murders. *Ladies Home Journal, 87*, p. 52+.

(Case Report - A. Rackley)

Who killed Alex Rackley? (1970, March 30) *Newsweek, 75*, p. 22.

(Case Report - Yablonski)

Just friends; Yablonski murders. (1970, Feb. 21) *New Republic, 162*, p. 10-11.

(Unnatural Death)

Concealed unnatural death. (1970, Feb. 14) *British Medical Journal, 1*, 384.

(Case Reports - Yablonski)

Hand from the grave; murder of the Yablonski family. (1970, Feb. 2) *Time, 95*, p. 11.

(Case Report - Richard Mattingly, Sr.)

Muffin: Daughter charged with murder of Richard Mattingly, Sr. (1970, Jan 26) *Newsweek, 75*, p. 21+.

(Case Report - Yablonski)

Fifth suspect: Murder of UMW executive J.A. Yablonski. (1970, Jan. 19) *Newsweek, 75*, p. 24.

(Case Report - Yablonski)

Lawrence, D. (1970, Jan. 19) Crime that shocked the nation; the murder of J. Yablonski. *US News, 68*, p. 80.

(Case Report - Murderer)

Gaddis, T.E. (1970) *Killer*. New York: Macmillan.

(Double Murder)

Matzler, A. (1970) "Portrait" of a double murder. 20957. J. 24, '70, 12, S. 616-619 (IBZ 1971).

(Murder)

Reinhardt, J.M. (1970) *Nothing left but murder*. New York: Johnson.

(Mafia Case)

Cameron, J.M. (1970) R. vs. Jewell: The mafia trial. *Med Leg J, 38*, 74-84.

(Case Report - Five Murders)

Davis, I., & Leblanc, J. (1970) *Five to die*. New York: Holloway.

(Baffling Murders)

Pearson, E. (1970) *Murders that baffled the experts*. New York: Signet.

(Murder Files)

Cuthbert, T.M. (1970) A portfolio of murders. 7430. vol. 116, '70. n. 530, p. 1-10 (IBZ 1971).

(Murder - Victorian)

Altick, R.D. (1970) *Victorian studies in scarlet*. New York: Norton.

(Case Report - C. Thompson)

Giese, D.J. (1969) *Carol Thompson murder case*. New York: Llewellyn.

(Case Report - Wylie-Hoffert)

Lefkowitz, B., & Gross, K.G. (1969) *Victims: The Wylie-Hoffert murder case and its strange aftermath*. New York: Putnam.

(Case Report - Improbable Events)

Kovac, T. (1968, March) Two improbable events (German). *Ther Gegenw, 107*, 346-348.

(Mini-car Murder)

The mini-car murder. (1968, Jan.) *Med Science and the Law, 8*, 54-55.

(Case Report - Murder Squad)

Joyner, W.B. (1968) *Murder squad*. New York: Tri-Ocean.

(Double Murder)

Kosyra, H. (1968) De Doppermorder Adolf Muller. 3647. Bd. 143, '68, H. 3-4, S. 61-66 (IBZ 1970).

(Case Report - Murder)

Simondi, M. (1968) Nota in margine ad una ricerca sull'omicidio. . ser. 4, an. lo, '68, p. 75-

82. (IBZ 1969).

(Case Report - Moors Murder)

Mars-Jones, W.L. (1968) The Moors murder. *Medicolegal Journal, 36*, 5-20.

(Case Report - Mass Murder)

Bruch, H. (1967, Nov.) Mass murder: The Wagner case. *American Journal of Psychiatry, 124*, 693-698.

(Case Report - Comb as Weapon)

Hendry, W.T., et al. (1967, Oct.) Stab wound of medulla by handle of metal comb. *Medical Science and the Law, 7*, 213-215.

(Parricide)

Moulun, R., et al. (1967, July) Sibling bondage: A clinical report on a parricide and his brother. *Bulletin of the Menninger Clinic, 31*, 229-235.

(Case Report - Louis Rosset)

Le meutre des Fivettes (Louis Rosset). 30202. vol. 21, '67, n. 4, p. 325-330 (IBZ 1968).

(Case Report - Murder)

Kilgallen, D. (1967) *Murder one*. New York: Random.

(Case Report - Art of Murder)

Gibson, W.B., (Ed.) (1967) *Fine art of murder*. New York: Grosset.

(Case Report - Manfred Jung)

If I had killed someone ... : The trial of Manfred Jung. 33077. J. 21, '67, n. 40, S. 72-75.

(Psychiatric Hospitalization)

Belleau, T., & Arsenian, J. (1967) Homicide and hospitalization: A case report. *Psychiatry*, 1967, 301, 1, Feb., 73-78. SA(1968), p. 955.

(Social Problems - Homicide)

Wolfgang, M.E., Ed. (1967) *Studies in murder*. New York: Harper.

(Accidental Deaths)

Pilleri, M., et al. (1966, Nov.-Dec.) On three cases of accidental death due to gunshot wounds from a rifle due to malfunctioning of the weapon. *Minerva Medicoleg, 86*, 307-309.

(Case Report - Murder by a Juvenile)

Kopkind, A. (1966, Aug. 12) Average American boy. *New Statesman, 72*, pp. 220-221.

(Case Report - David Riccio)

Fraser, A. (1966, April) Murder of David Riccio. *History Today, 16*, pp. 243-250.

(Case Report - Theft and Murder)

Enright, D.J. (1966, March 18) Few dollars and a radio (Clutter murders). *New Statesman, 71*, pp. 377-378.

(Double Murder)

Schmid, J. (1966) Teuflischer Doppelmord. 20957. J. 20, '66, 10, S. 542 (IBZ 1967).

(Double Murder)

Ehrlich, C. (1966) Doppelmord in westerwald. 20957. J. 20, '66, 3, S. IBZ 1967).

(Case Report - Sam Sheppard)

Seibert, C. (1966) Der seltsame Fall des Dr. Sam Sheppard. 20154. J. 21, '66, H. 17, S. 559-560 (IBZ 1967).

(Case Report - J.G. Wirsung)

Morgenstern, L. (1965, June) The murder of Johan Georg Wirsung. *Surgery, 57*, 906-907.

(Case Report - Domann Case)

Weber, F.R. (1965) Der Fall Domann. 20957. J. 19, '65, 5, S. 240-243 (IBZ 1966).

(Case Report - Mary McKinnon)

Miller, J.B. (1965) A cloud of witnesses or the trial of Mary McKinnon. 20132. vol. 10, '65, pt. 2, p. 117-136 (IBZ 1967).

(Murder - Historical)

Szondi, L. (1964, Fall) Thanatos and Cain. *American Imago, 21*, pp. 52-63.

(Case Report - Von Gudden)

Dewhurst, K. (1964, Aug.) The murder of Dr. von Gudden. *Practitioner, 193*, 220-227.

(Case Report - Murderer's Hatred)

Bigelow, N. (1964, July) "I 'ates yer one 'an hall". *Psychiatric Quarterly, 38*, 544-553.

(Case Report - Simcox)

Simcox case (double guilty to capital murder). (1964, March 7) *Economist, 210*, p. 871.

(Case Report - Murderers)

Feinberg, J. (1964, Feb. 27) On being, morally speaking, a murderer. *Journal of Philosophy, 61*, 158-171.

(Case Report - Phillips)

Miner, J.W. (1964, Jan.) Phillips case -- a new dimension in murder. *Journal of Forensic Science, 9*, 1.

(Murder Story)

Ambler, E. (1964) *Ability to kill.* New York: NAL.

(Case Report - "Born Alive")

Cannon, R.W. (1963, Nov.) Born alive. *Criminal Law Review*, p. 748.

(Murderers)

Simpson, K., & Acott, B. (1963) R. vs. Hamratty. The A6 murder. *Medicolegal Journal, 31,* 3-14.

(Case Report - Lewis Wolfe Murder)

Clements, A.V. (1962, June) State and Lewis Wolfe: A case history. *Albany Law Review, 26,* 187.

(Case Report - Little Elmer)

Trave, R. (1962, March) Little Elmer. *Michigan SB Journal, 41*, 11.

(Case Report - Psychology)

Psychology of strange killers. (1962) New York: CC Thomas.

(Family-style Murder)

Lipsig, F. (1962) *Murder, family style.* New York: Macmillan.

(Murder Book)

McComas, J.F. (1962) *Graveside companion.* Astor-Honor.

(Case Report - Smith)

Yahuda, J. (1960, Sept. 30) Smith's case. *Sol J, 104*, p. 771.

(Background Evidence)

Handler, J.F. (1960, Sept.-Oct.) Background evidence in murder cases. *Journal of Criminal Law, 51*, 317.

(Crime of Passion)

Rawlinson, P.A.G. (1959, July 3) Le crime passionel. *Sol J, 103*, p. 515.

(Case Report - Spilsbury)

Robinson, C.F. (1959, June 6) O. Magrath, Spilsbury, and homicides. *Journal of Maine Medical Association, 50*, 6.

(Case Report - A. von Droste)

Thomas, L.H.C. (1959, Jan) Die judenbuche by Annette von Droste-Hulshoff. *Modern Language Review, 54*, pp. 56-65.

(Case Report - J. Ford)

Carsaniga, G.M. (1958, Fall) Truth in John Ford's broken heart. *Comparative Literature, 10,* 344-348.

(Case Report - Montesi)

Clark, C.D.L. (1958, March) Montesi case. *Criminal Law Review 1958*, 163.

(Case Report - Chicken Thief)

Morris, N. (1958, March) Slain chicken thief. *Sydney Law Review, 2*, 414.

(Henderson Murder)

Jones, C.E. (1957, Oct.) Fielding's true patriot and the Henderson murder (with text of Fielding letter). *Modern Language Review, 52*, 498-503.

(Vickers Case)

Vickers case (Regnia v. Vickers, 1957, 3 W L R 326). (1957, Oct.) *L Q Review, 73*, 464.

(Murder Story)

Murderers and the unruly horse. (1957, June 7) *Law Times, 107*, 358.

(Plea of Innocence)

Not guilty. (1957, April) *Man B Times, 29*, p. 45.

(Case Report - Leyra Case)

Fraenkel, O.K. (1957, Spring) Leyra case. *Criminal Law Review, 4*, 83.

(Houseboat Twins)

Houseboat twins case. (1957, Feb.) *Criminal Law Review 1957*, 80.

(Crimes of Passion)

Ancel, M. (1957, Jan.) Crime passionel. *L Q Review, 73*, 36.

(Case Report)

Gloning, I., et al. (1957) A case of corporeal metamorphognosy (German). *Wein Zschr Nervenh, 14*(2-3), 228-235.

(Pierre Dion Murder)

Leblond, S. (1956, Sept.) Murder of Pierre Dion (French). *Laval Med, 21*(7), 1010-1017.

(Case Report - Ratcliffe)

Radzinowicz, L. (1956, April) Ratcliffe murders. *Camb Law Journal 1956*, 39.

(Case Report - George Wythe)

Boyd, J.F. (1955, Oct.) Murder of George Wythe. *William & Mary Quarterly, sect. 3, 12*, 513-542.

(Murder Story)

Wellman, M.W. (1955) *Dead and gone*. Chapel Hill, NC: University of North Carolina Press.

(Case Report - Keshner)

Felony murder and the Keshner case. (1954, Dec.) *Brooklyn Law Review 1954*, 84-90.

(Towpath Case)

Mant, A.K. (1954, July-Sept.) Teddington towpath murders. *Journal of Forensic Medicine, 1*, 260-270.

(Towpath Case)

Walton, H.B., & Doherty, C. (1954, March) Towpath murder. *Criminal Law Review 1954*,

179-188.

(Case Report - Straffen Case)

Treitel, G.H. (1953, Jan.) Straffen case. *Modern L Review, 16*, 74-79.

(Thakur Khuman Singh Case)

Carstairs, G.M. (1953) The case of Thakur Khuman Singh: a culture-conditioned crime. *British Journal of Delinquency, 4*, 14-25.

(Case Report - France Report)

Drouin, P. (1952, Nov. 22) Apres plus de trois mois d'enquete, le mur de silence qui entoure le crime de Lurs n'a pu etre franchi. *France Illus, 371*, p. 536.

(Somnambulistic Homicides)

Morris, N. (1951, Aug.) Somnambulistic homicide: Ghosts, spiders, and North Koreans. *Res Judicatae, 5*, 29-33.

(Uncomfortable Murders)

Hitchler, W.H. (1951, Jan.) Uncomfortable murders. *Dick Law Review, 55*, 139-140.

(Case Report - Ruth Steinhagen)

Haines, W.H., & Esser, R.A. (1950) Case history of Ruth Steinhagen. *American Journal of Psychiatry, 106*, 737-743.

(Case Report - General)

Orr, C.B. (1949, July 16) Death on the road. *Just P, 113*, 443-444.

(Famous Murders)

Hirsch, R. (1949) *Crimes that shook the world.* Books for Libraries.

(Case Report - Motivation)

Greene, J.E. (1948) Motivations of a murderer. *Journal of Abnormal Soc Psychology, 43*, 526-531.

(Psychopathology)

Karpman, B. (1948) *Case studies of the psychopathology of crime,Vol. IV: cases 14-17.* Washington, DC: Washington Medical Science Press.

(Case Report - Mayer & Smith)

Hilling, H.H. (1947, May) The case of Decasto Earl Mayer and Mary Ellen Smith. *Washington Law Review, 22*, 79-109.

(Case Study - W. Heirens)

Kennedy, F. (1947) Psychiatric study of William Heirens. *Journal of Criminal Law and Criminology, 38*, 311-341.

(True Murder Story)

Montgomery, A.E. (1944, Sept.) An interesting case. *Lawyer, 8*, 22-24.

(Case Report - Parson's Tale)

Johnson, D.R. (1942, March) Homicide in the Parson's tale. *PMLA, 57*, 51-56.

(Stroud Case)

Hopkins, R.J. (1941, May) The Stroud case. *J B A Kansas, 9*, 373-381.

(Homicide)

Shea, L.W. (1940, Jan. 30) In bar of dower - - homicide. *Florida Law Journal, 14*, 19-21.

(Homicide)

Laub, B.R. (1939, July) A brief glance at murder. *Case and Commentary, 45*, 15-20.

(Case Study - Jud)

Garcon, M. (1937, July 25) La vraie historie de Jud (French). *Mercure Fr, 277*, 246-266.

(Murder Fine)

Hamil, F.C. (1937, July) Presentment of Englishry and the murder fine. *Speculum, 12*, 285-298.

(Seefeld Case)

Lange, J. (1937) Several criminological views concerning the Seefeld case (German). *Mschr KrimBiol, 28*, 37.

(Case Study - General)

Coulon, M. (1935, Feb. 15) Reflexions sur l'affaire Prince et quelques autres. *Mercure Fr, 258*, 63-82.

(Lennox-Maxwell Case)

Steele, S. (1935) The case of Lennox-Maxwell. *Notre Dame Law Journal, 9*, 141.

(Donald Murder Case)

Roughead, W. (1934) Mrs. Donald's crime: Or the force of circumstance. *Jurid Review, 46*, 355-399.

(Wieland Case)

Dreyfuss, K. (1934) The Wieland case (German). *Int Z Psychoanal, 20*, 210-240.

(Halsmann Case)

Storring, G. (1932) Opinion in the Halsmann case (German). *Arch f d Ges Psychol, 84*, 372-386.

(Dying Declaration)

Hankes, F.H. (1931, Nov.) Dying declarations (Cochrane v. Commonwealth (Ky.) 33 S W (2d)). *Kentucky Law Journal*, 20, 101-105.

(Case Report - Legal)

Zeal. (1931, June 13) *Just P, 95*, 371-372.

(Albert Lane Murder Case)

Arado, C.C. (1931, May) Albert Lane, murder. *Journal of Criminal Law, 22*, 98-107.

(Murder Story)

Engelhardt, L. (1931) Der gardien de la paix prevost (German and French). *Arch f Krim, 89*, 177-190.

(Case Report - J. Zell)

Mezeger, & Heess. (1931) The case of Julius Zell in Zweifelsberg (German). *Arch f Krim, 89*, 207-215.

(Case Report)

The risk of being murdered (Holden v. Premier Waterproof and Rubber Co., The Times) (1930, Dec. 20) *L T, 170*, 507-508.

(Case Report - Rex v. Fox)

Room 66 (Rex v. Fox). (1930, March 29) *Just P, 94*, 206.

(Case Report - Neckerman)

Wolff, F. (1930) The case of Neckerman (German). *Monatsscher f Krimpsychol u Strafrechtref, 4*, 212-226.

(Case Report - Voller)

Kolle, K. (1930) The case of Voller (German). *Monatsschr f. Krimpsychol u. Strafrechtsref, 4*, 226-236.

(Case Report - Friedlander Case)

Tumlirz, O. (1930) The case of Manasse Friedlander (German). *In Die Jugendlichen und ihre Erzieher. II. Manns Pad Mag, 1930, 1314*, 45-49.

(Killing Rights)

The right to kill. (1929, Dec. 21) *Sol J, 73*, 758-759; *Ir L T, 63*, 305 (1929, Dec. 21).

(Case Report - Hickman Case)

Bowers, P.E. (1929) William Edward Hickman. *Medical Journal and Records, 130*, 79-82, 139-142.

(Case Report - Louvel Case)

Levy-Valensi, J., & Rigot, D. (1929) Louvel the magnicide (French). *Hygiene Ment, 24*, 125-150.

(Case Report - Mulbuie case)

Roughead, W. (1928) The Mulbuie case, or when Adam delved. *Jurid Review, 40*, 111.

(Poe and Plagiarism)

Wigmore, J.H. (1928) Did Poe plagiarize *Murders in the rue morgue*? *Cornell Law Quarterly 15*, 219.

(The Murderer's Touch)

Riddell, W.R. (1927, Aug.) At the murderer's touch. *Journal of Criminal Law, 18*, 175-179.

(Violet Gibson Case)

Ferri, E. (1927) The personality of Violet Gibson (French). *Rev de Crim, 14*, 259-268.

(Murder Case)

Riddell, W.R. (1927) A strange murder case. *Journal of Criminal Law, 18*, 365.

(Case Report)

Danville, G. (1925, March 15) Le droit de tuer. *Mercrure Fr, 178*, 671-683.

(DeQuincey Case)

Roughead, W. (1924) A case for DeQuincey. *Jurid Review, 36*, 295.

(Varota Murder)

Taylor, R.C. (1923) The kidnapping and murder of the Varotta boy. *Virginia Law Review, 9*, 432.

(Lord Eglinton Murder)

Lovat-Frase, J.A. (1916) Murder of Lord Eglinton. *Jurid Review, 28*, 155.

(Schmidt Case)

White, W.A. (1914) Comments on the case of Father Johannis Schmidt. *Journal of Criminal Law, 5*, 84.

(Chantrelle Case)

The case of Eugene Chantrelle. (1907) *Law Notes, 11*, 50.

(Olivo Case)

Speranza, G.C. (1906) The case of Alberto Olivo. *The Green Bag, 18*, p. 26.

(Dr. Cream Case)

Chapin, H.G. (1902) The strange case of Dr. Cream. *The Green Bag, 14*, p. 426.

(Art of Murder)

Chapin, H.G. (1901) A study in the fine art of murder. *The Green Bag, 13*, p. 515.

(Abel's Murder)

Amram, D.W. (1901) The murder of Abel. *The Green Bag, 13*, p. 592.

(Sipido Case)

Speyer. (1900) Legal aspects of the Sipido case. *Journal Comp Leg, 2*, 434.

Murder News Stories

(Israel Massacre)

What the tapes show. (1990, Nov. 13) *Village Voice, 35*(46), pp. 25, 28+.

(Palestinian Massacre)

Emery, M. (1990, Nov. 13) New Evidence. *Village Voice, 35*(46), pp. 26-27.

(Pierson Murder)

Page, J.A. (1990, Nov. 9) A dangerous environment. *Commonwealth, 117*(19), pp. 660-662.

(Murder - Editorial)

The Bill at the Bailey. (1990, Nov. 2) *New Statesman & Society, 3*, p. 5.

(Wife Murder)

Baker, J.N. (1990, Oct. 8) Mississippi gothic (R. Hane arrested for murder of his wife). *Newsweek, 116*, p. 36.

(Murder - Christian Brando)

Gottlieb, J. (1990, Oct. 1) Mutiny from the Bounty. *Us*, pp. 38-44.

(Harwood Murder)

Manguel, A. (1990, Oct.) Killers in paradise. *Saturday Night, 105*(8), pp. 25-33.

(Newspaper)

Fitzgerald, M. (1990, Sept. 15) The all-crime newspaper. *Editor and Publisher, 123*(37), p. 44.

(Murder Victims)

Updike, J., et al. (1990, Sept. 10) Books. *New York, 23*(35), pp. 104-108.

(Murder - Chico Mendez)

Matthews, T. (1990, Sept. 3) A life under fire in Brazil. *Newsweek, 116*(10), pp. 62-64.

(Gay Murder)

Minkowitz, D. (1990, Aug. 28) Gay murder sparks march. *Village Voice, 35*(35), p. 15.

(Chico Mendes Murder)

Brooke, J. (1990, Aug. 19) Why they killed Chico Mendes. *New York Times Book Review*, p. 7.

(Murder of CBS Reporter)

Stuttaford, G. (1990, Aug. 17) The Polk conspiracy. *Publishers Weekly, 237*(33), p. 56.

(Aranow Murder)

Fishman, A.J. (1990, Aug.) Arrest in Aranow murder. *Motor Boating and Sailing, 166*, pp. 44-47+.

(Murder - Mendez)

Shoumatoff, A. (1990, Aug.) The second death of Chico Mendez. *Vanity Fair, 53*(8), pp. 68-82.

(Murderer - Female)

Colapinto, J. (1990, Aug.) By love obsessed. *Mademoiselle, 96*(8), pp. 188-191+.

(Renee Linton Murder)

Hopkins, E. (1990, Aug.) No place to hide. *Essence, 21*(4), pp. 66-68+.

(El Salvador Murders)

Cockburn, A., McKerrow, R. (1990, July 27) Death squads: The smoking gun speaks. *New Statesman & Society, 3*(111), pp. 14-15.

(Murder - Family)

Brower, M., & Tamerkin, C. (1990, July 23) A fanatical cult leader faces trial in Ohio for the brutal murder of a family of five. *People Weekly, 34*(3), pp. 45-47.

(Murder Trial)

Moments. (1990, July) *Life, 13*(9), pp. 6-16.

(Murderer - Author)

Stein, M.L. (1990, June 23) To publish or not to publish. *Editor and Publisher, 123*(25), pp. 22, 64.

(G. Bull Murdered)

A make-my-day superweapon (G. Bull murdered while planning to build cannon for Iraq). (1990, June 4) *US News and World Report, 108*, pp. 48-49.

(Menendez Murders)

Hamill, P. (1990, June) Murder on Mulholland. *Esquire, 113*(6), pp. 67-70.

(Verdict)

Hackett, G. (1990, May 28) No justice - no peace. *Newsweek, 115*(22), pp. 18-19.

(Male Murderer)

Buckley, L. (1990, May 28) A killing at Brand's house. *Newsweek, 115*(22), p. 25.

(Raymond Ray Murders)

Bergman, B. (1990, May 21) Anatomy of a tragedy. *Macleans, 103*(21), p. 20.

(El Salvador Murders)

Stahl, T.H. (1990, May 19) Don't overlook those network documentaries. *America, 162*(19), p. 505.

(Serial Killers)

Hunting humans. (1990, May 13) *New York Times Book Review*, p. 16.

(Salazar Murder)

Shannon, E. (1990, April 23) Snatching "Dr. Megele" (DEA agents capture H. Alvarez Machain). *Time, 135*, p. 27.

(Japanese Murderer)

Buruma, I. (1990, March 31) Consuming passion. *Spectator, 264*(8438), pp. 12-13.

(Menendez Family)

Poindexter, J. (1990, March 26) A Beverly Hills paradise lost (Menendez children accused of killing parents; cover story). *People Weekly, 33*, pp. 66-69+.

(Murderers - Paroled)

Bamforth, I. (1990, March 23) A conditional existence (review of T. Parker's *Life after life*). *Times Literary Supplement, 4538*, p. 324.

(Scarsdale Affair)

Pooley, E. (1990, March 19) Love and death (C. Warmus kills B.J. Solomon over fatal attraction affair in Scarsdale, NY). *New York, 23*, pp. 50-54+.

(Hawkins Murder)

Harrison, B.G. (1990, March) Women and Blacks and Bensonhurst (murder of Y. Hawkins evokes childhood memories). *Harper's, 280*, pp. 69-79+.

(Murderers - Interviewed)

Bamforth, I. (1990, March 23) A conditional existence (review of T. Parker's *Life after life*). *Times Literary Supplement*, p. 324.

(Salazar Murder)

Brown, M. (1990, March) Drug wars, news casualties. *Channels, 10*, p. 22.

(Family Murder)

Streshinsky, S. (1990, March) Angela: A story of innocence, hope, despair, and mass murder (slaying of A. Salcido and family in Boyes Hot Springs, CA). *Glamour, 88*, pp. 268-271+.

(Fatal Attraction)

Brower, M. (1990, Feb. 26) Death imitates art as police charge teacher Carolyn Warmus with a 'fatal attraction' killing (shooting of B.J. Soloman in Scarsdale, NY.). *People Weekly, 33*, pp. 81-83.

(Family Murder)

Park, J. (1990, Feb. 12) Helping TV's Blind Faith, a son confronts a murder in the family (R. Marshall, son of Toms River, NJ murder victim. *People Weekly, 33*, pp. 42-43.

(Boston Murder)

White Boston family sets up scholarship to ease racial tension. (1990, Feb. 12) *Jet, 77*(18),

p. 9.

(Family Murder)

Litwinn, S. (1990, Feb. 10-16) Reliving a family tragedy (Marshall family murder case reenacted in TV version of Blind Faith). *TV Guide, 38*, pp. 22-25.

(Y. Miller Murder)

Miller, J.B. (1990, Feb. 7-14) In the city, a tale of crime and punishment (82-year-old Y. Miller found murdered in New York City). *The Christian Century, 107*, pp. 116-117.

(Murderer Killed)

Pooley, E. (1990, Jan. 29) Death of a hood (G. Farace, murderer of DEA agent E. Hatcher, killed; cover story). *New York, 23*, pp. 26-33.

(Amazon Martyr)

Hewitt, B. (1990, Jan. 15) A martyr who died for the Amazon (C. Mendez Fihlo). *People Weekly, 33*, pp. 28-35.

(Nuns)

Dangerous highways. (1990, Jan. 15) *Time, 135*(3), p. 40.

(C. Mendez Murder)

Hecht, S., & Cockburn A. (1990, Jan./Feb.) Media misses real Amazon story (land ownership issue in C. Mendez murder). *Utne Reader*, pp. 126-127.

(Family Murderer)

Jacobi, M. (1990, Jan.) The mystery of the model husband. *Good Housekeeping, 210*(1), pp. 82-83+.

(Dead Girl)

Preston, G.A. (1990) Law and Crime: The dead girl. *Library Journal, 115*(35), 125.

(Terror)

Bieleski, L. (1990) Social Sciences: Law and Crime - - the blood covenant. *Library Journal, 115*(12), 112.

(Serial Murders)

Lindheimer, S.K. (1990) Law and crime: Freed to kill. *Library Journal, 115*(16), 103.

(Sir Harry Oaks)

Preston, G.A. (1990) Social Sciences: Law and Crime - - Conspiracy of crowns. *Library Journal, 115*(10), 150.

(Stanford White Murder)

Hart, J. (1989, Dec. 22) Our greatest architect. *National Review, 41*(24), pp. 41-42.

(South African Police)

Probing the hit squads. (1989, Dec. 18) *Time, 134*(25), p. 30.

(Feminism and Murder)

Gunning for feminism. (1989, Dec. 15) *New Statesman and Society, 2*(80), pp. 61-63.

(Curt Moore Murder)

Peretz, M. (1989, Dec. 11) Global reach. *New Republic, 201*(23), pp. 9-11.

(Serial Killings)

Turque, B., & Hammill, R. (1989, Dec. 4) A string of sixty murders. *Newsweek, 114*(23), p. 64.

(El Salvador)

Stahl, T.H. (1989, Dec. 2) Of many things. *America, 313*(17), p. 390.

(El Salvador)

Bilsky, A., et al. (1989, Nov. 27) Wave of terror. *Macleans, 102*(48), pp. 26-27.

(El Salvador)

Bloodstained El Salvador. (1989, Nov. 25) *Economist, 313*(7630), p. 45.

(Don Bass Murder)

Obituaries: Don Bass. (1989, Nov. 18) *The Sporting News, 208*(23), p. 54.

(Suicide/Homicide)

Billingsley, K.L. (1989, Nov. 18) An unsolved 'suicide'. *American Spectator, 263*(8419), pp. 14-15.

(Boston Murder)

Brower, M., et al. (1989, Nov. 13) A dark night of the soul of Boston. *People Weekly, 32*(20), pp. 52-55.

(Boston Murder)

The murder of a mother-to-be. (1989, Nov. 11) *Newsweek, 114*(19), p. 45.

(Journalists Killed)

Radolf, A. (1989, Nov. 11) Working under fire (journalists in danger). *Editor and Publisher, 122*(45), pp. 15, 34.

(Steve Moore Murder)

Obituaries: Steve Moore. (1989, Nov. 6) *The Sporting News, 208*(21), p. 57.

(Red Baron Murder)

Bernard, J. (1989, Nov. 4) Apollo aftermath. *Spectator, 263*(8417), p. 39.

(Youngest Murderer)

Anderson, C.E. (1989, Nov.) Grown-up crime, boy defendant: ten-year-old youth to be tried for murder as an adult. *ABA Journal, 75*, 26-27.

(Hunter Shooting)

Clark, E. (1989, Nov.) The killing of Karen Wood. *Yankee, 53*(11), pp. 94-99+.

(Pavlov Murder)

Theodoracopulos, T. (1989, Oct. 27) Greek farce. *National Review, 41*(20), pp. 25-26.

(Terrorism)

Halvey, D., & Livingstone, N.C. (1989, Oct. 23) An American soldier's death becomes a pawn in a terrorist power struggle. *US News and World Report, 107*(16), p. 21.

(Safdar Hami Murder)

Armistead, C. (1989, Oct. 13) Taking to the street. *New Statesman and Society, 2*(71), p. 44.

(Mexican Journalist Killed)

Jackson, S.F. (1989, Oct.7) Killing of Mexican journalists. *Editor and Publisher, 122*(40), pp. 14-15+.

(New York Murder)

Racism, 1989. (1989, Oct.) *Progressive, 53*(10), p. 10.

(Policemen Surrender)

Hornung, R. (1989, Sept. 19) The last caged panther. *Village Voice, 34*(38), pp. 10, 16.

(Hawkins Slaying)

NY gunman surrenders in Hawkins slaying: Blacks riot on Brooklyn bridge. (1989, Sept. 18) *Jet, 76*(24), pp. 7-8.

(Colombian Murders)

Rosenberg, T. (1989, Sept. 18) A mess in the Andes. *New Republic, 201*(12-13), pp. 23-26.

(Palestinian Killings)

The Intifada turns against itself. (1989, Sept. 16) *Economist, 312*(7620), pp. 41-42.

(Winnipeg Murder Case)

Kaihla, P., & Brosnahan, M. (1989, Sept. 11) A death in Winnipeg. *Macleans, 102*(37), p. 16.

(Huey Newton Murder)

Cleaver, K. (1989, Sept. 5) Huey without tears. *Village Voice, 34*(36), pp. 31-32.

(Bensonhurst)

Dobie, K. (1989, Sept. 5) The boys of Bensonhurst. *Village Voice, 34*(36), pp. 34-38.

(Activist Murder)

Johnson, T. (1989, Sept. 5) Armed and intellectually dangerous. *Village Voice, 34*(36), pp. 31-32.

(George Adamson Murder)

Manegold, C.S., & Shields, T. (1989, Sept. 4) Death in the African bush. *Newsweek, 114*(10), p. 32.

(Newton Murder)

Turque, B., & Wright, L. (1989, Sept. 4) A fast rise, a long fall. *Newsweek, 114*(10), p. 27.

(Peking Massacre)

Cheng, N. (1989, Aug. 4) China devours its children: Massacre in Peking. *National Review, 41*(14), pp. 28-31.

(Anthony Bee Murder)

Security manager for guy dead following dispute with New Edition's crew member. (1989, July 24) *Jet, 76*(16), p. 18.

(Mariana Gomez)

Benavides, M. (1989, July 10) The death of Mariana Gomez. *Christian Crisis, 49*, pp. 210-211.

(Emmett Till Murder)

Howard, J. (1989, July 3) A death in the delta: The story of Emmett Till. *Washington Monthly, 21*(5), 54-55..

(Beijing Massacre)

China's blood. (1989, July) *Life, 12*(8), pp. 38-46.

(Kantian Casuistry)

Herman, B. (1989, July) Murder and mayhem: Violence and Kantian casuistry. *Monist, 72*, 411-431.

(Mexico Murders)

Garcia, G. (1989, June 29) The believers. *Rolling Stone*, pp. 46-49+.

(Murderer - Hearns)

Hit man Hearns' brother charged in shooting of 'girlfriend' in Michigan. (1989, June 26) *Jet, 76*(12), pp. 51-52.

(Murder - Carlo Tresca)

Aaron, D. (1989, June 15) Who killed Carlo Tresca? *New York Review of Books, 36*(10), pp. 43-45.

(Murder - John Holmes)

Sager, M. (1989, June 15) The devil and John Holmes. *Rolling Stone, 554*, pp. 50-61+.

(Wilson Pineiro Murder)

Steif, W. (1989, June) Rural workers face murder. *Progressive, 53*(6), p. 26.

(Cub Reporter Murder)

Baker, R. (1989, June) Murder in Baltimore; woman, cub reporter, done in by brick. *W J R, 11*, pp. 28-30+.

(Baltimore Murder)

Baker, R. (1989, June) Murder in Baltimore: Woman, cub reporter done in by brick. *World Journalism Review, 11*, 28-30+.

(Ramon Salcido Murders)

The horror of it all; seven dead ... (Ramon Salcido murders) (from the Santa Rosa Press Democrat - editorial). (1989, May 31) *The Los Angeles Daily Journal*, p. 6.

(Jeffery MacDonald Case)

Garbus, M. (1989, April 21) My say - - McGinnis: A travesty of libel. *Publisher's Weekly, 235*(16), p. 69.

(Wife Murdered)

Hopkins, A. (1989, April 20) Nowhere to run. *Rolling Stone*, pp. 72-78+.

(Hillside Strangler Investigation)

Dillow, G. (1989, April 1) The cop who cared too much. *TV Guide, 37*(13), pp. 26-27.

(Colombia - Drug Dealers)

Colombia - no doves here. (1989, April 1) *Economist, 311*(7596), p. 38.

(Murder Threat - S. Rushdie)

The talk of the town: Notes and comment. (1989, March 6) *The New Yorker, 35*(3), p. 27.

(Murder Story)

Savadis, G.P. (1989, Winter) Ill met by moonlight. *Grand St, 8*, 229-230.

(Nigeria)

Katsfelt, N. (1989, Jan.) Rumours of Maitatsine: A note on political culture in Nigeria. *African Affairs, 88*, 83-90.

(El Salvador)

Hackel, J. (1989) 2 major universities devastated by latest upsurge in El Salvador's civil unrest, campus murders. *Chronicle of Higher Education, 36*(13), pp. A47, A50.

(Massacre in China)

Leatherman, C. (1989) American colleges and scholarly organizations condemn massacre, scramble to get their students and professors out of China. *Chronicle of Higher Education, 35*(40), A38-A39.

(Murder - Beijing)

Jacobson, R.L. (1989) Beijing University, before and after. *Chronicle of Higher Education,*

35(40), A34-A35.

(Massacre in Beijing)

Biemiller, L., et al. (1989) Defiance and death in Beijing. *Chronicle of Higher Education, 35*(40), A1, A35+.

(Warrington Dawson Murder)

Worthington, W.C., Jr. (1989) The man who killed Warrington Dawson. *American Journal of Forensic Science, 10*(1), 76-82.

(El Salvador Victims)

Dutcher-Walls, T. (1988, Nov. 30) Being evangelized in El Salvador. *Christian Century, 105*(36), pp. 1084-1085.

Safran, C. (1988, Nov. 22) The devil made me do it. *Woman's Day, 52*(1), pp. 146-153.

(Murder Story)

Roberts, Y. (1988, Nov. 18) A lottery of justice. *New Statesman & Society, 1*(24), pp. 10-12.

(Murder Story)

McGinniss, J. (1988, Nov. 17) Blind faith. *Rolling Stone*, pp. 73-85.

(Troops Kill in El Salvador)

They were defenseless peasants. (1988, Oct. 3) *Newsweek, 112*(14), p. 33.

(Delgado Case)

Murder in the cathedral. (1988, Oct. 3) *Time, 132*(14), p. 29.

(Murder of British Soldiers)

Waugh, A. (1988, Oct. 1) Why don't the poodles of the Press ask the main Gibraltar question. *Spectator, 261*(8360), p. 8.

(Killing Parents)

White man kills parents over his black girlfriend. (1988, Oct.) *Jet, 75*(3), p. 31.

(Carlo Tresca)

Death of an anarchist. (1988, Sept.) *Progressive, 52*(9), p. 31.

(Victim - Judge)

Kasindorf, J. (1988, Aug. 1) Last Judgment. *New York, 21*(30), pp. 24-33.

(Case Report - K. Swenson)

Neill, M. (1987, March 16) A made-for-TV movie brings biathlete K. Swenson face-to-face with her past. *People Weekly, 27*, pp. 76-78+.

(Case Report - Lennon Murder)

Gaines, J.R. (1987, March 2) In the shadows a killer waited (M. Chapman's murder of John Lennon) *People Weekly, 27*, pp. 50-52+.

(Manson Interview)

Healy, R. (1987, March) In Manson's eyes (interview with Charles Manson) *Life, 10*, pp. 54-56.

(Mass Murder)

Satchell, M. (1987, Dec. 21) Mass murder in the clouds (D.A. Burke and the crash of PSA 1771). *US News and World Report, 103*, pp. 14-15.

(Primed to Kill)

Hammer, J. (1987, Nov. 16) Primed to kill, an angry young man shoots his own sister's boyfriend, leaving two families in ruins (T. Umstadter kills G. Evans). *People Weekly, 28*, pp. 158-160+.

(Case Report - Peter Tosh)

Goldberg, M. (1987, Oct. 22) Reggae great Peter Tosh murdered. *Rolling Stone*, p. 24+.

(Case Report - Peter Tosh)

Reggae great Peter Tosh murdered. (1987, Sept. 28) *Jet, 73*, p. 62.

(Massacre - Hungerford)

Levis, B. (1987, Aug. 31) The market-day massacre (Hungerford, England). *Macleans, 100*, p. 20.

(Kid Killers)

Kid killers (teenage murders in Detroit). (1986, Dec. 22) *Time, 128*, p. 33.

(Prison Escape)

Jones, R.F. (1986, Sept. 22) An angry rebel's paradise lost (escape of murderer C. Dallas from Idaho prison). *People Weekly, 26*, pp. 34-39.

(Case Report - D. Fossey)

Smith, W.E. (1986, Sept. 22) Case of the gorilla lady murder (W. McGuire charged in murder of D. Fossey in Rwanda). *Time, 128*, p. 35.

(Case Report - Jennifer Levin)

VanBiema, D. (1986, Sept. 15) The violent death of Jennifer Levin sobers the preppie elite of New York. *People Weekly, 26*, pp. 56-58.

(Cannibalism and Satanism)

Tales of cannibalism and Satanic rites (child abuse case in Hamilton, Ontario). (1986, July 28) *Macleans, 99*, p. 42.

(Madman)

Trippett, F. (1986, July 21) The madman on the ferry (J Gonzales stabs people on the Staten Island Ferry). *Time, 128*, p. 33,

(Case Report - Allan Berg)

Beech Tree/Morrow book explores murder of Denver talk show host A. Berg. (1986, June 13) *Publisher's Weekly, 229*, p. 54.

(Case Report - Claude Dallas)

Stuart, R.P. (1986, April) Claude Dallas sued (convicted killer of Idaho game wardens). *Outdoor Life, 177*, p. 119.

(Jeffrey MacDonald Case)

Nasser, T.J., & Stombaugh, P. (1986, March) The Jeffrey MacDonald murders: A new look at the evidence. *The Police Chief, 52*(3), 96-99. Microforms and article copies available from UMI.

(Case Report - Castellano)

Pileggi, N. (1986, Jan. 6) After 'Big Paul' (Mafia's direction following murder of P. Castellano). *New York, 19*, pp. 20-25.

(DEA Agent)

US very frustrated over Mexico's handling of search for DEA agent's murderers. (1986) *Narcotics Control Digest, 16*(15), 8-9. Article copies available from UMI.

(Investigator Slain)

Avianca investigator slain. (1986) *Narcotics Control Digest, 16*(18), 3. Article copies available from UMI.

(Gangland Slayings)

Was the Phoenix matre D' slain gangland-style because he testified against Spilotro? (1986) *Organized Crime Digest, 7*(6), 10.

(FBI Shootout)

Two FBI agents killed, five wounded in Miami shootout. (1986) *Crime Control Digest, 20*(15), 10. Article copies available from UMI.

(Police Scandal)

Miami police officers charged with murder in drug scandal. (1986) *Criminal Justice Newsletter, 17*(2), 2-3.

(Murder of Professor)

A death in the family (murder of mafia boss P. Castellano). (1985, Dec. 30-1986, Jan. 6) *US News and World Report, 99*, p. 13.

(Mafia Murder)

Glynn, L. (1985, Dec. 30) Sudden death by gunfire (the murder of Paul Castellano). *Macleans, 98*, p. 46.

(Mafia Murder)

Stengel, R. (1985, Dec. 30) Slaughter on 46th Street (Mafia boss P. Castellano murdered). *Time, 126*, p. 17.

(Godfather's Fall)

Alpern, D.M. (1985, Dec. 30) A godfather's fall: Mob under fire (murder of P. Castellano). *Newsweek, 106*, pp. 20-23.

(Fatal Bombings)

Shipps, J. (1985, Nov. 13) The salamander and the saints (fatal bombings and forged Mormon documents linked to M. Hoffman). *Christian Century, 102*, pp. 1020-1021.

(Transsexual Murder)

McMurran, K. (1985, Oct. 21) Amelia Cave's dream of a new beginning ends in her murder by a would-be transsexual. *People Weekly, 24*, p. 111+.

(Capture of Night Stalker)

Plummer, W. (1985, Sept. 16) Night Stalker (capture of R. Ramirez). *People Weekly, 24*, pp. 42-45.

(Serial Killings)

Are serial killers on the rise? (1985, Sept. 9) *US New and World Report, 99*, p. 14.

(Charles Manson - Interview)

Kennedy, K. (1985, Sept.) Charles Manson (interview). *Harper's, 271*, p. 28-29.

(Night Stalker)

Givens, R. (1985, Aug. 26) The Night Stalker of LA. *Newsweek, 106*, p. 23.

(Sikh Terrorists)

Carlson, P., & Leviton, J. (1985, Aug. 6) Two suspected Sikh terrorists honed their combat skills at an Alabama war school (F. Camper's mercenary school). *People Weekly, 24*, pp. 46-49.

(Extradition)

When felons flee to foreign lands (attempt to extradite C. Ng from Canada). (1985, July 29) *US News and World Report, 99*, p. 10.

(Office Murder)

Press, A. (1985, July 8) Murder in the front office. *Newsweek, 106*, p. 58.

(Random Killing)

McKay, S. (1985, July 8) Coming to grips with random killing (serial murderers) *Macleans, 98*, pp. 44-45.

(Murder Recorded)

Seeing no evil (murder of K. Nagano recorded on Japanese TV). (1985, July 1) *Time, 125*, p. 35.

(Macabre Case)

Haden-Guest, A. (1985, June 24) The macabre case of the man in the mask and the shadowy world of Crospo (murder of E. Vesti). *New York, 18*, pp. 30-41.

(Murder Fascination)

Collins, D. (1985, June 24) Most dramatic story ever: The fascination with murder. *US News and World Report, 98*, p. 64.

(Case Report - Alton Coleman)

Alton Coleman and friend found guilty of Ohio killing. (1985, May 27) *Jet, 68*, p. 39.

(Dungeons and Dragons)

Shuster, W.G. (1985, May 17) Critics link a fantasy game to 29 deaths (Dungeons and Dragons and teen-age deaths). *Christianity Today, 29*, p. 64+.

(Obsession)

Morrisroe, P. (1985, March 18) Obsession: The murder of an elusive beauty (G. Senty murders P. Lantos in New York City). *New York, 18*, pp. 38-44.

(Confession)

Drake, R., & Grogan, D.W. (1985, March 18) After 20 years of cat and mouse, coy killer Phil Adams volunteers one confession too many. *People Weekly, 23*, pp. 83-84+.

(Atlanta's Children)

Smith, V.E. (1985, Feb. 18) Atlanta's nightmare revisited (W.B. Williams and murders of Black children). *Newsweek, 105*, p. 31.

(Endless Party)

Mahon, G. (1985, Feb. 11) Mike Milken's endless party. *New York, 18*, pp. 42-48.

(Wayne Williams)

Atlanta responds angrily as a TV show pens an old wound (questions of W. Williams guilt in child murders case) (1985, Feb. 11) *People Weekly, 23*, p. 62.

(Case Report - A. Berg Murder)

Singular, S. (1985, Jan. 31) Talked to death (murder of talk show host Allan Berg). *Rolling Stone*, pp. 38-41.

(Mass Murder)

Gomez, L. (1985, Jan.) Ninety minutes at McDonald's (mass murder committed by J. Huberty in San Ysidro, CA). *Life, 8*, pp. 76-84+.

(Dr. E. Rogers Smith)

Buchanan, P.H., Jr. (1985) Courting disaster: Recollections of an Indiana judge about Dr. E. Rogers Smith. *Indiana Medicine, 78*(8), 660.

(Police Killings)

Hackler, J.C., & Janssen, C.T. (1985) Police killing in perspective. *Canadian Journal of Criminology, 27*(2), 227-232.

(Godfathers' Arrest)

All five godfathers of NYC ruling mob families arrested; new charges in the "pizza case". (1985) *Narcotics Control Digest, 15*(5), 7. Article copies available from UMI.

(Aiding and Abetting)

Soloman, S., & Smith, J.C. (1984, Sept.) Case and comment: Aiding and abetting. *The Criminal Law Review 1984*, 549-550.

(Hong Kong)

Soloman, S. (1984, July) Case and comment: Hong Kong. *The Criminal Law Review 1984*, 424-425.

(Serial Killers)

Interstate parley on serial killers. (1984, Feb. 13) *Law Enforcement News, 10*, p. 3. Microforms and article copies available from UMI.

(Green River Murders)

Green River murders are a "complex, frustrating" case. (1984) *Crime Control Digest, 18*(41), 3-4.

(Mob Confession)

Mob boss encouraged Agca confession. (1984) *Security Systems Digest, 14*(13), 9-10. Article copies available from UMI

(FBI Search)

FBI searching for Aussie race car driver in multi-state kidnapping and murders. (1984) *Crime Control Digest, 18*(15), 8-9. Article copies available from UMI.

(Case Reports - Patricide in Cheyenne)

Prendergast, A. (1983, May 26) It's you or me Dad (Jahnke children murder their father in Cheyenne). *Rolling Stone*, pp. 41-44+.

(Case Reports - Sommersworth's Skeletons)

Shapiro, W. (1983, May 16) New England gothic: Skeletons in a trunk (Baby skeletons found in Sommersworth, NH). *Newsweek, 101*, p. 42.

(Case Reports - Lin Biao)

Willey, F. (1983, May 16) Was Lin Biao murdered? *Newsweek, 101*, p. 55.

(Case Report - G. Foat)

Lichtenstein, G. (1983, May 12) Female troubles (case of G. Foat). *Rolling Stone*, pp. 43-44+.

(Case Reports - Infant Death)

Webb, J. (May 9, 1983) Another death from digoxin (infant deaths at Toronto's Hospital for Sick Children). *Macleans, 96*, p. 18.

(Case Reports - G.M. Perry's Murder)

Morganthau, T. (1983, May 9) A very businesslike execution (murder of G.M. Perry). *Newsweek, 101*, p. 30.

(Case Reports - Sartawi's Murder)

Hirschfield, R. (1983, May 6) Peacemaker's death (murder of F. Sartawi). *Commonwealth, 110*, pp. 263-264.

(Case Reports - Hustler's Murder)

Burstein, D. (1983, May 2) Death of a hustler (Russian emigre Y. Brokhin in New York City.) *New York, 16*, pp. 24-29.

(Case Reports - Palestinian Murder)

. . . and of a man (murder of Palestinian moderate I. Sartawi). (1983, May) *New Republic, 188*, p. 8.

(Case Reports - von Bulow Affair)

Wright, W. (1983, May) The von Bulow affair (excerpts). *Good Housekeeping, 196*, 140-141+.

(Case Report - Sartawi Murdered)

Ehrenreich, B. (1983, April 30) Murder at the S.I. (I. Sartawi murdered at the Socialist International meeting). *Nation, 236*, pp. 530-531.

(Case Report - PLO Murder)

Snuffing out a PLO voice of moderation. (1983, April 18) *Newsweek, 101*(42).

(Case Report - Delia Murder)

Wadler, J. (1983, April 14) Mary in the lavender pumps (D. Delia transsexual murder case). *Rolling Stone*, pp. 25-28+.

(Justifiable Homicide)

Difonzo, L. (1983, April 11) Justifiable homicide (N. Sindona ties his father to the unsolved murder of G. Ambrosoli). *New York, 16*, pp. 30-33.

(Case Report - John Belushi's Death)

McKay, S. (1983, April 4) Facing up to the future (C. Smith arrested in connection with J.

Belushi's death). *Mclean's, 96*, p. 16.

(Case Report - Miller Kills Mother)

A family's nightmare in posh Palos Verdes (M. Miller kills mother). (1983, April 4) *Newsweek, 101*, p. 27.

(Case Report - Atlanta Child Murderer)

Englade, K. (1983, March 28) A murder mystery still unsolved (Atlanta child murder W. Williams). *Macleans, 96*, p. 8.

(Case Report - Wilson's Murder)

Eisler, D. (1983, March 7) Duelling with deadly affidavits (J.A. Wilson's murder in Regina, Sask.) *Macleans, 96*, p. 19.

(Case Report - Patricide in Wyoming)

Janos, L. (1983, March 7) On a windswept Wyoming an abused son kills a father to bring peace to a family (Jahnke children murder father in Cheyenne, WY). *People Weekly, 19*, pp. 34-36.

(Case Report - B. Garland)

Smith, A. (1983, March) I just killed my girlfriend (case of B. Garland and R. Herrin). *Esquire, 99*, pp. 23-24.

(Case Report - Blacks in Miami)

Morganthau, T. (1983, March 28) Cops versus Blacks in Miami. *Newsweek, 101*, p. 18.

(Case Report - G. Kahl)

Salholz, E. (1983, Feb. 28) A Midwest manhunt and a far-out Posse (case of G. Kahl). *Newsweek, 101*, p. 24.

(Case Report - Murder in Chinatown)

Unlucky 13 (murders in Seattle's Chinatown). (1983, Feb. 28) *Time, 121*, p. 25.

(Case Report - Marshals Murdered)

America's guerrillas: Tax resisters (federal marshals murdered by the Posse Comitatus). (1983, Feb. 28) *US News and World Report, 94*, p. 8.

(Case Report - Chinatown Massacre)

Beck, M. (1983, Feb. 28) A massacre in Chinatown (Seattle). *Newsweek, 101*, p. 24.

(Case Report - Abduction after Murder)

Sarjeant, P. (1983, Feb. 7) Charges of abduction (kidnapping of S. Thatcher after murder of her mother in Regina, Sask.) *Macleans, 96*, p. 11.

(Case Report - Argentine Military)

Chelala, C.A. (1983, Feb. 5) The Argentine military turns on its own. *Nation, 236*, p. 139-140.

(Case Report - Steven Linscott)

Frame, R. (1983, Feb. 4) The strange case of Steven Linscott (case in Oak Park, IL). *Christianity Today, 27*, pp. 42-44+.

(Case Report - A. Nee Murder)

Tofani, L. (1983, Jan./Feb.) Murder's tragic aftermath (effect on family of victim A. Nee). *Saturday Evening Post, 255*, p. 36+.

(Case Report - Teamster Lawyer Murder)

The silencers (Teamster lawyer A. Dorfman murdered in Chicago). (1983, Jan. 31) *Time, 121*, p. 29.

(Case Report - J. Wilson Murder)

Eisler, D. (1983, Jan. 31) Killed in the second attempt (murder of J. Wilson in Regina, Sask.) *Macleans, 96*, p. 13.

(Murders in Chicago)

Morganthau, T. (1983, Jan. 31) A gangland hit in Chicago (murder of A.M. Dorfman). *Newsweek, 101*, pp. 27-28.

(Case Report - Memphis Shootout)

Angry aftermath of a shootout (police shootout with religious cult in Memphis). (1983, Jan. 31) *Time, 121*, p. 33.

(Case Report - J. McDonald Case)

Goldstein, W. (1983, Jan. 28) 1970 murder spree probed in *Fatal Vision* (Jeffery McDonald case). *Publisher's Weekly, 223*, pp. 69-70.

(Case Report - G. Foat)

Lerner, M.A. (1983, Jan. 24) An activist with an active past (case of G. Foat). *Newsweek, 101*, pp. 30-31.

(Case Report - G. Foat)

Murder charge (California NOW president G. Foat). (1983, Jan. 24) *Time, 121*, p. 27.

(Case Report - New York Murders)

Wolfe, L. (1983, Jan. 17) The transsexual, the bartender, and the Jewish-American princess (D. Delia murder case in New York). *New York, 16*, pp. 28-35.

(Case Report - H. Appledorf Murder)

McCall, C. (1983, Jan. 10) The fateful odyssey of three teenage runaways may take them to Florida's death row for murder (murder of Professor H. Appledorf in Gainesville). *People Weekly, 19*, pp. 67-68+.

(Case Report - Manila Connection)

Stamets, J. (1983, Jan.) The Manila connection (anti-Marcos labor activists murdered in Seattle). *Progressive, 47*, pp. 20-21.

(Case Report - Murder of Amish Woman)

Shattered calm (murder of Amish woman I. Huyard by J. Herr in New Holland, PA). (1983, Jan 3) *Time, 121*, p. 51.

(Murder)

Murder spree in Jolliet, IL leads to wave of fear. (1983) *Crime Control Digest, 17*(34), 7.

(Corrupt Police)

Clawson, P.M. (1983) Ex-Hell's Angel tells senators about corrupt police; describes drug trafficking by bikers. *Narcotics Control Digest, 13*(7), 2-3.

(Mafia Crackdown)

Judge murdered by mafia as crackdown on heroin traffickers continues in Sicily. (1983) *Organized Crime Digest, 4*(8), 6-7. Article copies available from UMI.

(Case Report - A. Walsh)

Adam Walsh: Killed because security guard lacked sense. (1983) *Crime Control Digest, 7*(43), 3.

(Case Report - Sutcliffe Case)

Prins, H.A. (1983) Diminished responsibility and the Sutcliffe: Legal, psychiatric, and social aspects (a 'layman's view'). *Medical Science and the Law, 23*(1), 17-24.

(Murder Investigation)

Gray, M. (1982, Dec. 13) Olson's fast trip to the coast (using convicted murderer C.R. Olson's help in British Columbia crime solving. *Macleans, 95*, p. 15.

(Filicide in Cheyenne)

It made terrible sense. (1982, Dec. 13) *Time, 120*, p. 34.

(Case Report - El Salvador)

Payne, K. (1982, Dec. 4) The strange ordeal of Hans Christ (El Salvador murder case). *Nation, 235*, p. 577+.

(Case Report - Argentine Murders)

An echo of Dachau from Gran Bourg (unidentified corpses found in Argentine cemetery). (1982, Nov. 15) *Newsweek, 100*, p. 68.

(Murder in Tchula, MS)

Settling scores (former mayor E.J. Carthas involved in racially motivated murder in Tchula, MS). (1982, Nov. 8) *Time, 120*, p. 30.

(Case Report - Richard Arnot)

Daly, E. (1982, Nov. 29) Sex and death in the desert (involvement of British subject Richard Arnot in Saudi Arabian murder). *Macleans, 95*, p. 34.

(Case Report - El Salvador Murders)

Step forward (ruling that National Guardsmen accused in murder of American missionaries must stand trial in El Salvador). (1982, Nov. 29) *Time, 120*, p. 48.

(Murder - Neo-Nazi)

Alpern, D. (1982, Nov. 22) A neo-nazi faces charges of murder (P.B. Warthan of Oroville, CA). *Newsweek, 100*, p. 87+.

(Case Report - Guatemala)

Brett, D.W. (1982, Oct. 30) A teacher and a martyr in Guatemala (Christian Brother J.A. Miller killed in Guatemala). *America, 147*, pp. 253-255.

(Case Report - E. Jopson Murder)

O'Hare, J.A. (1982, Oct. 30) Of many things (E. Jopson killed by government troops in the Philippines). *America, 147*, inside cover.

(Case Report - Argentina)

Lemoyne, J. (1982, Oct. 25) The dirty war strikes the elite (murder of M. Dupont in Argentina). *Newsweek, 100*, p. 87.

(Case Report - El Salvador)

Slow justice (AFL-CIO's investigation in 1982 murder of Americans in El Salvador). (1982, Oct. 18) *Time,120*, p. 38.

(Case Report - Baby Sitter)

Chandler, D. (1982, Oct. 11) Real-life Dr. Quincy tracks down a murder suspect (implicating baby sitter C. Falling in Florida children's deaths). *People Weekly, 18*, pp. 139-140.

(Case Report - Claus von Bulow)

Harrison, B.G. (1982, Oct.) The fatal charm of Claus von Bulow. *McCalls, 110*, pp. 102-103+.

(Case Report - Murder)

Shames. J. (1982, Oct.) Flesh and blood (J. Youmans accused by his sister of murder thirty years after crime) *Esquire, 98*, pp. 63-67+.

(Case Report - R. Johnson Murder)

Zwarun, S. (1982, Sept. 27) The grisly conclusion to a summer mystery (murder of R. Johnson family in British Columbia). *Macleans, 95*, p. 15.

(Case Report - Mafia Murders)

Shock therapy (C.A. Dalla Chiesa murdered by mafia hitmen in Palermo). (1982, Sept. 20)

Time, 120, p. 47.

(Case Report - Atlanta Murders)

Keerdoja, E. (1982, Sept. 20) Atlanta killer: A life of isolation (W. Williams in jail). *Newsweek, 100*, p. 18+.

Case Report - E. Hartman's Murder)

Trillin, C. (1982, Sept. 20) U.S. Journal: Grundy County, Iowa (murder of Esther Hartman by her husband Lawrence). *New Yorker, 58*, p. 98+.

(Case Report - H. Appledorf)

Lerner, M.A. (1982, Sept. 20) The junk-food murder (murder of Professor H. Appledorf in Gainesville, FL). *Newsweek, 100*, p. 34.

(Case Report - Mafia Murders)

Gilbert, S. (1982, Sept. 20) Striking back at the mafia (murder of Gen. C.A. Dalla Chiesa). *Macleans, 95*, p. 25.

(Case Report - Witness Murder)

More troubles for Donovan (murder of witness N. Masselli). (1982, Sept. 13) *Time, 123*, pp. 17-18.

(Case Report - Witness Murder)

Axthelm, P. (1982, Sept. 13) Donovan and a dead witness (murder of N. Masselli). *Newsweek, 100*, p. 32.

(Case Report - Keeping Murderers Jailed)

Adelson, S. (1982, Sept. 13) Emerging from her grief (Gwen Tate crusades to keep Sharon's murderers in jail). *People Weekly, 18*, p. 80+.

(Case Report - M. Doyle)

Gray, M. (1982, Sept. 6) Sudden death under Sec. 449 (M. Doyle charged with murder in scuffle with cottagers attempting a citizen's arrest in Takla Lake, BC). *Macleans, 95*, p. 15.

(Case Report - Witness Murdered)

Message for a mobster (murder of N. Masselli, witness in the investigation of R.J. Donovan). (1982, Sept. 6) *Time, 120*, p. 18.

(Case Report - Historical Homicide)

Balderson, T. (1982, Sept.) The sad, shattered life of Thera Sickles (murder of P.B. Kay by D. Sickles in 1859). *American History Illustrated, 17*, pp. 40-45.

(Case Report - J. Pius Murder)

Kornbluth, J. (1982, Aug. 30, 1982, Sept. 6) Trouble boys (murder of J. Pius in Smithtown, Long Island). *New York, 15*, pp. 32-39 and pp. 41-46+.

(Case Report - Fugitive Murderer)

Keenan, B. (1982, Aug. 30) Rebuked for keeping a friend (resignation of Irish Attorney General P. Connolly after capture of fugitive killer M. MacArthur). *Macleans, 95*, pp. 24-25.

(Case Report - Fugitive Murderer)

Willey, F. (1982, Aug. 30) The A.G.'s houseguest (arrest of M. MacArthur, murder suspect and friend of Attorney General P. Connolly in Ireland). *Newsweek, 100*, p. 48.

(Case Report - C.E. Watts)

Peer, E. (1982, Aug. 30) A mass killer cops a plea (case of C.E. Watts). *Newsweek, 100*, pp. 29-30.

(Case Report - Mass Murder)

Body count (mass slayings in Texas). (1982, Aug. 23) *Time, 120*, p. 12.

(Case Report - Matricide)

A case of Mommy dearest? (C. Kipp accused of murdering his mother by mailing her a book bomb in Brooklyn). (1982, Aug. 23) *Time, 120*, p. 15.

(Case Report - A. Fiore Murder)

Count, E., et al. (1982, Aug. 16) A message for Tony (murder of A. Fiore by brother-in-law in New York City). *New York, 15*, pp. 27-32.

(Case Report - R.A. Baldwin's Murder)

The man who would be king? (M. Richards charged in murder of R.A. Baldwin to prevent Baldwin from disclosing plot to take over Marin County, CA). (1982, Aug. 2) *Newsweek, 100*, p. 22.

(Case Report - E.J. Carthan)

McNatt, R. (1982, Aug.) Railroading in Tchula (Black mayor E.J. Carthan charged with murder) *Black Enterprise, 13*, p. 18.

(Case Report - Journalist's Murder)

Nelson, A. (1982, July 24-31) One way to kill the story (murder of Dutch journalists in El Salvador). *Nation, 235*, pp. 75-78.

(Case Report - Shrock's Murder)

Starr, M. (1982, July 26) The case of the missing professor (N. Schrock murder on Highway 15 in Mexico). *Newsweek, 100*, p. 25-26.

(Case Report - Canada Rape-Murder)

Riley, S. (1982, July 26) Sudden fear and loathing (rape-murder in Canada). *Macleans, 95*, pp. 47-48.

(Case Report - Breslin)

Beck, M. (1982, July 19) A killer who slipped through the system (case of J.F. Breslin). *Newsweek, 100*, p. 28.

(Case Report - Bowles Murder)

Daly, M. (1982, July 19) The end of the rainbow (murder of G.W. Bowles in a Columbia Ave. boutique, New York City). *New York, 15*, pp. 28-33+.

(Case Report - Hoffa Murder)

Hoffa outgunned (A. Provenzano alleged to have ordered Hoffa's murder). (1982, July 5) *Time, 120*, p. 29.

(Case Report - Idaho Murders)

Zumbo, J. (1982, July) Fugitive captured in game wardens' murders (capture of C. Dallas for Idaho murders). *Outdoor Life, 170*, p. 82+.

(Case Report - Parolees)

Anderson, I. (1982, June 28) Death delivered on parole (murders committed by parolees in Canada) *Macleans, 95*, p. 15.

(Case Report - Peterman Murder)

Hall, S.M. (1982, June 21) A teenager's traffic tickets end in a jailhouse tragedy and Boise, Idaho wonders why (murder of C. Peterman by fellow inmates). *People Weekly, 17*, pp. 36-37.

(Case Report - Peterman Murder)

Abramson, P. (1982, June 21) Cops and kids in Boise (jailhouse murder of C. Peterman). *Newsweek, 99*, p. 42.

(Case Report - Guatemala)

Specktor, M. (1982, June 5) Revolution and the Church in Guatemala. *America, 146*, pp. 440-441.

(Case Report - Chapman)

Salk, L. (1982, June) John Lennon's killer talks about his father (excerpt from My father, my son). *McCalls, 109*, p. 116.

(Case Report - Frank Lynching)

Wall, J.M. (1982, May 12) Anti-Semitism and the Sinai withdrawal (revelations concerning L. Frank lynching case of 1915). *Christian Century, 99*, p. 555.

(Case Report - Paraguay Torture)

Nadler, E. (1982, May 8) Paraguay torture in US courts (J. Filartiga's success in having case of his son's murder in Paraguay brought to trial in the United States). *Nation, 234*, pp. 551-552.

(Case Report - R. Vicker's Murder)

Press, A. (1982, May 3) Where to kill with impunity (death row prisoner indicted for jailhouse murder). *Newsweek, 99*, p. 88+.

(Case Report - El Salvador Killings)

Stone, I.F. (1982, May 1) Deadly silence (absence of media coverage on the killing of four Dutch journalists in El Salvador). *Nation, 234*, p. 515.

(Case Report - Mob Murders)

Posner, M. (1982, April 26) The price of crossing the mob (murder of M. Barbera and three CBS employees in New York City). *Macleans, 95*, pp. 44-45.

(Case Report - Grandfather's Murder)

Alpern, D.M. (1982, April 5) Who killed grandfather? (accusations against F. Schreuder and son in murder of her father F.J. Bradshaw). *Newsweek, 99*, p. 34.

(Case Report - R. Hunne)

Wunderli, R. (1982, April) Pre-reformation London summoners and the murder of Richard J. Hunne. *Journal of Ecclesiastic History, 33*, 209-224.

(Case Report - El Salvador)

Rogal, K. (1982, March 29) Reporters as targets (four Dutch journalist murdered in El Salvador). *Newsweek, 99*, p. 32.

(Case Report - Sikh Murders in Toronto)

'Go in peace' and then six shots (courtroom murder by Sikh fanatic in Toronto). (1982, March 29) *Macleans, 95*, p. 27.

(Case Report - American Diplomat's Murder)

Lewis, P. (1982, Feb. 1) The CIA prepares for battle (murder of American diplomat C.R. Ray in Paris). *Macleans, 95*, pp. 32-33.

(Case Report - C.R. Ray's Murder)

Murder on Boulevard Emile-Augier (murder of C.R. Ray). (1982, Feb. 1) *Time, 119*, p. 54.

(Case Report - Transsexual Murderers)

Milliken, A.D. (1982) Homicidal transsexuals: Three cases. *Canadian Journal of Psychiatry, 27*(1), pp. 43-46.

(Case Report - Boston Murders)

Rizzo, N.D. (1982) Murder in Boston: Killers and their victims. *International Journal of Offender Therapy and Comparative Criminology, 26*(1), 36-42.

(Case Report - Dr. Leonard Arthur)

Reg. vs. Dr. Leonard Arthur (letter) (1982) *Medical Journal of Australia, 2*(12), 558-560.

(Case Report - Hinkley)

Falk, V.S. (1982) Roosevelt/Reagan - Schrank/Hinkley (editorial). *Wisconsin Medical Journal, 81*(8), 9-10.

(Reidsville Murders)

Inmate violence kills three at Reidsville (GA). (1982) *Corrections Digest, 8*(3), 4. Article copies available from UMI.

(Case Report - Wagner)

Bantam, P. (1982) The case of Wagner, a primary school teacher (French). *Information Psychiatrique, 58*(5), 669-681.

(Case Report - Atlanta Murders)

Greaves, G.B., et al. (1982) Atlanta psychology, and the second siege: Report to APA by the Georgia Psychological Association's ad hoc Resource Committee on murdered and missing children. *American Psychologist, 37*(5), 559-568.

(Case Report - Scott-Elliot)

The Scott-Elliot murders. (1982) *Medical Legal Journal, 50*(4), 140-158.

(Case Report - Florida)

Feeling the heat in South Florida: An interview with Police Chief Kenneth Harms of Miami. (1981, Nov. 23) *Law Enforcement News, 20*, 8-11.

(Atlanta - Evidence Unattained)

Atlanta: More victims, no clues. (1981, Jan. 19) *Newsweek, 97*, p. 29.

(Case Report - B.C. Welch, Jr.)

Weiss, M.J., & Mills, B.K. (1981, Jan. 19) Suburban DC family man turns out to be a suspected killer and robbery baron (B.C. Welch, Jr. case). *People Weekly, 15*, p. 30-33.

(Miami Murders)

Dade eclipses 1980 murder total while South Miami crime drops. (1981) *Law Enforcement News, 7*(22), 5. Article copies available from UMI.

(Case Report - Aryan Brotherhood)

Aryan Brotherhood inmates "kill to get in, die to get out". (1981) *Corrections Digest, 12*(25), 1,4. Article copies available from UMI.

(Police Shootings)

Geller, W.A. (1981) Shootings of and by Chicago police: Uncommon crises, Part I: Shootings by Chicago police. *The Journal of Criminal Law and Criminology, 72*(4), 1813-1866.

(Case Report - Jonestown Massacre Reactions)

Hoyt, M.F. (1981) Observations regarding patients' reactions to the Jonestown massacre and the

Moscone-Milk assassinations. *Journal of the American Academy of Psychoanalysis, 9*(2), 303-309.

(Atlanta Murders)

Clark, M., & Smith, V.E. (1980, Dec. 22) Epidemic of murder (CDC investigation of Black child murder in Atlanta). *Newsweek, 96*, p. 62.

(Atlanta Manhunt)

Leviton, J. (1980, Nov. 10) Grieving mother spurs the hunt for the child killer who is terrorizing Atlanta (Work of C. Bell). *People Weekly, 14*, pp. 57-58.

(Atlanta Murders)

Beach, B.H., & Boyce, J.N. (1980, Nov. 3) Terror on Atlanta's South-side (death or disappearance of Black children). *Time, 116*, p. 67.

(Case Report - Familial Murder)

McCully, R.S. (1980) Satan's eclipse: A familial murderer six years later. *British Journal of Projective Psychology and Personality Study, 25*(2), 13-17.

(Case Report - Kavanagh's Murder)

Winney, T.J. (1979) The murder of Brian Harry Kavanagh: Homicide involving an unusual identification of the victim. *Australian Police Journal, 33*(3), 161-180.

(Case Report - Corpse Stealing)

Pueschel, K. (1979) Murder, suicide, and corpse stealing (German). *Arch Kriminol, 164*(1-2), 31-35.

Case Reports - By Place

(Case Report - El Salvador)

Arnson, C.J. (1990, Nov. 19) Conscience vote. *Nation, 251*(17), p. 584.

(Case Report - El Salvador)

Long, T., & Smyth, F. (1990, Nov. 13) Release the Jesuit tapes. *Village Voice, 35*(46), pp. 18, 22.

(Case Report - Kuwait)

Bilski, A. (1990, Oct. 22) Witness to terror. *Macleans, 103*(43), pp. 32.

(Case Report - Israel)

Massacre on the Mount. (1990, Oct. 13) *Economist, 317*(7676), pp. 15-16.

(Case Report - South Africa)

Ungar, S.J. (1990, Oct. 8) Death in South Africa: a newspaper editor as target. *US News &*

World Report, 109(8), p. 38-39.

(Case Report - Mississippi)

Baker, J.N. (1990, Oct. 8) Mississippi Gothic. *Newsweek, 116*(15), p. 36.

(Case Report - Boston)

Collins, M. (1990, Sept. 8-14) For Boston, the wounds in this murder case still cut deep (Good night sweet wife, TV drama). *TV Guide, 38*, pp. 20-23.

(Case Report - New York)

Heimel, C. (1990, Sept. 4) I hate New York. *Village Voice, 35*(36), p. 53.

(Case Report - South Africa)

Johnson, R.W. (1990, Aug. 31) Anatomy of fear. *New Statesman & Society, 3*(116), pp. 36-37.

(Case Report - Brazil)

Melville, J. (1990, Aug. 24) Under the canopy. *New Statesman & Society, 3*(115), pp. 10-12.

(Case Report - South Africa)

Johnson, R.W. (1990, Aug. 17) South Africa: Dirty realism. *New Statesman & Society, 3*(114).

(Case Report - Guatemala)

Jones, L. (1990, July-Aug.) Murder in Guatemala. *New Left Review*, pp. 53-61.

(Case Report - El Salvador)

Smyth, F. (1990, July 31) The truth will win out. *Village Voice, 35*(31), pp. 19-22.

(Case Report - Kashmir)

Asia: The killing of hopes for peace in Kashmir. (1990, May 26) *Economist, 315*(7656), pp. 33-34.

(Case Report - El Salvador)

Norton, C. (1990, May 22) Troublesome priests. *Village Voice, 35*(21), pp. 19-22.

(Case Report - El Salvador)

Evidence missing (murder of Jesuits in El Salvador), (1990, May 16-23) *The Christian Century, 107*, pp. 522-523.

(Case Report - Atlanta)

Gunman kills 1, injures four in Atlanta shooting spree (J. Brady). (1990, May 14) *Jet*, 78, p. 38.

(Case Report - Chile)

Chile: Fixing the blame. (1990, May 12) *Economist, 315*(7654), p. 41.

(Case Report - South Africa)

South Africa: All manners of villainies. (1990, May 5) *Economist, 315*(7653), pp. 52-56.

(Case Report - Boston)

Wylie, E.M. (1990, May) Night raid on Boston. *Yankee, 54*(5), pp. 76-81+.

(Case Report - Washington, DC)

Murder in a 'model' city (Washington, DC). (1990, April 16) *US News and World Report, 108*, pp. 13-14.

(Case Report - Bensonhurst)

Black prosecutor quits NYC racial killing case (B. McIntyre withdraws from Bensonhurst case). (1990, April 16) *Jet, 78*, p. 4.

(Case Report - Peru)

Farrell, N. (1990, April 14) The shining path to destruction. *Spectator, 264*(8440), pp. 14-15.

(Case Report - El Salvador)

Amando Lopez: b. Feb. 6, 1936; d. Nov. 16, 1989. (1990, April 7) *America, 162*(13), pp. 340-341.

(Case Report - Texas)

Connock, A. (1990, April 2) Todd Broom gunned down a killer, and much of Texas wants to say thanks (shoots E. Edwards after witnessing him kill ex-girlfriend in Irving, TX). *People Weekly, 33*, pp. 46-47.

(Case Report - Beverly Hills)

Were millions the motive (Menendez sons accused of slaying parents in Beverly Hills). (1990, March 26) *Time, 135*, p. 24.

(Case Report - Beverly Hills)

Where there's a will, there's murder (Menendez parents murdered by children in Beverly Hills). (1990, March 26) *Newsweek, 115*, p. 21.

(Case Report - Ontario)

Jenish, D. (1990, March 26) Rumor and scandal (murder charges in Prescott, Ontario). *Macleans, 103*, p. 55+.

(Case Report - Guatemala)

Guatemala: Breaking the rules. (1990, March 24) *Economist, 314*(7647), pp. 44-45.

(Case Report - El Salvador)

Can this war ever end? (Slaying of Jesuits in El Salvador) (1990, March 23) *Commonwealth, 117*, pp. 180-183.

(Case Report - El Salvador)

'Ellacu': Ignacio Ellacuria - - b. Nov. 9, 1930; d. Nov. 16, 1989 - - Rector, Jesuit University. (1990, March 17) *America, 162*(10), p. 254.

(Case Report - El Salvador)

'Lolo": Joaquin Lopez y Lopez - - b. Aug. 16, 1918, d. Nov. 16, 1989 - - National Director, 'Fe y Algeria'. (1990, March 10) *America, 162*(9), p. 228.

(Case Report - El Salvador)

Straight talk for Cristiani. (1990, Feb. 5) *National Review, 42*(2), p. 18.

(Case Report - Australia)

Allen, G. (1990, Feb. 5) A scathing report (inquiry into 1971 conviction of D. Marshall in Sydney, N.S.). *Macleans, 103*, pp. 50-51.

(Case Report - El Salvador)

Robinson, L.S. (1990, Feb. 5) Taking the rod to the Class of '66 (military involvement in murder of Jesuits in El Salvador). *US News and World Report, 108*, p. 50.

Case Report - El Salvador)

McKillop, P. (1990, Jan. 22) Anatomy of a murder probe (Jesuits in El Salvador). *Newsweek, 115*, p. 40.

(Case Report - El Salvador)

Notes and comment (murder of Jesuit priests in El Salvador). (1990, Jan. 22) *The New Yorker, 65*, pp. 31-32.

(Case Report - El Salvador)

Stahl, T.H. (1990, Jan.20) Of many things (military involvement in murder of Jesuits in El Salvador). *America, 162*, p. 26.

(Case Report - El Salvador)

Drinan, R.F. (1990, Jan. 3-10) Reflecting on the Jesuit martyrs (El Salvador). *The Christian Century, 107*, pp. 5-6.

(Case Report - Brazil)

Revkin, A.C. (1990, Jan.) Murder in the Amazon (environmentalist C. Mendes). *Discover, 11*, pp. 30-32.

(Case Report - Kenya)

Hartley, A. (1990) A political murder? *Africa Report, 35*(2), 17-20.

(Case Report - England)

Scott, K.W.M. (1990) Homicide patterns in the West Midlands. *Medical Science and the Law, 30*(3), 234-238.

(Case Report - Howard Beach)

Nudo, D. (1990) Social Sciences: Law and Crime- - Incident at Howard Beach. *Library Journal, 115*(4), 104.

(Case Report - Romania)

Jacobson, R.L. (1990) Romanian students and professors are among the thousands of victims of violence in final days of Ceausescu regime. *Chronicle of Higher Education, 36*(16), p. A35.

(Case Report - Colombia)

Colombia: He made their day. (1989, Dec. 23) *Economist, 313*(7634-7635), p. 68.

(Case Report - Montreal)

Doerner, W.R., & Graff, J.L. (1989, Dec. 18) The man who hated women. *Time, 134*(25), p. 30.

(Case Report - Pakistan)

Pakistan: Blood drips on to the election. (1989, Dec. 18) *Economist, 309*(7571), p. 30.

(Case Report - Montreal)

Came, B., et al. (1989, Dec. 18) Montreal massacre. *Macleans, 102*(51), pp. 14-17.

(Case Report - Colombia)

Manning, S. (1989, Nov. 17) A battle to the death: Colombia vs. its cocaine cartels. *Scholastic Update, 122*(6), pp. 12-14.

(Case Report - Bensonhurst)

Stone, M. (1989, Nov. 6) What really happened in Bensonhurst?. *New York, 22*(44), pp. 46-56.

(Case Report - Lexington, KY)

Bell, B.K. (1989, Oct.) A golf great cut down in her prime. *Women's Sports & Fitness, 11*(8), p. 60.

(Case Report - Phillipines)

Base blackmail. (1989, Sept. 30) *Economist, 312*(7622), p. 31.

(Case Report - Tianamen Square)

Fincher, J. (1989, Fall) Zhao's fall, China's loss. *Foreign Policy, 76*, pp. 3-25.

(Case Report - Los Angeles)

Gregor, A. (1989, May 22) Death among the innocent (gang-related murders in Los Angeles) *Macleans, 102*, p. 38.

(Case Report - Mexico)

Woodbury, R. (1989, April 24) Cult of the Red-Haire Devil. *Time, 133*(17), p. 30.

(Case Report - Mexico)

Gibney, F., Jr. (1989, April 24) Ritual murder in Mexico. *Newsweek, 113(17), p. 55.*

(Case Report - South Africa)

South Africa: Monumental row. (1989, Jan. 7) *Economist, 310*, (7584), pp. 36-38.

(Case Report - Puerto Rico)

Steif, W. (1988, Dec.) Puerto Rico's death squad. *Progressive, 52*(12), pp. 40-42.

(Case Report - Mafia)

Hallenstein, D. (1988, Dec.) The mafia strikes back. *World Press Review, 35*(12), p. 55.

(Case Report - Alabama)

Dying confession. (1988, Nov. 16) *Christian Century, 105*(34), 1033.

(Case Report - Alabama)

Shaw, B., & Jaynes, G. (1988, Nov.) Murder in the Blackfoot Valley. *Life, 11*(13), pp. 177-186.

(Case Report - Mexico)

Reding, A. (1988, Nov.) How to steal an election: Mexico, 1988. *Mother Jones, 13*(9), p. 36.

(Case Report - Canada)

Harris, M. (1988, Nov.) Warts and all. *Saturday Night, 103*(11), pp. 20-25.

(Case Report - Colombia)

Colombia: All fall down. (1988, Sep. 3) *Economist, 309*(7571), p. 38.

(Case Report - New Mexico)

Student dies in shooting at Eastern New Mexico University. (1988) *Chronicle of Higher Education, 35*(12), A2.

(Case Report - Canada)

Murphy, G.K. (1988) Birchall and Benwell: Murder in a Canadian swamp. *American Journal of Forensic and Medical Pathology, 9*(3), 255-257.

(Case Report - Atlanta)

Headley, B.D. (1988) The "Atlanta tragedy" and the rule of official ideology. *UM Journal of Black Studies, 18*(4), 452-470.

(Case Report - Hungerford, England)

Ogden, C. (1987, Aug. 31) Wednesday, bloody Wednesday. *Time, 130*, p.27.

(Case Report - Palm Bay, FL)

Carnage at a shopping mall (W. Cruse's killing spree in Palm Bay, FL). (1987, May 4) *Macleans, 100*, p. 24.

(Case Report - Kenya)

Ndetei, D.M., et al. (1987) Some social-psychological characteristics of criminal homicide in Kenya. *East Africa Medical Journal, 64*(1), 17-30.

(Case Report - Oklahoma)

Kopvillem, P. (1986, Sept. 1) In cold blood (mass slayings by H.P. Sherrill in Edmond, OK). *Macleans, 99*, p. 27.

(Case Study - Milan, Italy)

Italy: The last tango in Milano (American fashion model T. Broome kills F. D'Alessio). (1986, June 9) *Newsweek, 107*, p. 28.

(Case Report - Idaho)

Johnson, T.E. (1986, April 14) Killer of the purple sage (C. Dallas escapes from Idaho jail). *Newsweek, 107*, p. 25.

(Case Report - Los Angeles)

Ueling, M.D. (1986, June 9) The LA slayer. *Newsweek, 107*, p. 28.

(Case Report - Los Angeles)

Homicide - - Los Angeles, 1970-1979. (1986) *MMWR, 35*(5), 61-65.

(Case Report - New York)

Tardiff, K., et al. (1986) Homicide in New York City. *Am J Pub Health, 76*(5), 413-426.

(Case Report - Florida)

Richman, A. (1985, Sept. 9) Shootout in the street (Florida feud between M. Booth and H. Bryant). *People Weekly, 24*, pp. 88-92+.

(Case Report - Montreal)

The Montreal murderer (child murders). (1985, July 1) *Macleans, 98*, p. 56.

(Case Report - Beverly Hills)

Starr, M. (1985, Jan. 7) Murder in Beverly Hills (J.H. Meier accused of murdering A.W. Netter). *Newsweek, 105*, p. 19.

(Case Report - Guatemala)

Burka, E.R. (1984) 'Murder in Guatemala' inappropriate? (letter) *New England Journal of Medicine, 311*(5), 337-338.

(Case Report - Guatemala)

Goldfeld, A.E. (1984) Murder in Guatemala (letter). *New England Journal of Medicine, 310*(18), 1186.

(Case Report - Atlanta)

Centerwall, B.S. (1984) Race, socioeconomic status, and domestic homicide, Atlanta, 1971-1972. *American Journal of Public Health, 74*(8), 813-815.

(Case Report - New Mexico)

Lapham, S.C., et al. (1984) Risk factors for victimization during the 1980 riot at the New

Mexico Penitentiary. *American Journal of Epidemiology, 119*(2), 218-226.

(Case Report - Quebec)

Beirne, A. (1982, Aug. 9) Three murders most foul (murders of guards during prison riot at Archambault Institution (Quebec). *Macleans, 95*, p. 14.

(Case Report - Montana)

Bishop, L.V., et al. (1982) Major crime in three rural counties of Montana, 1895-1915. *Journal of Police Science and Administration, 10*(1), 82-92.

(Case Report - Tennessee)

Two inmates killed in Tennessee prison. (1982) *Corrections Magazine, 8*(2), 4. Article copies available from UMI.

(Case Report - Washington, DC)

Morganthau, T., et al. (1980, Dec. 22) One-man crime wave (burglar B.C. Welch, Jr. accused in murder of M. Halberstam in Washington, DC). *Newsweek, 96*, p. 30.

(Case Report - El Salvador)

Sanction, T.A., & Willwerth, J. (1980, Dec. 22) Aftermath of four brutal murders (US investigation into allegations of government involvement in deaths of three American nuns and lay worker in El Salvador). *Time, 116*, p. 40.

(Case Report - El Salvador)

Newhagen, J. (1980, Dec. 22) El Salvador's only certainty: More bloodshed. *Business Week*, p. 38.

(Case Report - El Salvador)

Martyrs' message (murder of three US nuns and a social worker in El Salvador). (1980, Dec. 20) *Nation, 231*, p. 660.

(Case Report - Atlanta)

Morganthau, T., & Smith, V.E. (1980, Dec. 1) Atlanta goes on a manhunt (Black children). *Newsweek, 96*, p. 40+.

(Case Report - New York City)

Juvenile time bomb (case of severely disturbed boy accused of murder in New York City). (1980, Nov. 3) *New York, 13*, pp. 25-28.

(Blacks' Fears)

Williams, D.A., et al. (1980, Oct. 27) Fears of black America. *Newsweek, 96*, p. 46.

(Case Report - New York)

Williams, D.A., et al. (1980, Mar. 24) Lady and the doctor (J.S. Harris' arrest in H. Tarnower murder in New York). *Newsweek, 95*, pp. 41-42.

(Case Report - New York City)

Wolfe, L. (1980, Oct. 20) Tragedy on 89th Street (I. Schwartz' murder of her children and her suicide). *New York, 13*, pp. 41-44+.

(Case Report - New York City)

Williams, D.A., et al. (1980, Sept. 22) Omega 7's killers strike in New York (murder of F. Garcia Rodreguez, Cuban diplomat). *Newsweek, 96*, p. 35.

(Case Report - Maryland)

Khomeini's long arm reaches into US (murder of A.A. Tabatabai in Bethesda, MD). (1980, Aug. 4) *US News & World Report, 89*, p. 7.

(Case Report - New York City)

Harris, D. (1980. Aug. 17) Bloody end to a 60's dream (murder of A. Lowenstein in New York City). *New York Times Magazine*, pp. 34-37+.

(Case Report - Quebec)

Cotton, J. (1980, Aug. 4) Murder and the cathedral murder of Father R. Rinfret in Quebec). *Macleans, 93*, p. 18.

(Case Report - New York City)

O'Toole, L. (1980, Aug. 4) Phantom of the Met (murder of violinist H. Hagnes at Metropolitan Opera House in New York City). *Macleans, 93*, pp. 25-26.

(Case Report - New York City)

Murder at the Met by a phantom killer (Case of Hagens). (1980, Aug. 4) *Newsweek, 96*, p. 24.

(G.R. Guerin Case)

Boulton, M. (1980, June 16) Death in the family (arrest of G.R. Guerin in Toronto). *Macleans, 93*, 24-25.

(Case Report - Maryland)

Peterson, K. (1980, May 26) Frightened and angry, an elderly Maryland man guns down two of his teenage tormentors (case of R. Welzant). *People Weekly, 13*, pp. 73-74.

(Case Report - Bronx)

Finn, D. (1980, May) Reflections on my brother's murder (shooting of H. Finn by Black teenagers in Riverdale section of the Bronx). *Saturday Review, 7*, pp. 22-23.

(Case Report - Iran)

Honor over life (allegations of US Marine hostage's paternity in case of pregnant Teheran girl slain by brother). (1980, April 7) *Time, 115*, p. 34.

(Case Report - New York)

Bourgeois, P. (1980, March 24) Three into two won't go (arrest of J.S. Harris in H. Tarnower murder case in New York). *Macleans, 9*, p. 30.

(Case Report - New York City)

Tragic end of a long march (murder of A. Lowenstein in New York City). (1980, March 24) *Newsweek, 95*, p. 42.

(Case Report - New York City)

Pileggi, N. (1980, March 17) War on the cops (New York City). *New York, 13*, pp. 31-35.

(Case Report - Florida)

Gettinger, S. (1980, March 6) Case of Robert A. Sullivan. *Rolling Stone*, p. 50.

(Case Report - California)

Scobie, W. (1980, March 3) Killing Blacks doesn't count (racial killings in Butte County, CA). *Macleans, 93*, p. 42.

(Case Report - New York City)

Young, R. (1980, March) Death by stranger (New York City). *New York, 13*, pp. 37-38.

(Case Report - Pennsylvania)

Walter, G. (1980, Feb. 25) For the Johnson family, police say, crime was a way of life - - and then death (case of B.A. Johnston of Chester County, PA). *People Weekly, 13*, pp. 95-96+.

(Case Report - Montreal)

Becker, K. (1980, Jan. 28) Trail as cold as The Cat (unsolved mass murder at Gargantua Bar Salon in Montreal). *Macleans, 93*, p. 8.

(Case - Report - North Carolina)

Beck, M., & Carroll, G. (1979, Dec. 31) Strange case of Annie Perry; uncovering murder of E.L. Cameron in Raeford, NC). *Newsweek, 94*, p. 37.

(Case Report - New Jersey)

You can't go home again; murder of E.J. Stockton in her Mercer St. home, Trenton, NJ. (!979, Dec. 24) *Time, 114*, p. 23+.

(Case Report - Great Britain)

Crime; Yorkshire murderer. (1979, Oct. 15) *People Weekly, 12*, pp. 117-118.

(Case Report - Great Britain)

Striking again: Yorkshire ripper in Great Britain. (1979, Sept. 17). *Time, 114*, p. 49.

(Case Report - Harlem)

Harris, R. (1979, Aug.) Death almost destroys family; murder of G. William two sons in Harlem. *Ebony, 34*, pp. 57-60.

(Case Report - Brooklyn)

Christopher, R. (1979, July 23) As he sowed, so he reaped; murder of G. Galante in Brooklyn restaurant. *Macleans, 92,* p. 30.

(Case Report - Brooklyn)

Beck, M., et al. (1979, July 23) Death of a godfather; murder of G. Galante in Brooklyn restaurant. *Newsweek, 94,* p. 34+.

(Case Report - Brooklyn)

Death in the afternoon; G. Galante gunned down in Brooklyn. (1979, July 23) *Time, 114,* p. 41.

(Case Report - New York)

Tucker, C. (1979, July 7) End of the ostrich option; murders in Bedford, NY. *Saturday Review, 6,* p. 56.

(Case Report - San Antonio)

Carroll, R., & Donosky, L. (1979, June 11) Texas: killing a federal judge; killing of J.H. Wood in San Antonio. *Newsweek, 93,* p. 50.

(Case Report - Scotland)

Gray, J.W.R. (1979, June) The expulsion of Beard from Scotland: Murder north of the border. *The Criminal Law Review,* pp. 369-380.

(Anti-Castro Terrorists)

Omega 7: Murder of C. Muniz by anti-Castro terrorists in San Juan. (1979, May 26) *Nation, 228,* p. 590.

(Case Report - El Salvador)

Carroll, R., & Nater, T. (1979, May 21) El Salvador: Murder at the cathedral; shooting of demonstrators attempting to free leaders of Popular Revolutionary Bloc. *Newsweek, 93,* p. 47+.

(Case Report - Los Angeles)

McWilliam, C. (1979, May 19) Second thoughts; E. Love shooting by Los Angeles police. *Nation, 228,* 558.

(Case Report - Iran)

Death of an Ayatollah; murder of M. Motahari in Teheran. (1979, May 14) *Time, 113,* p. 42. *Nation, 228,* p. 558.

(Case Report - Iran)

Carroll, R., & Allaway, A. (1979, May 14) Islam vs. the left; killing of Ayatollah M. Motahari. *Newsweek, 93,* p. 66.

(Case Report - Connecticut)

Beck, M. (1979, April 30) Brutal robbery: break-in of Purolator Securities depot in Waterbury, CT. *Newsweek, 93,* p. 37.

(Case Report - B.A. Johnson)

Wooten, J. (1979, April 10) Murder in Wyeth country; case of B.A. Johnson in Chester County, Pa. *Esquire, 91*, pp. 50-52+.

(Case Report - Netherlands)

Death through the rear window; murder of British Ambassador R. Sykes in the Hague. (1979, April 2) *Newsweek, 93*, p. 53.

(British Ambassador)

Murder in the Hague; death of British Ambassador R. Sykes. (1979, April 2) *Time, 113*, p. 38.

(Case Report - Utah)

James, L.P. (1979, April) Great underground manhunt; or one Mexican versus the State of Utah. *Journal of the West, 18*, pp. 11-20.

(Case Report - Tennessee)

Trillin, C. (1979, March 12) US journal; Knoxville: C. Stevens convicted in the death of F. Cooper. *New York, 55*, pp. 110-117.

(Case Report - Cleveland)

Daddy killers? Murder of J. White in Cleveland. (1979, March 5) *Newsweek, 93*, p. 54.

(Case Report - Lebanon)

Clugston, M. (1979, Feb. 5) Red Prince dies by the sword; death of Abu Hassan in Beirut. *Macleans, 92*, pp. 30-31.

(Murder - San Francisco)

Fong-Torres, B. (1979, Jan. 25) Letter from San Francisco: Murder of Mayor G. Moscone and Supervisor Harvey Milk. *Rolling Stone*, pp. 45-46.

(Case Report - Illinois)

I do rotten, horrible things; mass murder of young men and boys by J.W. Gacy in Des Plains, Ill. (1979, Jan. 8) *Time, 113*, p. 23.

(Case Report - Lebanon)

Beirut Dr. death; G. Habash blamed in slaying of F.E. Meloy. (1979, Jan. 1) *Newsweek, 93*, p. 32.

(Case Report - San Antonio)

San Antonio jail officers, inmates, and others charged with strangulation of prisoner. (1979) *Crime Control Digest, 13*(30), 9-10.

(Case Report - California)

Another day of death; murder of Moscone and Milk in San Francisco. (1978, Dec. 11) *Time, 112*, pp. 24-26.

(Case Report - San Francisco)

Matthews, T., & Lubenow, G.C. (1978, Dec. 11) Day of the assassin; murder of G.Moscone and H.Milk. *Newsweek, 92*, pp. 26-28.

(Murder Virginia)

Gothic romance in old Virginia; case of M. Michaelides. (1978, Nov. 6) *Time, 112*, p. 51.

(Case Report - Manhattan)

Punk murder; murder by rock star Sid Vicious in Manhattan. (1978, Oct. 23) *Newsweek, 92*, p. 54.

(Case Report - France)

Strasser, S., & Sciolono, E. (1978, Oct. 16) Marseille massacre. *Newsweek, 92*, p. 52+.

(Case Report - Libya)

Lewis, P. (1978, Oct. 16) Death of a salesman; W. Lamberz in Libya. *Macleans, 91*, pp. 32-34.

(Case Report - Chicago)

Holt, D., & Simons, P.E. (1978, Sept. 18) Tip from beyond? T. Basa case in Chicago. *Newsweek, 92*, pp. 35-36.

(Murders - G. Tison)

Death in the desert; murders committed by the G. Tison family. (1978, Sept. 4) *Time, 112*, p. 19.

(Case Report - Wyoming)

Demaret, K. (1978, Aug. 28) Tough and corrupt Wyoming mountain town is shocked by the death of a good cop; Rock Springs. *People Weekly, 10*, pp. 28-30.

(Case Report - Chile)

Velasco, E. (1978, Aug. 19) Chile's fake amnesty; effect of extradition of Chileans in the Letelier case. *Nation, 227*, pp. 131-133.

(Case Report - Chicago)

Jackson, D.S. (1978, Aug. 7) Something fishy in Chicago; A. Accardo's vengeance slayings. *Time, 122*, p. 28.

(Case Report - Wyoming)

Holt, D., & Brinkley-Rogers, P. (1978, Aug. 7) Wide-open town; murder of M. Rosa in Rock Springs, WY. *Newsweek, 92*, p. 35.

(Case Report - Guatemala)

Brockman, J.R. (1978, July 29) Murder in Guatemala; case of H. Lopez. *America, 139*, p. 58.

(Case Report - New Hampshire)

Trillin, C. (1978, July 24) US journal; Manchester, NH; case of the H. Piasency family. *New*

Yorker, 54, pp. 67-71.

(Murder - San Quentin, CA)

Derry, A. (1978, July 10) California settles with $50,000 for Billingslea's prison murder; death at San Quentin. *New Times, 11*, p. 18.

(Case Report - Chicago)

O'Brien, J. & Baumann, E. (1978, June) Accused of murder by a voice from the grave; T. Basa case in Chicago. *Ebony, 33*, pp. 56-58+.

(Case Report - New York)

Kornbluth, J. (1978, May 7) Fatal romance at Yale; murder of B.G. Garland in Scarsdale, NY. *New York Times Magazine*, pp. 44-45+.

(Case Report - Nicaragua)

Wilson, R. (1978, May 4) To die in Managua: killing of P.J. Chamorro Cardenal. *Rolling Stone*, p. 34+.

(Harris Case - Moscow)

Strange case of Johnny Harris; Moscow's creation of American civil rights martyr. (1978, April 17) *Time, 111*, p. 37.

(Case Report - Los Angeles)

Strangler suspects; Los Angeles. (1978, April 10) *Newsweek, 91*, p. 42.

(Case Report - Belgium)

Nun's story; case of Sister Godfrida in Belgium. (1978, March 13) *Time, 111*, p. 51.

(Case Report - Nicaragua)

Lernoux, P. (1978, Jan. 28) Murder in Nicaragua; killing of P.J. Chamorro. *Nation, 226*, pp. 69-70.

(Case Report - Nicaragua)

Shotguns silence a critic; murder of P.J. Chamorro Cardenal in Managua, Nicaragua. (1978, Jan. 23) *Time, 111*, pp. 55-56.

(Case Report - Nicaragua)

Southerland, D. (1978, Jan. 23) Human rights payoff? Murder of P.J. Chamorro Cardenal in Managua. *New Republic, 178*, pp. 17-19.

(Case Report - Nicaragua)

Willey, F., et al. (1978, Jan. 23) Murder in Managua: Case of P.J. Chamorro Cardenal. *Newsweek, 91*, p. 34.

(Case Report - Los Angeles)

Williams, D.A. (1978, Jan. 9) Strangler's grip; Los Angeles. *Newsweek, 91*, pp. 24-26.

(Case Report - New Orleans)

Hernon, P. (1978) *A terrible thunder: The story of the New Orleans sniper.* New York: Doubleday.

(Murder Story)

Blackmore, J. (1978) The dowager and the hitman. *Police Magazine Illustrated, 1*(5), 2-3.

(Case Report - Los Angeles)

LA strangler. (1977, Dec. 19) *Time, 110*, p. 24.

(Case Report - Los Angeles)

Williams, D.A., & Brinkley-Rogers, P. (1977, Dec. 19) Strangler; Los Angeles murders. *Newsweek, 90*, p. 36.

(Case Report - New York City)

Victim # 21; murder of mafia lawyer, G. Gallina in New York City. (1977, Nov. 21) *Time, 110*, p. 39.

(Case Report - New York City)

Son of Sam - - the killer who terrorized New York. (1977, Nov.) *Reader's Digest, 111*, pp. 155-160.

(Case Report - Alabama)

Boeth, R., & Smith, V.E. (1977, Oct. 10) Arrest in Birmingham; charging R.E. Chambliss with 1963 church bombing. *Newsweek, 90*, p. 32+.

(Case Report - Los Angeles)

Fingering a .22-cal. killer; arrest of J. Ullo in Los Angeles. (1977, Sept. 26) *Time, 110*, p. 29+.

(Case Report - San Francisco)

Williams, D.A., et al. (1977, Sept. 26) Civil war in Chinatown; San Francisco. *Newsweek, 90*, p. 39.

(Case Report - Chicago)

Steele, R., & Harper, C.J. (1977, Aug. 15) Chop-shop war; mob murders in Chicago. *Newsweek, 90*, p. 22.

(Case Report - Texas)

Crews, H. (1977, Aug.) Climbing the tower; Austin, Texas site of 1966 murders by C. Whitman. *Esquire 88*, pp. 38-39.

(Case Report - California)

Williams, D.A., & Huck, J. (1977, July 18) Trash-bag murders; case of D.D. Hill and P.W. Kearney in California. *Newsweek, 90*, p. 22.

(Case Study - Louisiana)

Tomlinson, K.Y. (1977, July 9) Murder at Jupiter; political corruption and construction workers' union in Lake Charles. *Reader's Digest, 111*, pp. 115-119.

(Case Report - Alabama)

Alpern, D.M., & Smith, V.E. (1977, July 4) Seventh son; shooting of Rev. W. Maxwell in Alexander City, AL. *Newsweek, 90*, p. 21.

(Case Report - New Rochelle)

Matthews, T., & Agrest, S. (1977, Feb. 28) Nazi of New Rochelle; case of F. Cowan. *Newsweek, 89*, p. 30.

(Case Report - Ethiopia)

Shoot-out in the Dirgue; Ethiopia. (1977, Feb. 14) *Newsweek, 89*, p. 48.

(Case Report - Italy)

Cantoni, A. (1977) Examination of 41 cases of homicide in the provinces of Novara and Varcelli (Italian). *Rass Criminol, 8*(1-2), 151-180.

(Girl Scout Killer)

Girl Scout camp security tight; Locust Grove killer still free, Florida kidnapper caught. (1977) *Juvenile Justice Digest, 5*(13), 7.

(Case Report - J. Peiper)

Daley, R. (1976, Nov. 7) Case of the SS hero; J. Peiper case in Trave, France. *New York Times Magazine*, pp. 32-33+.

(Case Report - New York City)

Couple forewarned by police - - murdered by jealous boyfriend, New York's highest court holds city may be liable. (1976, Oct.) *AELE Law Enforcement Legal Liability Reporter, 46*, 6-7.

(Case Report - England)

Willey, F., & MacPherson, M. (1976, Aug. 23) Drowning pool; murder of E. Sidoli in Kentish town. *Newsweek, 88*, p. 52+.

(Case Report - Virginia)

Armbrister, T. (1976, Aug.) Code-99 emergency; coronary patients murdered at General Hospital, Petersburg, VA. *Reader's Digest, 109*, pp. 105-108.

(Case Report - Argentina)

Murders continue; killing of prominent exiles in Argentina. (1976, June 14) *Time, 107*, pp. 37-38.

(Murder - Georgia)

Barnes, M. (1976) *Murder in Coweta County.* Pleasantville, NY: Readers Digest Press.

(Becket's Murder)

Davis, R.A. (1976) Becket's murder at Canterbury. *Surg Gynecol Obstet, 142*(5), 753-764.

(Murder Stories)

Kelly, T. (1976) *Murders: The Capital's famous murder stories.* Washingtonian Press.

(Harlem Mosque Incident)

Devaney, J., & Grosso, S. (1976) *The ten thirteen conspiracy: The Harlem mosque incident.*

(Case Report - Arizona)

Three runaways meet double death in Arizona. (1976) *Juvenile Justice Digest, 4*(11), 5.

(Case Report - Georgia)

Barnes, M. (1976) *Murder in Coweta County.* Pleasantville, NY: Reader's Digest Press.

(Case Report - Texas)

Hunter slays man reported to have killed Texas trooper. (1976) *Crime Control Digest, 10*(48), 3.

(Case Report - Tennessee)

Tennessee tragedy stirs state to reevaluate child abuse program. (1976) *Juvenile Justice Digest, 4*(21), 1-2.

(Case Report - Baltimore)

A 46-year old Baltimore woman . . . (1976) *Juvenile Justice Digest, 4*(3), 7.

(Case Report - England)

A Gloucestershire murder (R vs. Brittle). (1976) *Medical and Legal Journal, 44*(2), 48-62.

(Case Report - Kallinger)

Joseph Kallinger gets life for three-state murder spree. (1976) *Juvenile Justice Digest, 4*(20), 10.

(Murder - P.C. Schofield)

Rowe, C. (1976) The murder of P.C. Schofield at Caterham, July 1974. *Med Leg J, 44*(1), 15-27.

(Case Report - Germany)

Zippelius, K. (1976) Carl Hau case a 'cause celebre' of the criminal history of Baden-Baden (German). *Arch Kriminol, 158*(3-4), 109-121.

(Case Report - Great Britain)

Stevens, M., & Barnes, J. (1975, Dec. 29) Panther at bay; arraignment of D. Neilson in Great Britain. *Newsweek, 86*, p. 35.

(Case Report - Philadelphia)

Murder in Philadelphia; death of J.S. Knight, III. (1975, Dec. 22) *Time, 106*, p. 22+.

(Case Report - Mississippi)

Shostak, D.A. (1975, Dec.) Crosby Smith; forgotten witness to a Mississippi nightmare; murder of E. Till. *Negro History Bulletin, 38*, pp. 320-325.

(Case Report - South Carolina)

Williams, D.A., & Smith, V.E. (1975, Nov. 10) Heavy traffic; police shootings of Blacks in South Carolina. *Newsweek, 86*, p. 37.

(Case Report - New England)

Trillin, C. (1975, Oct. 27) US journal; New England: Murder of J. Oi by restaurant partner A. Therrin. *New Yorker, 51*, p. 102+.

(Case Report - New York)

Moore, G. (1975, Sept.) Sniper! Get down! A. Barbaro and the shooting at Olean, NY high school. *Reader's Digest, 107*, pp. 69-74.

(Wounded Knee Ambush)

Weisman, J.D. (1975, Sept.) About that ambush at Wounded Knee. *Columbia Journalism Review, 14*, 28-31.

(Case Report - Chicago)

Salmans, S., et al. (1975, June 30) King of Chicago; gangland-style slaying of M.S. Giancana. *Newsweek, 85*, pp. 17-18.

(Case Report - Florida)

Trillin, C. (1975, March 17) US journal; Miami Beach: Murder of H. St. Jean. *New Yorker, 51*, pp. 98-105.

(Case Report - Montreal)

Death in the branch office; Montreal massacre. (1975, Feb. 3) *Newsweek, 85*, p. 31.

(Case Report - Maryland)

Indicted youth faces death in Maryland. (1975) *Juvenile Justice Digest, 3*(16), 2.

(Case Study - Pennsylvania)

Harrisburg, PA. - - Joseph Kallinger . . . (1975) *Juvenile Justice Digest, 3*(19), 8.

(Case Report - Los Angeles)

LA seeks the "head chopper". (1975) *Crime Control Digest, 9*(4), 6.

(Indicted Youth - Maryland)

Indicted youth faces death in Maryland. (1975) *Justice Justice Digest, 3*(16), 2.

(Case Report - England)

Murder most foul; Lucan murder case in London. (1974, Nov. 25) *Newsweek, 84*, p. 54.

(Case Report - Boston)

Culliton, B.J. (1974, Oct. 25) Manslaughter; the charge against Edelin of Boston City Hospital. *Science, 186*, pp. 327-328+.

(Case Report - Washington, DC)

Suppliant stranger; search for murderer of young girls in Washington. (1974, Sept. 23) *Time, 104*, p. 30.

(Case Report - Chicago)

Double-dealers's death; murder of Richard Cain in Chicago. (1974, Jan. 7) *Time, 103*, p. 29.

(Case Report - Memphis)

Meyer, G. (1974) *The Memphis murders.* Seabury, CT: Continuum Books.

(Case Report - Illinois)

Seaman, B. (1973, Dec. 17) High noon after nightfall; murder of J. Bolinger of Brooklyn, IL. *Time, 102*, p. 24.

(Case Report - Nebraska)

Nebraska gothic; murder of Edwin and Wilma Hoyt. (1973, Nov. 26) *Newsweek, 82*, p. 37.

(Case Report - California)

Murder in California; mass murder in the hamlet of Victor. (1973, Nov. 19) *Time, 102*, p.41.

(Case Report - Virgin Islands)

Panic among continentals; Virgin Islands murders. (1973, Aug. 27) *Time, 102*, pp. 21-22.

(Case Report - Houston)

Nicest person; murder of teenage boys near Houston, TX. (1973, Aug. 20) *Newsweek, 82*, p. 32.

(Case Report - Detroit)

Murder City: Detroit. (1973, April 16) *Time, 101*, p. 17.

(Case Report - California)

Murdersville, USA: Multiple killings in Santa Cruz, CA. (1973, March 5) *Newsweek, 18*, p. 30.

(Case Report - Washington, DC)

Muslim massacre of seven Hanafi Mussulman disciples in a Washington, DC commune. (1973, Jan. 29) *Newsweek, 81*, p. 29.

(Case Report - New Orleans)

Death in New Orleans. (1973, Jan. 22) *Time, 101*, pp. 20-21

(Case Report - New Orleans)

Battle of New Orleans. (1973, Jan. 22) *Newsweek, 81*, pp. 26-27.

(Case Report - New York)

Turns, D.M., & Gruenberg, E.M. (1973) An attendant is murdered: The state hospital responds. *Psychiatric Quarterly, 47*(7), 487-494.

(Case Report - Boston)

Bailey, O.T. (1972, April 3) Brahma, Parkman, and Webster: Murder in medical Boston. *JAMA, 220*(1), 70-74.

(Case Report - England)

Sereny, G. (1972) *The case of Mary Bell.* London: Eyre Methuen.

(Case Report - New York)

Astor, G. (1971, Dec. 12) New York ten; murdered policemen. *New York Times Magazine*, pp. 32-35.

(Case Report - California)

Death in the orchards; Yuba City, CA. (1971, June 7) *Time, 97*, p. 14.

(Case Report - California)

California's sub-culture; mass murders reported in Yuba City. (1971, June 7) *Nation, 212*, p. 740.

(Case Report - California)

Grisly harvest of the orchard; mass murder in Yuba City. (1971, June 11) *Life, 70*, pp. 38-39.

(Case Report - California)

Massacre at Yuba City. (1971, June 7) *Newsweek, 77*, pp. 28-29.

(Case Report - Iowa)

Trillin, C. (1971, Feb. 20) US Journal: Center Junction, Iowa; Jim, Tex, and the one-armed man. *New Yorker, 47*, pp. 100-102+.

(Case Report - California)

Egan, F. (1971, Jan.) Incident at Tragedy Springs; an unsolved mystery of the California Trail. *American West, 8*, pp. 36-39.

(Case Report - Harvard)

Thomas, H. (1971) *Murder at Harvard.* Cambridge, MA: HM.

(Case Report - England)

Burton, J. (1971) The Heathrow hijack death. *Medical-Legal Journal, 39*, 27-30.

(Ratcliffe Murders)

Critchley, T.A., & James, P.D. (1971) *The maul and the pear tree: The Ratcliffe Highway murders*. Crane-Russak Co.

(Mass Murder - Sequel)

Mass murder in Sequel; case of Ohta family. (1970, Nov. 2) *Time, 96*, pp. 10-11.

(Case Report - California)

Bloody breakout at San Rafael; with editorial comment. (1970, Aug. 21) *Life, 69*, pp. 2A, 30-34.

(Case Report - California)

Courthouse shoot-out; San Rafael, CA. (1970, Aug. 17) *Newsweek, 76*, p. 34+.

(Homicide - Ireland)

Hogan, B. (1970, Aug.) Funeral in Dublin. *The Criminal Law Review 1970*, 452.

(Case Report - Pennsylvania)

Trillin, C. (1970, June 27) US Journal: West Chester, PA; under cover police officer John Mervin arrested for murder. *New Yorker, 46*, pp. 42-44+.

(Case Report - New Jersey)

Wren, C.S., & English, M. (1970, March 10) Murder New Jersey style; Judy Kavanaugh case. *Look, 34*, pp. 43-47.

(Case Report - Uganda)

Tanner, R.E. (1970) *Homicide in Uganda*. Holmes & Meier.

(Case Report - Yakai)

Sato, B. (1969, Jan.) Reflections on the Yakai case (Japanese). *Journal of the Tokyo Medical College, 27*, 131-160.

(Case Report - Arizona)

Gilmore, J., & Zeiger, H.A. (1969) *Tucson Murders*. New York: Dial.

(Case Report - Chicago)

Voss, H.L., & Hepburn, J.R. (1968, Dec.) Patterns in criminal homicide in Chicago. *Journal of Criminal Law, 59*, p. 499.

(Case Report - Mississippi)

Huie, W.B. (1968) *Three lives for Mississippi*. New York: New American Library.

(Case Report - Canada)

Simpson, K. (1968) The case against Steven Truscott in Canada. *Medicolegal Journal, 36*(14), 58-71.

(Child Slayer)

Myers, S.A. (1967, Aug.) A 25-year survey of homicides involving preadolescent victims. *Archives of General Psychiatry, 17*, 211-213.

(Case Report - Boston)

Belleau, T., & Arsenian, J. (1967) Homicide and hospitalization: A case Report. *Psychiatry, 30*(1). 73-78.

(Case Report - Arizona)

Moser, D., & Cohen, J. (1967) *Pied Piper of Tucson.* New York: New American Library.

(Case Report - Boston)

Frank, G. (1967) *Boston Strangler.* New York: New American Library.

(Case Report - Germany)

Michalke, H. (1965) The Frankfurt murder of a young girl (German). 20957. J. 19, '65, 7, S. 359-363. (IBZ 66).

(Homicide - Dumbarton)

Goodall, T.M. (1965) The homicide of Dumbarton (German). 20957. J. 19, '65, 5, S. 280 (IBZ 1966).

(Case Report - Scotland)

Gillies, H. (1965) Murder in the west of Scotland. *British Journal of Psychiatry, 111*(480), 1087-1094.

(Case Report - Parkland)

Three patients at Parkland. (1964, Jan.) *Texas Journal of Medicine, 60*, 60-74.

(Homicide - Kentucky)

Moreland, R. (1964) Kentucky felony willful murder. *Kentucky Law Journal, 52*, 585.

(Case Report - England)

Rowland, J. (1963) *Murder mistaken.* London: Long.

(Case Report - Minnesota)

Trenerry, W.N. (1962) *Murder in Minnesota: A collection of true cases.* Minneapolis: Minnesota Historical Society.

(Case Report - Madagascar)

Ratandra, R., & Berthomieu, R. (1961) Pathological murder in Madagascar (French). *Ann Medicopsychol, 119*(2), 877-889.

(Case Report - Pennsylvania)

Moschzisker, M. (1960, March) Rockview revisited. *Pennsylvania Bar Association Quarterly, 31*, 273.

(Murder at Sea)

Muhlfeld, E. (1959, Nov.) Murder on the high seas; the mate Bram case. *Boston Bar Journal, 3*, 6.

(Homicide - Colonies)

Lewis, J. (1958, Oct.) Outlook for a devil in the colonies. *Criminal Law Review 1958*, 661.

(Homicide - Texas)

McGregor, C.B. (1953, Fall) Homicide charges in Texas. *Baylor Law Review, 6*, 40-58.

(Homicide - Pennsylvania)

Voluntary manslaughter in Pennsylvania. (1952, June) *Dick Law Review, 56*, 541-546.

(Homicide - Texas)

Davenport, J. (1947, June) Twenty years of homicide in Texas. *Texas Law Review, 25*, 634-640.

(Drowning Case - Dallas)

Allen, B. (1945, Oct.) The Gragg drowning case from Dallas (Gragg v. State (TX) 186 SW 2d. 243). *Texas Bar Journal, 8*, 454-455, 478-480.

(Case Report - Dakota Indians)

Goldfrank, E.S. (1943) Historic change and social character: A study of the Teton Dakota. *American Anthropology, 45*, 67-83.

(Murder - Middletown)

Bacon, G.W. (1937, Nov.) Murder in Middletown. *L Lib Journal, 30*, 540-543.

(Felony-Murder - New York)

Corcoran, T.L.J. (1937) Felony-murder in New York. *Fordham Law Review, 6*, 43.

(Murder - Japanese)

Japanese civilian murdered in almost same spot as Nakayama was killed last November. (1936, July 18) *China W R, 77*, 244+.

(Case Report - Oregon)

McNary, L.A. (1935, Dec.) Oregon's first reported murder case. *Oregon History Quarterly, 36*, 359-364.

(Case Report - Wisconsin)

Gillin, J.L. (1934, May) Wisconsin murderer. *Social Forces, 12*, pp. 550-556.

(Case Report - Russia)

Haensel, V. (1932, May-June) A "justified" murder in Russia. *Journal of Criminal Law, 23*, 90-92.

(Murder Mysteries)

Wallace, W.S. (1931) *Murders & mysteries: A Canadian series.* Hyperion.

(Murder - California)

Hagan, H.A. (1929, Nov.) A California saga. *Com L League Journal, 34*, 677-684.

(Murder - Rhode Island)

Phelps, H.A. (1928, Feb.) Rhode Island's threat against murder. Journal of Criminal Law, 18, 552-567.

(Murder - Smutty Nose)

Pearson, E., & Darwin, B. (1927, April 9) Two American murders; review of Murder at Smutty Nose. *Nation* (London), *41*, pp. 14-15.

(Case Report - Chicago)

The Loeb-Leopold murder of Franks in Chicago, May 21, 1924. (1924) *Journal of Criminal Law, 15*, 347.

(Case Report - Japan)

Roe, R. (1921) Japanese murder cases. *Virginia Law Review, 8*, 27.

(Case Reports - Sierra Leone)

Gray, A. (1916) Human leopards of Sierra Leone. *J Comp Leg, 16*, 195.

(Homicide - New York)

"Hon": The prefix -- a bit of history in New York State. (1898) *Alb Law Journal, 58*, 158.

Case Reports
Medicolegal

(Case Report - Premature Infant)

Anderson, C. (1990, June 22) Baby's death deemed homicide: Premature death held no bar to conviction. *New York Law Journal, 203*.

(Case Report - Physician Cleared)

Brahams, D. (1990) Medicine and the law: Doctor cleared of murder of cancer patients. *Lancet, 335*(8691), 718.

(Case Report - Post-Mortem)

Sperry, K. (1990) Anterior thoracic wall trauma in elderly homicide victims: The CPR defense. *American Journal of Forensic Science and Pathology, 11*(1), 50-55.

(Case Report - Medicolegal Deaths)

Thakur, C.P., et al. (1987, March) Relation between full moon and medicolegal deaths. *Indian Journal of Medical Research, 85*, 316-320.

(Case Report - Brain Death)

Lucas, B.A., et al. (1987) Brain death in a murder victim: A medicolegal dilemma. *Hospital*

Practitioner, 22(4), 251-153, 256-258, 263.

(Case Report - Infanticide)

Shiono, H., et al. (1986) Medicolegal aspects of infanticide in Hokkaido District, Japan. *American Journal of Forensic and Medical Pathology, 7*(2), 104-106.

(Case Report - Nielsen Affair)

Chambers, G. (1985) The Dennis Nielsen affair. *Medicolegal Journal, 53*(3), 134-147.

(Case Report - Corpses)

Erzinclioglu, Y.Z. (1985) The entomological investigation of a concealed corpse. *Medical Science and the Law, 25*(3), 228-230.

(Case Report - Post-Mortem)

Cordner, S.M. (1985) The role of the second post-mortem examination. *Medicolegal Journal, 53*(1), 24-28.

(Case Report - Homicidal Wounds)

Mandal, A.K., et al. (1984) Evaluation of antibiotic therapy and surgical techniques in cases of homicidal wounds of the colon. *American Surgeon, 50*(5), 254-257.

(Case Report - Police Homicide)

Sherman, L.W. (1980) Execution without trial: Police homicide and the constitution. *Vanderbilt Law Review, 33*(1), 71-100.

(Case Report - Police Shooting)

Fyfe, J.J. (1980) Geographic correlates of police shooting: A microanalysis. *Journal of Research on Crime and Delinquency, 17*(1), 101-113.

(Felony-Murder Rule)

State v. Jackson (NM) 589 P 2d. 1052: A solution to the felony-murder rule dilemma. (1979, Summer) *New Mexico Law Review, 9*, 433-441.

(Case Report - Case and Comment)

Jones, C., & Smith, J.C. (1979, July) Case and comment: Murder. *The Criminal Law Review*, 465-466.

(Case Report - Battered Child Syndrome)

Commonwealth vs. Cadwell ((Massachusetts) 372 N E 2d. 246): Deliberate premeditation, extreme atrocity and cruelty, and the battered child syndrome - - a new look at criminal culpability in Massachusetts. (1979, Spring) *New England Law Review, 14*, 812-847.

(Case Report - Gacy)

Matthews, T., & Maier, F. (1979, Jan. 8) Double life of a clown; J.W. Gacy murders. *Newsweek, 93*, p. 24+.

(Case Report - Capital Punishment)

Kleck, G. (1979) Capital punishment, gun ownership, and homicide. *Journal of Sociology, 84*(4), 882-910.

(Epileptic Murder)

Gunn, J. (1978, May) Epileptic homicide: A case report. *British Journal of Psychiatry, 132*, 510-513.

(Case Report - Case and Comment)

Jones, C., & Smith, J.C. (1978, March) Case and comment: Murder. *The Criminal Law Review*, 166-167.

(Case Report - Bodies Recovered)

The tell-tale body in the trunk. (1978) *Law Enforcement Journal, 8*(5), 9.

(Case Report - Murder)

Nash, J.R. (1978) Hardscrabble murder along the Mohawk. *Law Enforcement Journal, 8*(7), 5.

(Case Report - Johnson)

Johnson, J.R. (1978) People vs. Johnson: A retreat from the duty to retreat? *UD Law Review, 1*, 147-159.

(Case Report - Police)

Two Maryland police officers killed by juvenile detained for coin-box theft. (1978) *Juvenile Justice Digest, 6*(13), 4. Article copies available from UMI.

(Mulligan v. Queen)

Parker, G. (1977, Oct.) Mulligan v. The Queen (1976) 28 C C C 2d. 266. *Osgoode Hall Law Journal, 15*, 427-435.

(Paquette v. Queen)

Claxton, E. (1977, Oct.) Paquette v. The Queen (1976) 70 D L R 3d. 129. *Osgoode Law Journal, 15*, 436-446.

(Case Report - Patterson)

Patterson v. New York (97 Sup Ct. 2319): Defendant must carry burden of proof in affirmative defense. (1977, Fall) *National Journal of Criminal Defense, 3*, 289-301.

(Copy Cat Killings)

The carbon copy murders ... or murder in triplicate. (1977) *The Police Journal, 50*(2), 116-141.

(Case Study)

Delogu, T. (1977) Treatment of case B/2 published in file no. 3, July-Sept. 1975. Penal law, criminology, and specialization of the penal magistrate. *Quad Criminol Clin, 19*(1), 107-117.

(Lafcadio Case)

Kloss, R.J. (1977) The gratuitous act: Gide's Lafcidio case reconsidered. *Psychoanalysis Review, 64*(1), 111-134.

(Case Report - Decriminalization)

McGrath, J.P. (1976, Oct. 1) Case for decriminalizing murder; Omnibus anticrime bill. *National Review, 28*, pp. 1066-1067.

(Case Report - Duress)

Moran, T.J., & Smith, J.C. (1976, Sept.) Case and comment: Duress. *The Criminal Law Review 1976*, 563-565.

(Case Report - Malpractice)

Forbes, E.M. (1976) Malpractice and manslaughter: The case of Edwin Martin Van Butchell. *Connecticut Medicine, 40*(5), 323-325

(Case Report - Snipers)

Sniper to stand trial. (1976) *Juvenile Justice Digest, 4*(18), 8.

(Walter Rowland Trial)

Cecil, H. (1976) *The trial of Charles Rowland*. David & Charles.

(Case Report - Murder)

Katz, L.S. (1975, Fall) Defense of a homicide case. *National Journal of Criminal Defense, 1*, 235-254.

(Case Report - Police Killing)

Kobler, A.L. (1975) Figures (and perhaps some facts) on police killing of civilians in the United States, 1965-1969. *Journal of Social Issues, 31*(1), 185-191.

(Case Report - Physician)

Goldsmith, L.S. (1974, March-April) Physician acquitted of charges of murdering patient. *Journal of Legal Medicine, 2*, 47-48.

(Case Report - Amnesia)

Amnesia bid fails. (1974, Jan.-Feb.) *Journal of Legal Medicine, 2*, 55.

(Case Report - Poisoning)

Derobert, L. (1974) The work of Doctor Jacques Trivas: 2 cases of poisoning in the Parthenay area (1886-1888). *Med Leg Dommage Corpor, 7*(4), 301-302.

(Case Report -Firearms)

King, D.P. (1973) Firearms and crime. *Criminologist, 8*(28), 50-58.

(Case Report - Physicians)

Rabson, S.M. (1971, April 15) Doctors delinquent: The trials of two physicians charged with murder. *JAMA, 16*, 121-124.

(Murder Case)

Heller, J.R., et al. (1970, Summer-Fall) Summation in a murder case. *Tr Law Q, 7*, 26.

(Near-Homicide)

Matthew, J.R., et al. (1964, Dec.) Six and fourteen dysrythmia and the ego: A case of near homicide. *J Neuropsychiatry, 5*, 490-494.

(Case Studies)

Piedlievre, R. (1960, July-Aug.) Story of two crimes. *Ann Med Leg* (Paris), *40*, 364-365.

(Felony-Murder Rule)

Felony-murder rule (People v. Wood (NY) 186 NY S 2d. 141). (1959, Fall) *Mercer Law Review, 11*, 231.

(Case Report - Emmett Dunne)

Camps, F.E. (1959) The case of Emmett Dunne. *Medicolegal Journal, 27*, 156-161.

(Case Report - England)

Bathurst, M.E., & Price, D.E. (1958) Regina v. Kenneth Barlow. *Medical Legal Journal* (Cambridge, England), *26*(2), 58-70.

(Case Report - Police)

Felon's responsibility for killing of accomplice by resisting officer (Commonwealth v. Redline (PA) 137 A 2d 472). (1958, Spring) *Syracuse Law Review, 9*, 311.

(Case Report - Dr. Stopes)

Dr. Marie Stopes. (1958) *Medical Legal Journal* (Cambridge, England), *2*(12), 166-169.

(Case Report - Implied Malice)

Williams, J. (1957, Nov.) Grievous bodily harm and implied malice in murder (Regina v. Vickers, 1957, 3 W L R 326). *Modern Law Review, 20*, 633.

(Case Report - Due Process)

Constitutional Law: Due process: Elimination of intent or culpable negligence as an element of manslaughter (People v. Stuart (CA) 295 P 2d 426). (1957, May) *Oklahoma Law Review, 10*, 179.

(Case Report - Accessory)

Accessory after the fact to what? (1957, Aug.) *SALJ, 74*, 275.

(Case Report - Felonious Homicide)

Felonious homicide - - the expanding concept (Commonwealth (PA) v. Thomas (117 A 2d 204). (1957, Winter) *South Carolina Law Quarterly, 9*, 287.

(Case Report - Justifiable Homicide)

Felony murder - proximate causality - justifiable homicide - surviving felon's liability. (Commonwealth v. Thomas). (1956, Oct.) *UD Law Review, 34*, 58.

(Case Report - Objectivity)

Denny, W.E. (1956, July) Objectivity in murder (Regina v. Ward, 1956 1 Q B 351). *Modern Law Review, 19*, 414.

(Case Report - Excitomotor Abduction)

Ollivier, H., et al. (1956, March-April) Inexplicable homicidal excitomotor abduction, atypical prodrome of acute neuromeningococcal infection (French). *Ann Med Leg, 36*, 102-103.

(Violence Against Nature)

Granata, M. (1956, March-April) Signs of carnal violence against nature in homicide case. *Minerva Medicoleg, 76*, 55-57.

(Case Study - Dismemberment)

Ollivier, H., & Robert, F. (1956, Jan.-Feb.) Study apropos of case of dismemberment. *Ann Med Leg, 36*, 55-57.

(Case Report - Homicide)

Belbey, J. (1956) Forensic psychopathology: Homicide and robbery (Spanish). *Dia Med. B Aires, 28*(77), 2301.

(Case Report - Extenuating Circumstances)

Evans, S. (1955, Nov.) Extenuating circumstances. *SALJ, 72*, 385.

(Case Report - Castle Doctrine)

Duty to retreat - - 'castle' doctrine (Commonwealth (PA) v. Fraser 85 Atla 2d 126). (1952, Spring) *University of Pittsburgh Law Review, 13*, 595-597.

(Case Report - Murder)

Matthews, S. (1949-50, Winter) First degree murder-premeditation and deliberation (Jones v. United States, 175 F 2d 544). *Arkansas Law Review, 4*, 92-94.

(Case Report - Duty to Retreat)

Self defense- - duty to retreat from domicile before attack of guest (State v. Grierson (NH 69 Atl 2d 851). (1950, March) *University of Pennsylvania Law Review, 98*, 593-595.

(Case Report - Political Murder)

El-Rawy, M. (1947) Political murder (Egyptian). *Egyptian Journal of Psychology, 3*, 207-214.

(Case Report - Murder)

Almand, B. (1947, Aug.) The Ashburn murder case and military trial. *Georgia Bar Journal, 10*, 43-48.

(Case Report - Murder)

Unger, J. (1946, April) Constructive murder, the limits of (Rex vs. Jarmain, 1945, 2 All E R 613). *Modern Law Review, 9*, 72-75.

(Case Report - Unfaithful Wife)

Criminal law -- killing by husband of unfaithful wife -- murder or manslaughter (Rex v. Holmes, 1946 62 T L R 342). (1946, Aug., 1947, Feb.) *Australian Law Journal, 20*, 150-151, 384-385.

(Case Report - Manslaughter)

Manslaughter by negligence. (1943, May 14) *Sol J*, pp. 169-170.

(Case Report - Murder)

Rozan, W.Z. (1935, April) A study of the Reppin case (Reppin vs. People (Colorado) 34 Pac 2d 71). *Rocky Mountain Law Review, 7*, 209-213.

(Case Report - Insanity Defense)

Due process, validity of a statute abolishing insanity as a defense for murder (Sinclair v. State (Miss.) 132 So 581). (1931, June) *Virginia Law Review, 17*, 826-827.

(Gastonia Strikers)

The Gastonia strikers' case (State v. Beale (NC) 154 SE 605). (1931, May) *Harvard Law Review, 4*, 1118-1124.

(Case Report - Attempted Arrest)

Killing in attempt to arrest (State vs. Bute (SD) 234 N W 605). (1931, May) *Law Notes, 35*, 23.

(Case Report - Civil Wrong)

Death resulting from act amounting only to civil wrong (R. v. Baldessare (1930) 22 Cr App R 70). (1931, April) *Law Quarterly Review, 47*, 167-168.

(Intestate Victim)

An intestates murderer as next-of-kin (Re Pitts; Cox v. Kilsby, The Times, 26th Feb., 1931). (1931, March 28) *Sol J, 75*, 210.

(Case Report - Rouse)

The Rouse case. (1931) *Law Journal, 71*, 147,

(Case Report - Earnest Lyons)

McLemore, J.L. (1931) The strange case of Earnest Lyons who falsely confessed murder and suffered accordingly. *Virginia Law Review, 17*, 369.

(Constructive Felo de Se)

Constructive felo de se. (1930) *Law Times, 170*, 226.

(Case Report - Castle Doctrine)

Castle doctrine (Oney vs. Commonwealth, 225 KY 590, 9 S W 2d 723). (1929, July) *St. Louis Law Review, 14*, 437-439.

(Specific Intent)

Specific intent, what constitutes (Andrews v. State (GA) 138 SE 923; Chambliss v. State (GA) 139 SW 80). (1928, Dec.) *Michigan Law Review, 27*, 214-215.

(Case Report - Dying Declaration)

Admitting dying declaration that defendant shot deceased held prejudicial error where evidence against defendant was circumstantial (Steven vs. Commonwealth, 221 KY 222, 298 S W 678). (1928, March) *Kentucky Law Journal, 16*, 270-271.

(Case Report - Manslaughter)

Manslaughter, second degree, instruction (People vs. Santini, 221 App Div 139, 222 NY Sup 683). (1928, Jan.) *New York University Law Review, 5*, 73-74.

(Case Report - Homicide)

Phelps, H.A. (1928) Rhode Island's threat against murder. *Journal of Criminal Law, 18*, 552-567.

(Case Report - Pace Case)

The Pace case. (1928) *Law Journal, 66*, 26.

(Case Report - England)

Rex v. Browne and Kennedy. (1928) *Just P, 92*, 303.

(Case Report - Murder Defense)

Parkes, N. (1927, Dec. 3) Case of pathological drunkenness as insanity defense at murder trial. *L T, 164*, 441-442.

(Judge's Decision)

Judge Caverly's decision. (1924) *Dickinson Law Review, 29*, 1.

(Case Report - Murder)

Cummings, H.S. (1924) State v. Harold Israel. *Journal of Criminal Law, 15*, 406.

(Case Report - Murder)

Roughead, W. (1923) The secret of Ireland's eyes. *Jurid Review, 35*, 201.

(Case Report - Wall)

Simpson, T.B. (1923) Governor Wall. *Jurid Review, 35*, 154.

Case Reports
Famous Murders

(Case Report - Lennon)

Literati: Who killed John Lennon? (1989, Sept. 20) *Variety, 336*, (10), p. 151.

(Case Report - Teresa Carlo)

Gallagher, D. (1989) All the right enemies: The life and murder of Teresa Carlo. *Journal of American History, 76*(2), 647-648.

(Case Report - Chappaquidick)

Damore, L. (1988, Oct.) Senatorial privilege. *Conservative Digest, 14*(9), pp. 101-108.

(Case Report - Jack the Ripper)

Farson, D. (1988, Sept. 10) Ripping yarns. *Spectator, 261*(8357), pp. 13-14.

(Case Report - Jack the Ripper)

Rumbelow, D. (1988) *Jack the Ripper; the complete case book.* Chicago: Contemporary Books.

(Case Report - Organized Crime)

Philadelphia: Two more hits. (1986) *Organized Crime Digest, 7*(8), 7. Article copies available from UMI.

(Case Report - Serial Murder)

Holmes, R.M., & Deburdger, J.D. (1985) Profile in terror: The serial murderer. *Federal Probation, 40*(3), 29-34. Article copies available from UMI.

(Case Report - Belushi Death)

Belushi's death (C.E. Smith murdered). (1983, March 28) *Time, 121*, p. 21.

(Case Report - Ribicoff's Murder)

Sullivan, R. (1982, March 18) The murder that changed Los Angeles (murder of S. Ribicoff by F.J. Thomas). *Rolling Stone*, pp. 33-37+.

(Case Report - Col. Ray's Murder)

Brecher, J. (1982, Feb. 1) An American in Paris (killing of Lt. Col. C.R. Ray). *Newsweek, 99*, p. 50.

(Case Report - Yorkshire Ripper)

Kennedy, C. (1981, Jan. 19) Lynch-mob journalism (arrest of alleged Yorkshire Ripper P. Sutcliffe). *Macleans, 94*, p. 29.

(Case Report - Yorkshire Ripper)

Hang him! Arrest of P. Sutcliffe, alleged Yorkshire Ripper. (1981, Jan. 19) *Time, 117*, p. 39.

(Case Report - Yorkshire Ripper)

Hauptfuhrer, F. (1981, Jan. 26) Olivia Reivers has reasons to wonder: Was she the Yorkshire Ripper's last date? *People Weekly, 15*, pp. 70-71.

(Case Report - Yorkshire Ripper)

Brecher, J., & Clifton, T. (1981, Jan. 19) Break in the Ripper case (Yorkshire Ripper of Great Britain). *Newsweek, 97*, p. 50+.

(Case Report - Jack the Ripper)

Eckert, W.G. (1981) The Whitechapel murders. The Case of Jack the Ripper. *American Journal of Forensic Medical Pathology, 2*(1), 53-60.

(Case Report - Lennon)

O'Toole, L. (1980, Dec. 22) Legacy of Lennon (with editorial comment by P.C. Newman). *Macleans, 93*, pp. 3, 36-38+.

(Case Report - Lennon)

Hamill, P. (1980, Dec. 22) Death and life of John Lennon. *New York, 13*, pp. 38-50.

(Case Report - Lennon)

Mayer, A.J., et al. (1980, Dec. 22) Death of a Beatle. *Newsweek, 96*, p. 31-36.

(Case Report - Lennon)

Cocks, J. (1980, Dec. 22) Last day in the life . . . *Time, 116*, pp. 18-24.

(Case Report - Yorkshire Ripper)

Thirteenth victim (Yorkshire Ripper) (1980, Dec. 1) *Time, 116*, p. 47.

(Case Report - Althusser)

Marx and murder (case of L. Althusser). (1980, Dec. 1) *Time, 116*, p. 47.

(Case Report - H. Hagnes Murder)

Dance of death (murder of violinist H. Hagnes at Metropolitan Opera House in New York City). (1980, Aug. 4) *Time, 116*, p. 26.

(Case Report - Tarnower)

Van Gelder, L. (1980, Aug.) Scarsdale diet doctor murder case. *Ms, 9*, pp. 69-79.

(Case Report - Tarnower Murder)

Langdon, D., et al. (1980, March 31) Killing of Scarsdale diet doctor Herman Tarnower leaves a single haunting question: Why?. *People Weekly,13*, p. 40.

(Case Report - Tarnower Murder)

Haden-Guest, A. (1980, March 31) Headmistress and the diet doctor. *New York, 13*, front cover+.

(Case Report - Jack the Ripper)

Kennedy, C. (1979, July 9) Jack the Ripper's latest disciple; Yorkshire Ripper. *Macleans, 92*, p. 18.

(Case Report - Hillside Strangler)

Bianchi, K. (1979, May 7) Murderous personality; capture of alleged Hillside Strangler. *Time, 113*, p. 26.

(Case Report - Yorkshire Ripper)

Ripper's return; Yorkshire Ripper. (1979, April 23) *Time, 113*, p. 43.

(Case Report - Murder)

Terrible tales; views of D. Bloch. (1979, Feb. 5) *Time, 113*, p. 140.

(Case Report - Yorkshire Ripper)

Nally, M. (1979) Hunt the Ripper. *New Society, 48*(871), pp. 629-630.

(Case Report - Gig Young)

Gig Young's final act. (1978, Oct. 30) *Newsweek, 92*, p. 33.

(Case Report - Jimmy Hoffa Case)

Jimmy Hoffa's last ride. (1978, Sept. 30) *Time, 112*, p. 29.

(Case Report - Letelier)

McCarthy, A. (1976, Nov. 5) My task is to be alive: Death of O. Letelier. *Commonwealth, 103*, p. 710+.

(Case Report - Letelier)

Miller, J. (1976, Nov.) Orlando Letelier. *Progressive, 40*, pp. 7-8.

(Case Report - Letelier)

Red herring; Letelier murder. (1976, Oct. 23) *Nation, 223*, p. 388.

(Case Report - Letelier)

Almost unbearable; Letelier case. (1976, Oct. 16) *Nation, 223*, pp. 355-356.

(Case Report - Letelier)

Murder on embassy row. (1976, Oct. 13) *Christian Century, 93*, p. 851.

(Case Report - Letelier)

Moffitt, M. (1976, Oct. 2) Chile in my life; murder of O. Letelier. *New Republic, 175*, p. 9.

(Case Report - Letelier)

Death of a dissident (murder of O. Letelier). (1976, Oct. 4) *Time, 108*, p. 54.

(Case Report - Hill Case)

Thompson, T. (1976, Sept. 6) Story behind the book; *Blood and money*, Hill murder case; interview by B.Bannon. *Publisher's Weekly, 210*, p. 36.

(Case Report - Dr. X)

Clark, M., & Shapiro, D. (1976, March 22) Strange case of Dr. X; reopening of the New Jersey curare case. *Newsweek, 87*, pp. 85-86.

(Case Report - S. Mineo)

Williams, D.A., & Kasindorf, M. (1976, Feb. 23) Outcast; murder of S. Mineo. *Newsweek, 87*, p. 25.

(Case Report - Salisbury Crags Murder)

O'Brien, F.W. (1976) The Salisbury Crags murder: H.M. Advocate v. Ernst Dumoulin. *Medical Legal Journal, 44*(4), 110-125.

(Case Report - Mullendore Murder)

Kwitny, J. (1976) *The Mullendore murder case.* New York: Warner.

(Case Report - Barka Case)

Murder of Mehdi Ben Barka. (1975, Dec. 29) *Time, 105*, p. 21.

(Case Report - Mudgett Case)

Franke, D. (1975) *The torture doctor: The incredible but true story of Herman W. Mudgett, the most fiendish killer in the annals of American crime.* New York: Hawthorn.

(Case Report - Yablonski Murders)

Armbrister, T. (1975) *Act of vengeance: The Yablonski and their aftermath.* New York: Saturday Review Press.

(Case Report - Cambert)

Borowitz, A.I. (1974, Nov.) Lully and the death of Cambert. *Mus R, 35*, 231-239.

(Case Report - Houston)

Olsen, J. (1974) *The man with the candy: The story of the Houston mass murders.* S & S.

(Case Report - Boden Murders)

Swann, G.C. (1974) The Wayne Boden murders. *International Journal of Forensic Dentistry, 2*(4), 34-42.

(Case Report - Manson)

Bugliosi, V. (1974) *Helter Skelter: The true story of the Manson murders.* New York: Norton.

(Case Report - Montreal)

Bensley, E.H. (1973, Nov. 17) McGill University's most infamous medical graduate. *Canadian Medical Association Journal, 109*, 1024.

(Case Report - Dr. Parkman)

Sullivan, R. (1971) *Disappearance of Doctor Parkman: The Parkman-Webster murder.* New York: Little, Brown.

(Case Report - Boston Strangler)

Frank, G. (1971) *Boston Strangler*. New York: New American Library.

(Case Report - Murder)

Bucove, A. (1970, Feb.) Some further facts in the case of Mrs. B. *American Journal of Psychiatry, 126*, 1185.

(Case Report - Tucson Murders)

Gilmore, J., & Zeiger, H.A. (1970) *Tucson murders*. New York: Dial.

(Case Report - Carol Thompson)

Giese, D.J. (1969) *Carol Thompson murder case*. London: Llewellyn.

(Case Report - Wylie-Hoffert)

Lefkowitz, B., & Gross, K.G. (1969) *Victims: The Wylie-Hoffert murder case and its strange aftermath*. New York: Putnam.

(Krutzler Case Report)

Eidherr, W. (1968) Der fall Krutzler. 20957. J. 22, '68, 12, S. 673-675 (IBZ 1970).

(Case Report - Murder)

Capote, T. (1966) *In cold blood*. New York: Random House.

(Case Report - Phillips)

Miner, J.W. (1964, Jan.) The Phillips case: A new dimension in murder. *Journal of Forensic Science, 9*, 1-10.

(Case Report - Drummond Family)

Brutal crime that shocked France; the murder of the Drummond family. (1952, Aug. 16) *London News, 221*, p. 216.

(Case Report - Lindbergh Case)

Vance, R., Jr. (1943, Jan.) A critique of the Lindbergh case. *Kentucky Law Journal, 31*, 193-197.

(Case Report - Munnick Case)

The Munnick case (Munnick v. Rex). (1932, Aug.) *South African Legal Times, 1*, 180.

(Case Report - Rouse Case)

The Rouse case. (1931, Feb. 28) *Justice of the Peace, 95*, 130; *Legal Times, 171*, 177, 178-180.

Case Reports
Investigated Murders

(Police Investigations)

Keppell, R.D. (1989) *Serial murder: future implications for police investigations.* Cincinnati: Anderson.

(Case Report - Warrington Dawson)

Worthington, W.C., Jr. (1989) The man who killed Warrington Dawson. *American Journal of Forensic and Medical Pathology, 10*(1), 76-82.

(Case Report - David Roberts)

Ball, A.L. (1988, Sept. 19) Night and day: Is David Roberts a killer or a saint? *New York, 21*(37), pp. 44-52.

(Case Report - John Donald Merrett)

Murphy, G.K. (1985) Murder for profit: The case of John Donald Merrett. *American Journal of Forensic and Medical Pathology, 6*(4), 325-328.

(Case Report - Dakota Dragnet)

Dakota dragnet (Posse Comitatus member G. Kahl murders two US marshals). (1983, Feb. 28) *Time, 121*, p. 25.

(Case Report - Argentina)

Mitchell, J. (1982, Dec. 6) Exhuming a nightmare. *Macleans, 95*, pp. 44-45.

(Case Report - Homicide Solved)

Lewis, C.N. (1982) Psychological resolution of homicide after ten years. *Journal of Personality Assessment, 46*(6), 647-657.

(Case Report - Franklin Case)

Gaines, J.R. (1980, Nov. 24) On the tail of a murderous sniper suspect; the tangled life of Joseph Paul Franklin. *People Weekly, 14*, pp. 30-35.

(Case Report - Franklin Case)

Tracing the pattern of racial murder. (1980,Nov. 10) *Newsweek, 96*, p. 45.

(Case Report - Hoffa Case)

Shannon, E., & Lowell, J. (1980, July 14) Seeking a break in the Hoffa case. *Newsweek, 96*, pp. 14-15.

(H. Tarnower Murder)

Scarsdale diet doctor is killed and a private school headmistress is accused (murder of H. Tarnower). (1980, March 24) *People Weekly, 13*, p. 79.

(Case Report - Lindbergh)

Eckert, W.G. (1980) The Lindbergh case: A triumph in forensic investigation. *American Journal of Forensic and Medical Pathology, 1*(2), 151-153.

(Case Report - Abu Hassan)

Carroll, R. (1979, Feb. 5) Death of a terrorist; murder of Abu Hassan charged to Mossad, Israeli intelligence. *Newsweek, 93*, p. 61.

(Case Report - Homicide)

Gresham, G.A. (1977) Arrows of outrageous fortune. *Medical Science and the Law, 17*(4), 239-240.

(Case Report - Sexual Murder)

Maehly, A.C., et al. (1977) Zinc sulfate under the prepuce: Criminal trace in a sexual murder (German). *Arch Kriminol, 159*(5-6), 139-143.

(Case Report - Murder)

McClintock, F.H. (1976, July) Homicide. *British Journal of Criminology, 16*, 284-287.

(Murder Investigated)

Gelb, B. (1976, Feb.) On the track of murder; condensation. *Reader's Digest, 108*, pp. 196-200+.

(Case Report - Leontieff Murder)

Middendorff, W. (1976) The Tatjana Leontieff case (German) *Arch Kriminal, 159*(5-6), 163.

(Case Report - Infanticide)

Srch, M. (1976) Violent or sudden infant death (Czech). *Cesk Pediatr, 31*(1), 19.

(Case Report - Murder Investigation)

Zimmerman, P.D. (1975, Oct. 20) On the track of murder, by. B. Gelb (review). *Newsweek, 86*, p. 103.

(Case Report - New York Police)

Anatomy of a manhunt; search for the killers of New York City policeman. (1975, Oct. 6) *Time, 106*, p. 48+.

(Case Report - B. Anderson)

Gelb, B. (1975, Oct. 5) Who killed Beatrice Anderson? *New York Time Magazine*, pp. 24-25+.

(Case Report - Gossage Murder)

Lubenow, G.C. (1975, March 3) Amy and Eben; arrest of Eben Gossage for the murder of Amy Gossage. *Newsweek, 85*, p. 30.

(Case Report - Jack the Ripper)

Shuster, S. (1975) Jack the Ripper and doctor-indentification. *International Journal of*

Psychiatry, 6(3), 285-402.

(Analysis of Death)

Van Till D'Aulnis De Bourouill, A. (1975) How dead can you be? *Med Sci Law, 15*(2), 133-147.

(Case Report - Dismembered Corpse)

Smerling, M. (1974) Forensic and criminological aspects in solving a case of a dismembered corpse (German). *Arch Kriminol, 153*(5-6), 129-140.

(Case Report - Yablonski)

Fall of Tony Boyle; arrest for planning murder of Joseph Yablonski. (1973, Sept. 17) *Time, 102*, p. 27.

(Case Report - Yablonski)

Man at the top; W.A. Boyle arrested for Yablonski murders. (1973, Sept. 17) *Newsweek, 82*, p. 30.

(Case Report - Brazier Murder)

Harvey,R., et al. (1973, July) The Nicola Brazier murder: The role of handwriting in a large-scale investigation. *Journal of Forensic Science and Sociology, 13*, 157-168.

(Case Report - CID Files)

Andrews, A. (1973) *Intensive inquiries: Seven Chief Constables open CID files on their most remarkable murder investigations*. New York: St. Martin.

(Case Report - Trunk Murders)

Dobkins, J.D., & Hendricks, R.J. (1973) *Winnie Ruth Judd: The trunk murders and the strange events after*. New York: G&D.

(Case Report - Murder)

Clark, W.A. (1972) *The girl on the Volkswagen floor*. New York: Bantam.

(Case Report - Mearns Case)

Kerr, N.W., et al. (1971, Oct.) An identification by means of forensic odontology; the Mearns (Garvie) murder. *Journal of Forensic Science and Sociology, 11*, 223-225.

(Case Report - Poisoning)

Barrowcliff, D. (1971) The Stoneleigh Abbey poisoning case. *Medical Legal Journal, 39*, 79-90.

(Murder Attempt - Case Report)

Ender, K. (1970) Ein mordversuch? 20957. J. 24, '70, S. 85-87 (IBZ 1971).

(Robbery/Murder)

Ulonska, K. (1968) Ein gut geplanter raubmord. 20957. J. 22, '68, 5, S. 262 (IBZ 1969).

(Case Report - Clues)

Van Hecke, W. (1966, Jan.) Comments on a bite on a breast in a murder case. *Medical Science and the Law, 8*, 47.

(Case Report - Investigation)

Dominici, I. (1966) The de-rooted stone - two labels helped solve a murder (German). 20957. J. 20, '66, 11, S. 598-599 (IBZ 1967).

(Case Report - Investigation)

Reitberger, L. (1966) The murder of a policeman 100 years ago (German). 20957. J. 20, '66, 6, S. 295-296 (IBZ 1967).

(Case Report - Detection)

Kessler, W.F., & Weston, W.B. (1953) *Detection of murder*. Arco.

(Case Report - Poisoning)

Sweets, H.H., Jr. (1949, Sept.) Investigating suspected homicidal poisoning. *Kentucky State Bar Journal, 13*, 155-165.

(Simulated Murder)

Spelman, J.W. (1949, June) Simulated homicide; report of case of obstructive laryngeal papilloma in child. *American Journal of Clinical Pathology, 19*, 565-569.

(British Soldier's Trial)

Gillen, D.J. (1946, Feb.) "The trial of the British soldiers." Who shot Patrick Carr? A review of the testimony and record of Boston's most famous murder trial. *Law Society Journal, 12*, 48-58.

(Hauptmann Case Report)

Hall, S.G. (1936, March) Venue in the Hauptmann case (State v. Hauptmann (NJ) 180 Atl. 809). *Dick L Rev, 40*, 193-199.

(Case Report - Rouse Case)

The Rouse Motorcar murder - - a possible reconstruction. (1931) *South Africa Law Journal, 48*, 287.

Case Reports
Murder Mysteries

(Case Report - Mystery)

Where is the black queen? (unraveling chess code to solve probable murder of T. Terry in Ireland). (1990, Aug. 9) *Time, 136*, p. 37.

(Case Report - TV Help)

Wickens, B. (1990, Jan. 22) A mystery story (TV show Unsolved Mysteries, helps in arrest of fugitive D.H. Fisher in Canada). *Macleans, 103*, p. 41.

(Murder on Tour)

Maio, K. (1989) Murder on tour - A rock and roll mystery (review). *Wilson Library, 63*(7), 90.

(Murder Mystery)

Maio, K. (1989) Murder mystery and mayhem (review). *Wilson Library, 64*(4), 116-117.

(Case Report - Ripper Project)

Eckert, W.G. (1989) The Ripper project: Modern science solving mysteries of history. *American Journal of Forensic and Medical Pathology, 10*(2), 164-171.

(Tony Losacco Murder)

Barrett, W., & Hancock, L. (1988, Dec. 6) The mysterious death of a school board witness. *Village Voice, 33*(49), pp. 1, 10+.

(Case Report - Mystery)

Is the Tennessee pastor a murderer? (1988, Sept. 26) *Newsweek, 112*(13), p. 27.

(Case Report - Mysterious Death)

Karlen, N. (1985, Nov. 4) Nuclear-powered death? (mysterious death of J. Penley after expressing concern for safety at Watts Bar Nuclear Plant). *Newsweek, 106*, p. 29.

(Case Report - Mystery)

Conant, J. (1985, Oct. 28) The Mormon mystery (fatal bombings and forged church documents linked to M. Hoffman). *Newsweek, 106*, p. 44.

(Case Report - Mystery)

Rothschild, M. (1985, April) Who killed Manuel Buenda (prominent Mexican journalist). *Progressive, 49*, pp. 18-24.

(Case Report - Mystery)

Leavy, W. (1980, Dec.) Mystery of the disappearing Blacks. *Ebony, 36*, pp. 136-138+.

(Case Report - Mystery)

Bugliosi, V., & Hurwitz, K. (1979) *Till death us do part: A true murder mystery*. New York:

Bantam.

(Death by Murder)

Biggers, T.A. (1979) Death by murder; a study of women murderers. *Death Education, 3*(1), 1-9.

(Classic Mysteries)

The inspiration of the classic mystery: It's elementary (second of four parts). *Law Enforcement News, 5*(20), 13.

(Case Report - Mystery)

London mystery; murders involving W. Scott-Eliot household. (1978, Feb. 6) *Time, 111*, p. 44.

(Case Report - Mystery)

Dundee, J.W. (1978) Mysterious deaths in Ann Arbor. *Anesthesia, 33*(98), 752-753.

(Case Report - Mystery)

Salisbury, H.E. (1977, May) On an unsolved mystery; 1948 murder of G. Polk in Greece. *Progressive, 41*, pp. 24-25.

(J.S. Knight Case)

Alpern, D.M., & Michaud, S.G. (1975, Dec. 22) Call of the wild, case of J.S. Knight. *Newsweek, 86*, pp. 29-30.

(Case Report - Russia)

Malmstad, J.E. (1975, March) Mystery of iniquity; Kuzmin's Twmnye ulitsy rozhdaiut temnye mysli. *Slavic Review, 34*, 44-64.

(Case Report - Mystery)

Hardwicke, G. (1974) The Gorse Hall mystery - - a new look at an old case. *Medical Legal Journal, 42*(1), 14-20.

(Case Report - Mysteries)

Harvey, W., et al. (1968, Dec.) The Biggar murder: Dental, medical, police, and legal aspects of a case "in some ways unique, difficult, and puzzling". *Journal of Forensic Science and Sociology, 8*, 157-219.

(Case Report - Mysteries)

Williams, E. (1968) *Beyond belief.* New York: Random House.

(Case Report - Mystery)

Zierold, N. (1968) *Three sisters in black.* New York: Little Brown.

(Case Report - Mystery)

Pearson, E. (1967) *Murders that baffled the experts.* New York: Signet.

(Case Report - Mystery)

Friars, H. (1958) Murder of a village doctor: A true story. *Practitioner London, 180*(1078), 483-

487.

(Case Report - Mystery)

Shelley, H. (1956) A medico-legal mystery. *Cyprus Medical Journal, 8*(6), 331-338.

(Edwin Drood Mystery)

Phythian-Adams, W.J. (1946, April) The corpse in the cathedral: Or, the mystery of Edwin Drood. *Jurid Review, 58*, 37-50.

(Case Report - Mystery)

Mumbrue, D., & Price, E.G. (1945, Oct.) Strange sombrero; an authentic murder story from Montana. *Pacific NW Quarterly, 36*, 309-318.

(Case Report - Mystery)

Treadwell, C.A.L. (1942, Nov. 17) Murder at Galilee; an unsolved crime. *New Zealand Law Journal, 18*, 247-248.

(Case Report - General)

Knudson, J.K. (1939, April) Murder by the clock. *Washington U L Q, 24*, 305-358.

(Case Report - Mysteries)

Wallace, W.S. (1931) *Murders and mysteries: A Canadian series.* Hyperion.

(Case Report - Mystery)

Roughead, W. (1926) Constance Kent's conscience: A mid-Victorian mystery. *Jurid Review, 38*, 1.

(Case Report - Mystery)

Fitting the motive to the crime in the Halls-Mills "murder mystery". (1926, Sept.) *New York Law Review, 4*, 377-381.

Case Reports
Mental Illness

(Case Report - Capgras Syndrome)

Blount, G. (1986) Dangerousness of patients with Capgras syndrome (letter). *Nebraska Medical Journal, 71*(6), 207.

(Case Report - Homicide)

Kua, E.H., et al. (1984) Homicide and mental illness in Singapore. *Singapore Medical Journal, 25*(2), 61-63.

(Double Murder)

Parker, N. (1980, Nov.) Personality change after accidents - the report of a double murder. *British Journal of Psychiatry, 137*, 401-409.

(Case Report - Personality Change)

Parker, N. (1980) Personality change following accidents: The report of a double murder. *British Journal of Psychiatry, 137*(5), 401-409.

(Case Report - Psychopathology)

Quinsey, V.L., et al. (1980) MMPI profiles of men referred for a pretrial psychiatric assessment as a function of offense type. *Clinical Psychology, 36*(2), 410-417.

(Case Report - Murder on the Job)

Parker, N. (1979) Murder on the job; case report of a unique disaster. *Mental Health Soc, 5*(3-4), 231-240.

(Murder on the Job)

Freed, H.M., et al. (1979) Murder on the job; case report of a unique disaster. *Mental Health Soc, 5*(3-4), 231-240.

(Case Report - Necrophilia)

Lancaster, N.P. (1978) Necrophilia, murder, and high intelligence; a case report. *British Journal of Psychiatry, 132*, 605-608.

(Case Report - Son of Sam)

'Son of Sam': Implications for psychiatry. (1978) *American Journal of Psychiatry, 135*(1), 131.

(Case Report - Mass Murderers)

Campbell, B. (1976, May) Portrait of a mass killer. *Psychology Today, 9*, pp. 110-111+.

(Case Report - Patrick Mackay)

Clark, T., & Penycate, J. (1976) *Psychopath: The case of Patrick Mackay.* London: Routledge.

(Case Report - Depraved Mind)

Gegan, B.E. (1975, Spring) Case of depraved mind murder. *St. John's Law Review, 49*, 417-459.

(A. Moravia Case)

Culbertson, D., & Valley, J.A. (1975) Alberto Moravia's melancholy murderer: The conformist as personality type. *Literature and Psychology, 25*(2), 79-85.

(Jack the Ripper)

Shuster, S. (1975) Jack the Ripper and doctor-indentification. *International Journal of Psychiatry in Medicine, 6*(3), 385-402.

(Case Report - Murder)

Damio, W. (1974) *Urge to kill.* New York: Pinnacle.

(Case Report - Psychosis)

Oberdalhoff, H.E. (1974) Matricide in a schizophrenic psychosis: Case report. *Confinement Psychiatry, 17*(2), 122-131.

(Case Report - Mental Health)

Shelton, J.L., et al. (1973, April) Mental health intervention in a campus homicide. *Journal of American College Health Association, 21*, 346-350.

(Case report - Schizophrenia)

Chaumont, A.J., et al. (1966, March-April) An unusual murder: Decapitation and dismemberment of a North African by a schizophrenic butcher's apprentice (French). *Ann Med Leg, 46*, 143-148.

(Case Report - Epilepsy)

Fenton, G.W., et al. (1965, April) Homicide, temporal lobe epilepsy and depression: A case report. *British Journal of Psychiatry, 111*, 304-306.

(Case Report - Psychopath)

Trice, J.E., et al. (1963, Nov.) A psychopath who killed. *Journal Louisiana Medical Society, 115*, 379-382.

(Valleyfield Murders)

Greenland, C. (1962, Oct.) L'affaire shortis and the Valleyfield murders. *Canadian Psychiatric Association Journal, 7*, 261-271.

(Case Report - Psychodynamics)

Salzman, L. (1962, June) Psychodynamics of a case of murder. *Compr Psychiatry, 3*, 152-169.

(Case Report - Psychiatric)

Greenland, C. (1962) L'affair Shortis and the Valleyfield murders. *Canadian Psychiatric*

Association Assessment, 7, 261-271.

(Educational Futility)

Rowe, E.C. (1935) A case of educational futility. *Journal of Abnormal Sociology and Psychology, 30*, 237-255.

(Case Report - Sadism)

MacDonald, A. (1907) A sadistic murder. *Medical Legal Journal, 24*, 589.

Case Reports - With Motives

(Murderer's Vendetta)

Lady's honor; G. Quariuccio's vendetta against the Sicilian mafia. (1976, Dec. 20) *Time, 108*, p. 36.

(Crimes of Passion)

Gorder, E. (1974) *Murder my love: The great crimes of passion.* Playboy Press.

(Madeleine Smith)

Hartman, M.S. (1973, June) Murder for respectability: The case of Madeleine Smith. *Victorian Studies, 16*, 381-400.

(Robbery/Murder)

Weber, F.R. (1966) Murder case Seidel. Robbery and murder case solved within 24 hours (German). 20957. J. 20, '66, 6, S. 303-308 (IBZ 1967).

(M.A. Ferguson Case)

Paull, K.R., & White, J.E. (1965) The murder of Mary Ann Ferguson; a murder without reason (German). 20957. J. 19, '65, 10, S. 546-547 (IBZ 1966).

(Political Homicide)

Friedrich, P. (1962) Assumptions underlying Tarascan political homicide. *Psychiatry, 25*, 315-327.

(Malice)

Necessity for malice aforethought (Landers v. State (TX) 25 SW 868). (1930, Dec.) *Texas Law Review, 9*, 118-119.

Chapter 9
Homicide, Suicide, and Accidents
Statistics

(Homicides and Accidents)

Taff, M.L., & Boglioli, L.R. (1990) Deaths at the workplace: Accidents or homicides? *American Journal of Forensic Medicine and Pathology, 11*(1), 66-70.

(Suicide and Homicide - St. Valentine's Day)

Lester, D. (1990) Suicide and homicide on St. Valentine's Day. *Perceptual Motor Skills, 71*(3), 994.

(Epidemiology - Blacks)

Griffith, E.E., & Bell, C.C. (1989, Oct. 27) Recent trends in suicide and homicide among Blacks. *JAMA, 262*(16), 2265-2269.

(Statistics - Guns)

Magnuson, E., et al. (1989, July 17) 7 deadly days. *Time, 134*(3), pp. 30-61.

(Epidemiology)

Smith, K. (1989) Epidemiological - Study of suicide, homicides, and accidents, by P. Hollinger (book review). *B Menninger, 53*(4), 364-365.

(Epidemiology - Oklahoma)

Goodman, R.A., et al. (1989) Fatal injuries in Oklahoma: Descriptive epidemiology using medical examiner data. *Southern Medical Journal, 82*(9), 1128-1134.

(Homicide/Suicide - Comparison)

Rockett, I.R., & Smith, G.S. (1989) Homicide, suicide, motor vehicle crash, and fall mortality: United States' experience in comparative perspective. *American Journal of Public Health, 79*(10), 1396-1400.

(Population Growth)

Lester, D., et al. (1989) Association of population growth, technological development, and social integration on rates of personal violence (suicide and homicide). *Psychological Reports,*

64(2), 462.

(Statistics)

Lester, D. (1989) Suicide and homicide rates in Hungary and Czechoslovakia during the suppression of dissent. *Psychological Reports, 64*(2), 666.

(Baseball Players)

Topp, R. (1989) Major league baseball performances of players who were later suicides and homicide victims. *Perceptual Motor Skills, 69*(1), 272.

(Media Violence)

Lester, D. (1989) Media violence and suicide and homicide rates: Note. *Perceptual Motor Skills, 69*(3), 894.

(Statistics - Hungary and Czechoslovakia)

Lester, D. (1989) National suicide and homicide rates - correlates vs. predictors. *Social Sciences and Medicine, 29*(11), 1249-1252.

(Statistics - US)

Wilbanks, W. (1989) Violent deaths in the United States - An epidemiologic study of suicide, homicide, and accidents, by P. Hollinger (book review). *Contemporary Psychology, 34*(6), 591-592.

(Statistics - US)

Vogt, K.A. (1989) Subcultures of self- and other-directed violence: Suicide, homicide, and accidental death in the United States, 1980-1984. *Dissertation Abstracts International, A: The Humanities and Social Sciences, 50*(6), 1810-A. Available from UMI, Order # DA8921942.

(Suicide and Gun Ownership)

Lester, D. (1989) Gun ownership and suicide in the United States. *Psychology and Medicine, 19*(2), 519-521.

(Homicide and Suicide)

Lester, D. (1989) Geophysical variables and behavior .56: The spatial auto-correlation of states' suicide and homicide rates; *Perceptual Motor Skills, 68*(1), 218.

(Homicide and Suicide - South Africa)

Lester, D. (1989) Personal violence in South Africa. *Acta Psychiatr Scand, 79*(3), 235-237.

(Attitudes Towards Animals)

Lester, D. (1988, Dec.) Attitudes toward animals and personal violence (suicide and homicide). *Psychology Reports, 63*, 810.

(Personal Violence and Alcohol)

Lester, D. (1988, Oct.) Rates of personal violence (suicide and homicide), traffic fatalities, and alcohol consumption. *Psychology Reports, 63*, 570.

(Emigration and Violence)

Lester, D. (1988, April) Emigration rates and personal violence by suicide and homicide rates. *Psychology Reports, 62*, 610.

(Statistics)

Stack, S. (1988) Violent deaths in the United States - an epidemiological analysis of suicide, homicide, and accidents, by P. Hollinger (book review). *Contemporary Sociology, 17*(5), 691-692.

(Suicide/Homicide)

Yang, B.J., et al. (1988) The participation of females in the labor force and rates of personal violence (suicide and homicide). *Suicide and Life Threatening Behavior, 18*(3), 270-278.

(Statistics)

Lester, D. (1988) Strikes, suicide, and homicide: A cross-national analysis. *International Journal of Contemporary Sociology, 25*(1-2), 9-14.

(Homicide and Suicide - Firearms Availability)

Lester, D. (1988) Firearm availability and the incidence of suicide and homicide. *Acta Psychiatr Belg, 88*(5), 519-521.

(Statistics - Regional Variation)

Lester, D. (1988) Pockets of violence: A study of regional variation in suicide and homicide rates. *Acta Psychiatr Belg, 88*(5), 394-399.

(Personal Violence Rates)

Lester, D. (1988) Suicide and homicide rates and fluoride. *Psychological Reports, 61*(3), 802.

(Epidemiology - Violent Deaths)

Hollinger, P.C. (1987) *Violent deaths in the United States: An epidemiological study of suicide, homicide, and accidents*. New York: Guilford.

(Statistics - US)

Hollinger, P.C., et al. (1987) Suicide and homicide in the United States: An epidemiological study of violent death, population changes, and the potential for predictions. *American Journal of Psychiatry, 144*(2), 215-219.

(Income Inequality)

Lester, D. (1987) Relation of income inequality to suicide and homicide rates. *Journal of Social Psychology, 127*(1), 101-102.

(Statistics)

Lester, D. (1987) Occupational prestige and rates of suicide and homicide. *Perceptual Motor Skills, 64*(2), 398.

(Statistics - US)

Leads from the MMWR: Premature mortality due to suicide and homicide - - United States, 1984. (1987) *JAMA, 258*(13), 1711.

(Statistics - US)

Premature mortality due to suicide and homicide - - United States, 1984. (1987) *MMWR, 36*(32). 531-534.

(Geophysical Variables)

Lester, D. (1987) Geophysical variables and behavior: XLI. Regional variations of suicide and homicide rates by different methods. *Perceptual Motor Skills, 64*(3, part 2), 1074.

(Statistics)

Lester, D. (1987) Suicide and homicide rates on national holidays. *Psychological Reports, 60*(2), 414.

(Statistics - US)

Lester, D. (1987) Social integration, economic hardship, and rates of personal violence (suicide and homicide): 1933-1970 in the USA. *Psychological Reports, 60*(3, part 2), 1306.

(Quality of Life)

Lester, D. (1987) Quality of life and rates of suicide and homicide. *Percept Mot Skills, 64*(1), 94.

(Statistics - Portugal)

Ferreira de Castro, E., et al. (1986) Relation between suicide and homicide in Portugal from 1970-1982. *Acta Psychiatr Scand, 74*(5), 425-432.

(Statistics - Hispanic-Americans)

Smith, J.C., et al. (1986) Suicide and homicide among Hispanics in the Southwest. *Public Health Report, 101*(3), 265-270.

(Statistics - Geography)

Lester, D. (1986) Suicide and homicide rates: Their relationship to longitude and latitude and weather. *Suicide and Life Threatening Behavior, 16*(3), 356-359.

(Premature Mortality)

Premature mortality due to homicide and suicide -- United States, 1983. (1986) *MMWR, 35*(22), 357-360.

(Suicide/Homicide)

Lester, D. (1986) The interaction of divorce, suicide, and homicide. *Journal of Divorce, 9*(3), 103-109.

(Children and Handguns)

Schetky, D.H. (1985) Children and handguns. *American Journal for Disabled Children 139*(3), 229-231.

(Homicide/Suicide)

Check, W.A. (1985) Homicide, suicide, other violence gains increasing medical attention (news). *JAMA, 254*(6), 721-723, 727-728, 730.

(Statistics)

Hillard, J.R., et al. (1985) Accidental and homicidal death in a psychiatric emergency room population. *Hospital and Community Psychiatry, 36*(6), 640-643.

(Statistics - Finland)

Kivela, S.L. (1985) Relationship between suicide, homicide, and accidental deaths among the aged in Finland, 1951-1979. *Acta Psychiatr Scand, 72*(2), 155-160.

(Suicide and Homicide Rates)

Lester, D. (1985) Variation in suicide and homicide rates by longitude and latitude in the United States, Canada, and Australia. *American Journal of Psychiatry, 142*(4), 523-524.

(Statistical Surveillance)

Rosenberg, M.L. (1985) Surveillance for suicide, homicide, and domestic violence: Strengths, weaknesses, and issues. *Public Health Reports, 100*(6), 593-595.

(Suicide/Accident/Homicide Rates)

Wasserman, J.M. (1984, Dec.) The linkage of United States presidential elections, unemployment changes, and reductions in suicide, accident, and homicide rates. *Journal of Social Psychology, 124*, 115-117.

(Homicide and Suicide Rates)

Lester, D. (1984, Dec.) The association between the quality of life and suicide and homicides. *Journal of Social Psychology, 124*, 247-248.

(Homicide/Suicide - Switzerland)

Michaud, P.A. (1984) Epidemiology of violent deaths in Switzerland over a ten year period, with particular regard to adolescents and youths (French with English summary). *Schweis Med Wochenschr, 114*(5), 172-177.

(Murder/Suicide)

Cold, J. (1983) The epidemiology of abnormal homicide and murder followed by suicide.

Psychological Medicine, 13(4), 855-860.

(Fatal Accidents)

Wilbanks, W. (1982) Fatal accidents, suicide, and homicide: Are they related? *Victimology, 7*(1-4), 213-217.

(Homicide and Suicide)

Humphrey, J.A., & Kupferer, H.J. (1982) Homicide and suicide among the Cherokee and Lumbee Indians of North Carolina. *International Journal of Social Psychiatry, 28*(2), 121-128.

(Statistics)

Jarebinski, N., et al. (1982) Aspects of the problems of suicide and homicide in Belgrade. *Srp Arch Celok, 110*(9), 1035-1039.

(Statistics - Homicide and Suicide)

Palmer, S. (1980-81) Sex difference in criminal homicide and suicide in England and Wales and the United States. *Omega: Journal of Death and Dying, 11*(3), 255-270.

(Alcohol - Suicide and Homicide)

Lester, D. (1980) Alcohol/suicide, and homicide. *Journal for the Study of Alcohol, 41*(11), 1220-1223.

(Homicide and Suicide: Africa and England)

Thomson, L.G. (1980) Homicide and suicide in Africa and England. *Medical Science and Law, 20*(2), 99-103.

(Suicide, Homicide, and Accidents)

Holinger, P.C. (1980) Violent deaths as a leading cause of mortality: An epidemiological study of suicide, mortality, and accidents. *American Journal of Psychiatry, 137*, 472-476.

(Suicide, Homicide, and Accidents)

Holinger, P.C. (1979) Violent deaths among the young: Recent trends in suicide, homicide, and accidents. *American Journal of Psychiatry, 136*(9), 1144-1147.

(Statistics - Norway)

Reigstad, A. (1978) Deaths from accidents, suicide, and homicide in Norway and in the city of Oslo, 1951-1975 (Norwegian). *Tidsskr Nor Laegeforen, 98*, 1072-1075+, 1097.

(Media)

Phillips, D.P. (1978,) Airplane accident fatalities increase just after newspaper about murder and suicide. *Science, 201*, 748-750.

(Violence - Patterns)

Humphrey, J.A., & Kupferer, H.J. (1977) Pockets of violence: An exploration of homicide and suicide. *Diseases of the Nervous System, 38*, 833-837.

(Suicide, Homicide, and Accidents)

Humphrey, J.A. (1977) Social loss: A comparison of suicide victims, homicide offenders, and non-violent individuals. *Diseases of the Nervous System, 38*, 157-160.

(Homicide and Suicide)

Franke, R.H., et al. (1977) Suicide and homicide: Common sources and consistent relationships. *Social Psychology, 12*, 149-156.

(Homicide and Suicide)

Lester, D. (1974) A cross-national study of suicide and homicide. *Behavior Science Research, 9*(4), 307-318.

(Homicide and Suicide - Norway and France)

Lester, D. (1973) External restraints, suicide, and homicide: Comparison of Norway and France. *Perceptual Motor Skills, 36*, 646-653.

(Statistics - Homicide and Suicide)

Hirsch, C.S., et al. (1973) Homicide and suicide in a metropolitan county, I. Long-term trends. *JAMA, 223*, 900-905.

(Homicide and Suicide)

Lester, D. (1971) Suicide and Homicide: Bias in the examination of the relationship between suicide and homicide rates. *Social Psychiatry, 6*, 80-82.

(Suicide, Homicide, and Accident Trends)

Chen, A.J. (1969) Recent trend of deaths from unnatural causes (accidents, suicides, and homicides) in Singapore, 1961-1965. *Singapore Medical Journal, 10*, 72-82.

Homicide and Suicide
General

(Murder - Terri Hoffman)

Wright, R. (1990, Oct.) Love, death, and Terri Hoffman. *Good Housekeeping, 211*(4), pp. 62-69.

(Suicide and Homicide)

Kowalski, G.S., & Duffield, D. (1990, Spring) The impact of the rural population component on homicide rates in the United States: A county-level analysis. *Rural Sociology, 55*, 76-90.

(Boston Murderer)

Carlson, M., & Allis, S. (1990, Jan. 15) Hero, suspect, suicide. *Time,135*(3), p. 30.

(Depression and Violence)

Rosenbaum, M. (1990) The role of depression in couples involved in murder-suicide and homicide. *American Journal of Psychiatry, 147*(8), 1036-1039.

(Homicide and Suicide - Study)

Lester, D. (1990) Suicide, homicide, and the quality of life in various countries. *Acta Psychiatrica Scandinavica, 81*(4), 333-334.

(Homicide and Suicide)

Lester, D., & Frank, M.L. (1990) Suicide and homicide away from home. *American Journal of Forensic and Medical Pathology, 11*(4), 312-315.

(Homicide and Suicide - Arkansas)

Lester, D., & Frank, M.L. (1990) Suicide and homicide in rural areas: A study of Arkansas. *Psychology Reports, 66*(2), 426.

(Homicide and Suicide - Use of Knives)

Marcikic, M., & Mandic, N. (1990) Homicide-suicide by stabbing. *American Journal of Forensic and Medical Pathology, 11*(4), 312-315.

(Suicide and Homicide)

Lester, D. (1989, Dec.) Media violence and suicide and homicide rates. *Percpt Motor Skills, 69*, 894.

(Murder/Suicide)

Davidowitz, E. (1989, April) "Die mother, father, brother" (teenage Satan worshiper T. Sullivan kills mother then commits suicide in Sparta, NJ). *Redbook, 172*, pp. 132-134+.

(Homicide and Suicide)

Lester, D. (1989) Geophysical variables and behavior .56: The spatial auto-correlations of states' suicide and homicide rates; note. *Perceptual Motor Skills, 68*(1), 218.

(Statistics - South Africa)

Lester, D. (1989) Personal violence (suicide and homicide) in South Africa. *Acta Psych Scand, 79*(3), 235-237.

(Homicide/Suicide - U.S.)

Rockett, I.R.H., & Smith, G.S. (1989) Homicide, suicide, motor vehicle crash, and fall mortality: United States experience in comparative perspective. *American Journal of Public Health, 79*(10), 1396-1400.

(Homicide and Suicide Rates)

Lester, D. (1989) Immigration and rates of personal violence (suicide and homicide). *Psychology Reports, 65*(12, part 2), 1298.

(Homicide and Suicide - Use of Guns)

Lester, D. (1989) Use of handguns and long guns in suicide and homicide. *Psychological Reports, 65*(3), 938.

(Murder/Suicide)

Migler, R. (1988, Nov.) "Please! Please kill me!" *Good Housekeeping, 207*(5), pp. 160-161.

(Geophysical Variables)

Lester, D. (1988, April) Geophysical variables and behavior: Climate and personal violence (suicide and homicide). *Perceptual Motor Skills, 66*, 602.

(Homicide and Suicide)

Lester, D. (1988) Suicide and homicide during major sporting events, 1979-1984: Comment on Curtis, Loy, and Karnilowicz. *Sociology of Sport Journal,5*(3), 285.

(Homicide and Suicide- Restraints)

Rahav, G., et al. (1988) External restraints and suicide and homicide rates. *Psychological Reports, 62*(1), 317-318.

(Statistics)

Joffe, V.W. (1988) Adolescent suicide, homicide, and unintentional injuries. *Maryland Medical Journal, 37*(12), 955-958.

(Homicide and Suicide - Case Study)

Fain, D.B., et al. (1988) An unusual case of child abuse homicide/suicide. *Journal of Forensic Science, 33*(2), 554-557.

(Homicide or Suicide)

Suwanjutha, T. (1988) Direction, site, and the muzzle target distance of bullet in the head and neck at close range as an indication of suicide or homicide. *Forensic Science International, 37*(3), 223-229.

(Personal Violence)

Lester, D. (1988) Personal violence (suicide and homicide) on Friday the 13th. *Psychology Reports, 62*(2), 433.

(Homicide/Suicide and Religion)

Lester, D. (1988) Personal violence (suicide and homicide) and religion. *Psychology Reports, 62*(2), 618.

(Homicide and Suicide)

Lester, D. (1987) Geophysical variables and behavior XXXVI: Regional variation in suicide and homicide: Controls for weather and Southern culture. *Perceptual Motor Skills, 64*(2), 430.

(Statistics)

Lester, D. (1987) Month of birth of suicides, homicides, and natural deaths. *Psychological Reports, 60*(3, part 2), 1310.

(Homicide and Suicide)

Lester, D. (1987) Benefits of marriage for reducing risk of violent death from suicide and homicide for White and non-white persons: Generalizing Gove's findings. *Psychological Reports, 61*(1), 198.

(Suicide - Youth)

Hendin, H. (1987) Youth suicide: A psychosocial perspective. *Suicide & Life-Threatening Behavior, 17*(2), 151-165.

(Homicide and Suicide)

Lester, D. (1987) Status integration, suicide, and homicide. *Psychological Reports, 61*(2), 672.

(Homicide and Suicide - Easter)

Lester, D. (1987) Suicide and homicide at Easter. *Psychological Reports, 61*(1), 224.

(Homicide and Suicide - Study)

Lester, D. (1987) Suicide, homicide, and the quality of life: An archival study. *Suicide and Life Threatening Behavior, 16*(3), 389-392.

(Homicide and Suicide)

Range, L.M., et al. (1987) Community responses following suicide, homicide, and other deaths: The perspective of potential comforters. *Journal of Psychology, 121*(2), 193-198.

(Homicide and Suicide)

Lester, D. (1987) Religion, suicide, and homicide. *Social Psychiatry, 22*(2), 99-101.

(Homicide and Suicide)

Lester, D. (1987) Religiosity and personal violence: A regional analysis of suicide and homicide rates. *Journal of Social Psychology, 127*(6), 685-686.

(Homicide and Suicide - Analysis)

Lester, D. (`987) Substitution of method in suicide and homicide: A regional analysis. *Psychological Reports, 60*(1), 278.

(Violence - Hispanics)

Smith, J.C., et al. (1986) Suicide and homicide among Hispanics in the southwest. *Public Health Reports, 101*(3), 265-270.

(Violence - Indian Tales)

Lester, D. (1986) Aggression in Indian folktales and personal violence (suicide and homicide). *Psychology Reports, 58*(3), 974.

(Suicide and Homicide - Prisons)

Lester, D. (1986) Suicide and homicide in US prisons. *Psychological Reports, 61*(1), 126.

(Homicide and Suicide - Psychopathology)

Baker, G., et al. (1986) Seasonal births, academic achievement, and psychopathology (suicide and homicide): A regional analysis. *Psychological Reports, 59*(2, part 2), 742.

(Personal Violence)

Lester, D., & Georges, V.C. (1986) National character and rates of personal violence: Suicide and homicide. *Psychological Reports, 58*(1), 186.

(Suicide Pacts)

Fishbain, D.A. (1986) Suicide pacts and homicide (letter) *American Journal of Psychiatry, 143*(10), 1319-1320.

(Homicide and Suicide)

Lester, D. (1986) The birthday blues revisited: The timing of suicidal, homicidal, and natural deaths. *Acta Psychiatrica Scandinavia, 73*(3), 322-323.

(Homicide and Suicide - Theory)

Lester, D. (1986) Somatosensory theory and personal violence (suicide and homicide). *Journal of Social Psychology, 126*(5), 681-683.

(Homicide - Victim Study)

Lester, D. (1986) The distribution of sex and age among victims of homicide: A cross-national study. *International Journal of Social Psychiatry, 32*(2), 47-50.

(Suicide and Depression)

Lester, D. (1986) Level of depression in nations and their suicide rate. *Psychological Reports, 58*(3), 930.

(Murder/Suicide)

Bierma,V.D. (1985, Nov. 5) The suicide of Dan White brings a notorious San Francisco murder case to a bizarre end. *People Weekly, 24*, pp. 46-47.

(Homicide, Suicide, or Accident)

Perrot, L.J., et al. (1985) Asphyxiation by hanging in two young Hispanic children: Homicide, suicide, or accidental deaths? *American Journal of Forensic and Medical Pathology, 6*(4), 284-288.

(Murder/Suicide - Study)

Santoro, J.P., et al. (1985) The murder-suicide: A study of the post-aggressional suicide. *American Journal of Forensic and Medical Pathology, 6*(3), 222-225.

(Homicide and Suicide)

Lidberg, L., et al. (1985) Homicide, suicide, and CSF 5-HIAA. *Acta Psychiatrica Scandinavia, 71*(3), 230-236.

(Homicide and Suicide)

Schulte, J.L. (1985) Homicide and suicide associated with alkalisia and haloperidol. *American Journal of Forensic Psychiatry, 6*(2), 3-7.

(Homicide and Suicide)

Lester, D. (1985) Regional variation in suicide and homicide. *Suicide and Life Threatening Behavior, 15*(2), 110-116.

(Homicide and Suicide)

Lester, D. (1985) The quality of life in modern America and suicide and homicide rates. *Journal of Social Psychology, 125*(6), 779-780.

(Suicide)

Lester, D. (1985) The quality of life and suicide. *Journal of Social Psychology, 125*(2), 279-280.

(Homicide and Suicide)

Fishbain, D.A., et al. (1985) Female homicide-suicide perpetrators: A controlled study. *Journal of Forensic Science, 30*(4), 1148-1156.

(Sexual Jealousy and Suicide)

Lal, B.V., et al. (1985) Veil of dishonor; sexual jealousy and suicide on Fiji plantations. *Journal of Pacific History, 20*, 135-155.

(Homicide/Suicide - Victims)

Russell, L.G. (1985) Psychosocial characteristics of homicide and suicide victims. *Leg Med 1985*, 20-33.

(Statistics - Homicide and Suicide)

Boor, M., & Fleming, J.A. (1984) Reductions in suicide and accident levels prior to presidential elections are independent of unemployment effects. *Journal of Social Psychology, 124*(1), 119-121.

(Statistics)

Wasserman, I.M. (1984) The linkage of United States presidential elections, unemployment changes, and reductions in suicide, accident, and homicide rates. *Journal of Social Psychology, 124*(1), 115-117.

(Suicide or Homicide)

Pueschel, K., et al. (1984) Hanging: Suicide or homicide? (German) *Arch Krimin, 174*(5-6), 141-153.

(Murder and Attempted Suicide)

Lidberg, L., et al. (1984) 5-Hydroxyindolleactic acid levels in attempted suicides who have killed their children (letter). *Lancet, 2*(8408), 928.

(Cost of Violence)

Houk, V.W. (1983) Public health and cost implications of suicide, homicide, and criminal violence. *Texas Medicine, 79*(9), 6-7.

(Homicide-Suicide Pact)

Homicide-suicide pact: Charging survivor with aiding and abetting suicide rather than murder. (1983) *The Criminal Law Reporter: Court Decisions, 33*(24), 2511-2512.

(Murder/Suicide)

Allen, N.H. (1983) Homicide followed by suicide: Los Angeles, 1970-1979. *Suicide and Life Threatening Behavior, 13*(3), 155-165.

(Homicide and Suicide)

Lester, D. (1982) Conformity, suicide, and homicide. *Behavior Science Research, 17*(1-20), 24-30.

(Homicide and Suicide)

Palmer, S. (1982) *Homicide and Suicide*. New York: Lieber-Atherton.

(Statistics - Homicide and Suicide)

Lester, D. (1981) Freedom of the press and personal violence - a cross-national study of suicide and homicide. *Journal of Social Psychology, 114*(2), 267-270.

(Homicide, Suicide, and Accident - Relationship)

Wilbanks, W. (1980) Fatal accidents, suicide, and homicide: Are they related? Paper presented at the First World Congress of Victimology, held in Washington, DC, August 20-24, 1980.

(Homicide and Suicide - Alcohol's Role)

Lester, D. (1980) Alcohol and suicide and homicide. *Journal on the Study of Alcohol, 41*(11), 1220-1223.

(Snipers and Assassins - Suicide)

Danto, B.L. (1980) The boomerang bullet: Suicide among snipers and assassins. *International Journal Offender Therapy and Comparative Criminology, 24*(1), 41-57.

(Instigating Suicide)

Lanham, D.J. (1980) Murder by instigating suicide. *Criminal Law Review*, 215-221.

(Corpse Stealing)

Pueschel, K., & Brinkmann, B. (1979) Murder, suicide, and corpse stealing (German). *Arch Kriminol, 164*(1-2), 31-35.

(Temporal Variation)

Lester, D. (1979) Temporal variation in suicide and homicide. *American Journal of Epidemiology, 109*(5), 517-520.

(Police Science)

Carrington, F.G. (1978) Police science and administration book reviews. *Journal of Police Science Administration, 6*(1), 119.

(Police News)

Mishkin, B.D. (1978) Police news. *Law Enforcement Journal, 8*(10), 9.

(Suicide Among Murderers)

Danto, B.L. (1978) Suicide among murderers. *International Journal of Offender Therapy, 22*(2), 140-148.

(Homicide/Suicide Rates)

Phillips, D.P. (1978) Airplane accident fatalities increase just after newspaper stories about murder and suicide. *Science, 201*(4357), 743-750.

(Suicide, etc. - Norway)

Reigstad, A. (1978) Deaths from accidents, suicide, and homicide in Norway and in the city of Oslo, 1951-1975 (Norwegian). *Tidsskr Nor Laegeforen, 98*(23), 1072-1075, 1097.

(Book Reviews)

Book review. (1978) *Law Enforcement News, 4*(16), 7,9.

(Homicide and Suicide - Prediction)

Lester, D. (1977) Prediction of homicide and suicide: A test in a healthy risk-taking group. *Perceptual Motor Skills, 44*(1), 222.

(Suicide and Homicide - Destructive Behavior)

Palmer, S., & Humphrey, J.A. (1977) Suicide and homicide: A test of a role theory of destructive behavior. *Omega: The Journal of Death and Dying, 8*(1), 45-58.

(Homicide and Suicide - Relationship)

Franke, R.H., et al. (1977) Suicide and homicide: Common sources and consistent relationships. *Social Psychiatry, 12*(3), 149-156.

(Murder/Suicide)

Elwin, V. (1977) *Mafia murder and suicide.* London: Oxford Press.

(Homicide and Suicide - Riveting Guns)

Lenoir, L. (1977) Suicide and homicide by propulsive riveting guns (French). *Bull Med Leg Urg Med Cent Antipoisons, 20*(3), 211-215.

(Aspects of Aggression)

Henry, A.F., et al. (1977) *Suicide and homicide: Some economic, sociological, & psychological aspects of aggression.* Ayer Co.

(Homicide/Suicide - Studies)

Humphrey, J.H., et al. (1977) Pockets of violence: An exploration of homicide and suicide. *Diseases of the Nervous System, 38*(10), 833-837.

(Murder/Suicide - Case Report)

Wolff, G. (1976, July) Man who fell in love with death: Crosby-Bigelow murder and suicide - excerpt from *Black sun. Atlantic, 238,* pp. 37-46.

(Homicide and Suicide - Nazi Leaders)

Lester, D. (1976) Homicidal and suicidal impulses in the Nazi leaders. *Perceptual Motor Skills, 43*(3, part 2), 1316.

(Homicide and Suicide - Comparison)

Vigderhous, G. (1975) Suicide and homicide as causes of death and their relationship to life expectancy: A cross-cultural comparison. *Social Biology, 22*(4), 338-343.

(Homicide and Suicide - Police)

Police News (1975) *Law Enforcement Journal, 5*(7), 4.

(Homicide and Suicide - Police)

Mishkin, B.D. (1975) Police News. *Law Enforcement Journal, 5*(5), 20.

(Homicide and Suicide - Attitudes)

Weiss, J.M.A., & Perry, M.E. (1975) Transcultural attitudes toward homicide and suicide. *Suicide, 5*(4), 223-227.

(Homicide and Suicide)

Naeve, W. (1973) Suicides and homicides simulating an auto-erotic accident (German). *Arch Kriminol, 154*(5-6), 145-149.

(Homicidal Threat - Suicidal Action)

Rhine, M.W., & Mayerson, P. (1973) A serious suicidal syndrome marked by homicidal threats. *Life Threatening Behavior, 3*(1), 3-10.

(Homicide and Suicide - Relationship)

Humphrey, J.A. (1973) Homicide, suicide, and role relationships in New Hampshire. *Dissertation Abstracts International, 34*(5-A), 2789-2790.

(Homicide and Suicide - Age Relationship)

Lester, D. (1973) Suicide, homicide, and age dependency ratios. *International Journal on Aging and Human Development, 4*, 127-132.

(Homicide and Suicide - Trends)

Hirsch, C.S., et al. (1973) Homicide and suicide in a metropolitan county, I. Long-term trends. *JAMA, 223*, 900-905.

(Suicide and Homicide - Norway vs. France)

Lester, D. (1973) External restraints, suicide, and homicide: Comparison of Norway and France. *Perceptual Motor Skills, 36*(2), 646.

(Homicide and Suicide)

Lester, D. (1971) Suicide and homicide in open and closed societies. *Psychological Reports, 29*, 430.

(Suicide After Accidental Homicide)

Petit, G., et al. (1970) Suicide after involuntary pseudo-homicide in a traffic accident (French). *Med Leg Domm Corpor, 3*, 423-435.

(Homicide and Suicide - Theory)

Whitt, H. (1968) *The lethal aggression rate and the suicide-murder ratio: A synthetic theory of suicide and homicide*. Chapel Hill, NC: UNC Press.

(Homicide or Accident)

Iskrant, A.P. (1968) *Accidents and homicide*. Cambridge, MA: Harvard Press.

(Homicide and Suicide - Africa)

Bohannan, P., (ED.) (1967) *African Homicide and Suicide*. New York: Athenaeum.

(Homicide and Suicide - Causes)

Lester, D. (1967) Suicide, homicide, and the effects of socialization. *Journal of Personality and Social Psychology, 5*, 466-468.

(Homicide and Suicide - Responsibility)

Solomon, P. (1967) The burden of responsibility in suicide and homicide. *JAMA, 199*, 321-324.

(Homicide, Suicide, Accidents - Epidemiology)

Pai, D.N. (1967) Epidemiology of suicide, homicide, and accidents. *Indian Journal of Medical Science, 21*, 117-122.

(Homicide and Suicide - Comparison)

Hartmann, H. (1966) Suicide and homicide: An analysis in two countries. *Postgraduate Medicine, 40*, A20.

(Homicide, Suicide, and Economic Development)

Quinney, R. (1965) Suicide, homicide, and economic development. *Social Forces, 43*, 401-406.

(Homicide and Suicide)

Palmer, S. (1965) Murder and suicide in forty non-literate societies. 18620. vol. 56, ‘65 n3, 320-324 (IBZ 1967).

(Suicide - Wide-Spread)

Popella, E. (1964) On wide-spread suicide (German). *Arch Psychiat Nervenkr, 205*, 615-624.

(Homicide and Suicide - Automobile)

MacDonald, J.M. (1964) Suicide and homicide by automobile. *American Journal of Psychiatry, 121*(4), 366-370.

(Murder or Suicide)

Verbeek, G.J. (1964) Mord oder Selbstmord. 20957 J 18(8): 421-422 (IBZ 1965).

(Homicide and Suicide - Ceylon)

Wood, A.L. (1961) A socio-structural analysis of murder, suicide, and economic crime in Ceylon. *American Sociological Review, 26*, 744-753.

(Violent Deaths)

Porterfield, A.L. (1960, Dec.) Traffic fatalities, suicide, and homicide. *American Sociology Review, 25*, 897-901.

(Homicide and Suicide - WW II)

Zamcheck, N., & Geisler, M.A. (1960) Homicides and suicides of WW II: A critical analysis of 656 homicides and 1179 suicides. *Journal of Forensic Science, 5*, 84.

(Homicide - Motor Vehicle)

Homicide by motor vehicle - a survey and proposal. (1959) *Iowa Law Review, 44*, 558.

(Homicide and Suicide - Causes)

Suicide, homicide, and the socialization of aggression. (1958) *American Journal of Sociology, 63*(6), 651-661.

(Murder or Suicide)

Muller, M., & P.H. (1958) 2 strange cases of suicide caused by butcher knife and by strangulation with a cord; murder or suicide? (French) *Ann Med Leg, 38*(6), 428-432.

(Suicide - Gunshot)

Ricci, P.L. (1958) Study of various aspects of suicide caused by multiple gunshots (Italian). *Minerva Med Leg Tor, 78*(4), 145-148.

(Homicide and Suicide)

Gold, M. (1958) Suicide, homicide, and the socialization of aggression. *American Journal of Sociology, 63*, 651-661.

(Homicide and Suicide - Method)

Protigliatti, B.M. (1957) Frequency of homicides and suicides with side-arms and especially with pointed and edged arms in particular. (French). *Acta Med Leg Social Liege, 10*(3), 501-511.

(Homicide and Suicide)

Henry, A.F., & Short, J.F. (1954) *Suicide and Homicide: Some economic, sociological, and psychological aspects of aggression.* New York: Free Press of Glencoe.

(Homicide and Suicide - Ceylon)

Straus, J.H., & Straus, M.A. (1953) Suicide, homicide, and social structure in Ceylon. *American Journal of Sociology, 58*, 461-469.

(Suicide - Method)

Gunn, H.M. (1953) Suicide in a moving automobile on a highly traveled highway. *Journal of Criminal Law, 43*, 827-828.

(Homicide and Suicide - Combined Methods)

Tovo, S. (1952) Combined methods in suicide and in homicide. *Minerva Med Leg, 72*, 1-26.

(Murder and Suicide - General)

Elwin,V.M. (1950) *Murder and suicide.* London: Oxford Press.

(Homicide-Suicide Pact)

Suicide agreement (Rex v. Croft (1944), 1 K B 295). (1944) *South African Law Journal, 61*, 337-338.

(Murder/Suicide)

Elsasser, G. (1939) The problem of family murder and suicide (German). *Allg Z Psychiat, 110,* 207-219.

(Murder/Suicide)

Tweedle, S.A. Killing another in attempt to commit suicide (State v Campbell (IA) 251 N W 717). *St. Louis Law Review, 19,* 153-154 (1934); *Minnesota Law Review, 18,* 745-747 (1934); *Journal of Criminal Law, 25,* 124-126 (1934).

(Homicide or Suicide)

Kennard, K.S. (1922) Esther Willings case: Suicide or homicide. *Medical Legal Journal, 39,* 66.

(Murder/Suicide)

Larremore, W. (1913) Feo de de. Suicide. *American Law Review, 47,* 210.

(Suicidal Declarations)

Dahl, G.M. (1904) Suicidal declarations in homicide cases. *Cent Law Journal, 59,* 103.

(Murder or Suicide)

Mikell, W.E. (1903) Is suicide murder? *Columbia Law Journal, 3,* 379.

Accidents - General

(Accidental Overdoses)

Bailey, D.N., & Shaw, R.W. (1989) Cocaine- and methamphetamine-related deaths in San Diego County (1987): Homicides and accidental overdoses. *Journal Forensic Science, 34*(2), 407-422.

(Accidental Deaths)

Hilsop, T.G., et al. (1987) Accidental and intentional violent deaths among British Columbia native Indians. *Canadian Journal of Public Health, 78*(4), 271-274

(Accidents - Second Degree Murder)

Homicide -- automobile accidents -- second degree murder. (1984) *The Criminal Law Reporter: Court Decisions, 34*(14), 2266.

(Aggressive Driving)

Sivak, M. (1983) Society's aggression level as a predictor of traffic fatality rate. *Journal of Safety Research, 14*(3), 93-99.

(Accident)

Evidence did not require instruction on defense of accident or misadventure in homicide. (1980, June) *Reporter, 9*(3), 98-99.

(Homicides - DUI)

Murder convictions for homicides committed in the course of driving while intoxicated. (1977) *Cumb Law Review, 8*, 477-494.

(Accidental Deaths - Adolescents)

Foodman, A., & Estrada, C. (1977) Adolescents who commit accidental homicide: The emotional consequences to the individual, family, and community. *Journal of the American of Child Psychiatry, 16*(2), 314-326.

(Reckless Homicide - Case Report)

Smith, K.J.M (1973) Case of reckless homicide. *New Law Journal, 123*, 792-793.

(Accident or Homicide)

Popovic, D., et al. (1970) Accident or homicide. *Med Pregl, 23*, 235-237.

(Accident Reconstruction)

Durante, F. (1968) Dynamic reconstruction of a traffic accident (Italian). *Zacchia, 4*, 581-606.

(Murder or Suicide)

Usher, A. (1968) Murder or Suicide? *Medical Science and the Law, 8*(4), 260-261.

(Murder or Accident)

Ueno, S. (1966) Murder or accidental death? *Japanese Journal of Legal Medicine, 20*, 164-170.

(Homicide - Negligent)

Negligent homicide in Idaho. (1965) *Idaho Law Review, 2*, 96.

(Homicide - Involuntary Manslaughter)

Involuntary manslaughter in Kentucky: Past, present, and future. (1965) *Kentucky Law Journal, 53*, 770.

(Provoked Manslaughter)

Manslaughter: Adequacy of provocation in Missouri. (1965) *Missouri Law Review, 30*, 112.

(Homicide - Idaho)

Manslaughter in Idaho. (1965) *Idaho Law Review, 2*, 87.

(Homicide - Negligent)

Desch, S.C. (1963) Negligent murder. *Modern Law Review, 26*, 660.

(Vehicular Homicide)

Brett, P. (1953) Manslaughter and the motorist. *Australian Law Journal, 27*, 6-12, 89-101.

(Homicide - Occupational)

Giuliani, G. (1953) Homicide as occupational accident; unusual event; 20 observations (Italian). *Minerva Med Leg, 73*, 92-101.

(Negligent Murder)

Negligent murder in Kentucky. (1952) *Kentucky Law Journal, 41*, 88-94.

(Homicide - Kentucky)

Misdemeanor-manslaughter doctrine in Kentucky. (1952) *Kentucky Law Journal, 41*, 94-99.

(Vehicular Homicide)

Manslaughter by automobile in Florida. (1951) *University of Florida Law Review, 4*, 360-369.

(Voluntary Manslaughter)

Statutory voluntary homicide. (1950) *Kentucky Law Journal, 39*, 108-112.

(Manslaughter - Auto Races)

Wynne, E.C. Manslaughter, wanton, reckless murder at midget auto races. *B U Law Review, 30*, 430-432 (1950); *Virginia Law Review, 36*, 395-397.

(Homicide or Manslaughter)

Karaba, F.A. (1950) Negligent homicide or manslaughter - a dilemma. *Journal of Criminal Law, 41*, 183-189.

(Manslaughter Doctrine)

Johnston, J.J. (1949) Reexamination of the misdemeanor manslaughter doctrine. *Kentucky Law Journal, 38*, 118-127.

(Homicide - Categories)

Kinnaird, J.M. (1948) Manslaughter: Preliminary study of categories of voluntary manslaughter. *Kentucky Law Journal, 36*, 320-323.

(Murder or Manslaughter)

Bull, A. (1946) Murder or manslaughter? *South African Law Journal, 63*, 235-241.

(Vehicular Homicide)

Manslaughter-negligence - driver falling asleep (Rex vs. Scarth (1945) Q S R 38). (1945) *Australian Law Journal, 19*, 191.

(Homicide - Manslaughter)

Creme, W.T. (1938) Manslaughter in the second degree (State vs. Root (Ohio) 7 N E 2d

664). *Ohio State Law Journal, 4*, 234-237.

(Vehicular Homicide)

Brais, F.P. (1938) Motor manslaughter and kindred offenses: Criminal and civil responsibility. *Canadian Bar Association, 23*, 126-150.

(Homicide - Manslaughter)

Involuntary manslaughter, defendant driving automobile without a license (Commonwealth vs. Williams (PA) 1 Atl 2d 812). (1938) *University of Pittsburgh Law Review, 5*, 58-59.

(Vehicular Homicide)

Robinson, J.J. (1938) Manslaughter by motorists. *Minnesota Law Review, 22*, 755-788.

(Vehicular Homicide)

Admissibility of paraffin mold in murder prosecution (Commonwealth vs. Westwood (PA) 188 Atl 304). (1938) *Law Notes, 41*, 46.

(Vehicular Manslaughter)

Manslaughter on the road. (1937) *Legal Times, 183*, 371-373.

(Liability - Automobile Owner)

Manslaughter, liability of non-driving automobile owner (People vs. Rauch [NY]). (1937) *University of Chicago Law Review, 5*, 142-143.

(Vehicular Homicide - Case Report)

Motorists and manslaughter (Andrews vs. Director of Public Prosecutions (1937) A C 576). *Justice of the Peace, 102*, 8 (1938); *D W L Law Quarterly Review, 53*, 306-307 (1937).

(Vehicular Homicide)

Dean, P. (1937) Manslaughter and dangerous driving. *Law Quarterly Review, 53*, 380-387.

(Vehicular Homicide)

Manslaughter by negligence in the driving of a motor car. (1937) *Ir Legal Times, 71*, 281-284.

(Vehicular Homicide - Case Report)

Manslaughter on the roads (Andrews vs. Director of Public Prosecutions (1937) 2 All E R 552). *Justice of Peace, 101*, 277 (1937); *Sol, 4*, 103-104 (1937); *Justice Journal, 83*, 302 (1937).

(Homicide - Intent)

McIntyre, H.L. (1935) Murder without intent to kill (Tennant vs. State (AL) 155 So 885). *Journal of Criminal Law, 25*, 775-777.

(Vehicular Manslaughter)

Motor manslaughter - two vital points. (1934, July 14) *Just P, 98*, 461.

(Vehicular Homicide)

Manslaughter - what is an unlawful act (Rex vs. Dolynchuk (1934) I W W R 200). (1934) *Fortnightly Law Journal, 3*, 257-258.

(Vehicular Homicide)

Dangerous driving and manslaughter (Rex v. Stringer (1933) I K B 704). (1933) *Australian Law Journal, 7*, 125.

(Vehicular Homicide)

Manslaughter and dangerous driving. (1933) *Law Journal, 75*, 42.

(Homicide)

Killing not manslaughter. (1932) *C L J, 74*, 289-290.

(Homicide - Psychopathology)

Puyn, H. (1931) Contribution to the psychopathology of murder and manslaughter (German). *Allg Asch f Psychiat, 93*(1-2), 66.

(Manslaughter)

Manslaughter, joint responsibility (R. v. Baldessare (1930) 22 Cr App R 70 W N 193). *Camb L J, 4*, 217-218. (1931); *Justice of Peace, 94*, 454. (1931).

(Murder - Accidental)

Accidental killing in the commission of a felony (People v. Udwin (NY) 172 N E 489). *University of Pennsylvania Law Review, 79*, 224-225. (1930); *Michigan Law Review, 29*, 371-372. (1931).

(Homicide - Negligent)

Manslaughter, contributory negligence (State v. Eldridge (NC) 150 S E 125). (1928) *University of Cincinnati Law Review, 4*, 88-89.

(Vehicular Manslaughter)

Manslaughter by drivers. (1930) *L J, 70*, 118.

(Manslaughter)

An unusual manslaughter charge. (1930) *Sol J, 74*, 777.

(Criminal Assault)

Assault with intent to commit manslaughter (Lassiter v. State (FL) 123 So. 735). *Illinois Law Review, 25*, 332-333 (1930, Nov.); *Yale Law Journal, 39*, 428 (1930, Jan.); *N Y U Law Review, 7*, 531 (1929, Dec.).

(Manslaughter - Jury Instructions)

Failure to instruct that the time between previous difficulty and shooting was inadequate "cooling time" held not prejudicial where defendant was convicted of manslaughter (Highbarger v.

Commonwealth 225 KY 302, 10 S W 2d 286). (1929) *Kentucky Law Journal, 17*, 300-301.

(Manslaughter)

Involuntary manslaughter. (1929) *Law Society Journal, 1*, 6-11.

(Involuntary Manslaughter - Case Reports)

Williams, J.A., et al. Involuntary manslaughter,acts of necessity, impaired exemptions of public officers from ordinances regulating traffic and speed of vehicles (Lilly vs. State of West Virginia 29 F 2d 61). *Texas Law Review, 7*, 476-477. (1929); *Illinois Law Review, 24*, 243-245. (1929); *North Carolina Law Review, 7*, 485-487. (1929); *Temple Law Quarterly, 3*, 444-445. (1929).

(Vehicular Manslaughter)

Murder by automobile (Commonwealth v. McLaughlin, 293 PA 218). (1928) *Temple Law Quarterly, 3*, 81-82.

(Robbery/Murder - Rent Collector)

Oertel. (1928) The robbery and murder of the rent collector Todt (German). *Arch f Kriminol, 83*(3-4), 83.

(Manslaughter)

Aiding and abetting manslaughter (State v. Hopkins (WA) 265 Pac. 481). (1928, Nov.) *Michigan Law Review, 27*, 101-102.

Causes of Accidents

(Self-Defense)

Shanken, P. (1990, Sept. 3) Self-defense shooting cannot be manslaughter (Smith, in re) (PA). *Pennsylvania Law Journal, 13*, 9.

(DUI)

Goodman, S. (1990) Agony without ecstasy: Alcohol and violence. *Current Health*, 17(2), 28-29.

(Accidental Shootings)

McKinney, C.D., et al. (1990) Accidental deaths involving derringer handguns: A report of three cases. *Journal of Forensic Science, 35*(3), 730-734.

(Accident - Cause)

Anthony, S. (1988, Dec.) Unlucky Lindy. *Ms., 17*(6), p. 73.

(Strangulation - Accidental)

Koutselinis, A. (1988) Accidental sexual strangulation (author's reply; letter). *American Journal of Forensic and Medical Pathology, 9*(1), 92.

(Vehicular Homicide - DUI)

Drunk driver in fatal accident can be charged with second degree murder. (1982) *The Criminal Law Reporter: Court Decisions and Proceedings, 30*(15), 2286-2287.

(Vehicular Homicide)

Fisher, J.S. (1980) Reckless driving again. *New Law Journal, 130*, 1057-1059.

(Accidents - Causes)

Phillips, D.P. (1980, June) Airplane accidents, murder, and the mass media towards theory of imitation and suggestion. *Forces, 58*, 1001-1024.

(Manslaughter)

Dennis, I.H. (1980) Manslaughter by omission. *Current Legal Problems, 33*, 257-267.

(Accidental Death, Psychology)

Petti, T.A., & Wells, K. (1980) Crisis treatment of a preadolescent who accidentally killed his twin. *American Journal of Psychotherapy, 34*(3), 434-443.

(Vehicular Homicide)

Heintz, J.E. (1977) Pretrial strategy in a vehicular manslaughter case. *Pract Law, 23*, 63-80.

(Accidents and Alcohol)

Karaharju, E.O.& Stjernvall, L. (1974) The alcohol factor in accidents. *Injury, 6*(1), 67-69.

(Accidents)

Eckert, W.G. (1974) Fatal trauma: Medical and legal aspects. *Journal of the Kansas Medical Society, 75*(12), 366-369.

(Violence - Psychological Effects)

Lyons, H.A. (1973) The imbalance of society -- violence in Belfast: A review of the psychological effects. *Public Health* (London), *87*(6), 231-238; *Community Health, 5*(3), 163-168.

(Causes of Death)

Fourcade, J., et al. (1967, March-April) On a case of delayed death after a large transfixing heart wound (French). *Ann Med Leg* (Paris), *47*, 141.

(Involuntary Homicide)

Lopes, C. (1958) Involuntary homicide caused by a ricocheted bullet confirmed by medicolegal investigation (Port). *Gaz Med Port, 11*(1), 41-44.

(Mistaken Cause of Death)

Murder and mistake concerning cause of death. (1954) *Law Quarterly Review, 70*, 146-147.

Homicide and Suicide

(Murder/Suicide)

Murder/suicide evidence, photos are public records (Arkansas). (1989, Spring) *News Media and the Law, 13*, 7-8.

(Homicide/Suicide and Pain)

Fishbain, D.A., et al. (1989) Homicide/suicide and chronic pain. *Clinical Journal on Pain, 5*(3), 275-277.

(Homicide and Suicide)

Vock, R., et al. (1988) Determination of questionable suicide as a homicide by studies of criminal stains (German with English abstract). *Arch Kriminol, 181*(1-2), 12-18.

(Suicide - Markers)

Windus, G., et al. (1988) Proof value of matching markers for the complicated suicide (German with English Abstract). *Beitr Gerichtl Med, 46*, 335-338.

(Bullet Range)

Suwanjutha, T. (1988) Direction, site, and the muzzle target distance of bullet in the head and neck at close range as an indication of suicide or homicide. *Forensic Science International, 37*(3), 223-229.

(Murder/Suicide)

Lester, D. (1987) Murder followed by suicide in those who murder police officers. *Psychological Reports, 60*(3, part 2), 1130.

(Homicide and Suicide)

Lester, D. (1987) Murders and suicides: Are they polar opposites. *Behavioral Science and the Law (Special Issue: Homicidal Behavior), 5*(1), 49-60.

(Homicide and Suicide)

Lester, D. (1987) Occupational prestige and the rates of homicide and suicide. *Perceptual Motor Skills, 64*(2), 398.

(Murder/Suicide)

Kleiber, M. (1987) A suicide decision as a motive for murder -- an airplane as the murder weapon (German). *Arch Kriminol, 179*(5-6), 154-160.

(Suicide)

Lester, D. (1987) Suicide and sibling position. *Individual Psychology: Journal of Adlerian Theory, Research, and Study, 43*(3), 390-395.

(Suicide - Disguised)

McDowell, C.P. (1987) Suicide disguised as murder: A dimension of Munchausen syndrome. *Journal of Forensic Science, 32*(1), 254-261.

(Suicide)

Lester, D. (1986) Suicide: The concentration camp and the survivors. *Israel Journal of Psychiatry and Related Sciences, 23*(3), 221-223.

(Suicide Called Murder)

Reese, M. (1985, May 6) A tragedy in Santa Monica (parent-child suicide called murder; case of F. Kimura). *Newsweek, 105*, p. 10.

(Homicide and Suicide - Surveillance)

Rosenberg, M.L. (1985) Surveillance for suicide, homicide, and domestic violence: Strengths, weaknesses, and issues. *Public Health Report, 100*(6), 593-595.

(Homicide or Suicide)

Perrot, L.J., et al. (1985) Asphyxiation by hanging in two young Hispanic children - homicide, suicide, or accidental deaths? A review of pediatric hangings. *American Journal of forensic Medicine and Pathology, 6*(4), 284-288.

(Homicide/Suicide)

Copeland, A.R. (1985) Dyadic death - revisited. *American Journal of Forensic Science and Sociology, 25*(3), 181-188.

(Homicide or Mass Suicide)

Rowe, W.F. (1984) Discussion of 'George Armstrong Custer and the Battle of the Little Bighorn: Homicide or mass suicide?' (letter) *Journal of Forensic Science, 29*(3), 696-699.

(Homicide or Suicide)

Keiser-Nielsen, H. (1984) Was the incredible suicide by axe blows in reality a homicide (German with English abstract). *Z Rechtmed, 93*(2), 135-141.

(Homicide or Mass Suicide)

Spencer, J.D. (1983) George Armstrong Custer and the Battle of the Little Bighorn: Homicide or mass suicide? *Journal of Forensic Science, 28*(3), 756-761.

(Gunshot Self-Inflicted)

Kost-Grant, B.L. (1983) Self-inflicted gunshot wounds among Alaska Natives. *Public Health Reports, 98*(1), 72-78.

(Homicide/Suicide)

Allen, N.H. (1983) Homicide followed by suicide: Los Angeles, 1970-1979. *Suicide and Life Threatening Behavior, 13*(3), 155-165.

(Homicide and Suicide)

Koops, E., et al. (1982) Pattern of clinical findings and special findings in homicidal and suicidal strangulation (German with English Abstract). *Beitr Gerichtl Med, 40*, 129-133.

(Homicide or Suicide)

Madro, R. (1981) Death by strangulation - suicide or homicide (Polish with summaries in English and Russian)? *Arch Med Sadow Kryminol, 31*(2), 139-143.

(Suicide among Murderers)

Danto, B.L. (1980) The boomerang bullet: Suicide among snipers and assassins. *International Journal of Offender Therapy and Comparative Criminology, 24*(1), 41-57.

(Homicide/Suicide)

Palmer, S., & Humphrey, J.A. (1980) Offender-victim relationships in criminal homicide followed by suicide, North Carolina, 1972-1977. *Suicide & Life Threatening Behavior, 10*(2), 106-118.

(Dyadic Death)

Berman, A.L. (1979) Dyadic death: Murder-suicide. *Suicide and Life Threatening Behavior, 9*(1), 15-23.

(Depression and Homicide)

Hirose, S. (1979) Depression and homicide: A psychiatric and forensic study of four cases. *Acta Psychiatr Scand, 59*(2), 211-217.

(Murder or Suicide)

Rho, Y.M. (1978) Murder or suicide? *New York State Journal of Medicine, 78*(6), 965-967.

(Homicide and Suicide - Differences)

Humphrey, J.A. (1978) Devastating losses; differences between suicides and murderers. *Human Behavior, 7*, 61.

(Murder/Suicide)

Danto, B.L. (1978) Suicide among murderers. *International Journal of Offender Therapy and Comparative Criminology, 22*(2), 140-148.

(Role Interference)

Humphrey, J.A. (1978) Role interference: An analysis of suicide victims, homicide offenders, and non-violent individuals. *Journal of Clinical Psychiatry, 39*(8), 652-655.

(Murder/Suicide - Family)

Goldney, R.D. (1977) Family murder followed by suicide. *Austrian Forensic Science, 9*(3), 219-228.

(Homicide or Suicide - Stab Wound)

Stichnoth, E. (1977) Stab wounds in the heart: Homicide or suicide? (German) *Munster Kriminalistic, 31*(7), 317-319.

(Suicide or Crime)

Schynder-Kogel, V. (1977) Suicide or crime: A report of two cases (German with English abstract) *Beitr Gerichtl Med, 35*, 71-75.

(Social Loss)

Humphrey, J.A. (1977) Social loss: A comparison of suicide victims, homicide offenders, and non-violent individuals. *Diseases of the Nervous system, 38*(3), 157-160.

(Homicide or Suicide)

Bonte, W., et al. (1975) Foreign bodies in the pharynx: Homicide or suicide? (German) *Arch Kriminol, 156*(5-6), 160-168.

(Heart Stab)

Haarhoff, K., et al. (1975) Heart stab: Homicide or suicide? (German) *Arch Kriminol, 155*(3-4), 103-109.

(Murder or Suicide)

Bonte, W., & Bode, G. (1974) Differential diagnosis between murder and suicide in stab wounds of the cervical region (German). *Arch Kriminol, 154*, (1-2), 9-24.

(Homicide and Suicide)

Virkkunen, M. (1974) Suicide linked to homicide. *Psychiatric Quarterly, 48*(2), 276-282.

(Homicide or Suicide - Testing)

Lester, D. (1974) Distinguishing murders from suicides with the Rorschach. *Perceptual & Motor Skills, 39*(1, part 2), 474.

(Homicide and Suicide - Prediction)

Futrell, R.H. (1974) *An empirical test of a social structural model for the prediction of suicide and homicide*. Lawrence, KA: KU Press.

(Homicide and Suicide - Disguised)

Naeve, W. (1974) Suicides and homicides under the disguise of an autoerotic accident. (German) *Arch Kriminol, 154*(5-6), 145-149.

(Murder and Attempted Suicide)

Lester, D., et al. (1974) Murderers who have attempted suicide. *Psychology Reports, 35*(1 pt. 1), 238.

(Suicide Attempts and Assaults)

Connor, H.E., et al.. (1973) Comparative psychopathology of suicide attempts and assaults. *Suicide & Life Threatening Behavior, 3*(1), 33-50.

(Homicide or Suicide)

Barta, T. (1973) Neck injury from suicidal and homicidal intention (Slovak with English abstract). Cesk Otolaryngol, 22, 53-57.

(Homicide and Suicide)

Baden, M.M. (1972) Homicide, suicide, and accidental death among narcotic addicts. *Human Pathology, 3*, 91-95.

(Rorschach Tests)

Lester, D. (1972) Suicide, homicide, and color-shading response on the Rorschach. *Perceptual Motor Skills, 35*, 562.

(Homicide or Suicide)

Lester, D. (1971) Ellen West's suicide as a case of psychic homicide. *Psychoanalysis Review, 58*, 251-263.

(Homicide vs. Suicide)

Arcadio, F., et al. (1971) Death caused by multiple wounds: Homicide or suicide (French). *Med Leg Domm Corpor, 4*, 190-191.

(Homicide and Suicide - Indians)

Ogden, M., et al. (1970) Suicides and homicides among Indians. *Public Health Reports, 85*, 75-80.

(Suicide)

Chomakov, M.I. (1969) Postmortem retention of a knife in the hand in suicide. (Russian). *Sudebnomed Ekspert, 12*, 51-52.

(Homicide and Suicide)

Lalli, M., & Turner, S.H. (1968) Suicide and homicide: a comparative analysis by race and occupational levels. *Journal of Criminal Law, Criminology, and Police Science, 59*(2), 191-200.

(Murder or Suicide)

Usher, A. (1968) Murder or suicide? *Med Sci Law, 8*, 260-261.

(Homicide and Suicide - Hanging)

Chini, A. (1967) A case of homicide-suicide by hanging (Italian). *Zacchia, 3*, 102-115.

(Murder/Suicide)

West, D.J. (1966) *Murder followed by suicide*. Cambridge, MA: Harvard Press.

(Homicide and Suicide - Predictability)

Wilkerson, R.C. (1966) The physician's liability in suicide and homicide. *Medicolegal Bulletin, 157*, 1-5.

(Murder or Suicide)

Huijser, P.H.J. (1966) Mord oder selbstmord? 20957. J. 20, '66, 11, S. 598 (IBZ 1967).

(Human Violence)

Pokorny, A.D. (1965) Human violence: A comparison of homicide, aggravated assault, suicide, and attempted suicide. *Journal of Criminal Law, Criminology, and Police Science 56*(4), 488.

(Murder/Suicide)

Fiorentini, H., et al. (1965) Contribution to the study of post-homicidal suicide (French). *Ann Med Leg, 45*, 36-41.

(Murder or Suicide)

Gaulke, K. (1965) Mord or freitod? 20957. J. 19, '65, 6, S. 318-319 (IBZ 1966).

(Homicide and Suicide - Case Report)

Weiss, S.W. (1963) Cry wolf; a case study of suicide and homicide. *Delaware Medical Journal, 35*, 293-297.

(Murder/Suicide)

Neiberg, N.A. (1961) Murder and suicide. *Arch Crim Psychodyn, 4*, 253-268.

(Murder and Suicide)

Wolfgang, M.E. (1959) Suicide by means of victim-precipitated homicide. *Journal of Clinical Experience and Psychopathology, 20,* 335-349.

(Murder/Suicide)

Wolfgang, M.E. (1958) An analysis of homicide-suicide. *Journal of Clinical Experience and Psychopathology, 19*(3), 208-218.

(Murder and Suicide)

Reichard, S., & Tillamn, C. (1950) Murder and suicide as defenses against schizophrenic psychosis. *Journal of Clinical Psychopathology, 11,* 149-163.

(Homicide and Suicide - Psychoanalysis)

Rabin, A.I. (1946) Homicide and attempted suicide: A Rorschach study. *American Journal of Orthopsychiatry, 16,* 516-524.

(Homicide and Suicide)

Deb, A.K. (1946) Suicide and homicide in relation to sexual difficulties. *Ind Med Rec, 66,* 134.

(Murder Motive)

Weber, V. (1937) Suicide as a murder motive (German). *Mschr Krim Biol, 28,* 4.

(Joint Suicide/Murder)

Grzywo-Dabrowska, M. (1936) Joint suicide and murder followed by suicide (Polish). *Hig Psychiczn, 2,* 75-98.

(Homicide and Suicide)

Mills, C.A. (1934) Suicides and homicides in their relation to weather changes. *American Journal of Psychiatry, 91,* 669-677.

(Homicide and Suicide)

Ravicini, S. (1934) Homicide and suicide (Italian). *Difesa Soc, 7,* 367-374.

(Homicide and Suicide)

Raven, A. (1929) Murder and suicide as marks of an abnormal mind. *Sociology Review, 21*(3), 28-31.

Chapter 10
Legal Aspects
General

(Homicide and the Press)

Stein, M.L. (1990, Sept. 8) California judge upholds shield law in murder case. *Editor & Publisher, 123*(36), p. 26.

(Sentencing)

O'Brien, J. (1990, Aug. 29) Jurors lament vote to convict in death case: 4 request lenient term in upstate manslaughter. *New York Law Journal, 204*, 1.

(Murder Trial)

Hornung, R. (1990, Aug. 28) Black to the future. *Village Voice, 35*(35), p. 26.

(Jogger Trial)

Noel, P. (1990, Aug. 28) Legal lynching? *Village Voice, 35*(35), pp. 25, 27+.

(Murder Trial)

Trippett, F. (1990, Aug. 27) Guilty, guilty, guilty. *Time, 136*(9), p. 40.

(Central Park Jogger)

Kunen, J.S. (1990, July 30) Risen from near death, the Central Park jogger makes her day in court one to remember. *People Weekly, 34*(4), pp. 32-34.

(Murder Trial)

Smith, K.E. (1990, July 23) Old enemies, new questions. *Newsweek, 116*(4), p. 24.

(Attempted Murder)

Morales, E. (1990, July 17) Puerto Rican pride and Bronx prejudice. *Village Voice, 35*(29), pp. 23-24.

(Accusation)

Carlson, M. (1990, June 4) Daddy's little girl. *Time, 135*(23), p. 56.

(Successful Defense)

Taylor, N. (1990, June 4) Murphy's law. *New York, 23*(22), pp. 48-55.

(Sentencing)

Souter, D.H. (1990, Aug.) Souter's stern judgment on sentencing (excerpts from David H. Souter's sentencing statement of a drunk driver who killed 3 teenagers). *Legal Times, 13*, 10.

(Racial Trials)

Trebay, G. (1990, May 29) Full court press. *Village Voice, 35*(22), pp. 41, 60.

(Torch Murder)

Ivins, M. (1990, May) Small favors: A fairly normal Spring. *Progressive, 54*(5), p. 39.

(Convictions)

Spencer, G. (1990, March 30) Howard Beach convictions are affirmed: 3 separate rulings on jury challenges issued. *New York Law Journal, 203*, 1.

(Press Coverage)

Press allowed to cover juvenile hearing. (1990, March 18) *Editor & Publisher, 122*(11), p. 23.

(Steinberg Case)

Quinn, J. (1990, March 15) Social sciences -- law and crime: What Lisa knew. *Library Journal, 115*(5), 102.

(Workplace Liability)

Verespej, M.A. (1990, March 6) Execs could be tried for murder. *Industry Week, 238*(5), 61-62.

(Court Ruling)

Gordon, J.B. (1990, March 4) Appeals court lifts prior restraint. *Edit & Publish, 122*(9), p. 29.

(Hypnosis)

Orne, M.T., et al. (1990) Rock v. Arkansas: Hypnosis, the defendant's privilege. *International Journal of Clinical and Experimental Hypnosis, 38*(4), 250-265.

(Homicide - Letter)

Gordon, D. (1990) The issue is homicide: Letter. *Policy Review, 52*(Spring), 91.

(Courts)

Monkkonen, E.H. (1990) The American state from the bottom up: Homicide and courts. *Law and Society Review,, 24*(2), 521-531.

(Corporate Homicide)

Maakestad, W. (1990) Corporate homicide. *New York Law Journal, 140*(6447), 356-357.

(Larry Davis Case)

Epstein, J. (1989, Dec. 12) Can a guy who shot six cops get justice? *Village Voice, 34*(50), pp. 10, 12+.

(Ornie Convicted)

Hoffman, J. (1989, Dec. 5) His sister's keeper. *Village Voice, 34*(49), pp. 21-26.

(Homicide Laws)

Walter, D., et al. (1989, Nov.-Dec.) The importance of clarity in the law of homicide: The Wisconsin revision. *Wisconsin Law Review, 1989*, 1323-1393.

(Mistrial - Todd Bridges)

Jury acquits Todd Bridges of charges of attempted murder, manslaughter. (1989, Nov. 27) *Jet, 77*(8), pp. 36-37.

(Improper Instruction)

Illinois manslaughter instruction held improper. (1989, Nov. 22) *Chicago Daily Law Bulletin, 135*, 1.

(False Conviction)

Crosley, E., & Tunsley, R. (1989, Nov. 21) Guilty. *Women's Day, 53*(1), pp. 106-114.

(Assassination Ban)

Glass, A.J. (1989, Nov. 14) A loophole in ban on assassination? *Los Angeles Daily Journal, 102*, p. 6.

(Thin Blue Line)

Lassell, M. (1989, Oct. 19) Crossing the "thin blue line". *Rolling Stone, 563*, p. 30.

(Extradition)

Serrill, M.S., et al. (1989, Sept. 28) Passing the extradition test. *Time, 134*(12), p. 48.

(Conspiracy)

Smith, R.J. (1989, Sept. 26) Conspiracy to commit voodoo: Is Leroy Ivy charmed and dangerous? *Village Voice, 34*(39), pp. 37-41.

(Japanese Police)

Jackson, T. (1989, Sept. 11) The Tokyo chain saw massacre. *New Republic, 201*(11), 20-21.

(Euthanasia)

Nowell-Smith, P. (1989, Sept.) Euthanasia and the doctors -- a rejection of the BMA's report. *Journal of Medical Ethics, 15*, 124-128.

(Euthanasia)

A civil lawyer's first criminal case: One lawyer's transition (S. Rosenblatt and the Rosier euthanasia case). (1989, August) *Trial, 25*, pp. 22-26.

(Drug Statute)

Osran, T.N. (1989, Summer) Illinois drug-induced homicide statute: A tough state just got tougher. *Northern Illinois University Law Review, 9*, 537-574.

(Homicide Laws)

Eryl, D., & Yale, C. (1989, July) A year and a day in homicide (Great Britain). *Cambridge*

Law Journal, 48, 202-213.

('Thin Blue Line' Case)

Prendergast, A. (1989, April) The "thin blue line". *World Journalism Review, 11*, 18-22.

(Workplace Liability)

Bros, C.L. (1989, Spring) Afresh assault on the hazardous workplace: Corporate homicide liability for workplace fatalities in Minnesota. *William Mitchell Law Review*, 287-326.

(Joel Steinberg)

Gross, K. (1989, March 6) Denying his guilt, Joel Steinberg tells how he cared for the child he killed and the lover he beat. *People Weekly, 31*(10), pp. 71-77.

(Euthanasia)

Campbell, C.S. & Crigger, B.J., (Ed). (1989, Jan.-Feb.) Mercy, murder, and mortality: perspectives on euthanasia; special supplement. *Hastings Cent Rep, 19*(32).

(Moral Dilemma)

Cole, J.J. (1989) Moral dilemma: To kill or allow to die? *Death Studies, 13*(4), 393-406.

(Euthanasia)

Aartsen, J.G.M., et al. (1989) Mercy, murder, and morality: Letter. *Hast Cent R, 19*(6), 47-48.

(Colonial Africa)

Rathbone, R. (1989) A murder in the colonial Gold Coast: Law and politics in the 40's. *Journal of African History, 30*(3), 445-461.

(Criminal Injustice)

Mitchell, B. (1989) Homicide and criminal injustice. *New Law Journal*, 1450.

(Homicide - Appeals)

Appeals court overturns sentence in reporter's murder. (1988, Dec. 31) *Editor & Publisher, 121*(53), p. 9.

(Juries)

Jacoby, T. & Emerson, T. (1988, Dec. 5) Are juries colorblind? *Newsweek, 112*(23), p. 94.

(Extradition)

Howse, J. (1988, Oct. 31) The Charles Ng case. *Macleans, 101*(45), p. 57.

(New Trial)

Curriden, M. (1988, Oct. 1) The trial of an all-American. *ABA Journal, 74*, 84-88.

(Court Rulings)

Trends in the law: A death in the family. (1988) *ABA Journal, 74*, 92.

(Delayed Sentencing)

Defense to appeal shield law ruling. (1988, Aug. 20) *Editor & Publisher, 121*(34), 23.

(Acquittal)

Harrison, B.G. (1988, Aug.) Why Robert Chambers got away with murder. *Mademoiselle, 94*(8), p. 134.

(FBI)

Yost, S. (1988, Aug.) Nebraska skullduggery and the origin of the FBI. *American West, 25*(8), 58-62.

(Asylum)

Macrides, R.J. (1988, July) Killing, asylum, and the law in Byzantium. *Speculum, 63*, 509-538.

(Euthanasia)

Jonson, E.P. (1988) Euthanasia: Is it murder? *Australian Journal of Forensic Science, 21*(1), 26-33.

(Blame)

Gudjonsson, G.H., & Singh, K.K. (1988) Attribution of blame for criminal acts and its relationship with type of offense. *Medicine, Science, and Law, 28*(4), 301-303.

(Child Custody)

Mass, P. (1987, Oct.) The child custody murder (battle for P.A. Taylor). *Good Housekeeping, 205*, 154-155+.

(Escaping Blame)

Darrach, B. (1987, Feb. 16) Could they get away with murder? (E. Woodward and A. Woodward) *People Weekly, 27*, pp. 52-54+.

(Lynching)

Winn, B. (1987, Fall-Winter) Lynching on Wynn's hill. *Southern Exposition, 15*, pp. 17-24.

(Dying Declaration)

Wiecking, D.K. (1987) The dying declaration. *Medical Legal Bulletin, 36*(4), 1-6.

(Law Codes)

Henderson, R. (1987) Codification of the law of homicide. *Medical Science and Law, 27*(4), 229-240.

(Sentencing)

Thomas, D.A. (1986, Oct.) Case and comment: Sentencing. *The Criminal Law Review*, 3-4. Microforms and article copies available from UMI.

(Conviction Upheld)

Murder conviction affirmed due to consensual entry on arrest -- IL. (1986, Oct.) *Search and Seizure Bulletin*, 3-4. Microforms and article copies available from UMI.

(Police Liability)

No liability for murder after police left scene. (1986, July) *AELE Liability Reporter 1986*, 163, 11. Article copies available from UMI.

(Manslaughter)

Knapman, L. & Smith, J.C. (1986, July) Case and comment: Manslaughter. *The Criminal Law Review*, 468-470.

(Evidence)

Knapman, L., et al. (1986, June) Case and comment: Evidence. *The Criminal Law Review*, 394-397.

(Ethics)

Griew, E. (1986, March) Reducing murder to manslaughter: Whose job? *Journal of Medical Ethics, 12*(1), 18-23.

(Corporations)

Maakstad, W.J. (1986, Winter) States' attorneys stalk corporate murderers: Can corporations commit murder? *Business and Society Review*, 21-25.

(Medical Limits)

The limits of medical care (letter). (1986, Jan. 9) *New England Journal of Medicine, 314*(2), 120-121.

(Mandatory Sentencing)

Dell, S. (1986) The mandatory sentence and section 2. *Journal of Medical Ethics, 12*(1), 28-31.

(Defenses)

Homicide -- defenses -- prayer. (1986) *The Criminal Law Reporter: Court Decisions, 39*(13), 2240.

(Sentencing Accomplices)

Ruling on sentencing accomplices. (1986) *Corrections Digest, 17*(3), 4-5.

(Homicide and Assault)

Crimes/offenses: Homicide -- assault. (1986) *Criminal Law Monthly, 5*(10), 8. Article copies available from UMI.

(Courts and Press)

Kene, P.E. (1986) *Murder, courts, and the press: Issues in free press/fair trial.* With a forward by Franklin S. Haiman. Southern Illinois University Press.

(Plea Bargaining)

Pritchard, D. (1986) Homicide and bargained justice: The agenda-setting effect of crime news on prosecutors. *Public Opinion Quarterly, 50*(2), 143-159.

(Intent)

Homicide -- poisoning -- intent. (1986) *The Criminal Law Reporter: Court Decisions, 39*(17), 2324.

(Evidence)

Rao, V.J. (1986) Patterned injury and its evidentiary value. *Journal of Forensic Sciences, 31*(2), 768-772.

(Felony Murder)

Homicide - felony-murder - possession of weapon. (1986) *The Criminal Law Reporter: Court Decisions, 38*(14), 2273.

(Premeditation)

Homicide - premeditation - inference from manual strangulation. (1986) *The Criminal Law Reporter: Court Decisions, 39*(10), 2175.

(Sentencing)

How many years does a murder conviction bring behind bars? Less than seven, BJS finds. (1986) *Corrections Digest, 17*(8), 7-8. Article copies available from UMI.

(Sentencing)

Judge gives probation to man, 85, who killed neighbor, while officials sought imprisonment. (1986) *Corrections Digest, 17*(14), 7-8. Article copies available from UMI.

(Legal Decisions)

Legal decisions: Homicide. (1986) *Inside Drug Laws, 3*(3), 15.

(Court Decisions)

Jury instructions -- lesser included offenses -- fundamental error. (1986) *The Criminal Law Reporter: Court Decisions, 39*(20), 2378.

(Lesser Offenses)

Homicide -- lesser included offenses. (1986) *The Criminal Law Reporter: Court Decisions, 32*(18), 2387.

(Guilty Pleas)

Guilty pleas -- voluntariness -- notice of elements of offenses. (1986) *The Criminal Law Reporter: Court Decisions, 38*(20), 2384.

(Assault)

Homicide -- assault. (1986) *The Criminal Law Monthly, 6*(2-3), 16-17.

(Evidence - Value)

Rao, V.J. (1986) Patterned injury and its evidentiary value. *Journal of Forensic Sciences, 31*(2), 768-772.

(Corporate Liability)

Spiegel, D.R. (1985, Nov.) The liability of corporate officers. *American Bar Association Journal, 71*, 48, 50.

(Ethics)

Hamilton, J.R. (1985) Murder into manslaughter: Letter. *Journal of Medical Ethics, 11*(3), 160.

(Assault)

Crimes/Offenses: Homicide -- assault. (1985) *Criminal Law Monthly, 5*(6), 14.

(Conviction Upheld)

Man's conviction upheld in fight/murder death. (1985) *Crime Control Digest, 19*(49), 9. Article copies available from UMI.

(Homicide - Prosecution)

Radelet, M.L., & Pierce, G.L. (1985) Race and prosecutorial discretion in homicide cases. *Law and Society Review, 19*(4), 587-621.

(Euthanasia)

Weinfeld, J. (1985) Active voluntary euthanasia- should it be legalized? *Medicine and Law, 4*(2), 101-111.

(Euthanasia)

Lusthaaus, E.W. (1985) Involuntary euthanasia and current attempts to define persons with mental retardation as less than human. *Mental Retardation, 23*(3), 148-154.

(Mock Juries)

Osborne, Y.H., & Rappaport, N.B. (1985) Sentencing severity with mock jurors: Predictive validity of three variable categories. *Behavioral Science and the Law, 3*(4), 467-473.

(Military Justice)

Dunlap, C.J., Jr. (1985) Military justice system and command accountability. *Military Review, 65*(2), 45-53.

(Euthanasia)

Pohlmeier, H. (1985) Suicide and euthanasia- special types of partner relationships. *Suicide and Life Threatening Behavior, 15*(2), 117-123.

(Patient Care)

Dresser, R.S., & Boisaubin, E.V., Jr. (1985) Ethics, law, and nutritional support. *Archives of Internal Medicine, 145*(1), 122-124.

(Euthanasia)

Siegler, M., & Weisbard, A.J. (1985) Against the emerging stream: Should fluids and nutritional support be discontinued? *Archives of Internal Medicine, 145*(1), 129-131.

(Right to Die)

Uzych, L. (1985) Right to die developments in the United States. *Medicine and Law, 4*(4), 347-350.

(Manslaughter)

Syrota, G. (1984, Aug.) Manslaughter -- The impact of Caldwell. *The Criminal Law Review*, 476-479.

(Sentencing)

Thomas, D.A. (1984, July) Case and comment: Sentence. *The Criminal Law Review*, 431-440.

(Infanticide)

O'Donovan, K. (1984, May) The medicalization of infanticide. *The Criminal Law Review*, 259-264.

(Sentencing)

Thomas, D.A. (1984, April) Case and comment: Sentence. *The Criminal Law Review*, 242-249.

(Common Law)

Hall, J.C. (1984) Deadly force: The common law and the Constitution. *FBI Law Enforcement Bulletin, 53*(4), 26-31.

(Expert Testimony)

Ruth-Behr, B. (1984) Judgment criteria of adolescent psychiatrists giving expert testimony in homicide cases (German). *Zeitschrift fur Kinder- und Jugendpsychiatrie, 12*(2), 144-160.

(Police Liability)

City not liable for off-duty officer's shooting over daughter's alleged involvement. (1984) *AELE Liability Reporter 1984. 141*, 12.

(Manslaughter - Drugs)

UCMJ -- Involuntary manslaughter -- drug overdose. (1984) *The Criminal Law Reporter, 35*(21), 2388-2389.

(Victimization - Racial)

Gross, S.R., & Mauro, R. (1984) Patterns of death: An analysis of racial disparities in capital sentencing and homicide victimization. *Stanford Law Review, 37*(11), 27-153.

(Racial Discrimination)

Paternoster, R. (1984) Prosecutorial discretion in requesting the death penalty: A case of victim-based racial discrimination based on the study of 300 homicides in South Carolina. *Law and Society Review, 18*(3), 437-478.

(Common Law)

Hall, J.C. (1984) Deadly force: The common law and the Constitution. *FBI Law Enforcement Bulletin, 53*(4), 26-31.

(Bite-Mark Evidence)

Karazulas, C.P. (1984) The presentation of bite-mark evidence resulting in the acquittal of a man after serving seven years in prison for murder. *Journal of Forensic Science, 29*(1), 355-358.

(Negligent Manslaughter)

Mens Rea in gross negligent manslaughter. (1983, Dec.) *The Criminal Law Review*, 776-786.

(Manslaughter)

Briggs, A. (1983, Dec.) In defense of manslaughter. *The Criminal Law Review*, 549-550.

(Legislation - Self-Defense)

O'Brien, N.C. (1983, Sept.) Excessive self-defense: A need for legislation. *The Criminal Law Quarterly, 25*(4), 441-457.

(Sentencing)

Thomas, D.A. (1983, June) Case and comment. *The Criminal Law Review*, 406-411.

(Self-Defense)

Case for liberalizing the use of deadly force in self-defense. (1983, Spring) *University of Puget Sound Law Review, 6*, 237-284.

(Homicide Laws - Virginia)

Should Virginia put the planning back into the premeditation required for murder? (1983, Winter) *Washington & Lee Law Review, 40*, 341-359.

(Defense Tactics)

Wilson, T.W. (1983) Defense tactics under the new death penalty sentencing procedure. *Advocate, 15*(6), 300-324.

(Certification)

Certification -- Illinois. (1983) *Juvenile & Family Law Digest, 15*(3), 108-109.

(Forensics)

Tiberti, S., & De Stefano, M.G. (1983) Forensic aspects of homicide (Italian). *Riv Tossicol Sper Clin, 13*(1-6), 119-127.

(Homicide - Great Britain)

Dell, S. (1982, Dec.) Homicide Act, 1957 (Great Britain): Diminished responsibility reconsidered. *The Criminal Law Review*, 809-818.

(Felony Murder)

Common-law felony murder doctrine judicially abolished in Michigan: People vs. Aaron, 299 N

W 2d 304. (1982, Fall) *Washington University Law Quarterly, 60,* 1197-1211.

(Homicide Law - West Germany)

Monson, R.A. (1982, Fall) West German statute of limitations on murder: A political, legal, and historical exposition. *American Journal of Comparative Law, 30,* 605-625.

(Capital Punishment)

Koenig, D.M. (1982, Summer) Capital punishment and crimes of murder. *Loyola (Chicago) Law Journal, 13,* 817-840.

(Sentencing)

Thomas, D.A. (1982, April) Case and comment: Sentence. *The Criminal Law Review,* 245-246.

(Homicide Law - Islamic)

Homicide (Islamic law): If it were an Islamic court. (1982, Feb.) *Economist, 282,* p. 62.

(Death Penalty)

Wickert, J.H. (1982, Winter) Death penalty and vicarious felony murder: Non-trigger man may not be executed absent a finding of intent to kill. *Journal of Criminal Law & Criminology, 73,* 1553-1571.

(Sentencing)

Hackler, J., et al. (1982) A comparison of sentencing strategies for violent crime in Columbus, Ohio and Edmonton, Alberta. *Canadian Journal of Criminology, 24*(2), 173-190.

(Prior Testimony)

Prior testimony becomes admissible after defendant murders witness. (1982) *The Criminal Law Reporter: Court Decisions and Proceeding, 30*(19), 2373-2375.

(Felony Murder - Michigan)

Michigan Supreme Court uproots the felony murder rule. (1981, Fall) *UMKC Law Review, 50,* 112-127.

(Corporate Liability)

Hickey, J.M. (1981, Spring) Corporate criminal liability for homicide: The controversy flames anew. *California Western Law Review, 17,* 465-492.

(Sentencing)

Thomas, D.A. (1981, Feb.) Case and comment: Sentencing. *The Criminal Law Review,* 119; (1981, March), 187-194.

(Manslaughter Law)

Manslaughter law may be applied to killing by use of trap gun. (1981) *The Criminal Law Reporter: Court Decisions and Proceedings, 30*(6), 2120-2122.

(Murder Trial - Primitive)

Wasserman, K.T. (1981) Case study of an intriguing "primitive" murder trial: Financial settlement between the murderer and the victim's family. *Bulletin of the American Academy of Psychiatry & the Law, 9*(4), 275-284.

(Felony Murder)

Felony murder - death of a participant in a felony. (1981) *The Criminal Law Reporter: Court Decisions and Proceedings, 29*(21), 2459.

(Death Penalty)

Constitutionality of the mandatory death penalty for life-term prisoners who murder. (1980, Oct.) *NYU Law Review, 55*, 636-670.

(Jury Instructions)

Murphy, A.A. (1980, Fall) Suggested standard jury instructions on criminal murder. *Dick Law Review, 85*, 1-19.

(Zimbabwe - Arrest)

Sanction, T.A., & Hawthorne, P. (1980, Aug. 18) First test (arrest of Minister of Manpower E. Tekere for murder of white farm manager in Zimbabwe). *Time, 116*, pp. 30-31.

(Control of Military)

Greer, D.S. (1980, Summer) Legal control of military operations- a missed opportunity. *Northern Ireland Law Quarterly, 31*, 151-159.

(Modern Problems)

Stone, F.F. (1980, June) Modern problems in ancient dress. *Tulane Law Review, 54*, 812-829.

(Trial - Idi Amin)

Wood, W.P. (1980, May 14) Trial of Idi Amin (widening jurisdiction of Genocide Convention to include mass murder). *Christian Century, 97*, 549-552.

(Homicide - Corporate)

Swigert, V.L., & Farrell, R.A. (1980-81) Corporate homicide: Definitional processes in the creation of defiance. *Law and Sociology Review, 15*, 161-182.

(Life for Death)

Mewshaw, M. (1980) *Life for death.* New York: Doubleday.

(Sentencing)

Decisions on sentencing: Offenses against the person. (1980) *The Criminal Law Quarterly, 23*(1), 34-37.

(Spousal Homicide)

Bonnie, R.J., et al. (1980) The spousal homicide syndrome: Legal implications. *Bulletin of the American Academy of Psychiatry and Law, 8*(4), 431-444.

(Murder - Historical)

Higginbotham, D., & Price, W.S., Jr. (1979, Oct.) Was it murder for a white man to kill a slave? Chief Justice Martin Howard condemns the peculiar institution in North Carolina (with text of address). *William & Mary Quarterly, 36*, 593-601.

(Murderers' Rights)

Barring slayers' acquisition of property rights in Virginia: A proposed statute. (1979, Fall) *University of Richmond Law Review, 14*, 251-277.

(Right to Live)

Fletcher, G.P. (1979, Summer) Right to life. *Georgia Law Review, 13*, 1371-1394.

(Guilt and Responsibility)

Hepworth, M., et al. (1979, Winter) Confession, guilt, and responsibility. *British Journal of Law and Sociology, 6*, 219-234.

(Homicide - Southern Attitudes)

Brown, R.M. (1979, Jan.) Southern violence- regional problem or national nemesis? Legal attitudes toward southern homicide in historical perspective (comment by D.R. Nolan). *Vanderbilt Law Review, 32*, 225-259.

(Test Faking)

Hinton, J.W., et al. (1979) Test faking relating to a hormonal index of murderous propensity. *International Journal of Offender Therapy, 23*(3), 257-261.

(New Selections)

Nash, J.R. (1979) Cons, killing, and kidnap featured in new selections. *Law Enforcement News, 5*(10), 11.

(Literature Review)

Simpson, A.E. (Ed.) (1979) The literature of criminal justice: The violent offender. *Law Enforcement News, 5*(9), S24-S25.

(Homicide - Defendants)

Ending 'heroic' medical measures didn't absolve defendants of murder. (1979) *The Criminal Law Reporter: Court Decisions and Proceedings, 25*(25), 2546-2548.

(Corporate Homicide)

Corporate homicide: A new assault on corporate decision making. (1979) *Notre Dame Law Review, 54*, 911-924.

(Felony Murder)

MacKinnon, P. (1979) Path of felony murder: Joyce vs. The Queen (1978) 42 C C C 2d, 141 in the British Columbia Court of Appeal. *Ottawa Law Review, 11*, 509-517.

(Court Decisions)

Barnet, B.S. (1979) Stereotypes and dispositions for criminal homicide. *Criminology, 17*(2), 139-158.

(Case Report - Sid Vicious)

Segell, M. (1978, Dec. 14) F. Lee Bailey to defend Sid Vicious. *Rolling Stone*, p. 15.

(Death Penalty - South Carolina)

King, D.R. (1978, Dec.) Brutalization effect: Execution publicity and the incidence of homicide in South Carolina. *Social Forces, 57*, 683-687.

(Direct Evidence)

Jury instructions - reasonable doubt - "don't need to know" instruction is not reversible error when conviction is based on direct evidence. (1978, Dec.) *Mississippi Law Journal, 49*, 985-993.

(Legal Disposition)

Farrell, R.A., & Swigert, V.L. (1978, Autumn) Legal disposition of inter-group and intra-group homicides. *Sociology Quarterly, 19*, 565-576.

(Murder Under Duress)

Cross, R. (1978, Fall) Murder under duress. *University of Toronto Law Journal, 28*, 369-380.

(Attempted Murder)

Attempt: Murder. (1978, June) *IACP Law Enforcement Legal Review, 72*, 10.

(Military Clashes)

Lynch, A.C.E. (1978, May) British subjects' involvement in foreign military clashes. *The Criminal Law Review 1978*, 257-268.

(Prior Record)

Farrell, R.A., & Swigert, V.L. (1978, Spring) Prior offense record as a self-fulfilling prophecy. *Law and Society Review, 12*, 437-453.

(Books for Lawyers)

Dolan, M.M. (1978, Jan.) Books for lawyers. *American Bar Association Journal, 64*, 96.

(Homicide - Accomplice)

Liability of an aider and abetter for aggravated murder in Ohio. (1978) *Ohio State Law Journal, 39*, 214-237.

(Accessory)

Murder - solicitation - accessory - principal. (1978) *The Criminal Law Reporter: Court Decisions and Proceedings, 23*(2), 2046.

(Jury Instructions)

Jury instructions- lesser included offenses - statute of limitations. (1978) *The Criminal Law Reporter: Court Decisions and Proceedings, 23*(22), 2499.

(Poisoning)

Leinzinger, E.P., et al. (1978) Medicolegal aspects of poisoning (German with English summary). *Arch Toxicol, 39*(3), 199-209.

(Burden of Proof)

Burden of proving affirmative can be placed on defendant. (1978) *Mercer Law Review, 29*, 875-883.

(Jury Instructions)

Supreme Court: Homicide - omission of an instruction on causation. (1977, Oct.) *IACP Law Enforcement Legal Review, 64*, 14.

(Felony Murder - Accomplice)

Burns, P., & Reid, R.S. (1977, March) From felony murder to accomplice felony attempted murder: The rake's progress complete? *Canadian Bar Review, 55*, 75-105.

(Criminal Law Revisions)

Elliot, D.W. (1977, Feb.) Offenses against the person: The criminal law revision committee's working paper. *Criminal Law Review 1977*, 70-78.

(Running Amok)

Schmidt, K., et al. (1977, Winter) Running amok. *International Journal of Social Psychiatry, 23*(4), 264-274.

(Defensive Theory)

Refuting the defensive theory with prior acts of misconduct. (1977, Winter) *Baylor Law Review, 29*, 163-171.

(Survival and Law)

Webster, M.H. (1977) Machine-assisted survival and the law. *Rho Cent Afr J Med, 23*(12), 275-284.

(Life Insurance)

Disposition of life insurance proceeds when owner-beneficiary murders the insured. (1977) *Maine Law Review, 29*, 126-148.

(Death Penalty)

Jurek execution postponed by Supreme Court decision. (1977) *Corrections Digest, 8*(2), 4. Article copies available from UMI.

(State of Mind)

Relative relevance - a limitation on the use of state-of-mind testimony in homicide prosecutions. (1977) *Utah Law Review 1977*, 85-102.

(Book Reviews)

Book reviews. (1977) *Police Journal, 50*(3), 299-300.

(Right to Life)

Hostler, J. (1977) The right to life. *Journal of Medical Ethics, 3*(3), 143-145.

(Penalty of Death)

Jayewardene, C.H. (1977) Penalty of death. Lexington Books.

(Crime Report)

1976 crime report released. (1977) *Crime Control Digest, 11*(39), 6. Article copies available from UMI.

(Homicide - Case Report)

Is a house a castle? (1976, Fall) *Connecticut Law Review, 9*, 110-135.

(Workplace Homicide)

If an employee is murdered while at work can his widow collect death benefits? (1976, Sept.) *Protection Management, 2138*, 2-3.

(Reprieve - Florida)

Holiday for homicide: Florida's reprieve for killers of Cammarata. (1976, May 31) *Time, 107*, p. 46.

(Legal Right to Die)

Steele, W.W., Jr. (1976, March-April) Legislative proposal for a legal right to die. *Criminal Law Bulletin, 12*, 140-164.

(Murderer's Estate)

Descendent's estates - forfeitures of property rights by slayers. (1976) *Wake Forest Law Review, 12*, 448-465.

(Murder Trial)

Humphries, S.V. (1976) Murder trial in the outback. *Central Africa Journal of Medicine, 22*(6), 123-124.

(Guns)

Dyer, D.L. (1976) Guns, crime, and the law: A case for the defense. First of a three part series. *Law Enforce Journal, 6*(8), 6-7.

(Homicide Book)

Connery, D. (1976) *Guilty until proven innocent*. New York: Putnam.

(Duty to Warn)

Annas, G.J. (1976) Confidentiality and the duty to warn. *Hastings Cent Rep, 6*(6), 6-8.

(Police News)

Police news. (1976) *Law Enforcement Journal, 6*(6), 18; *Law Enforcement Journal, 6*(2), 19.

(Literature Review)

Professional literature. (1976) *Corrections Digest, 7*(12), 4-5.

(Witnesses - Youths)

Youngsters witness murder, after-effects dramatic. (1976) *Juvenile Justice Digest, 4*(10), 3.

(Fright Death - Indictment)

Youth indicted for murder after man dies of fright. (1976) *Juvenile Justice Digest, 4*(17), 5.

(Homicidal Behavior)

Mecir, J. (1976) Homicidal behavior of persons older than nineteen years. *Ceskoslovenska Psychiatrie, 72*(6), 374-383.

(Forensic Psychiatry)

Henn, F.A., et al. (1976) Forensic psychiatry: Diagnosis and criminal responsibility. *J Nerv Ment Dis, 162* (6), 423-429.

(Homicide - France)

LeTourneau, G. (1976) Le projet de loi C-407 et la possibilite d'eliminer les offenses substantives de meurtre et d'homicide involuntaire coupable. *C de D, 17*, 493-502.

(Verdicts - England and Wales)

Scott, I.R. (1975, Autumn) Verdicts in murder cases in England and Wales. *Northern Ireland Law Quarterly, 26*, 153-176.

(Jurisprudential Dialogue)

D'Amato, A. (1975, June) Elmer's rule: A jurisprudential dialogue. *Iowa Law Review, 60*, 1129-1146.

(Supreme Court)

Dobbs, G.B. (1975, Spring) Murder in the Supreme Court: Appeals from the hanging judge. *Arkansas Law Review, 29*, 47-70.

(Fatal Acts)

Felon's responsibility for the fatal acts of a non-felon. (1975) *Chicago-Kent Law Review, 52*, 184-195

(Police News)

Miskin, B.D. (1975) Police news. *Law Enforcement Journal, 5*(11), 19.

(Simulated Jurors' Judgments)

Hendrick, C., & Shaffer, D.R. (1975) Murder: Effects of number of killers and victim mutilization on simulated jurors' judgments. *Bull Psychonomic Soc, 6*(3), 313-316.

(Court Decisions)

News briefs. (1975) *The Criminal Law Reporter: Court Decisions & Proceedings, 17*(14), 2284.

(Fatal Trauma)

Eckert, W.G. (1974) Fatal trauma: Medical-legal aspects. *Journal of Kansas Medical Society, 75*(12), 366-369.

(Law Enforcement - Politics)

Bent, A.E. (1974) *The politics of law enforcement.* Lexington, MA: D.C. Heath.

(Police Illegalities)

Takagi, P.A. (1974) A garrison state in 'democratic' society. *Crime Soc Justice, 1*, 27-33.

(Prosecutor Defense)

Adelson, Lester. (1974) *The Pathology of murder.* C.C. Thomas.

(Legal Sanctions)

Boydell, C.L., & Grindstaff, C.F. (1974) Public opinion towards legal sanctions for crimes of violence. *Journal of Criminal Law and Criminology, 65*(1), 113-116.

(Death Penalty)

Glaser, D., & Zeigler, M.S. (1974, Oct.) Use of the death penalty versus outrage at murder. *Crime and Delinquency, 20*, 333-338.

(Manslaughter)

Westling, W.T. (1974, Summer) Manslaughter by unlawful act: The "constructive" crime which serves no constructive purpose. *Sydney Law Review, 7*, 211-223.

(Property Acquisition)

Youdan, T.D. (1973, April) Acquisition of property by killing. *Law Quarterly Review, 89*, 235-259.

(Criminal Attitudes)

Homans, S.S. (1973) Charged with murder: Six men discuss their attitudes towards trial. *Massachusetts Journal of Mental Health, 3*(4), 4-32.

(Two Trials)

Skelhorn, N. (1973) Two unconnected trials for one murder. (1973) *Medical Legal Journal, 41*, 102-113.

(Medicolegal Systems)

Schneider, V. (1973) Current medicolegal systems in the United States. *J Leg Med, 73*(4), 313-

320.

(Homicide - Lawyer's Look)

Latimer, H.R. (1972, Jan.) Murder: A lawyer's look. *Journal of the Canadian Bar Association, 3*, 4.

(Simulated Jurors)

Vidmar, N. (1972) Effects of decision alternatives on the verdicts and social perceptions of simulated jurors. *J Personal Soc Psychol, 22*(2), 211-218.

(Criminal Liability)

Strict vicarious criminal liability for the acts of a victim. (1972) *Capital University Law Review, 1*, 232-246.

(Preliminary Hearings)

Theis, W.H. (1971, March) Preliminary hearings in homicide cases: A hearing delayed is a hearing denied. *Journal of Criminal Law, 62*, 17.

(Murder Trial - Lessons)

Jagusch, H. (1971) Lehren eines mordprozesses (Vera Bruhne). 25159. J. 24: 2198-2206, '71. (IBZ 1973).

(Medicolegal Aspects - Norway)

Giertsen, J.C. (1970, Oct.) Forensic pathology in Norway, 1960-1964: Medicolegally examined homicides (Norwegian). *Tidsskr Nor Laegeforen, 90*, 1862-1863.

(Gun Battle - San Rafael)

Professor's guns: Gun battle at Marin County courthouse, San Rafael, CA. (1970, Aug. 24) *Time, 96*, p. 13.

(Yablonski Case)

McGinniss, J. (1970, Jan. 23) Yablonski murders: A challenge to leadership among mine workers. *Life, 63*, pp. 36-37.

("Italian Divorce")

'Italian divorce' is on the way out. (1970) *Law Enforcement Journal, 8*(4), 9.

(Poverty)

McGovern, W.M. , Jr. (1969, Nov.) Homicide and the succession to poverty. *Michigan Law Review, 68*, 65.

(King's Pardon)

Hurnard, N.D. (1969) *King's pardon for homicide before A.D. 1307.* London: Oxford U. Press.

(A-9 Murder - Case Report)

Whittet, M.M. (1968, June) Medicolegal considerations of the A-9 murder. *British Journal of*

Medical Psychology, 41, 125-138.

(Murder Trial)

Judd, J. (1968) *Dawn of doubt: The Jack Kirschke murder trial.* Brandon.

(Poisoning - Medicolegal Aspects)

Ueberschlag, H., et al. (1966, Jan.-Feb.) Medicolegal aspects of a case of disulfiram poisoning. *Ann Med Leg* (Paris), *46*, 45-47.

(Felony Murder)

Felony murder - happy hunting ground of prosecutors. (1966, Winter) *University of Miami Law Review, 21*, 457.

(Criminal Responsibility)

Criminal responsibility for death of a co-felon. (1965, May) *Hastings Law Journal, 16*, 620.

(Life Policies)

Wickens, P.C. (1965, March) Life policies and homicide. *Australian Law Journal, 38*, 363.

(Witch Murder)

Seidman, R.B. (1965, Jan.) Witch murder and mens rea: A problem of society under radical social change. *Modern Law Review, 28*, 46.

(Justice Pursuit)

McGilvary, J.D. (1965) *Pursuit of justice*. Tri-Ocean.

(Murder Trial)

Prozesse - Mord: Maus und mann (German). (1964) 33077. J. 18: 69-71 '64. (IBZ 1965).

(Murder Trial - Witnesses)

Rosenthal, A.M. (1964) *Thirty-eight witnesses.* New York: McGraw.

(Felony-Murder Doctrine)

James, P.A. (1963, Fall) Felony-murder doctrine. *Criminal Law Quarterly, 1*, 33.

(Property Rights)

Scott, M.F.C. (1963, Summer) Effect of homicide on property rights. *Tasmanian U L Rev, 1*, 817.

(Unlawful Act)

Bingham, E.M. (1962, Nov.) Homicide by any unlawful act. *Tasmanian U L Rev, 1*, 670.

(Homicide - Marital)

Cormier, B.M. (1962) Psychodynamics of homicide committed in a marital relationship. *Correct Psychiat J Soc Ther, 8*(4), 187-194.

(Sentencing - Racial Factors)

Bullock, H.A. (1961, Nov.-Dec.) Significance of the racial factor in the length of prison sentences. *Journal of Criminal Law, 52*, 411.

(Psychiatry and Law)

Wiseman, F. (1961, Oct.) Psychiatry and law: Use and abuse of psychiatry in a murder case. *American Journal of Psychiatry, 118*, 289-299.

(Capital Punishment - Review)

Gold, L.H. (1961, Oct.) Psychiatric review of capital punishment. *Journal of Forensic Sciences, 6*, 465.

(Death Penalty - Perspectives)

McCafferty, J.A. (1961, Oct.) Death sentence and then what? *Crime & Delinquency, 7*, 363.

(Criminal Responsibility)

Puxon, M. (1961, Oct.) Collective responsibility for violence. *Sol J, 105*, 844.

(Death Penalty)

Murdy, R.G. (1961, Sept.) Moderate view of capital punishment. *Federal Probation, 25*, 11.

(Voluntary Manslaughter)

Insurance: Effect of probate code section 258: Participation in proceeds by beneficiary convicted of voluntary manslaughter (Davis v. Aetna Life Ins. Co. 279 F 2d. 304). (1961, Aug.) *California Law Review, 49*, 571.

(Death Sentence)

King, R. (1961, July) Some reflections on do-it-yourself capital punishment. *American Bar Association Journal, 47*, 668.

(Multiple Offender)

Remington, F.J. (1961, July) Charging, convicting, and sentencing the multiple criminal offender. *Wisconsin Law Review 1961*, 528.

(Fair Trial)

Oberer, W.E. (1961, May) Does disqualifications of jurors for scruples against capital punishment constitute denial of fair trial on issue of guilt? *Texas Law Review, 39*, 545.

(Jury Verdict)

Jurors and the sanctity of their verdicts. (1961, April) *West Virginia Law Review, 63*, 261.

(Death Penalty)

Gottlieb, G.H. (1961, Spring) Testing the death penalty. *Southern California Law Review, 34*, 268.

(Anti-Crime Bill)

Murray, J.W. (1961, March 11) Criminal justice bill in committee. *Justice of the Peace, 125*, 143.

(Sentencing - California)

Sentencing criminals in California - a study in haphazard legislation. (1961, March) *Stanford Law Review, 13*, 340.

("Reasonable Man" Doctrine)

Howard, C. (1961, Jan.) What color is the "reasonable man"? *Criminal Law Review 1961*, 41.

(Corpus Delicti - Alabama)

Proof of corpus delicti in Alabama. (1960, Fall) *Alabama Law Review, 13*, 147.

(Murder - Degrees)

Capital murder or manslaughter? (1960, June) *Legal Times, 229*, 323.

(After the Fact)

Burchell, E.M. (1960, May) Murder: The accused joining in after the fatal injury inflicted. *S A L J, 77*, 140.

(Felony-Murder - New York)

New York's felony-murder held limited to killing by actual perpetrators of felony (People v. Wood, 186 N Y S 2d. 141). (1959, Fall) *Syracuse Law Review, 11*, 102.

(Murder and Robbery)

Capital murder and robbery. (1959, April) *Sol J, 103*, p. 277.

(Infanticide)

Adelson, L. (1959, Jan.) Some medicolegal observations in infanticide. *Journal of Forensic Science, 4*, 60.

(Trial - Preparation)

Strauss, S. (1958, Oct.) Prosecutor prepares for a murder trial. *Pennsylvania Bar Association Quarterly, 30*, 61.

(Murder - Degrees)

Snelling, H.A. (1958, Summer) Alternative verdict of manslaughter. *Australian Law Journal, 32*, 137.

(Felony-Murder)

In general - defendant not guilty of felony-murder for death of co-felon justifiably shot by policeman (Commonwealth v. Redline (PA) 137 A 2d. 472). (1958, June) *Harvard Law Review, 71*, 1565.

(Offense - Murder)

Hartt, E.P. (1958, May-Aug.) Parties to the offense of murder. *Criminal Law Quarterly, 1*, 60, 178.

(Reasonable Man)

Lowe, J.T. (1958, May-June) Murder and the reasonable man. *The Criminal Law Review 1958*, 289, 374.

(Malice)

Turner, J.W.C. (1958, Jan.) Malice implied and constructive. *The Criminal Law Review 1958*, 15.

(Felony-Murder Doctrine)

Critical analysis of the felony-murder doctrine. (1957-1958) *Rev Jur U P R, 27*, 383.

(Murder Prosecutions)

Erisman, F., & Woodley, K.K. (1957, Dec.) Included offenses: Murder prosecutions in general. *Texas Bar Journal, 20*, 686.

(Implied Malice)

Murder and implied malice. (1957, Dec.) *Law Journal, 107*, 807.

(Homicide and Abortion)

Homicide and abortion in England and Ireland. (1957, Oct.-Dec.) *Journal of Criminal Law, 21*, 362.

(Manslaughter)

Snelling, H.A. (1957, July) Manslaughter upon chance-medley. *Australian Law Journal, 31*, 102.

(Provocation)

Wolfgang, M.E. (1957, May-June) Victim-precipitated criminal homicide. *Journal of Criminal Law, 48*, 1.

(Constructive Manslaughter)

Williams, G. (1957, May) Constructive Manslaughter. *Criminal Law Review 1957*, 293.

(No Body)

Failure to find the body in cases of homicide. (1957, March-April) *Ir L T, 91*, 85.

(Felony Murder)

Felony murder as a first-degree offense: An anachronism retained. (1957, Jan.) *Yale Law Journal, 66*, 427.

(Murder - Acquittal)

Von Hentig, H. (1957) Problems of acquittal in trials for murder (German). *J C B Mohr, 64*, 3-80.

(Manslaughter)

Snelling, H.A. (1957, Jan.-1956, Dec.) Manslaughter by unlawful act. *Australian Law Journal, 30*, 382.

(Manslaughter)

Misdemeanor manslaughter and its application in New York State. (1956, Dec.) *Brooklyn Law Review, 23*, 102.

(Responsibility)

Morris, N. (1956, Nov.) Felon's responsibility for the lethal acts of others. *University of Pennsylvania Law Review, 105*, 50.

(Homicide - Urban)

Bensing, R.C., et al. (1956, Oct.) Some legal, economic, and social aspects of homicide in an urban area. *Journal of Forensic Science, 1*, 87.

(Felony-Murder)

Ludwig, F.J. (1956, Fall) Foreseeable death in felony-murder. *University of Pittsburgh Law Review, 18*, 51.

(Homicide and Alcohol)

Wolfgang, M.E., & Strohm, R.B. (1956, Sept.) Relationship between alcohol and criminal homicide. *Quarterly Journal of the Study of Alcohol, 17*, 411-425.

(Common Purpose)

Evans, S. (1956, Aug.) Note on common purpose. *S A L J, 73*, 335.

(Mistaken Killing)

Prevezer, S. (1956, June) Murder by mistake. *The Criminal Law Review 1956*, 375.

(Corpus Delicti)

Coaker, J. (1956, May) Corpus delicti: Murder with no trace of a body. *S A L J, 73*, 181.

(Involuntary Manslaughter)

New test for involuntary manslaughter in California (People v. Penny 285 P 2d 926). (1956, May) *Stanford Law Review, 8*, 463.

(Felony Murder)

Felony murder: A new trend. (1956, March) *Kansas Law Review, 4*, 455.

(Highway Murders)

French, S. (1956, Feb.) Magistrates and the murders in Ratcliffe Highway. *The Criminal Law Review 1956*, 90.

(Sleepwalking)

Podolsky, E. Somnambulistic homicide. *Law J, 12*, 57 (1956, Feb.);*Case and Comment, 60*, 28 (1955, Nov.Dec.)

(Felony Murder and Rape)

Statutory rape and the felony murder doctrine. (1956, Jan.) *Dick Law Review, 60*, 178.

(Manslaughter)

Snelling, H.A. (1955, July) Categories of manslaughter in New South Wales. *Australian Law Journal, 29*, 108.

(Manslaughter)

Meyers, A.C., Jr. (1954, Spring) Murder and non-negligent manslaughter: A statistical study. *St. Louis University Law Journal, 3*, 18.

(Murder - Degrees)

Degrees of murder. (1953, Nov.) *Justice P, 117*, 750-751.

(Survivorship Benefits)

Effect on wrongdoer's inheritance intestate and survivorship benefits. (1953, June) *Miami Law Quarterly, 7*, 524-535.

(Felony-Murder Rule)

Crum, C.L. (1952, April) Causal relations and the felony-murder rule. *Washington University Law Quarterly 1952*, 191-210.

(Reversible Error)

Reversible error in murder cases and the Pennsylvania Supreme Court. (1951, April) *University of Pennsylvania Law Review, 99*, 814-826.

(Premeditation)

Premeditation and deliberation - can they occur in an instant? (1951, Spring) *Montana Law Review, 12*, 72-81.

(Infanticide)

Pozzato, R. (1950, Nov.-Dec.) Infanticide by serious knife wound to liver; activity of wounded ; survival. *Minerva Medicoleg, 70*, 165-167.

(Premeditation)

Hitchler, W.H. (1950, Oct.) Willful, deliberate, and premeditated killings. *Pennsylvania Bar Association Quarterly, 22*, 84-89.

(Manslaughter)

Rosenstock, J. (1950, Feb.) Propriety of conviction of manslaughter where evidence shows murder of the second degree or nothing (People v. Powell (CA) 208 Pac. 2d. 974). *Southern California Law Review, 23*, 264-266.

(Murder - Degrees)

Blinn, K.W. (1950) First-degree murder - a workable definition. *Journal of Criminal Law, 40*, 729-735.

(Reversible Error)

Rosenthal, J.M. (1949, Oct.) Reversible error in homicide cases in Massachusetts, 1927-1949. *Massachusetts Law Quarterly, 34*, 45-62.

(Homicide Statutes)

Keedy, E.R. (1949, May) History of the Pennsylvania statute creating degrees of murder. *Pennsylvania Law Review, 97*, 759-777.

(Property Rights)

Young, M.G. (1949, April) Descendants' estates - property rights of slayers - legacies and powers of appointment - Pennsylvania amendatory statute. *Temple Law Quarterly, 22*, 443-445.

(Conflagrations)

Dutra, F.R. (1949, March-April) Medicolegal aspects of conflagrations. *Journal of Criminal Law, 39*, 771-777.

(Murder by Government)

Kempner, R.M.W. (1947, Sept.-Oct.) Murder by government. *Journal of Criminal Law, 38*, 235-238.

(Medicolegal Aspects)

Law of homicide by R.M. Perkins; Forensic Immunology, by W.C. Boyd; Marshalling of proofs in homicide cases, by F.T. Doyle; Postmortem examination in cases of suspected homicide, by M. Helpern. (1946, March) *Journal of Criminal Law, 36*, 391-522.

(Homicide Law)

Perkins, R.M. (1946, March) Law of homicide: Reprint. *Journal of Criminal Law, 36*, 391-454.

(Homicide - Official)

Tappan, P.W. (1946, Jan.-Feb.) Official homicide. *Law Guild Review, 6*, 400.

(Dangerous Act - Definition)

Turner, J.W., Jr. (1940, May) Is knowledge of danger necessary in murder by a dangerous act? *Kentucky Law Journal, 28*, 474-479.

(Constructive Malice)

Dean, P.H. Constructive malice in murder (Rex v. Stone (1937) 53 T L R 1046). *Law Quarterly*

Review, 54, 22-24 (1938, Jan.); *Camb Law Journal, 6*, 436-437 (1938).

(Jury Instructions)

Instructions to jury, degrees of offense (People v. Stevens (NY) 6 N E 2d 60). (1937, May) *Georgia Law Journal, 25*, 1043-1045.

(Nonfeasance)

Crytzer, H.B. (1937) Homicide by nonfeasance. *Dickinson Law Review, 41*, 126.

(Homicide Law)

Wechsler, H., & Michael, J. (1937) A rationale of the law of homicide. *Columbia Law Review, 37*, 701, 1326.

(Murder Mentality)

Murder and mentality. (1936, Summer) *S A L J, 5*, 168.

(Murder - Degrees)

Pike, J.A. (1936, Jan.) What is second-degree murder in California? *Southern California Law Review, 9*, 112-136.

(Murder - Accessory)

Indictment as accessory before the fact held sufficent to sustain conviction as principal (Moore v. Lowe (WV) 180 SE 1). *Fordham Law Review, 5*, 164-166 (1936, Jan.); *West Virgina Law Quarterly, 42*, 67-69 (1935, Dec.); *Harvard Law Review, 49*, 340-341 (1935, Dec.).

(No Body)

Absence of body in homicide trials. *Fortnightly L J, 4*, 184 (1935); *L J, 78*, 249 (1934).

(Injury and Death - Time Limit)

Thomas, W.H., et al. Permissible duration of time between injury and death (People v. Brengard (NY) 191 NE 850). *Minnesota Law Review, 19*, 240-241 (1935, Jan.); *Law Notes, 38*, 52 (1935, Jan.); *St. John's Law Review, 9*, 200-202 (1934, Dec.); *Marquette Law Review, 19*, 48-49 (1934, Dec.); *Wisconsin Law Review, 10*, 112-114 (1934, Dec.); *Journal of Criminal Law, 25*, 632-634 (1934, Nov.-Dec.); *Brooklyn Law Review, 4*, 86-88 (1934, Oct.)

(Intestacies)

Benefits under intestacies of murdered persons. *Sol J, 78*, 829.

(Liability of Co-Conspirators)

Southworth, W.A. (1933, April) Homicide committed by conspirator during escape after robbery; liability of co-conspirators (State v. Terrell, Franklin, and Connor (La.) 144 So 488). *Cornell Law Quarterly, 18*, 439-442.

(Unlawful Act)

Homicide by an unlawful act (Rex v. Cahill) (1933, Feb.) *Fortnightly Law Journal, 2*, 237.

(Homicide - Felony)

Najarian, R. (1933) Homicide during the commission of a felony (People v. Walsh (NY) 186 N E 422). *Journal of Criminal Law, 24*, 598-600 (1933, Sept.-Oct.); *St. John's Law Review, 8*, 161-162 (1933, Dec.).

(Felony-Murder)

Wharton, I.L. (1933) Confusions - felony-murder. *St. John's Law Review, 7*, 328.

(Justifiable Homicide)

Haensel, V. (1932, May) Justifies murder in Russia. *Journal of Criminal Law, 23*, 90-92.

(Dying Declarations)

Leff, J., et al. Dying declarations (Wright v. State (AL) 135 So 636). *University of Cincinnati Law Review, 5*, 491-492 (1931, Nov.); *Georgia Law Journal, 2*, 118-119 (1932, Jan.); *New York University Law Quarterly Review, 9*, 357-359 (1932, March); *Southern California Law Review, 5*, 327-328 (1932, April); *Notre Dame Law, 7*, 529-534 (1932, May).

(Duty to Retreat)

Rothenburg, C. (1932, March) Duty to retreat "to the wall" (Gibson v. Commonwealth (KY) 34 SW 2d. 936). *Kentucky Law Journal, 20*, 362-366.

(Homicide - Humanitarian)

Buxton, J.T., Jr. (1932, Feb.) Humanitarian homicide. *Law Notes, 35*, 211-212.

(Reversible Error)

Baker, N.F. (1932) Reversible error in homicide cases. *Journal of Criminal Law , 23*, 28.

(Statute - Iowa)

Sufficiency of indictment under the Iowa Short Indictment Act (State v. Woodmansee (IA) 233 NW 725). (1931, Nov.) *Iowa Law Review, 17*, 107-109.

(Murderer's Rights)

Same murderer's rights under victim's intestacy (Re Pitts; Cox v. Kilsby (1931) 1 Ch. 546). (1931, July) *Law Quarterly Review, 47*, 320.

(Failure to Testify)

Inference from the defendant's failure to testify (State v. Gimbel (NJ) 151 Atl. 756). (1931, April) *Michigan Law Review, 29*, 783-784.

(Murdered Wife's Estate)

Estate of wife killed by husband (Re Pitts: Cox v. Kilsby). (1931, March) *Legal Times, 171*, 204-206.

(Famous Jury Charges)

Famous jury charges. (1930, Dec.) *South Jersey Law Society Dictum, 3*, 20-29.

(Murder Law - Texas)

Raymond, J.A. (1930, April) What constitutes murder in Texas? *Texas Law Review, 8*, 391-398.

(Murderer's Rights)

Pearce, E. Murder of ancestor as affecting right to inherit. *Title News, 9*, 15-17 (1930, Feb.); *Law Notes, 31*, 9 (1927).

(Murder Laws - Italy)

Italy puts teeth in murder laws. (1930, Feb.) *Fla S B A L J, 3*, 47.

(Legalized Murder)

Legalized murder of a fleeing felon. (1929, April) *Virginia Law Review, 15*, 582-586.

(Defense - Epilepsy)

Grant, A.R., & Allan, S.M. (1929) Post-epileptic automatism as a defense in a case of murder. *Journal of Mental Science, 75*, 311.

(Constructive Murder)

Constructive murder. (1929) *Law Journal, 67*, 450.

(Insurance Policy)

Mintz, C. (1929) Of the insured as a defense to a suit on a life insurance policy. *St. John's Law Review, 3*, 230.

(Crime Victims)

The victims of crime. (1928, Feb.) *Law Notes, 31*, 202.

(Murder - Degrees)

Murder in the first degree, contemporaneous felony (People v. Moran, 246 NY 100, 158 N E 35). *St. John's Law Review, 2*, 89-90 (1927, Dec.); *N Y U Law Review, 5*, 84-85 (1928, Jan.); *Georgia Law Journal, 16*, 266-268 (1928, Feb.).

(Dying Declaration)

Deceased's statements to person finding him fatally wounded held made in extremis and admissible as dying declaration, if otherwise competent (Fletch Smith and Elisha Short v. Commonwealth, 216 KY 832). (1927, May) *Kentucky Law Journal, 15*, 360-361.

(Homicide - Adultery)

Killing of wife taken in adultery not justified (Billing v. State (TX) 277 S W 687). *Texas Law Review, 4*, 383 (1926, April); *Medical Legal Journal, 43*, 92 (1926, June)

(Homicide - Trespasser)

Criminal liability for the homicide of a trespasser. (1923) *Illinois Law Quarterly, 5*, 244.

(Defense - Letter)

Pious defense of murder; Pascal's seventh letter. (1921, Jan.) *Spectator, 126*, 131-132.

(Mercy Killing)

Murder of mercy. (1920, Dec.) *Law Notes, 33*, 163.

(Murder Trial)

Riddell, W.R. (1919) International murder trial. *Journal of Criminal Law*, 10, 176.

(Property Rights)

Lenicheck, A.E. (1919) Homicide as affecting the devolution of property. *Marquette Law Review, 4*, 34.

(Murder - Jurisdiction)

Keedy, E.R. (1912) The jurisdiction of English judicial officials in murder cases. *Illinois Law Review, 7*, 316.

(Delay of Execution)

Ralston, R. (1912) Charging the jury in a trial for murder and delay in the execution of murderers. *American Law Review, 46*, 397.

(Character of Victim)

Beauchesne, A. (1906) Bad character of the deceased. *Canadian Law Review, 5*, 93.

(Inheritance)

Disinherision for murder. (1905) *Mad L J, 15*, 163.

(Murder Law - India)

Mukerji, S.C. (1904) Law relative to murder in British India. *Alla L J, 1*, 65, 81, 105, 129.

(Murder Law - Roman-Dutch)

Nathan, M. (1902) Roman-Dutch law of homicide. *S A L J, 19*, 115.

(Duty to Retreat)

Browne, I. (1899) Duty of retreating in homicide. *Cent L J, 48*, 5.

Criminal Law

(Criminal Law)

Ballot, R. (1990, Fall) Criminal law - homicide - defendant is entitled to a jury charge on passion/provocation when, under an objective standard, there was both adequate provocation and an insufficient time for defendant to regain composure prior to slaying. *Seton Hall Law Review, 20*, 971-975.

(Ruling - Manslaughter)

Rees, T., & Smith, J.C. (1990, Aug.) Manslaughter - change of plea following judge's ruling - 'unlawful' act leading to death - whether carrying offensive weapon 'unlawful' act (Great Britain). *The Criminal Law Review*, 588-589.

(Indictment)

Fishman, J.A. (1990, Aug.) Arrest in arrow murder. *Motor Boat &Sail, 166*(2), pp. 44-47+.

(Murder Charge)

Wylie, E.M. (1990, May) Night raid on Boston. *Yankee, 54*(5), pp. 76-81+.

(Rape Shield Laws)

Abrams, R. (1990, April 29) Linda Fairstein v. Rape. *New York Times Magazine*, p. 16.

(Conspiracy)

Barwick, S. (1990, April 7) Mr. King's other island. *Spectator, 264*(8439), pp. 22-23.

(Menendez Case)

McCullaugh, J. (1990, March 24) Menendez brothers charged with murder of parents. *Billboard, 102*(12), pp. 6, 85.

(Teen Slayings)

Colford, S.W. (1990, March 19) Athlete endorsements fouled by slayings. *Advertising Age, 61*(12), p. 64.

(Attempted Murder)

Morris, D. (1990, March) "They're going to kill me!" *Reader's Digest, 136*(815), pp. 118-124.

('Fatal Attraction')

Brower, M., et al. (1990, Feb. 26) Death imitates art as police charge teacher Carolyn Warmus with a 'fatal attraction' killing. *People Weekly, 33*(8), pp. 81-83.

(Murder - England)

McFadyean, M. (1990, Feb. 23) The heavy wait. *New Statesman & Society, 3*(89), pp. 12-14.

(DEA Murder)

Busting the brass. (1990, Feb. 12) *Time, 135*(7), p. 25.

(Homicide - Book Review)

Lewin, T. (1990, Jan. 5) Justifiable homicide, by C. Gillespie (book review). *The Los Angeles Times, 12*, p. 7.

(Vehicular Manslaughter)

Coutts, J.A. (1989, Nov.) Sentence for motor manslaughter. *J of Crim Law, 53*, 447-448.

(Criminal Injustice)

Mitchell, B. (1989, Oct. 27) Homicide and criminal injustice. *New Law Journal*, 1450.

(Manslaughter - Liability)

Manslaughter: A new liability? (1989, Aug. 4) *Health and Safety Information Bulletin*, 2-4.

(Felony-Murder)

Carrizosa, P. (1989, June 12) Cocaine case tests rule on felony-murder; prosecutors want to charge dealers for user's overdose; state justice will decide. *The Los Ang Daily Journal*, p. 1.

(Steinberg Case)

Wise, D. (1989, Feb. 1) Day after Steinberg trial - topic among lawyers. *N Y Law J, 201*, 1.

(Alzheimer's Disease)

Lesco, P.A. (1989) Murder/suicide in Alzheimer's disease. *Journal of the American Geriatrics Society, 37*(2), 167-168.

(Battered Women)

Conway, Z.D. (1989) Factors predicting verdicts in cases where battered women kill their husbands. *Law and Human Behavior, 13*(3), 253-269.

(Attempted Murder)

News exec's stepson found guilty of attempted murder. (1988, Dec. 31) *Editor & Publisher, 121*(53), p. 10.

(Extradition)

O'Farrell, E. (1988, Dec. 12) Facing extradition. *Macleans, 101*(51), p. 1.

(Set Free)

English, B., et al. (1988, Dec.) Crime and punishment (U.S.A.). *Reader's Digst, 133*(6), pp. 43-48.

(Sentencing - Proportion)

Fox, R.G. (1988, Dec.) The killing of Bobby Veen: The High Court (Australia) on proportion in sentencing. *The Criminal Law Journal, 12*, 339-366.

(Camarena Trial)

Justice for Camarena. (1988, Oct. 3) *Time, 132*(14), p. 29.

(Court Rulings)

Trends in the law: A death in the family. (1988) *ABA Journal, 74*, 92.

(Serial Murderer)

O'Hara, J. (1987, July 20) Epidemic of murder Vancouver, B.C.: Thought to be linked to Washington State serial murderer. *Macleans, 100, p.* 12.

(Supreme Court)

Appelbaum, P.S. (1987) The empirical jurisprudence of the United States Supreme Court. *American Journal of Medicine and Law, 13*(2-3), 335-349.

(Sexual Homicide)

Schorsch, E. (1987) Legal assessment of sexual homicide. *Beitr Sexual Forsch, 62*, 117-126.

(Worker's Deaths)

Can managers serve jail terms for workers' deaths caused by toxic fumes? (1986, Nov.) *Corporate Security,* p. 8. Microforms and article copies available from UMI.

(Crime Scene)

Nevling, F.M. (1986) Protect the scene and more. *Law and Order, 34*(10), 53-57. Article copies available from UMI.

(Murder Scene)

No liability for murder after police left scene. (1986) *AELE Liability Reporter 1986*(163), 11.

(Secret Things)

Penven, D.S. (1986) Things done in secret. *Law and Order, 34*(7), 33-34. Article copies available from UMI.

(Burden Shifted)

Presumption that shifted production burden to defendant was constitutional. (1986) *The Criminal Law Reporter: Court Decisions, 38*(14), 2267-2269.

(Accomplices - Sentencing)

Ruling on sentencing accomplices. (1986) *Corrections Digest, 17*(3), 4-5. Article copies available from UMI.

(Homicide Act)

Loftin, K. (1986) Anomalies of Section 2 of the Homicide Act of 1957. *Journal of Medical Ethics, 12*(1), 24-27.

(Warning - Parole)

Warning: stay away from the bay (D.J.White's parole ends for murder of George Moscone and Harvey Milk). (1985, Jan. 21) *Newsweek, 105*, p. 38.

(Feticide - Judicial)

Barrazotto, M.E. (1985-1986) Judicial recognition of feticide: Usurping the power of the legislature? *Journal of Family Law, 24*(1), 43-58.

(Organized Crime)

Paul Castellano assassinated in New York City. (1985) *Organized Crime Digest, 6*(12), 7.

(Double Jeopardy)

Double jeopardy: Collateral estoppel. (1985) *The Criminal Law Reporter: Supreme Court Decisions, 38*(7), 2137-2138.

(Charges Dropped)

Lower courted ordered to drop murder charges against physicians by Court of Appeals of the State of California. (1985) *Conn Med, 49*(10), 675-680.

(Malpractice)

Cashion, A.L. (1985) Tarasoff duty to warn: Malpractice if you do, malpractice if you don't? *U.S. Navy Medicine, 76*(1), 22-24.

(Manslaughter - Caldwell)

Manslaughter - the impact of Caldwell? A reply. (1984, Aug.) *The Criminal Law Review*, 479-480.

(Tape Recording)

Ashman, A. (1984, July) What's new: Florida court suppresses tape recording of murder. *American Bar Association Journal, 70*, 114.

(Provocation)

Miethe, T.D. (1984, July-Aug.) The impact of victim provocation on judgments of legal responsibility: An experimental assessment. *Journal of Criminal Justice, 12*, 4.

(Abortion)

Wright, G. (1984, June) The legality of abortion by prostoglandin. *The Criminal Law Review*, 347-349.

(Liability - Dispute)

City and officers could be liable for alleged improper handling of domestic dispute involving off-duty officer with firearm: County and sheriff settle suit. (1984, May) *AELE Liability Reporter*, 11-12.

(Employer Liability)

Employer not liable for murder by employee. (1984) *Security Law Newsletter, 4*(8), 84-85.

(Defenses -Jury)

Defenses--extreme emotional disturbance: Jury Instructions. (1984) *The Criminal Law*

Reporter: Court Decisions, 35(19), 2342.

(Homicide - Liability)

Case reversed and city not liable for officer's shooting and killing his relatives with service revolver. (1984) *AELE Liability Reporter 1984*(137), 6-7.

(Study - Arms)

Copeland, A.R. (1984) The right to keep and bear arms -- a study of civilian homicides committed against those involved in criminal acts in metropolitan Dade County from 1957-1982. *Journal of Forensic Sciences, 29*(2), 584-590. Article copies available from UMI.

(Spontaneous Births)

Mitchell, E.K., & Joseph, D.H. (1984) Spontaneous births into toilets. *Journal of Forensic Sciences, 29*(2), 591-596.

(Testimony - Expert)

Expert testimony inadmissible to distinguish murder, manslaughter. (1984) *The Criminal Law Reporter: Court Decisions, 35*(8), 2137-2138.

(Liability - Domestic)

No liability to officers at domestic dispute where father killed his child. (1984) *AELE Liability Reporter 1984*(139), 9.

(Termination of Rights)

Parental rights termination -- incarceration. (1984) *The Family Law Reporter, 10*(15), 1208.

(Immunity - Liability)

Liability and immunity issues. (1984) *Mental and Physical Disability Law Reporter, 8*(4), 402-403.

(Fetus - Definition)

The fetus under criminal law is considered a complete human being from onset of labor pains. (German) (1984) *Fortschr Med, 102*(10), 92.

(Manslaughter)

Briggs, A. (1983, Dec.) In defense of manslaughter. *The Criminal Law Review*, 764-775.

(Homicide - Comment)

Caryl-Thomas, E., & Smith, J.C. (1983, Aug.) Case and comment: Homicide. *The Criminal Law Review*, 549-550.

(Homicide - Comment)

Mott, G., & Smith,J.C. (1983, June) Case and comment: Homicide. *The Criminal Law Review*, 393-395.

(Decision - Fetus)

Destruction of unborn fetus does not constitute murder. (1983, April 19) *The Family Reporter: Court Opinions, 9* (24), 2380-2382.

(Sentencing)

Thomas, D.A. (1983, April) Case and comment: Sentence. *The Criminal Law Review,* 268-278.

(Homicide Act - Malice)

Uglow, S. (1983, March) Implied malice and the Homicide Act of 1957. *Modern Law Review, 46*, 164-177.

(Homicide Rule)

Homicide--'Year-and-a-day' rule. (1983, Feb.) *The Criminal Law Reporter: Court Decisions, 32*(19), p. 2407.

(Manslaughter - Degree)

Attempt - intent -second degree manslaughter. (1983, Jan.) *The Criminal Law Reporter: Court Decisions,23,*(1), pp. 50-60.

(Mens Rea)

Senate Bill 54: Legislative attack on mens rea defense. (1983, Winter) *U S F Law Review, 17,* 307-332.

(Provocation)

Wasik, M. (1983, Jan.) Cumulative provocation and domestic killing. *The Criminal Law Review 1982*, pp. 29-37.

(Legal Case Report)

Gudjonsson, G.H., et al. (1983) A specific recognition deficit in a case of homicide. *Medical Science and Law, 23*(1), 37-40.

(Self-Defense)

Gold, A.D. (1983) Notes and comments: Excessive self-defense. *The Criminal Law Quarterly, 25*(3), 290-291.

(Self-Defense)

O'Brien, N.C. (1983) Excessive self-defense: A need for legislation. *The Criminal Law Quarterly, 25*(4), 441-457.

(Murder - Degrees)

Notes and comments: Indictment -- second degree murder. (1983) *The Criminal Law Quarterly, 25*(3), 291-293.

(Doctors' Liability)

Doctors aren't criminally liable for "pulling plug" on comatose patient. (1983) *The Criminal Law Reporter: Court Decisions, 34*(6), 2119-2120.

(Manslaughter - Rule)

Manslaughter -- year-and-a-day rule. (1983) *The Criminal Law Reporter: Court Decisions, 32*(23), 2499.

(Police Practices)

Stranger homicide rise signals need for changes in police practice. (1983) *Police and Security Bulletin, 15*(1), 1. Article copies available from UMI.

(Certification - Juvenile)

Certification - treatable as juvenile - United States. (1983) *Juvenile and Family Law Digest, 15*(7), 237-239.

(Murder Conviction)

Review of a murder conviction. (1983) *Crime Control Digest, 17*(44), 9. Article copies available from UMI.

(Retrial)

Ruling on retrial for murder. (1983) *Crime Control Digest, 17*(44), 9. Article copies available from UMI.

(Self-Defense)

Debaisieux, T., & Pirlot, G. (1983) Self-defense: Legitimate defense or legitimate violence. (French) *Annales Medico-Psychologiques, 141*(7), 777-783.

(Felony-Murder)

Dietz, M. (1983) *Killing for profit: The social organization of felony-murder.* Nelson-Hall.

(Murder Trial)

Rowell, L. (1982, Nov. 29) Update from Tchula. *Chr & Crisis, 2*, 373-374.

(Homicide Law Reform)

Weisbrot, D. (1982, Oct.) Homicide law reform in New South Wales. *Criminal Law Journal, 6*, 248-268.

(Felony-Murder Doctrine)

Common-law - felony-murder doctrine judicially abolished in Michigan: People v. Aaron (299 NW 2d. 304). (1982, Fall) *Washington University Law Review, 60*, 1197-1211.

(Sentence - Comment)

Case and comment: Sentence. (1982, May) *The Criminal law Review*, 319-320.

(Felony-Murder Rule Abolished)

Criminal law - felony murder rule - the common-law felony murder rule is abolished in Michigan (People v. Aaron 299 NW 2d. 304). (1982, Spring) *U Det J Urb Law, 59*, 428-439.

(Mercy Killing)

Leng, R. (1982, Jan. 28) Mercy killing and the CLRC. *New Law Journal, 132*, 76-78.

(Affirmative Defense)

Haddad, J.B. (1982) Allocation of burdens in murder/ voluntary manslaughter cases: An affirmative defense approach. *Chicago-Kent Law Review, 59*, 23-66.

(Psychiatric Testimony)

Lesse, S. (1982) The psychiatrist in court - theater of the absurd. *American Journal of Psychotherapy, 36*(3), 287-291.

(Prosecution - Feticide)

Killing of seven-month-old fetus can't be prosecuted as murder. (1982) *The Criminal Law Reporter, 31*(24), p. 2511.

(Evidence - Sufficiency)

Homicide -- sufficiency of evidence -- failure to find victim's body. (1982) *The Criminal Law Reporter: Court Decisions, 32*(2), 2033.

(Drunk Drivers)

Sentencing -- drunk drivers -- manslaughter. (1982) *The Criminal Law Reporter: Court Decisions, 32*(10), 2033.

(Law Reform - California)

"Special circumstance" provision of California murder law struck down. (1982) *The Criminal Law Reporter: Court Decisions, 31*(16), 2325-2326.

(Self-Defense Claim)

Homicide - voluntary manslaughter - jury's rejection of self-defense claim. (1982) *The Criminal Law Reporter: Court Decisions and Proceedings, 31*(6), 2122.

(Provocation)

Weber, J.K. (1981, July-Sept.) Some provoking aspects of voluntary manslaughter law. *Anglo-American Law Review, 10*, 159-179.

(Mens Rea - N. Ireland)

Jackson, J.D. (1981, Summer) Mens rea of murder in Northern Ireland. *Northern Ireland Law Quarterly, 32*, 175-187.

(Provocation - Papua New Guinea)

Wilson, K. (1981, June) Provocation in Papua New Guinea. *Criminal Law Journal, 5*, 128-135.

(Criminal Law Doctrine)

Foreman, P., et al. (1981, Spring) Submitting the law of parties in a Texas criminal prosecution. *Baylor Law Review, 33*, 267-283.

(Diminished Capacity)

Criminal law - confusion in the concept of diminished capacity and the use of mental impairment to reduce degree of conviction in Massachusetts. (1981, Winter) *Western New England Law Review, 3*, 583-608.

(Mental Imbalance)

Bentil, J.K. (1981, Jan. 23) Mental imbalance and diminished responsibility in homicide. *Sol J, 125*, 54-56.

(Habeas Corpus)

Habeas corpus - manslaughter - confusing state law. (1981) *The Criminal Law Reporter: Court Decisions and Proceedings, 28*(16), 2373.

(Homicide - Property Rights)

Decedents' estates - homicide - property survivorship rights. (1981) *The Family Law Reporter: Court Opinions, 7*(12), 2184.

(Self-Defense - Reasonable Man)

Donovan, D.A., et al. (1981) Is the reasonable man obsolete? A critical perspective on self-defense and provocation. *Loyola University Law Review, 14*, 435-468.

(Criminal Intent)

Intoxication doesn't negate intent required for voluntary manslaughter. (1981) *The Criminal Law Reporter: Court Decisions and Proceedings, 30*(3), 2058-2059.

(Felony-Murder)

Fletcher, G.P. (1980/1981) Reflections on felony-murder. *Sw U L Review, 12*, 413-429.

(Law Revision)

Wells, C. (1980, Nov.) Criminal law revision committee, 14th report: Offenses against the person - homicide. *Modern Law Review, 43*, 681-691.

(Marital Relationship)

Criminal law - marital relation creates a duty of care between spouses - a spouse has a duty to summon medical aid when the other is in a condition necessitating immediate medical attention. (1980, Fall) *Dick Law Review, 85*, 173-181.

(Homicide - Search Warrants)

Hausknecht, B.D. (1980, Fall) Homicide scene exception to the fourth amendment warrant requirement: A dead issue? *Journal of Criminal Law and Criminology, 71*, 289-299.

(Duress)

Dennis, I.H. (1980, April) Duress, murder, and criminal responsibility. *Law Quarterly Review, 96*, 208-238.

(Felony-Murder Law)

Criminal law - homicide - felony-murder - felon is culpable for murder in the first degree under Maryland's felony-murder statute when police officer kills kidnapped hostage used by felon as human shield. (1980, Spring) *University of Baltimore Law Review, 9*, 508-523.

(Felony-Murder)

Criminal law - felony-murder - results from the shooting of one bystander by another. (1980, Spring) *Mo L Rev, 45*, 326-337.

(Legal Process)

Swigert, V.L., & Farrell, R.A. (1980) Speedy trial and the legal process. *Law and Human Behavior, 4*(3), 135-145.

(Euthanasia)

Kary, C. (1980) A moral distinction between killing and letting die. *The Journal of Medicine and Philosophy, 5*(4), 326-332.

(Criminal Law - Comparison)

Rengier, R. (1980) Should murder be taken out of the category of intentional killing? Comparative essay about the laws of Austria, Switzerland, and Germany. 38706, bd. 92, '80, h. 2, s. 459-480 (IBZ 1982).

(Law Reform)

Hogan, B. (1980) Reform of the law of homicide. *UNB Law Journal, 29*, 9-25.

(Brain Death)

Brain death: The emerging common law definition in criminal homicide. (1979, Spring) *Western State University Law Review, 6*, 295-309.

(Defense - Hypnosis Witness)

Leblang, T.R. (1979) Hypnosis of witness becomes focus of murder defense. *Legal Aspects of Medical Practice, 7*(4), 31-33.

(Year and a Day Rule)

Wiecking, D.K. (1979) The year and a day rule: A medical and legal anachronism. *Medical-Legal Bulletin, 28*(1),

(Defense - Drunkenness)

Step backward: The drunkenness defense in Morris v. R. (1979) 10 C R 259. (1980/1981) *Sask L Rev, 45*, 351-360.

(Psychiatric Testimony)

Criminal law - first degree murder - psychiatric testimony admissible on issue of intent. (1979) *Wisconsin Law Review 1979*, 628-660.

(Capital Murder)

O'Connor, P. (1979, Winter) Capital murder and the Supreme Court. *Irish Jurisprudence, 14*, 329-333.

(Year and a Day Rule)

Year and a day rule: Has its time run out? (1978-1979, Winter) *Creighton Law Review, 12*, 683-695.

(Criminal Law - Defense)

Criminal law: Impossibility as a defense. (1978, Spring) *Brooklyn Law Review, 44*, 667-673.

(Felony-Murder Rule)

Felony-murder rule: In search of a viable doctrine. (1978, Spring) *Catholic Law, 23*, 133-162.

(Felony Murder)

Criminal law - felony murder - felon not liable for killing committed by person other than himself or accomplices. (1978, Winter) *Rutgers Camden Law Journal, 9*, 368-374.

(Non-Capital Murder)

Criminal law: Non-capital murder: Duress: Whether the defense of duress under sections 17 or 7(3) of the criminal code is available to a party to the offense under section 21(2). (1978) *Ottawa Law Review, 10*, 214-223.

(Emotional Distress)

Del. revives law on murder defendant's emotional distress defense. (1978) *The Criminal Law Reporter: Court Decisions and Proceedings, 23*(9), 2189-2191.

(Law Reforms)

Smith, J.C. (1978) Some problems of the reform of the law of offenses against the person. *Current Legal Problems, 31*, 15-29.

(Year and a Day Rule)

Murder - common-law - year-and-a-day rule. (1978) *The Criminal Law Reporter: Court Decisions and Proceedings, 23*(21), 2475.

(Criminal Law - Defense)

Criminal law - the trend away from legal impossibility as a defense. (1978) *Wake Forest Law Review, 14*, 243-258.

(Manslaughter - Motor Vehicle)

Criminal law - implied repeal by section 31-232 (negligent homicide law) of that part of section 6-

58 (involuntary manslaughter statute) that states "or by any culpable neglect or criminal carelessness" insofar as it affects deaths resulting from the operation of a motor vehicle. (1978) *Land and Water Law Review, 13*, 595-611.

(Capital Murder)

Criminal law - capital murder - vicarious liability requires a finding of capital murder when a non-felon kills a peace officer in response to a felon's lethal provocation. (1978) *St. Mary's Law Journal, 10*, 195-204.

(Defense - Affirmative)

Criminal law - affirmative defenses - burden of proof. (1978) *New York Law Society Law Review, 23*, 802-812.

(Verdict)

King, D.P. (1978) 'And is this the verdict of you all?' *Police Journal, 51*(1), 115-116.

(Unlawful Killing)

Liability of parties to unlawful killing under the criminal code. (1977, Dec.) *University of Queensland Law Journal, 10*, 1-14.

(Justification)

Cohen, M.A. (1977, June-Oct.) Justification and excuse in the Judaic and common law: The exculpation of a defendant charged with homicide (student note) [letter]. *New York University Law Review, 52*, 599-628, 970-973.

(Felony-Murder Doctrine)

Merger doctrine as a limitation on the felony-murder rule: A balance of criminal law principles. (1977, Summer) *Wake Forest Law Review, 13*, 369-396.

(Legal Reform)

Lambert, J.L. (1977, June) Reform in the law of homicide. *New Law Journal, 127*, 571-573.

(Criminal Procedure)

Criminal procedure - statutory construction - simple assault not a lessor included offense of criminally negligent homicide. (1977, May) *American Journal of Criminal Law, 5*, 247-255.

(Legal Reform)

Farrier, D. (1977, March) Criminal law revision committee working paper on offenses against the person. *Modern Law Review, 40*, 206-215.

(Homicide - Law)

Swigert, V.L., & Farrell, R.A. (1977, Feb.) Normal homicides and the law. *American Sociology Review, 42*, 16-32.

(Criminal Procedure)

Criminal procedure: Uncorroborated confession of felony in the felony-murder prosecution. (1977, Winter) *Brooklyn Law Review, 43*, 541-545.

(Law and Violence)

Masamura, W.T. (1977) Law and violence: A cross-cultural study. *Journal of Anthropology Research, 33*, 391-399.

(Death Penalty)

Criminal law - constitutional law - death penalty - evidence - intent of an aider and abettor to commit felony murder may be presumed from a conspiracy to commit the accompanying felony. (1977) *University of Cincinnati Law Review, 46*, 630-640.

(Felony-Murder Rule)

Assault leading to homicide may be used to invoke felony-murder rule. (1976, Fall) *Mercer Law Review, 28*, 371-376.

(Felony-Murder)

Criminal law: Felony-murder under the new murder statutes. (1976, Spring) *Oklahoma Law Review, 29*, 445-454.

(Felony-Murder Rule)

Criminal law - People v. Hickman (IL) 319 NE 2d. 511 - defining the felon's accountability under the felony-murder rule. (1976, Spring) *Loyola University Law Journal, 7*, 529-545.

(Felony-Murder Statutes)

Adlerstein, J.A.C. (1976) Felony-murder in the new criminal codes. *American Journal of Criminal Law, 4*(3), 249-274.

(Diminished Capacity)

Criminal law - first-degree murder - evidence of diminished capacity inadmissible to show lack of intent. (1976) *Wisconsin Law Review 1976*, 623-641.

(Differential Treatment)

Swigert, V., & Farrell, R.A. (1976) *Murder, inequality, and the law: Differential treatment and the legal process*. Lexington Books.

(Felony-Murder Rule)

Constitutional limitations upon the use of statutory criminal presumptions and the felony-murder rule. (1975, Fall) *Missouri Law Journal, 46*, 1021-1040.

(Self-Defense)

Criminal law - self-defense - a duty to retreat - the rule now hits home. (1975, Fall) *Suffolk University Law Review, 10*, 100-115.

(Drug Laws)

Weissman, J.C. (1975, Fall) Imposing homicide liability for death-producing drug law violations. *California Western Law Review, 12*, 102-121.

(Torts)

Torts - exoneration under justifiable homicide statute does not preclude possibility of damages in subsequent civil suit for wrongful death. (1975, Fall) *Texas Tech Law Review, 7*, 219-227.

(Criminal Law - Jamaica)

Hucker, J. (1975, July-Sept.) Jamaican criminal law: The judicial contribution. *Anglo-American Law Review, 4*, 257-270.

(Definition of Death)

Law of homicide: Does it require a definition of death? (1975, June) *Wake Forest Law Review, 11*, 253-268.

(Prior Crimes)

Criminal law - admissibility of prior crimes governed by prosecution's need for evidence notwithstanding absence of proof of commission of prior crimes. (1974, Summer) *Suffolk University Law Review, 8*, 1316-1333.

(Due Process)

Criminal procedure - preaccusation delay as violation of due process: Absence of statute of limitations is factor to be weighed against murder defendant's allegations of actual prejudice. (1974, May) *Washington Law Review, 49*, 973-985.

(Death by Choice)

Maguire, D.C. (1974, Feb.) Death, legal and illegal: Excerpts from *Death by choice*. *Atlantic, 233*, 72-74+.

(Due Process)

Due process and supremacy as foundations for the adequacy rule: The remains of federalism after Wilbur v. Mullaney (473 F 2d. 943). (1974) *Maine Law Review, 26*, 37-92.

(Felony-Murder Rule)

Taming the felony-murder rule. (1973, Fall) *Santa Clara Law, 14*, 97-117.

(Felony-Murder Rule)

Felony-murder - elimination of the element of scrambling possession for application of the felony-murder rule to robbery. (1973, Fall) *Santa Clara Law, 14*, 188-194.

(Criminal Law - Suicide)

Parry-Jones, W.L. (1973, April) Criminal law and complicity in suicide and attempted suicide. *Medical Science and Law, 13*(2), 110-119.

(Psychiatric Evidence)

Criminal law - psychiatric evidence ruled admissible in murder prosecution to determine whether defendant acted in heat of passion. (1973, Winter) *Dick Law Review, 77*, 435.

(Vicarious Liability)

Criminal law - vicarious liability - robber convicted of murder when robbery victim killed accomplice. (1971-1972, Nov.-Jan.) *West Virginia Law Review, 74*, 204.

(Juvenile Delinquency)

Criminal law - juvenile delinquency proceeding - right to trial by jury - the New York Court of Appeals has overruled the New York Supreme Court, Appellate Division, which held that the sixth and fourteenth amendments require a jury trial in a family court proceeding charging one juvenile with being a juvenile delinquent based on an act which if committed by an adult would constitute a felony and thus entitle him to a jury trial. (1971, Summer) *Duquesne Law Review, 9*, 681.

(Model Code)

Moreland, R. (1971, Summer) Reexamination of the law of homicide in 1971: The model penal code. *Kentucky Law Journal, 59*, 788.

(Vicarious Liability)

Criminal law - felony-murder - vicarious liability - a felon can be held responsible for a murder committed be a fear-motivated victim - responsibility is based on a theory of vicarious liability and not felony-murder. (1971, Spring) *St. Mary's Law Journal, 3*, 158.

(Felony-Murder)

Criminal law - homicide - felony-murder - causation - degree of proof. (1971, Spring) *Duquesne Law Review, 9*, 542.

(Feticide)

Criminal law - feticide - the unborn child as a "human being". (1971, Feb.) *Tulane Law Review, 45*, 408.

(Fetal Destruction)

Role of the law of homicide in fetal destruction. (1971, Feb.) *Iowa Law Review, 56*, 658.

(Criminal Responsibility)

Parker, G. (1971) Evolution of criminal responsibility. *Alberta Law Review, 9*, 47.

(Participant in Crime)

Criminal liability of a participant in crime for the death of a fellow participant. (1971) *Syracuse Law Review, 22*, 1065.

(Defense - Alcoholism)

Criminal law: Alcoholism as a defense. (1970, Fall-Winter) *Marquette Law Review, 53*, 445.

(Felony-Murder Rule)

Criminal law - murder - felony murder rule. (1970, Fall) *Duquesne Law Review, 9*, 122.

(Felony-Murder Rule)

Criminal-law: Foreseeability and the felony-murder rule. (1970, Fall) *Arkansas Law Review, 24*, 342.

(Provocation)

English, P. (1970, May) What did section three do to the law of provocation? *Criminal Law Review 1970*, 249.

(Law Reform)

Cross, R. (1969, June) Proposals for the reform of the law of murder. *University of Western Australia Law Review, 9*, 50.

(Criminal Code)

Riess, P. (1969) Die neufassung des mordes in regierungsentwurf 1962 eines neuen strafgesetzbuches in kriminologischer und kriminalstatistischer Sicht. 24232 J. 52, '69, H. 1, S. 28-41. (IBZ 1971).

(Homicide Law)

Cross, R. (1968, Dec.) Necessity knows no law. *Tasmania University Law Review, 3*, 1.

(Violent Offenses)

Hadden, T. (1968, Oct.) Offenses of violence: The law and the facts. *The Criminal Law Review 1968*, 521.

(Law of Homicide)

Stroud, R.S. (1968) *Drakon's law on homicide.* University of California Press.

(Mens Rea)

Walker, R.J. (1967, Sept.) Mens rea in manslaughter. *New Law Journal, 117*, 950.

(Homicide Law)

Hooper, R.J. (1967, March) Some anomalies and developments in the law of homicide. *UBC Law Review, 3*, 55.

(Vehicular Manslaughter)

Criminal law - participant in drag race guilty of manslaughter for automobile death resulting during the race. (1967, Winter) *San Diego Law Review, 12*, 161.

(Psychiatry and Law)

Biggs, J., Jr. (1967) *Guilty mind, psychiatry, and the law of homicide.* Baltimore: Johns

Hopkins.

(Law - U.K.)

Marc, G. (1967) "Le Murder Act" des 1965 et le droit anglais de l'homicide. 30560. n. s., t. 22, '67, n. 4, p. 843-850. (IBZ 1969)

(Unlawful Act)

Buxton, R.J. (1966, April) By any unlawful act. *Law Quarterly Review, 82*, 174.

(Ethics)

Shuchman, P. (1966, Spring) Ethics and the problem of necessity. *Temple Law Quarterly, 39*, 279.

(Felony-Murder Rule)

Felony-murder rule - a reexamination. (1965, Spring) *Santa Clara Law , 5*, 172.

(Criminal Responsibility)

Osborough, N. (1965, March) Homicide and criminal responsibility bill (N.I.) 1963. *Northern Ireland Law Quarterly, 16*, 73.

(Legal Justice)

Freedman, L.Z. (1965) Psychiatry and law by L.H. Oswald (review). *Progr Neurol Psychiat, 20*, 608-611.

(Criminal Assault)

Pittman, D.J., & Handy, W. (1964, Dec.) Patterns in criminal aggravated assault. *Journal of Criminal Law, Criminology, and Police Science, 55*(4), 462-470.

(Legal Reform)

Schmalzbach, O.R. (1964, Aug.) The reform of the law of homicide. *Medical Journal of Australia, 2*, 221-224.

(Law)

The armor of the law. (1964, March) *New England Journal of Medicine, 271*, 516-517.

(Homicide Law)

Williams, J.E.H. (1964, Feb.) Developments in the law of homicide 1954-1963. *The Criminal Law Review 1964*, 84.

(Year and a Day Rule)

Present status of the year and a day rule. (1964, Jan.) *New York University Intra Law Review, 19*, 133.

(Historical Law)

MacDowell, D.M. (1963) *Athenian homicide law in the age of the orators*. Barnes & Noble.

(Law and Medicine)

Blease, W.L. (1962, Dec.) The relations between law and medicine. *British Journal of Clin Pract, 16*, 794-795.

(Mens Rea)

Turpin, C.C. (1962, Nov.) Mens rea in manslaughter. *Cambridge Law Journal 1962*, 200.

(Intent)

Criminal law - homicide - intent to kill is presumed from use of deadly weapon (State v. Preis (AZ) 362 Pac. 2d. 660. (1962, Fall) *Arizona Law Review, 4*, 109.

(Law Reform)

Danforth, F.W., Jr. (1962, June) Model penal code and degrees of criminal homicide. *American University Law Review, 11*, 147.

(Corpus Delicti)

Perkins, R.M. (1962, March) Corpus delicti of murder. *Virginia Law Review, 48*, 173.

(Year and a Day Rule)

Criminal law - homicide - death resulting more than a year and a day after assault (Commonwealth v. Ladd (PA) 166 A 2d. 501). (1962, Feb.) *North Carolina Law Review, 40*, 327.

(Tort Concept)

Use of the tort liability concept of proximate cause in cases of criminal homicide. (1962, Jan.-Feb.) *Nw U L Review, 56*, 791.

(Criminal Intent)

Criminal law - felony-murder - an anomaly in the intent element of robbery. (1962, Winter) *Rocky Mountain Law Review, 34*, 243.

(Criminal Law)

Criminal law - involuntary manslaughter - proximate cause (Commonwealth v. Root (PA) 170 A 2d. 310). (1962, Winter) *B U Law Review, 42*, 140.

(Year and a Day Rule)

Criminal law - judicial legislation in abolishing the year and a day rule (Commonwealth v. Ladd (PA) 166 A 2d. 501). (1961, Nov.) *Georgia Bar Journal, 24*, 280.

(Vicarious Liability)

Criminal law - involuntary manslaughter - presence as a prerequisite to liability for permitting an incompetent to drive an automobile (People v. Marshall (MI) 106 NW 2d. 842). (1961, Nov.) *Michigan Law Review, 60*, 102.

(Homicide Law - Ohio)

Criminal law - involuntary manslaughter (State v. Kotapish (OH) 171 NE 2d. 505). (1961, Fall)

Iowa Law Review, 47, 168.

(Year and a Day Rule)

Criminal law - homicide - year and a day rule abolished (Commonwealth v. Ladd (PA) 166 A 2d. 501). (1961, Summer) *Iowa Law Review, 46*, 883.

(Year and a Day Rule)

Criminal law - year and a day rule - since judiciary may alter common law rules of evidence, a killing may be deemed culpable homicide though death does not occur within a year and a day (Commonwealth v. Ladd (PA) 166 A 2d. 501). (1961, June) *Virginia Law Review, 47*, 880.

(Heat of Passion)

Criminal law - heat of passion - inclusive and exclusive nature (People v. D'Andrea, 207 N Y S 2d. 215) (1961, April) *Brooklyn Law Review, 27*, 351.

(Presumption of Malice)

Criminal law - the abolition of the presumption of malice and second degree murder (Commonwealth ex rel Johnson v. Myers (PA) 168 A 2d. 295). (1961, Spring) *Temple Law Quarterly, 34*, 336.

(Vicarious Liability)

Criminal law - manslaughter - automobile owner's vicarious responsibility (People v. Marshall (MI) 106 NW 2d. 842). (1961, Spring) *Wayne Law Review, 7*, 483.

(Criminal Law - Case Report)

Criminal law: Prejudicial character of charge that all homicides presumed felonious (Gardner v. State (GA) 114 SE 2d. 852). (1961, Feb.) *Georgia Bar Journal, 23*, 413.

(Legal Reform)

Gardiner, G. (1961, Feb.) Point about the Homicide Act. *New Statesman, 61*, 206+.

(Tort Concept)

Criminal law - causation - tort concept or proximate cause is inapplicable in criminal prosecution (Commonwealth v. Root (PA) 170 A 2d. 310). (1961-1962, Winter) *Vill Law Review, 7*, 297.

(Year and a Day Rule)

Criminal law - homicide - year and a day rule abandoned (Commonwealth v. Ladd (PA) 166 A 2d. 501). (1961, Winter) *Arizona Law Review, 3*, 294.

(Year and a Day Rule)

Abolition of the year and a day rule: Commonwealth v. Ladd. (1961, Jan.) *Dick Law Review, 65*, 166.

(Felony-Murder)

Criminal law - felony murder - homicide perpetrated by one other than the felon (People v. Wood (NY) 167 NE 2d. 736). (1960, Dec.) *Brooklyn Law Review, 27,* 161.

(Criminal Responsibility)

Criminal law - criminal responsibility of felon for homicide perpetrated by stranger during commission of felony (People v. Wood (NY) 167 NE 2d. 736). (1960, Dec.) *Missouri Law Journal, 32,* 121.

(Corpus delicti)

Criminal law - murder - proof of corpus delicti by circumstantial evidence (People v. Scott, 1 Cal. Rptr. 600). (1960, Dec.) *California Law Review, 48,* 849.

(Intent)

Williams, G. (1960, Nov.) Criminal law - murder - presumption of intent (D.P.P. v. Smith (1960) 3 W L R 546). *Cambridge Law Journal 1960,* 140.

(Corpus delicti)

Evidence - criminal law - circumstantial evidence sufficient to establish corpus delicti (People v. Scott, 1 Cal. Rptr. 600). (1960, Oct.) *Vanderbilt Law Review, 13,* 1290.

(Felony-Murder)

Criminal law - felony-murder - defendant not guilty of murder when killing committed by third person who is not defendant's co-felon (People v. Wood, 195 N Y S 2d. 133). (1960, Aug.) *Georgia Bar Journal, 23,* 107.

(Corpus Delicti)

Criminal law - homicide - proof of corpus delicti by circumstantial evidence (People v. Scott, 176 Cal. App. 504). (1960, Summer) *Iowa Law Review, 45,* 902.

(Vehicular Manslaughter)

Criminal law - involuntary manslaughter conviction affirmed against joy racer (Commonwealth v. Root (PA) 156 A 2d. 895). (1960, Summer) *Maryland Law Review, 20,* 299.

(Murder Evidence)

Criminal law - murder - evidence - proof of corpus delicti by circumstantial evidence (People v. Scott, 176 Cal. App. 504). (1960, June) *American University Law Review, 9,* 158.

(Corpus delicti)

Criminal law - corpus delicti in homicide - absence of body (People v. Scott 176 Cal. App. 504). (1960, June) *Tulane Law Review, 34,* 820.

(Felony-Manslaughter)

Criminal law - felony-manslaughter doctrine - immediate killer not the felon (State v. Garner (LA)

115 S 2d. 855). (1960, April) *Tulane Law Review, 34*, 612.

(Religious Beliefs)

Criminal law manslaughter conviction for failure to provide medical aid to child because of religious belief reversed (Craig v. Maryland 155 A 2d. 648). (1960, Spring-Summer) *Depaul Law Review, 9*, 271.

(Evidence - Circumstantial)

Criminal law - murder - circumstantial evidence (State v. Scott, 176 Cal. App. 504). (1960, Spring) *Mercer Law Review, 11*, 388.

(Drunk Driving)

Criminal law - homicide by drunken driving - liability of passenger (Eager v. State (TN) 325 SW 2d. 815). (1960, Spring) *Tenn Law Review, 27*, 417.

(Circumstantial Evidence)

Criminal law - corpus delicti held sufficent for murder conviction. (1960, Spring) *Maryland Law Review, 20*, 180.

(Felony-Murder)

Criminal law - acquittal for felony murder not bar to subsequent prosecution for the underlying felony (People ex rel Santangelo v. Tutaska, 192 N Y S 2d. 350). (1960, Spring) *Syracuse Law Review, 11*, 290.

(Heat of Passion)

Criminal law - homicide - heat of passion - self-defense - imminence of danger (State v. Jones (KS) 167 NE 2d. 736). (1960, Winter) *Washburn Law Journal, 1*, 146.

(Felony-Murder)

Criminal law - homicide - felony-murder (People v. Wood, 186 N Y S 2d. 141). (1960, Winter) *South Carolina Law Quarterly, 12*, 368.

(Legal Interpretation)

Elliott, D.W. (1960, Jan.) Interpretation of the homicide act of 1957. *Criminal Law Review 1960*, 5.

(Murder - First-Degree)

Criminal law - murder of the first degree - plea of guilty - abuse of discretion by the trial court (Commonwealth v. Green (PA) 151 A. 2d. 241). (1959, Fall) *Temple Law Quarterly, 33*, 103.

(Presumption of Innocence)

Criminal law - presumption of innocence (Commonwealth v. Edwards (PA) 147 A 2d. 313). (1959, Aug.) *Hastings Law Journal 11*, 89.

(Culpable Negligence)

Criminal law - manslaughter - murder or manslaughter - self-defense - excessive force (Queen v. Howe (1958) A L R 753). (1959, May) *M U L R, 2,* 113.

(Self-Defense)

Criminal law - homicide - murder or manslaughter - excessive force in self-defense - onus on Crown (Queen v. Buffalo (1958) A L R 746). (1959, May) *M U L R, 2,* 115.

(Felony-Murder)

Criminal law - homicide - murder under felony-murder rule (Commonwealth v. Redline (PA) 137 A 2d. 472). (1959, April) *Missouri Law Review, 24,* 266.

(Intent)

Criminal law - intoxication and specific intent in homicide prosecution (State v. Youngblood (LA) 106 S 2d. 689). (1959, Feb.) *Louisiana Law Review, 19,* 524.

(Felony-Murder Rule)

Torcia, C.E. (1959, Jan.) Clarification of the felony-murder statute? *Dick Law Review, 63,* 119.

(Murder - First-Degree)

Criminal law - first degree murder - judge's power to comment on issue of punishment (People v. Friend (CA) 327 P 2d. 97). (1959, Jan.) *UCLA Law Review, 6,* 149.

(Intoxication)

Criminal law - voluntary intoxication as a defense to murder (State v. Youngblood (LA) 106 S 2d. 689). (1958-1959) *Loyola Law Review, 9,* 243.

(Culpability)

Criminal law - culpability requirement of the drunk-driving-death statute (Goodell v. People (CO) 327 P 2d. 279). (1958, Dec.) *Rocky Mountain Law Review, 31,* 104.

(Homicide Act)

Gooderson, R.N. (1958, Nov.) Criminal law - Homicide Act 1957 - diminished responsibility (Regina v. Spriggs (1958) 1 Q B 270; Regina v. Matheson (1958 1 W L R 474). *Cambridge Law Journal 1958,* 140.

(Felony-Murder Rule)

Criminal law - felon's responsibility under felony-murder rule for acts of third persons (Commonwealth v. Redline (PA) 137 A 2d. 472). (1958, Fall) *Temple Law Quarterly, 32,* 117.

(Manslaughter - Case Report)

Criminal law - accessory before the fact of manslaughter (Stacy v. State (AR) 306 SW 2d. 852). (1958, Fall) *Arkansas Law Review, 12,* 402.

(Felony-Murder Rule)

Criminal law - felony-murder rule - felon not guilty of murder where co-felon killed by policeman (Commonwealth v. Redline (PA) 137 A 2d. 472). (1958, Summer) *University of Pittsburgh Law Review, 19*, 808.

(Death of Co-Felon)

Criminal law - death of co-felon in perpetration of arson as felony-murder (Commonwealth v. Bolish (PA) 138 A 2d. 447). (1958, Summer) *Fordham Law Review, 27*, 281.

(Murder Evidence)

Criminal law - murder - evidence sufficent to infer deliberation and premeditation (People v. Steward (CA) 318 P 2d. 806). (1958, June) *Vill Law Rev, 3*, 565.

(Felony-Murder)

Criminal law - felony-murder - guilt of robber for the justifiable killing of his accomplice by a policeman (Commonwealth v. Redline (PA) 137 A 2d. 472). (1958, May) *Michigan Law Review, 56*, 1197.

(Negligence)

Criminal law - evidence - homicide - negligence - evidence of prior accidents at the intersection are inadmissible in negligent homicide cases to show that the intersection was unusually dangerous (Coate v. State (TX) 306 SW 2d. 727). (1958, May) *Texas Law Review, 36*, 664.

(Justifiable Homicide)

Criminal law - justifiable homicide - prevention of a felony or a felon's escape (Queen v. McKay (1957) A L R 648). (1958, May) *M U L R, 1*, 401.

(Provocation)

Criminal law - murder - provocation - test of effect of provocation on mind of reasonable man - reasonable man not to be invested with the physical peculiarities of the accused. (1958, April) *Fac Law Review, 16*, 133.

(Felony-Murder Rule)

Criminal law - felony-murder doctrine (Commonwealth v. Redline (PA) 137 A 2d. 472). (1958, Spring) *Maryland Law Review, 18*, 169.

(Diminished Responsibility)

Diminished responsibility; the law of homicide. (1958, Feb.) *Economist, 186*, 390.

(Heat of Passion)

Criminal law - homicide - heat of passion. (1958, Feb.) *Oklahoma Law Review, 11*, 73.

(Felony-Murder Rule)

Criminal law - felony-murder rule - responsibility for death of fellow arsonist (State v. Morran

(MT) 306 P 2d. 679). (1957, Fall) *Montana Law Review, 19*, 63.

(Co-Felon's Death)

Criminal law - responsibility of felon for death of co-felon (Commonwealth v. Thomas (PA) 117 A 2d. 204). (1957, Summer) *University of Florida Law Review, 10*, 230.

(Estoppel and Malice)

Some aspects of malice and estoppel in the criminal law (Mraz v. The Queen (1955) A L R 929). (1957, June) *Sydney Law Review, 2*, 337.

(Criminal Law - Case Report)

Criminal law - homicide - defendant only eye witness (Reed v. State (MS) 91 S 2d. 269). (1957, May) *Mississippi Law Review, 28*, 234.

(Second-Degree Murder)

Criminal law - second-degree murder held an offense punishable by death for purposes of statute of limitations (State v. Brown (NJ) 126 A 2d. 161). (1957, May) *University of Pennsylvania Law Review, 105*, 1000.

(Justifiable Homicide)

Criminal law - justifiable homicide to prevent adultery (Scroggs v. State (GA) 93 SE 2d. 583). (1957, May) *Georgia Bar Journal, 19*, 521.

(Involuntary Manslaughter)

Criminal law - involuntary manslaughter - unlawful act as basis of conviction (State v. Strobel (MT) 304 P 2d. 606). (1957, Spring) *Montana Law Review, 18*, 218.

(Public Policy)

Robinson, H.L. (1957, March) Random thoughts on the rule of public policy that the law does not permit crime to pay. *U B C Legal Notes, 2*, 455.

(Homicide Bill)

Field-Fisher, T.G. (1956, Dec.) Homicide bill. *L J, 106*, 788.

(Mens Rea)

Fridman, G.H.L. (1956, Oct.) Two cases of mens rea. *Sol, 23*, 269.

(Felony-Murder)

Criminal law - homicide - robbery - felony-murder doctrine applied to justifiable homicide (Commonwealth v. Thomas (PA) 117 A 2d. 204). (1956, Oct.) *Texas Law Review, 34*, 1092.

(Felony-Murder Doctrine)

Criminal law - death of co-felon - felony-murder doctrine (Commonwealth v. Thomas (PA) 117 A 2d. 204) (1956, Fall) *Miami Law Quarterly, 11*, 145.

(Felony-Murder Rule)

Recent extensions of felony-murder rule. (1956, Summer) *Indiana Law Review, 31*, 534.

(Indictment)

Criminal law - indictment for murder of woman - rape alleged and immediate death - direction to jury - that manslaughter open-direction erroneous - Crimes Act 1901-1951 (NSW) ss. 5, 18- Criminal Appeal Act 1912 (NSW) s. 6 (Mraz v. The Queen (1955) A L R 929). (1956, June) *Res Judicatae, 7*, 334.

(Misdemeanor Manslaughter)

Criminal law - misdemeanor-manslaughter - death of tenants caused by violation of Multiple Dwelling Law (People v. Nelson (NY) 128 NE 2d. 391). (1956, June) *New York University Law Review, 31*, 1128.

(Co-Felon's Death)

Criminal law - felony-murder - criminal responsibility of felon for death of co-felon (Commonwealth v. Thomas (PA) 117 A 2d. 204). (1956, June) *New York University Law Review, 31*, 1125.

(Co-Felon's Death)

Criminal law - felony-murder - killing of co-felon (Commonwealth v. Thomas (PA) 117 A 2d. 204). (1956, June) *Louisiana Law Review, 16*, 804.

(Statutory Interpretation)

Criminal law - felony-murder - statutory interpretation (Commonwealth v. Thomas (PA) 117 A 2d. 204). (1956, June) *West Virginia Law Review, 58*, 415.

(Arson Death)

Criminal law - arson - strict application of the felony-murder doctrine (Commonwealth v. Bolish (PA) 113 A 2d. 464). (1956, May) *Hastings Law Journal, 7*, 314.

(Homicide of Co-Felon)

Criminal law - felony-murder - homicide of co-felon (Commonwealth v. Thomas (PA) 117 A 2d. 204). (1956, May) *Vill L Rev, 1*, 351.

(Negligence Requirement)

Criminal law - the negligence requirement for involuntary manslaughter (Trujillo v. People (CO) 292 P 2d. 980). (1956, April) *Rocky Mountain Law Review, 28*, 409.

(Felony-Murder Rule)

Criminal law - murder under felony-murder rule (Commonwealth v. Thomas (PA) 117 A 2d. 204). (1956, April) *Missouri Law Review, 21*, 172.

(Felony-Murder Rule)

Criminal law - homicide - application of felony-murder rule when non-felon kills felon (Commonwealth v. Thomas (PA) 117 A 2d. 204). (1956, April) *North Carolina Law Review, 34*, 350.

(Felony-Murder Rule)

Criminal law - felony-murder - D held for death of co-felon killed by robbery victim (Commonwealth v. Thomas (PA) 117 A 2d. 204). (1956, April) *Rocky Mountain Law Review, 28*, 412.

(Felony-Murder Rule)

Criminal law - application of felony-murder rule sustained where robbery victim killed defendant's accomplice (Commonwealth v. Thomas (PA) 117 A 2d. 204). (1956, Spring-Summer) *De Paul Law Review, 5*, 298.

(Felon's Liability)

Criminal law - felony-murder - liability of felon for death of co-felon (Commonwealth v. Thomas (PA) 117 A 2d. 204). (1956, Spring) *Arkansas Law Review, 10*, 221.

(Felony-Murder Rule)

Criminal law - felony-murder rule - liability for death of co-felon (Commonwealth v. Thomas (PA) 117 A 2d. 204). (1956, Spring) *Mercer Law Review, 7*, 391.

(Catathymic Crisis)

Criminal law - homicide - catathymic crisis as a defense. (1956, Spring) *Temple Law Quarterly, 29*, 386.

(Felony-Murder)

Criminal law - under the felony-murder doctrine, felons are guilty of first-degree murder of an accomplice who is killed by the victim of the felony (Commonwealth v. Thomas (PA) 117 A 2d. 204). (1956, March) *Georgia Law Journal, 44*, 529.

(Felony-Murder Rule)

Criminal law - the felony-murder rule (Commonwealth v. Thomas (PA) 117 A 2d. 204). (1956, March) *Western Reserve Law Review, 7*, 200.

(Felony-Murder Rule)

Criminal law - felony-murder - drunken driving as a felony. (1956, Feb.) *Oklahoma Law Review, 9*, 58.

(Felony-Murder - Case Report)

Criminal law - homicide - felony-murder - proximate cause - responsibility for death of co-conspirator in the perpetration of arson (Commonwealth v. Bolish (PA) 113 A 2d. 464).

(1956, Feb.) *Minnesota Law Review, 40*, 267.

(Felony-Murder Doctrine)

Criminal law - extension of felony-murder doctrine (Commonwealth v. Thomas (PA) 117 A 2d. 204). (1956, Winter) *Temple Law Quarterly, 29*, 205.

(Felony-Murder Rule)

Criminal law - felony-murder rule (Commonwealth v. Thomas (PA) 117 A 2d. 204). (1956, Jan.) *Howard Law Journal, 2*, 132.

(Multiple Dwelling Law)

Criminal law - conviction for homicide arising from violation of Multiple Dwelling Law upheld despite lack of notice to owner of violation (People v. Nelson (NY) 128 NE 2d. 391). (1956, Jan.) *New York University Law Review, 2*, 129.

(Felony-Murder Doctrine)

Criminal law - felony-murder doctrine as applicable to killing of accused's co-felon by intended victim of robbery (Commonwealth v. Thomas (PA) 117 A 2d. 204). (1956) *Washington & Lee Law Review, 13*, 193.

(Felony-Murder Rule)

Criminal law - felony-murder rule - application to the justifiable killing of an accomplice by the intended victim (Commonwealth v. Thomas (PA) 117 A 2d. 204). (1956) *Michigan Law Review, 54*, 860.

(Criminal Manslaughter)

Criminal law - misdemeanor manslaughter - necessity for notice of statutory violations (People v. Nelson (NY) 128 NE 2d. 391). (1955-1956, Winter) *Fordham Law Review, 24*, 688.

(Felony-Murder Rule)

Criminal law - homicide - felony-murder rule - criminal liability (Commonwealth v. Thomas). (1955-1956, Winter) *University of Kansas City Law Review, 24*, 155.

(Murder - Automobile)

Criminal law - homicide arising out of the use of automobiles. (1955, Nov.) *Oklahoma Law Review, 8*, 466.

(Felony-Murder Doctrine)

Criminal law - felony-murder doctrine (Commonwealth v. Bolish (PA) 113 A 2d. 464). (1955, Fall) *University of Pittsburgh Law Review, 17*, 101.

(Involuntary Manslaughter)

Criminal law - homicide - involuntary manslaughter (Graves v. Commonwealth (KY) 273 SW 2d. 380). (1955, Summer) *Sw L J, 9*, 365.

(Involuntary Manslaughter)

Criminal law - involuntary death from fright (Graves v. Commonwealth (KY) 273 SW 2d. 380). (1955, Summer) *Kentucky Law Journal, 43*, 548.

(Drunken Driving)

Criminal law - second-degree murder - homicide by drunken driving (Rogers v. State (TN) 265 SW 2d. 559) (1955, April) *Tennessee Law Review, 23*, 896-899.

(Legal Aspects)

Edwards, J.L.J. (1955, April) Legal aspects. *Criminal Law Review 1955*, 205-215.

(Second-Degree Murder)

Criminal law - second-degree murder instruction held prejudicial to defendant in statutory first-degree felony-murder trial (Green v. U.S. 218 F 2d. 856). (1955, April) *Virginia Law Review, 41*, 385-387.

(Felon's Death)

Criminal law - felony-murder - death of a felon in the perpetration of the crime (Commonwealth v. Bolish (PA) 113 A 2d. 464). (1955, Winter) *Rutgers Law Review, 10*, 446.

(Felony-Murder)

Criminal law - homicide - felony-murder committed in perpetration of arson - proximate cause - death of accomplice. (1955, Jan.) *Dick Law Review, 59*, 183-188.

(Corpus Delicti)

Criminal law - homicide - corpus delicti held sufficiently established by circumstantial evidence where motive, admissions, and unnatural death of deceased pointed to guilt of defendant (Opanowich v. Commonwealth (VA) 83 SE 2d. 432). (1954, Dec.) *Virginia Law Review, 40*, 1109-1111.

(Commentary)

Edwards, J.L.J. (1954, Dec.) Another view. *Criminal Law Review 1954*, 898-906.

(Provocation)

Odgers, F.J. (1954, Nov.) Criminal law - murder or manslaughter - provocation. *Cambridge Law Journal 1954*, 165-168.

(Provocation)

Cooper, A.M. (1954, Nov.) Criminal law - homicide - provocation - objective and subjective elements - effect of accused's state of intoxication - consideration of degree of violence used. *Canadian Bar Review, 32*, 1023-1027.

(Justifiable Homicide)

Criminal law - justifiable homicide to prevent commission of felonies. (1954, Aug.) *Oklahoma*

Law Review, 7, 344-347.

(Mens Rea and Actus Reus)

Burchell, E.M. (1954, Aug.) Murder - mens rea and actus reus. *S A L J, 71*, 285-286.

(Vehicular Manslaughter)

Criminal law - manslaughter - violation of motor vehicle statute (State v. Hugh (DE) 101 Atl. 2d. 355. (1954, May) *Catholic University Law Review, 4*, 133-135.

(Mens Rea)

Williams, G. (1954, May) Murder - mens rea - mistake of fact. *Modern Law Review, 17*, 271-272.

(Murder - Premeditated)

Criminal law - homicide - murder committed by lying in wait (People v. Thomas (CA) 261 Pac. 2d. 1; People v. Byrd (CA) 266 Pac. 2d. 505). (1954, May) *California Law Review, 42*, 337-345.

(Vehicular Homicide)

Criminal law -- homicide - prosecutions for motor vehicle homicide. (1954, March) *Nebraska Law Review, 33*, 456-462.

(Provocation)

Edwards, J.L.J. (1953, Oct.) Doctrine of provocation. *Law Quarterly Review, 69*, 547-550.

(Felony-Murder Doctrine)

Criminal law - application of murder-felony doctrine where homicide was the act of a non-participant in the felony (Miers v. State (TX) 251 SW 2d. 404). (1953, June) *Michigan Law Review, 51*, 1241-1243.

(Intent to Kill)

Criminal law - homicide - presumption of intent to kill although no deadly weapon is used (Henry v. State (TX) 246 SW 2d. 891). (1953, April) *Texas Law Review, 31*, 432-433.

(Malice)

Criminal law - constructive malice. (1952, April) *Law Journal, 102*, 229-230.

(Felony-Murder Rule)

Crum, C.L. (1952, April) Causal relations and the felony-murder rule. *Washington University Law Quarterly 1952*, 191-210

(Murder - Degrees)

Odum, J.E. (1952, Jan.) Criminal law - homicide perpetrated by poisoning not necessarily confined to murder in the first degree (Houlton v. State (AL) 48 So. 2d. 11). *Alabama Law, 13*, 54-57.

(Homicide Law)

Moreland, R. (1952) *Law of homicide.* Bobbs.

(Self-Defense)

Criminal law - defense of person in Texas. (1951, Oct.) *Texas Law Review, 29*, 960-962.

(Constructive Murder)

Willis, J. (1951, Aug.-Sept.) Constructive murder - Canadian law compared with law in England and United States - history and effect of section 260(d) of Criminal Code (Rowe v. The King (1951) 100 CCC 97). *Canadian Bar Review, 29*, 784-796.

(Intent to Kill)

Criminal law - intent in first-degree murder (Commonwealth v. Thompson (PA) 79 Atl. 2d. 401). (1951, June) *Dick Law Review, 55*, 405.

(Intent to Kill)

Murder - intent to kill as affecting degree of murder. (1951, April) *Southern California Law Review, 24*, 288-302.

(Manslaughter)

Misdemeanor manslaughter doctrine under modern statutes. (1951, March) *Kentucky Law Journal, 39*, 342-246.

(Involuntary Manslaughter)

Kentucky's concept of involuntary manslaughter. (1951, March) *Kentucky Law Journal, 39*, 351-352.

(Law Digest)

Barlow, T.B. Digest of law of murder and culpable homicide. *S A L J, 68*, 57-77 (1951, Feb.); *S A L J, 67*, 393-410 (1950, Nov.).

(Homicide - First Degree)

Criminal law - murder in the first degree in perpetration of felonies - definition of the felonies (Common wealth v. Maloney (PA) 73 Atl. 2d. 707). (1950, Oct.) *Dick Law Review, 55*, 80-82.

(Manslaughter)

Hatfield, G.W., Jr. (1949, Nov.) Misdemeanor-manlslaughter doctrine: Effect of "unlawfulness of the act" on liability for manslaughter. *Kentucky Law Journal, 38*, 129-134.

(Self-Defense)

Cagle, A.S. (1949, March) Imperfect self-defense. *Kentucky Law Journal, 37*, 334-337.

(Legal Reform)

Vesey-Fitzgerald, S.G. (1949) Reform of law of murder. *Current Legal Problems, 2*, 27-46.

(Criminal Homicide)

Thom, D.A. (1949) Juvenile delinquency and criminal homicide. *Journal of Maine Medical Association, 40,* 176-180.

(Trial Jury)

Linde, H. (1948, Dec.) Criminal law - first-degree murder - discretion of jury to choose between life imprisonment and death penalty (People v. Williams (CA) 195 Pac. 2d. 393). *California Law Review, 36,* 628-634.

(Autopsy)

Criminal law - autopsy as an essential in proving corpus delicti (Commonwealth v. Haley (PA) Atl. 2d. 62). (1948, Oct.) *Temple Law Quarterly, 22,* 230-232.

(Unborn Child)

Adcock, H.H. (1948, Fall) Criminal law - unborn child as subject of homicide (Singleton v. State (AL) 35 So. 2d. 375). *Alabama Law Review, 1,* 91-94.

(Manslaughter - Voluntary)

Mann, A. (1948, May) Criminal law - are there circumstances other than provocation which may "reduce" murder to manslaughter? *Kentucky Law Journal, 36,* 443-453.

(Intent to Kill)

Lynn, R.J. (1948, Spring) Criminal law - murder - intent to kill (State v. Salter (OH) 78 NE 2d. 575). *Ohio State Law Journal, 9,* 352-354.

(Manslaughter)

Becraft, C.E. (1948, Feb.) Criminal law - manslaughter - effect of violation of statute or ordinance on criminal negligence (State v. Nix (LA) 31 So. 2d. 1). (1948, Feb.) *Michigan Law Review, 46,* 566-568.

(Conspiracy - Case Report)

Brown, C.B. (1947, Fall) Criminal law - conspiracy (Mondier v. State (AR) 198 SW 2d. 177). *Arkansas Law Review, 1,* 304-306.

(Murder - Degrees)

Hitchler, W.H. (1947, March) Criminal law - degrees of murder - willful, deliberate, and premeditated killings (Commonwealth v. Jones (PA) 50 Atl. 2d. 317). *Dick Law Review, 51,* 183-184.

(Year and a Day Rule)

Whittle, J.A. (1947, Feb.) The year and a day rule (Head v. The State (GA) 24 SE 2d. 145). *Georgia Bar Journal, 9,* 320-322.

(Felony-Murder Evidence)

Criminal law - felony-murder evidence - intent - summation to jury (People v. Levan (NY) 64 NE 2d. 341). (1947, Feb.) *Brooklyn Law Review, 13*, 53-56.

(Required Intent)

Hess, R.K. (1947, Jan.) Criminal law - required intent - "Russian Poker" (Commonwealth v. Malone (PA) 47 Atl. 2d. 445). *Dick Law Review, 51*, 133-135.

(Provocation)

Criminal law - murder provocation (Holmes v. Director of Public Prosecutions (1946) A C 588). (1947) *Cambridge Law Journal, 9*, 378.

(Murder - First Degree)

Criminal law - first degree murder - mental deficiency not to be considered by jury if defendant's legal irresponsibility is not shown (Fisher v. United States 66 Sup. Ct. 1318). (1946, July) *Temple Law Quarterly, 20*, 155-156.

(Murder - Degrees)

Kopald, J.S. (1946, July) Criminal law - murder - distinction between first and second degrees. *Southern California Law Review, 19*, 417-423.

(Homicide Law)

Perkins, R.M. (1946, March-April) Law of homicide. *Journal of Criminal Law, 36*, 391-454.

(Personal Violence)

Criminal law - felony involving personal violence - use of loaded firearm a violent measure - death of victim caused by inadvertent discharge of firearm held to be murder (Rex v. Jarmain (1946) 1 K B 74). (1946) *Cambridge Law Journal*, 243-244.

(Homicide - Psychiatric Aspects)

Davidson, G.M. (1946) Psychiatric aspects of the law of homicide. *Psychiatric Quarterly Supplement, 20*, 30-49.

(Statute of Limitations)

Rae, W.G. (1945, Nov.) Criminal law - murder - statute of limitations (State v. Patriarca (RI) 42 Atl. 2d. 54). *B U L Rev, 25*, 372-373.

(Mens Rea)

Funk, A.E., Jr. (1945, May) Mens rea in the early law of homicide. *Kentucky Law Journal, 33*, 312-315.

(Suicide Pact)

Criminal law - murder - accessory before the fact - 'suicide pact' - survivor not present at suicide of other party - countermanding of agreement (Rex v. Croft (1944) K B 295). (1945)

Cambridge Law Journal, 9, 120-121.

(Jury Power)

Kivari, C. (1944, Sept.) Criminal law - jury's power to fix penalty - instructions by trial court with reference to (People v. Kolez (CA) 145 Pac. 2d. 580). *Southern California Law Review, 18,* 52-54.

(Proximate Cause)

Criminal law - homicide - proximate cause (People v. Goodman 44 NY Supp. 2d. 715). (1944, May) *Fordham Law Review, 13,* 104-109.

(Reversal of Judgment)

Criminal procedure - murder - reversal of judgment because of court's statement that conspiracy existed (People v. Jackson (NY) 52 NE 2d. 945). (1944, April) *St. John's Law Review, 18,* 124-125.

(Medical Negligence)

Criminal law - manslaughter - negligence of medical practitioner (Akerle v. The King (1943) A C 255). (1944) *Cambridge Law Journal, 8,* 323-324.

(Manslaughter)

Martin, G.A. (1943, June) Criminal law - voluntary and involuntary manslaughter - unlawful acts (Rex v. Larkin (1943) 1 All E R 217). *Canadian Bar Review, 21,* 503-505.

(Murder Trial)

Trial for murder - evidence consistent only with murder - whether judge should direct jury that they may return verdict of manslaughter (Rex v. Surridge (1942) 42 S R (N.S.W.) 278). (1943, April) *Australian Law Journal, 16,* 365.

(Homicide - Negligent)

Sayles, R.A. (1943, Jan.) Criminal law - negligent homicide - interpretation of Vehicle Code Section 500, as amended in 1941 (People v. Young (CA) 129 Pac. 2d. 353). *Southern California Law Review, 16,* 103-106.

(Murder and Manslaughter)

Murder and manslaughter (Rex v. Roberts (1942) 1 All E R 187). (1942, Oct.) *Law Quarterly Review, 58,* 446-448.

(Murder - First Degree)

Murder in the first degree, evidence, corroboration of accomplice's testimony (People v. Goldstein (NY) 34 NE 2d. 362). (1941, Nov.) *St. John's Law Review, 16,* 131-133.

(Involuntary Manslaughter)

Criminal law - homicide - involuntary manslaughter - negligence required (Commonwealth v.

Aurick (PA) 19 Atl. 2d. 920). *Temple University Law Quarterly, 16*, 96-98 (1941, Nov.); *Dick Law Review, 46*, 59-60 (1941, Oct.).

(Attempted Felony)

Criminal law - murder - homicide - attempted commission of felony (Commonwealth v. Guida (PA) 148 Atl. 501). (1941, Oct.) *Dick Law Review, 46*, 58-59.

(Sentencing)

Kassel, P.J. (1941, Oct.) Felony-murder, sentencing, recommendation of life imprisonment by jury not binding on court (People v. Cole (NY) 35 NE 2d. 503). *Brooklyn Law Review, 11*, 108-114.

(Murder - Second Degree)

Presumption of second-degree murder (State v. Davis (WA) 108 Pac. 2d. 641). (1941, July) *Washington Law Review, 16*, 162-163.

(Murder - First Degree)

Mintz, C.R. (1941, April) Crimes, murder in the first degree, defendant has no duty to retreat before slaying person who feloniously assaults him (People v. Ligouri (NY) 31 NE 2d. 37). *Columbia Law Review, 41*, 733-738.

(Robbery/Murder)

Murder in the perpetration of or attempting to perpetrate robbery (Commonwealth v. Kelly (PA) 10 Atl. 2d. 431). (1940, Feb.) *Temple University Law Quarterly, 14*, 284-287.

(Prior Threats)

Criminal procedure - homicide - evidence of dangerous and prior threats (State v. Stracner (LA) 187 So. 571). (1940, Jan.) *Louisiana Law Review, 2*, 376-378.

(Felony-Murder Doctrine)

Felony-murder doctrine: Are all the robbers guilty of murder when one kills another during the perpetration of the robbery? (People v. Cabaltero (CA) 87 Pac. 2d. 364). (1939, July) *California Law Review, 27*, 612-615.

(Felony-Murder Case)

Anderson, H.G. (1939, May) Charging the degrees of crime in felony-murder cases. *Brooklyn Law Review, 8*, 411-424.

(Murder - First Degree)

Myers, T.I. (1939, April) Murder in the first degree in the perpetration of felonies; definition of the felonies. *Dick Law Review, 43*, 194-203.

(Presumption of Murder)

Criminal law - homicide - presumption of murder - reasonable doubt (Commonwealth v. Kluska

(PA) 3 Atl. 2d. 398). *Temple University Law Quarterly, 13*, 394-397.

(Negligent Homicide)

Kahn, R.L. (1939, March) Criminal law - negligent homicide - degrees of negligence (People v. Warner (CA) 80 Pac. 2d. 737). *Southern California Law Review, 12*, 317-319.

(Aiding and Abetting)

Turner, J.W. (1939, March) Aiding and abetting - moral duty to act (Wright v. Commonwealth (1938) 272 KY. 77). *Kentucky Law Journal, 27*, 355-357.

(Felony-Murder)

James, J.D. (1939, Jan.) Killing in attempt to commit felony (State v. Wright (MO) 112 SW 2d. 571). *Missouri Law Review, 4*, 76-78.

(Manslaughter)

Manslaughter - death resulting from the commission of a misdemeanor (Commonwealth v. Samson (PA) 196 Atl. 564). (1938, Dec.) *Minnesota Law Review, 23*, 95-96.

(Felony-Murder)

Criminal law - homicide - committed in perpetration of felony - degree (State v. Roach (NJ) 197 Atl. 33). (1938, April) *Temple Law Quarterly, 12*, 408-409.

(Felony-Murder - Punishment)

Asip, E.F. (1938, April) Recent penal law provisions in relation to punishment for felony-murder (legislation). *St. John's Law Review, 12*, 373-377.

(Murder Law)

Mullins, C. (1938, July) Our law of murder. *Law Journal, 86*, 22-23.

(Homicide Law)

Michael, J., & Wechsler, H. (1937, Dec.) Rationale of the law of homicide. *Columbia Law Review, 37*, 1261-1325.

(Ancient Law)

Morrow, G.R. (1937, July) Murder of slaves in Attic law. *Class Philos, 42*, 210-227.

(Homicide Law)

Wechsler, H., & Michael, J. (1937, May) Rationale of the law of homicide. *Columbia Law Review, 37*, 701-761.

(Nonfeasance)

Crytzer, H.B. (1937, Jan.) Homicide by nonfeasance. *Dick Law Review, 41*, 126-132.

(Hearsay - Exceptions)

Hearsay - exceptions to the hearsay rule - statements of facts against penal interests (State v. Voges (MN) 266 NW 265). (1937, Jan.) *Minnesota Law Review, 21*, 181-191.

(Legal Status)

Bedwell, C.E.A. (1937) The legal status of voluntary. *Med-Leg & Crim Rev, 5*, 1.

(Child-Murder)

Gummersbach, H. (1937) The criminological and legal evaluation of child murder (German). *Mschr Krimbiol, 28*, 364.

(Appeal and Error)

Appeal and error - bills of exception - scope of (Miller v. State (TX) 84 SW 2d. 459). (1936, June) *Texas Law Review, 14*, 545-546.

(Criminal Law Case Report)

Criminal law - homicide (People v. Pace (IL) 198 NE 319). (1936, May) *University of Cincinnati Law Review, 10*, 330-331.

(Property Acquisition)

Wade, J.W. (1936, March) Acquisition of property by willfully killing another - a statutory solution. *Harvard Law Review, 49*, 715-755.

(Drunk Driving)

Pike, J.A. (1936, Jan.) Criminal law - statutory interpretation - death caused by drunk driving - Penal Code (1935) 367e, Vehicle Code (1935), 501. *So Cal Law Rev, 9*, 142-149.

(Statute Modification)

Gosline, R.B. (1935, Dec.) Validity of statute allowing modification of criminal verdict by appellate court (Turk v. State (OH) 194 NE 425) *Ohio State University Law Review, 2*, 44-46.

(Double Guilt)

Mortal wound by one and infliction of injury by another which hastens the death makes both guilty of murder (Payne v. Commonwealth (KY) 75 SW 2d. 14). (1935, April) *Temple Law Quarterly, 9*, 347-348.

(Dying Declaration)

Uncorroborated dying declaration of victim - identification of defendant (People v. Ludkowitz (NY) 194 NE 688). (1935, May) *St. John's Law Review, 9*, 411-413.

(Liability of Felon)

Perlstein, S.A. (1934, July-Aug.) Liability of robber for death caused by shot of third person (Wilson v. State (AR) 68 SW 2d. 100). *Journal of Criminal Law, 25*, 283-285.

(Recantation of Testimony)

Dyche, G.F. (1934, July-Aug.) Murder - recantation of testimony by state's principle witness (Commonwealth v. Gwizdowski (MA) 188 NE 383). *Journal of Criminal Law, 25*, 285-287.

(Criminal Responsibility)

Cohen, J., et al. Responsibility for failure to perform affirmative acts (Rex v. Russell (1933) Vict. L R 59). *Journal of Criminal Law, 25*, 287-289 (1934, July-Aug.); *West Virginia Law Quarterly, 40*, 387-390 (1934, June); *Wisconsin Law Review, 9*, 424-425 (1934, June).

(Double Jeopardy)

Absell, L. (1934, June) Double jeopardy as applied to grades of first-degree murder (Commonwealth v. Alessio (PA) 169 Atl. 764). *Dick Law Review, 38*, 276-280.

(Homicide - Accessory)

Hill, D.K. (1934, May-June) Murder - conviction of accessories to the felony (People v. Ryan (NY) 189 NE 225). *Journal of Criminal Law, 25*, 126-128.

(Hearsay Rule)

Wise, D.F., & Hippenmeyer, R.S. Hearsay rule - conditions under which exceptions may be made in favor of dying declaration (Shepard v. United States, 54 Sup. Ct. 22). *Wisconsin Law Review, 9*, 196-198. (1934, Feb.); *University of Pennsylvania Law Review, 82*, 290-292 (1934, Jan.); *Notre Dame Law, 9*, 256-258 (1934, Jan.); *Columbia Law Review, 34*, 175.

(Year and a Day Rule)

Blau, H., et al. Common law rule, that death must occur in a year and a day, has been abrogated (People v. Legeri, 266 NY Supp. 86). *Cornell Law Quarterly*, 19, 306-311 (1934, Feb.); *St. John's Law Review, 8*, 162 (1933, Dec.).

(Criminal Responsibility)

Omission to act - non-interference with murder of children and wife's suicide (Rex v. Russell (1933) Vict. L R 59) (1934, Jan.) *Harvard Law Review, 47*, 531-532.

(Corpus Delicti)

The corpus delicti in murder. (1934) *Scot Law Review, 50*, 101.

(Manslaughter)

Insurance and manslaughter. (1933, May) *Legal Times, 175*, 337-338.

(Criminal Responsibility)

Grover, R.L. Legal cause and criminal responsibility (Stephenson v. State (IN) 179 NE 633). *Michigan Law Review, 31*, 659-682 (1933, March); *University of Pennsylvania Law Review, 81*, 189-194 (1932, Dec.); *Journal of Criminal Law, 23*, 649-651 (1932, Nov.-Dec.); *Harvard Law Review, 45*, 1261-1262 (1932, May).

(Evidence - Sufficiency)

Criminal law and procedure - sufficiency of information (State v. Stone (WA) 13 Pac. 2d. 427). (1933, March) *Michigan Law Review, 31*, 728-730.

(Sentencing)

Weidel, M. (1933, Jan.-Feb.) Murder - sentence - consideration of prior related acts (People v. Corry (IL) 181 NE 603). *Journal of Criminal Law, 23*, 845-846.

(Murder by Beneficiary)

Murder of the insured by the beneficiary - who may recover. (1933) *Minnesota Law Review, 17*, 759.

(Co-Conspirators)

Southworth, W.A. (1933) Homicide committed by conspirator during escape after robbery - liability of co-conspirators. *Cornell Law Quarterly, 18*, 439.

(Withdrawal of Verdict)

Wiedel, M. (1932, Nov.-Dec.) Murder - withdrawal of verdict-form - less than unanimous verdicts (People v. Brothers (IL) 180 NE 442). *Journal of Criminal Law, 23*, 651-654.

(Defense of Property)

Homicide in defense of property. (1932, Sept.) *Law Journal, 74*, 142-143.

(Manslaughter)

Katz, A.R. (1932, July-Aug.) Manslaughter - accessory before the fact (Ra v. Commonwealth (KY) 43 SW 2d. 694). *Journal of Criminal Law, 23*, 287-289.

(Reversible Error)

Baker, N.F. (1932, May) Reversible error in homicide cases. *Journal of Criminal Law, 23*, 28-50.

(Aiding and Abetting)

Requirements of knowledge in an instruction on "aiding and abetting" (State v. Miner (IA) 238 NW 594). (1932, May) *Iowa Law Review, 17*, 520-532.

(Murder Charge)

Murder charge - expression of opinion (Commonwealth v. Nafus, 303 PA 418). (1932, April) *Temple Law Quarterly, 6*, 417-418.

(Murder Trial)

Murder - participation of trial judge in trial (Commonwealth v. Del Giorno, 303 PA 509). (1932, April) *Temple Law Quarterly, 6*, 418-419.

(Public Policy)

Public policy in its application to statute law (Re Pitts (1931) 1 Ch. 546). (1932, Feb.) *Sol J, 76*, 118-119.

(Intestacy)

Intestacy - murder of intestate - murderer's right to distributive share (In re Pitts (1931) 1 Ch.

546). *Law Quarterly Review, 48*, 20-21 (1932, Jan.); (letter) *Australian Law Journal, 5*, 203-204 (1932, Oct.); *Australian Law Journal, 5*, 161 (1931, Sept.); *Canadian Bar Review, 9*, 504-506.

(Homicide - Justifiable)

Herzog, C.E. (1932, Jan.) Criminal law - justifiable homicide - killing a supposed felon (People v. Doody (IL) 175 NE 436). *Illinois Law Review, 26*, 587-589.

(Murder by Beneficiary)

Murder of insured by beneficiary of life insurance policy (Meyer v. Johnson (CA) 2 Pac.2d. 456). (1932, Jan.) *California Law Review, 20*, 210-212.

(Poisoning - Attempted)

Criminal law - prosecution for poisoning not resulting in fatality. (1930, Nov.) *Michigan Law Review, 29*, 87-93.

(Intent to Kill)

Serhant, J.E. (1930, Nov.) Criminal law - assault with intent to murder - specific intent (Hawkins v. State (TX) 29 SW 2d. 384). *Journal of Criminal Law, 21*, 452-453.

(Felony-Murder)

Donlon, E.J. (1929, Dec.) Felony-murder and the Jones Law. *St. John's Law Review, 4*, 93-99.

(Unwritten Law)

The "unwritten law". *Crim L, 18*, 365-371 (1927, Nov.); *Sol J, 71*, 257-258 (1927, April).

(Legal Reform)

Modified murder law? (1927, May) *Outlook, 59*, 481-482.

(Penal Code - India)

The law relating to homicide in the Indian penal code. (1927) *Allahabad Law Journal, 25*, 17.

(Common Law vs. Code)

Violence causing death - common law and code (Rex v. Elnick, 53 D N R 298). (1927, Jan.) *Canadian Bar Review, 5*, 68-74.

(Manslaughter)

Accessory before the fact in manslaughter (State v. McVay (RI) 132 Atl. 436). *Harvard Law Review, 40*, 321-332 (1926, Dec.); *Michigan Law Review, 25*, 72-73 (1926, Nov.).

(Manslaughter)

Manslaughter - mens rea (People v. Mulcahy, 318 IL 332). (1926, April) *Illinois Law Review, 20*, 835-836.

(Jury Charge)

Cornish, L.C. (1920) Charge to a jury in a recent murder trial. *Maine Law Review, 13*, 87.

(Comparative Law)

Lobingier, C.S. (1918) Homicide concept: A study in comparative criminal law. *Journal of Criminal Law, 9*, 373-377.

(Judicial Decrees)

Crossley, F.B. (1914) Executive nullification of judicial decrees. *Journal of Criminal Law, 4*, 464.

(Homicide - Classification)

Dykes, D.O. (1913, July) Homicide - classification of homicide - a study of comparative law. *American Law Review, 47*, 528-535.

(Trial Recommendations)

Scott, F. (1912) A few points as to the administration of the criminal law suggested by the McNamara trial. *New Jersey Law Journal, 35*, 4.

(Murder Law)

Some points in the law of murder. (1903) *Justice of the Peace, 67*, 519, 530.

(Parental Liability)

Lee, J.H.S. (1901) Is a parent liable at common law on a charge of manslaughter for negligently omitting to furnish medical attendance to his child? *Am L, 9*, 565.

(Christian Science)

Purrington, W.A. (1899) Christian Science and the law. *Am L, 7*, 5.

(Parental Liability)

Parents and the criminal law. (1898) *Ir L T, 32*, 1.

Legal Case Reports

(Family Trial)

Edmiston, S. (1990, Nov.) Daddy's girl. *Glamour, 88*(11), pp. 228-231+.

(Charges Reinstated)

Homicide charges reinstated against Warren motorcyclist (Commonwealth (PA) vs. Cagle). (1990, Oct. 15) *Pennsylvania Law Journal-Reporter, 13*, 9.

(Conviction Reversed)

Use of recanted testimony forces conviction reversal (Commonwealth v. Brady (PA)). (1990, Oct. 15) *Pennsylvania Law Journal-Reporter*, 9.

(Halcion Suit)

Seager, S. (1990, Sept. 4) Man blames Halcion in wife's slaying; suits, complaints say sleeping pill induces violence; first California criminal case. *Los Angeles Daily Journal, 103*, p. 1.

(Colorado Trial)

Fitzgerald, M. (1990, Aug. 11) Witness identifies reporter as killer, then recants. *Editor & Publisher, 123*(32), p. 11.

(Sentencing)

Souter, D.H. (1990, Aug. 6) Souter's stern judgment on sentencing (excerpts from David H. Souter's sentencing statement of a drunk driver who killed 3 teenagers). *Legal Times, 13*, 10.

(Manslaughter)

Rees, T., & Smith, J.C. (1990, Aug.) Manslaughter - change of plea following judge's ruling - 'unlawful' act leading to death - whether carrying offensive weapon 'unlawful' act. *Criminal Law Review*, 588-589.

(Walker Case)

Shapiro, M. (1990, July 23) A lifeline of letters. *New York, 23*(28), p. 22.

(New Evidence)

Underwood, N. (1990, July 9) A freedom crusade (new evidence raises questions about conviction of D.Milgaard for 1969 murder in Saskatoon, Sask.) *Macleans, 103*, p. 39.

(Liability - Hospital)

Shanken, P., & Harris, B.R. (1990, June 4) Pa. hospital may be liable for discharging murderer. *Pennsylvania Law Journal-Reporter*, 9.

(Doctor Cleared)

Brahams, D. (1990, March 24) Doctor cleared of murder of cancer patient. *Lancet, 335*(8691),

718.

(Uneven Justice)

Bruning, F. (1990, Feb. 5) The race factor in a brutal killing. *Macleans, 103*(6), p. 11.

(Trial - Canada)

Solursh, L.P., & Meyer, C.A., Jr. (1990) After the trial: Abusing the expert - a Canadian case report. *Medicine and Law, 9*(6), 1202-1205.

(Peden Case)

Cordner, S. (1990) The Peden case and expert witnesses. *Medical Journal of Australia, 153*(11-12), 643-644.

(Computers)

Forker, A. (1990) The use of computers in criminal proceedings: A case report. *Forensic Science International, 46*(1-2), 15-16.

(Charges Dropped)

Dyer, C. (1990) SHO has murder charges dropped. *British Medical Journal, 300*(6727), 768-769.

(Police - Manslaughter)

Miami cop who killed two blacks and incited riot guilty of manslaughter. (1989, Dec. 25) *Jet, 77*(12), pp. 4-5.

(Trial - Parents)

Spencer, G. (1989, Dec. 18) Panel orders parents to stand trial for 'drinking' death of teenage son. *New York Law Journal, 202*, 1.

(Not Guilty)

Hoffman, J. (1989, Dec. 5) His sister's keeper. *Village Voice, 34*(49), pp. 21-26.

(Killer Manhunt)

Taylor, G.W. (1989, Nov. 27) Blood on the cross. *Macleans, 102*(48), p. 71.

(Manitoba Trial)

Underwood, N., & Brosnahan, M. (1989, July 10) Unhealed wounds. *Macleans, 102*(28), p. 41.

(Homicide - Faith Healing)

Anderson, C.E. (1989, July) When faith healing fails: Jurors convict Florida Christian Science couple of murder death of child. *ABA Journal, 75*, 22.

(Verdict)

Fisk, M.C. (1989, June 25) Verdict on Michigan judge's killing raises furor. *The National Law Journal, 11*, 14.

(Justice)

Weller, S. (1989, June) Justice at last (J. Pikul found guilty). *Ms, 17*, p. 75.

(Witness)

Brower, M. (1989, April 24) The littlest witness may say about her friend's killing (four-year-old J. Royal to testify against M. Ward in Miami trial). *People Weekly, 31*, pp. 108-110.

(Conviction Overturned)

Conviction overturned in brutal killing (new trial ordered for Reginald Mahaffey). (1989, April 20) *Chicago Daily Law Bulletin, 135,* 1.

(Mistrial)

Fitzgerald, M. (1989, April 1) Judge declares mistrial in murder case; city's news story. *Editor & Publisher, 122*(13), 23.

(Murder - J. Mendez)

Costikyan, B. (1989, March 20) Park Avenue gothic. *New York, 22*(12), 46-54.

(Hunting Death)

Chambers, M. (1989, Jan. 30) (Maine) On trail of truth in a hunting death. *The National Law Journal, 11*, p. 13.

(British Homicide)

Douglas, G.R. (1989) Murder and manslaughter in the Crown Court. *Law Society's Gazette, 86*(7), 19-20, 23.

(Right to Die)

Holley, D.M. (1989) Voluntary death, property rights, and the gift of life. *Journal of Religion & Ethics, 17*, 103-121.

(Crown Court)

Douglas, G.R. (1989) Murder and manslaughter in the Crown Court. *Law Society's Gazette, 86*(7), 19-20, 23.

(Burden of Proof)

Dixon, J., & Lizotte, A.J. (1989) The burden of proof- southern subculture of violence- explanations of gun ownership and homicide: Note. *American Journal of Sociology, 95*(1), 182-187.

(Sentence Overturned)

Appeals court overturns sentence in reporter's murder. (1988, Dec. 31) *Editor & Publisher, 121*(53), p. 9.

(Attempted Murder Conviction)

News exec's stepson found guilty of attempted murder. (1988, Dec. 31) *Editor & Publisher, 121*(53), p. 10.

(Beating Charges)

Supremacists arrested in Portland beating death. (1988, Dec. 12) *Jet, 75*, p. 17.

(Extradition)

O'Farrell, E. (1988, Dec.12) Facing extradition. *Macleans, 101*(51), p. N1.

(Sentence Condemned)

Allen, G., & Kavanaugh, P. (1988, Dec. 3) A sentence on trial. *Macleans, 101*(41), p. 15.

(Terrorist Trial)

Doerner, W.R., & Graff, J. (1988, Sept. 26) Chipping away at terrorism. *Time, 132*(13), pp. 41-44.

(New Evidence)

More good news for Lipscomb. (1988, Sept. 2) *Christianity Today, 32*(12), p. 47.

(Not Guilty Plea)

He pleads not guilty. (1988, Aug. 6) *Editor & Publisher, 121*(32), p. 36.

(Euthanasia)

Jordan, P. (1988, Aug.) Murderer of model husband? *50 Plus, 28*(8), pp. 22-25+.

(Euthanasia)

Wolinsky, A. (1988, Jan.-Feb.) Euthanasia. *Humanist, 48*, p. 24+.

(Tudor Law)

Robison, W.B. (1988) Murder at Crowhurst: A case history in early Tudor law enforcement. *Criminal Justice History: An International Annual, 9*, 31-62.

(Original Suspect)

Bloomfield, J. (1988) The original suspect. *Medical Science and the Law, 28*(4), 286-290.

(Innocence Proven)

Zuckerman, I. (1987, Oct. 19) Auguries of innocence (K. Buckner posthumously cleared of murdering his family in Ecklund, MO.). *Time, 130*, p. 21.

(Injustice)

Gee, M. (1987, Oct. 19) Exploring an injustice (inquiry into Sydney, N.S. conviction of D. Marshall). *Macleans, 100*, p. 29.

(Homicide - Antebellum)

Gorn, E.J. (1987, Sept.) "Good-bye boys, I die a true American": Homicide, nativism, and working-class culture in antebellum New York City. *Journal Of American History, 74*, 388-410.

(Jean Harris)

Harrison, B.G. (1987, Aug.) The lady killer: Should Jean Harris go free? *Mademoiselle, 93*,

p. 164.

(Sentence Extended)

Deaf-mute must stay in mental hospital for 1971 slaying in Chicago (D. Lang case). (1987, June 8) *Jet, 72*, p. 17.

(Brian Spencer Accused)

Dexter, M.P. (1987, May 11) The case against Brian Spencer (accused of M. Dalfo's murder in Palm Beach Gardens, FL.). *Sports Illustrated, 66*, pp. 98-102+.

(Murder - S. Bryant)

Hubner, J., & Gruson, L. (1987, April 9) Dial om for murder (involvement of guru Bhaktipada in murder of S. Bryant). *Rolling Stone*, pp. 53-54+.

(Don Arrow's Murder)

Hammer, J. (1987, March 30) Don Arrow's murder leaves Miami wondering: Were 'Cigarettes' hazardous to his health? *People Weekly, 27*, pp. 75-76+.

(Corporate Homicide)

Tasini, J. (1987, March 2) A death at work can put the boss in jail (homicide conviction against Sabine Consolidated, Inc.). *Business Week*, pp. 37-38.

(Murder - D. Fossey)

Trainer, B., & Maranto, G. (Eds.) (1987, Feb.) I didn't kill Diane, she was my friend (murder of gorilla protector D. Fossey). *Discover, 8*, pp. 28-32+.

(Cleared)

Alabama man cleared of murder 15 years later (case of B.J. Lester). (1987, Jan. 19) *Jet, 71*, p. 26.

(Witness Examination)

Becker, T.G. (1987) Cross-examination of expert witness. *Air Force Law Review, 27*, 119-123.

(Cross-Examination)

Johnston, M.W. (1987) Cross-examination of the accused. *Air Force Law Rev, 27,* 133-140.

(S. Linscott Case)

Steve Linscott's emotional roller-coaster ride continues (murder case in IL.). (1986, Nov. 21) *Christianity Today, 30*, p. 31.

(Court Review - Lang)

High Court orders review of deaf mute Donald Lang. (1986, Nov. 3) *Jet, 71*, p. 24.

(Conviction Affirmed)

Murder conviction affirmed due to consensual entry on arrest-- IL. (1986, Oct.) *Search and Seizure Bulletin*, 3-4.

(Parole Controversy)

Conn, N.H. (M. Story, Ed.) (1986, Sept.) Stalked by a killer (fight against parole of murderer R.M. Ellard). *Reader's Digest, 129*, pp. 59-63.

(Jean Harris)

Reed, J. (1986, Aug. 18) The strange case of Jean Harris (bid for clemency). *U.S. News & World Report, 101*, pp. 51-52.

(Sentence - Woman)

Woman sterilized to get a lesser sentence (case of D.A. Williams). (1986, Aug. 11) *Jet, 70*, p. 36.

(T. Cimo Case)

Harris, A. (1986, July 7) Tony Cimo served three years for avenging his murdered parent: He says time was well spent. *People Weekly, 26*, p. 149.

(Jean Harris Case)

An ailing Jean Harris has suffered enough, or so says her son, who is fighting to free her from prison. (1986, July 7) *People Weekly, 26*, p. 149.

(Murder - Case and Comment)

Pigott, M., & Smith, J.C. (1986, July) Case and comment: Murder. *The Criminal Law Review*, 470-471.

(Sentence - Controversy)

Gray, M. (1986, June 30) A new bid for freedom (controversy over manslaughter sentence given to Canadian B. Curtis in N.J.) *Macleans, 99*, pp. 38-39.

(Charges Dropped)

Black man cleared of wrongful murder charge (T. Ferrer of the Bronx, N.Y.). (1986, June 9) *Jet, 70*, p. 38.

(Evidence)

Knapman, L., et al. (1986, June) Case and comment: Evidence. *The Criminal Law Review 1986*, 394-397.

(Jean Harris Case)

Alexander, S. (1986, April 7) The case for Jean Harris. *New York, 19*, pp. 44-49

(Habeas Corpus)

Accessory to murder--habeas corpus petition denied--8th Circuit. (1986, March) *Arrest Law Bulletin*, 6-7.

(Intent)

Pigott, M., & Smith, J.C. (1986, March) Case and comment: Intent. *The Criminal Law*

Review 1986, 180-183.

(Conviction Overturned)

Jones, K.L. (1986, Feb.) Murderous dream (overturn of S. Linscott's conviction in Oak Park, IL.). *Omni, 8*, p. 87.

(Criminal Law)

McCullough, L.A. (1986, Winter) International and domestic criminal law issues in the Achille Lauro incident: A functional analysis. *Naval Law Review, 36*, 53-108.

(Witness)

Jones, D.P., et al. (1986) Can a three-year-old child bear witness to her sexual assault and attempted murder. *Child Abuse & Neglect, 10*(2), 253-258.

(Supreme Court)

Carr, J. (1986) Overview of recent Supreme Court decisions on the fourth amendment. *Search and Seizure Law Report, 13*(8), 57-64.

(Probation Sentence)

Judge gives probation to man, 85, who killed neighbor, while officials sought imprisonment. (1986) *Corrections Digest, 17*(14), 7-8. Article copies available from UMI.

(Police Testimony)

Police illegality results in exclusion of witness' testimony. (1986) *The Criminal Law Reporter: Court Decisions, 38*(17), 2323-2325.

(Death Penalty)

Capital defendant cannot bar presentation of mitigating evidence. (1986) *The Criminal Law Reporter: Court Decisions, 38*(17), 2325-2326.

(Sentencing - Length)

How many years does a murder conviction bring behind bars? Less than seven, BJS finds. (1986) *Corrections Digest, 17*(8), 7-8. Article copies available from UMI.

(Indifference)

Homicide -- defenses -- justification -- depraved indifference murder. (1986) *The Criminal Law Reporter: Court Decisions, 39*(13), 2240.

(Possession of Weapon)

Homicide -- felony murder -- possession of weapon. (1986) *The Criminal Law Reporter: Court Decisions, 38*(14), 2273.

(Charge Dropped)

Attempted murder raps dropped for N.Y.'s Goetz. (1986) *Law Enforcement News, 12*(3), 7. Article copies available from UMI.

(Defense Burden)

Presumption that shifted production burden to defense was constitutional. (1986) *The Criminal Law Reporter: Court Decisions, 38*(14), 2267-2269.

(Richardson v. State))

You be the judge: Richardson v. State. (1986) *The Law Officer's Bulletin, 10*(20) 118.

(State v. Mauro)

You be the judge: State v. Mauro. (1986) *The Law Officer's Bulletin, 10*(17), 100-101.

(State v. Saylor)

You be the judge: State v. Saylor. (1986) *The Law Officer's Bulletin, 11*(4), 23.

(State v. Williams)

You be the judge: State v. Williams. (1986) *The Law Officer's Bulletin, 10*(15), 88.

(Tarasoff Modified)

Sargent, M. (1986) Tarasoff decision modified. *ADAMHA N, 12*(1), 12.

(Warrantless Search)

Warrantless felony routine arrest-- AR. (1985, Dec.) *Arrest Law Bulletin*, 2-3. Microforms and article copies available from UMI.

(Right to Life - Downs)

Gunn, M.J., & Smith, J.C. (1985, Nov.) Arthur's case and the right to life of a Down's Syndrome child. *The Criminal Law Review 1985*, 705-715.

(Lawsuit Dismissed)

Judge dismisses lawsuit by Wayne Williams' parents. (1985, Oct. 21) *Jet, 69*, p. 26.

(Hillside Strangler)

O'Brien, D. (1985, Oct.) Convicting the hillside stranglers (excerpts from *Two of a kind*). *Good Housekeeping, 201*, pp. 97-100+.

(Conviction Overturned)

Court nixes conviction of N.Y. '.22-calliber killer' (case of J.G. Christopher). *Jet, 68*, p. 37.

(Trial - Doctor)

Breu, G. (1985, July 15) In a chilling case, a doctor stands trial after his son's shooting (case of J.D. Cavaness). *People Weekly, 24*, pp. 113-114.

(Verdict)

Cahan, V., et al. (1985, July) A murder verdict jolt business (employee exposure to cyanide at Film Recovery Systems plant). *Business Week*, pp. 24-25.

(Slain Cager)

Slain high school cager's family files $10 million wrongful-death lawsuit (case of B. Wilson).

(1985, May 27) *Jet, 68*, p. 38.

(Charges Dropped)

N.Y. man, who killed alleged newsstand robber, cleared of all charges (case of A. Frederick). (1985, April 22) *Jet, 68*, p. 40.

(Sentence - Protest)

Mother protests sentence given daughter's killer (case of C. Gray). (1985, April 8) *Jet, 68*, p. 38.

(Court Judgment)

Rare court judgment in love-murder case enrages deceased's kin (family of C. Gray protests light sentence given to E. Strother). (1985, March 11) *Jet, 67*, pp. 12-13.

(Death Penalty)

Willimon, W.H. (1985, March 6) Following Jesus (murder of 8-year-old girl J.K.H. Fewel, provokes capital punishment contemplation). *Christian Century, 102*, pp. 236-237.

(Defense - Moral)

Johnson, J.T. (1985) Threats, values, and defense: Does defense of values by force remain a moral possibility? *Parameter, 15*(1), 13-25.

(Justice System)

Bloom, J.D., et al. (1985) Halfway around the world to prison: Vietnamese in the Oregon criminal justice system. *Medicine & the Law, 4*(6), 563-572.

(Conspiracy)

Conspiracy--attempt--Parkes. (1985) *Criminal Law Monthly, 5*(5), 21.

(Wife-Killing)

Man sentenced in wife-torching. (1985) *Crime Victims Digest, 2*(11), 10.

(Homicide and Assault)

Crimes/offenses: Homicide -- assault. (1985) *Criminal Law Monthly, 5*(6), 14.

(Case Law)

Archibald, T., & Epstein, M. (1985) R. v. Bains and Grewal: A postscript to Ancio. *The Criminal Law Quarterly, 28*(1), 23-27.

(AIDS Case)

AIDS carrier arraigned on murder charges for spitting. (1985) *Crime Control Digest, 19*(50), 8-9.

(Conviction Upheld)

Man's conviction upheld in fight/murder death. (1985) *Crime Control Digest, 19*(49), 9. Microforms and article copies available from UMI.

(Robbery/Murder)

Cook, P.J. (1985) Is robbery becoming more violent? An analysis of robbery/murder trends since

1968. *The Journal of Criminal Law and Criminology, 76*(2), 480-489.

(Double Jeopardy)

Double jeopardy--collateral estoppel. (1985) *The Criminal Law Reporter: Court Decisions, 38*(21), 2137-2138.

(Amnesia)

Parwatikar, S.D. (1985) The detection of malingered amnesia in accused murderers. *Bulletin of the American Academy of Psychiatry & the Law, 13*(1), 97-103.

(State v. Reladan)

You be the judge: State v. Reladan. (1985) *The Law Officer's Bulletin, 10*(2), 9.

(Drunk Driving)

MADD pushes for murder charges in fatal drunk driving cases. (1985) *Criminal Justice Newsletter, 16*(24), 2-3.

(Murder Trial - Delay)

Murder -- delay of trial -- Maryland. (1984, Sept.) *Arrest Law Bulletin,* 8.

(Euthanasia)

MacKinnon, P. (1984, Sept.) Euthanasia and homicide. *The Criminal Law Quarterly, 26,* 4.

(Caldwell Impact)

Ashall, P.A. (1984, Aug.) Manslaughter - the impact of Caldwell? *The Criminal Law Review,* 467-476.

(Caldwell Impact)

Syrota, G. (1984, Aug.) Manslaughter: The impact of Caldwell (reply). *The Criminal Law Review*, 476-479.

(Murder Trial - Indians)

Svingen, O.J. (1984, July) The case of Spotted Hawk and Little Whirlwind: An American Indian Dreyfus affair. *Western History Quarterly, 15,* 281-297.

(Law - Ambiguity)

White, W.D. - (1984, Summer) Medical homicide: Clarity in law, ambiguity in practice. *South Atlantic Quarterly, 83,* 243-258.

(Murdered Damages)

What's new. Parents of murdered child get no damages from killer. (1984, Mar.) *American Bar Association Journal, 70,* 136, 138.

(Medical)

Lo, B. (1984) The death of Clarence Herbert: Withdrawing care is not murder. *Annals of Internal Medicine, 101*(2), 248-251.

(Homicide - Medical)

Reaves, L. (1984) Cutting off the IV: It's not murder, Court says. *American Bar Association Journal, 70,* 3.

(Murder Scene - Search)

Warrantless reentry, search of murder scene wasn't unreasonable. (1984) *The Criminal Law Reporter: Decisions, 35*(1), 2007-2008.

(Diminished Responsibility)

Williams, N.L., & Smith, J.C. (1984) Case and comment: Diminished responsibility. *The Criminal Law Review*, 553-554.

(U.S. v. Cherry)

You be the judge: U.S. v. Cherry. (1984) *The Law Officer's Bulletin, 8*(24), 142.

(Liability)

No liability to bar owner who shot and killed off-duty police officer mistaken as aggressor in fight. (1984) *AELE Liability Reporter 1984,* 141, 11.

(Emotional Defense)

Defenses -- extreme emotional disturbance -- jury instructions. (1984) *The Criminal Law Reporter: Court Decisions, 35*(19), 2342.

(Indictments)

Department of Justice secures indictments in killing of P.R. terrorists. (1984) *Crime Control Digest, 18*(6), 9-10. Microforms and article copies available from UMI.

(Recklessness)

Malice needed for murder not inferable from drunk driver's recklessness. (1984) *The Criminal Law Reporter: Court Decisions, 36*(6), 2098-2100.

(Liability)

Case reversed and city not liable for officer's shooting and killing his relatives with service revolver. (1984) *AELE Liability Reporter 1984,* 137, 6-7. Article copies available from UMI.

(Liability)

Homicide -- corporation's liability for manslaughter. (1984) *The Criminal Law Reporter: Court Decisions, 34*(14), 2266.

(Reckless Homicide)

Homicide -- jury instructions -- reckless homicide. (1984) *The Criminal Law Reporter: Court Decision, 36*(6), 2110.

(Battered Wife)

Bad instruction on self-defense dooms battered wife's homicide conviction. (1984) *The Criminal Law Reporter: Court Decisions, 35*(19), 2331-2332.

(Conviction - Police Officer)

Supreme Court upholds conviction of ex-NYPD Knapp Commission officer. (1984) *Crime Control Digest, 18*(9), 9-10. Microforms and article copies available from UMI.

(Homicide - Involuntary)

Homicide--involuntary manslaughter--"year and a day" rule. (1984) *The Criminal Law Reporter: Court Decisions, 34*(20), 2374.

(Corporate Liability)

7-11 may be liable for employee's murder. (1984) *Security Law Newsletter, 4*(2), 18.

(Search for Killer)

Montana sheriff invests own money in search for killers. (1984) *Crime Control Digest, 18*(42), 6. Article copies available from UMI.

(Students and Law)

Students and the law. (1984) *Campus Law Enforcement Journal, 14*(5), 8. Microforms and article copies available from UMI.

(Sentencing)

Thomas, D.A. Case and comment: Sentence. *The Criminal Law Review*, 431-440 (1983, July); 406-411 (1983, June); 242-249 (1984, April).

(Gross Negligence)

Mens Rea in gross negligent manslaughter. (1983, Dec.) *The Criminal Law Review*, 776-786.

(Verdict - PTSD)

Grant, B.L., & Coons, D.J. (1983) Guilty verdict in a murder committed by a veteran with post-traumatic stress disorder. *Bulletin of the American Academy of Psychiatry and Law, 11*(4), 355-358.

(Homicide - Co-Worker)

Missouri court allows suit in murder by co-worker. (1983) *Security Law Newsletter, 3*(9), 6.

(Brink's Robbery/Murder)

Brink's holdup slayers sentenced to 75-year terms. (1983) *Security Systems Digest, 14*(21), 10. Article copies available from UMI.

(Conviction - Review)

Review of a murder conviction. (1983) *Crime Control Digest, 17*(44), 8-9. Article copies available from UMI.

(Retrial)

Ruling on re-trial for murder. (1983) *Crime Control Digest, 17*(44), 9. Article copies available from UMI.

(Convicted)

Brinks' robbers convicted. (1983) *Security Systems Digest, 14*(19), 9-10. Microforms and article copies available from UMI.

(Verdict - Guilty)

Defendant may be found both guilty and insane, Maryland holds. (1983) *The Criminal Law Reporter: Court Decisions, 34*(2), 2028-2029.

(Liability - Doctors)

Doctors are not criminally liable for "pulling plug" on comatose patient. (1983) *The Criminal Law Reporter: Court Decisions, 34*(6), 2199-2120.

(Parole)

Los Angeles DA wins round in stopping killer's parole. (1983) *Crime Control Digest, 17*(26), 8. Article copies available from UMI.

(Court Decisions)

Dispositions--length of time--United States. (1983) *Juvenile and Family Law Digest, 15*(8), 279-280.

(Conviction Upheld)

Court upholds conviction of drug kingpin. (1983) *Narcotics Control Digest, 13*(9), 8. Article copies available from UMI.

(Defining Death)

Homicide--brain death--removal of organs for transplant--trial court's refusal to define death. (1983) *The Criminal Law Reporter, 34*(3), 2052-2053.

(Fetus)

Killing of seven-month-old fetus can't be prosecuted as murder. (1983) *The Criminal Law Reporter: Court Decisions, 33*(2), 2024-2025.

(Teen Slayings)

Suspect sought in "snuff-film" slayings of teenage girls. (1983) *Juvenile Justice Digest, 11*(16), 6. Article copies available from UMI.

(Child-Killings)

Suspect held in child killings. (1983) *Juvenile Justice Digest, 11*(15), 10. Microforms and article copies available from UMI.

(Sentence - Idaho)

Youth sentenced in Idaho for cellmate's torture death. (1983) *Juvenile Justice Digest, 11*(11), 5. Microforms and article copies available from UMI.

(People vs. Marcy)

Extreme indifference murder: The impact of People vs. Marcy (628 p 2d. 69 Colorado). (1982, Fall) *University of Colorado Law Review, 33*, 102.

(Self-Defense)

Criminal law - perfecting the imperfect right of self-defense - State v. Norris, 279 S E 2d. 570 (NC). (1982, Spring) *Campbell Law Review, 4*, 427-446.

(Defense - Military Courts)

Nagle, J.F. (1981, Spring) Inconsistent defenses in criminal cases. *Military Law Review, 92*, 77-128.

(Military Justice)

CAL rejects remaining arguments against former Army doctor's murder convictions. (1982) *The Criminal Law Reporter: Court Decisions, 31*(23), 2482-2484.

(Law Invalidated - Colorado)

Colorado's murder by extreme indifference law invalidated. (1981) *The Criminal Law Reporter: Court Decisions and Proceedings, 29*(3), 2049-2051.

(Police Killings)

Sherman, L.W. (1980, Jan.) Execution without trial: Police homicide and the constitution. *Vanderbilt Law Review, 33*, 71-100.

(Witness' Verification)

Mistleberger, K. (1980) Establishing the time of the offense in murder cases: Only five correct statements from 17 witnesses. *Kriminalistik, 34*(3), 139-141.

(Murdering Heir)

Maki, L.J., & Kaplan, A.M. (1980) Elmer's case revisited: The problem of the murdering heir. *Ohio State Law Journal, 41*, 905-971.

(Case Report)

Farrell v. Secretary of State for Defense. (1980) *WLR, 1*, 172.

(Self-Defense)

Imperfect self-defense. (1980) *Advocate, 12*(1), 40-42.

(Culpable Homicide)

Middendorff, W. (1980) Criminologic evaluation of a culpable homicide case (German). *Kriminolgische Auswertung Einer Fahrlassien Totung Blutalkohol, 17*(4), 259-275.

(Burden of Proof)

McLane, M.W. (1979, July-Aug.) Burden of proof in criminal cases: Mullaney and Patterson (Patterson v. New York, 97 Sup Ct. 2319). *Criminal Law Bulletin, 15*, 346-352.

(Legal Case Report - Georgia)

Fleming, R. (1979, May) Georgia justice and Dessie Woods: A case of Black v. White. *Encore, 8*, 44-45.

(Brain Death)

Guthrie, L.B. (1979, Jan.-Feb.) Brain death and criminal liability. *Criminal Law Bulletin, 15*, 40-61.

(Euthanasia)

Menzel, P.T. (1979) Are killing and letting die morally different in medical contexts? *Journal of Medical Philosophy, 4*(3), 269-293.

(Unarmed Client)

'My client was not even armed'. (1979) *Police Magazine, 2*(4), pp. 2-3.

(Longest Term)

The longest term ever served: 'Forget me? (1979) *Corrections Magazine, 5*(1), 42-43.

(Military Courts)

Courts of military review decisions. (1979) *Advocate, 11*(5), 253-258.

(Conviction Upheld)

Negligent homicide upheld. (1979) *Reporter, 8*(4), 141.

(Felony Murder Doctrine - Michigan)

Till- (People v. Till (MI) 263 NW 2d. 586), Wright- (People v. Wright (MI) 262 NW 2d. 917), and Thompson (People v. Thompson (MI) 265 NW 2d. 632): Recent developments concerning the felony murder doctrine in Michigan. (1978, Fall) *Detroit College of Law Review, 519-544.*

(Letelier Case)

Strasser, S., et al. (1978, Aug.) Pinochet's dilemma: DINA members indicted in Letelier killing. *Newsweek, 92*, p. 31.

(Euthanasia)

Skegg, P.D.G. (1978, July) Termination of life-support measures and the law of murder. *Modern Law Review, 41*, 423-436.

(Need for Symmetry)

Doherty, J.J. (1978, May) Strange fate of two men named David (People v. Muir (IL) 349 NE 2d. 423; People v. Trinkle (IL) 353 NE 2d. 18): The need for symmetry in the criminal law.

Illinois Bar Journal, 66, 518-519+.

(Burden of Proof)

Patterson v. New York (97 Sup Ct. 2319): Criminal procedure - the burden of proof and affirmative defenses. (1978, Spring) *University of Toledo Law Review, 9*, 524-545.

(Due Process)

Mulaney and Patterson (Patterson v. New York, 97 Sup. Ct. 2319): Due process protections and the defendant's burden of proving affirmative defenses. (1978, Winter) *Williamette Law Review, 15*, 85-103.

(Case Report - On the Job)

Freed, H.M., & Gandell, R. (1978) Murder on the job: Case report of a unique disaster. *Mental Health Soc, 5*(3-4), 231-240.

(Family Courts)

In the family courts: The Queen v. C. (1978) *Canadian Journal of Family Law, 1*(1), 159-160.

(Burden of Persuasion)

Allen, R.J. (1977, Nov.) Restoration of In re Winship: A comment on burdens of persuasion in criminal cases after Patterson. *Michigan Law Review, 76*, 30-63.

(Collateral Estoppel)

Owens, W.C., Jr. (1977, Fall) People v. Taylor: Collateral estoppel in criminal cases- key principles and policies. *Hastings Constitutional Law Quarterly, 4*, 747-755.

(Case Report - California)

Pizano v. Superior Court (138 Cal. Rptr. 363): California's Fifth Circuit misconstrues the Gilbert causation guidelines. (1977, Fall) *Western State University Law Review, 5*, 77-91.

(Conviction Overturned)

Through the looking-glass: Conviction of R. Williams overturned. (1977, April) *National Review, 29*, 428.

(Quinlan Case)

Collester, D.G., Jr. (1977, Winter) Death, dying, and the law: A prosecutorial view of the Quinlan case. *Rutgers Law Review, 30*, 304-328.

(Supreme Court)

Allen, R.J. (1977, Jan.) Mullaney v. Wilbur (95 Sup Ct. 1881): The Supreme Court and the substantive criminal law - an examination of the limits of legitimate intervention. *Texas Law Review, 55*, 269-301.

(Deferred Sentence)

Kahn, J.P. (1977, Jan.) Afternoon in purgatory: Sentence deferred in Alabama: Pre-trial hearing of J.L. Clausell. *Harper, 254*, 26-27.

(Commentary)

Williams, G. (1977) Commentary on R. vs. Dudley and Stephens. *Cambrian Law Review, 8*, 94-99.

(Case Report - San Francisco)

Rich, T.S. (1976, Spring) People v. Antick (CA) 539 Pac. 2d. 43. *University of San Francisco Law Review, 10*, 675-681.

(Euthanasia)

Euthanasia: The physician's liability. (1976, Fall) *John Marshall Journal, 10*, 148-172.

(Affirmative Defense - Patterson)

People v. Patterson (NY) (347 NE 2d. 8981): Constitutionality of New York's affirmative defense of extreme emotional disturbance. (1976, Fall) *St. John's Law Review, 51*, 158-180.

(Common Law)

State v. Evans (MD) 362 A 2d. 629- a frontal attack on the common law of murder. (1976, Fall) *University of Baltimore Law Review, 6*, 95-112.

(Franconia Case)

Marston, G. (1976, Jan.) Centenary of the Franconia case- the prosecution of Ferdinand Keyn. *Law Quarterly Review, 92*, 93-107.

(Euthanasia)

Robertson, J.A., & Fost, N. (1976) Passive euthanasia of defective newborn infants: Legal considerations. *Journal of Pediatrics, 88*(5), 883-889.

(Murder Cases - Defense)

Gilboy, J.A. (1976) The dilemma of seeking bail and preparing a defense in murder cases: Perspectives and practices of Chicago defense lawyers. *Journal of Criminal Law & Criminology, 67*(3), 259-272.

(Felony Murder Doctrine)

People v. Hickman (IL), 319 N E 2d 511: Journey to the logical limits of the felony-murder doctrine. (1975-1976, Winter) *John Marshall Journal, 9*, 517-532.

(Euthanasia)

Option of death! Euthanasia: An issue for the seventies. (1975, Fall) *USFV Law Review, 4*, 301-316.

(Law Commission)

McCall-Smith, A. (1975, July) Law commission and the proxy bomber. *Philos Q, 25*, 266-270.

(Supreme Court)

Summaries of docketed cases. (1975) *The Criminal law Reporter: Supreme Court Proceedings, 17*(2), 4014-4016.

(Issue Estoppel)

Campbell, M.W. (1974, Oct.) Issue estoppel in criminal cases, with special reference to Brown v. Robinson. *Australian Law Journal, 48*, 469-479.

(Homicide Victim - Robber)

Alvin Taylor v. The Superior Court of Alameda County, (CA) 477 P 2d 131: Criminal responsibility for a death inflicted by the robbery victim. (1972, March) *Williamette Law Journal, 8*, 128.

(Coppolino Case)

Bailey, F.L., with A. Aronson, Ed. (1971, Nov.) F. Lee Bailey's strangest murder case; excerpt from *The defense never rests*. *Lady's Home Journal, 88*, pp. 122-123+.

(Sheppard Case)

Bailey, F.L., with A. Aronson, Ed. (1971, Oct.) F. Lee Bailey's *The defense never rests*; Sheppard case; excerpts from *The defense never rests*. *Lady's Home Journal, 88*, 93-95+.

(Legal Limbo)

Murder in legal limbo; case of U.S. v. Escamilla. (1970, Sept.) *Time, 96*, p. 58.

(Feticide Case)

Keeler case (Keeler v. Superior Court, 80 Cal. Rptr. 865): Feticide as murder. (1970, Spring) *Catholic University Law Review, 19*, 372.

(Multiple Murder)

Usher, A. (1967, Oct.) The case of the disemboweled doll- a multiple murder. *Med Sci Law, 7*, 211-212.

(Case Report)

In warm blood: Some historical and procedural aspects of Regina v. Dudley and Stephens. (1967, Winter) *University of Chicago Law Review, 34*, 387.

(Case Reports - Trial)

Rosenthal, A.M. (1964) *Thirty-eight witnesses*. New York: McGraw-Hill.

(Felony Murder - Case Report)

Criminal Law: Applicability of felony murder rule where bystander killed by person other than the felon, People v. Harrison, 1 Cal Rptr 414; People v. Wood (NY), 167 N E 2d 736. (1960, Dec.) *California Law Review, 48*, 847.

(Felony Murder)

Criminal law - felony murder - former jeopardy (People ex rel Santangelo v. Tutuska, 192 N Y S 2d 350). (1960, April) *Brooklyn Law Review, 26*, 299.

(Constructive Theory)

Constructive trust theory applied where murderer of testator is legatee (In re Wilson's Will (WI) 92 N W 2d 282. (1960, Jan.) *Wisconsin Law Review 1960, 127.*

(Homicide Law)

Richardson, L.F. (1960) *Statistics of deadly quarrels*, Q. Wright and C.C. Lienau, Eds. Boxwood.

(Insurance)

Insurance - homicide - a new mode of changing beneficiary (Robbins v. Prudential Ins. Co, 168 F Supp. 668. (1959, Spring) *Alabama Law Review, 11*, 360.

(Robbery/Murder)

Williams, J.E.H. (1959, July) Murder in the course of theft (Regina v. Jones (1959) 2 W L R 190. *Modern Law Review, 22*, 426.

(Negligent Homicide)

Klein, S.A. (1958, April) Negligent homicide under article 134, UCMJ. *Judge Advocate General Journal 1958*, 7.

(Responsibility)

Mental responsibility in homicide act (Regina v. Spriggs (1958) 2 W L R 162). (1958, April) *Law Quarterly Review, 74*, 173.

(Criminal Abortion)

Criminal abortion and manslaughter: Five year sentence on doctor. (1958, May 24) *British Medical Journal, 5081*, 1242-1248.

(Homicide - Malice)

Smith, T.B. (1957, July) Malice in murderland. *S L T 1957*, 129.

(Felony Murder Doctrine)

Felony murder doctrine-shooting of co-felon by victim of armed robbery (Commonwealth v. Thomas (PA) 117 A 2d. 204). (1957, April) *Southern California Law Review, 30*, 357.

(Epilepsy and Crime)

Vizioli, R., et al. (1957, Jan.-March) Epilepsy and criminality, case report (Italian). *Ospedale Psichiatrico (Napoli), 25*(1), 117-123.

(Trial - Doctor)

Lister, J. (1957) Doctor on trial. *New England Journal of Medicine, 256*(22), 1054-1055.

(Homicide Act - Case Reports)

Armitage, A.L., et al. Homicide Act. *Cambridge Law Journal 1957*, 183 (1957, Nov.); *Criminal Law Review 1957*, 282 (1957, May); *Journal of Criminal Law* (London), *21*, 370 (1957, Oct.-Dec.); *Modern Law Review, 20*, 381 (1957, July).

(Felony Murder Doctrine)

Proximate cause and furtherance of design- felony murder and guilt of one felon for the death of his accomplice (Commonwealth v. Thomas (PA) 117 A 2d. 204). (1956, Summer) *Maryland Law Review, 16*, 249.

(Felony Murder Doctrine)

Murder- the felony murder rule (Commonwealth v. Thomas (PA) 117 a 2d. 204). (1956, April) *NDL Review, 32*, 140.

(Manslaughter)

Landlord convicted of manslaughter for violation of Multiple Dwelling Act notwithstanding lack of personal notice (People v. Nelson (NY) 128 N E 2d 391). (1956, Jan.) *Albany Law Review, 20*, 115.

(Duty of Jury)

Homicide - duty of jury to find extenuating circumstances before imposing life imprisonment for first degree murder (People v. Byrd (CA) 266 Pac. 2d 505). (1954, June) *UCLA Law Review, 1*, 598-602.

(Drummond Trial)

Drummond murders trial (photographs with text). (1954) *Illustrated London News, 225*, p. 940.

(Self-Defense)

Criminal law - murder - self-defense - duty of defendant when attacked in place of business (State v. Baratta (IA) 49 N W 2d 866). *Dick Law Review, 57*, 254-256 (1953, March); *Iowa Law Review, 37*, 593-596 (1952, Summer).

(Officer's Right)

Reexamination of the right of an officer to kill a fleeing suspected felon. (1952, Jan.) *Kentucky Law Review, 40*, 192-199.

(Homicide Law)

Moreland, R. (1952) *Law of homicide*. Bobbs.

(Psychology Case Reports)

Schroder, J. (1952) Psychology of homicide on basis of 35 cases observed at Psychiatric Clinic of Basel University. *Schweiz Arch Neurol u Psychiat, 69*, 287-320.

(Reversible Error)

Reversible error in murder cases and the Pennsylvania Supreme Court. (1951, April) *University of Pennsylvania Law Review, 99*, 814-826.

(Manslaughter - Involuntary)

Kentucky's concept of involuntary manslaughter. (1951, March) *Kentucky Law Journal 39*, 351-352.

(Murder - Degrees)

Keedy, E.R. (1950, Dec.) Problem of murder in the first degree: Fisher v. United States. *University of Pennsylvania Law Review, 99*, 267-292.

(Criminal Law)

Commonwealth v. Maloney (PA) 73 Atl. 2d. (1950, Oct.) *Dick Law Review, 55*, 80-82.

(Murder and Manslaughter)

Kennedy, G.D. Autrefois acquit - case report (Rex v. Pascal (1949) 95 CCC 288). *Canadian Bar Review, 28*, 689-698 (1950, July); *Canadian Bar Review, 27*, 968-972 (1949, Oct.)

(Murder - Degrees)

Hitchler, W.H. (1950, March) Murder in the first degree (Commonwealth (PA) v. Bey 70 Atl 2d 343). *Dick Law Review, 54*, 353.

(Felony Murder - Doctrine)

Barrett, J.N.Jr., & Quinn, E.J., Jr. Felony murder doctrine - death caused by shot fired by felon or third person (Commonwealth v. Alameida (PA) 68 Atl 2d 595). *B U L 30*, 422-425 (1950, June); *Catholic University Law Review, 1*, 46-47 (1950, May); *Temple University Law Quarterly, 23*, 423-425 (1950, April); *University Of Pennsylvania Law Review, 98*, 431-433 (1950, Feb.)

(Homicide Cases)

Harlan, H. (1950) Five hundred homicides. *Journal of Criminal Law and Criminology, 40*, 736-752.

(Murder - Degrees)

Matthews, S. (1949-50, Winter) First degree murder - premeditation and deliberation (Jones v. United States 175 F 2d 544). *Arkansas Law Review, 4*, 92-94.

(Constructive Murder)

Turner, A.L. (1949, Dec.) Constructive murder in England and Australia. *University of Western Australia Annual Law Review, 1*, 295-302.

(Murder Trial - Procedures)

Acker, A.E. (1949, Oct.) Admission of prior, unrelated crimes in first-degree murder cases

(Commonwealth (PA) v. De Pofi 66 Atl 2d 649). *Dick Law Review, 54*, 55-61.

(Reversible Error)

Rosenthal, J.M. (1949, Oct.) Reversible error in homicide cases in Massachusetts, 1927-1949. *Massachusetts Law Quarterly, 34*, 45-62.

(Supernatural - Case Report)

Williams, G.L. Homicide and the supernatural. *Law Quarterly Review, 65*, 491-503 (1949, Oct.); *Connecticut Bar Journal, 23*, 159-172 (1949, June).

(Road Death)

Orr, C.B. (1949, July) Death on the road. *Justice of Peace, 113*, 443-444.

(Homicide - Premeditated)

Mattson, L.H. (1949, June) Interpretation of willful, deliberate, and premeditated murder by Pennsylvania and New Jersey courts (Commonwealth (PA) v. Chapman 58 Atl 2d 433). *Dick Law Review, 53*, 292-297.

(Burden of Proof)

Burden of Proof- unconsciousness (People v. Hardy (CA) 198 Pac. 2d. 865). (1949, June) *Texas Law Review, 27*, 857-859.

(Case Report)

Tovo, S. (1949, Jan.-June) By cutting blows. *Zacchia, 12*, 81-95.

(Murderer - Co-Tenant)

Tenancy by the entirety - disposition of property where one co-tenant murders the other (Grose v. Holland (MO) 211 S W 2d 464). (1948, Nov.) *Missouri Law Review, 13*, 463-466.

(Manslaughter - Case Report)

Gillespie, J.R. (1948, Nov.) Origin and development of "chance medley" in the law of manslaughter. *Kentucky Law Journal, 37*, 86-90.

(Murderer - Co-Tenant)

Fant, C.E. (1948, Fall) Husband and wife- tenancy by the entirety- murder of one tenant by the other as affecting title of property (Grose v. Holland (MO) 211 SW 2d 464). *Alabama Law Review, 1*, 100-102.

(Burden of Proof)

First degree murder - burden of proof (People v. Bjornsen (CA) 180 Pac. 2d 443. (1948, March) *California Law Review, 36*, 132-133.

(Murder Trial)

Miller, R.B. (1947, Aug.) H.M. Advocate v. Thomas Leith; a murder trial of 1847. *Jurid Review, 59*, 131-145.

(Jury Charge - Case Report)

Goldberg, L. (1947, May) Charge to the jury in Commonwealth v. Goodale. *L Soc J, 12*, 542-604.

(Unintentional Homicide)

Davis, O.C. (1947) Medicolegal aspects of unintentional homicide. *M Press, 218*, 125-127.

(Felony Murder Doctrine)

Cadmus, F.T., III (1946, Oct.) Beginning and end of attempts and felonies under the statutory felony murder doctrine. *Dick Law Review, 51*, 12-26.

(Murder Accessory)

Hogan, M.T. (1946, Jan.) Murder and accessory before the fact as distinct crimes (State v. Patriarca (RI), 43 Atl 2d 54). *University of Detroit Law Journal, 9*, 109-111.

(Arson/Murder)

Jackson, R.M. (1946) Moot case on murder and arson. *Cambridge Law Journal, 9*, 154-158.

(Felony Murder)

Felony murder - nature and continuance of the underlying felony (People v. Luscomb (NY) 55 N E 2d 469). (1944, Nov.) *Fordham Law Review, 13*, 243-248.

(Murder Case Report)

Hitchler, W.H. (1944, Oct.) Murder in the first degree (State v. Severns (KS) 148 Pac. 2d. 488). *Dick Law Review, 49*, 30.

(Murderers - Study)

Banay, R.S. (1943, July-Aug.) Study of twenty-two men convicted of murder in the first degree. *Journal of Criminal Law, 34*, 106-111.

(Statutory Reform)

Tincher, M.M. (1942, May) Proposed statutory reform in the law of negligent homicide in Kentucky. *Kentucky Law Journal, 30*, 341-359.

(Hong Kong - Law)

Fraser, J.A. Hong Kong legislation, 1938. *J Comp Leg 3d. ser., 23*, 140-141 (1941, Aug.); *Journal Comp Leg 3d. ser., 22*, 144-146 (1940, July).

(Jury Charge)

Crimes - charge to jury concerning powers of Court of Pardons (State v. Leaks (NJ) 17 Atl. 2d. 550). (1941, Dec.) *University of Newark Law Review, 7*, 81-86.

(Death - Year and a Day)

Zacharias, W.F. (1941, March) Why death in a year and a day? *Chi-Kent Law Review, 19*, 181-187.

(Death - Year and a day)

Murder - death within a year and a day (State v. Manny Moore, Sup. Ct. Docket no. 35, 998 (LA) 1940). (1941, Feb.) *Tulane Law Review, 15*, 306-308.

(Unwritten Law)

Graham, J.H., Jr. (1940, Nov.) Justification by the unwritten law (Neece v. State (OK) 104 Pac. 2d. 568). *Notre Dame Law Review,* 16, 68-71.

(Trial)

Chisolm, J. (1940, May) Our first trial for murder; the King v. Peter Cartcel. *Canadian Bar Review, 18*, 385-389.

(Unwritten Law)

Pansing, T.R. (1940, March) Unwritten law in defense to homicide. *Nebraska L B, 19*, 146-150.

(Slayer's Claim)

Defeasance of slayer's claim to property or contract rights accruing at victims's death, unintended or non-criminal killing (Eisenhardt v. Siegel (MO) 119 SW 2d. 810). (1939, Feb.) *Washington University Law Quarterly, 24*, 277-279.

(Robbery/Murder)

Hitchler, W.H. (1938, Jan.) Murder in the commission of robbery (Commonwealth v. Stelma (1937) 327 PA 317). *Dick Law Review, 42*, 85-86.

(Felony Murder)

Homicide in the commission of a felony, relationship required between the felony and the killing (State v. Metalski (NJ) 185 Atl. 351). (1937, Feb.) *Minnesota Law Review, 21*, 333-334.

(Improbable Cause)

Tipton, S.V. (1937, April) Death resulting from improbable cause (State v. Frazier (MO) 98 S W 2d 707). *Missouri Law Review, 2*, 228-229.

(Dying Declaration - Case Report)

McLaws, D.P. (1937, Feb.) Dying declarations, not a charge of homicide, exclusion of "narrative" (Carl Schwartzenhaeur v. His Majesty the King (1935) 2 WWR 146). *Alberta Law Quarterly, 2*, 45-49.

(Burden of Proof)

Burden of proof in charges of murder (Woolmington v. Director of Public Prosecutions (1935) A C 462, 25 Cr. App. R 72). *Legal Times, 179*, 403-404 (1935, June); *L J, 79*, 378-379 (1935, June); *Just P, 99*, 383 (1935, June); *Sol J, 79*, 428 (1935, June); *Irish Legal Times, 69*, 171-173 (1935, June); *South African Legal Times, 4*, 144-145 (1935, July); *Camb Law Journal, 6*, 107-108 (1936).

(Transfer of Intent)

Chisolm, D.H. (1936, Nov.) Transfer of intent, retention of defense (State v. Batson (MO) 96 SW 2d. 384). *Missouri Law Review, 1*, 356-357.

(Felony and Burglary)

Stimson, H.I. (1936, Jan.-Feb.) Felony murder, burglary, entry with intent to commit larceny (State v. Hauptmann (NJ) 180 Atl. 809). *Journal of Criminal Law, 26*, 759-762.

(Effect of Arrest)

Nieman, C.E. (1935, April) Liability of confederate, effect of arrest (People v. Bongiorno (IL) 192 NE 856). *Wisconsin Law Review, 10*, 400-402.

(Acts and Declarations)

Klima, W.J. (1935, Jan.) Co-defendants, acts, and declarations in general (People v. Wysocki (MI) 255 NW 160). *Notre Dame L, 10*, 212-214.

(Charges)

Recent murder charges. (1934, Dec.) *Sol J, 1*, 238.

(Force of Circumstances)

Roughead, W. (1934) Mrs. Donald's crime; or the force of circumstances. *Jurid Review, 46*, 355.

(Murder - Degrees)

First degree murder, constructive intent (State v. Glover (MO) 50 S W 2d 1049, 1053; State v. Meadows (MO) 51 S W 2d 1033). (1933, June) *St. Louis Law Review, 18*, 350-352.

(Mistaken Identity)

Arado, C.C. (1933, March-April) Mistaken identity in a murder case. *Journal of Criminal Law, 23*, 1020-1026.

(Resisting Arrest)

Dickey, J.S. (1933) Culpable homicides in resisting arrest. *Cornell Law Quarterly, 18*, 373.

(Unlawful Act)

Causal relation between defendant's unlawful act and death. (1933) *Michigan Law Review, 31*, 659.

(Case Report - Indiana)

Scott, O.F. (1931, May-June) People of the State of Indiana v. Virgil and Kirkland. *Medico-Legal Journal, 48*, 84-88.

(Non-Feasance)

Cross, M.L. (1931, April) Criminal nonfeasance (State v. Harrison (NJ) 152 Atl. 867). *B U L Rev, 11*, 273-276.

(Intent)

Murder - constructive intent - necessity for concurrence of minds of jury in findings (State v. Flathers (SD) 232 NW 51). (1931, April) *Southern California Law Review, 4*, 324-325.

(Indictment - Short Form)

Crimes, procedure, constitutionality of the short form of indictment (State. v. Rector (SC) 155 SE 385). (1931, March) *Michigan Law Review, 29*, 636-637.

(Defense of Another)

Crimes - killing in defense of another (Brummet v. Commonwealth (KY) 31 SW 2d. 391). (1931, March) *Kentucky Law Journal, 19*, 258-259.

(State of Mind)

Admissibility of subsequent statements of accused as showing state of mind at time of crime (Karsner v. Commonwealth (KY) 32 SW 2d. 43). (1931, Feb.) *Virginia Law Review, 17*, 379-384.

(Guilty Plea)

Plea of guilty in murder charges. (1931) *Law Times, 172*, 383.

(Irresistible Impulse)

Irresistible impulse as a defense to criminal prosecution (Davis v. State (TN) 28 SW 2d. 993). (1930, Dec.) *Tenn L Rev, 9*, 57-59.

(Hearsay Rule - Exception)

Admissibility of opinion contained in a declaration admissible under an exception to the hearsay rule (Powell v. State (TX) 21 SW 2d. 728). (1930, Dec.) *Texas Law Review, 9*, 99-100.

(Homicide Indictments)

Korfist, N.A. (1930, Nov.) Homicide indictments (Ware v. State (OK) 288 Pac. 374). *Journal of Criminal Law, 21*, 451-452.

(Change of Venue)

Carlson, J.A. (1930, Nov.) Change of venue, discretionary power of trial court (Whiteside v. State (TX) 29 SW 2d. 399). *Journal of Criminal Law, 21*, 449-451.

(Self-Defense)

Duffy, R.E. (1930, Nov.) Circumstances governing right of person attacked to stand his ground - duty to retreat - question of fact for jury (Frank v. United States 42 Fed. 2d. 623). *Notre Dame Law, 6*, 128-129.

(Right to Kill)

Pearson, K.G. (1930, June) Right to kill in making arrests. *Michigan Law Review, 28*, 957-976.

(Parricide - Case Report)

Roughead, W. (1930) The edge of circumstance; a problem in parricide. *Jurid Rev, 42*, 99.

(Solicitation)

Solicitation to commit murder as attempt to commit (State of Missouri v. Davis 6 SW 2d. 609). (1928, Dec.) *Law Ser Mo Bull, 40*, 45-49.

(Right to Inherit)

Pearce, E. (1927, April) Murder of ancestor as affecting right to inherit (In re Taylor (WA) 250 Pac. 456). *Law Notes, 31*, 9-11.

(Conspirator)

Liability of conspirator for homicide committed by co-conspirators after his arrest and during their flight (Commonwealth v. Dorris, 8 Pa. D & C 210). (1927, Feb.) *Harvard Law Review, 40*, 651; *University of Pennsylvania Law Review, 75*, 361-365.

(Legal Reform)

Robbins, A.H. (1914) The Becker case as suggesting certain reforms in criminal procedure. *Cent L J, 78*, 307.

(Burrell-Oates Case)

Crowell, C.T. (1912) The Burrell-Oates case. *Journal of Criminal Law, 3*, 407.

(Homicide - Case Report)

Constructive murder. (1905) *Justice of the Peace, 69*, 614.

(Self-Defense)

Beale, J.H., Jr. (1903) Homicide in self-defense. *Columbia Law Review, 3*, 526.

Interpretation of the Law

(Self-Defense)

Shanke, P. (1990, Sept. 3) (Pennsylvania) Self-defense shooting cannot be manslaughter (In re Smith). *National Law Journal, 13*, 9.

(Murderer - Child)

Mustain, G. (1990, May 14) Can a child be convicted of murder? *National Law Journal, 13*, 8.

(Texas - Todd Broom)

Connock, A. (1990, April 2) Todd Broom gunned down a killer, and much of Texas wants to say thanks. *People Weekly, 33*(13), pp. 46-47.

(Self-Defense)

Wells, C. (1990) Domestic violence and self-defense. *New Law Journal, 140*(6441), 127-128.

(Psychological Defense)

Ewing, C.P. (1990) Psychological self-defense: A proposed justification for battered women who kill. *Law and Human Behavior, 14*(6), 579-594.

(Battered Women)

Greenwald, J.P., et al. (1990) Psychological self-defense jury instructions: Influence on verdicts for battered women defendants. *Behavioral Science and Law, 8*(2), 171-180.

(Self-Defense - Psychological)

Morse, S.J. (1990) The misbegotten marriage of soft psychology and bad law: Psychological self-defense as a justification for homicide. *Law and Human Behavior, 14*(6), 596-618.

(Unlawful Death)

Bentil, J.K. (1989, Oct. 6) Unlawfully occasioning another's death without physical contact. *Solicitor's Journal, 133*, 1250-1253.

(Provocation)

Rees, T., & Smith, J.C. (1989, Oct.) Homicide Act of 1957 - section 3 - direction on provocation - reference to age of defendant - whether provocation has to be considered only after other elements of murder. *The Criminal Law Review 1989*, 736-738.

(Justice - Miscarriage)

Reich, C. (1989, April) Lisa: Betrayed by the law. *Glamour, 87*(4), p. 195.

(Battered Women)

Follingstad, D.R., et al. (1989) Factors predicting verdicts in cases where battered women kill their husbands. *Law and Human Behavior, 13*(3), 253-269.

(Battered Women)

Gillespie, C.K. (1989) *Justifiable homicide: Battered women, self-defense. and the law.* Columbus, OH: Ohio State University Press.

(Mandatory Sentence)

Samuels, A. (1989) The mandatory life sentence for murder. *Justice of the Peace, 153*(18), 287-288.

(Contempt Charges)

Contempt charge upheld by Court. (1988, Aug. 13) *Editor & Publisher, 121*(33), p. 23.

(Psychiatric Guide)

Goldstein, R.L., et al. (1988) The psychiatrist's guide to right and wrong: Judicial standards of wrongfulness since M. Naghten. *Bulletin of the American Academy of Psychiatry and Law, 16*(4), 359-367.

(Infanticide)

Osborne, J.A. (1987) The crime of infanticide: Throwing out the baby with the bath water. *Canadian Journal of Family Law, 6*(1), 47-59.

(Manslaughter)

Knapman, L., & Smith, J.C. (1986, July) Case and comment: Manslaughter. *The Criminal Law Review*, 468-470.

(Homicide - Commentary)

Pigott, M., & Smith, J.C. (1986, July) Case and comment: Murder. *The Criminal Law Review 1986*, 470-471.

(Intent)

Pigott, M., & Smith, J.C. Case and comment: Intention. *The Criminal Law Review 1986*, 400-403 (1986, June); *The Criminal Law Review 1986*, 180-183 (1986, March).

(Defense - Production)

Presumption that shifted production burden to defendant was constitutional. (1986) *The Criminal Law Reporter: Court Decisions, 38*(14), 2267-2269.

(Depraved Indifference)

Homicide - defenses - justification - depraved indifference murder. (1986) *The Criminal Law Reporter: Court Decisions, 39*(13), 2240.

(Weapon Possession)

Homicide - felony-murder - possession of weapon. (1986) *The Criminal Law Reporter: Court Decisions, 38*(14), 2273.

(Fundamental Error)

Jury instructions - lessor included offenses - fundamental error. (1986) *The Criminal Law Reporter: Court Decisions, 39*(20), 2378.

(Legal Reform)

Davies, C., & Eugene, T. (1986) Tactic of legal reform: Learning from the recent past. *The Howard Journal of Criminal Justice, 25*(1), 25-32. Article copies available from UMI.

(Battered Women)

Blackman, J., & Brickman, E. (1985) The impact of expert testimony on trials of battered women who kill their husbands. *Behavioral Science and Law, 2*(4), 413-422.

(Warrantless Arrest)

Warrantless felony routine arrest - Ark. (1985, Dec.) *Arrest Law Bulletin*, 2-3.

(Reckless Homicide)

Homicide -- jury instructions -- reckless homicide. (1984) *The Criminal Law Reporter: Court Decisions, 36*(6), 2110.

(Homicide Rule)

Homicide - involuntary manslaughter - "year and a day" rule. (1984) *The Criminal Law Reporter: Court Decisions, 34*(20), 2374.

(Provocation)

Miethe, T.D. (1984) The impact of victim provocation on judgments of legal responsibility: An experimental assessment. *Journal of Criminal Justice, 12*(4), 407-414.

(Accidental Killing)

No liability to bar owner who shot and killed off-duty police officer mistaken as aggressor in fight. (1984, Sept.) *AELE Liability Reporter 1984,* (141), 11.

(Guilt and Insanity)

Defendant can be found both guilty and insane, Maryland holds. (1983) *The Criminal Law Reporter: Court Decisions, 34*(2), 2028-2029.

(Corporate Liability)

Homicide -- Corporation's liability for manslaughter. (1983) *The Criminal Law Reporter: Court Decisions, 34*(3), 2052-2053.

(Self-Defense)

O'Brien, N.C. (1983) Excessive self-defense: A need for legislation. *The Criminal Law Quarterly, 25*(4), 441-457.

(Murderers - Women)

Husain, A., et al. (1983) A study of young-age and mid-life homicidal women admitted to a psychiatric hospital for pre-trial evaluation (Summary in French). *Canadian Journal of Psychiatry, 28*(2), 109-113.

(Diminished Responsibility)

Dell, S. (1982, Dec.) Diminished responsibility reconsidered. *Criminal Law Review*, 809-818.

(Victim's Statements)

Beckett, J.S. (1982, Dec.) Speaking from the grave: A homicide victim's antecedent accusatory statements about the defendant. *Illinois Bar Journal, 71*, 250-256.

(Battered Wife)

Partially determined imperfect self-defense: The battered wife kills and tells why. (1982, Fall) *Stanford Law Review, 34*, 615-638.

(Heat of Passion)

Dressler, J. (1982, Summer) Rethinking heat of passion: A defense in search of a rationale. *Journal of Criminal Law & Criminology, 73*, 421-470.

(Vehicular Homicide)

Homicide - death by auto statute - stillborn fetus. (1982) *The Criminal Law Reporter: Court Decisions and Proceeding, 30*(24), 2478-2479.

(Defense - Duress)

Sornarajah, M. (1981, July) Duress and murder in Commonwealth criminal law. *International & Comparative Law Quarterly, 30*, 660-681.

(Capital Murder)

California court discusses 'flight' for purposes of capital murder law. (1981) *The Criminal Law Reporter: Court Decisions and Proceedings, 29*(26), 2557-2558.

(Battered Wives)

Rittenmeyer, S.D. (1981) Of battered wives, self-defense, and double standards of justice: A research note. *Journal of Criminal Justice, 9*(5), 389-395.

(Battered Wife)

Battered spouse syndrome as a defense to a homicide charge under the Pennsylvania Criminal Code. (1980, Nov.) *Villanova Law Review, 26*, 105-134.

(Battered Women)

Brown, L.R. (1980, Fall) The admissibility of expert testimony on the subject of battered women. *Criminal Justice Journal, 4*(1), 161-179.

(Case Report - Legal)

Farrell v. Secretary of State for Defense (1980) 1 W L R 172. (1980, Sept.) *Modern Law Review, 43*, 591-594.

(Case Report - Legal)

R. v. Bohan and another (1979) 5 N I J B. (1980, Summer) *No Ire L Q, 31*, 173-176.

(Case Report - Legal)

Johns v. The Queen (1980) 54 A L J R 166. (1980, June) *Mel U L Rev, 12*, 425-428.

(Battered Women)

Criminal law - evidence - expert testimony relating to subject matter of battered women admissible on issue of self-defense. (1980) *Seton Hall Law Review, 11*, 255-264.

(Battered Wife)

Berkman, A.S. (1980, Nov.) The State of Michigan versus a battered wife: A case study. *Bull Menninger Clin, 44*(6), 603-616.

(Self-Defense)

Gold, A.D. (1979) Self-defense - excessive force. *The Criminal Law Quarterly, 21*(4), 438-440.

(Battered Wives)

Does wife abuse justify homicide? (1978, Sept.) *Wayne Law Review, 24*, 1705-1731.

(Battered Women)

Battered Women Syndrome: A potential defense to a homicide charge. (1978, Fall) *Pepperdine Law Review, 6*, 213-229.

(Battered Women)

Eisenberg, A.D., & Seymour,E.J. (1978, July) Self-defense plea and battered women. *Trial, 14*, 34-42.

(Burden of Proof)

Criminal law - evidence - defendant in criminal trial has burden of proof in establishing affirmative defense. (1978, June) *Creighton Law Review, 11*, 1299-1320.

(Affirmative Defenses)

Constitutionality of affirmative defenses after Patterson v. New York (97 Sup. Ct. 2319). (1978, April) *Columbia Law Review, 78*, 655-678.

(Burden of Proof)

Shifting the burden of proving self-defense with analysis of related Ohio law. (1978, Spring) *Akron Law Review, 11*, 717-762.

(Battered Wives)

Fiora-Gormally, N. (1978) Battered wives who kill. Double standard out of court, single standard in? *Law and Human Behavior* 2(2), 133-165.

(Battered Women)

Dvoskin, J. (1978) Legal alternatives for battered women who kill their abusers. *Bulletin of*

American Academy of Psychiatry and Law, 6(3), 335-354.

(Burden of Proof)

Constitutional criminal procedure - due process - burden of proof - affirmative defenses. (1977-1978) *Duquesne Law Review, 16*, 457-468.

(Excessive Self Defense)

Kovacs, D. (1977, Dec.) Excessive self-defense in homicide cases: Some fundamental problems in Australian law. *Mon L R, 4*, 50-70.

(Deadly Force)

Moore, E. (1977, Nov.) Texas Penal Code of 1974, section 9.32: Deadly force in defense of person. *Texas Bar Journal, 40*, 951-954.

(Provocation)

Lee, J.A. (1977, July) Self-defense, provocation, duress. *Australian Law Journal, 51*, 437-449.

(Duress)

Wasik, M. (1977) Duress and criminal responsibility. *The Criminal Law Review 1977*, 453-464.

(Duress)

Beaumont, J. (1976, Oct.) Duress as a defense to murder. *Dalhousie Law Journal, 3*, 580-594.

(Burden of Proof)

Constitutional law - the burden of proof for affirmative defenses in homicide cases. (1976, Summer) *Wake Forest Law Review, 12*, 423-433.

(Right to Kill)

Bonventre, P., et al. (1975, Sept.) Right to kill: Justifiable homicide . *Newsweek, 86*, p. 69.

(Legal Reform)

Sornarajah, M. (1975, April) Commonwealth innovations on the law of provocation. *International & Comparative Law Quarterly, 24*, 184-204.

(Self-Defense)

Elliot, I.D. (1973, Oct.) Excessive self-defense in Commonwealth law: A comment. *International & Comparative Law Quarterly, 22*, 727-740.

(Duress)

O'Regan, R.S. (1972, Nov.) Duress and murder. *Modern Law Review, 35*, 596.

(Self-Defense)

Sornarajah, M. (1972, Oct.) Excessive self-defense in Commonwealth law. *International and Comparative Law Quarterly, 21*, 758.

(Self-Defense)

Smith, P. (1972, Sept.) Excessive self-defense - a rejection of Australian initiative? *Criminal Law Review 1972*, 524.

(Duty to Retreat)

Self-defense - duty to retreat - retreat from the porch of one's own home not required. (1972, Spring) *Seton Hall Law Review, 3*, 532.

(Civil Disturbance)

Murray, C.R. (1971, Fall) Civil disturbance, justifiable homicide, and military law. *Military Law Review, 54*, 129.

(Self-Control - Loss)

Samuels, A. (1971, March) Excusable loss of self-control in homicide. *Modern Law Review, 34*, 163.

(Duty to Retreat)

Criminal law - homicide - self-defense - the duty to retreat. (1970, Winter) *Duquesne Law Review, 9*, 313.

(Homicide - Justifiable)

Hinshaw, R.G. (1968, July-Aug.) Justifiable homicide. *California State Bar Journal, 43*, 541.

(Excessive Defense)

Howard, C. (1968, July) Two problems in excessive defense. *Law Quarterly Review, 84*, 343.

(Self-Defense - South Carolina)

Self-defense in South Carolina. (1967) *South Carolina Law Review, 19*, 823.

(Self-Defense - Judgment)

Self-defense or murder? (1966, Fall) *Idaho Law Review, 3*, 142.

(Legal History)

Brown, B.J. (1963, Oct.) Demise of chance-medley and the recognition of provocation as a defense to murder in English law. *American Journal of Legal History, 7*, 310.

(Provocation)

Armitage, A.L. (1963, April) Manslaughter - provocation (Lee Chu-Chuen v. Queen (1962) 3 W L R 1961). *Cambridge Law Journal 1963*, 17.

(State of Mind)

West, L.C. (1963) Proving fear as a state of mind in homicide cases. *Military Law Review 1963*,129.

(Manslaughter)

Parker, G.E. (1963) Plea of self-defense resulting in manslaughter. *Alberta Law Review, 3*, 16.

(Provocation)

Homicide in defense and under provocation (Regina v. Porritt (1961) 1 W L R 1372). (1962, April) *Law Quarterly Review, 78*, 166.

(Self-Defense)

Snelling, H.A. (1960, Sept.) Killing in self-defense. *Australian Law Journal, 34*, 130.

(Defense - New)

Morris, N. (1960, April) New qualified defense to murder. *Adelaide Law Review, 1*, 23.

(Closing Argument)

Henry, J.W., Jr. (1960, Jan.) Tennessee v. Walsh Jones: The closing argument for the defense. *ABA Journal, 4*, 52.

(Provocation)

Gooderson, R.N. (1959) The defense of provocation. *Medicolegal Journal, 27*, 57-63.

(Self-Defense)

Brown, B. (1958, Sept.) Self-defense in homicide from strict liability to complete exculpation. *Criminal Law Review 1958*, 583.

(Self-Defense)

Rosenszweig, S. (1956, March-April) Unconscious self-defense in an uxoricide. *Journal of Criminal Law, 46*, 791.

(Killing Burglar)

Can you kill the burglar? (1952, Aug.) *Law Journal, 102*, 467-468.

(Self-Defense)

Statutory study of self-defense of others as excuse for homicide. (1952, Spring) *University of Florida Law Review, 5*, 58-62.

(Duty to Retreat)

Duty to retreat - "castle" doctrine (Commonwealth v. Fraser (PA) 85 Atl. 2d. 126). (1952, Spring) *University of Pittsburgh Law Review, 13*, 595-597.

(Self-Defense - Historical)

Historical development of self-defense as an excuse for homicide. (1951, May) *Kentucky Law Journal, 39*, 469-471.

(Self-Defense)

Defense of third persons as excuse for homicide. (1951, May) *Kentucky Law Journal, 39*, 460-463.

(Self-Defense)

Retreat to the wall doctrine of self-defense. (1951, March) *Kentucky Law Journal, 39*, 353-357.

(Self-Defense)

Crimes - homicide - self-defense - imminency of danger (People v. Byars, 97 NY Supp. 2d 346). (1951, Jan.) *Albany Law Review, 15*, 124-126.

(Duty to Retreat)

Ganim, G.W. Self-defense - duty to retreat from domicile before attack of guest (State v. Grierson (NH) 69 Atl. 2d 851). *B U L Review, 30*, 282-283 (1950, April); *University of Pennsylvania Law Review, 98*, 593-595 (1950, March).

(Evidence - Victim's Character)

Storey, J.D., & Miller, J.M., Jr. Admissibility of evidence of deceased's good character in homicide case in which accused relies on self-defense (Lee v. Commonwealth (VA) 49 S E 2d 608). *Arkansas Law Review, 3*, 464-466 (1949, Fall); *Washington & Lee Law Review, 6*, 224-229 (1949).

(Defense - Case Report)

Johnston, J.P. (1949, Jan.) Defense available in Kentucky to peace officer who kills misdemeanant (Scott v. Commonwealth (KY) 204 SW 2d. 432). *Kentucky Law Journal, 37*, 182-186.

(Self-Defense)

Yeager, J.J. (1948, Nov.) Perfect and imperfect self-defense - effect of fault of defendant upon rights of self-defense. *Kentucky Law Journal, 37*, 117-121.

(Burden of Proof)

Bailey, R.E. (1948, July-Aug.) Burden of proving self-defense in homicide cases (Jones v. Commonwealth (VA) 45 SE 2d. 908). *Journal of Criminal Law, 39*, 188-192.

(Self-Defense)

Stumberg, G.W. (1942, Nov.) Defense of person and property under Texas criminal law. *Texas Law Review, 21*, 17-35.

(Self-Defense)

Self-defense - loss of right when assailant abandons attack (People v. Booker (IL) 38 N E 2d 32). (1942, April) *Minnesota Law Review, 26*, 662-664.

(Self-Defense)

Blackman, A.J. (1941, March) Self-defense, instructions (People v. Kinowacki (CA) 103 Pac. 2 203; People v. Campanella (CA) 103 Pac. 2d 193). *Southern California Law Review, 14*, 342-344.

(Provocation)

Provocation. *Justice of the Peace, 103*, 5 (1939, Jan.); *Law Journal, 84*, 61-62 (1937, July).

(Self-Defense)

Baker, H.H. (1938, June) Homicide and self-defense. *Tennessee Law Review, 15*, 288-299.

(Provocation)

Defenses - provocation - effect of provocation by one other than victim (Rex v. Manchuk (1937) 4 D L R 737). (1938, March) *Harvard Law Review, 51*, 928-929.

(Self-Defense)

Avakian, S. (1937) Prosecution for homicide - self-defense - admissibility of character and threats of victim. *California Law Review, 25*, 459.

(Self-Defense)

Self-defense - extent of the right in one who is the aggressor (Baussell v. Commonwealth (VA) 181 SE 453). (1936, March) *Minnesota Law Review, 20*, 433-434.

(Drunkenness)

Arado, C.C. (1936) Drunkenness as an excuse for murder. *Journal of Criminal Law, 26*, 703.

(Self-Defense)

Logan, J.C. (1935) Imperfect self-defense. *St. Louis Law Review, 20*, 131-140.

(Defense of Property)

Dawson, E. (1934, March) Homicide in defense of property. *Kentucky Law Journal, 22*, 450-452; Page, C.F. (1932, March) *Kentucky Law Journal, 21*, 93-95.

(Trial - Homicide)

Absence of body in homicide trials. (1934) *Law Journal, 78*, 249.

(Defense of Property)

Defenses - right to kill or injure in defense of property - spring guns (State v. Plumlee (LA) 149 So. 425). (1933, Dec.) *Minnesota Law Review, 18*, 77-79.

(Self-Defense - Provocation)

Coad, C. (1932, June) Self-defense - provocation (State v. Woodham (SC) 160 S E 885). *Oregon Law Review, 11*, 401-405.

(Defense of Property)

Homicide in defense of property. (1932) *Law Journal, 74*, 142.

(Defense of Property)

Hume, W. (1931, Nov.) Homicide in defense of personal property (Commonwealth (KY) v. Beverly, 34 S W 2d 941). *Kentucky Law Journal, 20*, 95-96.

(Self-Defense)

Shepherd, A.B. (1931, May) Right of self-defense by an officer who kills while attempting an illegal arrest. *Law Notes, 35*, 29-31.

(Self-Defense)

Temp, A.B. (1931, Jan.) Self-defense (State v. Plain (LA) 129 So. 730). *Law Quarterly, 5*, 294.

(Duty to Retreat)

Herndon, R.L., & Stadelman, G. (1930, June) Duty to retreat from deadly assault (debate). *Oregon Law Review, 9*, 469-489.

(Duty to Retreat)

Levine, A. (1930, June) Self-defense - the duty to retreat (People v. Williams (IL) 169 NE 190). *Wisconsin Law Review, 5*, 500-503.

(Self-Defense)

Insulting words as depriving the defendant of the excuse of self-defense (State v Davis (IA) 228 NW 37). (1930, April) *Iowa Law Review, 15*, 372-373.

(Self-Defense)

O'Connor, L.A. (1929, Nov.) Right of self-defense does not accrue to person until he has availed himself of all means in his power to decline combat (Commonwealth v. Trippi (MA) 167 N E 354). *Notre Dame Law, 5*, 98.

(Guest's Duty to Retreat)

Self-defense - guest's duty to retreat (Lawler v. State (AL) 117 So. 605). (1929, Nov.) *Illinois Law Review, 24*, 336-339.

(Self-Defense)

Duty to retreat before killing in self-defense (State v. Dills (NC) 146 SE 1). (1929, Aug.) *Temple Law Quarterly, 3*, 443-444.

(Defending Family)

Right of father, in defense of sons fleeing from still, to kill officer attempting arrest (Fagan v. State (TX) 14 SW 2d. 839). (1929, Aug.) *Law Notes, 33*, 92-93.

(Reputation of Victim)

Bates, R.E. (1929, April) Reputation of victim on the issue of self-defense in Missouri. *St. Louis Law Review, 14*, 259-276.

(Self-Defense)

Randolph, B.P. (1929, April) Self-defense - violent acts of deceased (State v. People (WV) 145 SE 389). *West Virginia Law Quarterly, 35*, 293-295.

(Self-Defense)

Person feloniously attacked need not retreat, but may stand ground and kill adversary if necessary (Jones v. State (AL) 116 So. 896). (1929, March) *Alabama Law Journal, 4*, 216-218.

(Self-Defense)

Braus, M. (1928, June) Justifiable homicide, killing in necessary defense of person (Fixico v. State (OK) 263 Pac. 171). *Cornell Law Quarterly, 13*, 623-627.

(Defense - Intoxication)

Sears, K.C. Intoxication as a defense (People v. Koerber, 244 NY 147, 155 NE 97). *Illinois Law Review, 23*, 159-166 (1928, June); *St. John's Law Review, 1*, 208-209 (1927, May).

(Burden of Proof)

Wilson, W.K. (1928, April) Burden of proof - self-defense (State v. Horner (ND) 215 NW 277). *Dakota Law Review, 2*, 173-174.

(Duty to Retreat)

Duty to retreat (State v. Sipes (IA) 209 NW 458). *Virginia Law Review, 13*, 431 (1927, Nov.); *Law Notes, 31*, 12 (1927, April); *Iowa Law Review, 12*, 171-175 (1927, Feb.)

(Defense of Brother)

Right of person, entering quarrel to commit homicide in defense of brother, held dependent on brother's right of self-defense (Noble v. Commonwealth, 217 KY 556, 290 SW 330). (1927, Nov.) *Kentucky Law Journal, 16*, 71-72.

(Self-Defense)

Duty to retreat and self-defense. (1927, Nov.) *Justice of the Peace, 91*, 860.

(Provocation)

Self-defense - aggression or provocation of attack (State v. Clay (IA) 210 NW 904). (1927, April) *Iowa Law Review, 12*, 304-305.

(Self-Defense)

Right of self-defense by officer attempting illegal arrest (Willinson v. State (Miss.) 108 So. 711). (1927, Feb.) *Law Notes, 30*, 212.

(Right to Defend)

Right to defend person not a relative (Wilkes v. State (TX) 280 S W 786). (1927, Jan.) *Minnesota Law Review, 11*, 170-171.

(Self-Defense - Angry Words)

Self-defense - effect of insulting and opprobrious words (Scott v. Commonwealth (VA) 129 SE 360). (1926, May) *Virginia Law Review, 12*, 602-604.

(Self-Defense)

Self-defense instruction properly qualified, where there was evidence defendant invited combat (Doneghy v. Commonwealth 208 KY 500). (1926, March) *Kentucky Law Journal, 14*, 257-258.

(Tort and Murder Law)

Walton, G.L. (1914) The claim of unconsciousness in tort and murder cases. *Journal of Criminal Law, 2*, 663.

(Defense - Strategy)

Wigmore, J.H. (1912) The limit of counsel's legitimate defense. *Virginia Law Review, 17*, 743.

(Homicide Excuse)

Stephen, H.L. (1901) Superior orders as excuse for homicide. *Law Quarterly Review, 17*, 87.

Criminal Law by States (Alphabetical)

(Cases of Intent - Alabama)

Simmons, B.W. (1945, Oct.) Alabama cases on homicidal intent. *Alabama Law, 6*, 414-419.

(Psychiatric Evaluation - Alaska)

Bloom, J.D. (1980) Forensic psychiatric evaluation of Alaska native homicide offenders. *International Journal of Legal Psychiatry, 3*(2), 163-172.

(Criminal Code - Arizona)

Hagen, T. (1978) Preparatory, homicide, and assault crimes of Arizona's criminal code: Some potential issues. *Arizona Law Review, 20*(3), 643-667.

(Homicide Law)

Preparatory, homicide, and assault crimes of Arizona's new criminal code: Some potential issues. (1978) *Arizona Law Review, 20*, 643-667.

(Homicide Responsibility - Arizona)

Prospective homicidal responsibility for the heroine dealer in Arizona. (1975) *Arizona State Law Journal 1975*, 97-110.

(Court Petition - Arkansas)

Vickie Lorene Rock, petitioner v. Arkansas: On Writ of Certiorari to the Supreme Court of Arkansas. (1990) *International Journal of Clinical and Experimental Hypnosis, 38*(4), 219-238.

(Felony-Murder - California)

California doctrine of felony-murder: An enigma wrapped up in a riddle. (1975, Winter) *UCLA Law Review, 7*, 150-161.

(Intent Doctrine - California)

Rethinking the specific-general intent doctrine in California criminal law. (1975, Sept.)

California Law Review, 63, 1352-1378.

(Homicide - Book)

Davidson, B. (1971) *Indict and convict: Crime and law enforcement in California, an inside story*. London: Michael Joseph.

(Felony-Murder - California)

Merger and the California felony-murder rule in California. (1972, Dec.) *UCLA Law Review, 20*, 250.

(Felony-Murder Rule - California)

Limitations on the applicability of the felony-murder rule in California. (1971, May) *Hastings Law Review, 22*, 1327.

(Criminal Responsibility - California)

Criminal responsibility for the death of a co-felon: Taylor v. Superior Court of Alameda County, 477 P 2d 131. (1971, Spring) *California Western Law Review, 7*, 522.

(Felony-Murder - California)

Criminal law: California's "vicarious murder" theory extends felony-murder doctrine. (1971, Spring) *Val U Law Review, 5*, 676.

(Feticide - California)

Criminal law - killing an unborn but viable, fetus is not murder under section 187 of the California penal code. (1971) *Syracuse Law Review, 22*, 828.

(Felony-Murder Rule - California)

Vicarious murder; ruling of California Supreme Court in The Taylor case. (1970, Dec. 21) *Time, 96*, p. 61.

(Infanticide - California)

Infanticide in California: The impact of Keeler v. Superior Court of Amador County, 470 P 2d 617, and the September 17, 1970, amendment to Penal Code Section 187. (1970, Fall) *California Western Law Review, 7*, 272.

(Felony-Murder - California)

California Supreme Court assaults the felony-murder rule. (1970, May) *Stanford Law Review, 22*, 1059.

(Felony-Murder Rule - California)

California rewrites felony-murder rule. (1966, Feb.) *Stanford Law Review, 18*, 690.

(Legal History)

Momboisse, R.M. (1962, Sept.-Oct.) Early California justice - first murder trial. *California State Bar Journal, 37*, 736.

(Mens Rea - California)

Mens rea and murder by torture in California. (1958, July) *Stanford Law Review, 10*, 672.

(Homicide - California)

Criminal law - murder by lying in wait in California (People v. Merkouris, 297 P 2d 999). (1956, Nov.) *Hastings Law Journal, 8*, 100.

(Criminal Negligence)

Criminal law - criminal negligence - interrelation of California Penal Code sections 20 and 192 (People v. Penny (CA) 285 P 2d. 926). (1956, July) *Southern California Law Review, 29*, 509.

(Criminal Negligence - California)

Criminal law - involuntary manslaughter - California standard of conduct for criminal negligence (People v. Penny, 285 P 2n 926). (1956, Feb.) *UCLA Law Review, 3*, 254.

(Homicide Law - California)

Clarification of homicide law in California from recent decisions. (1949, Fall) *Hastings Law Journal, 1*, 32-41.

(Proximate Cause - California)

Focht, J.L., Jr. (1938, Nov.) Proximate cause in the law of homicide with special reference to California cases. *Southern California Law Review, 12*, 19-53.

(Homicide Law - California)

Pike, J.A. (1936) What is second-degree murder in California? *Southern California Law Review, 9*, 112.

(Criminal Code - Colorado)

Quinn, J.R. (1972) Homicide under the Colorado Criminal Code. *Denver Law Journal, 49*,137.

(Corpus Delicti - Connecticut)

Corpus delicti rule in Connecticut (State v. Douchette, 157 A 2d 487). (1930, June) *Connecticut Bar Journal, 34*, 177.

(Year-and-a-Day Rule - Florida)

Edwards, H.P. (1946, Nov.) The year-and-a-day rule in Florida criminal law. *Florida Law Journal, 20*, 296-298.

(Specific Intent - Illinois)

Specific intent made more specific: A clarification of the law of attempted murder in Illinois. (1978, Fall) *DePaul Law Review, 28*, 157-170.

(Felony-Murder - Illinois)

Criminal law - felony-murder - the merger doctrine is rejected in Illinois. (1976, Dec.) *Southern*

Illinois University Law Journal 1976, 575-591.

(Felony-Murder - Illinois)

Felony murder in Illinois: Extension beyond justification. (1960, Spring) *University of Illinois Law Review 1960*, 158.

(Felony-Murder - Kansas)

Criminal law - felony-murder in Kansas - the prosecutor's new device. (1977, Fall) *Kansas Law Review, 26*, 145-160.

(Homicide Laws - Kansas)

Rees, W.L. (1946, July) Kansas laws relating to homicide - suggested revisions. *Kansas Judicial Council Bulletin, 20*, 79-90.

(Vehicular Homicide - Kentucky)

Criminal law - murder by auto: Kentucky's hard-line stance against drunken drivers. (1978) *Northern Kentucky Law Review, 5*, 279-286.

(Homicide Law - Kentucky)

Moreland, R. (1962, Fall) Kentucky homicide law with recommendations. *Kentucky Law Journal, 51*, 59.

(Suggested Statute - Kentucky)

Moreland, R. (1953, Jan.) Suggested homicide statute for Kentucky. *Kentucky Law Journal, 41*, 139-177.

(Statutory Degrees - Kentucky)

Stegmaier, H.I. (1934, March) Statutory degrees of homicide in Kentucky. *Kentucky Law Journal, 22*, 455-459.

(Homicide Statutes - Louisiana)

Brown, O. (1978, Spring) Louisiana's murder statutes - their past and future. *Southern University Law Review, 4*, 165-174.

(Homicide Statutes - Louisiana)

Rault, G.A., Jr. (1973, Fall) On Louisiana's new homicide statutes: Purpose, constitutionality, and problems of interpretation. *Loyola Law Review, 19*, 563-578.

(Felony Manslaughter Doctrine - Louisiana)

Criminal law - the felony manslaughter doctrine in Louisiana (State v. Garner, 115 S 2d 855). (1960, June) *Louisiana Law Review, 20*, 752.

(Statutory Interpretation - Louisiana)

Criminal law - statutory interpretation - possibility of nullification of reform by common law approach in interpreting La. Criminal Code of 1942 (State v. Harper 17 So 2d 260). (1944,

June) *Tulane Law Review, 18*, 639-646.

(Presumption of Malice - Maine)

Constitutionality of the common law presumption of malice in Maine. (1974, Nov.) *B U Law Review, 54*, 973-1005.

(Year and a Day Rule - Maryland)

Criminal law - judicial affirmance of the validity of the-year-and-a-day rule in Maryland. (1974, Fall) *University of Baltimore Law Review, 4*, 186-196.

(Homicide Laws - Maryland)

Developing law of intentional murder in Maryland (Chisley v. State, 95 Atl. 2d 577). (1953, Fall) *Maryland Law Review, 13*, 327-337.

(Due Process - Massachusetts)

Wire, G.E. (1929) Massachusetts homicide trial according to due process of law. *American Law Review, 63*, 86-117.

(Michigan's Law)

Vaugman, T. (1990, Jan.) Michigan's "uncommon law" of homicide. *Cooley Law Review, 7*, 1-18.

(Felony-Murder Rule - Michigan)

Criminal law - Michigan Supreme Court abrogates common law felony-murder rule: People v. Aaron, 299 N W 2d 304. (1981, Dec.) *Suffolk University Law Review, 15*, 1304-1323.

(Felony-Murder Doctrine - Michigan)

Demise of the felony-murder doctrine in Michigan. (1981, Fall) *Wayne Law Review, 28*, 215-238.

(Felony-Murder Rule - Michigan)

Does Michigan have a felony-murder rule? (1980, Feb.) *Michigan Bar Journal, 59*, 97-99+.

(Felony-Murder Doctrine - Michigan)

Saltzman, A. (1978, Nov.) Felony-murder doctrine in Michigan. *Wayne Law Rev, 25*, 69-82.

(Duty to Retreat - Michigan)

People v. Johnson, 254 N W 2d 667: A retreat from duty to retreat? (1978, Spring) *Detroit College Law Review 1978*, 147-159.

(Jury Instructions - Michigan)

Koenig, D. (1974, Nov.) Jury instructions for jurors: Proposals for the simplification of Michigan instructions on murder. *Wayne Law Review, 21*, 1-30.

(Criminal Code - Michigan)

Homicides under the Michigan Criminal Code (Revised). (1968, Summer) *Wayne Law Review,*

14, 904.

(Marshall Case - Michigan)

Marshall (MI) 106 NW 2d. 842. (1961, Dec.) *Minnesota Law Review, 46*, 414.

(Felony-Murder Rule Missouri)

Criminal law - felony-murder rule in Missouri - the underlying felony need not be inherently dangerous. (1976, Fall) *Missouri Law Review, 41*, 595-603.

(Manslaughter - Missouri)

Criminal law - instructing on manslaughter - eliminating the presumption of malice in Missouri homicide cases . (1973, Winter) *Missouri Law Review, 38*, 105.

(Criminal Law - Missouri)

Cisal, L.E. (1933, Dec.) Criminal homicide in Missouri. *Kansas City Law Review, 2*, 25-27.

(Murder Intent - Nebraska)

Criminal law - homicide - is a purpose or an intent an indispensable element of murder in Nebraska? (1954) *Nebraska Law Review, 33*, 481-491.

(Homicide Law - New Jersey)

New Jersey statute providing for mandatory life sentence for first-degree murder upheld. (1979) *Criminal Law Bulletin, 15(3)*, 255.

(Conviction Overturned - New Jersey)

Criminal law - homicide - New Jersey abrogates common law "year-and-a-day" rule; decision not given retroactive effect - defendant's conviction overturned. (1979) *Seton Hall Law Review, 10*, 389-406.

(Year and a day Rule - New Jersey)

Criminal law - homicide - New Jersey Superior Court rejects the "year-and-a-day" rule in homicide prosecutions. (1978, Spring) *Dick Law Review, 82*, 601-608.

(Statute of Limitations - New Jersey)

New Jersey five-year statute of limitations doesn't govern first-degree murder. (1977) *The Criminal Law Reporter: Court Decisions and Proceedings, 22*(13), 2285-2286.

(Felony-Murder - New Jersey)

Criminal law - homicide - felony-murder - felons can be held responsible under the New Jersey murder statute for the death of an innocent party killed by police attempting to apprehend the felons. (1970, Spring) *Rutgers Law Review, 24*, 591.

(Manslaughter - New Mexico)

Romero, L.M. (1982, Spring) Sufficiency of provocation for voluntary manslaughter in New Mexico: Problems in theory and practice. *New Mexico Law Review, 12*, 747-789.

(Affirmative Defense)

Criminal law: Affirmative defenses in criminal trials - what are the limits after Patterson v. New York (97 Sup. Ct. 2319)? (1978, Spring) *Oklahoma Law Review, 31*, 411-422.

(Reasonable Doubt)

Affirmative criminal defenses - the reasonable doubt rule in the aftermath of Patterson v. New York (97 Sup. Ct. 2319). (1978) *Ohio State Law Journal, 39*, 393-413.

(Death Penalty - New York)

NY strikes down law prescribing death for killers of cops, prison employees. (1977) *The Criminal Law Reporter: Court Decisions and Proceedings, 22*(10), 2211-2213.

(Heroin Deaths - New York)

Heroin deaths: Homicidal responsibility of the seller in New York. (1973) *Albany Law Review, 37*, 497.

(Penal Law - New York)

Gegan, B.E. (1966, Winter) Criminal homicide in the revised New York penal law. *New York Law Journal, 12*, 565.

(Criminal Law - New York)

Byrn, R.M. (1964, Dec.) Homicide under the New York penal law. *Fordham Law Review, 33*, 173.

(Felony-Murder Statute - New York)

Criminal law - construction of New York felony-murder statute - rejection of proximate cause theory (People v. Wood, 167 N E 2d 736). (1961, Jan.) *Albany Law Review, 25*, 153.

(Corpus Delicti - New York)

Corpus delicti in the New York law of homicide. (1957, Dec.) *Brooklyn Law Review, 24*, 71.

(Murder Doctrine - New York)

Criminal law: The misdemeanor-manslaughter doctrine in New York (People v. Nelson, 128 N E 2d 391). (1956, Summer) *Cornell Law Quarterly, 41*, 722.

(Felony-Murder - New York)

Criminal law - felony-murder - New York rules on charging degrees of homicide (People v. Lunse, 278 NY 303). (1938, Nov.) *New York University Law Quarterly Review, 16*, 151-155.

(Felony-Murder - New York)

Corcoran, T.L.J. (1937, Jan.) Felony murder in New York. *Fordham Law Review, 6*, 43-74.

(Murder - Degrees - New York)

Right of defendant in New York to a charge of lesser degrees in felony-murder cases. (1937, May) *Brooklyn Law Review, 6*, 455-461.

(Felony-Murder - New York)

Ellegaard, G.R. (1936, April) A reconsideration of the felony murder doctrine in New York. *St. John's Law Review, 10*, 253-263.

(Felony-Murder Doctrine - New York)

Arent, A.E., & MacDonald, J.W. (1935, April) The felony-murder doctrine and its application under the New York statutes. *Cornell Law Quarterly, 20*, 288-314.

(Legal Decisions - New York)

Whether a confession is voluntary or not is a question of law (People v. Barbat, 172 N E 458). (1930) *St. John's Law Review, 5*, 123-124.

(Criminal Law - North Carolina)

Criminal law - a further erosion of the retreat rule in North Carolina. (1976, Winter) *Wake Forest Law Review, 12*, 1093-1101.

(Felony-Murder Rule - Ohio)

Felony-murder rule in Ohio. (1956, Winter) *Ohio State Law Journal, 17*, 130.

(Homicide Law - Oklahoma)

Criminal law - justifiable homicide in defense of another: Oklahoma's anachronistic statute. (1982, Winter) *Oklahoma Law Review, 35*, 141-150.

(Revise States - Oregon)

Oregon's revised murder statutes: The regressive impact of court-appointed counsel for indigent defendants. (1977) *Oregon Law Review, 56*, 702-714.

(Felony-Murder Doctrine - Oregon)

Felony-murder doctrine under the Oregon code of 1971. (1972, Spring) *Oregon Law Review, 51*, 603.

(Vehicular Homicide - Pennsylvania)

McVardell, V.S. (1989, Summer) Evidence: Victim's intoxication in vehicular homicide. *Temple Law Review, 62*, 783-791.

(Psychiatric Testimony - Pennsylvania)

Commonwealth v. McClusker, 292 2d 286: The use of psychiatric testimony in Pennsylvania homicide trials. (1973, Fall) *Temple Law Quarterly, 47*, 156-171.

(Felony-Murder Rule)

Criminal law - proximate cause theory of felony-murder given final burial in Pennsylvania. (1970, Summer) *Syracuse Law Review, 21*, 1321.

(Year and a Day Rule - Pennsylvania)

Criminal law - murder - year-and-a-day rule rejected in Pennsylvania (Commonwealth v. Ladd, 166

A 2d 501). (1962, Oct.) *Vanderbilt Law Review, 14*, 1532.

(Murder Trial - Pennsylvania)

Admission of a defendant's convictions in a first-degree murder trial as information for jury in Pennsylvania - an undue concession to expediency. (1959, Fall) *Temple Law Quarterly, 33*, 89.

(Felony-Murder Rule - Pennsylvania)

Criminal law - felony-murder rule - a felon's guilt for deaths caused by others - the rule in Pennsylvania. (1958, June) *Villanova Law Review, 3*, 518.

(Killing of Felon - Pennsylvania)

Criminal law - killing of felon by police officer during perpetration of robbery does not make co-felon criminally responsible under Pennsylvania felony-murder rule (Commonwealth v. Redline, 137 A 2d 472). (1958, June) *University of Pennsylvania Law Review, 106*, 1176.

(Justification - Tennessee)

Justifiable homicide in Tennessee. (1961, Winter) *Tennessee Law Review, 28*, 265.

(Involuntary Manslaughter - Tennessee)

Criminal law - involuntary manslaughter - criminal liability for gross or wanton negligence. (1954, June) *Tennessee Law Review, 23*, 437-440.

(Homicide Statutes - Texas)

Scofield, G.R. (1980, March) Due process in the United States Supreme Court and the death of the Texas capital murder statute. *American Journal of Criminal Law, 8*, 1-42.

(Felony-Murder - Texas)

Criminal law - a defendant who intentionally commits a felony during which a bystander is killed by another bystander reasonably attempting to stop that felony commits an intentional killing within the meaning of section 19:02(a), (1), of the Texas penal code. (1978, Spring) *Texas Tech Law Review, 9*, 633-644.

(Intent to Kill - Texas)

Blansett v. State 556 S W 2d 322: Texas redefines the intent to kill. (1977, Fall) *National Journal of Criminal Defense, 3*, 317-328.

(Capital Murder - Texas)

Crump, D. (1977, March) Capital murder: The issues in Texas. *Houston Law Review, 14*, 531-581.

(Homicide Statutes - Texas)

Hvass, C.T. (1945, Dec.) Texas homicide statutes of 1927 - inconsistencies of application. *Texas Law Review, 24*, 83-88.

(Malice - Virginia)

Has the Burger Court dealt a death blow to the presumption of malice in Virginia? (1976, Spring) *University of Richmond Law Review, 10*, 687-705.

(Homicide Laws - Virginia)

A loophole in the Virginia homicide statutes. (1938, Feb.) *Virginia Law Review, 24*, 459-462.

Pleas of Negligence

(Conscious Negligence)

Fukushima, H., et al. (1990) A case of death due to dragging by a car: Establishment of a homicide because of conscious neglect. *Japanese Journal of Legal Medicine, 44*(2), 186-189.

(Extreme Recklessness)

Hoffheimer, M.H. (1989) Intoxication and extreme recklessness murder: Presenting and preserving the issues. *Criminal Law Bulletin, 25*(2), 123-138.

(Physician's Negligence)

Physician negligent in discharging mental patient who murdered family. (1984) *Journal of the Mississippi State Medical Association, 25*(10), 276, 284.

(Reckless Homicide)

Strobel, L.P. (1981, Winter) Reckless homicide. *American Business Law Journal, 18*(4), 588.

(Homicide - Reckless)

Strobel, L.P. (1980, Dec.) Reckless homicide: Ford's Pinto trial. *American Bar Association, 66*, 1547-1549.

(Reckless Driving)

Fisher, J.S. (1980, Nov.) Reckless driving again. *New Law Journal, 130*, 1057-1059.

(Prosecution)

Bourque, P. (1980, June) Proof of the cause of death in a prosecution for criminal negligence causing death. *Criminal Law Quarterly, 22*, 334-343.

(Manslaughter - Nursing)

Kalisch, P.A., et al. (1980) The 'Angel of Death': The anatomy of 1980's major news story about nursing. *Nursing Forum, 19*(3), 212-241.

(Involuntary Manslaughter)

Goldsmith, J.M. (1979) Involuntary manslaughter: Review and commentary on Ohio law. *Ohio State Law Journal, 40*, 569-602.

(Manslaughter)

Squire, L.E., & Painter, R. (1978, Oct.) Manslaughter and omissions to act. *New Law Journal, 128*, 994-997.

(Constructive Manslaughter)

Clarkson, C.M.V. (1978) Drunkenness, constructive manslaughter, and specific intent. *Modern Law Review, 41*, 478-483.

(Diminished Capacity)

Arenelia, P. (1977, Oct.) Diminished capacity and diminished responsibility defenses: Two children of a doomed marriage. *Columbia Law Review, 77*, 827-865.

(Homicide - Degrees)

Farrier, M.D. (1976, July) Distinction between murder and manslaughter in its procedural context. *Modern Law Review, 39*, 414-431.

(Manslaughter)

Manslaughter: The resting place of several former statutes. (1976, Summer) *Arkansas Law Review, 30*, 213-221.

(Causes - Alcohol)

Mayfield, D. (1976) Alcoholism, alcohol, intoxication, and assaultive behavior. *Disorders and Diseases of the Nervous System, 37*(5), 288-291.

(Reckless Murder - Commonwealth)

Sornarajah, M. (1975, Oct.) Reckless murder in commonwealth law. *International & Comparative Law Quarterly, 24*, 846-861.

(Victim - Alcoholic)

Choi, F.Y. (1975) Death in young alcoholics. *Journal of the Study of Alcoholism, 36*(9), 1224-1229.

(Cause - Alcoholism)

Haberman, P.W., & Baden, M.M. (1974) Drinking, drugs, and death. *International Journal of Addiction, 9*(6), 761-763.

(Causes - Alcoholism)

Westermeyer, J., & Bearman, J. (1973) A proposed social indicator system for alcohol-related problems. *Prev Med, 2*(3), 438-444.

(Victim - Bystander)

Felony murder - felon not responsible for accidental death of bystander shot by police. (1970, Summer) *Dick Law Rev, 74*, 756.

(Medical Quack)

Nahum, L.H. (1964, July) The first recorded murder conviction of a medical quack. *Connecticut Medicine, 28*, 492-495.

(Negligent Driving - Responsibility)

Edwards, E.J. (1964, Jan.) Owner's responsibility for homicide for the negligent driving of his car by another. *Australian Law Journal, 37*, 289.

(Murder by Motorist)

Murder by motorist (Staggs v. State (TN) 357 S W 2d 52). (1963, Spring) *Washington & Lee Law Review, 20*, 148.

(Vehicular Homicide)

Fallacy and fortuity of motor vehicle homicide. (1962, June) *Nebraska Law Review, 41*, 793.

(Reckless Homicide)

Homicide - defendant's unlawful or reckless conduct must be direct cause of death to constitute involuntary manslaughter (Commonwealth v. Root (PA) 170 A 2d 310). (1962, Winter) *Maryland Law Review, 22*, 78.

(Manslaughter)

Homicide - manslaughter - causal connection between act and death under misdemeanor-manslaughter rule (People v. Marshall (MI) 106 N W 2d 842). (1962, Jan.) *Notre Dame Law Review, 38*, 127.

(Intoxicated Driver)

Manslaughter: Automobile owner who permitted intoxicated person to drive not responsible for fatal collision (People v. Marshall (Michigan) 106 NW 2d. 842). (1961, Dec.) *Minnesota Law Review, 46*, 414.

(Gross Negligence)

Negligent homicide - its elusive standard of gross negligence. (1961, Fall) *Williamette Law Journal, 1*, 627.

(Negligent Homicide)

Collings, R.A., Jr. (1961, May) Negligent murder - some state-side footnotes to Director of Public Prosecutions v. Smith. *California Law Review, 49*, 254.

(Vehicular Homicide)

Death caused by drag racing - criminal liability of the participants. (1961, Winter) *Syracuse Law Review, 13*, 279.

(Merger Doctrine)

Doctrine of merger in felony-murder and misdemeanor-manslaughter. (1960, Dec.) *St. John's*

Law Review, 35, 109.

(Military Law)

Munster, J.H., Jr., & Larkin, M.A. (1958, Dec.) Negligent homicide in military law. *California Law Review, 46*, 782.

(Negligent Homicide)

Snelling, H.A. (1958, Jan.) Manslaughter by negligent act or omission. *Australian Law Journal, 31*, 630.

(Homicide - Negligent)

Stevens, T.L. (1957, Feb.) Manslaughter and negligent homicide. *Judge Advocate General Journal 1957*, 15.

(Defense - Psychology)

Neustatter, W.L. (1956, July-Dec.) Depression as a defense to murder. *Acta Med Leg Soc, 9*(3-4), 169-179, 181-186.

(Homicide - Provocation)

Williams, J.E.H. (1954, Sept.) Murder- provocation and drunkenness. *Modern Law Review, 17*, 457-459.

(Manslaughter)

Involuntary manslaughter - defense of unavoidable accident (State v. Peckham (WI) 56 N W 2d 835). (1953, Fall) *Marquette Law Review, 37*, 185-188.

(Negligent Manslaughter)

Negligent manslaughter in Kentucky (Mayre v. Commonwealth, 240 S W 2d 852). (1952, Jan.) *Kentucky Law Journal, 40*, 233-237.

(Vehicular Homicide)

Manslaughter by automobile in Florida. (1951, Fall) *University of Florida Law Review, 4*, 360-369.

(Degree of Negligence)

Degree of negligence necessary to sustain a conviction of involuntary manslaughter (State v. Barnett (SC) 63 S E 2d 57). (1951, June) *South Carolina Law Quarterly, 3*, 503-505.

(Multiple Causes)

Manslaughter from plural causes (People v. Cox (Colorado) 228 Pac. 2d. 163). (1951, April) *Rocky Mountain Law Review, 23*, 488-490.

(Homicide Laws)

Misdemeanor manslaughter under state statutes. (1951, March) *Kentucky Law Journal, 39*, 346-350.

(Involuntary Manslaughter - Kentucky)

Kentucky's concept of involuntary manslaughter. (1951, March) *Kentucky Law Journal, 39*, 351-352.

(Homicide - Case Studies)

Hitchler, W.H. (1951, Jan.) Uncomfortable murders. *Dick Law Review, 55*, 139-140.

(Homicide - Degrees)

Rosenstock, J. Propriety of conviction of manslaughter where evidence shows murder of the second degree or nothing (People v. Powell (California) 208 Pac. 2d. 974). *California Law Review, 38*, 934-938 (1950, Dec.); *Southern California Law Review, 23*, 264-166 (1950, Feb.)

(Negligent Homicide)

McElhenny, W.B. (1950, Dec.) Negligent homicide. *Kansas Judicial Council Bulletin, 24*, 172-175.

(Manslaughter - Voluntary)

Statutory voluntary manslaughter. (1950, Nov.) *Kentucky Law Journal, 39*, 108-112.

(Manslaughter - Voluntary)

Voluntary manslaughter under state statutes - Kentucky. (1950, Nov.) *Kentucky Law Journal, 39*, 113-119.

(Homicide - Degrees)

Karaba, F.A. (1950, July-Aug.) Negligent homicide or manslaughter- dilemma. *Journal of Criminal Law, 41*, 183-189.

(Autrefois Acquit)

Kennedy, G.D. Murder and manslaughter - autrefois acquit. *Canadian Bar Review, 28*, 689-698 (1950, July); *Canadian Bar Review, 27*, 968-972 (1949, Oct.).

(Time of Commission)

Lafitte, G.W. Negligent homicide - time of commission (State v. Masino (LA) 43 So. 2d 685). *Albany Law Review, 14*, 224-226 (1950, June); *Louisiana Law Review, 10*, 539-541 (1950, May); *Virginia Law Review, 36*, 680-682 (1950, June).

(Recklessness - Auto Races)

Wynne, E.C. Manslughter- wanton reckless conduct- what is the standard? (Comm. v, Sostilio (Massachusetts) 89 NE 2d. 510). *Boston University Law Review, 30*, 430-432 (1950, June); *Virginia Law Review, 36*, 395-397 (1950, April).

(Insanity Plea)

Weihofen, H. (1950, May) Eliminating the battle of experts in criminal insanity cases.

Michigan Law Review, 48, 961-982.

(Homicide - Historical Aspects)

Coldiron, W.H. (1950, May) Historical development of manslaughter. *Kentucky Law Journal, 38*, 527-550.

(Involuntary Manslaughter)

Morse, H.N. (1950, Feb.) Involuntary manslaughter proviso in Georgia. *Georgia Bar Journal, 12*, 285-288.

(Manslaughter Doctrine)

Johnston, J.J. (1949, Nov.) Reexamination of the misdemeanor manslaughter doctrine. *Kentucky Law Journal, 38*, 118-127.

(Unlawfulness of Act)

Hatfield, G.W., Jr. (1949, Nov.) Misdemeanor-manslaughter doctrine: Effect of "unlawfulness of the act" on liability for manslaughter. *Kentucky Law Journal, 38*, 129-134.

(Burden of Proof)

Kugle, W.H., Jr. (1949, June) Burden of proof - unconsciousness (People v. Hardy (CA) 198 Pac. 2d. 865). *Texas Law Review, 27*, 857-859.

(Insanity Plea)

Larkin, J.J. (1949, May) "Partial insanity" as a means of reducing an intentional homicide to voluntary manslaughter. *Kentucky Law Journal, 37*, 412-416.

(Involuntary Manslaughter - Pennsylvania)

Miller, G.T. (1948, Oct.) Involuntary manslaughter by malfeasance in Pennsylvania. *Dick Law Review, 53*, 46-56.

(Objective Test)

Sparks, B.M. (1947) Negligent murder: Should the objective test be applied in negligent murder cases? *Kentucky Law Journal, 35*, 242-251.

(Corpus Delicti)

Jackson, G.L. (1946, Feb.) Corpus delicti - criminal negligence (Bowie v. Comm. (Virginia) 35 S E 2d. 345). *Georgia Bar Journal, 8*, 326-327.

(Murder or Manslaughter)

Murder or manslaughter? (1946, Jan.) *Legal Times, 201*, 15-16.

(Murder or Manslaughter)

Bull, A. (1946, Jan.) Murder or manslaughter? *Canadian Bar Review, 24*, 13-17.

(Negligent Manslaughter)

Moreland, R. (1944, March) Negligent manslaughter statutes. *Kentucky Law Journal, 32*, 235-

238.

(Negligence)

Moreland, R. (1944, Jan.) Character of negligence in murder. *Kentucky Law Journal, 32*, 139-154.

(Negligence - Kentucky)

Stephenson, H. (1943, March) Negligent involuntary manslaughter in Kentucky- standard of care required. (1943, Mar.) *Kentucky Law Journal, 31*, 284-286.

(Negligence)

Standard of conduct required under amended negligent homicide statute (People v. Young (CA) 129 Pac. 2d. 353). (1943, Mar.) *California Law Review, 31*, 215-220.

(Criminal Negligence)

Criminal negligence - involuntary homicide statutes- Louisiana criminal code (State v. Vinzant (LA) 7 So. 2d. 917). *Louisiana Law Review, 5*, 136-141.

(Plea of Negligence)

Manslaughter - negligence - statutory construction (State v. Hedges (WA) 113 Pac. 2d 530). (1942, July) *Washington Law Review, 17*, 175-177.

(DUI)

Fogle, L.H., Jr. (1941, July) Manslaughter by operation of automobile while intoxicated, construction of word "operation" (Barrington v. State (FL) 199 So. 320). *Florida Law Journal, 15*, 267-268.

(Negligence)

Gates, Sir F. (1941, June) Negligent homicide and loss of expectation of life. *Law Journal, 91*, 235.

(Negligence)

Berrey, R.G. Standard of care required under negligent homicide and manslaughter statutes (People v. Pociask (CA) 96 Pac. 2d 788). (1940, May). *California Law Review, 28*, 518-521; *Southern California Law Review, 13*, 509-511.

(Intoxication Defense)

Coleman, S. (1940, May-June) Intoxication in mitigation of murder (O'Neil v. State (Indiana) 22 NE 2d. 825). *Journal of Criminal Law, 31*, 72-77.

(Negligence of Victim)

Contributory negligence of victim of negligent homicide. (1940, Feb.) *New York Law Review, 74* , 88-90.

(Felony Murder Doctrine)

Turner, J.W., Jr. (1940, Jan.) Felony murder doctrine distinguished from criminal negligence. *Kentucky Law Journal, 28*, 218-223.

(Negligent Homicide)

Tincher, M. (1939, Nov.) Negligent murder. *Kentucky Law Journal, 28*, 53-61.

(Negligent Manslaughter)

Kunc, C.C. (1939, June) Negligent homicide and manslaughter in Nebraska. *Nebraska L B, 18*, 196-204.

(Criminal Negligence)

Vogeler, A.R. (1939, Jan.) Standard of care in criminal negligence: Manslaughter. *Kentucky Law Journal, 27*, 221-225.

(Criminal Negligence)

Turner, J.W., Jr. (1939, Jan.) Criminal negligence - is it subjective or objective in homicide cases (People v. Rauch and Washington)? *Kentucky Law Journal, 27*, 229-233.

(Homicide - Jurisdiction)

Woodall, R.A. (1938, Nov.) Jurisdictions adopting the tort standard of care in criminal negligence. *Kentucky Law Journal, 27*, 111-115.

(Manslaughter)

Manslaughter conviction of motor vehicle owner for death caused by defective brakes (People v. Rauch and Washington, Queens County, NY Court). (1937, June) *Yale Law Journal, 46*, 1411-1415.

(Culpable Negligence)

Culpable negligence, degree of negligence required (People v. Hoffman). (1937, May) *Fordham Law Review, 6*, 309-312.

(Negligent Homicide)

Riesenfeld, S.A. (1936, Nov.) Negligent homicide: A study in statutory interpretation. *California Law Review, 25*, 1-40.

(Reckless Driving)

Justiciary, reckless driving (Paton v. His Majesty's Advocate S L T 298). (1936, Sept.) *Jurid Review, 48*, 275-276.

(DUI)

Riesenfeld, S.A. (1936, July) Homicide committed through the operation of a motor vehicle while intoxicated. *California Law Review, 24*, 555-573.

(Manslaughter - Theory and Practice)

Manslaughter: Theory and practice. (1936, July) *Sol J, 3*, 158.

(Manslaughter - Degrees)

Involuntary manslaughter - degree of negligence (Commonwealth v. Gill (PA) 182 Atl. 103). (1936, May) *Temple Law Quarterly, 10*, 327-328.

(Liability)

Liability of, for negligence of nurses and doctors. (1936) *Canadian Bar Review, 14*, 699.

(Vehicular Homicide)

Involuntary manslaughter, death caused while driving without a license. (1935, Nov.) *Temple Law Quarterly, 10*, 67-71.

(Reckless Driving)

Reagan, J.A., Jr. Manslaughter inflicted in commission of misdemeanor, merger of reckless driving with the homicide (People v. Grieco (NY) 193 N E 634). *St. John's Law Review, 9*, 385-390 (1935, May); *Columbia Law Review, 35*, 446-448 (1935, March).

(Criminal Negligence)

Manslaughter, liability of third parties for driver's criminal negligence (State v. Lewis (WV) 174 SE 483). (1934, Dec.) *New York University Law Quarterly Review, 12*, 303-304.

(Guilt of Defendant)

Lyne, J.C. (1931, Nov.) Defendant's guilt where death is caused by non-attention to wound inflicted by defendant (Commonwealth v. Kilburn (KY) 34 SW 2d. 728). *Kentucky Law Journal, 20*, 93-94.

(Manslaughter - Involuntary)

Involuntary manslaughter. (1929) *Massachusetts Law Society Journal, 1*, 6.

(Manslaughter - Negligence)

Manslaughter by negligence (People v. Crossan (CA) 261 Pac. 531). (1928, May) *Michigan Law Review, 26*, 820-821.

(Physician Negligence)

Murder and manslaughter, intervening negligence of physician causing death (Hall v. State (IN) 159 N E 420). (1928, April) *Temple Law Quarterly, 2*, 281-282.

(Manslaughter - Involuntary)

Involuntary manslaughter, causal connection between unlawful quality of the act and the homicide (Keller v. State (TN) 299 S W 803). (1928, March) *Harvard Law Review, 41*, 669-670.

(Negligence - Case Report)

Negligence, respondent superior (Moreland v. State (GA) 139 SE 77). (1928, Jan) *Harvard Law*

Review, 41, 398-399.
(Drunkenness)
Kesler, J.C. (1927, June) First degree murder, drunkenness as a defense (State v. Ross 193 NC 25). *North Carolina Law Review, 5*, 363-365.
(DUI)
Holland, R.B. (1926, June) Criminal responsibility in Texas for death caused by one driving car while under influence of liquor. *Texas Law Review, 4*, 497-499.
(Manslaughter - Negligence)
Manslaughter by negligence. (1925) *Sol J, 69*, 739.
(Homicide - Liability)
Lee, J.H.S. (1902) Liability of parent at common law on charge of manslaughter for negligently omitting to furnish medical attendants to child because of religious disbelief in the efficacy of medicine. *Cent Law Journal, 55*, 44.

Capital Punishment

(Death Row)
MacNamara, M. (1990, Nov.) Playing for time. *Vanity Fair, 53*(11), pp. 80-92.
(Execution - J. Girratano)
Hooker, S. (1990, Oct. 29) Unreasonable certainty: The killing of Joe Girratano. *Nation, 251*(14), pp. 485-386.
(Woman Sentenced)
Stuttaford, G. (1990, Sept. 21) Nonfiction: Early Graves. *Publisher's Weekly, 237*(38), p. 61.
(Death Penalty - Miss.)
Blacks fight to save life of Miss. teen on death row (S. Butler). (1990, Aug. 13) *Jet, 78*, p. 12.
(Governor's Decision)
Shapiro, W. (1990, May 28) A life in his hands. *Time, 135*(22), pp. 23-24.
(Sentencing - Murderers)
Death by gun: One year later (conviction and sentencing of murderers). (1990, May 14) *Time,*

135, 30-31.

(Trial - Mumia Abu-Jamal)

Deacon, K. (1990, April 23) Pennsylvania justice: The killing of Mumia Abu-Jamal. *Nation, 250*(16), pp. 556-559.

(Murder - Baghdad)

Murder in Baghdad. (1990, April 9) *New Republic, 202*(15), pp. 7-8.

(Juvenile Punishment)

Bieler, G.M. (1990, Spring) Death to be not proud: A note on juvenile capital punishment. *New York Law School Journal on Human Rights, 7*, 179-213.

(Baghdad Hanging)

Fielding, N. (1990, March 23) Profit and loss. *New Statesman & Society, 3*(93), p. 15.

(Execution - California)

Kaplan, D.A., & Wright, L. (1990, Feb. 19) Breaking the death barrier. *Newsweek, 115*(8), pp. 72-73.

(Victim - Old Lady)

Miller, J.B. (1990, Feb. 7) In the city, a tale of crime and punishment. *Christian Century, 107*(5), pp. 116-117.

(Death Penalty)

Kaplan, D.A. (1990, Jan. 22) Death rides a judicial roller coaster. *Newsweek, 115*(4), p. 55.

(Death Row - Interviews)

Shirley, D. (1990) *Death row: Interviews with inmates, their families, and opponents of capital punishment*. London: McFarland & Co.

(Death Penalty and Race)

Keil, T.J., & Vito, G.F. (1990) Race and the death penalty in Kentucky murder trials: An analysis of post-Gregg outcomes. *Justice Quarterly, 7*(1), 189-207.

(Capital Punishment)

Spradling, K.K., & Murphy, M.D. (1990) Capital punishment, the constitution, and the Uniform Code of Military Justice. *Air Force Law Review, 32*(1), 415-430.

(Death Penalty)

Constitutionality of the death penalty under the Uniform Code of Military Justice. Intoccia, Maj. G.F. (1990) *Air Force Law Review, 32*(1), 395-413.

(Death Penalty Law)

Biskupic, J. (1989, Oct. 28) Senate passes death penalty for murders by terrorists. *Congressional Quarterly Weekly Report, 47*(43), 2882.

(Time Analysis)

Bailey, W.C., & Peterson, P.D. (1989, Oct.) Murder and capital punishment: A monthly time-scale analysis of execution publicity. *American Sociological Review, 54*, 722-743.

(Juvenile Punishment)

Eth, S., & Schowalter, J. (1989, May) Resolved: There is no special developmental consideration in adolescence mitigating against capital punishment for those who committed murder under eighteen years of age. *Journal of the American Academy of Child and Adolescent Psychiatry, 28*(5), 450-454.

(Death Penalty)

Murder most foul. (1989, May) *Progressive, 53*(5), p. 10.

(Murder and Mercy)

Fenigsen, R., et al. (1989) Mercy, murder, and morality: Reply (letters). *Hastings Cent Rev, 19*(6), 50-52.

(Juvenile Punishment)

Skovron, S.E., et al. (1989) The death penalty for juveniles: An assessment of public support. *Crime & Delinquency, 35*(4), 546-561.

(Death Penalty)

Keil, T.J., & Vito, G.F. (1989) Race, homicide severity, and the death penalty: A consideration of the Barnett scale. *Criminology, 27*(8), 511-535.

(Capital Punishment)

Kahn, E., et al. (1989) Focus: Capital punishment. *South African Journal of Criminal Justice, 2*(2), 137-250.

(Human Rights)

When the state kills . . . the death penalty. (1989) New York: Amnesty International.

(Death Penalty - Costs)

Criminal justice: Limited data available on costs of death sentences. (1989) Washington, DC: U.S. Government Accounting Office.

(Tison v. Arizona)

Friedman, A.H. (1989) Tison v. Arizona: The death penalty and the non-triggerman - the scales of justice are broken. *Cornell Law Review, 75*(1), 123-157.

(Capital Punishment)

Capital Punishment. (1989) Rockford, MD: National Institute of Justice.

(Arson/Murder - Sentence)

Tenn. minister gets death in an arson-murder case. (1988, Oct. 17) *Jet, 75*(3), p. 54.

(Juvenile Punishment)

Ricotta, D.J. (1988) Eighth Amendment - the death penalty for juveniles: A state's right or a child's injustice? *Journal of Criminal Law & Criminology, 79*(3), 921-952.

(Death Penalty)

Kling, L. (1988) Constitutionalizing the death penalty for accomplices to felony murder. *American Criminal Law Review, 26*(2), 463-490.

(Death Penalty - Females)

Streib, V.L., & Sametz, L. (1988) *Capital punishment of female juveniles.* Paper presented at 1988 Annual Meeting of the American Society of Criminology.

(Killer - P. Cooper)

Bruning, F. (1987, Oct. 26) Countdown to the electric chair (18-year-old killer P. Cooper). *Macleans, 100,* p. 13.

(Death Penalty - Juvenile)

Ogloff, J.R. (1987) The juvenile death penalty: A frustrated society's attempt for control. *Behavioral Sciences & the Law, 5*(4), 447-455.

(Death Sentence - Juvenile)

Ellison, W.J. (1987) State execution of juveniles: Defing "youth" as a mitigating factor for imposing less than death. *Law & Psychology Review, 11*(2), 1-38.

(Capital Punishment)

Capital Punishment. (1985) *Criminal Justice Newsletter, 16*(15), 7-8.

(Execution - Nevada)

Nevada executes inmate. (1985) *Corrections Digest, 16*(26), 10. Microforms and article copies available from UMI.

(Death Row)

Philpott, T. (1984, June 4) Services asked to remove 5 from death row. *Air Force Times, 44,* p. 4.

(Death Sentence)

Philpott, T. (1984, Feb. 6) Death-sentencing changes not retroactive. *Air Force Times, 44,* p. 4.

(Capital Punishment)

Capital punishment. (1984) *Criminal Justice Newsletter, 15*(14), 7; *15*(17), 6.

(Death Penalty)

Carlson, N.A. (1984) Capital punishment - murder of police officer - knowledge of officer's status. *The Criminal Law Reporter: Court Decisions, 35*(25), 2460.

(Death Penalty)

Texas legislature proposing death for mass murderers. (1984) *Corrections Digest, 15*(16), 9.

(Juvenile Punishment)

Imposition of death penalty upon juvenile isn't unconstitutional. (1984) *The Criminal Law Reporter: Court Decisions, 35*(23), 2409-2410.

(Teen Offender)

Maryland appeals court upholds death penalty for teenage offender. (1984) *Juvenile Justice Digest, 12*(17), 4,6.

(Personality - Diagnosis)

Allison, R.B. (1984) Difficulties diagnosing the multiple personality syndrome in a death penalty case. *Int Clin Exp Hyp, 32*(2), 102-117.

(Capital Punishment)

Bailey, W.C. (1984) Murder and capital punishment in the nation's Capital. *Justice Quarterly, 1*(2), 211-213.

(Racial Discrimination)

Paternoster, R. (1984) Prosecutorial discretion in requesting the death penalty: A case of victim-based racial discrimination. *Law & Society Review, 18*(3), 437-478.

(Death Penalty)

Capital punishment - aggravating circumstances - commission of murder in heinous or depraved manner. (1983) *The Criminal Law Reporter: Court Decisions, 34*(9), 2172.

(Death Penalty)

Archer, D., et al. (1983) Homicide and the death penalty: A cross-national test of a deterrence hypothesis. *The Journal of Criminal Law and Criminology, 74*(3), 991-1013.

(Death Penalty)

Lempert, R. (1983) Capital punishment in the 80's: Reflections on the symposium. *The Journal of Criminal Law and Criminology, 74*(3), 1101-1114.

(Death Penalty)

Baldus, D.C. (1983) Comparative review of death sentences: An empirical study of the Georgia experience. *The Journal of Criminal Law and Criminology, 74*(3), 661-753.

(Deterrence Research)

Bailey, W.C. (1983) Disaggregation in deterrence and death penalty research: The case of murder in Chicago. *The Journal of Criminal Law & Criminology, 74*(3), 827-859, 991-1013.

(Deterrent - Short-Term)

McFarland, S.G. (1983) Is capital punishment a short-term deterrent to homicide? A study of the effects of four recent American executions. *The Journal of Criminal Law & Criminology, 74*(3), 1014-1032.

(Death Penalty)

Paternoster, R. (1983) Race of victim and location of crime: The decision to seek the death penalty in South Carolina. *The Journal of Criminal Law & Criminology, 74*(3), 754-785.

(Officers' Murders)

Carlson, N.A. (1983) Murders of officers at Marion Pen. call for death penalty. *Corrections Digest, 14*(25), 6-7. Microforms and article copies available from UMI.

(Execution - Florida)

Florida executes inmate. (1983) *Corrections Digest, 14*(25), 10. Microforms and article copies available from UMI.

(Death Penalty Needed)

Need for federal death penalty cited in officers' slayings. (1983) *Corrections Digest, 14*(24), 1-2. Microforms and article copies available from UMI.

(Death Penalty)

Philpott, T. (1982, Dec. 20) Soldier faces death sentence. *Air Force Times, 43*, p. 1+.

(Death Penalty)

Kobbervig, W., et al. (1982, July) Deterrence and the death penalty: A comment on Phillips. *American Journal of Sociology, 88*(1), 161-164.

(Death Penalty)

Tifft, L. (1982, Summer) Capital punishment research policy and ethics: Defining murder and placing murderers. *Crime and Social Justice, 17*, 61-68.

(Death Penalty)

Bailey, W.C. (1982, Feb.) Capital punishment and lethal assaults against police. *Criminology, 19*, 608-625.

(Judge's Discretion)

Foley, L.A., et al. (1982) The discretion of prosecutors, judges, and juries in capital cases. *Criminal Justice Review 1982, 7*(2), 16-22.

(Death Penalty)

Radelet, M.I. (1981, Dec.) Racial characteristics and the imposition of the death penalty. *American Sociological Review, 46*, 918-927.

(Punishment)

Eigen, J.P. (1981, Autumn) Punishing youth homicide offenders in Philadelphia. *Journal of Criminal Law & Criminology, 72*(3), 1072-1093.

(Death Penalty)

Phillips, D.P. (1981, Spring) Strong and weak research designs for detecting the impact of capital punishment on homicide. *Rutgers Law Review, 33*, 790-798.

(Death Penalty)

Russelburg, J. (1981, March-April) UCMJ death penalty: A constitutional assessment. *Advocate, 13*(2), 74-88.

(Homicide - Sentencing)

Indictments, convictions, sentences. (1980) *Organized Crime Digest, 1*(2), 3-4. Microforms and article available from UMI.

(Death Penalty)

Dawson, M. (1980) Is the death penalty in the military cruel and unusual? *Judge Advocate General Journal, 31*(1), 53-73.

(Death Penalty)

Hancock, C. (1979, April) Perils of calibrating the death penalty through special definitions of murder. *Tulane Law Review, 53*, 828-873.

(Sentencing Upheld)

Life imprisonment upheld where innocent man slain in revenge killing. (1979) *Criminal Law Bulletin, 15*(1), 105-106.

(Sentencing - Decisions)

Decisions on sentencing: Offenses against the person. (1979) *Criminal Law Quarterly, 21*(3), 270-280.

(Capital Punishment)

Kleck, G. (1979) Capital punishment, gun ownership, and homicide. *American Journal of Sociology, 84*(4), 882-910.

(Death Sentence - Race)

Killers of white persons by far the most likely to draw a death sentence. (1979) *Jail Administration Digest, 2*(3), 10. Article copies available from UMI.

(Death Penalty)

Wells, C. (1978, Nov.) Death penalty for provocation? *Criminal Law Review, 1978*, 662-672.

(Homicidal Threat)

Anable, W.R. (1978, Nov.) Homicidal threat as grief work. *Psychiatric Opinions, 15*(11), 43-47.

(Death Penalty Laws)

First-degree murder statutes and capital sentencing procedures: An analysis and comparison of statutory systems for the imposition of the death penalty in Georgia, Florida, Texas, and Louisiana. (1978, Fall) *Loyola Law Review, 24*, 709-751.

(Death Punishment)

Karge, S.W. (1978, Summer) Capital punishment: Death penalty for murder. *Journal of Criminal Law and Criminology, 69*, 179-196.

(Capital Punishment - England)

Polinsky, A.M., & Wolpin, K.I. (1978, May) Capital punishment and homicide (with reply by A.M. Polinsky). *American Econ R Pa & Proc, 63*, 422-427, 435-436.

(Crime and Capital Punishment)

Barnett, A. (1978, Winter) Crime and capital punishment: Some recent studies. *Journal of Criminal Law, 6*(4), 291-303.

(Death Penalty - Constitutionality)

Constitutionality of imposing the death penalty for felony murder. (1978, Jan.) *Houston Law Review, 15*, 356-386.

(Homicide - Degrees - Sentencing)

Life without parole for first degree murder is constitutional. (1978) *The Criminal Law Report: Court Decisions and Proceedings, 23*(8), 2165-2166.

(Prison Inmates)

Capital punishment - murder by inmate serving life sentence. (1978) *The Criminal Law Report: Court Decisions and Proceedings, 23*(14), 2314-2315.

(Deterrent Effect)

Forst, B.E. (1977, May) Deterrent effect of capital punishment: A cross-state analysis of the 1960's. *Minnesota Law Review, 61*, 743-767.

(Law Examination)

Rico, J.M. (1977) (Capital punishment, a critical examination of Bill C-84). *Canadian Journal of Criminology and Corrections, 19*(2), 230-242.

(Imprisonment)

Wisconsin high court says murderers need not ever be imprisoned. (1977) *Corrections Digest, 8*(8), 3.

(Death Penalty)

Jayewardene, C.H. (1977) *Penalty of death.* Lexington Books.

(Capital Murder)

Crump, D., & Jacobs, G. (1977) *Capital murder.* Texian.

(Homicide - Ser.tencing)

Wisconsin court says killers can be placed on probation. (1977) *Crime Control Digest, 11*(13), 4. Article copies available from UMI.

(Homicide Book)

Connery, D. (1977) *Guilty until proven innocent.* New York: Putnam.

(Mandatory Death Sentence)

Bedau, H.A. (1976, Spring) Felony-murder rape and the mandatory death penalty: A study in discretionary justice. *Suffolk University Law Review, 10*, 493-520.

(Death Penalty - Perspectives)

Zimring, F.E., et al. (1976, Winter) Punishing homicide in Philadelphia: Perspectives on the death penalty. *University of Chicago Law Review, 43*, 227-252.

(Rape/Murder - Death Penalty)

No death penalty for murder during rape in Massachusetts. (1976) *Crime Control Digest, 10*(1), 3-4.

(Differential Sentencing)

Kelly, H.E. (1976) A comparison of defense strategy and race as influences on differential sentencing. *Criminology, 14*(2), 241-249.

(Homicide - Sentencing)

Shaw, A.M.N. (1976) The penalty for murder and judges' recommendations. *Howard Journal of Penology and Crime Prevention Charts, 15*(2), 31-49.

(Sentencing)

Ashworth, A.J. (1975, Oct.) Sentencing in provocation cases. *Criminal Law Review, 1975*, 553-563.

(Capital Punishment)

Bailey, W.C. (1975) Murder and capital punishment: Some further evidence. *American Journal of Orthopsychiatry, 45*(4), 669-688.

(Capital Punishment)

Solomon, G.F. (1975, July) Capital punishment as suicide and as murder. *American Journal of Orthopsychiatry, 45*(4), 701-711.

(Capital Punishment)

Capital punishment reduction. (1975) *The Criminal Law Reporter: Court Decisions and Proceedings, 18*(14), 2308.

(Homicide Sentencing)

The penalty for murder. (1975) *Criminal Law Quarterly, 17*(4), 327-328.

(Death Penalty - Unconstitutional)

Massachusetts holds death penalty for rape-murder unconstitutional. (1975) *The Criminal Law Reporter: Court Decisions, 18*(14), 2303-2307.

(Death Penalty - Utah)

Utah declines to alter death penalty. (1975) *IACP Law Enforcement Legal Litigation Report, 52*, 5-7.

(Death Penalty - Case Report)

Diamond, B.L. (1975) Murder and the death penalty: A case report. *American Journal of Orthopsychiatry, 45*(4), 712-722.

(Death Penalty)

Bailey, W.C. (1974, Sept.) Murder and the death penalty. *Journal of Criminal Law, 65*, 416-423.

(Death Penalty - Outrage)

Glaser, D., & Zeigler, M.S. (1974, Oct.) Use of the death penalty v. outrage at murder. *Crime & Delinquency, 20*, 333-338.

(Sentencing)

Blake, L.W. (1973, Sept.) The sentence for murder: The case for retribution. *New Law Journal, 123*(5615), 862-864.

(Death Penalty)

Lester, D. (1973, July) Homicides and the death penalty. *JAMA, 225*, 313.

(Capital Punishment)

Burton, H., & Wolfe, E. (1973) *Pile-up on death row.* New York: Doubleday.

(Death Penalty - Canada)

Morrison, W.A. (1973) Criminal homicide and the death penalty in Canada: Time for reassessment and new directions - towards a typology of homicide. *Canadian Journal of Criminology & Corrections, 15*(4), 367-396.

(Capital Punishment)

Smith, L.M. (1972, Oct.) Reversible error in first degree murder convictions: The Modesto rule reexamined. *University of San Francisco Law Review, 7*, 1.

(Capital Punishment)

Sellin, T.E. (1967) *Capital punishment.* New York: Harper & Row.

(Death Penalty)

Dangl, J. (1966) Family council issues death sentence (German). 20957. J. 20, '66, 7, s. 378-379. (IBZ- 67)

(Murder Charge)

Kelly, V. (1965) *Charge is murder.* Tri-Ocean.

(Reduced Punishments)

Trial courts' power to reduce punishments fixed by juries in first degree murder trials. (1962, May) *Hastings Law Journal, 13*, 474.

(Capital Punishment)

Capital and non-capital murder. (1962, April) *Fac Law Review, 20*, 53.

(Law of Murder)

Law of murder and the death sentence. (1956, June) *Justice of the Peace, 120*, 83.

(Capital Punishment)

Graves, W.F. (1956) A doctor looks at capital punishment. *Medical Arts & Science, 10*(4), 137-141.

(Penalty)

Penalty for murder. (1948, July) *Law Times, 206*, 34-35.

(Punishment)

Gregory, T. (1946, Sept.) Murder is murder and the guilty can be punished. *ABA Journal, 32*, 544-549.

(Trial)

Deloria, E.D. (1944) Dakota treatment of murderers: Reprisal killing, trial by ordeal, or adoption of the murderer in place of his victim. *American Philosophical Society Proceedings, 88*(5), 368-371.

(Felony Murder)

Pollack, L. (1942, June) Felony murder: Effect of jury's failure on recommendation of life imprisonment under section 1045-a of the penal law (People v. Hicks (NY) 38 NE 2d. 482). *Cornell Law Quarterly, 27*, 565-569.

(Sentencing)

Sentence for first degree murder at court's discretion (Commonwealth v. Irelan (PA) 17 Atl. 2d. 897). (1941, May) *Dick Law Review, 45*, 328-330.

(Sentencing)

Graham, D.M. (1935, July) Evidence to be considered by jury in mitigation of punishment (State v. Barth (NJ) 176 Atl. 183). *Journal of Criminal Law, 26*, 282-286.

(Death Sentence)

Argument and conduct of counsel, death sentence (State v. Bradley (WA) 27 Pac. 2d 737). (1934, April) *Washington Law Review, 8*, 194.

(Homicide - Degrees)

The penalty in Pennsylvania for murder in the first degree. (1933) *Temple Law Quarterly, 7*, 330.

(Capital Punishment - Germany)

Kramer, K. (1932) (Murder and capital punishment Hesse, 1817-1929). *Monatssch f Krimpsychol u Strafrechstref, 23*, 129-176.

(Guilty Plea)

Plea of guilty in murder charges. (1931, Dec.) *Law Journal, 72*, 383.

(Guilt or Innocence)

Zieidler, C.F. (1931, April) Guilty or not guilty? (editorial) *Marquette Law Review, 15*, 164-167.

(Homicide - Judgment)

Death resulting from unlawful act (Letner v. State (TN) 155 Tennessee 624, 299 SW 1049). (1928, Dec.) *Tennessee Law Review, 7*, 51-53.

(Capital Punishment)

Hollander, B. (1928, July) Capital punishment. *Engl Review, 47*, 79-86.

(Life and Death)

Davies. Problems of life and death. *Sol J, 71*, 919 (1927, Dec.); *Sol J, 71*, 833, 856 (1927, Oct.-Nov.).

(Death Sentence - Appeal)

Riddell, W.R. (1926, June) Appeal of death and its abolition. *Michigan Law Review, 24*, 786-808.

(Death Penalty)

Sutherland, E.H. (1925, Feb.) Murder and the death penalty. *Journal of Criminal Law, 15*, 522-529.

(Capital Punishment)

Ralston, R. (1912, May) Charging the jury in a trial for murder and delay in the execution of murderers. *American Law Review, 46*, 397-434.

(Mercy)

Mercy and murder. (1907, March 30) *Spectator, 98*, 491-492.

(Capital Punishment - Austria-Hungary)

Shipley, M. (1907, March) Homicide and the death penalty in Austria-Hungary. *American Statistical Association, 10*, 253-259.

Plea of Insanity

(Mental Disorders)

Lindheimer, S.K. (1990) Law and crime: Murder of innocence. *Library Journal, 115*(13), 124-125.

(Homicide - Insanity)

Wortis, J. (1990) Getting away with murder. *Biology and Psychiatry, 28*(7), 555.

(Homicide - Insanity)

McGovern, C.M. (1990) Homicidal insanity from 1800-1985 by I. Colazzi (book review). *Journal of American History, 76*(4), 1238-1239.

(Homicidal Insanity)

McGovern, C.M. (1990) Homicidal insanity, by I. Coliazzi (book review). *Journal of American History, 76*(4), 1238-1239.

(Postpartum Psychosis)

Moss, D.C. (1988, Aug. 1) Postpartum psychosis defense. *ABA Journal, 74,* 22.

(Insanity Pleas - Illinois)

Wettstein, R.M., & Mulvey, E.P. (1988) Disposition of insanity acquitees in Illinois. *Bulletin of the American Academy of Psychiatry and Law, 16*(1), 11-24.

(Homicide - Insanity)

Spiegel, A.D. (1988) Temporary insanity and premenstrual syndrome: Medical testimony in an 1865 murder trial. *New York State Journal of Medicine, 88*(9), 482-492.

(Homicide - Insanity)

Brooks, S.A. (1988) What price insanity? *Canadian Journal of Psychiatry, 33*(2), 118-124.

(Insanity of Condemned)

Petty, J.R. (1988) Insanity of the condemned: The physician's dilemma. *Journal of Neurology and Orthopedic Medical Surgery, 9*(1), 77-80.

(PMS)

Spiegel, A.D. (1988) Temporary insanity and premenstrual syndrome: Medical testimony in an 1865 murder trial. *New York State Journal of Medicine, 88*(9), 482-492.

(Madness - Legal Problem)

Kunen, S. (1987, Oct. 5) Excercizing her right to madness, accused killer Gena Spero poses a legal problem without a solution (pleading insanity). *People Weekly, 28,* pp. 115-116+.

(Sane v. Insane)

Packer, I.K. (1987) Homicide and the insanity defense: A comparison of sane and insane murderers. *Behavioral Sciences and the Law, 5*(1), 25-35.

(Insanity Plea - Legislation)

Hamilton, J.R. (1986) Insanity legislation. *Journal of Medical Ethics, 12*(1), 13-17.

(Hinkley Trial)

Halpern, A.L. (1984) Further comments on the insanity defense in the aftermath of the Hinkley trial. *Psychiatry Quarterly, 56*(1), 62-69.

(Insanity - 19th Century)

Pankrantz, L.D. (1984) Murder and insanity: 19th century perspectives from the *American Journal of Insanity*. *International Journal of Offender Therapy and Comparative Criminology, 28*(1), 37-43.

(Ultimate Conflict)

Bluestone, H., & Travin, S. (1984) Murder: The ultimate conflict. *American Journal of Psychoanalysis, 44*(2), 147-167.

(Diminished Responsibility)

Dell, S., & Smith, A. (1983) Changes in the sentencing of diminished responsibility homicides. *British Journal of Psychiatry, 142*(1), 20-34.

(Insanity Plea)

Kahn, M.W., et al. (1981) Hospitalization versus imprisonment and the insanity plea. *Criminal Justice and Behavior, 8*(4), 483-490.

(Insanity Plea - Wisconsin)

Restricting the admission of psychiatric testimony on a defendant's mental state: Steele v. State (WI), 294 N W 2d 2. (1981) *Wisconsin Law Review 1981*, 733-789.

(Insanity)

Madness, responsibility, and the law (editorial). (1981) *Nature, 291*(5814), 367-368.

(Mental Illness)

Rondepierre, J. (1980) A rapist/murderer guillotined in 1969: Comments on the state of his brain. *Ann Med Psychol, 138*(10), 1237.

(Familicide)

Malmquist, C.P. (1980) Psychiatric aspects of familicide. *Bulletin of the American Academy of Psychiatry and Law, 8*(3), 298-304.

(Psychiatry and Law)

Bell, C.C. (1980) Interface between psychiatry and the law on the issue of murder. *Journal of the National Medical Association, 72*(11), 1093-1097.

(Offense Neutralization)

Minor, W.W. (1980) The neutralization of criminal offense. *Criminology, 18*(1), 103-120.

(Insanity Defense)

Easson, W.M. (1980) Myxedema psychosis - insanity defense for murder. *Journal of Clinical Psychiatry, 41*(9), 316-318.

(Insanity - Study)

Smith, R. (1980) Scientific thought and the boundary of insanity and criminal responsibility. *Psychology and Medicine, 10*(1), 15-23.

(Emotional Disturbance)

Proof of extreme emotional disturbance in Oregon murder prosecutions: A constitutional analysis. (1979) *Oregon Law Review, 58*, 98-118.

(Insanity Pleas - Due Process)

Burden of proof for extreme emotional disturbance and insanity: The deterioration of due process. (1979) *Temple Law Quarterly, 52*, 79-101.

(Murderer - Mentally Ill)

Pasewark, R.A., et al. Characteristics and dispositions of persons found not guilty by reason of insanity in New York State, 1971-1976. (1979) *American Journal of Psychiatry, 136*(5), 655-660.

(Homicide - Insanity)

Murder rap for mental patients. (1979) *Law Enforcement Journal, 8*(6), 2. Article copies available from UMI.

(Insanity Defense)

Uhlin, D.M. (1978) The use of drawings for psychiatric evaluation of a defendant in a case of homicide. *Mental Health Soc, 4*(1-2), 61-78.

(Capital Punishment)

Dix, G.E. (1978) Participation by mental health professionals in capital murder sentencing. *International Journal of Law and Psychiatry, 1*(3), 283-308.

(Insanity Defense)

Hoch, E.M. (1978) Devana. *Journal of Psychiatry and Law, 6*(3), 403-427.

(Murder Evidence)

Criminal law- murder- evidence- psychiatric testimony- specific intent - diminished capacity. (1977-1978) *Duquesne Law Review, 16*, 129-137.

(Diminished Capacity)

Prison conditions and diminished capacity - a proposed defense. (1977, Fall) *Santa Clara Law*

Review, 17, 855-883.

(Insanity Defense)

Burden of proof and the insanity defense after Mullaney v. Wilbur (95 Sup. Ct. 1881). (1977) *Maine Law Review, 28*, 435-469.

(Homicide - Mental Illness)

Herjanic, M., et al. (1977) Forensic psychiatry: Female offenders. *American Journal of Psychiatry, 134*(5), 556-558.

(Mental Illness)

Henn, F.A., et al. (1977) Forensic psychiatry: Anatomy of a service. *Comparative Psychiatry, 18*(4), 337-345.

(Emotional Disturbance)

Affirmative defenses after Mullaney v. Wilbur (95 Sup. Ct. 1881): New York's extreme emotional disturbance. (1976, Summer) *Brooklyn Law Review, 43*, 171-199.

(Burden of Proof)

Constitutional limitations on allocating the burden of proof of insanity to the defendant in murder cases. (1976, May) *Boston University Law Review, 56*, 499-521.

(Mental Health Law)

Brooks, A.D. (1976) Mental health law. *Adm Ment Health, 4*(1), 94-97.

(Murder - Mental Illness)

Medlicott, R.W. (1976) Psychiatric aspects of murder and attempted murder. *New Zealand Medical Journal, 83*(555), 5-9.

(Insanity Defense)

McGlynn, R.P., et al. (1976) Sex and race as factors affecting the attribution of proof of insanity to the defendant in murder cases. *Journal of Psychology, 93*(1), 93-99.

(Diminished Capacity)

Diminished capacity: The middle ground of criminal responsibility. (1975, Summer) *Santa Clara Law, 15*, 911-938.

(Mental Condition)

Milte, K.L., et al. (1975, April) Abolition of the crime of murder and of mental condition defenses. *Australian Law Journal, 49*, 160-172.

(Mental Disease)

Criminal law- mental disease or defect reducing the degree of crime- Missouri changes the rule. (1975, Spring) *Missouri Law Review, 40*, 361-368.

(Manslaughter - Involuntary)

Diminished capacity and non-statutory involuntary manslaughter- diminished capacity due to mental defect or mental illness can reduce homicide to involuntary manslaughter. (1974, Fall) *Santa Clara Law, 15*, 210-217.

(Legal Aspects)

Brennan, K.S.W. (1973) Legal aspects of community psychiatry. *Community Health, 5*(3), 169-175.

(Mental Illness)

Hafner, H., & Boker, W. (1973) Acts of violence committed by mentally deranged persons. *Dtsch Med Wschr, 98*(43), 2005-2011.

(Legal Competence)

Ciccone, J.R., et al. (1973) Incompetency to stand trial: A difference of opinion. *Journal of Forensic Science, 18*(10), 380-384.

(Felony-Murder)

Busch, J.P., & Fulgoni, D.J. (1972, June) Diminished capacity applied to the felony-murder rule. *Legal Bulletin, 47*, 291.

(Defense - Psychiatric)

Tanay, E. (1972) Forensic psychiatry in the legal defense of murder. *Journal of Forensic Science, 17*(1), 15-24.

(Sanity)

Hahn, J.K. (1972) *Legally sane*. Chicago: Regnery.

(Insanity Plea)

Kahn, M.W. (1971, Nov.) Murderers who plead insanity: A descriptive factor-analytic study of personality, social, and history variables. *Genet Psychological Monograph, 84*, 275-360.

(Psychiatric Ruling)

Malik, A. (1970) Analysis of cases of homicide forensic-psychiatric rulings (Polish). *Psychiatr, 4*, 549-555.

(Psychiatric Judgment)

Weigand, G. (1969, July) Is helping weak fellow citizens psychopathic or criminal? Comments of an involved on audacious psychiatric theories (German). *Nervenarzt, 40*, 325-326.

(Psychiatric Evaluation)

Bourke, J.P. (1969) *Insanity and injustice*. Milton, Australia: Jacaranda Press.

(Responsibility)

Topp, D.O. (1968) Homicide and responsibility. *Medicolegal Journal, 36*, 124-136.

(Diminished Responsibility)

Power, D.J. (1967, Oct.) Diminished responsibility. *Medical Science and Law, 7*, 185-191.

(Insanity Defense)

Kahn, M.W. (1967, Aug.) Correlates of Rorschach reality adherence in the assessment of murderers who plead insanity. *J Project Techn, 31*, 44-47.

(Murderer- Psychiatry)

Biggs, J., Jr. (1967) *Guilty mind: Psychiatry and the law of homicide.* Baltimore: Johns Hopkins.

(Diminished Responsibility)

MacRae, A.K. (1964, March) Diminished responsibility and treatment: A Scottish psychopath. *Journal of Forensic Science and Sociology, 4*, 173-174.

(State of Mind)

Required state of mind under Wisconsin's manslaughter statute. (1963, July) *Wisconsin Law Review, 1963*, 636.

(Diminished Responsibility)

Williams, J.E.H. (1962, Jan.) Diminished responsibility- satisfactory developments (Rose v. Queen (1961) 2 WLR 506; Regina v. Terry (1961) 2 WLR 961). *Modern Law Review, 25*, 83.

(Psychiatric Aspects)

Neustatter, W.L. (1960) Psychiatric aspects of diminished responsibility in murder. *Medicolegal Journal, 28*, 92-101.

(Evidence - Diminished Responsibility)

Evidence of diminished responsibility (Regina v. Mathson (1958) 1 WLR 474). (1958, July) *Law Quarterly Review, 74*, 343.

(Diminished Responsibility)

Williams, J.E.H. (1958, May) Homicide Act of 1957 and diminished responsibility- abdication of responsibility? (Regina v. Spriggs (1958) 2 WLR 162). *Modern Law Review, 21*, 318.

(Mental Illness)

Robert, P. (1958) Homicides and mental disorders according to 80 psychiatric expert testimonies for military courts of the expeditionary forces in the Far East (French). *Ann Med Leg, 38*(1), 3-12.

(Criminal Insanity)

Weihofen, H. (1950, May) Eliminating the battle of experts in criminal insanity cases. *Michigan Law Review, 48*, 961-982.

(Partial Insanity)

Larkin, J.J. (1949, May) "Partial insanity" as a means of reducing an intentional homicide to voluntary manslaughter. *Kentucky Law Journal, 37*, 412-416.

(Insanity)

Cohen, L.H., & Coffin, T.E. (1946, Nov.-Dec.) Patter of murder in insanity; a criterion of the murderer's abnormality. *Journal of Criminal Law, 37*, 262-287.

(Insanity)

Laub, B.R. (1946, Dec.) Insanity as a defense to homicide in Pennsylvania. *Temple Law Quarterly, 20*, 345-357.

(Insanity - Burden of Proof)

Barry, J.V. (1939, Oct.) Defense of insanity and the burden of proof. *Res Judicatae, 2*, 42-49.

(Diminished Responsibility)

Roughead, W. (1939, Sept.) Killing no murder; or, diminished responsibility. *Jurid Rev, 51*, 217-253.

(Insanity - Burden of Proof)

Allen, J.D. (1939, March) Burden of proof when defense is insanity (Noelke v. State (IN) 15 N E 2d 950). *Kentucky Law Journal, 27*, 348-350.

(Insanity - Burden of Proof)

Burden of proof of insanity as a defense (State v. Green (UT) 40 Pac. 2d 961). (1935, June) *Rocky Mountain Law Review, 7*, 289-291.

(Insanity Plea)

Recognition of the honor defense under the insanity plea. (1934, March) *Yale Law Review, 43*, 809-814.

(Guilty Plea)

Zelkowich, S. (1933, Sept.-Oct.) Murder, plea of guilty by person presumed to be insane (People v. Varecha (IL) 186 NE 607). *Journal of Criminal Law, 24*, 604-606.

(Insanity - Burden of Proof)

Murder, burden of proof, and insanity (State v. Kudzinowski (NJ) 147 Atl. 453). (1930, Aug.) *Temple Law Quarterly, 4*, 395-396.

(Insanity - Degree of Guilt)

Insanity as affecting degree of guilt (People v. Troche (CA) 273 Pac 767). (1929, July) *St.*

Louis Law Review, 14, 439-449.

(Insanity Defense)

Insanity as defense, burden of proof, degree of proof required (Clark v. State (GA) 145 S E 647). (1929, June) *Minnesota Law Review, 13*, 731-732.

(Damages Recoverable)

Damages recoverable for wrongful killing by homicide are punitive, plea of insanity presents valid defense in action for damages for homicide (Parke v. Dennard (AL) 118 So 396). (1929, Jan.) *Alabama Law Journal, 4*, 117-118.

(Insanity Defense)

Insanity as defense, irresistible impulse (State v. Buck (IA) 219 N W 17). (1928, Dec.) *Minnesota Law Review, 13*, 64-65.

(Feeble-mindedness)

Haines, T.H. (1921) A feeble-minded homicide in Mississippi. *Journal of Criminal Law, 12*, 76.

(Insanity)

Bowlby, F.H. (1911) Insanity as a defense for murder. *Case and Comment, 17*, 491, 534.

Intent to Kill

(Bronx Shooting)

Neely, K. (1990, Oct. 18) Rapper indicted in Bronx shooting. *Rolling Stone, 589*, p. 30.

('Sister's Keeper' Case)

Hoffman, J. (1989, Dec. 19) 'Sister's keeper' sentenced. *Village Voice, 34*(51), p. 37.

(Homicide - Assault)

Homicide - assault. (1986) *Criminal Law Monthly, 6*(2-3), 16-17. Article copies available from UMI.

(Corporate Liability)

Spiegel, D.R. (1985, Nov.) The liability of corporate officers. *ABA Journal, 71*, 48, 50.

(Intent)

Sornarajah, M. (1981, Dec.) Common intention and murder under the criminal codes. *Canadian Bar Review, 59*, 727-749.

(Malice)

Duff, R.A. (1979, July) Implied and constructive malice in murder. *Law Quarterly Review, 95*, 418-444.

(Murder - Attempted)

Attempted murder: Should specific intent to kill be required? (1979, Spring) *Baylor Law Review, 31*, 243-252.

(Intent to Kill)

Heilbrun, A.B., Jr., et al. (1978, Spring) Impulsive and premeditated homicide: An analysis of subsequent parole risk of the murderer. *J of Criminal Law &Criminology, 69*, 108-114.

(Psychiatric Evidence)

Psychiatric evidence was admissible to negate defendant's intent to kill. (1978) *The Criminal Law Reporter: Court Decisions and Proceedings, 23*(11), 2239-2241.

(Intent to Kill - Case Report)

Taylor, R.M. (1978) Cranial evidence of attack with intent to kill. *New Zealand Dental Journal, 74*(388), 215-217.

(Intoxication Defense)

Defendant's intoxication may negate premeditation, Minnesota says. (1978) *The Criminal Law Reporter: Court Decisions and Proceedings, 22*(21), 2464-2465.

(Intent)

Murder on the mind. (1978) *Law Enforcement Journal, 8*(9), 11. Article copies available from UMI.

(Malice)

Constitutional law - due process - burden of proof - presumption of malice in homicide prosecution violates due process. (1976) *University of Cincinnati Law Review, 45*, 144-150.

(Amnesia)

Sadoff, R.L. (1974) Evaluation of amnesia in criminal legal proceedings. *Journal of Forensic Science, 19*(1), 98-101.

(Malice)

Buxton, R. Malice aforethought. *Modern Law Review, 37*, 676-681 (1974, Nov.); *New Law Journal, 123*, 984-986 (1973, Nov.).

(Provocation)

English, P. (1973, Dec.) Provocation and attempted murder. *Criminal Law Review 1973*, 727-736.

(Retribution)

Blake, L.W. (1973, Sept) Case for retribution. *New Law Journal, 123*, 862-864.

(Intent)

Burns, P. (1973) Attempted murder- specific intent to kill- recklessness- constructive malice. *UBC Law Review, 8*, 364-374.

(Imputed Criminal Intent)

Ross, H., & Williams, J.E.H. (1967, July) Law commission: Imputed criminal intent. *Modern Law Review, 30*, 431.

(Intent to Kill)

Imputing act and intent in felony-murder cases: An elaborate fiction. (1966, March) *Connecticut Bar Journal, 40*, 107.

(Malice)

Luby, E.D. (1964, Aug.) Murder with malice. *Michigan State Bar Journal, 43*, 39.

(Justification - Police)

Robin, G.D. (1963, June) Justifiable homicide by police officers. *Journal of Criminal Law, 54*, 224.

(Malice - Transferred)

Gooderson, R.N. (1962, April) Murder- transferred malice- defenses not expressly pleaded (Regina v. Porritt (1961) 1 WLR 1372). *Cambridge Law Journal 1962*, 6.

(Murder - Premeditation)

Deliberation and premeditation in first degree murder (Cummings v. State (MD) 165 Atl. 2d 886). (1961, Fall) *Maryland Law Review, 21*, 349.

(Intent)

Assault with intent to murder- necessary for actual intent to cause death (Wimbush v. State (MD) 165 A 2d. 886). (1961, Summer) *Maryland Law Review, 21*, 254.

(Diminished Responsibility)

Ellis, C.J. (1960, July) Jury's responsibility in assessing diminished responsibility. *Lancet, 2*, 103.

(Provocation)

Gooderson, R.N. (1959) The defense of provocation. *Medicolegal Journal, 27*, 57-63.

(Malice)

With malice aforethought: R. v. Vickers reconsidered. (1958, Nov.) *Criminal Law Review 1958*, 714.

(Culpable Homicide)

Lansdown, A.V., & Burchell, E.M. (1958, March) Intentional killing yet culpable homicide: Two recent decisions. *S A Law Journal, 75*, 154.

(Impulsive Murder)

Brenner, F. (1953, Dec.) Impulsive murder and the degree device. *Fordham Law Review, 22*, 274-297.

(Robbery/Murder)

Killing while in commission of attempted robbery-proof of intent to kill (State of Ohio v. Farmer 102 NE 2d. 11). *University of Cincinnati Law Review, 21*, 201-203.

(Evidence - Intent to Rob)

Evidence - felony-murder - admissibility of other crimes to show common scheme and intent to rob (People v. Coefield (CA) 236 Pac. 570). (1952, April) *Brooklyn Law Review, 18*, 322-325.

(Murder - Degrees)

Murder - intent to kill as affecting degree of murder. (1951, April) *Southern California Law Review, 24*, 288-302.

(Uncommunicated Threats)

Evidence of uncommunicated threats in excusable homicide cases. (1951, Spring) *Arkansas Law Review, 5*, 207-213.

(Intent)

Premeditation and deliberation- can they occur in an instant? (1951, Spring) *Montana Law Review, 12*, 72-81.

(Statutory Intent)

Creech, C. (1950, March) Statutory intentional murder. *Kentucky Law Journal, 38*, 441-458.

(Intentional Murder)

Cagle, A.S. (1950, March) Intentional murder at common law and under modern statutes. *Kentucky Law Journal, 38*, 424-440.

(Intent - Effect of Battery)

Reigler, N.W. (1949, Jan.) Intentional homicide - effect of battery by deceased in reducing or excusing the offense. *Kentucky Law Journal, 37*, 187-191.

(Deliberation)

Presumption of deliberation and premeditation - the doctrine of Hunter Hill's case (Thomas v. Commonwealth (VA) 41 S E 2d 476). (1947) *Virginia Law Review, 33*, 531-538.

(Responsive Verdict)

Ernest, G.D., Jr. Attempt as a responsive verdict (State v. Love (LA) 26 So 2d 156; State v. Ferrand (LA) 27 So 2d 174). *Tulane Law Review, 21*, 281-285. (1946, Dec.); *Louisiana Law Review, 7*, 127-133 (1946, Nov.).

(Implied Malice)

Funk, A.E., Jr. (1946, Jan.) Implied malice in the law of murder, the development of the doctrine of. *Kentucky Law Journal, 34*, 160-162.

(No Intent)

Shapiro, E.B. (1942, March) Murder in the second degree based on an assault and battery without intent to kill (People v. Efstathiou (CA) 118 Pac. 2d. 22). *Southern California Law Review, 15*, 371-372.

(Homicide Decision)

Shapiro, E.B. (1942, March) Murder in the second degree based on an assault and battery without intent to kill (People of California v. Efstathiou, 118 Pac. 2d 22). *Southern California Law Journal, 15*, 371-372.

(Intent)

Repko, J.S. (1942) Premeditation and deliberation in the law of murder. *Duke Bar Association Journal, 10*, 36-45.

(Provocation)

Murder and provocation (Mancini v. Director of Public Prosecutions, 192 LT 213). (1941, Nov.) *Legal Times, 192*, 221-222.

(Intent)

Murder in the first degree, killing in the commission of robbery (Commonwealth v. Frisbee (PA) 20 Atl. 2d 285). (1941, May) *Dick Law Review, 46*, 55.

(Liability)

Frosh, S.B. (1941, Jan.-Feb.) Unnecessary killing by the overzealous peace officer (Woods v. Commonwealth (KY) 139 SW 2d. 439). *Journal of Criminal Law, 31*, 601-604.

(Unintentional Act)

Wilner, I. (1939, May) Unintentional homicide in the commission of an unlawful act. *University of Pennsylvania Law Review, 87*, 811-836.

(Felony-Murder)

Dupee, E.H., Jr. (1938, May-June) Felony-murder, intent to commit felony after homicide (Commonwealth v. Stelma (PA) 192 Atl. 906). *Journal of Criminal Law, 29*, 136-139.

(Resisting Arrest)

Kean, A.W.G. (1937, Nov.) Homicide in resisting arrest. *Kentucky Law Journal, 26*, 50-54.

(Irresistible Impulse)

"Irresistible impulse" (Sodeman v. The King, 10 Aust. L J 161). *Law Journal, 81*, 432-433 (1936, June); *Australian Law Journal, 20*, 130-136 (1936, Aug.).

(Attempt to Commit)

Attemp to commit murder - the line between preparation and attempt (People v. Miller (CA) 42 Pac. 2d. 308). (1936, April) *Columbia Law Review, 36*, 676-678.

(Acquisition of Property)

Wade, J.W. (1936) Acquisition of property by willful killing of another - a statutory solution. *Harvard Law Review, 49*, 715.

(Attempted Arrest)

MacIntosh, J.C. (1935, Jan.) Killing in attempting to effect arrest. *South African L T, 4*, 7-8.

(Arson)

Stellman, W.J., & Day, R.S., Jr. (1935, May) Homicide committed in perpetration of arson, necessity of intent to kill (Turk v. Ohio, 194 N E 425). *Journal of Criminal Law, 26*, 126-128.

(Malice)

Perkins, R.M. (1934, Feb.) A reexamination of malice aforethought. *Yale Law Journal, 43*, 537-570.

(Presumption of Malice)

Waterman, J.F. (1932, March) Presumption of malice from proof of the killing, burden of proof in the rebuttal (State v. Mangino (NJ) 156 430). *Journal of Criminal Law, 22*, 907-909.

(Motive)

Day, C.E. (1931, May) Motive, defendant's knowledge of the facts (State v. Potter (233 NW 650). *Dakota Law Review, 3*, 386-387.

(Assault - Case Report)

Assault with intent to kill, what constitutes intent (People v. Wilson (IL) 174 NE 398). (1931, June) *St. Louis Law Review, 16*, 331-332.

(Jury Agreement)

Necessity of jury's agreement that defendant intended to kill deceased and not another (State v. Flathers (SD) 232 NW 51). (1931, Feb.) *St. Louis Law Review, 16*, 331-332.

(Self-Defense)

Chadbourn, J.H. (1929, June) Self-defense, duty to retreat, reasonableness of appearance of necessity (State v. Dills 196 NC 457). *North Carolina Law Review, 7*, 460-462.

(Jury Verdict)

Although defendant started fight, as he did not use deadly weapons, nor intended to kill, nor knew of such intention by others, he was not guilty of aiding in committing homicide (Warren v. Commonwealth (KY) 1 SW 2d 774). (1928, May) *Kentucky Law Journal, 16*, 354-355.

(Specific Intent)

Assault with intent to kill, specific intent (Andrews v. State (GA) 138 SE 923). (1928, Jan.) *Yale Law Journal, 37*, 384-385.

(Specific Intent)

Specific intent as essential element (Springer v. State (GA) & Battle v. State (GA) 139 SE 159). (1927, Dec.) *Georgia Law Review, 1*, 51.

(Malice)

Homicide - presumption of malice from fact of homicide with deadly weapon (Owens v. State (GA) 136 S E 530). (1927, May) *Minnesota Law Review, 11*, 562-563.

(Right to Kill)

Right to kill a burglar. (1926, July) *Sol J, 70*, 826.

(Presumption of Malice)

Buford, E.P. (1922) Presumption of malice in the law of murder. *Virginia Law Review, 8*, 178.

(Malice - Defined)

Curtis, H.J. (1910) Malice aforethought, in definition of murder. *Yale Law Journal, 19*, 639.

Legal Provocation

(Provocation - Lack of)

Birch, D.J., & Esdale, M. (1989, Oct.) Homicide Act 1957, sect. 3 - ruling that there was no evidence of provocation. *Criminal Law Review 1989*, 740-741.

(Duress)

Miller, J.C. (1981) Duress and homicide. *Criminal Law Journal, 5*(2), 76-83.

(Provocation - New South Wales)

Sharma, K.M. (1980, June) Provocation in New South Wales: From Parker to Johnson. *Australian Law Journal, 54*, 330-343.

(Law of Provocation)

English, P. (1979, Feb.-March) New developments in the law of provocation. *Sol J, 123*, 119-121; 139-140.

(Provocation)

English, P. (1978, Oct.) Provocation and the reasonable man test in England and New Zealand. *New Zealand University Law Review, 8*, 169-175.

(Reasonable Man)

Painter, R.W. (1977, July) Provocation, the reasonable man and the criminal law revision committee. *New Law Journal, 127*, 708-710.

(Provocation Doctrine)

Ashworth, A.J. (1976, Nov.) Doctrine of provocation. *Cambridge Law Journal,* 35, 292-320.

(Provocation)

Wood, J.C. (1975) Recent judicial decisions: Everyone provokes. *The Police Journal, 48*(3), 252-254.

(Provocation - Other Countries)

O'Regan, R.S. (1972, July) Ordinary men and provocation in Papua and New Guinea. *International and Comparative Law Quarterly, 21*, 551.

(Insurance Claim - Suit)

Insurance - felonious killing of insured by beneficiary - plea of guilty admissible in subsequent civil suit (Smith v. Southern Nationa Life Ins. Co. (LA) 134 S 2d. 337). (1962, April) *Tulane Law Review, 36*, 579.

(Provocation - Australia)

Howard, C. (1960, Jan.-Feb.) Provocation and homicide in Australia. *Australian Law Journal,*

33, 323, 355.

(Murder Trial)

Marsack, C.C. (1959, Oct.) Provocation in trials for murder. *Criminal Law Review 1959*, 697.

(Manslaughter)

Snelling, H.A. (1958, March) Manslaughter under provocation. *Australian Law Journal, 31*, 790.

(Provocation - New Law)

Eddy, J.P. (1958, Dec.) New law of provocation. *Criminal Law Review 1958*, 778.

(Provocation)

Burchell, E.M. (1958, Aug.) Provocation: Subjective or objective? *S A L J, 75*, 246.

(Provocation)

Provocation reducing murder to manslaughter. (1955, July) *Law Journal, 105*, 404.

(Provocation)

Homicide upon provocation. (1955, Aug.) *Law Times, 220*, 78.

(Provocation - Resentment)

Atiyah, P.S. (1954, Sept.) Relation between the provocation and the resentment. *Modern Law Review, 17*, 459-461.

(Defending Others)

Barry, J.V. (1951, May) Defense of third persons as excuse for homicide. *Kentucky Law Journal, 39*, 460-463.

(Provocation - Manslaughter)

Manslaughter - criminal and forceful relations with spouse as provocation (State v. Martin (SC) 57 SE 2d. 55). (1950, Summer) *University of Pittsburgh Law Review, 11*, 709-711.

(Provocation)

Provocation in murder cases. (1949, Nov.) *Sol J, 93*, 685.

(Provocation Defense)

Barry, J.V. (1949, Oct.) Defense of provocation: *Res Judicatae, 4*, 129-143.

(Manslaughter)

Gillespie, J.R. (1949, March) Provocation- assault and battery as sufficient provocation to reduce an intentional homicide to manslaughter. *Kentucky Law Journal, 37*, 311-315.

(Manslaughter)

Miller, H.B. (1948, May) Suggested classification of 'provocation' in manslaughter cases. *Kentucky Law Journal, 36*, 482-485.

(Provocation)

Killing no manslaughter. (1932) *Law Journal, 78*, 289 (1932)

(Provocation)

Upon provocation. (1930) *Law Journal, 70*, 351.

Chapter 11
Assassination
General

(Murder of Alfred Herrhausen)

Friedman, A. (1990, March) Death of a Europower. *Vanity Fair, 53*(6), pp. 164-170+.

(Mail-Bomb Murder)

A new lead in the racial bomb attacks. (1990, Feb. 5) *Newsweek, 115*(6), p. 21.

(Ahmed Abdallah Assassination)

Hartley, A. (1990) Paradise lost. *Africa Report, 35*(1), 37-40.

(Death Squads)

Meldrum, A. (1990) The assassination bureau. *Africa Report, 35*(2), 42-44.

(Murder of General Secretary)

Stuttaford, G. (1989, Nov. 24) Nonfiction: Report on the murder of the General Secretary. *Publisher's Weekly, 236*(21), p. 63.

(Political Shooting)

Kinsley, M. (1989, Oct. 23) We shoot people, don't we? *Time, 134*(17), p. 118.

(Murder in Greece)

Taki. (1989, Sept. 30) Murder most foul. *Spectator, 263*(8412), pp. 48-49.

(Guatemala)

Guatemala: The president vanishes. (1989, July 8) *Economist, 312*(7610), pp. 46-48.

(Assassination - Pakistan)

Epstein, E.J. (1989, June) How General Zia went down. *Vanity Fair, 52*(6), pp. 42-60.

(Government-Sponsored Homicide)

Tyson, B. (1989, April 12) Assassination in Brazil (land reform activist J.F. Alevino). *The Christian Century, 106*, pp. 347-348.

(Government-Sponsored Homicide)

Madelin, H. (1987, Nov. 28) Assassination in South Lebanon (French Jesuit A. Masse).

America, 157, pp. 397-398.

(Government-Sponsored Homicide)

The same old assassins (slaying of Salvadoran human-rights activist H. Anaya). (1987, Nov. 20) *Commonwealth, 114*, p. 646.

(Government-Sponsored Homicide)

Friesen, D. (1987, Oct. 14) Leandro Alejandro: Victim of militarism (Phillipines). *Christian Century, 104*, pp. 877-878.

(Political Killings)

Nairn, A. (1987, March) The Contras' little list; American mercenary J. Adams discloses assassination plots against Nicaraguan leaders by the Contras. *Progressive, 51*, pp. 24-26.

(Assassination Attempt - Pope John Paul II)

Sheils, M., et al. (1985, May 25) Again the shadow of a gunman. *Newsweek, 97*, pp. 22-26.

(Mafia Killings)

Two Chicago mobsters hit; Japan's "godfather" slain. (1985) *Organized Crime Digest, 6*(2), 8. Article copies available from UMI.

(Assassination - Colombia)

Colombia's president declares "state of siege" following Justice Minister's assassination. (1984, May 2) *Narcotic Control Digest, 14*(9), 3-4. Article copies available from UMI.

(Assassins - Study)

Would-be assassins studied. (1984, March 26) *Law Enforcement News, 10*(6), 7. Article copies available from UMI.

(Danger to Police)

Acosta, H.A. (1983) Minimizing the danger to police and public officials. *Law Enforcement News, 9*(7), 6,11. Article copies available from UMI.

(Assassination - Turkish Attache)

Janigan, M. (1982, Sept. 6) Assassination with vengeance (murder of Turkish military attache A. Atikat by Armenian terrorists in Ottawa). *Macleans, 95*, p. 12.

(Drug Trafficking)

Heffernan, R., et al. (1982) Homicides related to drug trafficking. *Federal Probation Quarterly, 46*(3), 3-7. Article copies available from UMI.

(Mafia - Italy)

Italy's top anti-terrorist expert assassinated by mafia hitmen. (1982) *Organized Crime Digest, 3*(9), 1,6; *Security Systems Digest, 13*(18), 7; *Narcotics Control Digest, 12*(19), 5-6. Article copies available from UMI.

(Assassination - Threats)

Threats against the President - sufficiency of evidence. (1982) *The Criminal Law Reporter: Court Decisions, 31*(17), 2360.

(Assassination)

Schmookler, A. (1982) Assassinations: The problem is not that the world is sick. *Terrorism 1982, 5*(4), 367-369.

(Assassination)

Cooper, H.H. (1982) Expecting the unexpected. *The Police Chief, 49*(4), 54-55. Article copies available from UMI.

(Assassination Attempt - Pope John Paul II)

Adler, J., et al. (1981, May 25) Man with the gun (M.A. Agca). *Newsweek, 97*, pp. 36-38.

(Assassination Attempt)

Posner, M. (1981, April 13) America'a high noon mentality. *Macleans, 94*(3), pp. 23-27.

(Assassination)

The escalating incidence of assassination. (1981) *Security Letter Part II, 11*(24), 2. Article copies available from UMI.

(Assassination)

Guatemala: It's not the place to go, State Department advises. (1981) *Security Systems Digest, 12*(25), 7.

(Assassination)

American security training, money, did not save President Sadat. (1981) *Security Systems Digest, 12*(21), 1, 3-4. Article copies available from UMI.

(Assassination - Prevention)

Report: How to stop assassinations. (1981) *Security Systems Digest, 12*(25), 6. Article copies available from UMI.

(Assassination)

Post-arrest statements by alleged presidential assailant suppressed. (1981) *The Criminal Law Reporter: Court Decisions and Proceedings, 30*(9), 2165-2168.

(Assassins)

Cooper, H.H.A. (1979) Terroristic fads and fashions: The year of the assassin. *Chitty's Law Journal, 27*(3), 92-97.

(Assassination - Presidential)

Weinstein, E.A. (1976) Presidential assassination: An American problem. *Psychiatry, 39*(3),

291-293.

(Assassinations without Motives)

Gallemore, J.L., Jr. (1976) 'Motiveless' public assassins. *Bulletin of the American Academy of Psychiatry and the Law, 4*(1), 51-57.

(Art and Assassination - Russia)

Fetzer, L. (1975, Jan.) Art and assassination: Garshin's Nadezhda Nikolaevna. *Russian R, 34*, 55-65.

(Assassination - Political)

Donoghue, M.A. (1975) *Assassination: Murder in politics.* New York: Major Books.

(Diagnosing Assassins)

Westermeyer, J., et al. (1974, June) Letter: Caveats on diagnosing assassins. *American Journal of Psychiatry, 131*, 722-723.

(Assassination Threats)

Pontius, A.A. (1974) Threats to assassinate the king-president while propitiating mother: Some aspects of dangerousness. *Journal of Analytic Psychology, 19*(1), 38-53.

(Assassination - Laos)

Westermeyer, J. (1973, May) Assassination in Laos: Its psychosocial dimensions. *Archives of General Psychiatry, 28*, 740-743.

(Assassination - Laos)

Westermeyer, J. (1973) Assassination and conflict resolution in Laos. *American Anthropologist, 75*(1), 123-131.

(Murder and Assassination)

Ellis, A., & Gullo, J.M. (1971) *Murder and assassination.* New York: Stuart.

(Assassination)

Ullrich, J. (1970) Ein mordanschlag? 20957. 24(3): 150-152 (IBZ 1971).

(Assassinations - US Presidents)

Weisz, A.E. (1969) American Presidential assassinations. 11235. 30: 659-668 '69 (IBZ 1971).

(Assassinations - Presidential)

Edelman, M., et al. (1969) Presidential assassinations: Their meaning and impact on society. 12599. 79: 199-221 '69 (IBZ 1971).

(Psychiatric Aspects)

Dorpat, T.L. (1968, Oct.) Psychiatric observations on assassinations. *Northwest Med, 67*, 976-979.

(Assassination - MLK)

Walker, H.I. (1968, Sept.) Some reflections on the death of Dr. Martin Luther King - a commentary on white racism. *Journal of the National Medical Association, 60*, 396-400.

(Assassins - Psychology)

Abrahamsen, D. (1967, Oct.) A study of Lee Harvey Oswald: Psychological capability of murder. *Bulletin of the NY Academy of Medicine, 43*, 861-888.

(Oswald, Psychology of)

Progoff, I. (1967, May) The psychology of Lee Harvey Oswald: A Jungian approach. *Journal of Individual Psychology, 23*, 37-47.

(Assassins)

Kaplan, J. (1967, May) Assassins. *Stanford Law Review, 19*, 1110.

(Oswald)

Chaplin, J.P. (1967, May) Commentary on three Oswald interpretations. *Journal of Individual Psychology, 23*, 48-52.

(Oswald)

Ansbacher, H.L. (1966, Fall) Lee Harvey Oswald: An Adlerian interpretation. *Psychoanalysis Review, 53*, 55-68.

(Assassination - Presidential)

Scott, M.E. (1966, April) Paradoxical reaction to Presidential assassination. *Virginia Medical Monthly, 93*, 217-218.

(Assassinations - Presidential)

Hastings, D.W. (1965, Dec.) The psychiatry of Presidential assassination: Garfield and McKinley. *Applied Theory, 7*, 113-115.

(Assassinations - Wartime)

Kelly, J.B. (1965, Oct.) Assassination in wartime. *Military Law Review, 30*, 101.

(Assassinations - Presidential)

Hastings, D.W. (1965, July) The psychiatry of Presidential assassinations: Truman and Kennedy. *Lancet, 85*, 294-301.

(Assassinations - Presidential)

Cole, D.L. (1965, Feb.) Affiliative behavior at the time of the President's assassination. *Psychological Reports, 16*, 326.

(Assassinations - Presidential)

Kirschner, D. (1965, Jan.) The death of a President: Reactions of psychoanalytic patients. *Behavioral Science, 10*, 1-6.

(Assassinations)

Williams, J. (1965) Assassinations. *Medicolegal Journal, 33*, 93-104.

(Assassinations - Study)

Robinson, G.W. (1965) A study of political assassinations. *American Journal of Psychiatry, 121*, 1060-1064.

(Assassination - Presidential)

Rothstein, D.A. (1964, Sept.) Presidential assassination syndrome. *Archives of General Psychiatry, 11*, 245-254.

(Assassination Attempt)

Schmidt, E. (1931) Prehistory of an attempted assassination (German). *Int Zsch f Indiv-Psychol, 5*, 358-367.

(Social Dangers)

Gaultier, P. (1927, Nov.) Un grave danger social; le droit a l'assasssinat. *R Politic et Litt, 65*, 691-692.

(Victim's Son)

Sarcey, Y. (1925, March) L'exception confirme la regle; pathetique roman de cette jeune actrice polonaise, assassinant son ami. *Annales Polit et Litt, 84*, 221-222.

Assassination of Presidents and Head of State

(Assassination - Colombia)

'We have sent so many to their tomb' (assassination of presidential candidate C. Pizzaro of Colombia). (1990, May 7) *Newsweek, 115*, p. 32.

(Assassination - Sweden)

Pettersson, G. (1990) The impact of the Palme murder on Sweden. *Scandinavian Review, 78*(1), 17-22.

(Assassination - Henry III)

Greengrass, M. (1989, Nov.) The assassination of Henry III. *History Today, 39*, pp. 11-17.

(Assassination - JFK)

Davis, J.M. (1989) *Mafia kingfish: Carlos Marcello and the assassination of JFK.* New York: McGraw-Hill.

(Assassination - I. Gandhi)

Varma, V.K., et al. (1989) Assassination of Indira Gandhi: Impact on psychiatric patients. *American Journal of Psychiatry, 43*(1), 77-86.

Assassination - Sweden)

Sweden: Just him? (1988, Dec. 24) *Economist, 309*(7582-7583), p. 59.

(Assassination - JFK)

Reston, J., Jr. (1988, Nov. 28) Was Connally the real target? *Time, 132*(22), pp. 30-41.

(Assassination - I. Gandhi)

India: Judgment time. (1988, Oct. 29) *Economist, 309*(7574), pp. 36-37.

(Assassination - Sweden)

Sweden: The even more secret police. (1988, Aug. 20) *Economist, 308*(7564), pp. 41-42.

(Assassination - Sweden)

Stadt, V.D., & Dominique, C. (1988, Aug.) Regional Report: Europe - - Palme Plot. *World Press Review, 35*(8), p. 34.

(Assassination Threats)

Griffith, E.E.H., et al. (1988) Institutional response to inpatient's threats against the President. *Hospital and Community Psychiatry, 39*(11), 1166-1171.

(Assassination - Colombia)

Colombia judge murdered. (1986) *Narcotic Control Digest, 16*(16), 6-7. Microforms and article copies available from UMI.

(Assassination - JFK)

Wilber, C.G. (1986) The assassination of the late President John F. Kennedy: An academician's thoughts. *American Journal of Forensic Science, 7*(1), 52-58.

(Assassination - Sikh Leader)

Johnson, M. (1985, Sept. 2) "A man of peace has fallen" (assassination of Sikh leader H.S. Longowal). *Time, 126*, p. 30.

(Assassination - Sikh Leader)

Andreson, H. (1985, Sept. 2) A murder in the Punjab (assassination of Sikh leader). *Newsweek, 106*, p. 36.

(Assassination - Sikh Leader)

Quinn, H. (1985, Sept. 2) Murder in the temple (leader H.S. Longowal assassination). *Macleans, 98*, p. 19.

(R. Gandhi)

Gee, M. (1985, May 27) Twarting a murder plot (against R. Gandhi). *Macleans, 98*, p. 31.

(Assassination - Gandhi)

Deming, A. (1985, May 27) A plot to assassinate Gandhi. *Newsweek, 105*, p. 36.

(Assassinations - Colombia)

Colombia-US extradition treaty may have sparked massacre. (1985) *Narcotics Control Digest, 15*(23), 6. Article copies available from UMI.

(Assassination - JFK)

Koenig, B.E. (1985) Acoustic gunshot analysis - the Kennedy assassination and beyond. *International Criminology Policy Review, 40*(384), 2-11.

(Presidential Assailants)

Felthous, A.R. (1985) Fates of assailants of US Presidents. *Journal of Forensic Science, 30*(1), 31-36.

(Assassination - Lincoln)

Library redisplays contents of Lincoln's pockets from night of his assassination. (1985) *Library of Congress Information Bulletin, 44*(7), 30-31.

(Assassination - I. Gandhi)

Reagan, R., & Schultz, G.P. (1985) Assassination of India's Prime Minister. *Department of State Bulletin, 85*(2094), 40-41.

(Assassination Plot - US Ambassador)

Plot to kill US Ambassador in Bolivia discovered, foiled. (1984) *Narcotics Control Digest, 14*(25&26), 7-8.

(Assassination - Lincoln)

An historical remembrance: The life and death of Abraham Lincoln. (1984) *Security Letter, Part I, 14*(3), 2. Article copies available from UMI.

(Assassination Plot - Honduras)

FBI thwarts plot to kill Honduran President financed by drug trafficking ring. (1984) *Narcotics Control Digest, 14*(23), 6-7; *Security Systems Digest, 15*(24), 3-4. Article copies available from UMI.

(Assassination Attempt - Reagan)

Konig, H.D. (1984) Birth of a hero: Reagan's self-dramatization following the attempted 1981 assassination (German with English abstract). *Psyche, 38*(2), 152-174.

(Assassination - Attempted)

Quarles, R., et al. (1983, Fall) News diffusion of assassination attempts on President Reagan and Pope John Paul II. *Journal of Broadcasting, 27*, 387-394.

(Media Study)

Jeffers, L.W., & Quarles, R. (1983, Winter) A panel study of news diffusion. *Journalism Quarterly, 60*, 722-725.

(Assassination Attempt - Reagan)

Taylor, S., Jr. (1982, July 26) Questions of John Hinkley's sanity: Assassin's case awash in uncertainties. *The New York Times, 131*, pp. A7-A8.

(Assassins - Presidential)

Cain, S. (1982) The psychodynamics of the presidential assassins and the examination of the theme: Graphic variables of their threatening correspondence. *Forensic Science International, 19*(1), 39-50.

(Assassination - JFK)

Ramsey, N.F., et al. (1982) Reexamination of acoustic evidence in the Kennedy assassination. *Science 1982, 218*(4568), 127-133.

(Assassination - Sadat)

Drozdiak, W. (1981, Oct. 19) Four suicidal killers succeed in slaying Sadat and stunning the world. *Time, 118*, pp. 14-18.

(Assassination Attempt)

Hinkley case - why it's dragging. (1981, Aug. 31) *US News & World Report, 91*, p. 7.

(Assassination Attempt - John Paul II)

Morrow, L. (1981, May 25) Hand of terrorism, a Pope of peace falls victim to a vengeful gunman. *Time, 117*, pp. 10-11.

(Assassination Attempt)

Sidey, H. (1981, April 27) That show-must-go-on spirit. *Time, 117*, p. 26.

(Assassination Attempt - Reagan)

Magnuson, E.D. (1981, April 13) Six shots at a nation's heart: Again a moment of madness threatens a President and tarnishes the US. *Time, 117*(15), pp. 24-38.

(Assassination - Anwar Sadat)

Reagan, R., & Haig, A., Jr. (1981) Death of Egyptian President Anwar Sadat. *Department of State Bulletin, 81*(2056), 67.

(Assassination Plots)

Khadafy planning to kill Reagan, other US officials, *Newsweek* reports. (1981) *Security Systems Digest, 12*(24), 1-6. Article copies available from UMI.

(Assassination - Prevention)

Executive protection. The Sadat assassination. When the principle refuses protection. (1981) *Security Letter, Part I, 11*(20), 5. Article copies available from UMI.

(Assassination - JFK)

Wilber, C.G. (1978) *Medicolegal investigation of the President John F. Kennedy murder*. Springfield, IL: Thomas.

(Potempa Murder)

Bessel, R. (1977, Sept.) Potempa murder. *Central European History, 10*, 241-254.

(Assassination - Lincoln)

Greenwood, R.D. (1977) The last hours of President Lincoln: A historical notation. *Military Medicine, 1*, 59-60.

(Assassination - Lincoln)

Mudd, R.D. (1977) Medical aspects of the Lincoln assassination. *Maryland State Medical Journal, 26*(7), 55-65.

(Assassination Threats)

Bort, R.F. (1977) Threats to the President revisited. *Forensic Science, 9*(3), 173-178.

(Assassination - Kennedy - Reaction)

Biller, W.A. (1977) Suicide related to the assassination of President John F. Kennedy. *Suicide and Life Threatening Behavior, 7*(1), 40-44.

(Assassination - Kennedy - Connally Wounded)

Nichols, J. (1977) The wounding of Governor John Connally of Texas, November 22, 1963. *Maryland State Medical Journal, 26*(10), 20.

(President's Kin)

Greene, H. (1976, Dec.) All the President's kin (review article). *Times Literary Supplement, 3092*, p. 1600.

(Chilean Assassination)

Carroll, R., et al. (1976, Oct.) Long arm of DINA? Killing ex-Chilean ambassador O. Letelier in Washington, DC. *Newsweek, 88*, pp. 59-60.

(Assassination - Presidential)

Weinstein, E.A. (1976) Presidential assassination: An American problem. *Psychiatry, 39*(3), 291-293.

(Assassination - JFK)

Lattimer, J.K. (1976) An experimental study of the backward movement of President Kennedy's head. *Surg Gyn Ob, 142*(2), 246-254.

(Assassination - JFK)

Wecht, C.H. (1975) Why is the Rockefeller Commission so single-minded about a lone assassin in the Kennedy case? *Journal of Legal Medicine, 3*(7), 22-25.

(Assassination - Kennedy - Medical Evidence)

Wecht, C.H., & Smith, R.P. (1974) The medical evidence in the assassination of President John F. Kennedy. *Forensic Science, 3*(2), 105-128.

(Kennedy's Autopsy)

Wecht, C.H. (1974) Pathologist's view of Kennedy's autopsy: An unsolved case. Ninth anniversary of assassination. *Med Trial Tech Q Ann, 10*, 42-52.

(Assassination - Kennedy - Theories)

Lattimer, G., et al. (1974) The Kennedy-Connally one bullet theory: Further circumstantial and experimental evidence. *Medical Times, 102*(11), 33-56.

(Assassination - Garfield)

Gorton, D.A. (1972, July) The Garfield assassination, 1881. *Medical Times, 100*, 126-127.

(Assassination - Kennedy - Ballistic Studies)

Lattimer, J.K (1972, April) Could Oswald have shot President Kennedy? Further ballistic studies. *Bulletin of the New York Academy of Medicine, 48*, 513-524.

(Assassination Attempt - Archbishop Makarios)

Grant, J. (1972) The attempted assassination of Archbishop Makarios: A forensic science case study. *Medical Legal Journal, 40*, 42-52.

(Assassination - JFK)

Olson, D., et al. (1971, Oct.) Photographic evidence and the assassination of President John F.

Kennedy. *Journal of Forensic Science, 16*, 399-419.

(Assassination - Lincoln)

Lattimer, J.K. (1970) The wound that killed Lincoln. *Illinois Medical Journal, 138*, 514-517.

(Assassination - Kennedy - Response)

Ginsparg, S.L., et al. (1969, Sept.) Reactions of young people to the Kennedy assassination. The significance of characteristic patterns of individual response. *Bulletin of the Menninger Clinic, 33*, 295-309.

(Assassination - Symbolic Aspects)

Weinstein, E.A., et al. (1969, Feb.) Symbolic aspects of Presidential assassinations. *Psychiatry, 32*, 1-11.

(Threatening the President)

Threatening the President: Protected dissenter or potential assassin. (1969) *Georgia Law Journal, 57*, 553.

(Assassination - Kennedy - Theories)

Lattimer, J.K. (1968, Dec.) The Kennedy-Connally single bullet theory: A feasibility study. *Int Surgery, 50*, 524-532.

(Assassination - Kennedy - Warren Commission)

Hamsher, J.H., et al. (1968, July) Interpersonal trust, internal-external control, and the Warren Commission report. *Journal of Personality and Social Psychology, 9*, 210-215.

(Assassination - National Illness)

Correspondence: A national illness? Letters from psychiatrists and psychologists on the assassination of Robert F. Kennedy. (1968, July) *Northwest Med, 67*, 650-661.

(National Trauma)

Nierenberg, H.H. (1968, Spring) Ego disturbance following a national trauma. *Psychoanalysis Review, 55*, 128-134.

(Assassination - JFK)

Barnum, M.C. (1966, Nov.-Dec.) An occupational therapist's observations concerning President Kennedy's assassination; with ramifications for understanding loss. *American Journal of Occupational Therapy, 20*, 280-285.

(Assassination - JFK)

Appelbaum, S.A. (1966, Fall) The Kennedy assassination. *Psychoanalysis Review, 53*, 69-80.

(Mourning the Loss - JFK)

O'Toole, J.K. (1966, Oct.) Mourning a president. The reactions of a group of emotionally disturbed adolescent girls to the assassination of JFK. *Psychiatric Quarterly, 40*, 737-755.

(Assassination - Kennedy - Medical Evidence)

Wecht, C.H. (1966, July) A critique of the medical aspects of the investigation of President Kennedy. *Journal of Forensic Science, 11*, 300-317.

(Assassination JFK)

Schwartz, J. (1966, July) A legal demurrer to the Report of the Warren Commission. *Journal of Forensic Science, 11*, 318-329.

(Assassination - JFK)

Osterburg, J.W. (1966, July) The Warren Commission: Report and hearings. A commentary on issues of importance in the study of investigation and criminalistics. *Journal of Forensic Science, 11*, 261-271.

(Assassination - JFK)

Leopold, R.L., et al. (1966, July) The Kennedy assassination. *Pennsylvania Medicine, 69*, 55-56.

(Assassination Attempts - Roosevelts)

Hastings, D.W. The psychiatry of presidential assassination: IV. Truman and Kennedy. *Applied Therapy, 8*, 155-171 (1966, Feb.); Part 3, The Roosevelts. *Applied Therapy, 8*, 53-65 (1966, Jan.).

(Assassination - JFK)

Tuchler, M.I. (1966) Psychiatric observations on the Warren Commission report. *Journal of Forensic Science, 11*289-299.

(Assassination - JFK)

Suinn, R.M. (1966) Note: Guilt and depth of reaction to the death of a president. *Psychoanalysis Review, 53*, 81-82.

(Assassination - Medical Aspects)

Brooks, S.M. (1966) *Our murdered Presidents: The medical story*. New York: Fell.

(Assassination - Statutes Against)

Forkosch, M.D. (1965, June) Presidential murder: The constitutionality of making it a federal crime. *SW Law Journal, 19*, 229.

(Assassination - Psychosocial Pathology)

Freedman, L.Z. (1965, June) Assassination: Psychopathology and social pathology. *Postgrad Med, 37*, 650-658.

(Assassination and Assassination Attempts)

Hastings, D.W. The psychiatry of Presidential assassination, Jackson and Lincoln. *Lancet, 85*, 93-100 (1965, March); *Applied Therapy, 7*, 993-1015+ (1965, Nov.).

(Assassination - Reaction)

Wrightsman, L.S., et al. (1965, Feb.) Reactions to the President's assassination and changes in philosophies of human nature. *Psychology Reports, 16*, 159-162.

(Assassination - JFK)

Katz, J. (1964-1965, Winter) On the death of the President: President Kennedy's assassination. *Psychoanalysis Review, 51*, 661-664.

(JFK - Reactions)

Kirschner, D. (1964-1965, Winter) Some reactions of patients in psychotherapy to the death of the president (Kennedy, J.F.). *Psychoanalysis Review, 51*, 665-669.

(Assassination - JFK)

Official autopsy report on President Kennedy. (1964, Oct.) *JAMA, 190*, 98-100.

(Assassination - Kennedy - Jurisdiction)

Assassination of the President: Jurisdictional problems. (1964, Fall) *Syracuse Law Review, 16*, 69.

(Assassination Syndrome)

Rothstein, D.A. (1964) Presidential assassination syndrome. *Archives of General Psychiatry, 11*(3), 245-255.

(Lincoln's Conspirators)

Gray, J.A. (1911) The fate of Lincoln's conspirators. *Med Leg J, 29*, 126.

Chapter 12
Prevention and Control
General

(New York City)

Barrett, W. (1990, Oct. 2) Panic and the police panacea. *Village Voice, 35*(40), 11-12.

(New York City)

Morganthau, T. (1990, Sept. 17) New York's nightmare. *Newsweek, 116*(12), p. 35.

(Forecasting - China)

Stuttaford, G. (1990, April 13) Forecasts: Nonfiction -- China rising. *Publishers Weekly, 237*(15), p. 51.

(Catholic Anti-Semitism)

Thorne, E.D. (1990. March 9) We cannot hide you from Jesus. *Commonwealth, 117*(5), pp. 142-144.

(Campus Crime)

Hodge, M., & Blyskal, J. (1989, Oct.) Who says college campuses are safe? *Reader's Digest, 135*(10), pp. 141-148.

(Revisionists)

Andreyev, C. (1989, July 15) Revising the revisionists. *Spectator, 263*(8401), pp. 30-31.

(Rumors)

Jeffery, D. (1989, Sept. 23) LIVE acts to squelch rumors. *Billboard, 101*(38), pp. 5,100.

(Crime Suppression)

O'Sullivan, J. (1989, Oct. 13) Do the right thing -- suppress crime. *National Review, 41*(19), p. 13.

(Wife Killing)

Besse, S.K. (1989) Crimes of Passion: The campaign against wife killing in Brazil, 1910-1940. *Journal of Social History, 22*(4), 653-666.

(Crime Education)

Steacy, A., & Laderette, B. (1988, Aug. 1) Murder in a small town. *Macleans, 101*(32), pp. 44-46.

(Homicide - Information)

Leads from the MMWR: Premature mortality due to homicides -- United States, 1968-1985. *JAMA, 260*(14), 2021,2026.

(Homicide - Prevention)

Wilson, P.R. (1988) 'Stranger' child-murder: Issues relating to causes and controls. *Forensic Science International, 36*(3-4), 267-277.

(Confidentiality)

Crofts, Y.B. (1988) Confidentiality - An ethical dilemma. Balancing the 'duty to warn' against the right to privacy. *AAOHN Journal, 36*(8), 346-348.

(Drowning - Prevention)

Wintemute, G.J., et al. (1988) The epidemiology of drowning in adulthood: Implications for prevention. *American Journal of Preventive Medicine, 4*(6), 343-348.

(Response to Violence)

Depue, R.L. (1986) American response to an era of violence. *FBI Law Enforcement Bulletin, 55*(12), 2-5.

(Research and Development)

Ult, L.R., Jr. (1986) NCAVC's research and development program. *FBI Law Enforcement Bulletin, 55*(12), 6-8.

(Anti-Drug Legislation)

California Attorney General urges enactment of package of strong anti-drug bills. (1986) *Narcotics Control Digest, 16*(18), 7-8. Microforms and article copies available from UMI.

(Dying and Bereavement)

Rynearson, E.K. (1986) Psychological effects of unnatural dying on bereavement. *Psychiatric Annals, 16*(5), 272-275.

(Criminology)

Rogers, R., & Wettskin, R.M. (1985) Relapse in NGRI outpatients: An empirical study. *International Journal of Offender Therapy and Comparative Criminology, 29*(3), 227-236.

(Murderer - Psychotherapy)

Oberkirch, A. (1985) Psychotherapy of a murderer: Excerpts. *American Journal of Psychotherapy, 39*(4), 499-514.

(Alcohol)

Kristenson, H., & Trell, E. (1985) Alcohol-related problems in a Swedish community. *Alcohol & Alcoholism, 20*(1), 27-29.

(Preventing Homicide)

Herndon, W. (1985) Two models for preventing Black-on-Black homicide. *ADAMHA N, 11*(12), 7.

(Homicide Prevention)

Michaud, P.A. (1985) Violent deaths among adolescents in Switzerland: From epidemiology to prevention. *Pediatrician, 12*(1), 28-36.

(Manslaughter - Sentencing)

Instead of jail, she is sentenced to a religious community (A.M. O'Brien convicted of manslaughter and sent to Catholic community People of Hope in New Hampshire). (1983, March 18) *Christianity Today, 27*, p. 23.

(Crime Prevention)

Security news briefs. (1982) *Security Systems Digest, 13*(18), 9-10. Article copies available from UMI.

(Crime Prevention)

Security news briefs. (1982) *Security Systems Digest, 13*(17), 9-10. Article copies available from UMI.

(Police Risk)

Zunno, F.A. (1982) The risk of murder for police. *International Criminal Police Review, 37*(354), 6-8.

(Crime Prevention)

Security News Briefs. (1982) *Security Systems Digest, 13*(7), 10. Article copies available from UMI.

(Crime Prevention)

Lewis, D.A., & Salem, G. (1981, July) Community crime prevention: An analysis of a developing strategy. *Crime and Delinquency, 27*, 405-421.

(Minority Issues)

Minority researchers discuss key issues. (1981) *Justice Assistance News, 2*(2), 10-11.

(Homicide - Prevention)

Back to prohibition. (1981) *Organized Crime Digest, 2*(4), 8. Microforms and article copies available from UMI.

(Crime Prevention)

Curtis, A.L. (1980) HUD's crime prevention program. *Public Health Report, 95*(6), 558.

(Homicide Prevention)

Iverson, D.C. (1980) Homicide prevention from the perspective of the Office of Health Promotion. *Public Health Report, 95*(6), 558.

(Homicide Prevention)

Allen, N.H. (1980) *Homicide: Perspectives on prevention.* New York: Human Sciences Press.

(Homicide - Control)

Sorrels, J., Jr. (1980) What can be done about juvenile homicide? *Crime & Delinquency, 26*(2), 152-161.

(Prevention Priorities)

Holliday, B.G. (1980) Advocacy for life: Mandates, models, and priorities for prevention. *Public Health Reports, 95*(6), 558.

(Homicide - Prevention)

Locklear, J. (1980, Nov.) Churches in Buffalo respond to race murders with a rally, extra prayer meetings, and a call for reason. *Christianity Today, 24*, pp. 52-53.

(Narcotics - Control)

Are narcotics to blame? (1979) *Narcotics Control Digest, 9*(23), 8.

(Homicide Trends)

Kleck, G. (1979) *Homicide, capital punishment, and gun ownership: An aggregate analysis of U.S. homicide trends from 1947-1976.* Champaign, IL: University of Illinois.

(Homicide - Prevention)

Parker, R.N., & Smith, M.D. (1979) Deterrence, poverty, and type of homicide. *American Journal of Sociology, 85*(3), 614-624.

(Homicide - Prevention)

Prevention of homicide (editorial). (1979) *British Medical Journal, 1*(6166), 774.

(Terrorism - Response)

Civeletti, B.R. (1979) Terrorism: the government's response. *FBI Law Enforcement Bulletin, 48*(1), 19-22.

(Mafia and the FBI)

Gage, N. (1977, Oct. 2) Has the mafia penetrated the FBI? *New York Times Mag,* pp. 14-16.

(Maximum Security)

King, B. (1977) Maximum security vital for Maddux' protection. *Quarterly Journal of Corrections, 1*(2), 55.

(Prevention - Editorial)

Relman, A.S. (1977) More than sutures and transfusions. *New England Journal of Medicine, 297*(10), 552-553.

(Homicide Literature)

Marcus, M., et al. (1976) *Police consolidation - a selected bibliography.* Washington, DC: National Criminal Justice Reference Service.

(Treatment - Youth)

King, C.H. (1976) Counter-transference and counter-experience in the treatment of violence-prone youth. *American Journal of Orthopsychiatry, 46*(1), 43-52.

(Prevention - Case Report)

Gaines, J.R., Jr. (1975, July 7) Pine Ridge shoot-out: Killing of two FBI agents on South Dakota Indian Reservation. *Newsweek, 86*, pp. 15-16.

(Aggression Control)

Lester, D., et al. (1974) Murder and the control of aggression. *Psychology Reports, 34*(3), 706.

(Child-Murder - Prevention)

Lansky, S.B., et al. (1974) Prevention of child-murder: A case report. *Journal of the American Academy of Child Psychiatry, 13*(4), 691-698.

(Penal Code Revision - Tennessee)

Homicide: An enlightened step forward in revitalization of the Tennessee penal code. (1974, Spring) *Tennessee Law Review, 41*, 687-718.

(Prevention)

Lester, D. (1972) The prevention of homicide. *Crisis Intervention, 4*(4), 105-111.

(Homicide and the Family)

Boudouris, J. (1971) Homicide and the family. *Journal of Marriage and the Family, 33*(4), 666-676.

(Homicide Treatment - Ancient)

Genauer, M. (1970) *The treatment of homicide in the Talmud.* University of Washington.

(Social Problems)

Brearly, H.C. (1969) *Homicide in the United States.* Montclair, NJ: Patterson-Smith.

(Threats)

MacDonald, J.M. (1967, Oct.) Homicidal threats. *American Journal of Psychiatry, 124*, 475-482.

(Solving Murders)

Pearson, E. (1967) *Murders that baffled the experts.* Signet.

(Train Murder)

Nagre, A.D. (1966) An effective control (murder in the train). 20957. 20, '66, 276-277 (IBZ 1967).

(Witnesses)

Rosenthal, A. (1964) *Thiry-eight witnesses.* McGraw.

(Homicide - Prevention)

Mead, M. (1964) Cultural factors in the cause and prevention of pathological homicide. *Bulletin of the Menninger Clinic, 28*(1), 11-22.

Prevention and Prediction

(Measuring Crime)

MacKensie, D.L. (1990) *Measuring crime large-scale, long-range efforts.* Albany, NY: State University of New York Press.

(Racial Motivations)

The business of us all. (1989, Sept. 22) *Commonweal, 116*(16), pp. 484-485.

(Video Restrictions)

Fujita, S. (1989, Sept. 16) Tokyo murders lead to call for video restrictions. *Billboard, 101*(37), p. 59.

(Campus Security)

Wright, R. (1989, Sept. 5) Crime on campus. *Family Circle, 102*(12), pp. 13-18.

(Homicide - Prediction)

Browne, A., & Williams, K.R. (1989) Exploring the effect of resource availability and the likelihood of female-perpetrated homicides. *Law & Society Review, 23*(1), 75-94.

(Prevention)

Spivak, H., et al. (1989) Practitioners' forum: Public Health and primary prevention of adolescent violence. The violence prevention project. *Violence Victims, 4*(3), 203-212.

(Predictors)

Lester, D. (1989) National suicide and homicide rates: Correlates versus predictors. *Social Science and Medicine, 29*(11), 1249-1252.

(Prevention)

Dyer, C. (1989) Public interest and a psychiatrist's duty of confidentiality. *British Medical Journal, 299*(6711), 1301.

(Violence - Control)

Silverman, M.M. (1988) Control of stress and violent behavior: Mid-course review of the 1990 health objectives. *Public Health Report, 103*(1), 38-49.

(Prevention)

Bell, C.C. (1987) Preventive strategies for dealing with violence among Blacks. *Community Mental Health Journal, 23*(3), 217-228.

(Prevention)

Thomas, C.W. (1987) Pride and purpose as antidotes to Black homicidal violence. *Journal of the National Medical Association, 79*(2), 155-160.

(Homicide - Prevention)

Mitlohner, M. (1987) Etiology of homicide and possibilities of its prevention (German with English abstract). *Cesk Zdrav, 35*(3), 133-139.

(Intercultural Therapy)

Tobin, J.J. (1986) Counter-transference and failure in intercultural therapy. *Ethos, 14*(2), 130-143.

(Prevention)

Lunde, D.T. (1986) Murder and madness: Suggestions for homicide prevention. Second Annual Symposium in Psychiatry and Law, Maui, Hawaii, 1984. *American Journal of Forensic Psychiatry, 7*(2), 40-47.

(Intervention)

Kirk, A.R. (1986) Destructive behaviors among members of the Black community with a special focus on males: Cause and methods of intervention. Special Issue - The Black male: Critical counseling, developmental, and therapeutic issues, III. *Journal of Multicultural Counseling and Development, 14*(1), 3-9.

(Education)

Teach the children well (murder of J.D. Levin). (1986, Sept. 13-20) *American, 155*, p. 111.

(Prevention)

Black doctors can prevent murders: Experts. (1986, Aug. 11) *Jet, 70*, p. 30.

(Homicide - Predictor)

Hollander, N. (1986) Physical abuse as a predictor of child homicide. *Texas Medicine, 82*(6), 21-23.

(Violence - Prediction)

Steadman, H.J. (1986) Predicting violence leading to homicide. *Bulletin of New York Academy of Medicine, 62*(5), 570-581.

(Prevention)

Selden, D.R. (1986) Preventing murder (letter). *Hospital Community Psychiatry, 37*(11), 1160.

(Anti-Gang Efforts)

Anti-gang drive credited with drop in teen killings. (1986) *Juvenile Justice Digest, 14*(4), 2-3. Article copies available from UMI.

(Victim Evaluation)

Miller, K., et al. (1985) A group for families of homicide victims: An evaluation. *Social Casework, 66*(7), 432-436.

(Physician Impact)

Glasser, M., et al. (1985) The impact of psychotherapists and primary physicians on suicide and other violent deaths in rural areas. *Canadian Journal of Psychiatry, 30*(3), 195-202.

(Corrections - Research)

Conrad, J.P. (1985) Research and development in corrections: The lifer's life. *Federal Probation, 49*(4), 60-62.

(Saving the Children)

Graham, V.M. (1984, Sept.) To save the children. *Airman, 28*(9), C2.

(Execution)

Conrad, J.P. (1984) Terminating the executioner: How the empiricist can help. *Federal Probation, 48*(2), 59-62.

(Violence - Control)

Silver, B.J., et al. (1984) The 1990 objectives for the nation for control of stress and violent behavior: Progress report. *Public Health Report, 99*(4), 374-384.

(Violence - Epidemiology)

Disease researchers studying epidemiology of violence. (1984) *Criminal Justice Newsletter, 15*(17), 5-6.

(Corrections - Research)

Conrad, J.P. (1984) News of the future: Research and development in corrections. *Federal Probation, 48*(2), 59-62. Article copies available from UMI.

(Legislation - Impact)

Jolin, A. (1983) Domestic violence legislation: An impact assessment. *Police Science & Administration, 11*(4), 451-456.

(Minimizing Danger)

Acosta, H.A. (1983) Minimizing the danger to police and public officials. *Law Enforcement, 9*(7), 6,11. Article copies available from UMI.

(Crime Prevention)

Lewis, D., & Salem, G. (1981, July) Community crime prevention: An analysis of a developing strategy. *Crime & Delinquency, 27*, 405-421.

(Homicide - Prevention)

Allen, N.H. (1981) Homicide prevention and intervention. *Suicide and Life Threatening Behavior, 11*(3), 167-179.

(Homicide - Prediction)

McDonald, A., & Paitrich, D. (1981) A study of homicide: The validity of predictive test factors. *Canadian Journal of Psychiatry, 26*(8), 549-554.

(Crime Stoppers)

Martinez, D. (1981) *FBI Law Enforcement Bulletin, 50*(9), 5-6.

(Advice)

Don't be a dead hero. (1981, March-April) *Post Life, 14*(5), pp. 13-14.

(Homicide - Prediction)

McDonald, A., et al. (1981) A study of homicide: The validity of predictive test factors. *Canadian Journal of Psychiatry, 26*(8), 549-554.

(Homicide Prevention)

Allen, N.H. (1981) Homicide prevention and intervention. *Suicide and Life Threatening Behavior, 11*(3), 167-179.

(Prevention)

Schlesinger, L.B. (1981) Homicide: Perspectives on prevention, by N.H. Allen (book review). *Journal of Personality Assessment, 45*(5), 547.

(Prevention)

Holliday, B.G. (1980) Advocacy for life: Mandates, models, and priorities for prevention. *Public Health Report, 95*(6), 558.

(Homicide Prevention)

Iverson, D.C. (1980) Homicide prevention from the perspective of the office of Health Promotion. *Public Health Report, 95*(6), 558.

(Crime Prevention)

Curtis, L.A. (1980) HUD's crime prevention program. *Public Health Report, 95*(6), 558.

(Remarks)

Klerman, G.L. (1980) Concluding remarks (to special section on crime prevention). *Public Health Report, 95*(6), 561.

(Planning and Research)

Rajan, V.N. (1980) Crime victimization research program and policy planning in developing countries. *Victimology, 5*(2-4), 193-200.

(Rescue Fantasies)

Selkin, J. (1976) Rescue fantasies in homicide-suicide. *Suicide and Life Threatening Behavior, 6*(2), 79-85.

(Homicidal Behavior - Prediction)

Sendi, I.B., & Blomgren, P.G. (1975) A comparative study of predictive criteria in the predisposition of homicidal adolescents. *American Journal of Psychiatry, 132*(4), 423-427.

(Homicide Prediction - Rorschach)

Lester, D., et al. (1975) Prediction of homicide with the Rorschach. *Journal of Clinical Psychology, 31*(4), 752.

(Homicidal Behavior - Prediction)

Miller, D., et al. (1974) The prediction of adolescent homicide: Episodic dystcontrol and dehumanization. *American Journal of Psychoanalysis, 34*(3), 187-198.

(Threats)

MacDonald, J.M. (1967) Homicidal threats. *American Journal of Psychiatry, 124*, 475-482.

(Homicide - Prevention)

Blackman, N., et al. (1963, March) The sudden murderer: Clues to preventive interaction. *Archives of General Psychiatry, 8*, 289-294.

(Medical Emergency)

De Leon, C.A. (1961, Sept.) Threatened homicide - a medical emergency. *Journal of the National Medical Association, 53*, 467-472.

Gun Control

(Firearm Availability)

Vadakan, V. (1990) Homicide rates and firearm availability (letter). *JAMA, 264*(17), 2210-2211.

(Gun Control)

Lester, D. (1990) Capital punishment, gun control, and personal violence (suicide and homicide). *Psychological Reports, 66*(1), 122.

(Firearms - Australia)

Ellard, J. (1990) Guns and violence in Australia (I: Reply). *Medical Journal of Australia, 153*(2), 118.

(Firearms - Australia)

Bradbury, R. (1990) Guns and violence in Australia (II). *Medical Journal of Australia, 153*(2), 119.

(Firearms - Australia)

Ellard, J. (1990) Guns and violence in Australia (II: Reply). *Medical Journal of Australia, 153*(2), 119-120.

(Firearm Availability)

Lester, D. (1990) Relationship firearm availability and primary and secondary murder. *Psychology Reports, 67*(2), 490.

(Homicide)

McNamara, J.D. (1989, May) A nation of certified killers. *Harper's, 278*(1668), pp. 58-59.

(Gun Regulation)

Lapierre, W. (1989, April) Tough justice could have averted Stockton shooting. *American Hunter, 17*(4), p. 1

(Handgun Regulation)

Blackman, P.H., et al. (1989) Handgun regulations, crime, assaults, and homicide: A tale of two cities. *New England Journal of Medicine, 320*(18), 1214-1217.

(Firearms - New Jersey)

Fife, D., & Abrams, W.R. (1989) Firearms' decreased role in New Jersey homicides after a mandatory law. *Journal of Trauma, 29*(11), 1548-1551.

(Homicide - Handguns and Long guns)

Lester, D. (1989) Use of handguns and long guns in suicide and homicide. *Psychology Reports, 65*(3, part 1), 938.

(Gun Ownership)

Dixon, J., & Lizotte, A.J. (1989) The burden of proof - Southern sub-culture of violence: Explanation of gun ownership and homicide & note. *American Journal of Sociology, 95*(1), 182-187.

(Handgun Regulation)

Stolinsky, D.C. (1989) Handgun regulations, crime, assaults, and homicide: A tale of two cities & letter. *New England Journal of Medicine, 320*(18), 1215-1216.

(Homicide - Method)

Abrams, W.R. (1989) Firearms decreased role in New Jersey homicides after a mandatory sentencing law. *Journal of Trauma, 29*(11), 1548-1551.

(Gun Control)

Ticer, S. (1989) Handgun regulations, crime, assaults, and homicide - a tale of two cities & letter. *New England Journal of Medicine, 320*(18), 1216.

(Gun Control)

Sproule, C.F., & Kennette, D.J. (1989) Killing in the U.S.A. and Canada, 1977-1983: Further evidence for the effectiveness of gun control. *Canadian Journal of Criminology, 31*, 245-251.

(Firearms Statistics)

Tsuda, R., et al. (1989) Statistical survey of medicolegal activities for the murderous and accidental death (40 cases) by use of firearms (German with English abstract). *Isaku Kenkyu, 59*(1), 23-28.

(Handgun Availability)

Wintemute, G.J. (1988) Handgun availability and firearm mortality. *Lancet, 2*(8620), 1136-1137.

(Gun Control)

Sloan, J.H., et al. (1988) Handgun regulations, crime, assaults, and homicide: A tale of two cities. *New England Journal of Medicine, 319*(19), 1256-1262.

(Homicide - Method)

Barlow, H.D., et al (1988) More on the role of weapons in homicidal violence. *Medicine and the Law, 7*(4), 347-358.

(Firearm Availability)

Wintemute, G.J. (1988) Handgun availability and firearm mortality (letter). *Lancet, 2*(8630), 1136-1137.

(Gun Control)

Howard, M. (1986, Winter) Husband-wife homicide: An essay from a family law perspective.

Law and Contemporary Problems, 49, 63-88.

(Gun Control)

Lester, D., & Murrell, M.E. (1986) The influence of gun control laws on personal violence. Special issue: Law and Psychology. *Journal of Community Psychology, 14*(3), 315-318.

(Guns and Alcohol)

Abel, L. (1986) Guns and blood alcohol levels among homicide victims. *Drug and Alcohol Dependency, 18*(3), 253-257.

(Gun Control - Costs)

Lizzotte, A.J. (1986) The costs of using gun control to reduce homicide. *Bulletin of the New York Academy of Medicine, 62*(5), 539-549.

(Gun Control)

Zimring, F.E. (1986) Gun control. *Bulletin of the New York Academy of Medicine, 62*(5), 615-621.

(Firearms - Deaths)

Kellerman, A.L., & Reay, D.T. (1986) Protection or peril? An analysis of firearm-related deaths in the home. *New England Journal of Medicine, 314*(24), 1557-1560.

(Gun Control)

Baker, S.P. (1985) Without guns, do people kill people (editorial)? *American Journal of Public Health, 75*(6), 587-588.

(Firearms - Deaths)

Alexander, G.R. (1985) Firearm-related fatalities: An epidemiological assessment of violent death. *American Journal of Public Health, 75*(2), 165-168.

(Gun Control - Laws)

Lester, D. (1985) Handgun control laws, suicide, and homicide (letter). *American Journal of Psychiatry, 142*(1), 144.

(Homicide - Method)

Baima-Ballone, P.L. (1984) Homicide with firearms in Turin and environs in the last three years (1981-1983) (Italian with English summary). *Minerva a Medicolegal Arch Antropol Crim, 104*(3), 91-97.

(Firearms - Deaths)

Abu Al Ragheb, S.Y. (1984) Firearm fatalities in Jordan. *Medical Science and the Law, 24*(3), 213-221.

(Gun Ownership - Rights)

Copeland, A.R. (1984) The right to keep and bear arms -- a study of civilian homicides committed against those involved in criminal acts in metropolitan Dade County from 1957 to 1982. *Journal of Forensic Science, 29*(2), 584-590.

(Handguns)

Handguns used to kill over 9,000 persons in 1983, report says. (1984) *Crime Control Digest, 18*(37), 6-7. Article copies available from UMI.

(Handguns)

Handguns: An American obsession (special section). (1982, Oct. 18) *People Weekly, 18*, pp. 26-31.

(Gun Control)

Lester, D., et al. (1982) The preventive effect of strict gun control laws on suicide and homicide. *Suicide & Life Threatening Behavior, 12*(3), 131-140.

(Gun Control)

Kluin, K.F. (1982) Gun control: Is it a legal and effective means of controlling firearms in the United States? *Washington Journal, 21*(2), 244-265.

(Gun Control)

Conklin, B.R. (1981) Gun deaths: Biting the bullet on effective control (United States). *Public Affairs Report, 22*, 1-7.

(Homicide - Regional Differences)

Ruben, E.R., et al. (1981) Homicide in five Southern states: A firearms phenomenon. *Southern Medical Journal, 74*(3), 272-277.

(Firearms Law)

Massachusetts firearms law assessed. (1980) *Just Assist N, 1*(5), 15.

(Gun Control)

Detroit murder rate drops in '79, police credit new anti-gun law. *Security Systems Digest, 11*(1), 5-6.

(Handguns and Homicide)

Access to handgun turns young, tormented mind into cold-blooded killer. (1978) *Juvenile Justice Digest, 6*(11), 4. Article copies available from UMI.

(Gun Control)

Gendreau, G., & Harridge, C.T. (1977) The control of crimes committed with firearms: Jamaican experience (Italian). *Quad Crim Clin, 19*(1), 65-94.

(Gun Control)

El Guebaly, N., & Leo, M. (1977) Alcoholism and gun control. *Canadian Psychiatric Association Journal, 22*(5), 243-251.

(Gun Control)

Mahler, A.J., et al. (1977) Firearms and gun control: A public health concern. *New England Journal of Medicine, 297*(10), 556-568.

(Handguns)

Browning, C.H. (1976) Handguns and homicide: A public health problem. *JAMA, 236*(19), 2198-2200.

(Gun Control)

Phillips, L., et al. (1976) Guns, crime, and the law: Minimizing losses and the cost of control. *Journal of Legal Studies, 5*, 463-478.

(Guns and the Law)

Guns, crime, and the law: A case for the defense (second in a series). (1976) *Law Enforcement Journal, 6*(9), 5-6.

(Gun Control)

Pistol regulations in the 50 states: Better check the gun laws in each state first. (1973) *Law Officer, 6*(5), 45-47.

(Handguns)

Pasternack, S.A. (1973) The American connection: Handguns and homicide. *Medical Annals, DC, 42*, 369-373.

(Gun Control)

Edwards, J.G. (1972) Murder and gun control. *American Journal of Psychiatry, 128*, 811-814.

(Gun Control - Discussion)

Edwards, J.G. (1972) Commentary: Murder and gun control. *Wayne Law Review, 18*, 1335.

(Gun Control)

Seitz, S.T. (1972) Firearms, homicides, and gun control effectiveness. *Law and Society Review, 6*(4), 595-613.

(Murder Reduction)

Zimring, F. (1968) Is gun control likely to reduce violent killings? *University of Chicago Law Review, 35*(4), 721-737.

(Gun Registration)

Do laws requiring registration of privately owned firearms lower murder rate? (1958) *S T L J, 3*, 317.

Psychological or Mental Treatment

(Psychopathology - Treatment)

Treatment of psychopath convicted of manslaughter. (1990, Aug.) *Journal of Criminal Law, 54* 339-342.

(Psychological Treatment)

Schlesinger, L.B., & Revitch, E. (1990) Outpatient treatment of the sexually motivated murderer and potential murderer. *Journal of Offender Counseling, Services, and Rehabilitation, 15*(1), 163-178.

(Treatment - Adolescents)

Myers, W.C., et al. (1988) Characteristics and treatment of four homicidal adolescents. *Journal of the American Academy of Child and Adolescent Psychiatry, 27*(5), 595-599.

(Treatment - Traumatized Child)

Brown, M. (1987) Application of Horney theory in the treatment of a traumatized child. *American Journal of Psychoanalysis, 47*(1), 3-20.

(Medical Deterrents)

Nordlicht, S. (1986) Medical deterrents. *Bulletin of NY Academy of Medicine, 62*(5), 582-588.

(Post-Traumatic Stress Disorder)

Harry, B., et al. (1986) Post-traumatic stress disorder in murderers. *Journal of Forensic Science, 31*(2), 609-613.

(Psychotherapy)

Oerkirch, A. (1985) Psychotherapy of a murderer: Excerpts. *American Journal of Psychotherapy, 39*(4), 499-514.

(Psychotherapy)

Ishihara, K. (1985) Female crime and menstrual cycle: Case study of psychotherapy using skin potential activity biofeedback technique. *Japanese Journal of Criminal Psychology, 23*(1), 39-48.

(Hypnotic Relief)

Scneck, J.M. (1983) Hypnotic relief of guilt associated with murder of a parent. *International Journal of Electric Psychotherapy, 2*(1), 10-17.

(Psychotherapy)

Ishihara, K., & Yui, S. (1981) Psychotherapy of female psychiatric patients: Successful treatment of a foreign prisoner incarcerated for murdering her child who exhibited mutism. *Japanese Journal of Criminal Psychology, 18*(1-2), 19-24.

(Treatment of Behavior)

Bowerman, W.M. (1980) Paradoxical effects of Ritalin in adults. *Journal of Orthomol Psychiatry, 9*(3), 223-227.

(Crisis Therapy)

Brown, B. (1978, April) Town that grieved; Girardi murders; crisis therapy for Briarcliff Manor, NY. *Good Housekeeping, 186*, p. 135+.

(Deinstitutionalization)

Grunberg, F., et al. (1977) Homicide and the deinstitutionalization of the mentally ill. *American Journal of Psychiatry, 134*(6), 685-587.

(Homicide Prevention)

The American Psychiatric Association position statement on homicide prevention. (1973) *American Journal of Psychiatry, 130*, 391.

(Homicide Prevention)

Tanay, E. (1972) Psychiatric aspects of homicide prevention. *American Journal of Psychiatry, 128*(7), 815-818.

(Homicidal Impulses - Control)

Kuehn, J.L., et al. (1969) Management of the college student with homicidal impulses - the "Whitman syndrome". *American Journal of Psychiatry, 125*, 1594-1599.

(Violence - Prevention)

Hankoff, L.D. (1966) Psychiatric and public health aspects of the prevention and treatment of violence. *Journal of Hillside Hospital, 15*(2), 94-103.

(Fratricide - Treatment of Survivors)

Carek, D.J., et al. (1964) Treatment of a family involved in fratricide. *Archives of General Psychiatry, 11*, 533-542.

(Prevention of Delusion)

Lanzkron, J. (1961) Murder as a reaction to paranoid delusions in involuntary psychosis and its prevention. *American Journal of Psychiatry, 118*, 426-427.

(Psychoanalytic Treatment)

Williams, A.H. (1960) A psychoanalytic approach to the treatment of the murderer. *International Journal Psychotherapy, 41*, 532-539.

Deterrence Through Legislation

(Death Penalty)

Burns, R.E. (1990, April) The examined life: Killing is no way to stop murder. *U.S. Catholic, 55*(4), p. 2.

(Deterrence - Analysis)

Grogger, J. (1990) The deterrent effect of capital punishment - an analysis of daily homicide counts. *Journal of American Statistical Association, 85*(410), 295-303.

(Capital Punishment)

Lester, D. (1990) Capital punishment, gun control, and personal violence. *Psychological Reports, 66*(1), 122.

(Execution - Publicity)

Bailey, W.C. (1990) Murder, capital punishment, and television: Execution publicity and homicide rates *American Sociological Review, 55*(5), 628-633.

(Anti-Crime Bill)

Biskupic, J. (1990) Judiciary panel presses on in drafting anti-crime bill. *Congressional Quarterly Weekly Report, 48*(29), 2321-2323.

(Deterrence)

Deparle, J. (1989) The juice ain't no use. *Washington Monthly, 21*(4), pp. 32-33.

(Deterrence)

Lester, D. (1989) The deterrence effect of executions on murder - effect of different ways of measuring execution rates & note. *Perceptual & Motor Skills, 47*(1), 878.

(Capital Punishment)

Bailey, W.C. (1989) The deterrence effect of capital punishment during the 1950's. *Suicide & Life Threatening Behavior, 13*(2), 95-107.

(Capital Punishment)

Bailey, W.C. (1989) Murder and capital punishment: A monthly time-series analysis of execution publicity. *American Sociological Review, 54*(5), 722-743.

(Death Penalty)

Vito, G.F., et al. (1989) Death penalty issues. *Journal of Contemporary Criminal Justice, 5*(4), 181-255.

(Capital Punishment)

Harries, K.D. (1988) Regional variations in homicide, capital punishment, and perceived crime severity in the United States. *Geografiska Annaler, 70B*(3), 325-334.

(Capital Punishment)

Peterson, R.D., & Bailey, W.C. (1988) Murder and capital punishment in the evolving context of the post-Furman era. *Social Forces, 66*(3), 774-807.

(Legal Deterrents)

Kaplan, J. (1986) Legal Deterrents. *Bulletin of the NY Academy of Medicine, 62*(5), 601-614.

(Public Executions)

Green, S.T., et al. (1986) The last public execution in Glasgow: The case of Dr. Edward Pritchard, M.D. *Scottish Medical Journal, 31*(4), 256-260.

(Execution - Nevada)

Nevada executes killer. (1985) *Corrections Digest, 16*(26), 10.

(Death Penalty)

Burns, R.E. (1990, April) The examined life: Killing is no way to stop murder. *U.S. Catholic, 55*(4), 2.

(Deterrence)

Decker, S.H., & Kohfeld, C.W. (1984) A deterrence study of the death penalty in Illinois, 1933-1980. *Journal of Criminal Justice, 12*(4), 367-377. Microforms and article copies available from UMI.

(Deterrence)

McFarland, S.G. (1983) Is capital punishment a short-term deterrent to homicide? A study of the effects of four recent American executions. *The Journal of Criminal Law and Criminology, 74*(3), 1014-1032.

(Capital Punishment)

Lempert, R. (1983) Capital punishment in the 1980's: Reflections on the symposium. *The Journal of Criminal Law and Criminology, 74*(3), 1101-1114.

(Executions - Effects)

The effect of executions on homicides: A new look in an old light. (1983) *Crime and Delinquency, 29*(1), 88-115.

(Deterrence)

Forst, B. (1983) Capital punishment and deterrence: Conflicting evidence? *The Journal of Criminal Law and Criminology, 74*(3), 927-942.

(Deterrence)

Archer, D., et al. (1983) Homicide and the death penalty: A cross-national test of a deterrence hypothesis. *The Journal of Criminal Law and Criminology, 74*(3), 991-1013.

(Deterrence)

Bailey, W.C. (1983) Disaggregation in deterrence and death penalty research: The case of murder in Chicago. *The Journal of Criminal Law and Criminology, 74*(3), 827-859.

(Deterrence)

Yunker, J.A. (1982) Testing the deterrence effect of capital punishment: A reduced form approach. *Criminology, 19*(4), 626-649.

(Capital Punishment - Research)

Yunker, J.A. (1982) The relevance of the identification problem to statistical research on capital punishment. *Crime and Delinquency, 28*(1), 96-124.

(Deterrence)

Wasserman, I.A. (1981) Non-deterrent effect of executions on homicide rates. *Psychological Reports, 48*(1), 137-138.

(Deterrence)

Phillips, D.P. (1980) Deterrent effect of capital punishment: New evidence on an old controversy. *American Journal of Sociology, 86*, 139-148; Discussion, *American Journal of Sociology, 88*, 161-172 (1982).

(Execution - Gilmore)

Lester, D. (1980) Effect of Gary Gilmore's execution on homicidal behavior. *Psychological Reports, 47*(3, part 2), 1262.

(Death Penalty)

Haney, C. (1980) Juries and the death penalty: Readdressing the Witherspoon question. *Crime and Delinquency, 26*(4), 512-536.

(Deterrence)

Bowers, W.J., & Pierce, G.L. (1980) Deterrence or brutalization: What is the effect of executions? *Crime and Delinquency, 26*(4), 453-484.

(Deterrence)

Bailey, W.C. (1980) Deterrence and celerity of the death penalty: A neglected question in the deterrence research. *Social Forces, 58*, 1308-1333.

(Deterrence)

Bailey, W.C. (1980) Multi-variate cross-sectional analysis of the deterrent effect of the death penalty. *Social and Sociology Research, 64*, 183-207.

(Deterrence)

Bailey, W.C. (1979) Deterrence and the death penalty for murder in Oregon. *Willamette Law Review, 16*, 67-85.

(Deterrent Effect)

Bailey, W.C. (1979-1980) Deterrent effect of the death penalty: An extended time series analysis. *Omega: Journal of Death and Dying, 10*(3), 235-259.

(Deterrent Effect)

Avio, K.L. (1979, Nov.) Capital punishment in Canada: A time series analysis of the deterrent hypothesis. *Canadian Journal of Economics, 12*, 647-676.

(Effects of Executions)

Lester, D. (1979, Oct.) Deterring effect of executions on murder as a function of number and proportion of executions. *Psychology Reports, 45*, 598.

(Executions as Deterrents)

Lester, D. (1979, April) Executions as deterrents to homicides. *Psychology Reports, 44*, 562.

(Deterrent Effect - California)

Bailey, W.C. (1979, March) Deterrent effect of the death penalty for murder in California. *Southern California Law Review, 52*, 743-764.

(Capital Punishment)

Glaser, D. (1979, Winter) Capital punishment - deterrent or stimulus to murder? Our unexamined deaths and penalties. *University of Toledo Law Review, 10*, 317-333.

(Deterrent Effect)

Parker, R.N., & Smith, M.D. (1979) Deterrence, poverty, and type of homicide. *American Journal of Sociology, 85*(3), 614-624.

(Deterrent Effect - Ohio)

Bailey, W.C. (1979) The deterrent effect of the death penalty for murder in Ohio: A time series analysis. *Cleveland State Law Review, 28*(1), 51-81.

(Deterrent Effect)

Anyone who thinks the death penalty is not a crime deterrent is crazy. (1977-1978) *The National Sheriff, 29*(6), 15.

(Deterrent Effect - Utah)

Bailey, W.C. (1978, Winter) Deterrence and the death penalty for murder in Utah: A times series analysis. *Journal of Contemporary Law, 5*, 1-20.

(Homicide and Publicity)

Trilling Linker, C. (1977) *Homicide and publicity: A view of from the deterrence perspective.* Albany, NY: State University of New York, Albany.

(Deterrent Effect - Report)

Death penalty does not deter murder rate, First study shows. (1977) *Corrections Digest, 8*(22), 5-

6. Article copies available from UMI.

(Psychological Implications)

Rawlins, G.C. (1976) An exploratory study of some psychological implications of the death penalty as measured on the MMPI of convicted murderers. *Dissertation Abstracts International, 36*(11-B), 5813-5814.

(Legislative Deterrent)

Texas Law Enforcement Legislative Council. Legislation ... a deterrent to crime. (1975) *Texas Police Journal, 23*(2), 1-5, 18.

(Death Penalty)

Homicide: Black victims of, 5(1), 69 38; in Canada, and death penalty 10(2), 74 393; psychodynamics of, 8(1), 72 37; suicide, analysis by race and occupations, 5(1), 69 32. *Social Workers Reports Abstracts*, 1965-1974.

(Death Penalty - Canada)

Jayewardene, C.H.S. (1973) The death penalty and the safety of Canadian policemen. *Canadian Journal of Criminology and Corrections, 15*(4), 356-366.

(Deterrence)

Bean, F.D., & Cushing, R.G. (1971) Criminal homicide, punishment, and deterrence; methodological and substantive reconsiderations. *Social Science Quarterly, 52*(2), 277-289.

(Punishment and Deterrence)

Osborne, H.W. (1968) On crime, punishment, and deterrence. *Social Science Quarterly, 49*(1), 157-160.

(Law)

Cohen, L.H. (1952) *Murder, madness, and the law*. Cleveland: World Publishing Co.

Police Action

(Search and Seizure)

Waterman, G. (1991, Fall) Constitutional law: Search and seizure - post-search disclaimer of ownership, standing alone, does not constitute abandonment (case note). *North Dakota Law Review, 67*, 553-567.

(Media)

Officer in shooting need not be named (Maine). (1991, Fall) *News Media & the Law, 15*, 21-22.

(Teaneck Case)

Fleury, R.J. (1991, Sept. 26) Skirmish of the experts bedraggles Teaneck case (police shooting case in Teaneck, New Jersey). *New Jersey Law Journal*, p. 1.

(Conviction Upheld)

Adams, E.A. (1991, Sept. 19) Convictions upheld in bombing case: Radical group members' suppression claims denied (United Freedom Front). *New York Law Journal*, p. 1.

(Tracing Explosives)

Kolla, P. (1991, Sept.) Trace analysis of explosives from complex mixtures with sample pretreatment and selective detection. *Journal of Forensic Sciences, 36*, 1342-1359.

(Police Shootings)

Vogeler, W. (1991, Aug. 29) Routinely justified police shootings questioned (California). *Los Angeles Daily Journal*, p. B1.

(Supreme Court Decision)

Mynatt, J.P., Jr. (1991, Spring) Has the Supreme Court let the public sentiment shroud the Constitution? (case note) *American Journal of Trial Advocacy, 14*, 583-601.

(Taser Guns)

Kornblum, R.N., & Reddy, S.K. (1991, March) Effects of Taser in fatalities involving police confrontation (Taser gun). *Journal of Forensic Sciences, 36*, 434-448.

(Police Shootings)

Harding, R.W. (1991, Jan.-June) Twenty-five years of shootings by police: Past patterns and future trends (Australia). *Australia Journal of Forensic Sciences, 22*, 7-13.

(Detection of Murder)

Kostal, S. (1991, Jan.) Who killed Dexter Jacobson? (California) *California Lawyer, 11*, 28(8).

(Police Shootings)

Stone, I.C., et al. (1991, Jan.) Coordination of resources in officer-involved shootings. *Journal of Forensic Sciences, 36*, 40-46.

(Arrest)

Leerhsen, C. (1990, Nov. 19) Busting the prince of love. *Newsweek, 116*(21), p. 45.

(Police Violence)

Waddington, P.A.J. (1990, Oct.) 'Overkill' or 'minimum force'? *Crim Law Rev 1990*, 695-707.

(Murder Threat)

Magner, D. (1990) Alleged plot prompts extra security on some campuses. *Chronicle of Higher Education, 36*(25), A2.

(Police Homicide)

Taylor-Greene, E. (1989) The effects of police systems and their environment on police homicides: An explanatory analysis. *Dissertation Abstracts International, A: The Humanities and Social Sciences, 50*(4), 1099A.

(Police as Victims)

Lester, D. (1987) The police as victims: The role of guns in the murder of police. *Psychology Reports, 60*(2), 366.

(Serial Killers)

Interstate parley on serial killers. (1984) *Law Enforcement News, 10*(3), 1.

(Police Homicide)

Lester, D. (1982) Civilians who kill police officers and police officers who kill civilians: A comparison of American cities. *Journal of Police Science and Administration, 10*(4), 384-387.

(Police Force)

Wilson, J.Q. (1980) Police use of deadly force. *FBI Law Enforcement Bulletin, 49*(8), 16-21.

(Police Incompetence)

Vigilante 'white hand' slaps police for incompetence. (1980) *Law Enforcement News, 6*(6), 6.

(Jekyll-and-Hyde)

Bianchi, K. (1979, May 3) Jekyll-and-Hyde on the hillside: Arrest of alleged Hillside strangler. *Macleans, 92*, pp. 35-36.

(Police Officers)

Sherman, L.W., & Langworthy, R.H. (1979, Winter) Measuring homicide by police officers. *Journal of Criminal Law & Criminology, 70*, 546-560.

(Mass Murderers)

Kearney, P., & Hill, D. (1977, July 16) Twenty-eight, and counting...; arrest of mass murderers. *Time, 110*, p. 49.

(Violence against Police)

Violence against police and hostages erupts across several states. (1976) *Crime Control Digest, 10*(47), 9-10. Article copies available from UMI.

(Victim Advocates)

Houston, C. (1977) Victim advocate services: A programmed police response for crime victims. *Canadian Police Chief, 66*(1), 25-25.

(Killing of Police)

Daley, R. (1976) *To kill a cop.* Crown.

(Sheriff's Deputies)

Ft. Lauderdale sheriff's deputies. (1975) *Juvenile Justice Digest, 3*(13), 9.

(Police Responses)

Donovan, E.J., & Sullivan, J.F. (1974) Police response to family disputes. *FBI Law Enforcement Bulletin, 43*(9), 3-6.

(Deadly Force)

Use of deadly force in Arizona by police officers. (1973) *Law and Social Order 1973*, 481-495.

(Police Killings)

Logan, A. (1973, March) Around city hall: Murders of policemen in New York. *New Yorker, 49*, p. 76+.

(Protection of Police)

New drive against killers of police. (1973, Jan. 19) *U.S. News and World Reports, 74*, pp. 26-27.

(Deadly Force)

Policeman's use of deadly force in Illinois. (1971) *Chi-Kent Law Review, 48*, 252.

(Investigation)

Sanders, B. (1969) *They caught these killers.* Roy.

(Escape - Prevention)

Burchell, E.M. (1953) Killing to prevent prisoner's escape. *S A L J, 70*, 345-347.

(Deadly Force)

Killings by arresting officers in Texas. (1952) *Texas Law Review, 30*, 608-613.

(Deadly Force)

Felony murder - death caused by a police bullet (People vs. Podolski (Michigan) 52 N W (2d) 201).

(Self-Defense)

Hopkins, J.J. (1949) Illegal arrest as sufficient provocation to mitigate a homicide. *Ky Law*

Journal, 37, 316-321.

(Deadly Force)

Reexamination of the right of an officer to kill a fleeing suspected felon. (1949) *Ky Law Journal, 40*, 192-199.

(Self-Defense)

Gibbs, J.L. (1949) Right to kill in resisting an illegal arrest. *South Carolina Law Quarterly, 1*, 298-301.

(Deadly Force)

Iman, D.B. (1946) Criminal procedure: Killing of a misdemeanant who is forcibly resisting arrest (Scott vs. Commonwealth (KY.) 190 S W (2d) 345). (1946) *Ky Law Journal, 31*, 359-361.

(Self-Defense)

Howe, J.E. (1943) Homicide to prevent unlawful arrest. *Ky Law Journal, 31*, 359-361.

(Preventing Escape)

Making arrest or preventing escape of prisoner (Scarborough v. State (TN) 76 SW 2d. 106). *Tennessee Law Review, 13*, 195-197.

(Resisting Arrest)

Dickey, J.S. (1933) Culpable homicides in resisting arrest. *Cornell Law Quarterly, 18*, 373-390.

(Deadly Force)

Rogers, B. (1930) Right of officer to shoot and kill fleeing felon. *Law Notes, 34*, 66-70.

(Deadly Force)

Officer had no right to kill person resisting arrest for misdemeanor unless resistance was by armed force (Shelton vs. Commonwealth (KY.) 11 S W (2d) 125). (1929) *Ky Law Journal, 17*, 402-404.

(Degree of Force)

Degree of force which officer may lawfully use in making arrest for misdemeanor (Durham vs. State (IN.) 159 N E 145). *Indiana Law Journal, 3*, 479-480 (1928); *Minnesota Law Review, 12*, 539-540.

(Punishment - Rhode Island)

Phelps, H.A. (1928) Effectiveness of life imprisonment as a repressive measure against murder in Rhode Island. *American Statistical Association Journal, 23*(Sup), 174-181.

(Crime Prevention)

Pitman, O.H. (1928) When homicide committed to prevent commission of a crime is justifiable. *Texas Law Review, 6*, 184-189 (Feb.); *American Law Review, 62*, 265-271 (March-April).

(Customs Officers)

Justification, customs officers (Ex parte Dickson, 14 F 2d. 609). (1927, March) *Illinois Law Review, 747-748.*

Aftermath

(Murder of Rabbi)

Meir Kahane: Die by the sword. (1990, Nov. 10) *Economist, 317*(7680), p. 28.

(Aftermath)

Park, J. (1990, Nov. 19) As he copes with his son's murder rap, Marlon Brando is dealt a second blow; daughter Cheyenne's suicide try. *People Weekly, 34*(20), pp. 58-60.

(Homicide - El Salvador)

Roses in November. (1990, Nov. 9) *Commonwealth, 117*(19), pp. 628-629.

(Terrorism - Jerusalem)

Holy terror in Jerusalem. (1990, Oct. 27) *Economist, 317*(7678), p. 44.

(Elegy)

Hubbard, K. (1990, Oct. 15) Melanie Thernstrom's elegy to a murdered friend brings riches, praise, and unforeseen anger. *People Weekly, 34*(15), pp. 79-82.

(Aftermath - Brando Family)

Manso, P. (1990, Aug.) The Brando demons. *Vanity Fair, 53*(8), pp. 102-112.

(Aftermath - Bensonhurst)

Sullivan, A. (1990, July 2) The two faces of Bensonhurst (aftermath of Y. Hawkins murder; cover story). *The New Republic, 203*, pp. 13-16.

(Aftermath - Bensonhurst)

Brower, M. (1990, June 4) The racial murder of Y. Hawkins inflamed New York, forcing his parents to relive their anguish. *People Weekly, 33*(22), pp. 56-60.

(Trial - Aftermath)

Garneau, G. (1990, May 26) Journalists assaulted following N.Y. trial verdicts. *Editor & Publisher, 123*(21), 12, 50.

(Racial Tension)

Trippett, F. (1990, May 28) Broken mosaic. *Time, 135*(22), pp. 20-22.

(Aftermath - Kent State)

Dowling, C.G. (1990, May) Kent State. *Life, 13*(6), pp. 137-141.

(Aftermath - Hatred)

Kunen, J.S., et al. (1990, April 30) Hate flourishes on the street where the families of a killer and his victim still live. *People Weekly, 33*(17), pp. 58-60.

(El Salvador Murder)

Lacefield, P. (1990, Mach 23) Can this war ever end? Narrowed options in El Salvador. *Commonweal, 117*(6), pp. 180-183.

(Grief)

Gross, K. (1990, Feb. 19) After their daughter is murdered at college, her grieving parents mount a crusade for campus safety (death of J.A. Clery at Lehigh University). *People Weekly, 33*, pp. 113-114+.

(Reliving Tragedy)

Litwin, S. (1990, Feb. 10) Reliving a family tragedy. *TV Guide, 38*(6), pp. 22-225.

(Homicide - Gay Victim)

Massa, R. (1990, Feb. 6) Pols snub SI funeral. *Village Voice, 35*(6), p. 14.

(Victims - Support)

Brown, L., et al. (1990) *Victim support: Families of murder victims project (final report).* London: Victims' Support National Office.

(Grief)

Hambridge, J.A. (1990) The grief process in those admitted to regional secure units following homicide. *Journal of Forensic Sciences, 35*, 1149-1154.

(Aftermath - Concern)

Wilson, R. (1990) Officials of universities that have been targets of past killers view U. of Florida tragedies with horror and concern. *Chronicle of Higher Education, 37*(2), A33-A34.

(Family Violence)

Dyson, J.L. (1990) The effect of family violence on children's academic performance and behavior. *Journal of the National Medical Association, 82*(1), 17-22.

(Aftermath - Montreal)

Bergman, B., et al. (1989, Dec. 18) Sisterhood of fire and fury. *Macleans, 102*(51), pp. 18-19.

(Homicide - El Salvador)

O'Hare, J.A., & O'Donavan, L.J. (1989, Dec. 16) In solidarity with the slain Jesuits of El Salvador. *America, 161*(19), pp. 443-446.

(Nazis Trial)

Put Nazis on trial. (1989, Dec. 16) *Economist, 313*(7633), p. 18.

(Savagery - Churches)

Nemeth, M., & Gannon, J. Fear in the midst of war. *Macleans, 102*(49), p. 48.

(Aftermath - Holocaust)

Horrors past. (1989, Nov. 25) *Economist, 313*(7630), pp. 102-105.

(Law Suit)

Shooting victim's kin sue newspaper. (1989, Oct. 28) *Editor & Publisher, 122*(43), p. 27.

(Political Murder)

Peerman, D. (1989, Oct. 4) Evolution of a martyr. *Christian Century, 106*(28), 870-872.

(Aftermath)

Hope, J. (1989, Oct.) "My wife shouldn't have died." *Good Housekeeping, 209*(4), pp. 92-97.

(Aftermath - Forgiveness)

Shaver, J. (1989, Sept. 22) Daughter of Mason victims finds forgiveness. *Christianity Today, 39*(13), pp. 50-51.

(Politics - New York)

Barrett, W. (1989, Sept. 12) The politics of poison. *Village Voice, 34*(37), p. 18.

(Entertainment Industry Hit)

Jeffery, D. (1989, Sept. 2) LIVE takes stock after tragic loss of its CEO. *Billboard, 101*(35), pp. 3, 82.

(Passions)

Walder, J., et al. (1989, Jan. 23) The passions of Peter Bogdonovich. *People Weekly, 31*(3), pp. 56-62.

(Gay Violence)

Rist, D.Y. (1989, Jan. 9) Gleanings: Global gay bashing. *Utne Reader, 42*(2), p. 62.

(Mendez Murder - Aftermath)

Cockburn, A. (1989, Jan. 6) The man who loved trees. *New Statesman & Society, 2*(31), p. 19.

(Survivors)

Amick-McMullan, A., et al. (1989) Family survivors of homicide victims: Theoretical perspectives and an exploratory study. *Journal of Traumatic Stress, 2*(1), 21-35.

(Survivors)

McCune, N., & Donnelly, P. (1989) Children surviving parental murder. *British Journal of Psychiatry, 154*(889), 166-179.

(Grief)

Vargas, L.A., et al. (1989) Exploring the multidimensional aspects of grief reactions *American Journal of Psychiatry, 146*(11), 1484-1488.

(Psychological Scars)

Penna, D., et al. (1989) Southern Africa's children: The psychological scars. *Africa Today, 36*(2), 34-35.

(Aftermath)

North, C.S. (1989) Short-term psychopathology in eyewitness to mass murder. *Hospital and Community Psychiatry, 40*(12), 1293-1295.

(Survivors)

Cowles, K.V. (1988) Personal world expansion for survivors of murder victims. *West Journal of Nursing Research, 10*(6), 687-704.

(Bereavement)

Fraser, K.A. (1988) Bereavement in those who kill. *Medical Science and the Law, 28*(2), 127-130.

(Sentencing - Prediction)

Yang, B., et al. (1988) Predicting execution rates in the U.S.A. *Psychology Reports, 62*(1), 305-306.

(Genocide - Aftermath)

Bauman, Z. (1988) Sociology after the holocaust. *British Journal of Sociology, 39*(4), 469-497.

(Facing Murder)

Gampel, Y. (1988) Facing war, murder, torture, and death in latency. *Psychoanalysis Review, 75*(4), 499-509.

(Mourning)

Savin, D.L. (1987) The expression of mourning in an eight-year-old girl. *Clinical Social Work Journal, 15*(2), 121-135.

(Aftermath)

Collison, B., et al. (1987) After the shooting stops. Special issue: Counseling and violence. *Journal of Counseling & Development, 65*(7), 389-390.

(Grief)

Pynoos, R.S., et al. (1987) Grief reactions in school-age children following a snipe attack at school. *Israeli Journal of Psychiatry and Related Sciences, 24*(1-2), 53-63.

(Hungerford - Aftermath)

Burton-Bradley, B.G. (1987) The Hungerford massacre and its aftermath (letter). *British Journal of Psychiatry, 151*(866).

(Family Tragedy)

Prendergast, A. (1986, July) "You can't see my heart": One family's return from tragedy (Jahnke family three years after patricide in Cheyenne, WY). *Ladies Home Journal, 103*, p. 32+.

(Aftermath)

Kahn, M. (1986, Jan.) Emotional aftermath for policeman. *ADAMHA N, 12*(1), p. 9.

(Aftermath - Witness)

Malmquist, C.P. (1986) Children who witness parental murder: Post-traumatic aspects. *Journal of the American Academy of Child Psychiatry, 25*(3), 320-325.

(Aftermath - Witness)

Pynoos, R.S., & Spencer, E. (1986) Witness to violence: The child interview. *Journal of the American Academy of Child Psychiatry, 25*(3), 306-319.

(Cities - Decline)

Sampson, R.J. (1986) The contribution of homicide to the decline of American cities. *Bulletin of the New York Academy of Medicine, 62*(5), 562-569.

(Post-Traumatic Stress Disorder)

Harry, B., & Resnick, P.J. (1986) Post-traumatic stress disorder in murderers. *Journal of Forensic Sciences, 31*(2), 609-613. Article copies available from UMI.

(Akin Family)

Miss America: Old Ghosts (Akin family involvement in murders of civil rights workers in Mississippi, 1964). (1985, Oct. 7) *Newsweek, 106*, p. 35.

(Calming Fears)

Mayor Young heads effort to calm kids' fears after Atlanta child murders. (1985, Feb. 25) *Jet, 67*, pp. 58-59.

(Massacre - Aftermath)

Granberry, M., & Weinhouse, B. (1985, Jan.) The children of San Ysidro: Aftermath of a massacre. *Ladies Home Journal, 102*, pp. 59-60.

(Aftermath)

Flugge, I. (1985) After a murderous assault in a school class (German). *Praxis der Kinderpsychol und Kinder Psychiatr, 34*(1), 2-8.

(Aftermath - Children)

Eth, S., et al. (1985) Mental health consultation to a preschool following the murder of a mother and child. *Hospital and Community Psychiatry, 36*(1), 73-76.

(Aftermath - Suicide)

James, D., & Hawton, K. (1985) Overdoses: Explanations and attitudes in self-poisoners and significant others. *British Journal of Psychiatry, 146*(5), 481-485.

(Aftermath - Victims' Families)

Getzel, G.S., & Masters, R. (1984) Serving families who survive homicide victims. *Social Casework, 65*(3), 138-144.

(Bereavement)

Rynearson, E.K. (1984) Bereavement after homicide: A descriptive study. *American Journal of Psychiatry, 141*(11), 1452-2454.

(Witness - Child)

Pynoos, R.S., & Eth, S. (1984) The child as witness to homicide. *Journal of Social Issues, 40*(2), 87-108.

(Aftermath - Therapy)

Zeanah, C.H., et al. (1984) A young child who witnessed her mother's murder: Therapeutic and legal considerations. *American Journal of Psychotherapy, 38*(1), 132-145.

(Tylenol Scare - Aftermath)

Dershewitz, R.A. (1984) The effect of the Tylenol scare on parents' use of over-the-counter. *Clinical Pediatrics, 23*(8), 445-448.

(Aftermath - Parents)

Getzel, G.S., & Masters, R. (1983) Group work with parents of homicide victims. *Social Work with Groups, 6*(2), 81-92.

(Grief)

Rosenblatt, P.C. (1983) Grief and involvement in wrongful death litigation. *Law & Human Behavior, 7*(4), 351-359.

(Stress)

Braddock, H.O. (1982) Children and stress: The Atlanta child murder crisis. *Journal of Non-White Concerns in Personal & Guidance, 11*(1), 24-32.

(Aftermath)

Barnett, A. (1982) Learning to live with homicide: A research note. *Journal of Criminal Justice, 10*(1), 69-72.

(Aftermath - Organization)

Leerhsen, C. (1982, April 12) Parents of murdered children (Organization); parents of slain children. *Newsweek, 99*, p. 84.

(Aftermath - Treatment)

Pruett, K.D. (1979) Home treatment for two infants who witnessed their mother's murder. *Journal of the American Academy of Child Psychiatry, 18*(4), 647-657.

(Aftermath - Psychotic Reaction)

Arboleda, F. (1981) Post-homicide psychotic reaction. *International Journal of Offender Therapy & Comparative Criminology, 25*(1), 47-52.

(Aftermath - Treatment)

Cottreax, J. (1981) Grief therapy and cognitive restructuring in a depressed woman acquitted of justifiable homicide. *Behavioral Psychotherapy, 9*(3), 194-199.

(Aftermath - Social Costs)

Dennis, R.E. (1980) Social costs to families and communities. *Public Health Reports, 95*(6), 556.

(Survivors)

Danto, B., et al. (1980) *Homicide and survivors.* Thantatology Service Series.

(Arson Aftermath)

Traini, R. (1979) The aftermath of arson. *Security Gazette, 21*(9), 37, 39. Article copies available from UMI.

(Aftermath - Family, etc.)

Foodman, A., & Estrada, C. (1977) Adolescents who commit accidental homicide: The emotional consequences to the individual, family, and community. *Journal of the American Academy of Child Psychiatry, 16*(2), 314-326.

(Aftermath - Yablonski Murders)

Armbrister, T. (1975) *Act of vengeance: The Yablonski murders and their aftermath.* New York: Saturday Review Press.

(Aftermath - Family)

Burgess, A.W. (1975) Family reaction to homicide. *American Journal of Orthopsychiatry, 45*(3), 391-398.

(Homicidal Disputes)

Henderson, D.F. (1964) Settlement of homicide disputes in Sakya (Tibet). *American Anthropology, 66*(5), 1099-1105.

(Biblical Concept)

Greenberg, M. (1959, June) Biblical concept of asylum. *Bib Lit, 78,* 125-132.

(Aftermath - Conversion)

Foxe, A.N. (1943) Post-homicidal contrition and religious conversion. *Psychiatric Quarterly, 17,* 565-578.

Subject Index

-A-

- B -

-D-

-E-

-F-

- G -

-H-

-I-

-J-

- K-

- L -

-Q-

-R-

- S -

-T-

- U -

-V-

-W-

-X-

-Y-

-Z-

AUTHOR INDEX

-A-

- B -

-C-

-D-

-E-

-G-

-H-

-I-

-J-

-M-

-N-

-O-

-Q-

-R-

-S-

-T-

-U-

-V-

-W-